TAIWAN

A New History

TAIWAN

A New History

Murray A. Rubinstein
EDITOR

An East Gate Book

M.E. Sharpe
Armonk, New York
London, England

An East Gate Book

Copyright © 1999 by M. E. Sharpe, Inc.

All rights reserved. No part of this book may be reproduced in any form
without written permission from the publisher, M. E. Sharpe, Inc.,
80 Business Park Drive, Armonk, New York 10504.

Photographs by Patricia Loo unless otherwise noted

Library of Congress Cataloging-in-Publication Data

Taiwan : a new history / Murray A. Rubinstein, ed.
    p.   cm. — (Taiwan in the modern world)
    "An East gate book."
    Includes index.
    ISBN 1-56324-815-8 (alk. paper). —
    ISBN 1-56324-816-6 (pbk. : alk. paper)
    1. Taiwan—History.   2. Taiwan—Politics and government—1945–
    3. Taiwan—Civilization.   I. Rubinstein, Murray A., 1942–
    II. Series.
    DS799.5.T353   1998
    951.24′905—dc21   98-6043
    CIP

Printed in the United States of America

The paper used in this publication meets the minimum requirements of
American National Standard for Information Sciences—
Permanence of Paper for Printed Library Materials,
ANSI Z 39.48-1984.

BM (c)	10	9	8	7	6	5	4	3	2	1
BM (p)	10	9	8	7	6	5	4	3	2	1

Contents

Introduction

Murray A. Rubinstein

Taiwan's past is encountered wherever one travels on this small, crowded, and, perhaps, overdeveloped island. To understand the dramatic and sometimes chaotic chronicle that is Taiwan's history, one must first gain some sense of place and some appreciation for how geography helped to define this island's multilayered past—from sites that reflect the island's present, on to places that reflect the dawn of the island's written history as home of Australasian immigrants, as new-found home of land-hungry southeastern Chinese settlers, and as one of the two island frontiers of imperial China.

Taipei is the heart of this modern Taiwan, the island's bustling, traffic-clogged, major city, which hosts the national government of this political entity dominated by the Nationalist Party (Kuomintang—KMT) that continues to call itself the Republic of China (ROC). There are located the government's executive offices, cabinet ministries, legislative assemblies, highest courts, and examination and "control" branches.[1] Here are also the homes of the island's major electronic media, three government-dominated television stations, and the major newspapers. Here, too, in the city and its nearby suburbs are three of the island's major public universities: National Taiwan University (T'ai-ta), Taiwan Political Affairs University (Cheng-ta), and Taiwan Normal University (Shih-ta). The city also serves as a cultural hub. Thus the major museums—the world-renowned Palace Museum, the Museum of History, and the Taipei Museum of Modern Art—are in or near the city. The state's two largest memorials *cum* cultural centers, the performance halls of Chiang Kai-shek Memorial and the Sun Yat-sen Memorial Hall—are, respectively, in the city's governmental and financial districts.

The sprawling city and suburbs that make up the Taipei special administrative district are both the center of national development and the stronghold of the "ethnic" mainlander (*wai-sheng jen*) population that still dominates the organs of the central government. Taipei thus can be seen as a city approaching the world-class status that befits the hub of a state that is a small, but still dynamic, East Asian economic and political power center. Another, and in many ways very different, Taiwan can be found to the south of this increasingly sophisticated city.

Our journey into Taiwan's past begins here in Taipei, at the front gate of the park that houses the Chiang Kai-shek Memorial. In March 1990 this gate and the steps of a nearby theater were the site of a dramatic sit-in staged by students of the ROC's major universities. These students were demanding political change and, following in the footsteps of Peking University students at Tiananmen Square ten months before, attempting to pressure their government and induce it to promise constructive reforms. Conscious of the events in Beijing (Peking), and well aware of the worldwide reaction to these events, the regime leaders remained calm and, through an intermediary, negotiated a peaceful settlement with the students. This settlement paved the way for the formation of the National Consultative Assembly.[2] This meeting, held early in the summer of 1990, brought together people of diverse backgrounds and opinions and promoted the discussion of many of the major political problems that faced Taiwan as it attempted to democratize.

Just to the south and west of Taipei's urban core lies the suburb of Pan-ch'iao. Here, amid the choking sprawl that is typical of the nearby suburbs of Taipei and the other large cities of the island, is a large square block that is a refuge from the crowded neighborhood. It is surrounded by a window to the quieter times when Taiwan was a prefecture of the Ch'ing empire: the walled complex that was the home of the Lins, one of the two large and powerful landlord/gentry families that shared the same surname. The estate, once neglected, has been refurbished, and visitors can obtain a published guide to the buildings, gardens, and pavilions of the complex. Wandering through these grounds, one can tune out the modern city and imagine the world in which these gentry on the Ch'ing maritime frontier lived.

Beyond Pan-ch'iao lies the countryside and, farther on to the south and east, the small town of San-hsia. This town and the cluster of villages nearby have a long and rich history and, unlike the case in many areas in Taiwan, Westerners have played a role in bringing this history to light. Anthropologists began to study the area in the 1960s and the 1970s, when the island was one of the few places with large Chinese populations where they could still do intensive, local-level ethnography. The area became home to such scholars as Arthur Wolf, Emily Martin Ahern, Stevan Harrell, Robert Weller, and P. Steven Sangren and the scholar/activist Linda Gail Arrigo.[3] Their work has become the window to Taiwanese rural and village society that is required reading for the new generation students of Taiwan and mainland society. Taiwanese scholars have also focused on this area, and this effort has had a marked impact on the life of the community. One scholar/activist has devoted himself—his time, his energy, and his personal resources—to the rebuilding and the refurbishing of the great temple that lies at the heart of the town of San-hsia. Through this project, the restoration of a major religious edifice, this man and his supporters are linking past and present and keeping alive a major piece of the town and the area's religious/cultural history.

Farther south, east of Taichung, is another monument to the island's past: the home of the other major Lin family, in Wu-feng. Here, present-day descendants of this powerful family still live in a large estate that defines in its own way the rise of a Fukien-like local Taiwanese gentry. The history of that family and their world has been powerfully evoked in a landmark piece of Western scholarship on Taiwan, Johanna Meskill's *A Chinese Pioneer Family*.[4] One of the things that Meskill demonstrates is that Wu-feng was once a frontier and that it represented a border where the Han Chinese immigrants from Fukien who settled Taiwan met the *yuan-chu-min* (also called *shang-ti jen*), the aborigine peoples who were the first settlers of the island.

Yuan-chu-min history, that of the island's southern Min speaking Han Chinese, is in evidence farther east, in Nan-t'ou county. After reaching the heart of Nan-t'ou city, the county's center of government and also home to Taiwan's provincial government, one can board a bus to ascend the mountains that dominate much of the central and eastern landscape of the island. Here, at the end of an ascending road consisting of over sixty switchbacks is the town of Wu-she. This is a *ping-ti jen* (plains people, or Han-Taiwanese) town a few kilometers west of the small *shan-ti jen* (or mountain people) village of Chun-yang, a village on the *yuan-chu-min* reservation (a system instituted by the Japanese). These two villages define the tragic past and the sad present of *yuan-chu-min* existence. It was in Wu-she that a violent *yuan-chu-min* revolt against the Japanese began in the late 1930s. The Japanese, who took over the island in 1895, imposed tight controls over contact between Han-Taiwanese and *yuan-chu-min* and did much to further suppress the mountain people. The revolt was the long-awaited *yuan-chu-min* response to this treatment. The revolt was put down with brutal efficiency, and many members of the local tribe were moved to other *yuan-chu-min* reservations on the island. A monument at the entrance to Wu-she marks the place where that revolt began. Some of the sons and daughters of those rebels still live in Chun-yang. The village reeks of poverty and desperation. Alcoholism is prevalent, and daughters are often sold into prostitution by their impoverished families. The miracle of Taiwan's development has largely passed these people by.

These two towns, so close but so far away from each other, are also useful symbols of another facet of the island's past and present—the Christian Church's presence in Taiwanese life.[5] Wu-she's main street is home to a Catholic church, pastored by a Western *shen-fu* (holy father) and members of the Maryknoll order. Catholic missionaries have been active in the area, and nearby Chun-yang has a sizable Catholic population. The village also is the home to two Protestant churches. One is Presbyterian, the largest and most influential of Taiwan's numerous Protestant denominations. The Presbyterians maintain their connections with the wider world of Western Protestantism. The other major Protestant church, the largest indigenous church on the island, the True Jesus Church (Chen Ye-su Chiao-hui) is independent of formal Western connections and has its roots in Shantung in northeastern China. Both the Presbyterian Church and the True Jesus Church focus their efforts on Han-Taiwanese and *yuan-chu-min* and thus are united by their willingness to serve the needs of these two, often antagonistic, populations.

South of Taichung is the old port town of Lu-kang. Here again we come face to face with Taiwan's past, sometimes in dramatic fashion. Founded in the seventeenth century, during the eighteenth and nineteenth centuries Lu-kang was an important port city with strong ties to Ch'uan-chou—the eighteenth-century classic but declining entrepôt of southern Min Fukien. It became the home of two major Ma-tsu temples. The first was founded at the turn of the century and had direct connections with the Ma-tsu *tsu-miao* (mother temple) in Mei-chou, the island home of the cult of the goddess. The second temple to T'ien-hou Shang-mu (the Heavenly Mother—one of a number of titles given this goddess) was founded, with support from the Ch'ing authorities, in the 1780s, after the quelling of a major rebellion, one of many that the island witnessed during its first century under the Manchus. Lu-kang also hosted major Wang-yeh (Plague God) temples and the Lung-shan Tzu, a major center of Buddhist devotion.

Thus this city retains living remnants of the island's past. Its Ma-tsu temples represent the southern Min roots of the island as well as the two major types of Ma-tsu temples—the popular and the official—found throughout Taiwan.

Two hours south of Lu-kang lies the agricultural heartland of the southwestern coastal plain. In this landscape of rice paddies, farms, and small factories are the small town of Hsin-kang and, 12 kilometers farther on, the larger town/religious center of Pei-kang. These two towns each claim primacy as the site of the island's first (and major) Ma-tsu temple, and this rivalry has spanned decades, if not centuries. Because of their prominence, each has served as the *tsu-miao* for many of the island's smaller Ma-tsu temples. Every weekend, pilgrims from a given temple visit each of these sites (even as other bands of pilgrims visit the Lu-kang T'ien-hou Kung). Pei-kang has had the better of its rival, though historians agree that Hsin-kang does have the greater claim of being "the first." The birthday of Ma-tsu is celebrated with great pomp by hundreds of thousands at Pei-kang. This celebration is a major event in the island's religious and cultural calendar. The ceremonies celebrating the birthday of the goddess are also important events at both Lu-kang and nearby Hsin-kang, but they do not approach the size or grandeur of the event in Pei-kang. These battles for primacy are important in the lives of the Taiwanese and are linked to the process of defining a "Taiwanese" identity in the face of the claims and pressures of the Nationalist regime for a larger Han-Chinese identity.

Farther to the south, at the southern tip of the island, lies Tainan and rural sites just outside the Tainan metropolitan area. An-ping, three centuries ago an islet on the Taiwan Strait, served as the headquarters of the Dutch East India Company. Here the Dutch, based in Batavia, built a fort and town which later expanded into the area of what would become the island's first major city. And here they developed a base and gradually expanded to the north along the coast and to the island's northern and eastern shores.

And here the Sino-Japanese pirate, and defender of the Ming regime, Cheng Ch'eng-kung (Koxinga), came with his thousands of troops in 1662 to wrest control of the area from the Dutch. He made the city the base for his efforts to continue to war against the Ch'ing and also developed the area, but as a military colony and as the home of a growing number of immigrants from nearby southern Min Fukien. Tainan today is a sprawling city, whose residents and administrators are deeply aware of the heritage of the past and of its continuing role as a center of Buddhism and popular religion. Thus on any street one can find many examples of the city's and the island's rich historical and cultural heritage.

To truly complete the journey and discover the roots of Taiwan's southern Min majority one would have to travel to the P'eng-hu islands (Pescadores) and then still farther west to the shores of southern Fukien and the cities and towns along the province's east-facing coast, which is where new history of Taiwan begins.

This book explores Taiwan's development from its formal beginnings as a political entity—a Dutch East India Company colony—to a home for a Ming-loyalist regime, to its centuries as a Ch'ing prefecture and province, to its half-century as a Japanese possession, and to fifty years as the home of the Kuomintang-controlled Republic of China.

Several themes run through this work. The first is that Taiwan's political history as well as its socioeconomic history and its religiocultural history are defined, in some measure, by the contours of China's larger, expansionist history. Over the millennia the Chinese needed to find new land for agriculture and new markets for commerce. These people moved into China's inner Asian frontier and to the offshore islands. In these frontier zones, traditional social and cultural patterns took root as the ethnic Chinese presence expanded. Taiwan was just such a frontier zone where these multilevel processes occurred.

The second theme is the relationship, both conflictual and cooperative, between the indigenous peoples—the early waves of immigrants from Southeast Asia and beyond who settled the plains and the mountains and lived in distinctive tribal linguistic groupings—and the Han peoples from southern Fukien and northern Kuangtung who migrated to the island after 1600. This racial and cultural relationship, with its tensions and accommodations, frames the Dutch takeover of the island, the Chinese settlement during the Cheng Ch'eng-kung decades and the Ch'ing centuries, and the Japanese half-century. Chinese/*yuan-chu-min* relations remain an ongoing problem in modern Taiwanese life.

The third theme is the impact of the West—and Japan as a unique Western surrogate—in Taiwanese history. The Dutch attempted to control the island and left some reminders of their presence. After 1860, the Western economic and political presence, the Presbyterian missionaries, and, after 1895, the Japanese all introduced modes of modernization that changed the face of Taiwan. As is now evident, these successive groups prepared the people of the island for the U.S.-directed socioeconomic change of the 1950s and the 1960s. How Taiwan was transformed by these waves of invasion and how the island has become—aside from Hong Kong—the most Westernized and modernized part of China is a topic that runs throughout this book.

The fourth theme is a problematic and controversial one: the development of a unique Taiwanese identity. The Chinese pioneers who came to Taiwan from southern Min-speaking regions of Fukien and the Hakka-dominated regions of Kuangtung bore with them cultures that were at the same time all-inclusive and regional. Taiwan's historical, political, economic, and sociocultural development was to a degree a product of larger trans-Chinese patterns that have their roots in the southern Min region of Fukien and, to a lesser extent, in the Mei-shan area of Kuangtung. However, as John Shepherd shows in Chapter 5, the largely male migration to the island created a society that was inherently unstable and, at first, unable to develop, at least along the lines of the society of the South China coast. The process of Mandarinization (or "inlandization" to use Li Kuo-chi's popularly accepted term), was a slow and painful one. Interethnic conflict among the Han immigrants as well as competition with the militant indigenous peoples who inhabited the western plains and the mountain interior retarded this sinification of the island. These ongoing conflicts transformed the life of Han-Chinese from Fukien and Kuangtung who had come to the island and created a raw frontier society that had to be policed heavily by a Ch'ing government reluctant to make the necessary expenditures or commitment of personnel. That Taiwan became a province only in the late nineteenth century reflects this fact. But how Chinese was Taiwan? What did Taiwan become, given its unique history? Did a very special culture, a hybrid culture, evolve over time?[6] As Taiwan was buffeted by the waves of invasion from Holland, from the Chinese mainland (some Taiwanese nationalists have suggested that China can be seen as an alien presence), from the Western mercantile imperialists, from Japan and, after 1945, from the mainlander-dominated regime of the Kuomintang and its savior, the United States, its people developed a society and culture that reflected the effects of or reactions to these varied outside sociocultural, political, and intellectual influences. What Taiwanese themselves have increasingly begun to assert is that, over time, they developed their own forms of economic enterprise, social structure, and modes of religious and cultural experience that reflect the multifaceted influences of their historical experience. Today they see their culture as unique. But how valid is this view? Are there challenges to this idea in the form of a larger, southern Min–centered identity?

The fifth and pervasive theme is the development of Taiwanese society and culture. Are they simply a variant of both the larger Chinese culture—the great tradition—and of southern Min culture and a product of both Western and Japanese influences, or are they something different and distinct from their complex origins, as Taiwanese now argue?

Here, then, is what this collaborative history does. Chapter 1 examines the physical lay of the land and then explores how it was transformed by the hand of man. Chapter 2 portrays prehistoric Taiwan, a Taiwan dominated by Austronesian aboriginal groups before 1600. Chapter 3 covers the Fukien homeland of most of the Chinese who came to Taiwan. Chapter 4 examines the southern Min and Hakka settlement and development of the island. It examines the impact of the Dutch and of their conqueror, Koxinga, on Taiwan's development as an island frontier. Chapter 5 explores the first and most difficult period of Ch'ing rule of Taiwan, the period from 1684 to 1780. Chapter 6 focuses on Taiwanese sociocultural, political, and economic development under a Ch'ing empire in decline, from 1780 to 1862. Chapter 7 covers the period from 1860 to 1895, discussing the impact of the West on the island and the attempts of the Ch'ing governors of the newly designated province of Taiwan to modernize their island. How the Japanese converted Taiwan into a model colony is dealt with in Chapter 8. Chapter 9 covers Taiwanese culture during the period of Japanese control, focusing on trends in literature. Chapter 10 discusses the painful years of retrocession and their violent conclusion. Chapter 11 narrates the years from 1949 to 1970. It follows the course of development of the only province the KMT was left with and examines the ROC, now more than ever a U.S. client state, by tracing the island's political evolution and rapid socioeconomic development during these critical years of regime consolidation, reform, and economic restructuring. Chapter 12 looks at Chinese religion on Taiwan and assesses its impact on the modernizing KMT-dominated nation-state. Next come three chapters that deal with Taiwan in the years from 1971 to 1996. Chapter 13 covers the island's economic development; Chapter 14 explores literature during the KMT decades; Chapter 15 on the *yuan-chu-min* in contemporary Taiwan, explores the evolution of modern aboriginal sociopolitical consciousness. Chapter 16 continues with politics: the Taiwanization of the KMT and the government and democratization under Chiang Ching-kuo and Lee Teng-hui. Chapter 16 focuses on Taiwan's diplomatic policy and the post-1987 opening toward the People's Republic of China. The epilogue focuses on the dramatic months from the winter of 1995 to the late spring of 1996 during which Taiwan became a showplace of democratic change and a target of venom from an embarrassed and enraged People's Republic.

Notes

1. The government of the ROC consists of five branches, two more than found in major Western democracies. The two additional branches deal with civil service appointments—the Examination Yuan—and the general surveillance of governmental func-

tions—the Control Yuan. On the details of the constitution, see *The Republic of China Yearbook 1993* (Taipei: Government Information Office, 1993), 716–731.

2. On the National Consultative Assembly, see Harvey Feldman, ed., *Constitutional Reform and the Future of the Republic of China* (Armonk, NY: M. E. Sharpe, 1991).

3. Emily Martin Ahern, *The Cult of the Dead in a Chinese Village* (Stanford: Stanford University Press, 1973); P. Steven Sangren, *History and Magical Power in a Chinese Community* (Stanford: Stanford University Press, 1987); Robert Weller, *Unities and Diversities in Chinese Religion* (Seattle: University of Washington Press, 1987).

4. Johanna Meskill, *A Pioneer Family on Taiwan* (Princeton: Princeton University Press, 1979).

5. This presence has been explored in Murray A. Rubinstein, *The Protestant Community on Modern Taiwan: Mission, Seminary, and Church* (Armonk, NY: M.E. Sharpe, 1991).

6. The complex theme of cultural hybridity is discussed at length in Robert J.C. Young, *Colonial Desire: Hybridity in Theory, Culture and Race* (London: Routledge, 1995).

TAIWAN

A New History

1

The Shaping of Taiwan's Landscapes

Ronald G. Knapp

A rice field in Ilan County, Taiwan.

"TAIWAN: TOO BIG TO IGNORE" proclaimed *The New York Times* in early 1990. Attaching apparent hyperbole to an area only a third the size of Virginia or a little smaller than Switzerland provokes one to ask just how such a small piece of the earth 160 kilometers (96 miles) away from the mainland of Asia overcame its seemingly overwhelming physical limitations. Today Taiwan remains, as it has always been, quite small in total area, yet it has clearly traversed a development path that has strikingly altered its natural environment and given shape to cultural landscapes that resonate both an inherited Chinese character and international elements. The transformation of Taiwan's landscapes is a compelling story that involved acknowledging and overcoming conspicuous constraints as well as seizing opportunities at critical times. In the process, "little" Taiwan indeed has become "too big" to ignore.

As background to the historical drama realized on Taiwan's stage that is the focus of this book, this chapter examines the changing geographical dimensions of Taiwan. At the outset, the island is presented as rather raw, geometrical *space*, distinguished in terms of Taiwan's absolute and relative location as well as distance and direction within a more extensive spatial framework. As it will become clear, these somewhat abstract attributes are actually nothing more than a geographical matrix that humans endow with meaning. In the process of transforming space, Taiwan has emerged as a distinctive and still-evolving *place*. It is this continuing dynamic shaping of selected aspects of Taiwan's landscapes that comprises the bulk of this chapter. Examining the shaping of *space* into *place* allows one to understand better the interlinked relationships among the elements of the physical environment—landforms, climate, and natural vegetation—and the economic, social, and political dimensions of the human enterprise over time that have imparted meaning to a specific portion of the earth's surface.

Locational Attributes

Among the festooned islands that embrace coastal East Asia, Taiwan lies closest to the mainland. Yet even with such seeming proximity, Taiwan remained obscure and relatively remote off the southeastern coast of China for most of its history. The location of a place has both absolute and relative meanings. From the perspective of Taiwan's *absolute location*—its latitude and longitude—the island shares characteristics with other places in the world. Straddling the Tropic of Cancer ($23^{1}/_{2}°$N)—some 2,600 kilometers (1,560 miles) north of the Equator—Taiwan is at the same latitude as the Bahama islands, Burma, Mexico, and, perhaps surprisingly, the Sahara and Arabian deserts; Taiwan shares some geographical characteristics of all these disparate areas. The island's subtropical latitudinal location has defined the basic elements of its climate, as discussed below. Taiwan's longitude, on the other hand, plays no role relative to the island other than simply to fix it at a unique location on the earth's surface some $120°$ east of the Greenwich meridian.

Clearly, it is Taiwan's changing relative location in relation to the coastal mainland, its place astride the arc of islands that rims the western Pacific Ocean basin from the Kuriles to Indonesia, and, in recent centuries, its position straddling the sea and air lanes that crisscross this part of the world that has been essential in the island's transformation. Once viewed as a rather remote and shadowy satellite along China's cultural flank, Taiwan has become today a pivot within "Greater China," an increasingly dynamic part of the global economy.

Until the early years of the seventeenth century, the island was populated by non-Han aboriginal groups as well as limited numbers of Han-Chinese migrants from the mainland. The commercial sweep of European interests—principally the Dutch but also the Spanish—into East Asia in the sixteenth century, however, served as a catalyst leading to the island's ensuing inclusion as a cultural and economic extension of southeastern China. Relative proximity, even though across unpredictable straits, led subsequently to substantial migration from Fukien and Kuangtung, the two facing Chinese provinces. Through arduous and intensive efforts between the seventeenth and nineteenth centuries, migrant peasants and fisherfolk transformed the coastal lowlands of the island into agricultural and settlement landscapes quite similar to those on the mainland across the strait. Although Taiwan's absolute location has not shifted, its relative location—its geographic circumstances—clearly has been subject to continual adjustment. As the twentieth century ends, Taiwan is no longer remote or isolated from either the Chinese mainland or Europe or the Americas but has become pivotal in the restructured global economy that has emerged.

The Physical Environment: Landforms, Climate, and Vegetation

Taiwan is a mountainous island with a prominent north/south longitudinally trending backbone. Two of the landform regions comprise hills and mountains that are tectonically quite active. On the east, the T'ai-tung Mountains between Hua-lien and T'ai-tung rise precipitously from the Pacific Ocean as coastal ranges with average elevations above 1,000 meters (1,100 yards, 3,300 feet). The uplifted and tilted Central Mountain Range, considered an outlier of similar mountains found across the strait in Fukien province, dominates the island with its imposing landscapes of deep gorges and soaring peaks. On its eastern flank, the Central Mountain Range rises abruptly to elevations over 4,000 meters (4,400 yards, 13,200 feet); more than forty crests exceed 3,000 meters (3,300 yards, 9,900 feet). Along its western slopes, the Central Mountain Range gives way less dramatically to mountain depressions, such as Sun Moon Lake and the intermontane alluvial basins that cradle the cities of Taipei and Taichung, as well as a wide band of hilly terrain that runs from the northeastern coast nearly to the water in the south.

Two other prominent physiographic regions encompass lowlands: the narrow

T'ai-tung Rift Valley in the east and the broader coastal alluvial plain on the west. The T'ai-tung Rift Valley, squeezed like a 140-kilometer-long (84-mile) slim cigar between the T'ai-tung Mountains and the Central Mountain Range, is but 2 kilometers wide in some places and never exceeds 7 kilometers at its broadest. Isolated from the densely populated western lowlands by the Central Mountain Range, this eastern valley was a "marginal region" throughout most of the island's history until the twentieth century, when Japanese policies brought concerted agricultural colonization to the region. Short rivers with steep gradients that pour from the mountains have produced alluvial fans composed of gravel that challenged humans as they set out to tame the region's agricultural potential through the construction of terraces. Throughout the valley floor, farmers have collected round river-borne rocks to form stone walls that are reminiscent of those encountered in New England. Wherever one stands in the rift valley, the fringing mountains are in view.

Extending some 300 kilometers (180 miles) from Tan-shui (Tan-sui) in the north to Ping-tung in the south, the larger Western Coastal Plain is rather monotonously flat, consisting of a series of coalesced alluvial fans that splay forth from the foothills. The relatively short, seasonally rapid rivers that flow from the uplands carry with them substantial rocks that are deposited somewhat haphazardly as the streams meander sluggishly across the plain on their way westward to the Taiwan strait. Narrowest in the north and widening substantially in its southern reaches, the Western Coastal Plain is at no place broader than 50 kilometers (30 miles).

Between the Western Coastal Plain and the Central Mountain Range, as mentioned briefly above, are coastal rolling hills and several intermontane basins. These areas, together with the Western Coastal Plain, are where most of Taiwan's population has lived, and where humans have crafted distinctive cultural landscapes as they have modified substantially the natural landscapes created by nature. The Taipei and Taichung basins are structural depressions with important rivers passing through them on the way to the sea. Draining the rimming hills surrounding the Taipei basin, the Tan-shui River also gave sailing ships entry upstream into the basin until increasing siltation blocked river passage except for very shallow draft vessels. The shallow Tatu River and its tributaries drain the Taichung basin. Both the Taipei and Taichung basins, as well as Sun Moon Lake, are embraced by foothills of the Central Mountain Range. These gently sloping foothills have provided important secondary areas for settlement.

Bisected by the Tropic of Cancer, a geographic reality that governs the intensity and pattern of solar energy reaching a place, Taiwan possesses a subtropical climate that is distinguished by both relatively high temperatures and substantial precipitation throughout the year. However, even as subtropical conditions dominate across the island, other significant factors actually function to modify local climates. The relative proximity of the massive continent of Asia, the warm Kuroshio current that moves north from the Equator, and the prominent high and rugged mountain core of the island all bear on modifying local climates from expected subtropical norms.

Most of Taiwan shares average annual temperatures that are clearly subtropical, with the result that growing seasons are long, nearly year round throughout the island. Highest temperatures all over the island are reached between June and August, when the sun's rays are most intense and the days are longest. Winter, as it is understood in the middle latitudes, does not occur in the lowlands of Taiwan, but for six months of the year days become shorter and the sun's rays are comparatively less intense. There is not much difference in mean annual temperature between northern and southern Taiwan, although in general one can note a change of about 1° C for each 1° of latitude. In the hot month of July, there is very little difference in temperature between north and south. On the other hand, in January or February, when southern Taiwan remains quite warm, the temperatures in northern Taiwan turn rather chilly because of the cool damp winds that blow across the Taiwan strait from the mainland. During this "winter" season, northern Taiwan becomes more like places found in middle latitude locations than a location crossed by the Tropic of Cancer. Wind velocities within powerful storms are especially great between November and February throughout the P'eng-hu islands and at exposed coastal locations in western Taiwan because of the dominance of high pressure over the Asia mainland. The seasonal steadiness as well as alternation of prevailing winds both have been important climatic variables to which early settlers on the island paid attention. Throughout eastern Taiwan between December and March, however, most places enjoy subtropical conditions because of the protection afforded by the Central Mountain Range, which acts as a formidable barrier to the winds that blow from the mainland. A further moderating influence on temperature extremes throughout coastal Taiwan is the Kuroshio ocean current, a warm northward flow of equatorial waters that divides into two streams as it passes the island. In the high mountains, as one might suspect, altitude leads to significant decreases in temperature. Here in upland areas, ice and snow appear even as the lowlands enjoy subtropical conditions.

East Asian monsoonal conditions of recurring seasonal wind flow—affecting in particular the patterns of rainfall—are governed by the alternating high and low pressure systems that form over the oceans and continent. There is a somewhat unusual pattern of alternating monsoonal seasons in northern and southern Taiwan, with dry and rainy periods occurring at opposite times during the year. Throughout southern Taiwan, the rainy season lasts from April to September, while in the north the rains come between October and March. Each of these rainy periods is followed by relative drought. In general, rainfall is greater in the south than in the north, and there are differences in the type of rainfall as well. Falling during the cooler months, rain in northern Taiwan is steady and not particularly intense, brought by the winds that flow from the Siberian High across the relatively warm East China Sea. The areas around Keelung and Hua-lien in northeastern Taiwan, for example, experience abundant cloudy days between November and March, when the Siberian outflow leads to day after day of depressing drizzle. In southern Taiwan, by contrast, the southwestern monsoonal winds carry with them abundant moisture that is released from thunderstorm downpours during the hot summers between June and September. Rainy days during the year, moreover, are more than 50 percent greater in eastern Taiwan than they are on the Western Coastal Plain. Along the Western Coastal Plain from Taipei in the north to Kao-hsiung in the south, there is a pronounced "winter" drought caused by the moisture-deficient outflow of air from the cold and dry high pressure system that dominates in East Asia at that time of year. In general, rainfall throughout Taiwan is considered sufficient for most domesticated crops. Clouds that pile up against the mountain slopes contribute to high humidity at ground level and reduce the appearance of the sun in these areas. Relative humidities all over the island generally are high and range from 75 to 80 percent year round.

Taiwan, like other coastal locations that front on the Pacific Ocean, experiences typhoons, or intense tropical cyclones, that periodically bring in their wake abundant rain as well as destructive winds. The two to three typhoons that strike coastal Taiwan every year always enhance annual rainfall. Sometimes they are also a very destructive natural force, rivaling earthquakes in terms of the catastrophic winds and short-term flooding that directly affect human life. Damage to double-cropped rice has been particularly significant over time, far exceeding the deleterious impact of either drought or disease. Eastern Taiwan receives the brunt of Pacific typhoons between May and October, and it is here, especially, that intense rainfall coupled with steep bare hill slopes have led to extensive flooding. While rainfall patterns have not been inhibiting factors in agricultural development on Taiwan, local differences have led to a variety of human responses in settlement and agricultural patterns as Chinese pioneers and indigenous groups opened up the island's potential and had to cope with regional differences and temporal variation.

Subtropical temperature and precipitation conditions historically supported a diverse ecosystem of vegetation and animals. Striking biodiversity, however, has been one of the principal victims of Taiwan's history of human occupation, bringing in its wake an almost total elimination of all natural vegetation and wild animals from lowland areas. This has been especially true along the Western Coastal Plain and within the various intermontane basins because of the demands of continuing cultivation and settlement. The mountainous core, however, is still cloaked with magnificent forest cover, much of which has had significant commercial value. Broadleaf evergreens give way to conifers and cedars at elevations above 1,500 meters. In spite of the substantial impact of human settlement on Taiwan, more than half the island remains covered with forests.

Population

Taiwan's diminutive size has been a constant throughout the island's history, but the same obviously cannot be said for its population. With 592 people per square kilometer, the island today is the second most densely populated place on earth, exceeded only by Bangladesh ($828/km^2$) and far in excess of other densely populated areas such as South Korea ($452/km^2$), the Netherlands ($379/km^2$), and Belgium ($334/km^2$) (Population Reference Bureau 1995). This density statistic is even more striking when one considers that the bulk of the 21 million people residing on the island today are concentrated along the narrow Western Coastal Plain and in several constricted intermontane basins.

Although there are no reliable statistics on Taiwan's population until the twentieth century, when the Japanese began taking regular censuses, fragmentary evidence makes it possible to reconstruct elements of Taiwan's historical demography. Until the seventeenth century, aboriginal groups with affinities to both Malayo-Polynesian and Chinese mainland origins comprised most of Taiwan's population, although archaeological evidence clearly shows other prehistoric peoples as well. As discussed in Chapter 2, these native groups, whose origins have been traced to Southeast Asia, occupied both the coastal lowlands and the island's uplands. Records indicate as many as 70,000 aborigines living in small dispersed villages on the Western Coastal Plain in the early years of Dutch occupation, but, because of Dutch colonial policies, new migrants from the China mainland quite quickly came to outnumber the native settlers. From the early seventeenth century to the Japanese occupation in 1895 and then again after 1945, Taiwan's overall population became dominated by Han Chinese as a result of significant in-migration from several locations across the Taiwan strait. Although the making of a Taiwanese identity and its relationship to broader issues of Chinese cultural identity are complex subjects beyond the scope of this chapter, it is useful to sketch the conditions out of which a diverse population arose. The varied ethnic composition of Taiwan's population must be acknowledged for many reasons, among which are important "mainland/Taiwanese" dichotomies that have long been recognized and debated (Siu 1993; Cohen 1994; Murray and Hong 1994).

There is evidence of limited numbers of Chinese migrants crossing the Taiwan strait to trade with the aborigines as early as six hundred years ago, yet substantial migration did not begin until around 1624 and then only in the wake of Dutch colonial designs on the island. Hazardous navigation, pirate depredation, and imperial maritime prohibitions limited sailing by Chinese along the southeastern coast. Yet the pull of increasing barter trading opportunities with the aborigines and the push of hardship along coastal China spurred small numbers of merchants and settlers to chance the voyage. By 1650, the Chinese immigrant population reached perhaps 25,000 as peasants suffering famine along the coastal mainland set sail for Taiwan in quest of productive virgin land. As a

Table 1.1

Population of Taiwan

1684	100,000
1905	3,039,751
1915	3,479,922
1925	3,993,408
1935	5,212,426
1945	6,560,000
1955	9,078,000
1965	12,628,000
1975	16,150,000
1985	19,258,000
1995	21,300,000

result of Dutch colonial efforts to promote agriculture and recruit Chinese settlers, the Chinese population grew to perhaps 50,000 by the end of the Dutch
occupation in 1664, while the Dutch colonialists themselves numbered only
about 2,800, 2,200 of whom were soldiers (Hsu 1980, 17). By 1905, nearly three
hundred years after Chinese migration began to grow substantially, the number
of Taiwan residents of Chinese origin—principally from Fukien and Kuangtung—
had burgeoned to 2,492,784 and, of course, there were no Dutch. The Japanese
census of 1905 showed only 82,795 "high mountain people," two and a half
centuries after the Dutch occupation (Barclay 1954, 16). Migration and population growth at these levels led to a substantial remaking of Taiwan's natural
landscapes. In the process, the island was incorporated into China's pale, sharing
basic cultural patterns and practices, even as it retained a frontier character
distinctive to "remote" Taiwan.

In the twentieth century, first under fifty years of Japanese occupation and
then under another fifty of Chinese sovereignty as the Republic of China, population growth continued at high rates (Table 1.1).

As the figures in Table 1.1 indicate, Taiwan's population doubled in the
forty years between 1905 and 1945 and then more than tripled in the following
forty years.

Settlement and Land Use

Seen as only a fragment of a significantly larger and certainly quite diverse
China, diminutive Taiwan might appear marginal to the great Chinese historical
tale, easily tamed by human actions. The contours of Taiwan's history before
substantial migration from the China mainland is now well known from archaeological research. During the two centuries after 1683, Han settlers established
villages across Taiwan's coastal plains, into the foothills, and even penetrated the
unruly rugged mountain spine. It is they who transformed the island over the

next three centuries from a rather remote location to one increasingly linked to China. Chiao-min Hsieh skillfully introduced the concept of "sequential occupancy" to the study of Taiwan's historical geography—the imprinting of landscapes by a succession of groups over time: aborigines, Dutch and Spanish, Chinese settlers, Japanese colonialists, and the Chinese again since 1945 (1964, 123–200). Yet, a nuanced reading of the settlement history of the island demands more than broad strokes to give form to discrete periods. In recent years, local historical studies have portrayed a much more variegated picture of the process of settlement.

Before the establishment of a Dutch colony on Taiwan, there was no intensive agriculture, and therefore settlement patterns simply reflected the hunting, fishing, gathering, and small-scale farming activities of diverse native tribes. Aborigines lived in the lowlands as well as the mountainous areas in small dispersed villages, as described in Chapter 2. Candidius offers a brief description of aboriginal life in the seventeenth century that reveals the relatively benign impact on the environment (1704, 472–473):

> They use neither horse, oxen nor plough: if the rice happens to come up thicker in one place than in another, they transplant it, which is not performed without a great deal of labour and pains; they know nothing of scythes and sickles, but make use of an instrument like a knife, wherewith they cut their corn halm by halm; neither do they thresh it, but the women hang in the evening two or three small bundles over the fire to dry, and rise early in the morning to stamp it for their use the next day, and this they repeat throughout the year. . . .
>
> They hunt several ways, either with nets, with small lances . . . or with bows and arrows . . . or else they lay traps, which they cover with earth, in those places where they know the deer or other wild beasts come in great numbers.

Fourteen distinct groups lived along the western and northern coastal areas, with another nine groups occupying locations in the Central Mountain Range and along the T'ai-tung Rift Valley (Wang 1980, 31–35). Efforts at taxing the native tribes as well as other, less direct means of control led some of the aborigines to elude the Dutch by withdrawing to areas beyond Dutch control. Through increasingly engaging the aborigines in trading deerskins and in accepting Christianity, the Dutch were able to affect native life in the villages (usually called *she* in Chinese), which were typically small compact settlements encircled by bamboo thickets.

While it does not appear that the brief Dutch interlude in Taiwan itself was fatally inimical to the life of the native tribes, it is clear that the arrival and advancement of increasing numbers of Chinese immigrants confronted the aborigines with a significant threat to themselves and their habitat. From 1630 onward, it was quite clear that the Dutch did not plan on developing the kind of

European colony being developed by them at the same time in North America (Hauptman and Knapp 1977). They disregarded the Ming court's restrictive maritime policy and recruited Chinese settlers from Fukien for their Taiwan colony. In order to promote farming, the Dutch provided Chinese settlers with land, oxen, seeds, implements, and money. Especially in the areas of what today is Tainan and adjacent areas of Kao-hsiung, the Dutch provided assistance in the development of water conservancy facilities to support the growing of rice, sugar cane, tea, hemp, and wheat—all crops with which the Chinese pioneers were familiar in their mainland communities. An effort was made to survey the island and to make maps, but most mapmakers captured no more than the mere outline of the island without the details of its filling in by Chinese pioneers. Several seventeenth-century European sketch maps gave cartographic definition to the island. Yet, in accentuating how limited the Dutch colony was, they revealed their obliviousness to the extent of Chinese settlement by showing most of the island as unexplored and uninhabited. Even European maps of the eighteenth century still failed to capture the spread of Chinese settlement, which by then had become considerable.

The Dutch presence in Taiwan was centered close to present-day Tainan, at Fort Zeelandia and Fort Provintia. The site for Fort Zeelandia was a sandspit called T'ao-yuan, chosen "for the convenience of loading and unloading vessels, [rather] than of the situation of the place" (Campbell 1903, 385). In the early years, Fort Zeelandia was simply surrounded by a mere wooden palisade, but by 1632, using cement from the Chinese mainland and stone and brick from Batavia in Indonesia, an imposing fortification was completed. To the east of Fort Zeelandia, an unwalled Chinese quarter took form on the islet. Because of limited space for expansion on the narrow spit and problems with water supply, a second fort, called Provintia, was built on the coastal plain several hundred meters across the inlet. The Dutch called this coastal area Sakam and the Chinese named it Ch'ih-k'an. It is clear that the Dutch looked outward toward the China mainland rather than to the island of Taiwan itself, seeing Fort Zeelandia and Fort Provintia as emporia—trading centers—and not nodes from which an islandwide urban and concomitant transportation network would emerge, at least as long as it was in Dutch control. The selection of the site for Fort Provintia nonetheless was fortuitous in that it secured a location whose primacy was to arise as the important Chinese city of Tainan emerged over the next two centuries.

Although Spanish interest in Taiwan actually predated that of the Dutch, it was not until 1626, when Spain perceived a threat to its interests in the Philippines, that the Spanish attempted to establish a presence in northern Taiwan. Spain declared the area around present-day Keelung as property of its king and established Castle San Salvador astride one of the island's best harbors. Two years later, their ships reached present-day Tan-shui, began the building of Fort Santo Domingo, and then sailed up the Tan-shui River into what today is called the Taipei basin. To facilitate the occupation of northern Taiwan, the Spanish constructed two simple roads that linked their two bases as a means to promote missionary work among the native inhabitants. In view of a Spanish population that never exceeded 500, difficulty adjusting to an inhospitable environment, and frequent skirmishes with the aborigines, Spanish interest weakened to the point that the Dutch were easily able to expel their colonial mercantile competitors from the island in 1642.

With the passing of twenty years, the Dutch interlude on Taiwan also was to end. The expulsion of the Dutch by the Ming loyalist Cheng Ch'eng-kung (Koxinga) in 1662 led to some two hundred years of attenuated Chinese jurisdiction over the island, first in a brief interval by the Cheng family and then, subsequently, through control—however weak—as part of the Ch'ing dynasty. While the level of actual Chinese administrative control varied, increasing numbers of Chinese peasant pioneers and traders continued to bring about a fundamental remaking of Taiwan's natural landscapes. Cheng Ch'eng-kung chose the Dutch Fort Provintia as his administrative seat and Fort Zeelandia, renamed An-p'ing, as his residence. More so than the Dutch, Cheng administrators encouraged Chinese settlers to move away from the coast into wilderness areas in order to reclaim new land. Cheng troops themselves were deployed in a military colonization effort that brought much of the Southwestern Coastal Plain under cultivation. In the area in what is today Tainan and Kao-hsiung, some thirty-seven compact villages took form. These villages constituted an embryonic rural settlement landscape, a volatile frontier economy based upon the production of salt and rice as well as an unstable rural society made up essentially of men. The encroachment of Han peasants—reaching 100,000 by the end of two decades of Cheng rule—into the natural habitats of the native tribes displaced the transience of shifting cultivation and hunting with the permanence of anchored settlement sites and an incised agricultural system based upon the control of water. Elsewhere on the island, aboriginal tribes retained their life-style, still little affected by the intrusion of Han Chinese.

Reclamation by Cheng military forces increased throughout the 1670s, but the early death of Cheng Ch'eng-kung as well as the ineffectual control of the island by his son and grandson provided only a brief interlude before imperial Ch'ing forces in 1683 were able to wrest the P'eng-hu islands and the Taiwan forts from the Cheng family. From the perspective of Chinese dynastic cycles, the capture of Taiwan resolved the conclusion of the Ming dynasty and confirmed the rise of the Manchu Ch'ing dynasty that had actually begun in 1644. Although Chinese were banned from crossing the strait from either Fukien or Kuangtung between 1656 and 1684 and peasants were forcibly removed from coastal locations to inland areas between 1660 and 1681, these restrictions actually had accomplished little in restraining those attracted by Taiwan's fertile soil and other opportunities. Hsu has argued that "the draconian Ch'ing policy [actually] compelled some people on the southeast coast of China to migrate to Taiwan" (1980, 24).

With Taiwan now clearly a part of Chinese territory, it was subdivided under the jurisdiction of Fukien province into one prefecture and three counties (*hsien*): Tai-wan prefecture, with Taiwan county (around present-day Tainan), Chu-lo county (around present-day Chia-yi), and Feng-shan county (around present-day Kao-hsiung). Just as under Dutch occupation, most migrants were beyond the control of Chinese officials, but in increasing numbers they spread their settlements northward from the southwestern coast until they occupied most of the lowlands. In their wake, the lowland tribes either yielded their hunting lands and sought refuge in the distant hills or assimilated through intermarriage with Han newcomers who were settling the lowlands. For the most part, difficult mountain terrain and strong resistance from the aboriginal groups there prevented Chinese pioneers from penetrating the rugged uplands. Yet, from time to time, mountain tribes raided Chinese farmsteads in the lowlands, with much bloodshed on both sides.

In an attempt to blunt the heightened violence, Chinese administrators sought to establish a clear boundary between the Han-settled areas of the coastal plain and the mountain areas inhabited by aborigines. A line of Chinese mountain military outposts was set up for defensive purposes against tribal forays and to prevent Han peasants from penetrating into aboriginal refuges in the mountains. By 1839, Chinese were prohibited by statute from entering tribal precincts, a condition that allowed the mountain tribes to maintain their life-styles well into the later part of the nineteenth century without being overwhelmed by Chinese migrants. A significant number of the Chinese settlers continued to spend part of the year on the island, before returning seasonally to their home village on the mainland. Varying natural conditions, distance from imperial authority, presence or absence of a threat from the native population, pioneer reclamation organiza-tion, among other influences, helped guide the substantial patterns of Chinese pioneer settlement and reclamation on the island (Knapp 1976). Chinese referred to those aborigines beyond the Chinese pale as *sheng fan* ("raw" or uncivilized aborigines) while those who became sinicized were known as *shu fan* ("ripened" or civilized aborigines).

Two centuries of Chinese agricultural colonization led to intensive cultivation of the western lowlands and the creation of cultural landscapes reminiscent of those across the Taiwan strait. On an island as small as Taiwan, it may come as a surprise that rural settlement patterns and cultural landscapes vary as much as they do. In both southern and eastern Taiwan nucleated villages predominate while in the northern parts of the island rural settlements are more dispersed with individual houses widely separated from each other. These differences reflect not only natural conditions, such as the availability of water, but also the degree of aboriginal threat at the time of village formation, and land tenure practices. At least one geographer has seen the seasonality of precipitation as the critical factor in guiding village form: "in the northern part of Formosa where there is a fair amount of rain in every month throughout the year people are free to select their abodes. But in the south where the dry season lasts as long as half a year

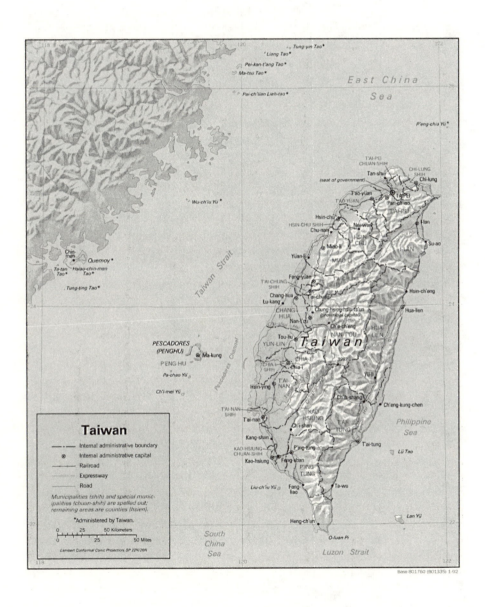

Map of Present-Day Taiwan

Figure 1. This late seventeenth-century Chinese map focuses on the southwestern plain, showing palisaded towns, numerous villages, and anchorages along the coast. In the north (on the left of the map), a walled outpost is shown.

Source: Unknown.

through the winter season when often there will be not a drop of rain for several months, water supply is a serious problem for the inhabitants" (Chen 1959). It has been asserted that settlement in grasslands, such as those in southern Taiwan, led to compact villages, while in forested areas villagers opted for scattered settlements. Environmental determinism of this type, however, has only limited use because settlers indeed frequently had a range of options open to them rather than the narrow constraint of an environmental straitjacket.

Scholars who have studied Chinese pioneer settlement strategies on the Taiwan frontier differ in their conclusions concerning the forms and structure of village settlements that emerged. For the most part, Chinese migrants to Taiwan came from Fukien and Kuangtung, where compact villages based on lineage relationships were the norm. One might assume that pioneers would have chosen to reconstitute a familiar village form if conditions allowed, even without a threat from natives or if water were readily available. Yet such was not always the case. When viewed broadly, it appears clear that migrants from these areas of the mainland came in somewhat successive waves that spread them in increasingly less satisfactory locations: Fukien pioneers from Ch'uan-chou settled along the lower coastal plain, those of Chang-chou origin occupied areas farther upslope but still on the plain. Those identified as belonging to the Chinese subethnic group known as the Hakka, or K'o-chia, moved into the more rugged foothills. Separate regions of settlement, some have said, reflect an attempt by homesteaders to avoid the inevitable conflict that would pit one group against another if settlement were more mixed under frontier conditions. In such a scenario, the Hakka—as latecomers—were forced to settle in the less favorable parts of the island. Yet it seems reasonable that Hakka, who actually were migrating from the hilly areas of Kuangtung, purposefully planted settlements in hilly areas of Taiwan that were similar to their home environments, rough and remote areas that other migrants might have found inhospitable.

On the southwestern plains—the present-day areas of Tainan and adjacent Kao-hsiung *hsien*—compact villages populated by Chinese settlers emerged from "state"-sponsored colonization because of both Dutch and Cheng family efforts during their brief interludes. Under the Dutch, all land that radiated out from Fort Zeelandia was vested in the name of the Dutch monarch as "crown land" and served to organize colonial settlement patterns. Attempting to go beyond trading deerskins, dried venison, and rattan with the aborigines, the Dutch promoted the growing of sugar by Chinese peasants. The deep wells needed to blunt seasonal water shortages provided the life-giving nodes for increasing numbers of nucleated Chinese villages that were established around the communal wellheads.

Upon the expulsion of the Dutch in 1662, Dutch "crown land" (*wang-t'ien*) was transformed into "government land" (*cheng-t'ien*) with the village life of peasants changing very little. The Cheng family, furthermore, promoted land reclamation through the opening up of outlying virgin land by military colonization. Some thirty-seven nucleated villages can be identified as having originated under these officially sanctioned Cheng settlement schemes (Hsu 1980, 25). The organization of other nucleated villages under Cheng family military colonization further helped increase the overall density of rural settlement in the southwest, but elsewhere on the island there was only isolated and random rural settlement by individual pioneers.

In virgin areas of northern Taiwan, rather remote from authority, unauthorized and often clandestine pioneer activity occurred, leading to a great variety of rural settlement forms. One important exception was on the T'ao-yuan plain, where, with imperial consent, a patent system led to a mixture of nucleated and dispersed rural settlement patterns that might appear at variance with the dictates of natural conditions. Here, rainfall was relatively abundant year round, with a summer maximum but only moderate amounts during the cool months of the year. Pioneer settlers clearly had more options in terms of village site selection than settlers in southern Taiwan, who, recruited by the Dutch or the Cheng family and mindful of the need for year-round sources of drinking water from wells, often lived in compact rural settlements as they did on the mainland. Early eighteenth-century pioneers entering the T'ao-yuan area, furthermore, were not tormented by hostile aborigines and thus had no critical need for easily protected nucleated settlements. The relative ubiquity of water in the T'ao-yuan area certainly provided settlers with a broad range of settlement options. Indeed, the first Chinese settlement in the area was a compact hamlet built immediately adjacent to Nan-k'ang *she*, one of four aboriginal villages surrounded by bamboo thickets on the plain. In time, the aboriginal village was absorbed into the Chinese village. Surrounding another aboriginal village, K'eng-tzu *she*, Chinese settlement, on the other hand, was rather dispersed with simple dwellings built some distance from each other. In some cases, migrating Hakka kinsmen, known for their clannishness, did form nucleated villages like their home villages on the mainland in the uplands of T'ao-yuan and nearby areas of Hsin-chu and Miao-li *hsien*.

For the most part, an imperially sanctioned patent system guided rural settlement on the T'ao-yuan plain, even though there existed at the same time settlement by individual pioneers who negotiated settlement and cultivation rights directly with aborigines or squatted on virgin lands. Ill-defined expanses of T'ao-yuan were granted individuals under patent or estate certificates (*k'en chao* or *chih chao*) that promised "ownership" if the land were reclaimed and cultivated. Because of the demands of wet-rice paddy cultivation, patentees were given a ten-year reclamation period until 1723, when the period was reduced to six years. Tax relief was granted for a three-year period in order to stimulate reclamation.

In order to carry out the resculpting of land and the creation of an articulated water conservancy system, patentees (*k'en-shou* or *yeh-hu*) recruited landless peasants from Fukien for frontier land reclamation, employing land tenure practices that were common on the mainland (Knapp 1980, 61 ff.). Patent-inspired land reclamation brought the *i-t'ien liang-chu* ("one field, two owners") system

Figure 2. **Probably based upon a crude sea chart, this eighteenth-century Dutch map of "Eyland Formosa" names many places along the island's coast. The drawing of the tributaries of several rivers reveals the fruits of expeditions into the interior uplands.**

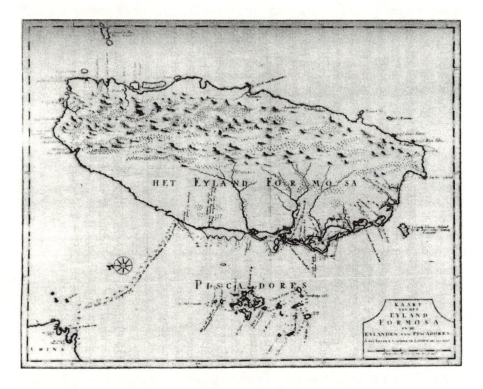

Source: C. Imbault-Huart. *L'ile Formose: Histoire et description.* Paris: Ernest Lerous, 1893, p. 33.

to Taiwan. Although the patentee retained proprietary title to the subsoil (*t'ien-ku, t'ien-ken,* or *t'ien-ti*), he transferred rights to the surface (*t'ien-p'i* or *t'ien-mien*) to a tenant. Surface and subsoil rights were independent of each other, and one could be alienated without affecting the other. Because patentees were usually absentee, tenant holders of subsoil rights could expand cultivable area and in general maximize their options. An annual rent payment, called *ta-tzu* ("primary rent") was paid to the patentee, also called *ta-tzu hu* ("primary rent keeper").

Domesticating Space

Villages are mappable spatial domains, organic entities that generally increase in size as the dwellings of residents expand and as other structures, including lineage or clan halls, temples, storage sheds, and other functional economic and social buildings, are added. The domestication of space involved the selection of propitious building sites, the process of construction itself, and the arrangement of rooms in dwellings in order to express normative hierarchical relationships within the family. Simple dwellings of bamboo, reed, or grass matting met the shelter needs of the earliest Chinese settlers, who were usually single males who saw themselves as transients on the island. Sketchy pictorial representations from the eighteenth century portray the common houses of early settlers nestled among the aboriginal *she*. Because they expected to return to their home villages on the mainland, the earliest pioneers required only simple shelter. As land was improved and water conservancy facilities expanded, it is likely that there was a transition from sojourner settlements made up of unrelated males occupying "temporary" shelters to more stable and permanent villages composed of families living in houses. It is revealing that the Chinese words for home and family (*chia*) are the same. The ideograph represents a roof sheltering a pig, a clear indication of the domestication of space and the prominence of the pig in household life. Over time, as resources allowed and domestic circumstances changed, more substantial dwellings were necessarily built using locally available materials and the peasants' own hands.

As is the case today in most areas of China, it is likely that simple rectangular dwellings sufficed during early stages of family formation in Taiwan. As the size and composition of households changed from nuclear to stem and, much later, joint or extended forms, this was revealed in the extent and structure of village dwellings that preserved balance, symmetry, and axiality, three fundamental characteristics of Chinese architecture in general. Balance and symmetry were maintained by having the rooms total odd numbers, usually one or three, and by placing a door in the center of the front wall. Axiality was embodied in the way space was organized to represent hierarchy, principally the seniority of generations living within the dwelling. As the number and sex of children as well as a family's fortunes changed, so did the construction of new space which was sometimes ordered to separate public from private space. Guided by idealized family norms in the nineteenth and twentieth centuries especially, some rural dwellings grew first to a U-shape, surrounding an open courtyard, and then later to much larger and complex ramified structures. Growth could be in either a lateral or forward direction, depending on the socioeconomic circumstances of a household. The houses of peasant farmers generally only lengthened laterally while the dwellings of ambitious gentry stretched to substantial depth, with numerous paired wings, built to house multiple generations and more than a hundred family members.

Construction of early Chinese dwellings, like those of the aborigines, was eased because of the abundance of bamboo and other grasses. Bamboo and wood splints could be used as struts and lathes to constitute walls, while rice straw and other grasses were tied using pliant rattan to fabricate a roof. Even in the middle

Figure 3. **Printed in a 1717 *Chu-lo hsien-chih* [Chu-lo county gazetteer], this perspective drawing shows the intermingling of Chinese and aboriginal settlement along the Western Coastal Plain. Chinese dwellings are set directly on the ground while those of the indigenous people are raised on pilings.**

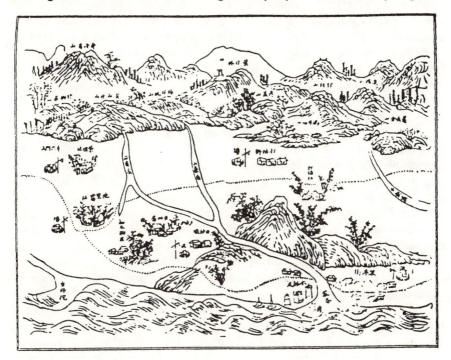

Source: Chen Meng-lin. *Chu-lo hsien-chih*, 1717.

of the twentieth century, bamboo-plaited walls covered with mud plaster exceeded all other walling material in rural dwellings. Adobe bricks, as in most areas of the China mainland, also have been common building materials in Taiwan. While kiln-dried bricks have existed on Taiwan since the late seventeenth century, they were generally restricted to the dwellings of the wealthy, who obtained them from shippers who used them as ballast on trips to the island. Even as recently as 1952, only some 10 percent of farmhouses were of fired brick. By 1958 this had increased to 25 percent as a result of the successful Land-to-the-Tiller program, which increased rural wealth (Kirby 1960, 149). Dwellings are humanized spaces that mirror the changing nature of families. No striking structural elements separate dwellings on Taiwan from their precursors on the mainland, yet the heterogeneity of settlements clearly reveals the substantial variety of forms that Chinese families and communities take as they populate an area. For most of Taiwan's history, dwellings and village settlements grew largely in response to increases in population and the intensification of rice production. In the fifty-odd years since 1945, however, Taiwan's predominantly village-based agricultural economy has been transformed into a mature, globally significant economy based upon capital- and technology-intensive industrialization. Taiwan's rural environments have been substantially recast in the process. The number of farm households fell from 51 percent in 1953 to less than 20 percent in 1990 as agriculture's share of the net domestic product decreased from 34 percent to only 4 percent. The dispersal of industry into Taiwan's villages has been a critical factor in this transition, at once raising farm household income because of off-farm, nonagricultural work for village laborers, but also making it possible for farmers to retain their residence in the countryside.

Village projects throughout the 1950s and 1960s that were promoted by the Chinese–American Joint Commission on Rural Reconstruction led to improvements in sanitation, health, and nutrition as well as transportation and communications, all of which contributed to reducing the disparity between urban and rural life. Over the past quarter century, the physical appearance of the countryside has changed dramatically. In a kind of village sprawl, increasing numbers of multistory structures serving as both residence and workshop have proliferated as the economic base of the countryside has changed dramatically. Abandoned and dilapidated older farmhouses, numerous shops, and newly built temples all alter the configuration of countless villages and proclaim as well rural affluence.

Many of Taiwan's villages today exhibit an untidy appearance, a disorder that stems from the volume of raw materials and refuse associated with manufacturing that are strewn throughout the countryside. There is, moreover, much contamination that is not simply relatively benign visual or noise pollution. Taiwan's Environmental Protection Administration revealed in 1987 that some 15 percent of farmland islandwide was contaminated by heavy metals disgorged into fields by wastewater that flowed from decentralized electroplating workshops. Unregulated pesticide, food processing, paper, and dyeing factories similarly have defiled drinking water sources all over the island. Small rural factories, often unregistered and unregulated, that disregard building and environmental protection codes have been major polluters in rural Taiwan over the past decade and a half, fouling not only productive paddy fields but also residential environments. Since the mid-1980s, there has been an increasing awareness of the environmental and social consequences of accelerating rural industrialization, and efforts have been made to ameliorate the accumulation of environmental damage from the past. Taiwan's villages today are patchworks of structures, transitional settlement forms in which residents are both farmers and factory workers.

Nodes and Linkages in Taiwan's Spatial Network

From the seventeenth century onward, the emergence of a village-based agricultural economy that transformed the island's landscapes was accompanied by an evolution of urban and transportation systems that both anchored and facilitated Taiwan's subsequent transition in the twentieth century. The evolving network of nodes (towns and cities) and linkages (transportation routes) from earliest times to the 1970s has been well described (Hsu, Pannell, and Wheeler 1980).

Some of China's first modern roads and railroads were constructed in Taiwan in the latter quarter of the nineteenth century. Yet it was left to the Japanese in the half century after 1895 to build on these incipient elements and articulate the construction of a comprehensive transport network linking the urban focal points. By 1906, Taiwan had in place the outline of a transportation system that was to serve the island's commercial needs well into the 1960s. Before 1874, cities, towns, and villages were poorly connected and insular in terms of connectivity. The extension of roads and rails increased connectivity as well as accessibility among urban centers, profoundly contributing to economic growth islandwide.

In recent decades, the accelerated expansion of metropolitan centers such as Taipei and Kao-hsiung has involved not only urban sprawl but the accompanying destruction of agricultural land. Taiwan's urban population was only 5 million in 1961, slightly over half the total population. Today, three-fourths of the island's population lives in urban or periurban areas with nearly 50 percent of the total population residing in the Taipei, Kao-hsiung, and Taichung metropolitan areas. Historically, much of Taiwan's urban growth was unplanned and accompanied by a relatively predictable assemblage of problems. Within cities and towns, nonexistent or ineffective zoning controls permitted rather chaotic cityscapes to emerge without the infrastructure necessary to provide for a reasonable quality of life. Recent years have seen government development plans structured so as to anticipate future needs, even though it is clear that problems are more obvious than are their solutions. The completion of the North–South Freeway in 1978 catapulted Taiwan's transportation system to modern levels by creating a modern limited-access transportation conduit that significantly alleviated the congestion that had increasingly clogged the existing two-lane highways. By 1986, freeway crowding and overloading on the rail system, however, forced attention on the need for further dramatic expansion of the transportation network. A complementary and costly northern freeway, running through quite rugged terrain, was subsequently completed in 1993, but it too served only to meet short-term needs.

Additional plans more recently have been directed at untangling an increasingly overtaxed situation. These involve the construction of high-speed road and railway systems that will encircle the island. In addition, continuing attention is being directed at new town construction and industrial zone formation, which are expected to mitigate overcrowding conditions that have grown worse as Taiwan's urban and rural economies continue to unfold. Too often, however, disorganized growth continues to outrun the policies and plans being developed to guide growth. Comprehensive plans for new projects all too often seem to lead

Figure 4. **Extracted from a Chinese atlas that reputedly follows the work of Jesuits, this 1862 map reveals substantial settlement not only in the basins but throughout the Western Coastal Plain.**

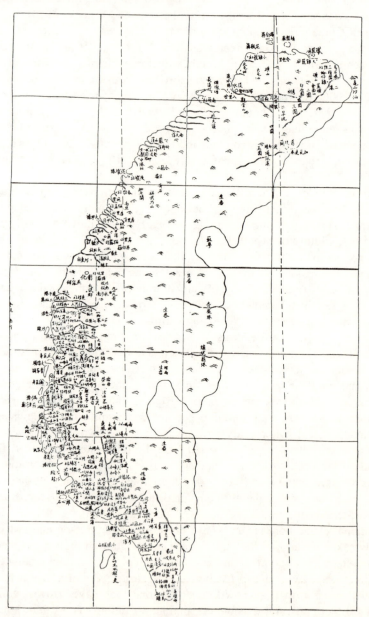

Source: C. Imbault-Huart. *L'ile Formose: Histoire et description.* Paris: Ernest Leroux, 1893, following p. 8.

to a resurgence of old problems. The financial and social costs of upgrading transport facilities today are hotly debated. The capital requirements necessary for the construction of intra- and interurban transport systems are staggering. The growth of population in recent decades has swamped the capacity of transportation facilities islandwide. Planners today beckon with schemes that will shrink distance significantly, perhaps reducing the time to travel overland from Taipei to Kao-hsiung to only ninety minutes.

No longer insignificantly small, no longer obscurely remote, Taiwan today is a place transformed. Spanning space has become less the issue than has the need to contract time. Seen as only a fragment of a significantly larger and certainly quite diverse China, Taiwan remains rather diminutive, but the island is hardly marginal to Chinese modernization. Taiwan's physical environment has been tamed and modified as an interconnected system of rural and urban settlements. A sophisticated economy and society has been linked well to the world beyond through the deployment of knowledge, capital, technology, and human resources. As a pivotal component of Greater China, Taiwan has indeed become too big to ignore.

References

Barclay, George W. 1954. *Colonial Development and Population in Taiwan*. Princeton: Princeton University Press.

Campbell, William, ed. 1903. *Formosa Under the Dutch: Descriptions from Contemporary Records*. London: Kegan Paul, Trench, Trubner.

Candidius, George. 1704. "A Short Account of the Island of Formosa in the Indies, Situated Near the Coast of China: and of the Manners, Customs, and Religions of the Inhabitants." In *A Collection of Voyages and Travels, Some First Printed from Original Manuscripts,* comp. Awnsham Churchill. London.

Chen Cheng-hsiang. 1959. *Atlas of Land Use in Taiwan*. Taipei: Fu-min Geographical Institute.

Ch'en Ch'iu-k'un [Chen Qiukun]. 1987. "Landlord and Tenant: Varieties of Land Tenure in Frontier Taiwan, 1680–1900." Ph.D. dissertation, Stanford University.

Cohen, Myron L. 1994. "Being Chinese: The Peripheralization of Traditional Identity." In *The Living Tree: The Changing Meaning of Being Chinese Today*, ed. Tu Weiming. Stanford: Stanford University Press.

Hauptman, Laurence M., and Ronald G. Knapp. 1977. "Dutch-Aboriginal Interaction in New Netherland and Formosa: An Historical Geography of Empire." *Proceedings of the American Philosophical Society* 121 (April): 166–182.

Hsieh, Chiao-min. 1964. *Taiwan—Ilha Formosa: A Geography in Perspective*. London: Butterworths.

Hsu, Wen-hsiung. 1980. "From Aboriginal Island to Chinese Frontier: The Development of Taiwan Before 1683." In Knapp, ed., *China's Island Frontier*, pp. 3–29.

Hsu, Yi-rong Ann, Clifton W. Pannell, and James O. Wheeler. 1980. "The Development and Structure of Transportation Networks in Taiwan: 1600–1972." In Knapp, ed., *China's Island Frontier*, pp. 167–201.

Kirby, E. Stuart. 1960. *Rural Progress in Taiwan*. Taipei: Chinese-American Joint Commission on Rural Reconstruction.

Knapp, Ronald G. 1976. "Chinese Frontier Settlement in Taiwan." *Annals of the Association of American Geographers* 66 (March): 43–59.

——. 1986. "The Rural Dwelling on China's Taiwan Frontier." In *China's Traditional Rural Architecture: A Cultural Geography of the Common House*, ed. Knapp. Honolulu: University of Hawaii Press, pp. 88–107.

Knapp, Ronald G., ed. 1980. *China's Island Frontier: Studies in the Historical Geography of Taiwan*. Honolulu: University of Hawaii Press.

Murray, Stephen O., and Keelung Hong. 1994. *Taiwanese Culture, Taiwanese Society*. Lanham, MD: University Press of America.

Population Reference Bureau. 1995. *1995 World Population Data Sheet*. Washington: PRB.

Shepherd, John R. 1981. "Plains Aborigines and Chinese Settlers on the Taiwan Frontier in the Seventeenth and Eighteenth Centuries." Ph.D. dissertation, Stanford University.

Siu, Helen F. 1993. "Cultural Difference and the Politics of Difference in South China." *Daedulus* 122.2 (Spring), no. 274: 19–43.

"Taiwan: Too Big to Ignore." 1990. *New York Times*, November 10, sec. A, p. 22.

Vertente, Christine, Hsu Hsueh-chi, and Wu Mi-cha. 1991. *Hsien-min te tsu-chi* [The authentic story of Taiwan]. Knokke, Belgium: Mappamundi.

Wang, I-shou. 1980. "Cultural Contact and the Migration of Taiwan's Aborigine: A Historical Perspective." In Knapp, ed., *China's Island*, pp. 31–54.

2

The Politics of Taiwan Aboriginal Origins

Michael Stainton

**An "Aborigine" practicing traditional crafts at the
Formosan Aboriginal Cultural Village.**

The past exists only in our present. This means that it is problematic both as history and as "history"—not just what we can know about the past but how our own cultural structures and intentionalities lead us to represent and interpret it. Malinowski's insight that history as myth is a charter for social action is now a standard assumption in the social sciences, especially anthropology.

Maurice Halbwachs noted: "The past cannot be reborn, but we can fathom what it was like, and we are most successful if we have at our command well established landmarks" (1997: 103). This reminds us that, while history as myth may be labile, there is a bedrock of somethingness—"landmarks"—that limits even as it becomes the basis for the inventedness of our constructions. When we deal with prehistory (or, more accurately, pretextual history) the problem is more complex in that we often do not have many well-established landmarks. Writing about the prehistory of the Pacific, John Terrell (1986: 9) highlights the problems of "landmarks" in his "rules of model building": "First we have got to decide what is important, that is, which features of the situation or problem being represented need to be included. Second, we must explain how all the features selected are believed to go together."

The question of the origin of the Austronesian languages and peoples of Taiwan is just such a case. Indeed, even the extent to which either of these exist as useful categories, or can be equated, is a matter of debate.[1] When landmarks are so contested, we do well to address models as a category of Malinowski's myths. Models or metaphors of science, or the social sciences, are like myths in that "they provide human beings with a representation of the world and the forces which are supposed to govern it" (François Jacob, quoted in Terrell 1986: 4).

This chapter explores theories of Taiwan aboriginal origins. My topic here is not the empirical "landmarks" but, rather, the social fact of how these contested landmarks of the distant past are used as charters for the present in Taiwan and China. I call this usage "the politics of Taiwan aboriginal origins." Nonetheless, there are landmarks, and it would be disingenuous to say that the linguistic and archaeological discoveries of the past sixty years in Taiwan and China have provided us with no landmarks on which constructions of Taiwan aboriginal origins can be based. However, readers who wish to pursue "the facts" are advised to read the debates raised in the books included in the reference list.

Just the Facts

Some uncontested landmarks are the following. There are today at least 380,000 people in Taiwan, now officially called "Taiwan Aboriginal Peoples," who are speakers of Austronesian languages. Their dozen extant, and dozen extinct, languages are agreed to be the most archaic of the Indonesian branch (at least) of that vast language family. Their cultures and physical attributes, which are quite varied, also identify them as Austronesian peoples. There have been human settlements in Taiwan since at least fifteen thousand years ago, in the palaeolithic age. By the seventeenth century there were several ethnolinguistically distinct groups settled in Taiwan. However, we cannot yet explain the development of such ethnic diversity.

In the early 1960s a series of site finds in Taiwan enabled archaeologists to organize these landmark discoveries into a pattern paralleling developments in ceramics in Southeast China, up to the beginning of the bronze age in China, after which the patterns diverge. This progression of "prehistoric ceramic horizons" from "corded ware" through "Lungshanoid" to "geometric"[2] is now generally uncontested. Clearly, contemporary model builders have more information on which to build models, but this still brings us back to the world of models as myths.

Three models of Taiwan aboriginal origins are presented here, as are two or three representative proponents for each model. These are not evaluated or deconstructed, but simply have their "politics" summarized at the ends of the sections.

Theories of Southern Origin

In 1889 the Dutch Indologist Hendrik Kern proposed the "southern origin" theory of the Austronesian languages. He suggested the bearers of this language family came from peninsular Southeast Asia and moved eastward through the Indonesian and Philippine archipelagos, northward to Taiwan, and eastward into the Pacific. In Kern's time Indonesia was a Dutch colony. Is it simply by coincidence that the suggestion of a Dutch Indologist privileges this area and ignores China? In the southern origin theory Taiwan is a dead end, valuable as a living museum of archaic Indonesian languages.

The southern origin theory was convincing to Canadian missionary George Leslie Mackay, who lived in Taiwan from 1872 to 1901. It is not likely that Mackay had time to read Kern, so we assume that he came to his conclusions independently. Mackay had a lively and informed interest in the ethnology of the island, especially its aboriginal inhabitants. He states that "the aboriginal tribes . . . are all descendants of settlers from around the Malay Archipelago" (1895: 94). He presented five arguments for this:

1. "Aboriginal tradition" of legends "that their forefathers came from a southerly direction";
2. "Consensus of foreign opinion" that "travelers see in the various tribes of Formosa the features and manners of the inhabitants of Luzon, Polynesia, the Malay Peninsula";
3. "Natural migration" of northward-flowing ocean currents, illustrated with instances of boats from the Philippines and Pelau washed onto Taiwan's shores;

4. "Habits and customs" including headhunting and tattooing;
5. "Physical features . . . characteristic of the islanders belonging to the lower races."

Mackay conjectures "that numerous adventurers, fishermen, and traders from the islands south and east of the China Sea, and others from the north and east of Formosa, with perhaps a few from the mainland, entered the island at intervals, and formed what is now called the aboriginal race, and that race is Malayan" (1895: 98).

Anthropologist Janet Montgomery McGovern, a student of R.R. Marett, spent the years 1916 to 1918 in Formosa.[3] She argued for "an Indonesian origin of the aborigines of Formosa" in similar terms. She mentions Amis legends and rituals commemorating the landing of ancestors in boats "from the south" (1922: 132). McGovern goes on to suggest that, because of centuries of isolation from their original stock and loss of seafaring skills, the Formosan aborigines are a "decadent" people. She further predicts, as did Mackay, that:

> It seems probable [that] under the dominance of the Japanese, the aborigines of Formosa will in a few decades, or, at the longest, in a century or two, cease to exist as a people. Unless, indeed, their dream of being rescued from the rule of both Chinese and Japanese by "White Saviours from the West" ever comes true. (1922: 198)

The Japanese saw themselves as saviors of these same aborigines, whom they fenced off from the Chinese areas of Taiwan, restricting all communication between the "savage areas" and the rest of Taiwan. Japanese anthropologists continued the southern origin tradition. Mabuchi Toichi did his life's work in Taiwan and is buried there. Mabuchi (1974: 66, 90) argued that waves of peoples migrated from Southeast Asia and that "aboriginal Formosa seems to represent an earlier, if not the earliest, phase of Malaysian cultures" (1974: 66). He recounts an Amis origin myth that says their ancestors came from Lan-yu, a small island southeast of Taiwan.

Miyamoto Nobuto also spent most of his working life in Taiwan. Miyamoto suggests that, while archaeological evidence is not yet conclusive as to the relationship between ancient culture sites and contemporary Taiwan aborigines, it seems likely that the ancestors of Taiwan's aboriginal people immigrated to Taiwan in the stone age (1985: 40).

Miyamoto also uses Ketagalan and Amis migration voyage myths to support the southern origin theory and notes that the Kavelan tribe of Ilan had similar accounts (1985: 74–75, 212). He recounts the origins of the Yami from the Batanes Islands north of Luzon and the convenience of the chain of islands from Luzon to Taiwan for ancient voyagers. He concludes: "Because of this we can affirm that all the aboriginal people of Taiwan immigrated to Taiwan via the aforesaid route. But if we wanted to propose which tribe immigrated at what time, we would have great difficulty." Like Mabuchi, Miyamoto had a strong emotional link with Taiwan; he wrote, "in the field of scholarship Taiwan is my birthplace" and to be among aboriginal people "is like returning to my own hometown" (1985: 222).

There are some common points of discourse between the Japanese and the Westerners, which I call the politics of the southern origin theory:[4]

- Taiwan as an isolated island, at the margins, an end of the line
- Aboriginal myths of origin as important evidence
- Successive waves of immigration, mainly from the south
- Aboriginal people as ancient remnants (even a doomed race)
- A discontinuity of present with ancient past
- The Asian (Chinese) mainland as generally irrelevant
- A conceptual and historical separation between China and Taiwan
- Aboriginal people as non-Chinese needing help from non-Chinese against the Chinese invaders
- Taiwan as home.

The southern origin theory thus arose and was promoted in situations in which an ethnic and political border was drawn between Taiwan and China, and more specifically between Taiwan Aboriginal Peoples as non-Chinese against the Chinese of Taiwan. This was clearly congenial for the Japanese colonial era, and for missionary or anthropologist foreigners who see themselves as friends of the oppressed.

I must confess that I have also supported the southern theory, so fitting neatly into this pro-Taiwan/help the aboriginals foreigners box! In my master's thesis in 1995 I wrote:

> The non-Chinese indigenous people of Taiwan are over 20 different Austronesian peoples who came to Taiwan in several migrations, most from the Philippines, over the past six thousand years. The archaeology, linguistics and anthropology of Taiwan Aboriginal peoples is voluminous in Chinese and Japanese, and it is not within the scope of this thesis to review this literature except to note how the very issue of origins has long been a part of the hegemonic discourse on Aboriginal people in Taiwan.

For aboriginal people in Taiwan, establishing the boundary between themselves and the Chinese was a constant issue in the period up to the early 1990s. ROC nationalist "history" insisted that they were "a branch of the Chinese nation." It is in this context that an article in the short-lived *Tai-yuan-jen* (Taiwan Indigenous People Alliance) published by Wu Ming-yi, an Amis historian and Presbyterian minister, presents the southern origin theory as fact (1988: 30).[5] The writer recounts the cultural similarities with local people encountered by Amis soldiers serving the Japanese in Southeast Asia, reports another Amis legend of origin about a couple blown to Taiwan from the south by a great flood, who "became the ancestors of the Taiwanese." Linking ancestors of the Amis to the Pei-nan culture stone coffin sites of east coast T'ai-tung, the article concludes that the direct ancestors of his Amis people were in Taiwan at least forty-five hundred years ago.

Drawing a line between Taiwan's prehistory and China is also a counterargument to Chinese claims that "Taiwan has been a part of China since ancient times." It should not be surprising, then, that Shih Ming, the doyen of Taiwan independence, who spent most of his life in exile in Japan, argued strongly in favor of the southern origin theory. In his *Four-Hundred-Year History of the Taiwanese People* Shih Ming pours contempt on theories of northern origin:

> To simply rely on [cultural similarities] is not enough to conclude that Taiwan aborigines without exception migrated from mainland China. If we look at the background of all these arguments, rather than saying they are seeking truth we should say that they are imitating scholarship in the mythogenesis of a political agenda. They arbitrarily seek to make out that from prehistoric times Taiwan has had a continuing and close relationship with mainland China. This kind of false scholarship, which tends to political advocacy is not worth discussing, and should be strongly refuted. (1980: 15)

We should note that Shih Ming's belief in southern origin also arises from his own "scholarship that tends to political advocacy," and this is exactly what makes it worth discussing here.

Theories of Northern Origin

In 1996 *People's Daily* (overseas ed., April 19, 1996, p. 5) carried a photo of and brief article on "A dugout canoe that drifted from Taiwan" and was on exhibit in the "Fukien and Taiwan Prehistoric Cultural Links" exhibit hall in the Tuang-shan Museum. The article suggests that "this canoe is probably several decades old, proving that Taiwan still has dugout canoes." In the text we also find the assertion:

> Anthropological data proves that the ancestors of the *Kao-shan-tzu* [high mountain people] in early times used dugout canoes as their maritime means of transport, coming from the continent [*ta-lu*] to Taiwan. The Ami people of eastern Taiwan still preserve ancient dugout canoes, and have legends that their ancestors came in this dugout canoe from the south of the continent.

While this popular report cannot represent serious Chinese scholarship, it does demonstrate in the extreme Terrell's "reduced amount of information believed to capture the essence of the situation" (1986: 9). The only dugout canoes in Taiwan are for tourist purposes on Sun Moon Lake; the Amis use bamboo rafts, and the Amis origin legend says they came from the south, or from Lan-yu. The dugout in question, if we accept the story, floated from the southeast toward China. None of this really matters since the story supports two a priori truths constant in Chinese minorities discourse, which, in circular form, validate this "evidence." The two truths are the continuing primitive nature of the "*Kao-shan-tzu,*" as ethnographic fossils, and their Chinese origin.

In 1929 Lin Hui-hsiang, an anthropologist at Amoy University, visited Taiwan and wrote a monograph for the Academia Sinica.[6] *The Primitive Aborgines of Formosa* is important as the first Chinese research on Taiwan Aboriginal Peoples. Lin's conclusions on their origins concur with Japanese views of his day—the primitive nature of the aborigines, and their southern origin:

> Taiwan's savage tribes [*fan-tzu*] migrated to the island in the stone age from the south seas [*Nan-yang*]. Having had very little contact with outside cultures until recent times they have preserved many original features, so truly are excellent representatives of primitive peoples [*wei-k'ai min-tzu*]. By studying these tribes we can hope to learn much about the situation of primitive peoples. (1930: Introduction)

> The savages belong to the Malay or brown race ... and the legends of the savages also talk about coming from the south, which confirms this. Most Japanese scholars hold this view, and from my own observations I firmly believe this is correct. ... The savage tribes definitely have migrated from the south seas, but their time of arrival must have been very early, because the whole island has stone age sites, both on the plains and in the mountains. Among the stone tools there is one kind of stone adze very similar to those discovered in Shensi, which might prove that the savage tribes who did not enter Taiwan have some relationship with the Han people of the continent. (1930: 1, 4)

Lin's acceptance of the southern origin theory seems unremarkable considering his training in the Philippines, and the fact that he based his conclusion mainly on Japanese materials. It is significant, however, that he clearly expresses one of the two basic assumptions of later Chinese discourse—the primitive nature of the "savage tribes" of Formosa. While he notes similarity between Taiwan and Shensi adzes, he places this information within his southern origin model. This again seems natural given the hegemony of this theory in 1929, but is significant in that he is working from his data and not from a "Chinese" nationalist program. Later Chinese writers take such similarity as immediate and unproblematic "proof" of the Chinese origins of Taiwan's peoples.

Lin's monograph also exhibits a significant feature that becomes standard in Chinese discussion of Taiwan Aboriginal Peoples. In an appendix he reviews the classic Chinese texts that appear to relate to Taiwan (presumably the referant of "Yi-chou" and "Liu-ch'iu"). Lin shows that he is more of a scholar than later

Chinese authors because he does not immediately draw a direct line to the present and conclude that this proves that Taiwan has been linked to China since ancient times. But this also relates Lin neatly to the politics of theories of origins—in 1929 China was not at war with Japan, and Taiwan was not considered a lost province of China. The ancient link was an interesting possibility raised in these texts, not a dogma to be affirmed.

By 1936 research into national minorities was a major theme of Chinese anthropology, and Lin wrote *Chinese Ethnohistory* (Chung-kuo min-tzu-shih). In Chapter 6, in his discussion of "which modern people are the Pai Yueh," he reviews a number of different possibilities (Lin 1936: 115ff). Among them are the possibility that their descendants are found in the southern Min people, who have many physical features different from those of northern Chinese (*Chung-yuan jen*). He then makes a new and interesting suggestion:

> So is it possible that there is a relationship between the Pai Yueh and the Malay race? While the Malay race must have moved south from the continent in early times, is it possible that some stayed? Today in Taiwan the savage tribes still retain the custom of tattooing, and belong to the Malay race. Their physical appearance has many similarities to modern Min-Yueh people, so might they be related to the ancient Yueh peoples? . . . Today in riverine estuaries of Fukien and Kwangtung are another Yueh people, the Tanka ("boatpeople"). Might some of them have left the Yueh tribes and set out on the seas? (1936: 117)

Lin presents this as conjecture, and is the first person to raise this possibility, now seriously pursued by linguist Robert Blust (Blust in Goodenough 1996: 117–137).

After liberation, Lin also published an article, "Research into Taiwan Stone-age Tools," which stated that one could conclude that Neolithic man in Taiwan had close relations with the southeast continental coast, and floated across the sea from the southeast continental coast (*Kao-shan-tzu chien-shih* 1982: 11). Taiwan was by then the unliberated province across the sea from that coast. It is to Lin's credit that he uses the geographic "southeast continental coast" rather than the nationalist "continental motherland," for which the Chinese nationalist "history" is taken to task by a Taiwan aboriginal voice (see the end of this chapter).

In Lin Hui-hsiang we see the development of the northern origin model as new data and new ideas are entered into the selection process. But we also can see that this development parallels the change in the political position of Taiwan in relation to China—from an island of no special import in 1929, to the search for roots of the Chinese nation in a period of nationalism being constructed against Japan in 1936, to the position of Taiwan as the unrecovered province of China after 1949.

That Taiwan is a timeless part of China has now become the basis of all Chinese "history" of aboriginal origins, both in China and Taiwan. For example,

Lin's research is presented in the 1982 *Kao-shan-tzu chien-shih* (Brief History of the Kao-shan Tribe), but the evolution of his ideas is elided, and a reader is given the impression that his 1930 monograph also argues the northern origin theory. How origins become teleology in PRC discussion of Taiwan aboriginal origins is neatly illustrated in the chapter headings of this 1982 work. Chapter 3 is "The Origin of the Kao-shan-tzu," while Chapter 8 is "The Kao-shan-tzu will ultimately return to the bosom of the motherland." A timeline at the end of the book also confirms the essential teleology of Chinese "history" of Taiwan (1982: 131). It begins in A.D. 230: "Sun Ch-uan of Wu sends Wei Wen and Chu-ko Cjoj with 10,000 people to Taiwan, and brings back several thousand Kao-shan-tzu." It ends in 1945 with "China recovers its own territory, Taiwan."

While we may see through the transparency of Chinese "history" of aboriginal origins, this is not the same as rejecting the northern origin theory as history. There is by now an accumulation of evidence to support arguments of "clearly defined Neolithic inputs from Fukien, and isolation beginning in post-Neolithic times," as archaeologist Richard Pearson says (in Chang et al. 1989: 111–136). Pearson also notes the many differences along with similarities in the evidence, which "suggest strong ethnic differentiation." He concludes cautiously that while "in general there does seem to be some continuing confirmation that Austronesian speakers did live in the Fukien area . . . the linguistic picture remains confused."

There is, however, no confusion whatsoever in the chapter on "*Kao-shan-tzu*" in *Chung-hua min-tzu* (Tian 1991). It begins by noting that "in ancient times Taiwan was (geologically) linked to the continental motherland [*tzu-kuo ta-lu*]," thus transforming geology into teleology. The first section of the chapter also proclaims: "Taiwan is an indivisible part of the territory of the motherland, the Kao-shan-tzu are a member of the great family of the Chinese nation [*Chung-hua min-tzu*]."

It then affirms that the 30,000-year-old "Tso Chen man" site near Tainan "belongs to a branch of Peking man, and they had paternal cousin links" (1991: 654). Contemporary Kao-shan-tzu are a branch of the ancient Yueh peoples, as proved by a long list of cultural similarities. This amazing linking of pre-sapiens Peking man of more than three hundred thousand years ago with a homo sapiens of thirty thousand years ago is a feat of genealogy exceeding even biblical begats, but is true in the same sense as sacred books are—revelations of higher truths.

Chinese anthropologists on Taiwan have also tended to support the northern origin theory.[7] One Taiwanese anthropologist, Chen Chao-ju, characterizes them:

> After these strongly nationalistic anthropologists came to Taiwan, their emphasis on "origins" [*yuan-liu*] did not weaken . . . their research interests in relation to *Kao-shan-tzu* fieldwork came out of the same mold as their ethnology on the mainland. Naturally their goal was hoping to demonstrate the genealogical and cultural relations of the *Kao-shan-tzu* with the Chinese nation [*Chung-hua min-tzu*]. . . . Such as Ling Shun-sheng, who, after coming to Taiwan, continued to advocate his so-called Circum-Pacific Cultural Contact hypothesis.

From the mainland period, when their efforts were to attach minorities to the Chinese nation, to Taiwan, where they worked at demonstrating the connections between *Kao-shan-tzu* and Chinese minorities, we can draw a sort of line of ethnic evolution:
Taiwan *Kao-shan-tzu* →
Chinese minorities →
Chinese orthodox traditions →
Han chauvinism. (Chen 1994: 27–36)

As Chinese, they also use historical records as evidence. A good example of this is archaeologist Huang Shih-chang (in Chang et al. 1989: 59–97):

The prehistoric archaeological record of Taiwan is marked by a seeming discontinuity between what may be termed an earlier stage of widespread cultural homogeneity, and a later stage of increasing heterogeneity through time . . . and that settlers came to Taiwan from a number of different points of origin. The archaeological record reveals the fact that these origins were from different parts of the greater southeastern coastal mainland. Historical records tell us that in ancient times this region was inhabited by the so-called "Pai Yueh" peoples.

Huang then uses references from *Spring and Autumn Annals, Huai-nan tzu, Han shu,* and *Shih chi* to construct this history:

Following Chin Shi-huang's unification of China he subsequently launched a military campaign to subjugate the Nan Yueh peoples in the south. During the reign of Han Wu Ti, a military campaign was again launched to attack the various Yueh peoples. Such internal and external military strife . . . created the conditions under which the Pai Yueh peoples may have been compelled to undertake large scale migrations. . . . Not only were the Pai Yueh Indonesian speaking peoples, I also believe this explains the origins of the native inhabitants of Taiwan. In fact, Ling (Shu-sheng) also stated: "We may now say with a certainty that as early as the pre-Christian era, the Yueh peoples migrated from the mainland to Taiwan."

On the other hand, in fieldwork, Taiwan anthropologists do not let "history" overdetermine their conclusions. The Taiwanese-born, but Shanghai-educated Chen Chi-lu presents an analysis of Paiwan glass beads and concludes that the "migratory date of the Paiwan into Formosa cannot be prior to the birth of Christ [during which chemically similar glass beads were prominent in Southeast Asia]. I do not consider China to be the source of Paiwan glass beads, because . . . other culture traits of the Paiwan also show close southern affinity" (1968: 366). Nonetheless, Chen follows that monograph with another supporting Ling's circum-Pacific cultural contact hypothesis, quoting Li Chi that "the source of the major art tradition of the whole Pacific basin is most probably to be found in the lost art of wood carving of China's past" (1968: 391).

The idea of Chinese origins has sometimes entered into aboriginal self-construction. An article in *Yuan-chu-min,* the paper of the Alliance of Taiwan Aborigines (see below), reported according to Kavalan's own legend, their ancestors drifted to Tamsui from Shanghai. However, before 1992 aboriginal elite opinion supported southern origins. The Chinese hegemonic project of making Taiwan aborigines part of the Chinese nation was incompatible with the developing counterhegemonic aboriginal project of affirming their distinct identity and political rights as indigenous people.

The politics of the northern origin theory, as developed through Chinese anthropologists, can be summed up as follows:

- China at the center, and a place of origin for cultures across the Pacific
- Taiwan as linked to the motherland from prehistoric times
- Chinese historiography as important evidence
- Migration from China bringing diversity
- Continuity of Taiwan's Austronesian past with the Chinese present
- Taiwan aborigines as part of the story of the expansion of the Chinese nation and destined to be reunited with it.
- Telescoping of time and space into a nationalist teleology.

The northern origin theory serves the needs of Chinese nationalist "history." More particularly, the theory as promoted in the People's Republic of China explicitly serves the project of reuniting Taiwan with China. Mainland Chinese research interest in Taiwan Aboriginal Peoples continues to grow as avenues are sought to use aboriginal concerns to promote reunification. Taiwan Aboriginal Peoples attend conferences and cultural festivals in China, and examine Chinese minorities policy as a way of critiquing the policies of the government on Taiwan. But most would agree with aboriginal legislator Lin T'ian-sheng, who in 1987 proclaimed in the Legislative Yuan that aboriginal people are the only true "Taiwanese." And this brings us to the third theory of Taiwan aboriginal origins.

Taiwan as Austronesian Homeland

In 1963 Isidore Dyen proposed that Formosa might be the place from which the Austronesian languages originated (in Chang 1963). He proposed that the place of origin of the Austronesian languages should be the place where the greatest number of language families is concentrated. With more than twenty languages in an area the size of Vancouver Island that constitute three of the oldest branches of the Indonesian group, Taiwan is logically the place to look for the origin of this language family. Dyen's proposal did not attract attention in Taiwan beyond linguists[8] until Peter Bellwood published "The Austronesian Dispersal and the Origin of Languages" in *Scientific American* in 1991.[9] Within a year, this theory was being advocated in aboriginal circles in Taiwan.

Bellwood's map in *Scientific American* has been reproduced in several aboriginal publications, and in a book on Taiwan prehistory published by the East Coast Scenic Area Administration. The map has become almost canonical in Taiwan.

This Dyen/Blust/Bellwood theory is essentially a refinement of the northern origin theory, positing an early neolithic immigration from southeastern China, and then independent development in Taiwan:

> one must consider very seriously the possibility that the expansion of the Austro-Tai language family began among Neolithic coastal rice-cultivating communities in south China. . . . Moving forward in time from Austro-Tai to its daughter, Austronesian, Robert Blust . . . favors a geographic expansion that began in Taiwan (the location of the oldest Austronesian languages, including Proto-Austronesian), then encompassed the Philippines, Borneo, and Sulawesi. (Bellwood 1991: 91)

How is it that a modified northern origin theory, proposed in the early 1980s, suddenly became canonical in Taiwan aboriginal discourse in 1991? A few landmarks of Taiwan's recent past can help explain this.

In December 1984 aboriginal activists organized the Alliance of Taiwan Aborigines (ATA, Yuan ch'uan hui). This marks the organizational beginning of the Taiwan Aboriginal People's political movement. The next year, the Government Information Office refused to let the ATA register its publication *Yuan-chu-min* (the Aborigine), because it had an "inappropriate title." These people were *shan pao* (mountain compatriots), *shan-ti-jen* (mountain people), "*Kao-shan-tzu*" or even "*Taiwan t'u-chu min-tzu*" (Formosan aborigines),[10] but not "Yuan-chu-min" (aboriginal people).

But "Yuan-chu-min" was here to stay, and soon became the center of contested discourses of origins. In a 1992 issue of *Lieh-jen Wen-hua* (which carried the Bellwood map), Tayal activist Walis Yugan reviewed the struggle over naming, which was at its height as he wrote:

> The first concern of the government is that this term "aboriginal people" will be used to oppose Chinese [Hua jen] immigrants and a Chinese government, and develop a trend to separatism. Secondly, it worried that the term "aboriginal" will involve xenophobia, using this name to act against Chinese immigrants, injuring the status and rights of the Chinese immigrants. Third, a foreboding that the term "aboriginal" already implies some political and empirical rights. (*Lieh-jen Wen-hua,* 18 [June 27, 1992]: 33)

While the first two fears were exaggerated, the third certainly was not. In 1988 the first national mobilization of aboriginal people, the Return Our Land movement, issued a statement beginning:

> The Aboriginal People of Taiwan ("Mountain People") are the first peoples to have lived on this island of Taiwan. Because of this, our right to the land is

absolute and a priori. Those lands which have been robbed by violence or deceit by the later occupying Han Chinese, or taken by successive governments by legal force, should by right be returned to us.

In the same year the first Taiwan aboriginal delegate took part in the UN Working Group on Indigenous Populations meeting in Geneva. He fought off an attempt by the PRC to make him change his title from "Alliance of Taiwan Aborigines" to "Alliance of Taiwan Aborigines, Province of China" and condemned the human rights abuses of the ROC against aboriginal people, including not letting them call themselves "aboriginal."

It was time to bring out the anthropologists. A chorus of senior anthropologists, mostly of Chinese rather than Taiwanese origin, argued that using *Yuan-chu-min* in place of *shan-ti-jen/shan-pao* was highly inaccurate. They advocated the term *hsien-chu-min* (first residents) or *tsao-chu-min* (early residents), to remove implications of "ab origio" and emphasize that the Austronesian inhabitants of Taiwan were only first in order of time. The implication of this unsuccessful attempt to block use of the term *yuan-chu-min* was that no special claims of aboriginal rights can be made, since everyone was an immigrant. The anthropologists appealed to archaeological record that there had been other peoples in Taiwan since the Palaeolithic age, and to the Saisiat myth, commemorated in their biennial "Dwarf Sacrifice" ritual, that their ancestors had destroyed a race of small people. This putative Negrito race, the anthropologists argued, were the real "aboriginal" people of Taiwan.

By mid-1991 the Return Our Land movement had evolved into an "Aboriginal Constitutional Movement" demanding use of the term "Taiwan Yuan-chu-min" and constitutional guarantees of aboriginal rights as proposed by the UN Working Group. All of Taiwan was now in the post–martial law, Lee Teng-hui era of democracy and political transformation. The law penalizing advocacy of Taiwan independence had been repealed. Taiwanese nationalism was in full flower, driving the political transformation.

In this heady time the July 1991 *Scientific American* with Bellwood's article and map arrived in Taiwan. Here, like a voice from the sky, was scientific proof that the Austronesian peoples of Taiwan were indisputably "aboriginal." Not only were they no longer immigrants, but

> Over the past five thousand years, Taiwan aboriginal people have established ten or twenty nations, in Africa, Southeast Asia, and the Pacific. Something we can be proud of before the whole world! (*Lieh-jen wen-hua* 18: 62)

Clearly aboriginal nationalists are equally capable of writing "history" as their Chinese interlocutors.

The best representative of the aboriginal Taiwan origin theory is a paper by Amis sociologist Tsai Chung-han, presented at a symposium in Peking in October 1993. Tsai is an Amis from T'ai-tung on the east coast of Taiwan, with a Ph.D. in sociology from Tokyo University. In 1986 he became a member of the legislature, symbolizing the new, democratic aboriginal face of the Kuomintang. In 1988 Tsai was one of the signers of the Return Our Land Common Statement cited above.

He begins his paper by reminding his Chinese listeners that, even if one argues that ancestors of Taiwan aboriginal people came from the continent, to which Taiwan was once linked in the ice age, "there was no Chinese mainland ten thousand years ago, only the Asian continent. So the correct statement is that Taiwan aboriginal people migrated from the southern part of the Asian continent" (Tsai 1993: 2).[11]

After reviewing the archaeological and linguistic evidence, Tsai critiques in detail each of the other two theories, ending with a strong attack on the "southern Yueh" hypothesis. His punch line is quite good:

> If the proto-Austronesian peoples came from mainland China, how is it that today in China there is not a single Austronesian people? Ethnic migration is essentially an expansion, and not a matter of the entire ethnic group departing from its ancestral territory. In the whole world there is no example of any such ethnic migration. (1993: 8)

He then presents the Dyen/Blust/Bellwood hypothesis, critiques traditional Chinese racist attitudes and terms toward other ethnic groups, and argues for the use of the term "Taiwan Aboriginal Peoples" (yuan-chu min-tzu), as opposed to "people" (yuan-chu-min).[12]

Finally he asserts that the Pei-nan megalithic culture is the direct ancestor of his own southern Amis clans and predicts that future archaeological discoveries will "continue to fill in the blanks of Taiwan Aboriginal Peoples' history and prove that the Ch'ang-pin Cave Culture [the Palaeolithic culture dated from 15,000 to 8,000 years ago, near Tsai's hometown] is also a cultural site of Taiwan Aboriginal Peoples" (1993: 16).

His paper appends the Bellwood map, and a glance at it will show why this theory is so popular in Taiwan. There, at the top of a great fan of migration, is Taiwan, labeled "number 1." Between China and Taiwan is a thick, impervious line delineating the Austronesian world from China.

The Taiwan origin theory, as seen through Tsai's article, can be compared to the southern and northern theories as follows:

- Taiwan at the center and a place of origins
- Taiwan's connection with China only in remote past
- A continuous thread of Taiwan aboriginal history
- Taiwan as homeland of the Austronesian diversity and expansion
- Aboriginal people as contributors to world culture

- Autochtonous origins from the Palaeolithic age
- Argument based on linguistics and archaeology with no use of Aboriginal myth or Chinese historiography.

There are several noteworthy points in this discourse. First, although it is "aboriginal," it is not "nativist" in that does not appeal to native knowledge—traditions or myths. Second, it has appropriated the theory of northern origin and turned it into an argument against that theory. But even more significant for the politics of aboriginal origins is that it is not solely an aboriginal discourse but a Taiwanese nationalist discourse. It appeared in a period when strong Taiwanese nationalism was forming ideas about a new, multicultural Taiwanese ethnic identity, which Democratic Progressive Party chair Hsu Hsin-liang termed a new people (*hsin-sheng min-tzu*). It affirms that Taiwan is a place where creative, new things happen, that Taiwan has only remote links with China, that Taiwan is "number 1," and that aboriginal identity is the heart of Taiwanese identity. Which leads us to the latest theory.

Aboriginal Genes Defining Taiwanese Identity

In February 1997 a message in an e-mail discussion group called the "Taiwan Future Discussion Group" made a startling assertion:

> The majority of Taiwanese are descendents of Austronesians (60%) and only a minor proportion of Taiwanese are the descendants of immigrants from mainland China, no matter [whether] they are speaking Holo, Hakka, Chinese, or English today. This is also supported by the recent biological research findings indicating that the blood DNA profiles of most Taiwanese are different from [those] of Chinese.

The assertion was made by a Taiwanese scientist in the context of an appeal for solidarity of Taiwanese with the aboriginal Yami people (now reclaiming their own name, Tau) on the island of Lan-yu (which they call Pongso no Tau) who "are our brothers in blood." This assertion sparked a vigorous debate and eventually a clarification by the researcher, whose work on the presence of blood immunotypes had led him to speculate that one factor could perhaps be present in 60 percent of the population of Taiwan, as most Taiwanese do have aboriginal ancestors. The man who drew a theory of origins from this was not deterred and continued to insist that genes as well as history are equally important in the makeup of a nation. The discovery of the English "Cheddar man" genetic link more than eight thousand years old only strengthened his conviction![13]

In *Imagined Communities* Benedict Anderson discusses how nineteenth-century postrevolutionary nationalism involves the revival of the past and a search for an aboriginal essence. He called this "reading nationalism genealogically." What could be less surprising than to hear that Taiwanese nationalism has also begun to seize upon aboriginal genealogy, based on the Taiwan origin theory, to establish an aboriginal essence for Taiwanese identity? The Internet discussant argues that "true respect to Taiwan history is the most solid basis of Taiwan nationalism, which justifies a republic to build, Taiwan."

Remembering the 1936 conjectures of Lin Hui-hsiang, and Blust's recent revival of the Austric hypothesis (in Goodenough 1996: 117–137), which suggest that both the Austronesians and the southern Min-speaking Chinese of Fukien and Taiwanese "Hoklo" are all descendants of the southern Yueh peoples, we can predict further evolution in Taiwanese nationalist "history." A new "history" might affirm a primordial "Taiwanese" identity encompassing both the Hoklo and the aborigines, and neatly exclude any "Chinese" or "Han" claims to Taiwan based on origins.

New myths arise to create new social charters, and the present continually writes new "history" to serve future desires. In April 1994 Lee Teng-hui made a speech at the first "Aboriginal Cultural Conference." In it he made the first use of the word "*Yuan-chu-min*" in official government speech, presaging the adoption of that term into the ROC Constitution a few months later. In his speech Lee said, "Aboriginal people in Taiwan must definitely not place themselves outside the whole society of Taiwan. People must have self-confidence and be far sighted, and no matter what, integrate into the larger whole of society bringing out the special characteristics of aboriginal people as part of the mainstream" (*World Journal,* Toronto, April 11, 1994, p. A15).

Depending on which theory of aboriginal origins this Japanese-educated Taiwanese-Hakka president of the Republic of China subscribes to, the implications of this exhortation are strikingly different. The politics of Taiwan aboriginal origins are ultimately the politics of Taiwan's future.

Notes

1. In fact it is this debate about which Terrell is writing in *Prehistory in the Pacific Islands.*

2. Most of these are discussed in the special Taiwan issue of *Asian Perspectives* 7 (1963), edited by Chang Kwang-chih. What Chang and his colleagues make of this pattern is discussed in this paper in the section on "theories of Chinese origin."

3. McGovern's book is a terrible hodgepodge of inaccuracies and hearsay, and if it was not an embarrassment to Marrett it certainly is to anthropologists today. It is however still in circulation, sold in Taiwan in reprint form.

4. Not all Japanese anthropologists subscribed to the southern origin theory. Tadeo Kano (cited in Chang 1963: 199) concluded that "the prehistoric cultures of Taiwan, on the whole, are related to the mainland cultures, but closer examinations reveal that the west coast exhibits heavy Southern Chinese colours, whereas the eastern coast is connected with southern Indochina (and) iron age cultures of the Philippines."

5. And as a Taiwan Presbyterian, Wu is at once heir to George Leslie Mackay and shares in the Taiwanese nationalist sentiments of the Presbyterian Church in Taiwan.

6. Lin began his study of anthropology at the University of the Philippines, returning to China with his M.A. in 1928.

7. Here I mean anthropologists born in China who came to Taiwan with the Republic of China. By "Taiwanese" I mean born in Taiwan, but not aboriginal. Chen's scathing attack is of course also political. Historical debate in Taiwan is sharply divided along lines of ethnic politics.

8. His article in *Asian Perspectives* (Chang 1963: 261–271) shows why. It is fairly technical linguistics, but also he mentions this as only one possible thesis and then spends most of the space trying to disprove the case, by exploring the idea that in fact all the aboriginal languages of Taiwan constitute a single family, which would mean that Taiwan does not fit his criteria for a linguistic homeland.

9. Bellwood first made this proposal in 1983. That version of his map was printed in a paper by K.C. Chang, "Taiwan Archaeology in Pacific Perspective" (in Chang et al. 1989: 93), where Chang called it a "reasonable hypothesis of migratory and diffusion routes." Chang remains true to the northern origin theory, however, emphasizing that "prehistoric Taiwan is a part of prehistoric Southeast China" (ibid.: 89).

10. While *t'u-chu min-tz'u* is usually translated in Taiwan academic publications as "Formosan aborigines," the Chinese term has a very different implication from *yuan-chu-min*, also translated as "aboriginal people or indigenous people." *T'u-chu*, literally "land adhering," is closer in sense to the older English anthropological usage "native" or "tribal," and was never used by Taiwan aboriginal peoples as a self-ascription, as was *shan-ti-jen*.

11. This is the language that was used by Lin Hui-hsiang, but not by his successors.

12. This is also the politics of aboriginality—as "peoples" they are a collectivity that theoretically enjoys the right of self-determination in UN discourse.

13. The positivist biologist commented, "British due respect to the scientific truth is sharply in contrast to ours . . . it may be fair to say that Taiwanese . . . are not used to respect to scientific truth yet."

References

Bellwood, Peter. 1991. "The Austronesian Dispersal and the Origin of Languages." *Scientific American* (July 1991): 88–93.

Chang Kwang-chih, ed. 1963. *Asian Perspectives: Bulletin of the Far-Eastern Prehistory Association* 7 (1963): 195–275.

Chang Kwang-chih, Li Kuang-chou, Arthur P. Wolf, and Alexander Yin Chien-chung, eds. 1989. *Anthropological Studies of the Taiwan Area*. Taipei: Department of Anthropology, National Taiwan University.

Chen Chao-ju. 1994. "Shih lun Taiwan jen-lei-hsueh ti kao-shan yen-chiu" (Taiwan Anthropological Research on Mountain Tribes). *Taiwan Indigenous Bimonthly* 6 (September 1994): 27–36.

Chen Chi-lu. 1968. *Material Culture of the Formosan Aborigines*. Taipei: Taiwan Museum.

Goodenough, Warren, ed. 1996. *Prehistoric Settlement of the Pacific*. Philadelphia: American Philosophical Society.

Halbwachs, Maurice. 1997. *La Mémoire Collective*. Edition critique établie par Gérard Namer; préparée avec la collaboration de Marie Jaisson. Paris: A. Michel.

Kao-shan-tzu chien-shih (Brief History of the Gaoshan Nationality). 1982. Foochow: Fukien jen-min ch'u-pan-she.

Lieh-jen Wen-hua. Vol. 18 (June 27, 1992). Published by Tayal teacher Walis Yugan in Taichung. Ceased publication. Special Section on Cheng-ming Yun-tung (Name Rectification Movement).

Lin Hui-hsiang. 1930. *The Primitive Aborigines of Formosa*. Shanghai: Academia Sinica, Monograph of the Institute of Social Sciences, no. 3.

———. 1936. *Chung-kuo min-tzu-shih* (Chinese Ethnohistory). Shanghai: Commercial Press.

Mabuchi, Toichi. 1974. *Ethnology of the Southwestern Pacific* Taipei: Orient Cultural Service, Asian Folklore and Social Life Monographs, no. 59.

McGovern, Janet B. Montgomery. 1922. *Among the Headhunters of Formosa*. London: Fisher Unwin.

Mackay, George Leslie. 1895. *From Far Formosa*. Toronto: Fleming H. Revell.

Miyamoto Nobuto. 1985. *Taiwan ti yuan-chu-min* (Taiwan's Aborigines). Taipei: Morning Star.

Shih Ming. 1980. *Taiwan-jen 400 nien shih* (Four-Hundred-Year History of Taiwanese People). San Jose: Paradise Culture Associates.

Stainton, Michael. 1995. "Return Our Land: Counterhegemonic Presbyterian Aboriginality in Taiwan." M.A. thesis, York University.

Tai-yuan-jen (Taiwan Indigenous People Alliance). No. 3 (December 16, 1988). Published by Amis historian Wu Ming-yi in Hua-lien. Ceased publication.

Terrell, John. 1986. *Prehistory in the Pacific Islands*. New York: Cambridge University Press.

T'ien Hsiao-hsiu, ed. 1991. *Chung-kuo min-chu* (The Chinese Nation). Pei-king: Hua-hsia chu-pan-she.

Tsai Chung-han. 1993. "Taiwan Yuan-chu-min-tzu chih ch'i-yuan" (The Origin of Taiwan Aboriginal Peoples). Paper presented at the Cultural Seminar at the Minorities Institute in Beijing, July 28, 1993.

Yuan pao (Aboriginal Post) (April 28, 1992). Published by Ju-k'ai activist Chao Kui-chung in P'ing-tung. Ceased publication. Includes articles on "The History of Migration of Taiwan's Austronesian Peoples" and "The Relationship of Taiwan's Pre-historic Cultures and Aboriginal People."

3

Up the Mountains and Out to the Sea

The Expansion of the Fukienese in the Late Ming Period

Eduard B. Vermeer

A view of the Fujianese countryside. *(Photo by M. Rubinstein)*

Fukien is a mountainous province on the southeastern coast of China. The local saying that it is "80 percent mountains, 10 percent water, and 10 percent farmland" characterizes not only its geography but also its traditional sources of living. The Wuyi mountain range separates Fukien from Kianghsi and Kuangtung. A second, parallel range of coastal mountains runs from the northeast to the southwest. Only in the north does the Min river valley provide access to Huichou and the Yangtze river basin. The other access route is the sea, where small river valleys and promontories face what is now called the Taiwan strait. Mountains, almost all of which have an altitude under 1,000 meters, and hills occupy 95 percent of Fukien. The remaining 5 percent of lowlands consist mostly of the small coastal alluvial plains formed by the In river, the Thing river, and the Chiu-lung river and the long, narrow river valleys of the interior.

These valleys and plains were settled by Han-Chinese immigrants fairly late in history. They displaced, or slowly integrated with, native peoples of whom we know very little. When Fukien became part of the Chinese empire during the T'ang dynasty and again under the Sung, many local traditions persisted. Its late and incomplete integration, the settlement by different waves of immigrants, and the difficult communications between the various river valleys explain the great social and linguistic diversity of Fukien. The earliest Chinese name for its native peoples, "the Seven Min (snakes)," was subsequently adapted as "the Eight In" and then stood for the eight different prefectures of Fukien—an illustrations of the civilizing strength of the Chinese, whose cultural heroes had killed the snakes in many districts. At the same time, it is a reminder that native traditions and diversity had not died.

In the glorious centuries of the Sung and Yuan dynasties, the malarial coastal areas were completely transformed. Monasteries and private investors drained the marshes, diked silt flats along the coast, and constructed irrigation canals. The military government built bridges and roads that made the coastal and river plains accessible over land, enabling a safe and cheap transportation of people and goods. The civil administration established walled county seats, postal stations, law and order, education, and other services. These expansive activities were supported by Fukien's growing agricultural production, fishery, industries, and overseas trade and helped to boost its commercial economy, population, and wealth. The destruction of the outward-oriented Yuan dynasty, which had brought such great benefits to Ch'uan-chou and other international ports in Fukien, brought an end to this boom.

After the Ming dynasty adopted a policy of sea closure and severely restricted commercial activities and the free movement of people, Fukien lost major sources of income and employment and went into a downward spiral. This situation was reversed only in the sixteenth century, with the opening up of new global and interregional trade flows, which brought merchant ships to the Chinese harbors and Fukienese ships to Japan and Southeast Asia. China's huge potential for exports of silk, tea, porcelain, and other goods could now be exploited because they could be paid for with American silver, Japanese copper, and Southeast Asian tropical products. However, this resurgence of Fukien was ridden with conflicts with the central government and with fierce competition and many small-scale or large-scale local wars. The process of opening up and commercial development was a very painful and often destructive one. It ripped Fukien apart and eventually drove many people overseas in search of a living. Both sides of the medal are part of our story of turbulent sixteenth-century Fukien.

Fishery

A Ming source noted 167 different types of fish and 90 types of other sea animals in Fukien. Some contemporary writers claimed that, in the coastal prefectures, more than half the population lived from the fishing industry, but this was true only for island inhabitants and villages with good access to the sea. In dried form, fish was sold in the interior and was a major source of animal protein. "People eat rice gruel, with fish as a sweetener, and do not dare to ask for meat."[1] The fishing industry might be divided into three segments.

First, fishery at sea brought the Fukienese beyond their own coastal waters to the rich fishing grounds in the Choushan archipelago in Chekiang, to Kuangtung and to Taiwan. The Fukienese fleets followed the migration of the ocean fish. Several thousand ships went north to the Choushan archipelago in autumn and winter, and returned south from there in March. This brought them into conflict with fishermen from Chekiang, and was one reason why piracy was difficult to eradicate. Successive schools of different fish arrived in Fukienese waters every month of the year, beginning with the two-pound "blow shark" *chüi-sha*.[2] While some species were popular because of their excellent taste or because they were easy to catch and could be found on most markets (such as the slender, six-feet-long hairtail fish, or *tai*), others were rarer and used for medicine or special occasions.

Second, possibly just as important in terms of employment, income, and nutrition was the catch of shrimp, clams, scallops, crabs, and other seafood on coastal silt flats or seaponds. Each area had its own specialties. For instance, the P'u-t'ien-ese were reported to value octopus most and also to collect "white pebble" shells for food. Oysters and other shells were widely used for building materials and as lime for improvement of saline soils.[3] Some of these products were artificially bred. In most cases, exploiters of such coastal grounds or waters had gained exclusive rights, which were jealously defended against intruders.[4] Gradual siltation of many coastal harbors forced part of the seafaring fishing villages to change over to smaller flat-bottom boats and exploitation of the silt flats or abandon their trade altogether.

Finally, probably of a declining importance because of population growth, land reclamation, irrigation projects, and overfishing, there was fishery by nets, traps, or otherwise in the rivers, streams, ponds, and canals of Fukien. Some of the fish was bred. "People collect fry of the Red Bream *hung-lien* from the river in spring, breed them in small ponds until they are over one foot long and then move them to larger ponds. They are fed with grass and harvested in the ninth month."[5]

Little is known about the quantities and numbers of people involved. One source refers to a Fukienese ocean fleet of five hundred to six hundred ships.[6] Taxes levied on fishermen give some indication. Around 1500, the Fukienese fishermen paid five times as much tax as those of Kianghsi province.[7] This shows the relative unimportance of freshwater fishing. The early Ming government instituted heavy taxes, which resulted in many fishermen leaving their villages and giving up their trade. Under the policy of sea closure, the population of the islands along the coast, many of whom depended on fishery for a living, was removed. The result was that a considerable part of the fishing trade was conducted without the consent of, or payment of taxes to, the authorities.

According to early Ming regulations, each fisherman had to pay taxes amounting to 1.5 *shih* of rice. The tax was converted in 1494 to 0.35 tael of silver per household; the total for Fukien amounted to 31,600 *shih,* which was converted to 7,100 taels. This tax base of about 21,000 fishermen households constituted only 4 percent of the total taxed households in Fukien province, the official number of which was 506,039 in 1491. In most coastal prefectures, the ratio of fishermen was higher: 7 percent of the population in Ch'uan-chou and in Hsing-hua; 5 percent in Foochow (a large part of which was in Fu-ch'ing), but (for reasons that are not clear) not so in Fu-ning or Chang-chou prefectures. The highest percentage of fish taxpayers, 11 percent of all households, was registered in the inland prefecture of Yen-p'ing (where Sha-hsien and Nan-p'ing had the highest fish taxes). Some prefectures levied freshwater fishing boat taxes separately and issued fish permits; in Foochow and Hsing-hua the latter two yielded 1,785 taels and 1,313 taels, respectively, which was more than the above-mentioned fisherman's tax.[8] These data are not easy to interpret, and we dare go no further than concluding that at the end of the fifteenth century, sea and inland fishery may have provided 5 to 15 percent of all employment in the counties along the sea or along the middle and lower reaches of the Min river. If we include employment in related industries and services, the figures are considerably higher.

Most types of fishery were seasonal, undertaken by men, and could be combined with maintaining a family farm. Nevertheless, there were many coastal villages where the entire economy revolved around fishery. The fishing industry had many backward and forward linkages: shipbuilding; manufacturing of ropes, nets, and sails; the timber trade and saw mills; provisions of crews; salt-making; production of various containers; processing and sales; and so on. All this was not just for the local market. Fishermen could move easily from one market to the other in search of better prices or lower taxes. Profits were high, but so was the cost of investment in ship and netting, and the risk of losing it all. The government offered little if any protection against piracy and robbers, and even the goddess of Ma-tsu was of little help against typhoons. Government interdictions against seafaring interrupted the regular catch and supply of fish and deprived many people of their income or source of food.

In ordinary times fish and other seafoods contributed a sizable amount of animal protein to the Fukienese diet, which must have benefited the general health situation. When the fish supply was ample, "a pound of fish costs only a few pennies. The rich fetch their fish with oxen-carts then, and conserve it for several years. The poor eat their fill of fresh fish, too."[9] The salted and dried fish could be kept for a long time and because of its low weight could be transported and traded in interior Fukien and other provinces.

Shipping Industry

Early observers from the West such as Marco Polo and Ibn Battuta were amazed at the size and strength of the Chinese junks and noted the peculiarities of their construction. Because of its flat bottom, with a central longitudinal timber substituting for the keel, the junk could navigate in shallow waters. The many bulkheads divided the vessel into compartments and added to its strength and safety. With a cross-beam at the bow and a prolonged stern deck, through which the rudder-post protruded, its deck space was quite large. The larger ships had four or more masts, with mat-and-batten lug-sails. There were many small cabins for the merchants, who accompanied their merchandise. Both construction and rigging were essentially different from Western ships. In the early Ming period, the treasure ships with which Cheng Ho sailed to South Asia and Africa had been 440 feet or maybe even 600 feet long, very broad, with nine masts, and accommodated between five hundred and a thousand men.[10] After imperial support for these overseas voyages stopped, such large vessels were no longer built. The largest vessels were those used in the official trade with the Ryukyuans, who tried to get the most out of the limited number of ships allowed. In the sixteenth century and later, ship sizes usually did not go beyond a length of 150 feet and a capacity of 400 tons.

The ship wharfs at Foochow had the advantage of many favorable conditions. There was timber for masts and hulls and local production of iron and hemp. Because of its fishery, Fukien had a long tradition of shipbuilding and repairs, even if the era of giant expeditions had ended. The wharfs had received a state monopoly on the manufacture of the official messenger ships for the Ryukyu islands. The commercial development of the Min river basin (particularly the silk goods manufacture, but also forestry and paper industries) provided a steady need for boats and ships. Moreover, because Fukien was a large producer of salt, many of the salt-carrying ships were built there. The Foochow wharfs could profit from their strategic and commercial location at the mouth of Fukien's largest river basin and proximity to the provincial capital.

One important shipyard was the official shipyard for Chinese Ryukyu messenger ships at Nant'ai. They were between 150 and 200 feet long, 26 to 30 feet wide, and perhaps more than 14 feet deep. They were made very strong by design by employing various techniques such as a double hull, separation of about 25 compartments, a low center of gravity, close-sealing, iron cords, use of high-quality timber for the masts and rudder, and high side-boards against billows. Although few in number because of their size and quality (and large overhead of management costs), they commanded prices of between 1,800 and 3,000 taels each, as against 80 or 90 taels for the ordinary Fu-ch'ing ship.[11] In return, the Ryukyuans themselves had many of their ships built or repaired in Foochow.

In 1567, the warship manufacturing of Foochow was moved from Ho-k'ou to Chieh yuan-chou and its scale was enlarged. In addition to the ships of the sea fortresses of the Foochow Naval Command, the fortresses of Feng-huo-men in Fu-ning, Nan-jih-shan in Hsing-hua, Wu-yu in Ch'uan-chou, and T'ung-shan in Chang-chou also had their ships manufactured there. The combined total of government ships, dispatch ships, and patrol ships that controlled the Fukien coastal waters numbered several hundreds in the Foochow area alone, so the total for Fukien must have been more than a thousand.[12]

Because during most of the Ming construction of civil ships above a certain size was not officially permitted, records are scarce. Particularly during times of pirate activities, ocean ships commanded very high prices, up to 300 or 400 taels. The coastal economy profited greatly from the various shipbuilding activities, legal or illegal. Because of the high costs of ocean-faring vessels, ships were often owned not by single individuals, but by groups of merchants or investors. But there were also large investors, who owned dozens of ships and boats.

Common types of ships were the Fukien ship, Kuangtung ship, coaster (*sha-ch'uan*), and crow-ship (*wu-ch'uan*). Another distinction is by use and size. Warships included six classes, the largest of which was the large Fukien-class ship, which could carry more than a hundred soldiers and had four decks. Compared to the Kuangtung-class vessel and coaster types of ship, it was sturdier, and with a depth of 12 feet, more able to withstand the high ocean waves in the South China Sea. However, it needed more wind to sail. Thus, it was of less use in shallow waters along the coast. It was supplemented by two smaller types, the patrol ship and the even smaller "winter ship."

Commercial ships and boats included, apart from fishing vessels, specialized carriers for salt, oxen, sugar, and grain. The largest ones, the "fish-shaped carriers" (*tiao-t'ao ch'uan*), were in use for long-distance ocean transport to Japan, the Philippines, Indochina, and elsewhere. The salt ships made in Foochow were about 25 feet long and carried about 100 tons of cargo; the "oxen ships" also carried almost 35 tons; flat-bottoms called "scrapers" were in use for carrying goods in shallow and interior waters. The boats carrying freight and passengers on the Min river had open or covered sterns and flat bottoms made of fir. Instead of a rudder, a large front paddle was used for steering. Boats traveled in groups, and were linked to each other with ropes when crossing rapids.[13]

The size and scope of Fukien's shipping industry was influenced by several factors. Commercial expansion and increased dependence of imports and exports raised the demand for transport vessels. The successive pirate wars and government interdictions of seafaring caused destruction of the existing fleet, both military and civil, and resulted in great fluctuations in demand and prices. Official government control and interdictions drove shipbuilding activities away from existing shipyards to new harbors such as Yue-kang and islets under pirate or smugglers' control. During the Ming, there are few if any signs of shortages of materials such as timber, and the connected industries continued to thrive.

Salt Production

Salt was an essential element in the preservation of food. Like elsewhere in China, its production and distribution was strictly controlled and heavily taxed by the government, which used it as a source of revenue. Originally, in Fukien salt was produced mainly by boiling brine. This technique was rather complicated and required large amounts of brine and wood fuel. Productivity was low, and cost was high; the large bamboo containers generally used could produce only about 100 kilograms per day. By the mid-Ming, in coastal areas wood fuel had become scarce, and a new method was adopted, sun-drying. Its advantages were simplicity and low operating costs. Now a single person could produce 100 kilograms a day. Cost was thereby reduced to two cash per pound, or only one-fifth of the boiling method in the 1630s.[14] However, the new technique required preparation of the saltwater, a considerable outlay of land, and careful maintenance; moreover, because of its increased seasonality, more storage facilities were needed. In the mid-sixteenth century, a number of saltfields along the coast were technically improved, with inlets, ridges, and a tile cover facilitating the collection of dried salt.

A century earlier, in 1448, the salt households of the four major saltfields in southern Fukien had had their levies of salt converted into obligatory supplies of food grain to the Yung-ning garrison in Ch'uan-chou and the Quemoy granary. Being short of food grain themselves, they used their income from private sales of salt to purchase grain elsewhere. In the mid-sixteenth century, their grain tax was converted into silver, too. The other three major saltfields in Fukien had similar conversions in practice, although without formal approval. The traditional salt households, which had been under an obligation to provide wood fuel from the mountains for salt manufacture, had their duties converted to a monetary tax. Most of the salt produced by the coastal fields entered the private market. While the traditional method was organized collectively, because of its economies of scale, and thus could be more easily controlled by the authorities, the new method of salt production could be done on a small scale just as well. All along the Fukien coast, but particularly in the south, illegal production of salt increased because it could easily find its way to markets elsewhere through smuggling. The government found it impossible to control salt households at the major saltfields when they engaged in private sales and even strikes or refusals to deliver salt. In recognition of this fact, it lifted its monopoly on sales in Hsing-hua, Ch'uan-chou and Chang-chou prefectures, but with the restriction that a merchant could trade only within a single prefecture. The salt households and other producers sold their product directly to salt merchants, and the latter bought salt permits and paid taxes—2 *fen* per 200 *chin*.[15] The official price was driven down by competition with the untaxed illegal product.

Because within China Fukien had been the first to adopt the new and cheaper salt collection methods, and because of its early commercialization and easy communications, it became a major supplier of salt to other Chinese provinces. However, the development of large-scale production and interprovincial sales was limited by the local competition of small producers, who could more easily evade taxes and levies than the Fukienese salt ships could.

Reclamation of Farmland and Irrigation

The natural processes of a slowly rising land mass and settlement of silt at the mouth of Fukien's rivers created favorable conditions for reclamation of farmland from silt flats along the coast. During the Sung, reclamation took place on a large scale. In order to be able to flush the salts out and keep the brackish underground water down, it was essential to have irrigation water, and such facilities were built at the same time. As a result, the newly constructed polder fields could give very high rice yields and became an important venue for capital investment. During the mid- and late Ming, problems of a secure supply of irrigation water became more pronounced. When new polders were added to the existing ones, they needed a share of the water supply. Intensification of cropping and the expansion of water-demanding crops such as sugar cane further raised the demand for water. Although average annual rainfall along the coast and in the plain areas is quite large, about 1,100 to 1,400 millimeter, its distribution over the year, and between years, is very uneven. In wet years, rainfall is 2.6 times as great as in dry years (P = 10,90). Moreover, in many places sources of water supply were shrinking because of denudation of upstream river basins and siltation.

The increasing shortages of irrigation water led late Ming and Ch'ing authors to the conclusion that, after a golden age of water conservancy construction in the Sung period, irrigation facilities had deteriorated during the Ming.[16] This view has been accepted as true by present local historians, but without real quantitative evidence. Lin Dingshui believes that although a certain number of irrigation projects were constructed in mountain areas during the Ming and Ch'ing periods, not many projects were new. Destruction was rather serious at that time, and in most places irrigation facilities had deteriorated already.[17] There are many reasons suggesting that such views are erroneous and that the long-term trend in Fukien was extension and further improvement of irrigation facilities.

Without additional irrigation water, Fukien could never have realized its increases in production of rice, sugarcane, mulberry leaves, tobacco, and other crops (newly introduced dryland food crops such as potatoes and maize became more common in most counties only since the mid-Ch'ing). The denudation of hills and mountains and soil erosion increased the irregularity of run-off, and thereby the need for human intervention in order to guarantee water supply to the crops. The expansion of farmland in hilly and mountainous areas created a need for construction of new facilities. As upstream users took more water for their crops, downstream supply became less and less secure. In order to maintain the same levels of output, downstream facilities had to be managed in a better way or additional facilities had to be created.

Local complaints about irrigation water supply demonstrate that water had become more scarce during the Ming because of its use elsewhere and higher water requirements of the crops. At the time, they were reminders that more attention needed to be given to maintenance. Increasing scarcities resulted in a greater number of reported or unreported drought disasters, even if they led to a fuller and more economical utilization of water resources. For instance, in the first half of the sixteenth century in Hsing-hua prefecture severe droughts, for which tax reduction was granted, occurred in the years 1499–1500, 1526, 1528, 1536–37, and 1541.[18]

The shortage of irrigation water led to conflicts between new and old water users. The farmers in the old irrigation district were often in the weaker position because they were smallholders and unable to fully defend their customary rights. Local officials had often been involved financially and bureaucratically in the reclamation projects and backed the land developers against local opposition. The new landowners and their prospective tenants had had to invest large amounts of capital and labor in building dikes and other infrastructure, reclaiming the land from the sea and improving the soil. They paid taxes for it and had considerable economic and social muscle. Nevertheless, being at the downstream end of irrigation canals and ditches meant that their newly gained farmland was dependent on the amount of water upstream users were willing to let through. Therefore, a compromise had to be struck and mutual agreements had to be upheld. In the initial phase, the local magistrate played an important role, but subsequently this task fell on the irrigation district, that is, the community of water users.

Water conservancy structures were vulnerable to natural and manmade disasters. At times, heavy rainfall caused landslides, river floods swept entire villages away and destroyed manmade structures and farm soils, and typhoons destroyed dikes, homes, and crops. As a sixteenth-century author noted, "The rivers of Fukien may be very violent and bring destruction easily. Therefore, bridges are strengthened with heavy beams."[19] If repairs were not undertaken quickly, the negative effects might be long-lasting. Major-scale repairs required a strong and effective local organization. Local disputes between lineages, a lack of funds in times of economic decline such as the 1620s and 1630s, or lack of government support could result in long periods of neglect. In some periods, the Ming government itself was to blame. For instance, in the early Ming period the stone covers of the sea dikes in Hsing-hua were taken away by military commanders who used the stones for the construction of fortifications.[20] In the sixteenth century, government and local communities built local fortifications against pirates or local robber bands, often in great haste, and most likely (there is no direct evidence) existing stone constructions suffered. When areas along the coast were declared forbidden territory and cleared, protective dikes and other infrastructure were no longer maintained and much farmland was lost.

Different Types and Qualities of Farmland

Contemporary sources distinguished several types of farmland, with different levels of productivity, rents, and taxes. Overall, farmland in Fukien was considered rather poor because most of it was in the hills and produced only one crop per year.

In coastal counties, the irrigated fields in the alluvial plain (*yang-t'ien*) had the highest quality, followed by the diked fields (*tai-t'ien*), which had been reclaimed from the sea since the Sung dynasty and equipped with irrigation canals. Next, there were the fields on river banks or abandoned river courses (*chou-t'ien*), which had easy access to surface and underground water, but sometimes were sandy and flood-prone. During the Ming period, all three types could produce two rice crops per year. The quality of "seafields" (*hai-t'ien*), that is, recently reclaimed and irrigated silt flats along the seashore, was very uneven: The soil was still salty, and often insufficient irrigation water could be secured to press down the brackish underground water. The dikes offered little protection against seepage of saltwater and were vulnerable to typhoons.

In the hills, there were sloping fields that might receive adequate amounts of rainfall (*shan-t'ien*) and terraced fields (*t'i-t'ien*).[21] Their productivity seldom reached the standards of the plains, and both were more vulnerable to drought spells. Because of their higher labor requirements for production and maintenance, production costs of the terraced fields were higher than those of other fields, and at times when labor was scarce or expensive or food grain prices were low, many such fields were abandoned. Erosion would follow. Particularly near urban centers, many of the hills were no longer fit for agriculture at the end of the Sung period.

In the inland areas of Fukien, almost all farmland belonged to the categories of mountain and terrace fields, which also included dry-farming fields. The latter, called *ti* ("land')' instead of *t'ien* ("watered field"), had the lowest yields, rents, and taxes. Nevertheless, in ordinary times the Fukienese mountain areas yielded a surplus of grain and industrial crops, which was traded with the coastal areas for cloth, salt, fish, silk, and imported products. The sixteenth-century growth of trade and wealth in the coastal region stimulated the expansion of farmland for the cultivation of grain and industrial crops in the interior. When, at the end of the Ming, less demanding food crops such as tubers became available and demand for industrial crops had increased, the dry-farming area was expanded also on poor soils along the coast. This probably reduced some of the pressure on existing farmland resources in the watered valleys and plains.

Land use in the mountains was wasteful and exploitative. "Mountain fields are not manured. Farmers burn the mountain vegetation and wait for rain, which washes the ashes unto the fields as fertilizer. In early spring, all mountains are on fire. Traveling over land, one sees burnt mountains which are bare and black, an ugly sight!"[22] Such fertilization practices were poor substitutes for the use of pig manure. However, because of the shortage of grain and other animal feed and the competition of seafood, Fukien's coastal areas had few pigs.

At the end of the Ming, people spoke of a crisis of resources. According to the gazetteer of Ch'uan-chou, "In recent years, population has increased every day. Mountains are too bare to find wood for making charcoal, lakes have been too exhausted for netting fish, one relies on sea ships for bringing food, and calls for food supplies from elsewhere." At the same time, it condemned the people for engaging in conspicuous consumption and noted that they were ashamed of wearing anything other than beautiful clothes.[23] This quotation shows how much the coastal Fukienese depended on the use of outside resources and services for their wealth, once local resources of timber and sloping farm soils had been exhausted. However, with a shrinking support from a hinterland that had never been very large to begin with, the coastal Fukienese became very vulnerable to outside developments in interregional and international shipping and trade. When the Chinese economy went into a downward spiral after 1620, Fukien suffered greatly.

Farmland Tenure Systems

According to Fu Yiling, permanent tenure became common during the Wanli period. Gu Yanwu noted that early in that period, a magistrate of Chang-chou had written that in Ch'ang-t'ai county irrigated farmland had just one owner, but in Lung-hsi, Nanking, and P'ing-ho counties three "owners" (*chu*).[24] The three "owners" were the landlord, who had bought the rent and paid the fixed grain tax and duties; the tax owner, who had bought the tax (*shui*), but did not pay the grain tax and duties; and the tenant, who worked the land and paid rent and taxes. As long as the tenant fulfilled his obligations, the landlord could not replace him. This permanent utilization right had been bought and could be sold, not necessarily by the farmer himself. In Foochow, urban residents bought such rights already in the Wanli period. The respective ownership rights were usually labeled "surface" (different counties using different names: *t'ien-p'i, t'ien-mien, ken-t'ien, fen-tü,* etc.) rights and "subsoil" (*t'ien-ku, liang-t'ien, mien-t'ien, mien-ti,* etc.) rights, and also small and large cropping rights (*hsiao ta miao* or *hsiao ta tsu*).[25] The different names clearly indicate that these were autonomous local developments without any government intervention. The shortage of grain made it attractive for urban residents and merchants to invest in farmland. At the same time, increased rural mobility and peasant unrest strengthened the tenants' position against urban and rural landlords, who found it difficult to personally manage their land. The influx of silver provided the necessary cash for a monetization of the respective land rights.

Permanent tenancy rights came about in different ways. One originated from the demise of the military colony system, when tenants began to cultivate land on behalf of the original soldiers. Another was more specific for Fukien in the mid- and late Ming. Originally, temple properties and those who had obtained registration as a monk enjoyed the privilege of a reduced tax status. However, during the sixteenth century both government and commercial interests in Fukien struck heavy blows at the strong and favored position of Buddhist and Taoist temples and their corporate landholdings. In the coastal regions, the scholar-official families with their newly increased wealth succeeded in breaking up most temple estates. As their lineages got stronger, they put up their own temples and endowed them with properties. In the mountains, the struggle for resources was often fought with violent means, between local gentry and newly established monasteries. Because of the repressive anti-Buddhist policies of the Taoist emperor Shih-tsung during the Chia-ching reign, and an apparent diminishing elite and popular support for traditional Buddhist organizations and beliefs during the late Ming, most Buddhist temples were forced to sell the majority of their landholdings and rent out much of the remainder. The Ming government raised taxes on these lands, which made its formal ownership unattractive.[26] Many owners and original farmers refused and fled, leaving the tenant in actual control if not ownership of the land. This phenomenon of intentional or unintentional unclarity of ownership was not limited to temple properties. Thus, in many cases permanent tenancy rights resulted from tax evasion by the original owners. As a contemporary author noted, it was difficult to know who exactly owned what. "Once the land has fallen into the hands of the tenants, the crafty ones evade rent and taxes, nothing is clear, and after the property has been transferred, the tenant is still around as a crouching tiger. Therefore one applies a strict ranking of the names of the three 'owners.' "[27]

The main stimulating factor for permanent tenancy rights was the landlords' demands for additional security in the form of a monetary deposit, which provided a guarantee against default. If a peasant was in arrears, the landlord could deduct his dues from the original deposit.[28] Once a tenant had established his position in this manner, he might rely on his deposit (locally called "fertilized soil silver" or *fen-t'u yin,* which indicates that the deposit was considered as compensation for the improved quality of the soil) to trade his rights for cash with others.

The effects of permanent tenancy rights were to stimulate farmland reclamation and improvement. Contracts often stipulated that tenants who reclaimed a plot of land and duly paid rent for some years would receive permanent tenancy rights and that their rents were fixed. Moreover, it stabilized rural tenancy relations and increased payments in cash. The tenant who held permanent tenancy rights held a commanding position, in between the landlord (to whom he paid a fixed rent) and the temporary tenants to whom he had leased his farmland, and about whom the landlord had no say.

Almost all farmland rents continued to be paid in grain. A study of Hui-chou showed that less than one percent of the rents were paid in cash before the Taiping, and even by the twentieth century, only a little over 10 percent of the rents in Fukien. Out of 707 collected land contracts in Fukien, partly from the Ming period but mostly from the Ch'ing period, only 15 percent had rents in cash. Almost all of the latter concerned mountain land, where cash crops were grown. This picture is confirmed by genealogies, which show a significant amount of rent payments in cash only with some special types of fields, such as common lineage properties.[29] One may conclude that, in the sixteenth century, rents for paddies were paid in kind, not in cash.

For both the tenant and the landlord there were some very good reasons for rent payment in grain, even if the tenant might have sufficient cash income from his multiple undertakings. While grain yields were fairly stable, their price in silver fluctuated considerably. The burden of rents expressed in kind was predictable, while those in cash were not, and the former could less easily be increased. Share-cropping arrangements reduced the risk for the tenant even further. For the landlords, rents in kind offered protection against the long-term inflationary tendency, and grain was easier to collect from the tenant than cash. Moreover, when individual tenants sold grain, transaction costs were higher and prices usually lower than when the landlord sold a much larger quantity of collected grain. Finally, because of the grain shortages of Fukien, landlords had to pay most of the grain tax in kind and deliver the grain to the local yamen anyway.

Privatization of Mountain Land

In recent years, local historians have collected and analyzed many land deeds from the Ming and Ch'ing periods. Their conclusion is that beginning in the mid-Ming mountain land in Fukien became private property and was devoted mainly to commercial crop production. The main causes of the privatization and commercialization of mountain land were the monetarization of Fukien's economy, an increasing demand for industrial products, and economic growth in general.[30] While this trend is undeniable, particularly since the Wanli period, because of the very limited coverage of such land contracts, it remains an open question to what extent village common rights persisted. By their very nature, common rights were seldom recorded. If they were, after privatization it was in nobody's interest to conserve their records.

The term *privatization* should not obscure the fact that much of this mountain land became property of lineages rather than of private individuals. Such lineage land remained collectively shared property that could not be sold by individuals at will. Also, the early land contracts were concluded mostly for commercial production and do not tell us how much mountain farmland was devoted to subsistence agriculture. In any case, the influx of seasonal labor into the mountain areas for industrial crop production, logging, burning charcoal, transport, and so on created a local demand for food grain. Mountain farmers and their families did not just produce for themselves, but took advantage of the new employment and marketing opportunities.

Local Markets

Around 1500, each county had several officially designated general and special markets. In coastal counties, there were dozens.[31] In spite of demographic and economic growth and specialization of production, with few exceptions along the coast their number increased only moderately or not at all during the sixteenth and seventeenth centuries. This seems to prove that most markets were capable of absorbing a larger turnover than they did and that most newly established commercial regions did not have a need for new market centers. This may have been the case for several reasons. Geographically, the number of possible overland and overseas trading routes in mountainous and land-locked Fukien was limited. During the commercially oriented periods of the Sung and Yuan dynasties, many periodic markets had already been set up, and their capacity could be increased simply by increasing their frequency. During the Ming period, prefectural and county governments tried to maintain their continuous supervision and control of markets, for reasons of tax revenues on product sales and to prevent smuggling and social disorder. They shifted most of the burden of collection and control of specialized markets to official brokers, who contracted for commercial tax payment and regular supplies of the product.

Most commercial products of the rural areas, whether indigo or tea from the mountains, sugar from the plains, or silk and porcelain, were produced in large quantities for the provincial, national, or international markets. Therefore, most trade was wholesale for specialized markets, and only part of its goods had been traded at small local markets first. Finally, the increasing rural unsafety made traders seek the relative protection of the walled towns, even if markets were often located immediately outside the city wall.

The *Li-chia* System and Corvée Services

Under the village responsibility (*li-chia*) system of the Ming dynasty, the government had ordered that a village head and unit head (*chia-shou*) be held responsible for village management. This included public affairs, law and order, and registration of population and farmland. Their most important responsibility was the payment of grain and head taxes. To that end, they might be required periodically to revise the registers of the tax-paying population (*huang-ts'e*). Moreover, they were held responsible for arranging the obligatory supply of goods (in principle, once every decade) and corvée services to the local and central authorities.[32] With the growth of local administration, such burdens became more heavy. At the same time, the growing mobility of labor and changes in local production made the corvée and tribute systems difficult to enforce and impractical.

In the early sixteenth century, measures were taken to establish these local burdens on a more objective and predictable footing and thereby curb abuses by local officials and village heads. In 1519, the Fukien provincial government replaced the obligatory supply of goods to the authorities by an annual fixed cash payment of 0.08 tael of silver per taxpayer (*ting*), the so-called eight cents system (*pa-fen fa*). The proceeds were used by the prefectural authorities for the purchase of the goods required by the central government. In 1557, a decision to forward only silver to the provincial tax bureau completed the monetization of this tax. Some districts such as Chang-chou reduced rates to 0.07 tael. Other districts (including Chang-chou) managed to bring also some small miscellaneous taxes under this new tax.[33]

Nevertheless, the supply of corvée services to the local government continued to exist. Particularly at the end of the Ming, when local government revenues fell because of the economic downturn, nonfinancial burdens of supply of goods and services increased again. For instance, there were growing complaints about the heavy burden of supplies of feed and grain to the official postal stations, each of which had scores of horses and personnel to be fed. Apparently, the burden of maintenance shifted toward the local population after their income declined. Also, there were irregularities. Hou Ch'iao-yuan noted that in his days, some people were registered as official taxpayers (*kuan-ting*), but others as private taxpayers (*ssu-ting*). The former paid about 0.3 tael per year, while the latter had to pay according to the number of people in their household and their wealth, as estimated by tax inspectors, "but those are not the real figures."[34]

Taxes and Local Government

Fukien and other southern provinces did not forward much tax grain to the capital. According to data for 1578, 536,000 *shih* of the annual tax grain (or 63 percent of the Fukien total of 850,000 *shih*) stayed within the province to feed the garrisons and pay for the local state apparatus. The largest contributors since the fifteenth century were Chien-ning and Foochow, followed by Chang-chou and Ch'uan-chou, these four prefectures paying between 166,000 and 109,000 *shih* of rice each. The three smaller prefectures of Yen-p'ing, Shao-wu, and

Hsing-hua paid between 60,000 and 86,000 each, and T'ing-chou and Fu-ning only about 30,000 *shih*. Before 1578, these official regular taxes had been lowered by 15 percent in Foochow and 10 percent in Ch'uan-chou, but subsequently they were restored to their previous level.[35] Although relative wealth and population numbers of the prefectures changed, grain taxes did not.

Chinese contemporary sources abound with complaints about the many, heavy, and unequal taxes and other burdens imposed by government and local yamen runners. However, because of our incomplete understanding of the size of population and economy of different counties, it is difficult to establish how heavy even the official tax burden was. If the coastal county of P'u-t'ien is a representative example, half the regular tax income was derived from the farm-land grain tax, and around 1600 this burden amounted to about one-fifth of the land rent and one-tenth of the average yield. This burden does not seem excessive. All other regular taxes combined (in descending order, corvées, fodder tax, principal silver, military equipment, and salt duties) supplied the other half. More than 85 percent of these taxes were used for the upkeep of local civil and military government.

What regular government services did the taxpayers get in return? The 1612 list of P'u-t'ien officials, institutions, and personnel gives a good idea of government functions and staff. Its administration had nine military and eight civil prefectural officials and four civil county officials. They were responsible for the Court of Justice, the supplies' room, the treasury, the police, the secretariat, the executioner's office, the Prefectural Hall, the County Hall, the archives, three granaries, the salt bureau and transport office, the grain mill inspectorate, the prison, the examination hall, three school libraries, the army inn, fifteen postal inns, five military posts, and some minor services. The total number of low-ranking personnel was 565 people, a hundred of which served in the military posts and fifty-five in the postal stations. This regular personnel comprised less than one percent of the working population.[36]

Official land and head taxes covered only part of the economic activities and did not keep up with the growth and diversification of the economy. The miscellaneous taxes were a much better indicator of economic growth, and the very different rates and burdens of official and unofficial local taxes and levies show that the local government apparatus and its finances grew at very different rates in different districts. It is therefore not necessarily correct to conclude, as contemporary writers did and some historians do, that the very different rates reflect increasing corruption or greed of officials and yamen runners at the end of the Ming period or an unfair distribution of unequal tax burdens between counties. It is clear, though, that certain economic activities and sectors were more heavily taxed than others and that people who lived closer to government or military centers or communication lines (such as the postal stations, which were considerably expanded during the sixteenth century, in response to pirate activities and increased trade) had to carry heavier burdens.

In periods of population growth and economic expansion, the increased government burdens could be met rather easily. In periods of economic and demographic contraction, such as the final decades of the Ming, the very inelastic taxes and levies necessary to sustain the government and military apparatus became a burden that weighed much more heavily on some districts than on others. Commercial cropping, trade, and industry were very dependent on changes in demand, and as soon as demand decreased because of economic and demographic decline, their capacity to pay taxes was greatly reduced. Thus, the commercially and industrially developed areas were affected most by such external changes.

Local Forts

During the mid- and late Ming, fortified villages or compounds in many areas of Fukien were built by private persons in response to the increasing rural unsafety caused by pirate attacks, mountain robbers, feuding between lineages or villages, and peasant uprisings. Of course, the government had some fortifications of its own, but its main concern was to protect the county capital. Some of these private fortifications may still be seen today. They had varying sizes and forms: square or circular, with an outer wall made from earth, brick, or stone, and usually one gate in front and an escape in the back. On the inside, there were rooms for several or several dozen families and storage, and a central place for cattle. They might be from one to four stories high, sometimes even higher. Their defenses were simple, but effective against raids by small groups. Their construction had to be approved by the local government, which in ordinary times would have had strong objections against civilian self-defense structures, but saw no reason not to comply in times of rebellions, war, and feuds.[37] Three types can be distinguished: the walled village, the stone fort, and the combined family compound. The second one was built as a temporary refuge in times of trouble and then was stacked with weapons and provisions. The other two were inhabited by several dozen or hundreds of people on a permanent basis and could provide temporary safety for many more if necessary. Most counties had dozens or hundreds of such fortifications.

As the scale of hostilities and bandit troubles increased, the smaller forts became inadequate and rural residents combined their resources and built larger protective structures. However, most continued to be built for the protection of one lineage only.[38] With the growth of commercial agriculture, handicraft production, and trade, there were more goods and lives to protect, and the growth of banditry in the sixteenth century may be seen as a sign of deepening divisions between local landowners and immigrant labor. Paradoxically, these forts often weakened the village as a social organization. Their effect was to strengthen the lineage as a social, economic, and even paramilitary organization, which defended the resources of its members against outsiders. More so than the village, the lineage shared a permanent common interest in the defense of its life and properties, and on that basis it could mobilize the necessary financial and labor resources.

Decline of Confucian Education and Buddhist Institutions, But Persistence of Religious Activities

Fukien used to have a reputation for its high level of Confucian education. During the Sung and Ming periods, both coastal and inland prefectures supplied a disproportionate number of successful graduates, and scholarship flourished. "The people from Chang-chou are very well educated. Of the fifty top scholars on the examination lists, most are from Chang-chou."[39] However, in the late Ming and Ch'ing periods the number of graduates in Fukien declined dramatically for several reasons. The rapid commercialization of the economy raised the income and status of merchants and made an official career less attractive. The dissatisfaction with and struggle against central government policies since the mid-sixteenth century may have played a role, too. Moreover, the destruction caused by the pirate wars and the Ming–Ch'ing transition affected the socioeconomic position of many great lineages. The general trend was for the old and new elites to become more supportive of local religious and social activities. This came at the expense not only of Confucianism, but also of the traditional Buddhist monasteries.

Fukien had many Buddhist and Taoist temples and monasteries as well as many local deities. Some of the larger temples dated back to the T'ang dynasty and had given rise to numerous daughter temples. Taoism was widespread, particularly in the Wu-yi mountains. Local deities included the gods of local mountains, rivers, and soil and protectors of towns. Temples were devoted to the Jade Emperor, the Secret Celestial Emperor, the Great Farming Emperor, the Dragon Emperor and dozens of geographically more limited deities such as Ma-tu, the Life-Protecting Emperor, the Woman of Lin-shui, the Kingly Father of the Five Prefectures, the General-Who-Founded-Chang-chou, the Holy King K'uo, Heavenly Teacher Chang, and many others.[40] Some places such as Chang-chou still had snake cults or other animistic cults. Islam had been wiped out almost completely at the end of the Yuan, but persisted in Ch'uan-chou and Foochow. Christian churches were built in many coastal cities and towns at the end of the Ming period and attracted a following that grew to hundreds of thousands. Religious fervor rose in times of disaster, as the following example shows.

In 1640, Foochow was struck by drought in spring and a typhoon in autumn. Many buildings and river boats were lost, and people killed. The Foochow population prayed to Wu-ti ("Five Emperor") and gave many offerings to invoke his help against an epidemic disease. They made paper boats, which Wu-ti could use to send pests away to the ocean. They offered sheep and pigs. Thousands took to the streets, chanting and beating drums. From the second to the eighth month, the city and villages were in a frenzy, until Provincial Governor Chang stepped in and strictly forbade all further activities.[41]

Even if such intervention by the magistrate was quite common, one should not overemphasize the opposition between "rational" Confucianism and religious cults. The Confucian magistrate had to lead the people, including in prayers for good harvests or rains. After a long period of drought "Sub-prefect Lo took pity on the people's sorrow. Devoutly, he prayed to the mountains and streams, but there was no answer. He inquired with the Dragon Lake of the Pei-hsi river . . . and had an engraved stone tablet erected there. . . . Some days later, he put up an altar and prayed . . . and immediately rains poured down."[42] Rather than opposing religious activities, which would have been socially explosive, the government tried to divert them or even use them for its own ends.

The cult of Ma-tsu is the best-known example. Her cult originated in P'u-t'ien, and during the Sung dynasty spread along the coast among seafarers and fishermen, with an important center of worship established on Mei-chou island. She promised protection against the dangers of the high seas. Admiral Cheng Ho promoted her as a rallying force in the early Ming. He built a large temple for her in Ch'ang-lo county, and many other ones along the southeast coast, claiming that she had blessed the expeditions of his fleet.[43] Her institutionalization in the Ming and Ch'ing as the "Heavenly Imperial Consort" and "Empress of Heaven" and her widespread popularity over Taiwan and the South Seas demonstrate the successful efforts of the Confucianist bureaucracy to contain Fukien's religious activities and direct them toward politically and socially acceptable goals.[44]

As for the traditional Confucian values, there is reason to believe that in late sixteenth- and early seventeenth-century Fukien, ideological and social values had shifted under the influence of urban and commercial growth, and outward-oriented maritime development. The government had a tradition of taking a stance against the power and influence of lineages and temples. To give just one example of a local official's request: "Only in Fukien there are so many temple fields. . . . In Hsien-yu, even a single monk in a small temple has 30 to 50 *shih* of grain, much more than the common people. Moreover, the latter pay all kinds of taxes. . . . I would like to ask permission to use the temple grain for support of the military."[45] While there may have been some popular support for such measures in the beginning, the continuous government repression of the very activities that Fukien valued most—overseas trade and religion—and its inability to offer adequate protection against outside threats must have left many southern Min people with negative feelings toward the state. Our predominantly Confucian source materials cannot reflect this. However, the enthusiastic support at all levels for local religious and social activities, and even for the Christian religion, and emigration overseas may be taken as a rejection of central orthodoxy and a confirmation of Fukienese local identities.

Population, Lineages, Gender, Adoption, and Migration

We have little idea of the population in Fukien during the Ming period. Registration was exclusively for tax and corvée purposes and covered only part of the population. Official figures dropped from 815,000 households with 3,917,000 people in 1393 to 506,000 households with 2,105,000 people in 1491. Almost a century later, in 1578, the registered number of households was slightly higher, but the number of people dropped further to 1,739,000. So far, no historian has been able to offer satisfactory explanations for this drop in absolute numbers or for the implied reduction of the average household size, which dropped from almost 5 to only 3.4. Both deviated from the trend in China as a country. The drop in households indicates a weakened base of central government taxes. This may have been caused by a weaker economy, higher local taxes, fewer taxable households, or a combination of all three. The much smaller household size (the average for China as a whole stood at almost six) might be explained by less careful counting (particularly of female adults) or by increased mobility of labor and division of families in Fukien. All this is most uncertain.

Between the mid-fifteenth and mid-sixteenth centuries, only in Foochow and Ch'uan-chou did the registered number of households significantly increase (from 46,000 to over 90,000, and from 23,000 to 33,000, respectively), but in other prefectures it remained about the same: Chien-ning a little over 100,000, Hsing-hua 24,000, T'ing-chou and Shao-wu 35,000 each. The numbers for Chang-chou and Yen-p'ing decreased (from 52,000 to 35,000 and from 64,000 to 53,000). The changes had little to do with actual changes in population numbers, but primarily reflected increases or decreases in political control and ability to perceive taxes. It is no coincidence that increases were largest in Foochow's suburban districts of Min-hsien and Hou-kuan, and Ch'uan-chou's Chin-chiang district, closest to the seats of provincial and prefectural governments.

Although the inferior position of women in family and society was a general phenomenon in China, according to contemporary sources it was more pronounced in Fukien than elsewhere. Female infanticide and sales of young daughters were common, but the extent to which they were practiced is unknown. Sources that mention, and always condemn, these customs date from the Ch'ing rather than the Ming period. Most likely, such practices, which meet the need to limit population growth, were strongest during times of perceived or objective overpopulation, that is, during late Ming and again during mid- and late Ch'ing. The custom of raising girls as servants in their prospective husbands' homes was a common strategy among the poor to reduce the costs of marriage, which rose along with local wealth *and* the shortage of women. The poorest men were able to marry only after many years of savings, or not at all. In addition, there were the long absences from home of men who had gone abroad as a sailor or trader, many of whom did not return.

China's traditional ideal was to maintain the extended family, with all generations under one roof. In practice, more often than not only the eldest son stayed with his parents, the younger sons setting up their own households. Thus, "stem families" with two or sometimes three generations were most common. It has been suggested that the early Ming household registration system and policies worked against the maintenance of extended families because the government recruited soldiers and salt carriers from households with more than one adult son and imposed heavier taxes on the rich. Thus, families divided property and split up in order to evade these burdens. In the next centuries, because of changes in the taxation and corvée systems, the number of people in a family did not matter very much any more, and the extended family made a comeback. In some cases, although formally property and family were divided, people continued to live together as an extended family.[46]

Clan genealogies by their very nature tend to emphasize the extended family and may not be representative of the poorer and less successful segments of Fukienese society. From an economic point of view, the extended family had some obvious advantages and disadvantages. In agriculture, pooling labor, cattle, and tools and sharing investments could raise their efficient use and spread individual risks, on the conditions that sufficient farmland and other employment opportunities were available. A large economic scale reduced the costs of acquisition of inputs (including loans) and sales of output and might enable the family to buy a loom or invest in other income-generating activities. Moreover, it might reduce the average cost of consumption (including housing) and fluctuations in income and provide some security during disasters or illness. Also, in times of turmoil, the extended family offered more safety against banditry and theft. However, the expansion of farming into the mountain areas, both for subsistence and for commercial crops (some of which had been introduced from overseas during the sixteenth and seventeenth centuries), and the increase of employment opportunities outside agriculture were economic incentives for young males to leave their families for a long period of time and finally establish a household elsewhere. As the economic activities of coastal and inland mountain regions tended toward specialization and differentiation, a pattern of labor migration emerged whereby many young males tried their luck in transport and trade, including overseas, and seasonal laborers moved from subsistence villages to commercial cropping areas. Generally speaking, these were movements from the inland river valleys into the hills and mountains and from inland areas to the coastal areas.

Particularly in the early phases of setting up an enterprise, which was too large to be handled by one family or lineage, the Fukienese had found a solution by establishing contractual lineages. These were based on blood ties at first, but later also on a territorial basis. The latter form of cooperation must have been particularly useful for the reclamation of silt flats along the coast from the Sung dynasty onward and again since the sixteenth century for the joint development of mountain land with an unclear or disputed ownership status. By joining lineages, conflicts were avoided and the entire community became a participant in the development of local resources. Finally, with the development of commercial ventures that required a great deal of capital, contractual lineages were established purely on the basis of business interests. Adoption of the lineage form provided a degree of stability, security of continued involvement of labor and capital, and financial risk sharing that an ordinary partnership could not guarantee. Moreover, the lineage had control and sanction mechanisms of its own and therefore had less need to appeal to the courts or other official intervention. It had the hierarchy and leadership structure for disciplining individual members. It could use its ancestral temple as a meeting hall for conducting its internal business and keeping accounts. Thus, the family and lineage organizations were most suitable vehicles not only for social affairs but also for economic enterprises.

One should be reminded here of the fact that in premodern societies death tolls are high. Even if, according to a calculation by Liu Ts'ui-jung, records of southern lineages show an average of almost two sons per father during the final century of the Ming, life-spans were short and only one out of four lived to become a grandfather.[47] Only the larger unit of the lineage and adoption could guarantee a continuation of the family line.

One such form specific to Fukien has received a great deal of attention: the practice of adoption of adult sons by overseas traders to serve as captains or trading agents on their ships.[48] This practice fitted within the prevalent family strategy in other economic sectors. Adult males who had not yet married made the largest net contribution to family income. Families feared losing their own sons, knowing how great the risks of seafaring were, and they might not have the right capacities or age. Moreover, the captains and agents in their service were entrusted with a great deal of capital and responsibilities and were usually far away and very difficult to control. Adoption into the family provided a guarantee against embezzlement or flight and secured the permanent allegiance to the family enterprise of persons who might be more capable and more experienced than one's own sons. For the employee, the permanent status of adopted son gave him a new and more affluent family backing and prospects of a share of the family wealth. In the absence of a sufficiently strong legal framework for the creation of long-term share-holding companies, the family as a more or less permanent institution provided an alternative in which risks could be shared, business expanded, profits reinvested, experience accumulated over many years, and employee allegiance assured. The practice of adoption secured the survival of the family business, and both sides, capital and labor, benefited from it.

Few existing genealogies of lineages refer to migration from Fukien to Taiwan before the Dutch, Cheng Chih-lung, and the Spaniards established bases there in the 1620s.[49] Apparently, even if late Ming Fukien suffered from overpopulation, heavy taxation, and other government burdens, and pestilences, crossing the Taiwan strait and settling in Taiwan were not safe and attractive enough. Because of government restrictions, Chinese emigrants overseas were insufficiently armed or organized for a strong defense of their newly created communities. The aboriginal tribes, most of whom were fierce hunters, and malaria and other unhealthy conditions associated with the original forests and marshes of Taiwan made any settlement a risky undertaking. Instead, the southern Min migrated to the Philippines and other Southeast Asian countries, where there was more trade and employment in agriculture and mining, some protection by Western powers, and where they felt safer—not always rightly so, as was demonstrated by the 1603 massacre of more than 20,000 Chinese in the Philippines.[50] A recent study of the Yen lineage from An-p'ing showed that the average age of death was thirty-nine for those members who emigrated to Southeast Asia and forty-four for those who went to Taiwan, while those who went to Kuangtung and other mainland destinations died at an average age of forty-nine. Marine accidents and massacres took a heavy toll. About 70 percent of the emigrants were already married, but almost none took their wives and very few married overseas.[51] "Some An-p'ing merchants do not return home for more than ten years, and if they do, they do not recognize their grown-up sons. This is because some of them leave immediately after the marriage ceremony with their pregnant wives remaing behind. . . . Nine out of ten families profit from the overseas trade with the Philippines."[52]

The Chinese government did not consider active involvement in private overseas ventures, military, commercially, or otherwise, but instead held fast to its interdiction of overseas migration and contacts with foreign peoples, which had been a source of so much trouble for the government in the sixteenth century. Only the disaster-ridden Ming–Ch'ing transition and Dutch encouragement and protection of Chinese settlers gave sufficient stimuli for migration.

The Military Dominance in Fukien

Because of the civil bias of most Chinese sources, historians of China tend to give insufficient attention to the military aspects of government and society. In sixteenth-century Fukien, which was considered a border region by the Ming court, the military presence was overwhelming and a dominating element in government, taxes and levies, and personnel.

In the early Ming, two commanderies had been established: One in Foochow controlled eleven garrisons in the coastal prefectures, and another in Chien-ning controlled five garrisons in the upper reaches of the Min river and the mountain prefectures. Most garrisons were located in the vicinity of major cities and lived in a walled compound. Including their subdivisions, the number of garrison soldiers totaled 48,200 according to two sixteenth-century sources, but totaled 102,400 according to the late Ming *Min Shu*.[53] It is not clear whether this difference is due to inaccuracy by the authors (military figures were secret at the time) or actual changes in numbers. Most likely, there was a slow decline from the fifteenth century because of the low income and status of soldiers. Their numbers seem to have hardly increased later, although they were much needed for military campaigns against the pirates. Their levels of training and morale were low. According to Gu Yanwu, "They could not even kill a chicken" and "took fright and wanted to run as soon as they heard a drum."[54] Instead, a people's militia system was created, which was much more flexible. If we take the example of P'u-t'ien county, in 1501 its regular bow soldiers were reduced to 400, but from 1512 on a force of 315 militiamen received regular pay. In 1537 they were divided into two alternating groups, each of which served and was paid for half a year.[55] When the experienced general Yu Ta-yu assumed command over the fight against the pirates in Fukien in 1562, he recruited several thousand local fighters from the mountains and islands of Ch'uan-chou and Chang-chou, because they were experienced and brave.[56] After the pirates' defeat, in 1572 in P'u-t'ien four garrisons were established manned with 602 soldiers from elsewhere—apparently the militia could not be sufficiently trusted, and their numbers were reduced to 112.[57]

The reason for the decline of the regular garrison forces may be found also in the growth of population numbers and wealth in the region. This increased the local government and villages' capability to hire soldiers themselves on a short-term basis if and as the need arose. A stone tablet records one such action by a prefect in Nan'an county in 1548: "The prefect established military barracks, assembled several warships, and recruited over one thousand naval soldiers. He dispatched officials in charge of civilian and military supplies. . . . He ordered Magistrate Ma to send ships and attack the pirates. Most were captured and killed. . . . Later, he ordered Magistrate Ma to go at night to all villages and collect more than a hundred strong people. He followed them in person, wearing armor and on horseback, and simply said: Those who retreat will die of their own volition!"[58] From the early sixteenth century onward, in addition to local governments, also local merchants, clans, and villages began to hire their own braves and construct their own defense works, with permission of the local civil authorities.[59] As a county official remarked, "The situation of the Japanese pirates is very unpredictable. The measures for protection of our land must be adequate. How can one rely on fortified villages if their fortifications are in disrepair? One should allow Mr. Ch'ao Yi to protect his family."[60]

Similar declines in numbers of personnel have been recorded for the navy patrols. In addition to the land defenses, the Ming had established forty-five naval patrols and five sea forts in Fukien: Fenghuomen near the border with Chekiang, Hsiao-ch'eng near Foochow, Nan-jih island in Hsing-hua, Wu-yu island (now called Quemoy), and Tung-shan at the border with Kuangtung. They were manned by soldiers drawn from the nearest garrisons and had a variety of ships for patrol and customs duties and for providing protection against pirates. For the sake of convenience and under the threat of pirates, they were moved from their exposed positions closer to land in the fifteenth and early sixteenth centuries. During the crisis of the 1550s, less than half their nominal force of almost 20,000 men was found to be present, a rate similar to other garrisons.[61] Chu Wan noted that most warships were nonexistent or unfit for action. General Ch'i Chi-kuang restored the five sea forts, but only three received regular soldiers, the other two being manned with local fighters.

Sea Interdiction and Pirates

The Ming prohibitions on ocean trade severely restricted Chinese trade and migration. Forbidden were the export of horses, cattle, military supplies, iron tools, copper cash, silk, and silk goods. The list shows the many concerns of the central government: It feared the supply of military goods to foreign enemies (horses, weapons), negative effects on China's agriculture (cattle) or the economy (copper cash), and a breakdown of government trade monopolies (horses, silk). Later, it flatly forbade all ships with two or more masts to trade overseas. Operating from forts established along the Fukien coast, navy patrols controlled the sea and harbors. The government could enforce its interdiction of overseas trade by a variety of means. Legal sanctions such as a hundred blows with the bamboo cane and confiscation of goods and ships were applied to those who broke the rules or had not been granted permits. Economic and social sanctions could be applied by using the collective responsibility system (*pao-chia*), under which family and *pao* heads were held responsible for the actions of their members. Village heads had to report migrants to the authorities. Ship captains had to report their crew and were held responsible for their return. Heavy taxes, inofficial levies by the military or local authorities, and customs procedures, whether designed to restrict trade or not, added to its cost. The same applies to regulations about maximum ship sizes, market restrictions, and so on. The combination of restrictive rules and measures had a very strong negative effect on overall overseas trade, even if some private trade could be carried on under the umbrella of the official tributary trade.

In the early Ming period, the tributary missions of the Ryukyuans became an important channel for trade with Japan and Southeast Asia. At first, the Ryukyuans received ships and sailors from China. Later, they became more independent and had their ships made and sailors recruited in Fukien. However, the growth of international trade in the sixteenth century, fueled by population increase, the new links with the Americas—through European traders—and economic growth in East Asia and elsewhere was so large that trade with outsiders could no longer be controlled by the Ming government or restricted to designated ports and tribute missions. Moreover, because international trade was in the best interest of China—notably by increasing overseas sales and import of much-needed silver to sustain China's economic growth—and benefited the merchants and shipping services of Fukien in particular, local authorities would have liked to turn a blind eye to private overseas trade and profit from it as much as they could. But the central government insisted that local governments should take action against what it had defined as smuggling and collusion with foreign enemies. After the abolition of the Office of Trading Ships, the interdiction of sea trade became more strict and more rigidly enforced. Thus, the private traders were forced into illegality and became smugglers and "pirates." They were driven by foreign demand for Chinese products, that was backed up by silver which the growing Chinese economy could put to good use.

Local effects of the overseas trade were manifold: the import of many new crops; commercialization of the economy; development of local handicraft production for export; specialization of agricultural export crops; monetarization of the economy (and development of rent payment in cash instead of in kind). The lesson of the sixteenth century should have been that liberalizing overseas trade was the only remedy against "piracy," because it changed smugglers into traders. However, the Ming court had many other concerns, particularly about defense against the Mongols and maintenance of unity and orthodoxy in the empire. Ch'ang Han, a scholar who had held high posts throughout China, including governorships of Kuangtung and Shanhsi, noted that those who ruled China knew about the exchange markets in the northwest, but were unaware of the overseas markets of southeastern China. Yet the latter were incomparably larger than the markets in the northwest and had great profits but no drawbacks.[62]

Chu Wan and Explosion of the Conflict

The conflict between local interests and the central government became most violent in the mid-sixteenth century.[63] In 1547, an imperial inspector of Chekiang recommended that all coastal prefectures of Chekiang and Fukien be brought under the unified military command of one official. Only in this way could the highly mobile pirates, who attacked now here, then there, be controlled. The court agreed that it was indeed necessary to take extraordinary measures and appointed Chu Wan as governor of Chekiang province and concurrently commander of the garrisons of the coastal prefectures of Fukien.

Chu Wan's strict measures against local officials and merchants who dared to send out ships and continue to trade with the Japanese and others quickly made him most unpopular with the Fukienese gentry and merchants and with those high court officials who profited from this trade. At first, the court consented to his policies of terror: Ships and warehouses were burnt, people were forced to inform on each other, and armies were sent to attack harbor towns and arrest merchants known to be trading with the foreigners. By executing several scores of leading merchants, he hoped to frighten others into abandoning their overseas trade. According to the theory held by him and others at the court, the pirate troubles would end only if the Chinese merchants would stop trading and offering shelter for their ships. Cut off from their outlets and provisions on the mainland, the pirates would have to stop or go elsewhere. Chu realized that many of the merchants had local political and financial backing and that this had to be stopped, too. "[Retired officials] gather fugitives and traitors and set up local rackets. They terrorize the region and intimidate officials. They provide capital, sailors and ships to overseas traders . . . and demand a 100 percent interest when the ships return with their cargoes, and an equal share of profits in excess of that."[64] What he failed to see is that by that time international and coastal trade had become so large and well established and so important to the

South Fukienese society and economy, that short of a military attack on Fukien by the regular armies, it could no longer be stopped. Army commanders who were sent in to fight the Japanese or Chinese "pirates" looked in vain for their enemies, as the latter were usually sheltered and supported by the local people. Local guerrillas and opposition could not be conquered short of destroying much of the Fukien coastal area with its population. As it turned out, unlike its successor in the Ch'ing dynasty, the Ming court was not prepared to go that far.

The local reaction was swift. The local elite, most of whom either directly participated in foreign trade or had heavily invested in it, claimed that Chu Wan overstepped his powers and hurt "the decent people" and their profitable trade. Such remonstrations found a willing ear in the intensively competitive Ming bureaucracy, and soon Chu Wan's powers were curtailed. Fearing impeachment, he killed himself in 1550. However, the discussions at the court between those for and those against compromise with the pirates and liberalization of trade lasted on.

When in 1551 even fishing boats were forbidden, local resistance exploded. Pirates and locally recruited Chinese, who had ties with local merchants and gentry, raided the coastal region and captured coastal forts and dozens of towns, including some county seats. The damage to the unprotected country done by pirates and government troops was most extensive. Tens of thousands of people died, their properties were destroyed, their fields inundated, and farmland laid to waste.[65] The conflict had now escalated to a point where the Ming government had to send in tens of thousands of troops. It took more than a decade before the force of the pirates had been broken and their island strongholds recaptured. In 1563 General Ch'i Chi-kuang retook Hsing-hua prefecture and drove the pirates out of Fukien. These successes provided the necessary political and military room for the court to approve a relaxation of the ban on shipping in 1567. Using warships collected and built in Fukien, and after having bought over the pirate chief Lin Tao-ch'ien, General Yu Ta-yu then annihilated Tseng Yi-pen and other pirates in Kuangtung.

If the court had had a greater understanding of the economic needs of the Fukienese and their predicament, it would have been readier to compromise at an earlier date, and pirate raids and military campaigns could have been avoided. Now the result was much suffering and damage, and the court's policies left Fukien and other provinces in a position where, on the mainland, most Fukienese could profit only indirectly and through illegal channels from the blooming international trade. Partly because of these unhappy experiences, partly for reasons of military defense, and possibly also because of competition between cities, Foochow and Hsing-hua insisted on maintaining the ban on overseas shipping, while Ch'uan-chou and Chang-chou favored its liberalization.[66]

Harbors: Yue-kang and Some Other Ports in the South

Ch'uan-chou's decline in the mid-Ming has been attributed to siltation of its harbor after the Yuan (partly owing to destruction of the vegetation cover along the Chin river) and to its inability to compete with harbors such as Yue-kang, which did not suffer from government control and taxes. In 1574, the government transferred its Fukien Shipping Bureau to Foochow. Thereafter, Yue-kang took over most of Ch'uan-chou's overseas trading activities.

The rise of Yue-kang illustrates the triumph of private southern Min traders over stifling government control. It had developed as a smuggler's harbor on the border of two counties. In 1566, it received formal recognition as a separate administrative unit, Hai-ch'eng county. The next year, the Ming government abolished the sea interdiction and allowed overseas trade. Yue-kang was appointed as the only harbor in China where private overseas trade was legal. Competitors on the China coast, such as the flourishing Shuang-yu harbor in the Chou-shan archipelago near Ning-po, had been eliminated by the Ming navy two decades earlier. Thus, Yue-kang's trade could increase dramatically, until 1613. Customs duties, which probably failed to capture most of this trade, increased from 3,000 silver taels to 35,100 taels, which was two-thirds of the Fukien total.[67] Part of this rise reflected rising tariffs, but most of it represented increased volumes. Various sources reported that "at least 70" and at most "more than 200" trading ships came to Yue-kang each year.[68] Ships went to Indochina, the Indonesian archipelago, the Philippines, Korea, the Ryukyus, Japan, and many other countries. Silk, porcelain, cotton cloth, tea, sugar, paper, fruits, and so on were main export items, and spices, gems, silver coins, rice, coconuts, beans, and many foreign products were imported.

Causes for Yue-kang's rise were many. Its heavily indented coastline with many natural shelters, creeks, and islets, made it an ideal place for safe and fast loading and unloading of goods. Most overseas trade was forbidden, and its position on the border of Long-hsi and Chang-p'u counties, away from major centers of government control, made it attractive to smugglers.[69] Its location near the mouth of the Chiu-lung river facilitated local trade and transport of people and goods. Moreover, the local economy in Chang-chou had flourished on the basis of agricultural land improvement and increased specialization in agriculture and handicraft industry, notably sugar production, tangerines, lychees, and other fruit, and later also tobacco. Considerable quantities of timber were still available in the upper basin of the Chiu-lung river for shipbuilding. The increased Fukienese production of silk goods, hemp cloth, indigo, iron, and fruit for national and international markets stimulated overseas trade and vice versa. However, the main reason for Yue-kang's rise is the growing trade between the Spanish from the Philippines and the Chang-chou merchants, who tried to escape from government interference and taxes in the three officially approved harbors of Ch'uan-chou, Foochow, and Canton.

Decline set in after 1621, after the government established customs control over Yue-kang and again forbade private overseas trade. Moreover, the aggression by the Dutch East India Company ships took its toll on Chinese junks and interrupted Chinese trade with Manila. In 1632, the Ming abolished its

Haich'eng Supplies Inspection Office, and thereafter most trade moved to Amoy, An-hai, and other harbors.

Amoy island, at the mouth of the Chiu-lung river, was a major naval base during the Ming. Its harbor offered the advantages of sufficient depth and a shelter against wind and waves behind some smaller islets such as Ku-lang-yu and Quemoy. It was the designated mooring place where the authorities inspected ships from Yue-kang and issued permits for overseas trade. When the Dutch began with their attacks on Chinese and Spanish ships, traders gravitated to the relative safety offered by the Amoy garrison and navy, and the island became a major bone of contention between the warring parties for several decades, for instance when in 1633 the Dutch burned Cheng Chih-lung's fleet but were severely beaten a month later.

An-hai had served the city of Ch'uan-chou as its main sea harbor during the Sung and Yuan dynasties. It received its name "Pacification of the Seas" only after its defenses had been strengthened with a city wall and a garrison in order to be able to cope with the pirate attacks of the Chia-ching period. By 1600, its mainly commercial population numbered more than 100,000 and conducted a lively trade with the Philippines and Japan, even at times when it had been declared illegal. Because An-hai was at some distance from Ch'uan-chou, it could conduct illegal trade more easily than other places could. Being the home-town of Cheng Chih-lung, it became one of the most important bases for his trading empire, and when he received an official commission as a general in 1628, he opened an office in An-hai. From An-hai a direct shipping line was maintained with Nagasaki. The town was heavily defended by Cheng Ch'eng-kung, and although it fell to the Ch'ing armies in 1647, he managed to regain and keep it until 1655. The town was destroyed by the Ch'ing a second time, and subsequent Ch'ing policies of sea closure killed its trade for good.

One northern harbor should be mentioned here because it suffered the same problems of government control. Sha-ch'eng in the northeast of Fu-t'ing county was a meeting point for the coastal trade between Chekiang and Fukien, and Fukien's most important naval base. Iron, fish, cotton, and silk were traded here, and ships bound for illegal destinations such as Japan used its harbor. In 1612, the Ming government ordered all vessels that traded between the provinces of Chekiang and Fukien to moor at Sha-ch'eng and transfer their goods there under the watchful eyes of the authorities. Offenders were to expect their ships and cargo to be confiscated. However, this ruling was not very effective, and direct trade continued to flourish.[70]

Taxes on Overseas Trade

Liberalization of overseas trade was never more than partial, and fiscal and administrative intervention continued to be serious constraints. When some overseas trade was legalized again in 1567, and Yue-kang designated as the sole official port in Fukien, ships were monitored and taxed by a system of permits.

Ship owners were taxed by the width of their ship, with rates of 5.5 taels per foot for ships wider than 17 feet and 5 taels per foot for those less than 17 feet wide. Ships bound for southern China seas paid 30 percent less than those bound for Japan. This method of taxation per foot of width was very regressive (with an increase in width, the carrying capacity increases many times more), and it is not known why such a system was adopted. It was simple, of course, and the cost of inspection and tax perception of large and small ships may have been not very different. However, it may also have reflected the government's carefulness not to antagonize the largest investors and preference for taxing the less powerful owners of smaller ships. In any case, the taxation method was a stimulus for the building of longer and larger ships and technological improvements in shipbuilding. Revenues went to the navy. In addition to the ship tax, a tax on cargo was levied from the merchants (who usually accompanied their cargo), the revenues of which went to the army. The total taxes from these two sources rose quickly from about 6,000 taels in 1575 to almost 30,000 taels in 1594. In addition, there were military exactions and inofficial levies, for example, a 150-tael surcharge on ships from the Philippines. At that time, ships for Yue-kang had to stop for inspection at the patrol stations of Wu-yu or T'ung-shan, and then get a customs permit at the Amoy Office. However, there was much bribery and smuggling. In 1593, the local authorities of Ch'uan-chou proposed dividing the tax receipts from Yue-kang's overseas trade between them and Chang-chou, but because people believed that such dual control would increase smuggling, it was not accepted.[71]

When the eunuch Kao-ts'ai became the tax collector in Fukien in 1599, merchants were ruthlessly fleeced. Originally, the taxes contributed by Yue-kang had provided for the garrison of Chang-chou and the budgetary expenses of local government. However, after the Ming emperor had sent his eunuchs, these taxes were siphoned off to the imperial treasury or private pockets. Finally the emperor had to abolish Kao-ts'ai's position, but the tax conflict with local authorities remained unresolved.

At the court, objections to a further relaxation of overseas trade remained strong, particularly after Hideyoshi's invasions of Korea in 1592. Ports were closed, defenses were strengthened, and officials called for an end to overseas trading. However, others noted that this would provoke rather than prevent collusion with the Japanese enemy and thought that the ban should be applied only on Japan.[72] The net effects on the Fukienese economy of the Korean campaigns and the ban on trading with Japan are difficult to measure. The requisitioning of ships and temporary interruption of trade must have hurt, but the additional attention to coastal defense, on both land and sea, gave a boost to local construction, shipbuilding, and employment.

Chinese Actions in the Philippines and the 1603 Massacre

In the 1570s, a total of seventy-five Chinese junks came to Manila. In the following decades until the end of the Ming, almost 1,700 junks, or an average of twenty-eight junks per year, were reported. This made it the major destination of southern Min traders and settlers.[73] In 1575, while the Spaniards were laying siege to a fort held by the Fukienese pirate Lin Feng in the Philippines, a Chinese naval officer who had been chasing the same pirate arrived in Manila. They agreed on joint action, and the Spaniards went with him to Foochow to plead their case for trade and missionary work. Then news arrived that Lin Feng had broken the siege and returned to the Fukienese waters with his pirate fleet. The negotiations were broken off, with bad feelings on both sides. Nevertheless, the number of settlers from southern Min continued to grow in the subsequent decades.

The next, much more unfortunate incident occurred in 1602–3. Upon the recommendation of a local Chinese investor, the Ming government gave a permit to the Fukien intendant in charge of business taxes and mining to mine for precious metals in the Chi-yi mountains on an offshore island—most likely not realizing that this territory was overseas and claimed by the Spanish. The arrival of the Chinese survey team made the Spaniards fear that a Chinese invasion was imminent and sparked a conflict that resulted in a massacre of the Chinese residents. These and other incidents reinforced the Ming government's conviction that it should not become involved beyond its traditional sphere of influence.

The massacre of the Chinese in the Philippines in 1603 made many traders flee to Fukien, and some years later Li Tan and other Fukienese merchants established a major presence in Nagasaki and Hirado. Their trade with Japan, the Philippines, the Dutch East Indies, and Taiwan stimulated the coastal economy of Fukien, which continued to boom until the 1620s. However, there was an increasing tendency to trade not from the mainland itself, but from islands off the coast or other countries.

Profits from Trade and Reinvestment in Other Sectors

Contemporary Chinese sources stated that the profit from overseas trade was very high, "tenfold." These accounts were written by scholars who frowned on such activities, not by businessmen. "The poor people living on the Fukien coast depend on the sea for a living. They catch fish and traffic salt. It is a living, but not at all rewarding. Only the simple and weak folks rely on this. The traitorous and domineering among the people board ships to search for profits overseas, and their profit is tenfold."[74] Actually, in ordinary years gross profits on trade between China and Japan or Southeast Asia were about 100 to 150 percent for high-value bulk goods such as silk and silk wovens, and 200 to 300 percent on low-value bulk goods such as sugar.[75] Profit margins were higher in times of war and for specialty products. There is insufficient data about cost and freight rates to calculate net margins for traders and ship owners. Risks, scarcities, and prices fluctuated a great deal, more so than in the coastal trade. However, ship owners might use their ships on the coastal transport routes whenever demand for overseas cargo was low. Considering the risks of the high seas, pirates, diseases, official exactions, fraud, and so on, one might expect annual net returns on capital to have been at least 30 to 40 percent in ordinary years, in order to make up for the losses in bad years.

Part of the profits derived from overseas trade were reinvested in buying farm-land and establishing strong ties with officials and the local community. The usual explanation for this diversion of capital from a high-profit sector to low-profit sectors is that the Chinese merchant wanted to buy respectability and lead a gentry life. As an individual, he had little recourse against official exactions, social pressures, or outright robbery, and he thought it wise to protect his family by establishing a firm political and social presence in the local community. While this explanation is not incorrect, it enumerates only one out of several forms of capital flows from overseas trade. For most Fukienese, overseas trade was a medium-term investment, a venture of one to two years. As overseas trade could not be expanded at will, often there was excess capital that had to find an outlet elsewhere for short or long periods.

In the short term, capital might go into speculation or conspicuous consump-tion. In 1524, Chang-chou experienced a craze for rare pigeons not unlike the later Dutch tulip mania. "The price of pigeons rose to a hundred *tael*. The spotted black and green ones were the most expensive, followed by the red with purple ones. At first, their price had been only one or two *tael*. Wild speculation arose. Finally, the government forbade the trade, but it did not stop. When the trade busted, some people lost a fortune."[76] Also funds had to be spent on protection of the increased wealth and properties against local and outside robbers. The de-structive pirate raids, which lasted to the 1560s, necessitated huge investments in rebuilding damaged city walls, yamens, bridges, temples, and other structures in the coastal region. Many of these were financed through extra public duties or by local communities. In addition, many private properties had to be repaired.

In the long term, much commercial capital was reinvested in building new houses, bridges, and temples. During the relatively peaceful period of 1580 through 1620, there was a rapid rise in construction of all sorts. Even prefectures such as Hsing-hua, which did not have much overseas trade, saw a building boom.[77] Also, part of the capital accumulated from overseas trade left China for good, being invested in agriculture, mining, trading, and other activities by Chi-nese emigrants in the Philippines and other Southeast Asian countries. Under-standably, both entrepreneurs and rentiers tried to reduce the high risks and vulnerability of having too many liquid assets in one place. Thus, they diversi-fied their undertakings and also bought farmland. As landlords, they might profit from rising land prices and also from the additional opportunity to supply export products. In some cases, they might want to recruit reliable laborers for local or overseas activities and find a most suitable source in their tenant households. Tenants were a primary target for the supply of loans—one of the more profit-able uses of short-term excess capital. In conclusion, even if ownership of farmland itself yielded only moderate profits from rents, it opened up other economic opportunities that might make it economically very rewarding. While the above economic arguments are sufficient in themselves, one may also consider socio-political explanations for reinvestment of profits from trade in other sectors.

Fu Yiling has studied the An-p'ing merchants, who played an important role in the raw silk trade for which the Philippines had become a center. Many developed from small traders into big businessmen. He notes several differences with their Western or inland Chinese counterparts. First, while Western merchants were risk-seeking and willing to go to faraway territories, the An-p'ing merchants concentrated on immediate income. Second, the sea-traders were partly linked with bureaucracy, but they did not have institutionalized political power such as the salt merchants had and therefore were incapable of protecting their position. Third, the An-p'ing merchant had close ties with his village lineage and his individual position was weak. Fourth, he maintained ties with agriculture and usually settled down in a rural area at the end of his career. As a trader noted, "For becoming rich, trade is better than agriculture; but for accumulation of virtue by conducting business, agriculture is superior."[78] Sometimes, merchants would pursue a scholarly career as well. For the above-mentioned reasons, accumulation of merchant capital remained limited.[79]

The Effect of Foreign Silver and the Seventeenth-Century Crisis

Silver was the main means of exchange in commercial transactions during the Ming period, and taxes had to be paid in silver, too. The main sources of silver were the state mines in the provinces of Chekiang and Yunnan, in Lung-hsi and P'u-ch'eng counties in Fukien, and illegal private mines. In the sixteenth century, with the arrival of Spanish silver from the Americas to Asia, foreign imports began to play a major role in China's supply of silver. Because most of it was brought from the Philippines by Fukienese traders, the monetarization of the economy started earlier in Fukien than in other Chinese provinces.

After the Spaniards had settled in Manila in 1571, they began to encourage Chinese merchant junks to come and trade Chinese silk for American silver. Most Chinese ships belonged to the southern Min, as they were already catering to their settlements in the Philippines. The Chinese trade grew to several dozens of junks per year and came to include sugar, porcelain, and spices. Via Manila, between 2 and 3 million pesos of silver flowed into China every year.[80]

Some Western scholars have linked the economic decline of the late Ming to the world crisis of the seventeenth century and given a prominent role in both to the diminished supply of silver from the Americas. The disruption of trade and interception of part of the flow of silver to Manila by Dutch and English captures of Spanish ships and Chinese junks in the 1620s and 1630s would have resulted in scarcity of silver in China, which drove the price of coppers up and created economic upheaval.[81] This theory is questionable for several reasons. First, the decline of the late Ming economy can be attributed to many other factors: costly wars in Korea and Manchuria, deterioration of standards of government, heavy and arbitrary taxation by eunuchs from Peking, a general breakdown of social order, low temperatures, and epidemics. Second, the improved Japanese silver mines were an important source of Chinese silver, and supply continued to grow until 1639. The Japanese were willing to pay more and more for Chinese silk: Nagasaki prices rose from 140–150 taels of silver per 100 *chin* around 1600 to 280 taels in 1622 and 550 taels in 1631. During the 1640s, Japan's annual imports of silk were between 100,000 and 200,000 *chin,* and prices fluctuated between 225 and 516 taels. According to contemporary Spanish estimates, about half of Japan's demand for raw silk was covered by imports.[82]

In the Nagasaki–Macao trade, apart from silks, porcelain and sugar were also exchanged for Japanese silver. Silver imports from this source increased from 15 to 20 tons per year in the 1590s to more than 70 tons during 1635–38, possibly totaling 1,650 tons between 1600 and 1639. From Goa and Manila came another 500 tons. Moreover, the direct China–Japan trade during that period was of a similar magnitude: a total of 350 official ships; a probably not much lower figure of private Japanese traders; and, most important of all, private trade carried by Chinese ships from Nagasaki and other harbors. In the 1640s, between thirty-four and ninety-seven Chinese junks arrived in Nagasaki each year. After 1635, Dutch exports of silver from Nagasaki rose to several dozens of tons per year. Together, Japanese silver exports had a marked increase from less than 100 tons per year until 1610 to 130 tons in 1630 and a peak of 200 tons in 1637. Moreover, there was an increasing amount of silver brought from Europe.

Therefore the European silver crisis did not affect China very much. Chinese imports depended mainly on the increasing silver production in Japan and growing trade in the East Asian region.[83] This goes *a fortiori* for Fukien, which was the main port of entrance of Japanese silver. The scarcity of silver in the late Ming was not due to supply reasons. Government diversion to unproductive purposes such as warfare and hoarding may have played a minor role. The shortage resulted primarily from the growth in foreign demand for Chinese products. More and more foreign silver was needed to pay for these exports and to finance the expansion of their production and trade in China.

Conclusion: Structural Changes and the Limits of Fukienese Expansion in the Late Ming

In the Ming period, Fukien's economic and social growth was based primarily on the new opportunities offered by the development of global and interregional trade. Fukien could draw on its strategic location on the southeastern coast, the seafaring tradition of its fishermen and regional traders, and the presence of ship wharfs and all the necessary materials for shipbuilding. Like Flanders and Holland in late medieval times, Fukien managed to overcome the fundamental politi-cal and economic weaknesses of a peripheral, divided, and resource-poor region by developing processing industries, shipping, and trade. Its mountain areas already had an industrial tradition of lumber, paper, iron, porcelain, printing, and so on. Its shipping services could transport raw materials, particularly silk, from Kiangnan at low cost, and deliver final products to national and international markets. At the periphery of the main centers of political power, the region witnessed the autonomous development of a number of harbors and industrial-commercial cities.

The major industries of spinning and weaving in coastal urban and rural areas relied mainly on imports and exported their produce. They capitalized on their low wages and immigrant labor from Fukien's interior areas. Thereby, they outcompeted other regions of China. There was fierce competition between cities and towns and between merchants, leading to strong organizations of interest groups. Both in urban and in rural areas, lineages became important concentra-tions of socioeconomic power and manifested their enhanced role in a display of wealth, religious, and social activities.

The organization of shipping and trade services was not just a downstream effect of Fukien's economic expansion. Rather, it was its major initiator and underlying strength. However, Fukien's trade- and service-based economic boom was critically dependent on a number of favorable conditions. To a certain extent, it was destroyed by its own success. The overseas trade attracted Japan-ese pirates, and the wealth of coastal cities invited marauding parties. In the early seventeenth century, European traders were major buyers, but they were also competitors, prone to piracy, and at times ruthless in their dealings with overseas Fukienese settlers. Worse than the external enemy it wished to keep at bay, the central government clamped down on both international and regional shipping and trade through strict regulations, unpredictable administrative interventions, and destructive military activities. Instead of receiving government support for their economic and social expansion and migration overseas, the southern Min were severely repressed. Although the official burdens and indiscriminate exac-tions could be sustained during the economic upswing, once China moved into a downward cycle of political insecurity, economic crises, and demographic con-traction after the 1620s, Fukien was the first to suffer. Its industries and trade were severely hurt, and part of its services moved elsewhere. The effects on the Fukienese were not just economic. The sixteenth and seventeenth centuries left a lasting tradition of distrust of government, concern for the social security of one's family, and realization that the world is a hostile place where one needs the protection of one's own kind.

Another long-lasting effect of the sixteenth-century internationalization of the Fukienese economy was diversification of its agriculture and opening up of the mountain areas. Tubers and maize from the New World and industrial crops were introduced in mountain regions and dry land areas along the coast. They

enabled internal specialization and exposed local communities to the opportunities and dangers of interregional and international trade and division of labor.
More intensive exploitation of mountain farmland required a growing number of
seasonal migrant-laborers and intensified local efforts to maintain or gain control
over resources. A common reaction to all this was to strengthen lineage organizations. Eventually, the cultivation of new food crops and tea was to increase
Fukien's capacity to sustain a larger population, but only after it had recovered
from the economic crisis and destruction of the Ming–Ch'ing transition.

At first, the southern Min went overseas for short periods, for fishing and
trade. Subsequently, when socioeconomic conditions in Fukien began to deterio-
rate, increasing numbers of the urban and rural young and poor went overseas,
too, in search of a precarious living as miners, foresters, or farmers in the thinly
populated Southeast Asian countries. Although some of them returned home,
many stayed on for most of their productive life, resulting in a permanent drain
of labor and capital resources from Fukien. Thus, a tradition of emigration from
southern Min villages to overseas Chinese communities was established, which
was based mainly on local or lineage ties. Emigrants took with them the localist
feelings, competition, and conflicts of their communities and cities back home.
Their traditional customs and gods became the cohesive force and center of
social activities in their new environment.

Notes

1. Memorial by Zheng Shanfu, *Ming jingshi wenbian*, vol. 150, pp. 12–13; He
Qiaoyuan, (1630) *Ming shu*, vol. 38, Record of customs: Quanzhou. Fuzhou, 1994, pp.
942–943.

2. Tu Benjun, "Minzhong hai cuoshu," in *Congshu jicheng,* vol. 1358 (Shanghai:
Commercial Press, 1939), p. 4.

3. Wang Shimou, *Min bu shu* (ca. 1586), pp. 20 and 21b.

4. Gu Yanwu, *Tianxia junguo libing shu*, Zhangpu county, vol. 94, chap. 4; "Record
of Products of the South," in *Min Shu*, vol. 150.

5. Wang Shimou, *Min bu shu*, p. 6.

6. "Record of fish and salt," in *Dinghaixian zhi* (Jiajing).

7. Wu Zhihe, "Mingdai yuhu yu yangzhi shiye," in *Mingshi yanjiu zhuankan*, vol. 2,
quoting the (Wanli) *Huidian.*

8. (Ming) *Wanli huidian*, vol. 19, Finance 6, Population 1; (Wanli) *Quanzhoufu zhi*,
vol. 7, pp. 2–9; *Min shu*, vol. 39, p. 971. Fish tax data refer to around 1485 and have been
calculated from individual counties given in Huang Zhongshao, "Provisions and Goods,"
Bamin tongzhi, vol. 20 (1491, repr. Fuzhou , 1989),. pp. 389–421.

9. (1771) *Xianyouxian zhi*, vol. 53, p. 1.

10. Joseph Needham, *Science and Civilisation in China*, vol. 4, pt. 3 (Cambridge:
Cambridge University Press, 1971), pp. 396–484.

11. Chen Jian and Chao Jianjun, "Mingdai Fuzhou zaochuanye kaolue," *Zhongguoshi
yanjiu*, no. 3 (1987): 147–155.

12. (Wanli) *Fuzhoufu zhi*, vols. 21 and 22.

13. Song Yingxing, *Tian gong kai wu* (1637; repr. Taipei, 1980, in English), p. 259.

14. "Salt taxes," *Ming shu*, vol. 39.

15. Zeng Ling, "Mingdai Zhonghouqi-di Fujian yanye jingji," *Zhongguo shehui jingji shi yanjiu*, no. 1 (1987): 53–68.

16. See, e.g., Chen Mao, *Puyang shuili zhi* (repr. Taiwan: Ch'eng-wen, 1973)

17. Lin Tingshui, "Tangyilai Fujian shuili jianshe gaikuang," *Zhongguo shehui jingji shi yanjiu*, no. 2 (1989): 73–78.

18. *(Xinghuafu) Putianxian zhi* (1758; repr. 1926), pp. 120 and 300–301.

19. Wang Shimou, *Min bu shu*, p. 18.

20. Chen Mao, *Puyang shuili zhi*, vol. 5, pp. 3–6.

21. *Haichengxian zhi*, vol. 4. (1633).

22. Wang Shimou, *Min bu shu*, p. 14b.

23. "Customs," in (Wanli) *Quanzhoufu zhi*, vol. 3.

24. Lin Xiangrui, "Fujian yongdianquan chengyin-di chubu kaocha," *Zhongguo shi yanjiu*, no. 4 (1982): 62–74; idem, "Yongdianquan yu Fujian nongye ziben zhuyi mengya," *Zhongguo shi yanjiu*, no. 2 (1985): 41–55; *Tianxia junguo libing shu*, vol. 93.

25. Yang Guozhen, "Ming–Qing Fujian tudi siren suoyouquan neizai jiegou-di yanjiu," in *Ming–Qing Fujian shehui yu xiangcun jingji*, ed. Fu Yiling and Yang Guozhen (Xiamen: Xiamen daxue chubanshe, 1987), pp. 30–68.

26. Tien Ju-k'ang, "The Decadence of Buddhist Temples in Fu-chien in Late Ming and Early Ch'ing," in *Development and Decline of Fukien Province in the Seventeenth and Eighteenth Centuries*, ed. E.B. Vermeer (Leiden: E.J. Brill, 1990), pp. 83–95.

27. Gu Yanwu, *Tianxia junguo libing shu*, chap. 93.

28. Lin Xiangrui, "Fujian yongdianquan chengyin-di chubu kaocha."

29. Chen Zhiping, "Ming–Qing Fujian huobi dizuzhi lun," *Zhongguo shehui jingji shi yanjiu*, no. 1 (1989): 56–64.

30. Yang Guozhen and Chen Zhiping, "Cong shanqi kan mingdai Fujian shandi-di siyouhua," in Fu and Yang, ed., *Ming–Qing Fujian shehui yu xiangcun jingji*, pp. 144–160.

31. *Bamin tongzhi*, vols. 14 and 15.

32. Population registers: taxes, in *Min shu*, vol. 39.

33. Population registers: payments to the authorities, in *Min shu*, vol. 39; Record of taxes: the land tax, in (Wanli) *Zhangzhou fuzhi*, vol. 8; and Record of taxes: miscellaneous taxes, in ibid., vol. 9.

34. Population registers: the census, in *Min shu*, vol. 39.

35. Liang Fangzhong, *Zhongguo lidai renkou, tiandi, tianfu tongji* (Shanghai: Shanghai renmin chubanshe, 1980), pp. 354, 356, and 443.

36. E.B. Vermeer, "The Decline of Hsing-hua Prefecture in the Early Ch'ing," in Vermeer, ed., *Development and Decline of Fukien Province*, pp. 156–160.

37. For the arguments used by the applicants and the authorities, see, e.g., the stone record on the reconstruction of the Zhao family fortified village in Zhangpu, in Eduard B. Vermeer, *Chinese Local History: Stone Inscriptions from Fukien in the Sung to Ch'ing Periods* (Boulder: Westview, 1991), pp. 30–33.

38. Yang Guozhen and Chen Zhiping, "Ming–Qing shidai Fujian-di tubao," *Zhongguo shehui jingji shi yanjiu*, no. 2 (1985): 45–57.

39. Wang Shimou, *Ming bu shu*, p. 18.

40. B.J. Ter Haar has given short descriptions of eight local cults in "The Genesis and Spread of Temple Cults in Fukien," in Vermeer, ed., *Development and Decline of Fukien Province*, pp. 349–396.

41. An, "Rongcheng jiwen" (1662?), in *Qingshi ziliao*, vol. 1 (Beijing: Zhonghua shuju, 1980), p. 2.

42. "Stone Tablet of the Happy Rains of Subprefect Luo Yiwo," in Vermeer, *Chinese Local History*, pp. 52–54.

43. "Stone Tablet of the Miracles Performed by the Heavenly Imperial Consort in Ch'ang-lo," in Vermeer, *Chinese Local History*, pp. 112–116.

44. For different theories about her origin, see Li Xianzhang, *Maso Shinkō no kenkyū* (Tokyo: 1979); and James L. Watson, "Standardizing the Gods: The Promotion of T'ien Hou Along the South China Coast, 960–1960," in *Popular Culture in Late Imperial China*, ed. D. Johnson et al. (Los Angeles: 1985), pp. 292–324.

45. *Xianyouxian zhi* (1771), p. 268.

46. Zheng Zhenman, "Ming–Qing Fujian-di jiating jiegou jiqi yanbian qushi," *Zhongguo shehui jingji shi yanjiu*, no. 4 (1988): 67–74.

47. Liu Ts'ui-jung, "A Comparison of Lineage Populations in South China," in *Chinese Historical Microdemography*, ed. Stevan Harrell (Berkeley: University of California Press, 1995), p. 102.

48. Customs, in *Min shu*, vol. 38.

49. Su Xinhong, "Ming–Qing shiji minnan renkou-di hailu wailiu," *Zhongguo shehui jingji shi yanjiu*, no. 4 (1987): 46–53.

50. "Pirate trouble," in (Qianlong) *Haichengxian zhi*, vol 18. Spanish sources mention a death toll of 15,000.

51. Wang Lianmao, "Migration in Two Minnan Lineages in the Ming and Qing Periods," in Harrell, ed., *Chinese Historical Microdemography*, pp. 183–214.

52. He Qiaoyuan, "Preface for the Celebration of Mother Yan," in *Jingshan quanji*, vol. 48 (Quanzhou Library ed.); and Customs, in *Min shu*, vol. 45.

53. Zhu Weigan, *Fujian Shigao* (Fuzhou: Fujian jiaoyu chubanshe, 1986), pp. 169–173.

54. "Military defense," in *Tianxia junguo libing shu*, vol. 93. Fujian 3.

55. *Xinghuafu putianxian zhi*, p. 299.

56. Zhu Weigan, *Fujian shigao*, vol. 2, pp. 225–226.

57. *(Xinghuafu) Putianxian zhi*, p. 299.

58. "Stone Record of the Pacification of the Pirates," in Vermeer, ed., *Chinese Local History*, pp. 17–23.

59. "Military Defense" (1700), in *Zhangpuxian zhi*, vol. 11 (repr. 1936); "Zhangzhoufu: Walled Defenses," in *Tianxia junguo libing shu*, vol. 93 Fujian 3.

60. "Stone Record on the Reconstruction of the Chao Family Fortified Village in Zhangpu," in Vermeer, *Chinese Local History*, pp. 30–33.

61. Bu Datong, *Bei wo tuji*, Baoyantang miji, ed. (Shanghai, 1922); and Regional Inspector Dan Lun's memorial in *Mingchen zouyi*, vol. 26.

62. Chang Han, "Songchuang mengyu" (ca. 1593), in *Wulin wangzhe yizhu*, vol. 4 1907).

63. A work in English discussing this period is So Kwan-wai, *Japanese Piracy in Ming China during the 16th Century* (East Lansing:Michigan State University Press, 1975). For elite views of the marauders in the Shanghai region, see John Meskill, *Gentlemanly Interests and Wealth on the Yangtze Delta* (Assoc. for Asian Studies Monograph no. 49, 1994), pp. 81–120.

64. Zhu Wan, *Piyu zaji* (1587 ed.), vol. 2, p. 26.

65. See Vermeer, "The Decline of Hsing-hua Prefecture in the Early Ch'ing," in Vermeer, ed., *Chinese Local History*, pp. 109–111.

66. Shen Defu, *Wanli ye hu bian* (ca. 1606), vol. 12 (repr. Beijing, 1959).

67. Zhang Xie, "Military and Civil Taxes," in *Dongxiyang kao*, vol. 7; and "Tax Collectors for the Emperor," in ibid., vol. 8.

68. *Tianxia junguo libing shu*, vol. 93; *Dongxiyang kao*, vol. 7.

69. (Qianlong) *Haichengxian zhi*, vols. 21 and 25.

70. Nie Dening, "Ming–Qing zhiji Fujian-di Minjian haiwai maoyi gangkou," *Zhongguo shehui jingji shi yanjiu*," no. 4 (1992): 39–45.

71. Chen Sidong, "Lüeshu Mingdai Fujian yanhai-di fanzou cuoshi," *Quanzhou wenshi*, vols. 6/7 (1982), pp. 125–127.

72. A synopsis of this debate is in Lin Renchuan, *Mingmo Qingchu siren haishang maoyi* (Shanghai: Huadong shifan daxue chubanshe, 1987), pp. 396–404.

73. Qian Jiang, "1570–1760 nian Zhongguo he lusong maoyidi fazhan ji maoyi edi zhansuan," *Zhongguo shehui jingji shi yanjiu*, no. 3 (1986): 69–78.

74. Mao Yuanyi, *Wu bei shi* (ca. 1621), vol. 214.

75. Lin Renchuan, *Mingmo Qingchu siren haishang maoyi*, pp. 267–272.

76. (Guangxu) *Zhangzhoufu zhi*, vol. 48, p. 7.

77. Vermeer, "The Decline of Hsing-hua Prefecture," pp. 101–161.

78. Li Guangjin, "Preface for Uncle Yuxi," in *Jing pi ji*, vol. 3 (Quanzhou Library ed).

79. Fu Yiling, "Mingdai Quanzhou Anping shangren shiliao jibu," *Quanzhou wenshi*, vol. 5 (1981), pp. 1–5.

80. William Atwell, "Notes on Silver, Foreign Trade, and the Late Ming Economy," *Ch'ing-shih wen-t'i* (December 1977).

81. William Atwell, "International Bullion Flows and the Chinese Economy Circa 1530–1650," *Past and Present*, no. 95 (1982): 68–90; Frederic Wakeman, "China and the Seventeenth-Century Crisis," *Late Imperial China*, no. 1 (1986): 1–26.

82. Fan Jinmin, "Ming–Qing shiqi Zhongguo dui Ri sizhou maoyi," *Zhongguo shehui jingji shi yanjiu*, no. 1 (1992): 28–37.

83. Ni Laien and Xia Weizhong, "Waiguo baiyin yu Mingdiguo-di bengkui," *Zhongguo shehui jingji shi yanjiu*, no. 3 (1990): 46–56.

4

The Seventeenth-Century Transformation

Taiwan Under the Dutch and the Cheng Regime

John E. Wills, Jr.

Statue of Ch'eng Ch'eng-kung. *(Photo by M. Rubinstein)*

The history of Taiwan seems to present some remarkable discontinuities. The long development of a maritime frontier for settlers from South China was altered around the edges by the opening of ports to trade and the whole island to foreign residence after the Arrow War. The occupation by Japan in 1895 was a more profound discontinuity. Then came the retrocession to Kuomintang China in 1945 and about two decades of cold war political repression and secure but modest beginnings of economic growth. The subsequent mounting pace of economic change, the rise of levels of education and of cosmopolitan connection, the demands of an articulate and sophisticated people, and the considerable political wisdom of Chiang Ching-kuo and those around him opened the way to the rich, messy, and vitally democratic Taiwan of today.

If we go back to the beginning of the age of the Fukien frontiersmen we find discontinuities every bit as startling. Taiwan in 1600 was on the outer edge of Chinese consciousness and activity, with little or no permanent Chinese settlement, visited only by fishermen, smugglers, and pirates, and only dimly reflected in the discussions and records of the officials who administered and patrolled the South China coast. It was inhabited largely by the Malayo-Polynesian peoples, called "aborigines" in the English-language literature. In the course of the seventeenth century, maritime Chinese, Japanese, Spanish, English, and Dutch warriors and traders all sought to settle on the great island, make it a commercial base, and profit from its riches. Its incorporation into the Ch'ing Empire in 1683 was another dramatic discontinuity; it almost immediately ceased to be a center of multinational maritime trade, and its southern Chinese frontier phase, slowly under way under the Dutch and the Ch'eng-kung regime, began in earnest.

The study of Taiwan in the seventeenth century places us at the intersection of two rapidly changing fields of scholarship. The involvement of seagoing Europeans, Chinese, and Japanese makes it a wonderful case study in what used to be called the history of European expansion in Asia but now, in recognition of the major and dynamic maritime roles of Asian peoples, more often is called the history of maritime Asia.[1] The other scholarly trend is the approach to the history of Ming and Ch'ing China, greatly indebted to Skinner's "macroregions" paradigm, that takes seriously the great variety of cultures, economies, and trajectories of change in different parts of the great empire.[2] Taiwan was in some ways part of "Maritime China," which does not quite fit yet does not quite violate the Skinner paradigm.[3] It also can be viewed as a very distinctive case of the phenomena of Chinese frontier expansion, which were very important for a number of other Ming–Ch'ing macroregions.[4]

The Wild Coast

As we learn more about the energy and tenacity of Chinese frontiersmen and the occasional, serious efforts of local elites and bureaucracies to bring newly settled areas fully within state and civilization, we are likely to find the history, or prehistory, of Taiwan more and more puzzling. The connections with China seem to go back a very long way. There are Neolithic sites on Taiwan that are closely related to those of the Chinese mainland.[5] The languages and cultures of the present-day "aboriginal" peoples of Taiwan suggest that their ancestors may have reached the island in the early stages of the dispersal of proto-Austronesian peoples from South China to the south and east.[6] One group even worships a millet god, for all the world like the ancestors of the Chou dynasty.[7] The Taiwan strait is only a hundred miles wide. This might have been daunting to Han dynasty seamen, but certainly not to those of the Sung who sailed to Southeast Asia and perhaps to India. So why didn't they get to Taiwan?

Except for records of the Three Kingdoms and Sui periods that refer to Taiwan or to the Ryukyu islands,[8] the earliest Chinese record we have of a visit to Taiwan is Wang Ta-yuan's *Tao-i chih-lueh* (1349).[9] Wang found substantial settlements of Chinese traders and fishermen in the P'eng-hu islands. Officers occasionally had been stationed there since about 1170, bringing the islands under the control of the Chinese state for the first time, but there is no record of Chinese settlement or political authority on Taiwan at this time. The early Ming rulers, reversing the positive policies toward seafaring characteristic of southern Sung and Yuan, withdrew their officials from P'eng-hu, attempted to evacuate all the people, and forbade all Chinese maritime activity. If any Chinese managed to remain in P'eng-hu or in the harbors of Taiwan they were completely outside the law and no record of them has been found.

The collapse of Ming maritime restrictions after 1550 was accompanied by a multifaceted upsurge of maritime activity. Probably the first effect on Taiwan and P'eng-hu was a revival of Chinese fishing. The Portuguese passing through the Taiwan strait to Japan called P'eng-hu the "Pescador" (Fisherman) islands. Ocean fishing has formed one of the most enduring links between Fukien and Taiwan. Very little can be known about it before the period documented by the Dutch. Brief references seem to link it to Wang-kang, Pei-kang, Tan-shui (Tamsui), and Keelung. Chinese fishermen probably spent weeks ashore at these places during fishing seasons, salting and drying their catch. These temporary settlements had to defend themselves against aborigine raids, but also may have been able to conciliate the local people with gifts of fish and salt; an early Dutch observer commented on the aborigines' meager fishing abilities and dependence on Chinese traders for supplies of salt. Fishing communities in P'eng-hu were reported to select their own headmen, and some kind of primitive democracy may well have prevailed in the fishing camps on the coast of Taiwan, as it did in those on the wild coast of Newfoundland in the same years.

After the limited legalization of Chinese maritime trade in 1567, a few licenses were given every year for voyages to Tam-sui and Keelung. The ships so licensed sometimes made illegal voyages to Japan, and, as Japanese maritime trade expanded, Japanese and Chinese sometimes met and traded in the harbors of Taiwan. The dramatic expansion and commercialization of the Japanese economy also gave Taiwan its first important market for exports, as Chinese traders bought deer hides from the aborigines for sale in Japan.

In the late 1500s many heavily armed ships—Chinese, Japanese, Portuguese, Spanish—passed through the Taiwan strait every year, and the strategic position of Taiwan and P'eng-hu attracted a good deal of attention. There were discussions in Japan in 1593 of an expedition to Taiwan. Eventually there was an exploratory expedition of Arima Harunobu in 1609 and the much larger but still unsuccessful effort of Maruyama Tōan in 1616.[10] The Tokugawa authorities still were discussing the possibility of expeditions against Taiwan and Luzon in the early 1630s. The Portuguese were much less interested; references to the island they called Formosa ("beautiful"), are scarce in their records, and their only known landing on it was the ten-week stay in 1582 of the survivors of a shipwreck.[11]

Far more important was the advance of Chinese organized force, both outlaw and official, toward Taiwan. Two major pirate leaders took refuge there from increasingly effective Ming defensive measures, Lin Tao-ch'ien in 1566 and Lin Feng in 1574.[12] Neither stayed long, but one of them or some other unknown Chinese or Japanese expedition so frightened the aborigines with their firearms that the local people fled to the mountains and recalled the incident decades later; it is recorded in Ch'en Ti's record of the Ming expedition there under Shen Yu-jung in 1603.[13] That expedition, part of a general reinforcement of coastal defenses begun in response to Hideyoshi's invasion of Korea, led to the re-establishment of a Ming military presence in P'eng-hu. Ch'en Ti's record says nothing about Chinese settlers on the Taiwan coast, but it is clear that there were Chinese traders or fishermen who could translate from an aboriginal language for him.

The years between 1600 and 1620 represented the peak of commercial activity, and one of the peaks of drama and disorder, in the history of the South China Sea.[14] Streams of silver from the mines of Japan and of South America—via Manila and Acapulco—flowed into China. At Manila a great massacre of Chinese residents in 1603 was followed immediately by a new appreciation of their indispensability and the peak years of their trade. Licensed "red seal ships" full of samurai and merchants traded to Vietnam, as far as the Malay peninsula, and caused much unease when they stopped at Macao. The Japanese domain of Satsuma conquered the Ryukyu islands. It is highly probable that there was a growing outsider presence on the coast of Taiwan. When the Dutch got there in 1622–24 they estimated that there were 1,000 to 1,500 Chinese on the Taiwan coast. This may have included a good many sojourners for the fishing or trading season, but it seems to represent an increase from the situation described by Ch'en Ti in 1603. And it soon became clear that the Dutch had blundered into the middle of a well-established nexus of Chinese-Japanese trade in at least one of the Taiwan ports.

Reports of two Dutch visitors to the big aboriginal village of Hsiao-lung (Soulang) in 1623 provide a fascinating picture of the Chinese presence before the arrival of the Dutch had changed anything.[15] Every house had one or more Chinese lodgers, whose main business was the purchase of deer skins and dried deer meat "for a trifle, because they [the aborigines] have no knowledge of money." The Chinese made the aborigines provide them with food, threatening to cut off their supply of salt if they did not do so. Li Tan explained that the Chinese imported salt from the mainland and did not manufacture it on the Taiwan coast so that the aborigines could not learn the process and break their dependence.

But these were pretty tentative beginnings for a convenient coast and a potentially rich agricultural hinterland just a hundred miles off the South China coast. It seems fair to say that, left to itself, the Chinese presence on Taiwan would have continued to grow in subsequent decades, but not nearly as fast as it did with the catalyst provided by the incursion of the Dutch East India Company. So where were all those tough Chinese frontier farmers and civilization-bringing bureaucrats who made their different contributions to China's expansion on several frontiers? We need to remember that Chinese maritime expansion up until this time was not propelled primarily by the overpopulation and land hunger that pushed so many out to Southeast Asia, the South Pacific, and the Americas from 1700 or 1750 on, but by commercial motives: a search for new markets for Chinese goods and for supplies of spices, incense woods, and other exotic consumer goods. And for seafarers of that kind, Taiwan, however close by, simply had not been an attractive destination.[16] On the other hand, it might be argued that since Sung times the trade of the South China Sea always had produced one major nexus where all parties could meet with a minimum of political complication: Ch'uan-chou in Fukien under the Southern Sung and Yuan, the Ryukyus for much of the Ming.[17] With the Ryukyus now under Satsuma control and the China coast increasingly unsettled, the shift to a Taiwan entrepôt might have gone a long way without the Dutch catalyst.

The Dutch and the Spanish

The Dutch made a first appearance in the P'eng-hu islands as early as 1604 and were told at that time that something might be worked out for trade with them, not on P'eng-hu but on the coast of Taiwan.[18] In 1622 they returned in force, having just been beaten off in a major attack on Macao, occupied one of the P'eng-hu islands, and set out to try to terrorize the Ming Empire into permitting them to trade, forcing their Chinese captives to work on a small fort.[19] The Ming authorities assembled a substantial fleet, pushed them back into the waterless peninsula on which their little fort stood, told them that they would have to leave P'eng-hu, which was imperial territory, and implicitly repeated their suggestion of almost twenty years before: Try Taiwan. Very active in these negotiations were Li Tan, the "captain" of the Chinese community in Hirado, Japan, and his subordinate, Cheng Chih-lung. Cheng may already have been influential in the

Chinese settlements on the Taiwan coast; as he rose to power on the Fukien coast in the late 1620s, he retained many forms of influence and apparently a few sources of revenue on Taiwan, under the noses of the Dutch or outside their sphere of power. When his son, Cheng Ch'eng-kung, came to oust the Dutch in 1661, he proclaimed that he was claiming his inheritance from his father.

The first Dutch post was on a sandbar at the mouth of a coastal bay; in the next year they bought from the local aborigines an area on the mainland side of the bay. On the sandbar they would build in the 1630s a formidable stone castle, Casteel Zeelandia; on the mainland a smaller brick fort, Provintia. Today the pile of rubble and a wall or two on the site of Casteel Zeelandia can be seen in An-p'ing-chen on the coast west of Tainan city, and a good deal more of Fort Provintia, Ch'ih-k'an-lou, in the city.[20]

The Dutch had come to the region looking for a base from which to seek to trade with China and Japan and to wage war on their enemies and anyone else whom they saw fit to bully; for those purposes P'eng-hu would have been almost as good as Taiwan. At first the aborigines and the Chinese settlers were seen as sources of trouble; only later were they seen as a source of revenue. In all lines of trade, and especially in trade between Japan and China, the Dutch were competitors of established Chinese and Japanese traders who had been using Taiwan as a rendezvous point for some years, and the potential for competition and conflict was very real. For the time being, however, the Dutch need not have been altogether unwelcome. They would help make Taiwan safe for traders and settlers; provide large supplies of pepper, sandalwood, and other tropical goods; and invigorate all lines of trade with new capital. Conditions on the South China coast were more and more unsettled, and the future of Japanese foreign trade was uncertain. If they treated other traders sensibly, the Dutch could have made their settlement a welcome island of commercial and political stability. But the Company's basic orientation was toward the use of force to obtain and enforce monopolies. Even in terms of that general policy, the Taiwan commanders so mismanaged things for ten years that they made enemies for themselves and aggravated the general disorder.

The rapidly changing situation among the Chinese with whom the Dutch interacted sometimes would have baffled the wisest policymaker and the most percipient observer. The Ming state, in deep systemic crisis composed of bankruptcy, court factionalism and eunuch power, Manchu invasion, and widespread rebellion, paid little attention to the local version of that crisis on the South China coast. Would-be sealords, often called pirates both by the Dutch and by the Ming officials, contended for control of the coast and its rich trade. Eventually it was Cheng Chih-lung who made himself indispensable to the Ming, received office from them, and came to dominate the South China coast with his fleets and control most of its trade. He had mediated the beginnings of the Dutch presence on Taiwan and early and late seems to have been eager to use his connections with them to advance his own power and trade. But the Dutch treated him very badly, holding him under arrest on one of their ships until he signed a trade agreement on their terms, constantly complaining that he was keeping others from trading with them, and finally burning some of his best ships in Amoy (Hsia-men) harbor in July 1633. But Cheng had forces in reserve, and in October 1633, 150 of his ships attacked eight Dutch warships off Quemoy (Ch'in-men), burned three, and the others fled. In 1635–36 the Dutch finally were ready to negotiate with him for stable arrangements for peaceful competition in the import of Chinese goods to Japan and for stable supply of Chinese goods to the Dutch on Taiwan.[21]

Japanese and Chinese traders had been meeting in the harbors of Taiwan before the arrival of the Dutch. A first Dutch effort to collect tolls from the Japanese on their trade was abandoned when the Japanese objected, but it had set a hostile atmosphere. In 1627 the Japanese demanded that the Dutch convoy them to the China coast or help them hire Chinese junks to go there and attempt to collect their debts. The Japanese were not at all welcome in China, and the Dutch quite sensibly refused. When the Japanese left they took with them a delegation of aborigines from Hsin-k'ang who apparently were going to offer sovereignty over their village to the Japanese government. The offer was rejected by the shogunate. When the Japanese came again in 1628 they came heavily armed. Pieter Nuyts, the new and inexperienced governor, insisted on searching their ships and removing all weapons and imprisoned the returning Hsin-k'ang delegation. Nuyts refused to let the Japanese leave until ships from Batavia called on their way to Nagasaki, so that the Dutch version of the Taiwan quarrels would be presented at the same time as any Japanese complaints. This detention was the last straw for the Japanese, who surrounded Nuyts's house and held him and his small son hostage at sword point until the Dutch council on Taiwan revoked the detention and agreed to other Japanese demands. The Tokugawa authorities were so incensed by this conflict that they imprisoned the Dutch at Hirado, stopped their trade, and demanded that the Dutch leave Taiwan. They showed some signs of relenting in 1630, but it was not until 1632, when Nuyts was sent to Japan and turned over to the authorities there to serve a term under house arrest, that trade was completely restored.

For purposes of trade with China and Japan, a post on the P'eng-hu islands would have served the Dutch almost as well as one on the coast of Taiwan. At first Taiwan and its aboriginal people seemed to be a source of difficulty, not opportunity. Relations with Hsin-k'ang remained wary after its leaders' involvement in the conflict with the Japanese. In 1629 the people of Ma-tou attacked a party of Dutch soldiers, the Dutch burned Ma-tou in retaliation, and Ma-tou warriors raided Hsin-k'ang. This conflict simmered until 1635, when more than four hundred Dutch soldiers arrived, Ma-tou was burned to the ground, and its elders came to the castle to sue for peace. The Dutch troops now made several more expeditions to the north and south of the castle, more villages submitted, and in February 1636 representatives of twenty-eight villages met in a council, a practice that would be regularized as the Dutch sphere of control widened. Thus the breakthrough toward a more peaceful environment for the castle and a wider sphere of influence on the island came in the same years as the ends of the conflicts with the Chinese and the Japanese.

The Dutch now were drawn much farther into domination of the great island by their response to the presence on its northern end, at Keelung and Tam-sui, of their Spanish enemies.[22] The Spanish had come from Manila to Keelung in 1626 and to Tam-sui in 1629. The area already was the scene of a good deal of Chinese and Japanese trade, but we have no record of conflict between those traders and the Spanish. The Spanish hoped to counter the strategic dominance of the Dutch in East Asian waters, attract Chinese trade to their outpost, and use it as a way-station for missionary penetration of China. Their efforts were shaped by the peculiar geography of the area. The Keelung fort was built on the west end of what is now called Ho-p'ing island, at the mouth of Keelung harbor. The harbor was an unusually fine safe anchorage. But it was closely ringed by mountains, and just beyond the mountains was the wide, populous plain of the Tam-sui river, which even then was said to produce a surplus of rice. Missionary efforts in that wider sphere inevitably led to involvement in wars between tribes. The little garrison's efforts to levy a tax of chickens and rice from every household caused more trouble. Meanwhile, the main fortress at Keelung did attract some traders from China, but the incessant winter rains caused much sickness. Once the Tam-sui garrison was abandoned in 1638, hostile tribesmen just over the ridge in the Tam-sui valley made Keelung very uncomfortable. The Manila authorities already were cutting their losses; in 1640 the Keelung garrison had only 50 Spanish soldiers, 30 Filipinos, 200 slaves, and 130 Chinese. In 1642 a force of more than five hundred Dutch soldiers took it, encountering little resistance.

The Dutch in their turn faced a good deal of resistance in the Tam-sui basin, but sent reinforcements that brought it under control in 1644 and then marched southward overland, crushing occasional resistance and receiving the submission of many villages. The number of villages over which the Dutch claimed sovereignty rose from 44 in 1644 to 217 in 1646, 251 in 1648, and 315 in 1650.[23] Headmen were named for each village and given robes and staffs of office, and summoned to annual regional councils where their disputes were mediated and they were exhorted to keep the peace among themselves and not attack the Chinese who were in the villages with Dutch permission. The people of Hsin-k'ang were converted to Christianity at least nominally by about 1630, and after 1635 missionary activity spread to Ma-tou and other villages. At least two aboriginal languages were given romanized forms, and basic Christian instructional materials were prepared in them. The struggle to make these conversions more than nominal, to root out the old "superstitions," was a long one. Female shamans, leading practitioners of the old cults, were exiled. Much attention was given to schools, in the hope that a properly educated younger generation would be purer Christians. Missionary ministers and schoolmasters often were the only

Dutch presence in an outlying village, more or less willingly performing quasi-governmental functions, sometimes causing trouble with the local people by their misconduct, resisting Company efforts to cut costs by reducing the missionary presence in outlying areas.

Hsin-k'ang was largely converted in the early 1630s, Ma-tou not long after. Near the end of Dutch rule, in 1659, many of the big villages under their authority had a school, and in many of them it was reported that half the people could recite their catechism.

The success of this missionary effort in just a few years with limited manpower is surprising, but some explanations can be suggested. From a religious background in which specific powers and spirits were approached for specific worldly benefits, the power of the Dutch arms had a great effect; there were not many "rice Christians" but quite a few "musket Christians." When a shrine or cult object was destroyed or a taboo violated and the violator lived and the crops grew, it seemed that the newcomers had a superior form of power that should be tapped. The new way of life of going to school and reading and writing also clearly had its uses and appeals. And, as John Shepherd has shown us, the Siraya, the people closest to Casteel Zeelandia, had a social and cultural organization that was stable and comfortable in isolation but vulnerable in the new situation.[24] Women did most of the growing of food. Young men hunted and went to war, taking heads from neighboring villages. Couples did not live together in their younger years, but husbands regularly spent the night with their wives. A pregnant wife could ruin a hunt, whether for deer or human heads, so all pregnancies were ended by massage abortion until women were in their late thirties, when their slightly older husbands ended their active participation in hunting and war. The resulting low number of births per woman kept the population stable at a low density, which helps to account for the great material comfort of aboriginal life and the good health and fine stature that impressed the Dutch, and also for the rather meager manpower available to resist invaders. The Dutch missionaries of course set out to abolish head-hunting, to change the marriage customs entirely, and to wipe out the culturally mandatory practice of abortion. In some villages they succeeded. Some women may have welcomed the possibility of having babies when they were younger and stronger, and of having their husbands around to help them in the fields. Some men probably were relieved not to be going out taking heads and risking their own, and still could go to war and even take heads sometimes as auxiliaries for the Dutch. Leadership and cultural dominance in the villages now was exclusively male, no longer shared with the female shamans.

From the beginning the Dutch had claimed 10 percent of any product of their zone in Taiwan, for example, of the Chinese fishing along the coast. The most important products for which such a tax was levied were deer meat and hides. The antlers and some other parts of the deer went into the Chinese medicine market. Most of the meat was salted and dried for sale in China. Most of the hides were sold in Japan, many of them by the Company. The spread of Chinese deer hunters, taking some deer themselves and buying more from the aborigines, had begun before the Dutch arrived. The Company sold licenses to Chinese hunters, collected a tenth of their take as a tax, and bought much of the rest. In 1645 the Company shifted to a system of competitive bidding for a "tax farming" license to the Chinese for the monopoly of trade in each aboriginal village that included all forms of trade, not just deer-hunting. This system was the commercial mainstay of Chinese frontier interaction with the aborigines until the Ch'ing period; the Dutch *pachter* (tax-farmer) passed into Chinese as *pak-she* (in Taiwan dialect; in Mandarin *p'u-she*). The scale of this deer trade was astonishing: more than 60,000 hides per year from the mid-1630s to 1659. Some of the closest zones were hunted out fairly quickly, but the trade spread, and the numbers shipped were highest for 1655–59.[25]

While some Chinese were living this rough frontier life, others were moving into the plains near the Dutch fort and building up a zone of Chinese-style intensive agriculture, growing rice and other food crops for local consumption and growing sugar cane for sale to the Company for the world market. Land-clearing and water control required substantial investments of capital and hired labor before the first crop. Several big merchants did a great deal of investing and organizing, setting up "parks" or plantations of about 20 morgen (45 acres) each.[26] The most interesting figure among them was Sung Ming-kang, or "Captain Bencon," formerly astute adviser of the fearsome Jan Pietersz Coen and first headman of the Chinese at Batavia, who resigned that post in 1635, came to Taiwan, and built himself a fine stone house there.[27] The Company had already been buying sugar grown in South China and probably continued to do so. It sold this sugar in Europe, Persia, and India. The market was very strong until the mid-1650s, when production began to revive in Brazil, followed by the West Indies. Sugar cultivation in Taiwan continued to grow, from about 1,500 acres in 1645 to an unsustainable peak of more than 9,000 in 1650 to more than 4,000 in 1657.[28]

These products of Taiwan, and the taxes on Chinese trade and Chinese residents, made marvelous supplements and supports for the Dutch presence there, but they were not its main purpose. Taiwan was supposed to be the Dutch access point to the China market and to the goods, especially raw silk and silk goods, that could be exported from China and sold in Japan at a great profit. Once the Dutch had come to their senses and decided to try to live at peace with Cheng Chih-lung, this trade expanded amazingly. The Japanese made a wonderful opening for them by prohibiting all Japanese maritime trade and expelling the Portuguese. The Chinese were the only competition the Dutch had in importing foreign goods to this vital, rapidly urbanizing country with its own sources of gold, silver, and copper. In the nineteen months ending in January 1639, Dutch Taiwan sent to Japan cargoes worth more than f4,600,000 ("f" stands for the Dutch guilder, figured at f3.5 = 1 tael in this period), well over a million taels; in August 1640 three Dutch ships left Taiwan for Japan with cargoes valued at f5,173,000.[29] Large cargoes of Taiwan sugar, Japanese copper, and much more were also being sent to the ports of India. The profits of trade in Taiwan, that is, the gains on pepper and other goods sold to the Chinese there, and the earnings from tolls and head taxes were quite respectable, but it was through the contribution to the trade with Japan that Taiwan had the greatest impact on the Company's balance sheets.

The collapse of the Ming in 1644 and the disorders that followed along the South China coast produced a wave of refugees to Taiwan. There was another surge in the 1650s as Cheng Ch'eng-kung consolidated his base on the Fukien coast and the Ch'ing increased their efforts to crush him. Dutch incomes from the work of all these Chinese and their head taxes increased. But Dutch collection of the head tax on the Chinese caused much resentment, especially when Dutch soldiers pounded on the doors of Chinese houses at night, engaged in petty thievery and extortion, and intruded into households where there were Chinese women. Also, in 1650 the sugar planters overplanted and complained of labor shortages, then cut back the next year and threw the field hands out of work. The result of these tensions and instabilities was the rebellion in 1652 led by Kuo Huai-yi.[30] This was a rebellion strictly of the rural poor; as soon as headmen of the Chinese community heard about it, they informed the Dutch. There may have been as many as 4,000 rebels, but they were very poorly armed and trained. They allowed Dutch musketeers to wade ashore and form up and broke almost as soon as the musket volleys began. Three days later the Company soldiers, now joined by aborigine auxiliaries, marched on a rebel gathering place in a valley a few miles to the north. Again the rebels broke at the first volley, and the aborigines joined enthusiastically in the massacre; more than 2,000 Chinese were killed.

There had been rumors that Kuo Huai-yi and the other rebels were linked to Cheng Ch'eng-kung, but this does not seem at all likely. As Cheng took drastic measures to get all Chinese shipping under his control and to strengthen himself against growing Ch'ing pressure he sometimes cut off trade with Taiwan, and the possibility of a hostile confrontation grew. In 1659 and 1660 the Ch'ing evacuated and devastated a wide stretch of coastal Fukien, making it really difficult for the first time for Cheng Ch'eng-kung on Amoy to get food and trade goods from the mainland. Cheng's great invasion up the Yangtze river to Nanking in 1659 was a spectacular failure.

In 1658 the Dutch Company on Taiwan reduced the fixed price it had paid for sugar.[31] The authorities in Batavia, facing major challenges in many parts of maritime Asia, had little force to spare to reinforce Taiwan. With a weak market for sugar and uncertain trade connections with China, it seemed a shaky asset at best. The governor on Taiwan, Fredrik Coyet, was reporting many rumors that Cheng Ch'eng-kung planned to expel the Dutch and take refuge on Taiwan, but the Batavia authorities, advised by an old factional opponent of Coyet, paid little attention. When they finally sent some reinforcements in the summer of 1660, the officer in charge of them looked around, saw no danger, and sailed away. On April 30, 1661, a huge Cheng fleet, hundreds of ships carrying more than 25,000 men, appeared off Casteel Zeelandia. Making his first landing not far from the fields where the Kuo Huai-yi rebels had been mowed down, Cheng was welcomed as a deliverer by many Chinese. "My father, Iquan [Cheng Chih-lung]," he proclaimed, "lent this land to the Dutch; now I come to reclaim it. And since it no longer is fitting for you to occupy my land, give it up, and I will raise you to high ranks and spare your lives, along with those of your wives and children."[32] Within a few weeks he had everything in control except Casteel Zeelandia. A few Dutch prisoners were executed and two were crucified. A new commander sent to replace Coyet arrived with flags flying but quickly sailed on to Japan. Some reinforcements arrived and did manage to enter the castle, but could not even push the Cheng forces out of the town under its walls. On January 25, 1662, Cheng forces took a little redoubt on a sand dune that commanded the walls of the castle. On February 1 a treaty was concluded and the Dutch were permitted to withdraw in peace, leaving all their goods and records.[33] Coyet, who had tried to warn Batavia of the danger, was made the scapegoat for the defeat, but it seems clear that nothing the Company could have done would have come close to enabling it to fend off Cheng's large and well-trained army. In the seventeenth century Europeans expected to conquer, not be conquered, outside Europe. News of the great defeat, and the name of Koxinga (Cheng Ch'eng-kung) in many forms, appeared in print in several European languages within just a few years.[34]

The Cheng Regime, 1661–1683

Taiwan had a Chinese ruler for the first time. It was not entirely clear what Cheng Ch'eng-kung intended to do next. Some of his erstwhile allies in resistance to the Ch'ing thought he was turning his back on that losing struggle. He acknowledged the authority of no prince of the Ming imperial house and may have been preparing to claim the succession himself as an adopted "Lord of the Imperial Surname"; he named Casteel Zeelandia Tung-tu ("Eastern Capital"), as if it might be the seat of an emperor. He commanded a ministate of impressive but rather narrow centralization, with an elaborate military organization, rudimentary civil administration of occupied areas, and a widespread commercial network in which the main lines, as far as we can tell, were monopolized by the Cheng family and their agents. The Cheng family, their merchant associates, the military commanders, and the common people all had benefited from the prosperity of trade links from such coastal centers as Amoy into China and the wide family estates on the mainland that characterized the early 1650s, and had suffered as the Ch'ing trade embargo and advances of military forces into coastal Fukien began to bite. Taiwan was as good as Amoy as a base for trade with Japan, Manila, and other points outside China, but that trade would be a sad remnant of past splendors if the China links were cut off. The great island had immense agricultural potential, but almost all of it would have to be opened up by backbreaking pioneer labor amid severe shortages of cloth and other consumer goods and occasionally of food. Thus it is quite understandable that quite a few followers of Cheng Ch'eng-kung preferred surrender to the Ch'ing to the challenges of the Taiwan frontier.

In 1662–64 the melodramas of Cheng family politics made Taiwan even less attractive to many Cheng family members and military commanders. The last months of Cheng Ch'eng-kung's life were dominated by a furious quarrel with his son and putative heir, Cheng Ching, still on Amoy, over his "incestuous" relationship with the wet nurse of a younger son. Cheng T'ai, a younger brother of Cheng Ch'eng-kung who was very important in the family's commercial operations, resisted Ch'eng-kung's orders to kill Ching and order Lady Tung, Ch'eng-kung's principal wife, to commit suicide. Cheng Ch'eng-kung slipped deeper into insanity and died on June 23, 1662. Generals on Taiwan tried to set up one Cheng Hsi as Ch'eng-kung's heir, but at the end of the year Ching crossed to Taiwan and defeated the Hsi faction. But by now Ching and T'ai both were negotiating behind each other's back for surrender to the Ch'ing. In February 1663 Ching and his commanders returned to Amoy. In July they imprisoned T'ai, who soon was murdered or committed suicide. T'ai's relatives and followers, perhaps one-fourth of the whole Cheng force, now surrendered to the Ch'ing. They provided much of the manpower, backed up by earlier defectors and Dutch warships, for the Ch'ing conquest of Amoy and Quemoy in November. Cheng commanders at other coastal outposts surrendered to the Ch'ing or fled to Taiwan early in 1664, so that the tension in the Cheng regime between commitment to Taiwan and attraction to the mainland was temporarily resolved, but at the cost of very substantial losses of leadership and manpower.[35] Cheng Ching's control was secure. His leading aides both were products of the lower coastal elite, mentioned among his first appointees after his father's death, each later tied to his ruler by the marriage of a daughter to a son of Cheng Ching: Ch'en Yung-hua in civil affairs and Feng Hsi-fan in military. A third important figure was one Liu Kuo-hsuan, who was from inland Fukien, had supported the wrong side in the succession struggle, spent the 1600s defending a base area near modern Chang-hua in central Taiwan,[36] and always stood a little apart but was a major supporter of the regime and probably its most effective commander down to its last days.[37]

The Ch'ing rulers sought to maintain momentum and put an end to maritime resistance by sending an expedition to conquer Taiwan. The key figure in these efforts was Shih Lang, who had defected from Cheng Ch'eng-kung's regime in 1646 and was one of the very few maritime experts in the very continental early Ch'ing regime. Adept at finding the right patron and maximizing his own power and freedom from the usual bureaucratic checks and balances, very much interested in trade and ready to cut a deal with anyone, a sort of mirror image within the Ch'ing state of the Cheng outlaw traders-mediators-sealords,[38] he is one of the key figures in the history of Taiwan in the seventeenth century. In September 1664 he, assisted by other former Cheng commanders, was ordered to command a large fleet of Ch'ing warships and cooperate with ships of the Dutch East India Company in an assault on Taiwan. The ships set out at the end of December but soon turned back, Shih explaining to the skeptical Dutch that the weather had been dangerous. After the Dutch ships returned to Batavia, Shih's fleet set out again in late May 1665, but it was scattered by a storm.

Thereafter the Ch'ing rulers lost interest in a direct conquest of Taiwan and sought to negotiate its surrender. Already in 1663 Cheng Ching had changed the name of his capital from Eastern Capital to Tung-ning (East Pacified), and seems to have been ready to discuss acknowledging Ch'ing suzerainty as a tributary state, on roughly the same terms as Korea. These negotiations continued off and on until 1669, and in their last phase involved Ming-chu, a fast-rising star of the K'ang-hsi emperor's new personal rule. But there was no precedent since the Five Dynasties for permitting tributary autonomy of a regime of Han Chinese language and culture. The Cheng regime had legitimized itself as part of the Ming loyalist resistance to the Ch'ing. Cheng Ching continued to use the reign period of the last Ming loyalist emperor, who was executed in Yunnan in 1662, and made it clear early and late that his peace terms were "not cutting the hair, not coming to the mainland." The Ch'ing certainly would have wanted to be free to move surrendered commanders around and break up their concentration. But for both sides the adoption and nonadoption of the queue was of central importance as a symbol of acceptance or nonacceptance of the Ch'ing mandate to rule. The focus on it here made it absolutely certain that no modus vivendi could be found. It is disconcerting to see in these tentative and always doomed negotiations the widening of the rift between maritime China and the Ch'ing empire, and the sharpening of a sense that there was no room for imperial recognition of partial autonomy of any group of Han Chinese, that all had to be complete subjects of a single political center, that the late imperial political tradition gave no support to any idea of "one empire, two systems."

Records of Dutch efforts to maintain a presence in the Taiwan strait after their rule of the great island ended in January 1662 offer a few sidelights on the strengthening grip of the Cheng regime. In January 1664 Cheng soldiers in the P'eng-hu islands attacked a Dutch landing party and then fled to Taiwan. Going on land in the area of modern Kao-hsiung, the Dutch engaged in very murky negotiations first with someone who may have been a dissident Cheng commander but more likely was simply trying to shake them down, and then with Cheng Ching's regime, which was willing to offer them trading posts in outlying areas but certainly was not interested in surrendering Tung-ning. In July 1664 a Dutch squadron found Cheng defenses on P'eng-hu much improved. Part of this squadron went on to reoccupy the old fortress at Keelung, as a counterweight to the Cheng presence and a possible center for trade with China. A Dutch garrison of 200 to 300 held on there until 1668. Sick, drunk, quarrelsome, crazy from the isolation and the rain, the Dutch soldiers managed to make some repairs on the fort. Cheng Ching took their presence as a threat and by 1665 had moved troops into the Tam-sui area. In May 1666 a force of more than 2,000 landed on the island where the Dutch fort stood, gaining surprise by a very bold landing on the shelving sandstone outer coast of the island. The badly outnumbered Dutch garrison shot at any Chinese who approached the fort but did not venture out. After ten days the Dutch were amazed to see the Cheng army boarding its ships and sailing away; they had probably not expected any prolonged resistance and had brought provisions for only ten days. Thereafter slower pressures did their work, as Chinese settled in the aborigine villages just over the hills in the Tam-sui valley, the Dutch bullied and alienated the nearby aborigine villages, and not a shred of trade was done with China. The Dutch garrison was withdrawn in 1668. The Cheng response very probably had accelerated the expansion of the regime's presence in the important Tam-sui area.[39]

Even before the Dutch finally surrendered Casteel Zeelandia, Cheng Ch'eng-kung had been busy receiving the homage of Chinese settlers and plains aborigines, surveying roads and land-holdings, and sending some of his soldiers out to farm on assigned lands. As more troops arrived from the mainland and Cheng Ching's regime stabilized, the systematic deployment of soldiers in "garrison fields" (t'un-t'ien) was very vigorously pursued. Land that had been reclaimed under the Dutch was treated as "official fields" and taxed at a high rate, basically a rent, not a tax. Much lower rates were levied on newly reclaimed land to encourage settlement and investment in land-clearing. Most of the Dutch structure of monopolies of trade with aborigine villages and collection of various categories of tax was maintained, but with fixed quotas, not competitive bidding. The Dutch had even given Cheng Ch'eng-kung lists of their lease-holders and debtors. The Cheng regime monopolized the export of deer hides and sugar, mostly to Japan. The deer hide trade seems to have approximately equaled the volumes under the Dutch, but the sugar trade was considerably smaller, since the urgent need for food produced a considerable shift from sugar cultivation to rice.[40]

Cheng Ch'eng-kung's army of invasion in itself represented a major increase in the Chinese population of Taiwan. More troops and civilians followed as Cheng Ching and others withdrew from the mainland. From the late 1650s on, there was a varying and unquantifiable stream of refugees from the ruthless Ch'ing coastal evacuation policies. But Taiwan was not healthy, the frontier work was very hard, and many returned to the mainland in the 1670s. In broad terms, it can be estimated that if the Chinese population of Taiwan under the Dutch was 30,000 to 50,000, under the Cheng regime it was 50,000 to 100,000. Even a mapping of the locations of military colonies shows an expansion of the zone of settlement around modern Tainan and a number of other small centers to the north and south. The almost unmappable presence of merchants in aborigine villages and pioneers pushing out on their own no doubt was affecting much more of the western plains and the Tam-sui area.

The change of regime and the increase in Chinese population must have put new pressures on the aborigines. The Cheng regime seems to have tried to prevent encroachment on its land by its military colonies, but it is not clear that it always managed to do so, and it cannot have avoided the many modes of frontier accommodation and clash that had begun before the Dutch and would continue under the Ch'ing. There was some talk of encouraging the aborigines to increase their grain production by plowing with oxen. Headmen were appointed over the villages. Some exulted over their release from the discipline of Dutch pastors and schoolmasters, but others preserved the practice of using the Roman alphabet to write their languages until the early nineteenth century. The Cheng regime made some efforts to replace Dutch projects of "civilization," establishing schools where aborigine children were to be taught the Chinese language and the basics of proper behavior. The prestige and magic of text and writing, the focus on male cultural and political leadership, the breaking of the web of magic and custom in favor of productivity, universalized religious and cultural values, and propriety—all were striking continuities from the Dutch civilizing project to that of the Chinese.[41]

Beginning in 1670, the British East India Company attempted to trade with the Cheng regime, first on Taiwan and later at Amoy.[42] The directors of the Company in London were interested in trade in temperate climates where the market for English woolens might be better than it was in India and Indonesia. They were especially interested in Japan and in sources of goods that might be sold in Japan, such as Taiwan sugar and deer hides. Their one voyage to Japan, in 1673, was turned away so firmly that they did not try again. But they still thought a good trade with Taiwan might open up proxy sales of English and Southeast Asian goods via Chinese merchants going from there to Japan, Manila, and the Chinese mainland. The possibility of buying Chinese gold and selling it in India or Europe, profiting from China's lower price of gold in terms of silver, also was attractive. The trade was managed from the English post at Banten (Bantam in most older books), west of Batavia on the north coast of Java. Their first voyage to Taiwan was in response to the arrival at Banten of an envoy sent by Cheng Ching, apparently one of several sent to Southeast Asian ports in 1668–69 to encourage everyone to come to Taiwan to trade. When the first English ship reached Taiwan in 1670, its merchants were very cordially received, a detailed "contract" on procedures was soon signed, and Cheng Ching gave the English a list of goods that he would buy from them every year. But the English soon found that Cheng Ching monopolized the export of sugar and deer hides and that they could not compete with the low prices at which Chinese merchants imported pepper and other Southeast Asian goods. A shift to Amoy when the Cheng forces reoccupied it produced only limited improvement. A few small cargoes were bought and sent to Banten, but they in no way compensated for the expense and the risk to ships in the South China Sea. For the historian the main interest of the whole episode is in the eyewitness accounts by the handful of

Englishmen who still were on Taiwan winding up the affairs of the trading post there when the Cheng regime finally collapsed in 1683.

Both Chinese and English sources make it clear that Cheng Taiwan was a hard frontier world and that many of its Chinese residents, having grown up not on frontier farms but in the urbanized consumer society of coastal Fukien, resented the hard life and the nearly total absence of cloth and other consumer goods. The regime, although impressively thorough in its promotion and taxation of agriculture, had been built up under Cheng Chih-lung and Cheng Ch'eng-kung on a base of the taxation and monopolization of maritime trade. Thus it is not surprising to find Cheng Ching sending trade promotion emissaries as far as Banten and monopolizing the export of sugar and deer hides to Japan. Taiwan must have been an especially welcome haven for merchants from the mainland and Southeast Asia when Ch'ing coastal evacuation policies were being harshly enforced in the 1660s. The results of this advantageous position and of the regime's energetic promotion of its foreign trade probably were substantial for their trade with many ports in Southeast Asia. They can be fairly well quantified for trade with Manila and Japan. Of 186 Asian ships recorded as reaching Manila between 1664 and 1683, 41 came from Taiwan. From 1664 to 1673, the proportion was 32 out of 101. The peak was 8 out of 18 in 1670.[43] For Chinese ships (including those from Southeast Asia) reaching Nagasaki between 1662 and 1683, out of 714, 201 were from Taiwan; peak years were 14 out of 33 in 1666 and 20 out of 38 in 1671.[44]

Despite all the Ch'ing prohibitions and drastic measures, trade between the Cheng regime and the mainland was never completely cut off. Any base on the coast would very much facilitate it. One Chinese source says that an outpost was re-established on Amoy as early as 1666. The English reported in 1670 that the Chengs had outposts on Amoy, Quemoy, and P'u-t'o-shan![45] And what about a return to military action on the mainland? Cheng Ching continued to use the reign period of the last Ming loyalist emperor, but it is not clear that his regime was committed to overthrowing the Ch'ing, even as a myth of self-legitimation. Certainly he had been ready to make peace with the Ch'ing if his people could keep the great island and their long hair. But a return to the mainland would be for many a return to longed-for home places and to all a chance for loot and glory in battle. The opportunity came with the outbreak in 1673 of the Rebellion of the Three Feudatories. Cheng Ching moved some of his forces to Amoy, and several local commanders in other coastal centers declared their allegiance to him. In 1674 Cheng moved his household and much of his administration to Amoy. Several local commanders in coastal areas came over to his side. The Cheng forces and their allies dominated the coastal areas from Hui-chou in Kwangtung to beyond Ch'uan-chou. Much of this expansion was at the expense not of the Ch'ing but of the rebellious feudatories, Keng Ching-chung in Foo-chow and Shang Chih-hsin in Canton. The Keng rebellion collapsed in 1676, and in 1677 Ch'ing forces swept south, taking most of the Fukien cities. Early in

1678 Cheng armies under Liu Kuo-hsuan counterattacked, threatening the important city of Chang-chou. But the Ch'ing changed its provincial leadership, built up its forces, and by the end of 1678 had driven the Cheng forces out of all their mainland holdings except one city. Cheng Ching still was on Amoy and his forces were causing a great deal of trouble in that area. The inexorable Ch'ing buildup continued, the last Cheng stronghold on the mainland fell, and on March 26, 1680, Cheng Ching and his commanders sailed from Amoy for Taiwan in demoralized confusion.[46]

The mainland venture had accomplished nothing except to divert manpower and resources from the building up of Taiwan. The regime was desperately short of funds, unable to pay its troops. And the new governor general of Fukien, Yao Ch'i-sheng, was a master of "pacification" tactics, rewarding surrendered Cheng soldiers and people, recommending turncoat officers for appointment under the Ch'ing. There were many stories of nearly successful efforts to assassinate Ching, to surrender Taiwan, and so on. At this point the Cheng regime dissolved in family melodrama. Cheng Ching died in March 1681. His eldest son, K'o-ts'ang, was the putative heir. He had been supported by Ch'en Yung-hua, who had been left in charge of the administration on Taiwan, and whose daughter was married to K'o-ts'ang. But Ch'en Yung-hua had died in 1680, and K'o-ts'ang, the product of his father's scandalous liaison with a wet nurse, was not acceptable to much of the Cheng family. Feng Hsi-fan managed his deposition and the appointment in his place of Cheng K'o-shuang, who was married to Feng's daughter. Feng was in complete control, except for the forces under Liu Kuo-hsuan. Liu was the focus of much of Yao Ch'i-sheng's "pacification" effort.

In 1682 Shih Lang was sent from Peking to resume his command over Ch'ing maritime forces and plan for the conquest of Taiwan. Yao Ch'i-sheng called for an attack on Taiwan in the north monsoon, but Shih argued successfully for the tactical advantages of a south monsoon attack.* Their arguments in memorials to the throne took up much of 1682, Shih pointing out his own lifelong expertise in sea warfare and Yao's limited understanding. Finally Shih was placed in sole charge of the expedition. In May 1683 he was ready. On July 12 his main fleet of 300 to 400 junks closed with Liu Kuo-hsuan's Cheng fleet near P'eng-hu. The Cheng fleet held up very well, and Shih was forced to break off the battle. On July 17 the Ch'ing fleet returned to the attack, and after a fierce and complex battle broke the Cheng resistance and occupied most of P'eng-hu. Liu reached Tung-ning two days later. It was clear that resistance was no longer possible. Many feared a general massacre when Shih's forces landed, but he held back, releasing prisoners and proclaiming that any Cheng soldier who wished to surrender would be taken into his forces at full pay. The effects of this on Cheng

---

*The southern or southwestern monsoon comes in the summer from Southeast Asia; the northern monsoon comes from the north in the winter.

soldiers whose pay had been erratic at best for years can be imagined. The Cheng authorities—that is, Feng Hsi-fan and Liu Kuo-hsuan making the decisions for Cheng K'o-shuang—sent envoys to discuss terms, and Shih sent envoys in return. The ordinary people adopted the Ch'ing queue, soon followed by the high officials. Shih Lang's army entered Tung-ning, evicted all the great men from their houses, and began extorting large sums of money from them on various pretexts.[47] But there was no massacre. Cheng K'o-shuang was taken to Peking and given a nonhereditary and powerless dukedom. Liu Kuo-hsuan was named to a very important position as one of the commanders of the garrison at Tientsin.[48]

Toward Ch'ing Rule

It was not at all clear what was to be done with Taiwan. It had never been part of the Chinese imperial state. Shih Lang met with Alexander van 's Gravenbroek, one of a small group of Dutchmen who had been held on Taiwan ever since the Cheng conquest of 1661–62, and asked him to ask his masters in Batavia how much they would pay to get Taiwan back; the latter were predictably uninterested.[49] At the end of 1683 Shih conferred with the other high officials of Fukien. There was some talk of abandoning Taiwan and evacuating its entire Chinese population. Shih argued vigorously that it would not be feasible to evacuate all of them, that an outlaw population would surely remain, and that a hostile power might move in and establish a base there.[50] His arguments carried the day. Taiwan became a prefecture of Fukien province, divided into two counties. Small garrisons would be rotated to it from the Fukien coast. The coast would be at peace, without the threat of a hostile presence just across the strait, and its ports could be opened to Chinese and foreign trade and to controlled emigration to Taiwan.

Thus the Ch'ing had decided to keep Taiwan largely to keep it out of the hands of trouble-making foreigners and dissident Chinese. But they saw from the beginning that it would be a headache, as every part of maritime China was for them. Eventually they would draw grain from it for the Fukien coastal garrisons, but at first it would produce nothing of sufficient value to offset the trouble it caused. Their administration would keep expenses and commitments as low as possible. This attitude toward Taiwan was a sharp contrast to that of the last two regimes, the Dutch and the Cheng, for whom Taiwan had been an essential base at a time when they were not welcome on the mainland. But the Dutch presence had been destabilized by the four-way tensions among the Europeans, the aborigines, the Chinese settlers, and Cheng Ch'eng-kung. Of these four only the aborigines were completely committed to Taiwan. For Cheng, the Chinese settlers, and the Dutch, its separateness from the mainland was a liability; the Dutch were also drawn away from it by opportunities and commitments elsewhere in maritime Asia. For the Cheng armies and their leaders after 1661, Taiwan was a refuge, but a pretty grim and deprived one. Many of them were quickly drawn back into mainland trade and politics after 1673, surrendered after 1680, or were quite ready to be returned to the mainland after 1683. In the new situation thereafter, the Ch'ing rulers' attitude toward Taiwan was negative and minimalist, but there was no impermeable barrier between it and Fukien, so that increasingly land-hungry frontier farmers could make their own decisions about going and coming back, going and settling down. No longer a vortex of power politics and world trade, Taiwan now would grow perhaps more slowly but certainly more securely as a distinctive Chinese frontier.

Notes

Abbreviations used in Notes

BDR: *Dagh-Register gehouden in't Casteel Batavia, 1628–1682*. 31 vols. Batavia: Landsdrukkerij, 1887–1931.

GM: W. Ph. Coolhaas, ed., *Generale Missiven van Gouverneurs-Generaal en Raden aan Heren XVII der Verenigde Oost-Indische Compagnie*. Rijks Gescheidkundige Publicatien, Grote Serie, vol. 104 et seq. The Hague: Nijhoff, 1960 – .

TW: *T'ai-wan wen-hsien ts'ung-k'an*. Taipei: Bank of Taiwan, 1958–.

ZDR: J.L. Blussé, M.E. van Opstall, and Ts'ao Yung-ho, eds., *De Dagregisters van het Kasteel Zeelandia, Taiwan. Deel I: 1629–1641*. Rijks Geschiedkundige Publicatien, Grote Serie, 195. The Hague: M. Nijhoff, 1986.

1. John E. Wills, Jr., "Maritime Asia, 1500–1800: The Interactive Emergence of European Domination," *American Historical Review* 98, no. 1 (February 1993): 83–105.

2. For a very effective summary of macroregional differences and trajectories, see Susan Naquin and Evelyn S. Rawski, *Chinese Society in the Eighteenth Century* (New Haven and London: Yale University Press, 1987), chap. 5.

3. John E. Wills, Jr., "Maritime China from Wang Chih to Shih Lang: Themes in Peripheral History," in *From Ming to Ch'ing: Conquest, Region, and Continuity in Seventeenth-Century China*, ed. Jonathan D. Spence and John E. Wills, Jr. (New Haven: Yale University Press, 1979), pp. 204–238.

4. See especially John Robert Shepherd, *Statecraft and Political Economy on the Taiwan Frontier, 1600–1800* (Stanford: Stanford University Press, 1993). This excellent work provides the fullest account of seventeenth-century Taiwan now available. My intellectual debts to it are only partly reflected in the citations in this chapter. In general I have tried to abbreviate my discussion of the themes on which Shepherd focuses and to give more detail on others. An earlier magisterial work from which I have learned much is Ts'ao Yung-ho, *T'ai-wan tsao-ch'i li-shih yen-chiu* (Taipei: Lien-ching, 1979).

5. Kwang-chih Chang, *The Archeology of Ancient China*, 4th ed. (New Haven and London: Yale University Press, 1986), pp. 228–233, 235, 289–292.

6. Shepherd, *Statecraft and Political Economy on the Taiwan Frontier*, p. 28.

7. Wayne H. Fogg, "Swidden Cultivation of Foxtail Millet by Taiwan Aborigines: A Cultural Analogue of the Domestication of *Setaria italica* in China," in *The Origins of Chinese Civilization*, ed. David N. Keightley (Berkeley, Los Angeles, and London: University of California Press, 1983), pp. 95–115.

8. "Liu-ch'iu yu Chi-lung-shan," TW, no. 196.

9. Laurence G. Thompson, "The Earliest Chinese Accounts of the Formosan Aborigines," *Monumenta Serica*, 23 (1963): 163–204.

10. Iwao Seiichi, "Shih-ch'i shih-chi Jih-pen-jen chih T'ai-wan chin-lueh hsing-tung" [The Japanese invasions of Taiwan in the seventeenth century], in *T'ai-wan ching-chi-shih pa-chi*, pp. 1–23. I have found very little information on Japanese trading in Taiwan before the arrival of the Dutch. Lin Ch'ien-kuang, "T'ai-wan chi-lueh," in *Hsiao-fang-hu-chai yu-ti ts'ung-ch'ao* [Collected geographical essays from the Hsiao-fang-hu studio: 1877, supplements to 1897], ed. Wang Hsi-ch'i, 9th collection, pp. 136–137, says Pei-hsien-wei, the Dutch Baxemboy, the sand-bar just north of Casteel Zeelandia, was one of the centers of their trade.

11. C.R. Boxer, *The Great Ship from Amacon: Annals of Macao and the Old Japan Trade, 1555–1640* (Lisbon: Centro de Estudos Históricos Ultramarinos, 1959), p. 44.

12. L. Carrington Goodrich and Chaoying Fang, eds., *Dictionary of Ming Biography* (New York and London: Columbia University Press, 1976), pp. 917–919, 927–930.

13. Thompson, "Earliest Chinese Accounts"; Shen Yu-jung et al., "Min-hai tseng-yen," TW, no. 56.

14. For a summary, see John E. Wills, Jr., "Relations with Maritime Europeans, 1514–1662," *Cambridge History of China*, vol. 8, in press, also to appear in Wills, ed., *China and Maritime Europe, 1500–1800: Trade, Settlement, Diplomacy, and Missions* (Cambridge University Press, nearing completion).

15. Leonard Blussé and Marius P. H. Roessingh, "A Visit to the Past: Soulang, A Formosan Village Anno 1623," *Archipel*, no. 27 (1984): 63–80.

16. This point was made and richly supported by evidence and argument by Leonard Blussé of Leiden University in his presentations to a symposium on seventeenth-century Taiwan funded by the Chiang Ching-kuo Foundation and held at the University of Southern California in November 1992.

17. The importance of the Ryukyus for this argument was emphasized by Professor Ts'ao Yung-ho of the Academia Sinica, Taiwan, at the November 1992 symposium.

18. W.P. Groeneveldt, *De Nederlanders in China, Eerste Deel: De Eerste Bemoeingen om den Handel in China en de Vestiging in de Pescadores (1601–1624)* (The Hague: Nijhoff, 1898); Chang Wei-hua, *Ming-shih Fo-lang-chi, Lu-sung, Ho-lan, I-ta-li-ya ssu-chuan chu-shih* (Peiping: *Yenching Journal of Chinese Studies* monograph series, no. 7, 1934), pp. 107–146.

19. "Ming-chi Ho-lan-jen chin-chu P'eng-hu ts'an-tang", TW, no. 154; BDR 1624–1625, pp. 1–26, 40–42, 139–146; J.L. Blussé, "The Dutch Occupation of the Pescadores (1622–1624)," *Transactions of the International Conference of Orientalists in Japan*, 18 (1973): 28–43.

20. The Dutch period is by far the best documented in the history of seventeenth-century Taiwan. This summary provides only a suggestion of the richness of the sources. It would be premature to attempt a full-scale treatment at this time, while the Dutch publication of the day-registers of Zeelandia Castle is not yet complete.

21. Leonard Blussé, "The VOC as Sorcerer's Apprentice: Stereotypes and Social Engineering on the China Coast," in *Leiden Studies in Sinology*, ed. W.L. Idema (Leiden: Leiden University Press, 1981), pp. 87–105; Blussé, "Minnan-jen or Cosmopolitan? The Rise of Cheng Chih-lung Alias Nicholas Iquan," in *Development and Decline of Fukien Province in the Seventeenth and Eighteenth Centuries*, ed. E.B. Vermeer (Leiden: E.J. Brill, 1990), pp. 245–264.

22. Much remains to be done in finding and using all the source material on this episode in ecclesiastical and Spanish governmental archives. For starting points see Shepherd, *Statecraft and Political Economy on the Taiwan Frontier*, pp. 56–59; ZDR, pp. 237–238; BDR, 1634, p. 284; 1636, pp. 287–288; 1640, pp. 110–120; 1645, pp. 128–129;

GM, vol. 1, pp. 229–230, 271–273, 709; F.R.J. Verhoeven, *Bijdragen tot de Oudere Koloniale Geschiedenis van het Eiland Formosa* (The Hague:Nijhoff, 1930), chaps. 4–7; José María Álvarez, O.P., *Formosa, Geografica e Historicamente Considerada* [Formosa, geographically and historically considered] (Barcelona, 1930), vol. 1, pp. 20–90.

23. GM, vol. 2, pp. 357, 455.

24. John Robert Shepherd, *Marriage and Mandatory Abortion Among the Seventeenth-Century Siraya*, American Ethnological Society Monograph Series, no. 6 (Arlington: American Anthropological Association, 1995).

25. Thomas O. Höllman, "Formosa and the Trade in Venison and Deer Skins," in *Emporia, Commodities, and Entrepreneurs in Asian Maritime Trade, c. 1400–1750*, ed., Roderich Ptak and Dietmar Rothermund, Beiträge zur Südasienforschung, Südasien-Institut, Universität Heidelberg, no. 141 (Stuttgart: Franz Steiner, 1991), pp. 263–290.

26. BDR, 1637, pp. 37–39.

27. BDR, 1636, pp. 152–153; BDR, 1637, pp. 37–39; B. Hoetink, "Soe Bing Kong: Het eerste hoofd der Chinezen te Batavia," in *Bijdragen tot de Taal-, Land-, en Volkenkunde van Nederlandsch Indië*, vol. 73 (1917), pp. 344–415.

28. Johannes Huber, "Chinese Settlers Against the Dutch East India Company: The Rebellion Led by Kuo Huai-i on Taiwan in 1652," in Vermeer, ed., *Development and Decline of Fukien Province*, pp. 276–279; BDR, 1645, p. 172; GM, vol. 3, p. 197.

29. ZDR, pp. 451, 499.

30. Huber, "Chinese Settlers."

31. GM, vol. 3, p. 198.

32. BDR, 1661, p. 489.

33. William Campbell, *Formosa Under the Dutch* (London: Kegan, Paul, Trench, and Trubner, 1903; repr. Taipei: Ch'eng-wen, 1967), pp. 318–328, 383–492; Inez de Beauclair, *Neglected Formosa*, trans. Frederick Coyett, ed. L. Blussé et al. (San Francisco: Chinese Materials Center, 1975); BDR, 1661, pp. 484–520.

34. Chikamatsu Monzaemon, *The Battles of Coxinga*, ed. and trans. Donald Keene, Cambridge Oriental Series, no. 4 (London: Taylor's Foreign Press, 1951), pp. 61–75; Donald F. Lach and Edwin J. Van Kley, *Asia in the Making of Europe*, vol. 3 (Chicago and London: University of Chicago Press, 1993), pp. 1820–1823.

35. John E. Wills, Jr., *Pepper, Guns, and Parleys: The Dutch East India Company and China, 1662–1681* (Cambridge: Harvard University Press, 1974), pp. 28, 41–43, 51–52, 72–74, 81–82.

36. Shepherd, *Statecraft and Political Economy*, p. 102.

37. Huang Tien-ch'uan, *Cheng Yen-p'ing k'ai-fu T'ai-wan jen-wu-chi* (Tainan: Haitung shan-fang, 1958), contains a convenient compilation of biographical information on these and other Cheng regime figures.

38. Wills, "Maritime China."

39. J.L.P.J. Vogels, "Het Nieuwe Tayouan: De Verenigde Oostindische Compagnie op Kelang, 1664–1668," Ph.D. dissertation, Rijksuniversiteit Utrecht, 1988.

40. Shepherd, *Statecraft and Political Economy*, chap. 4.

41. For a rich set of examples of similar shifts in early modern Southeast Asia, see Anthony Reid, *Southeast Asia in the Age of Commerce, 1450–1680* (New Haven and London: Yale University Press, 1988, 1993), vol. 2, chap. 3.

42. There is no account of this English trade in any language that makes use of all the material available in the India Office Library in London. My own attempt at a fuller account is contained in my *Toward the Canton System: Maritime Trade and Ch'ing Policy, 1681–1690*, forthcoming. Many of the important sources were published in Iwao Seiichi, *Shih-ch'i shih-chi T'ai-wan Ying-kuo mao-i shih-liao, T'ai-wan yen-chiu ts'ung-*

k'an, no. 57, ed. Ts'ao Yung-ho, Chou Hsien-wen, and Lai Yung-hsiang (Taipei: Bank of Taiwan, 1959); and M. Paske-Smith, *Western Barbarians in Japan and Formosa in Tokugawa Days, 1603–1868* (Kobe: 1930). See also H.B. Morse, *Chronicles of the East India Company Trading to China* (Oxford: Clarendon Press, 1926–1929; repr. Taipei, 1966), vol. 1, pp. 41–49.

43. Pierre Chaunu, *Les Philippines et le Pacifique des Ibériques (XVIe, XVIIe, XVIIIe siècles); Introduction méthodologique et indices d'activité* (Paris: S.E.V.P.E.N., 1960), pp. 164–169.

44. Iwao Seiichi, "Kinsei Nisshi bōeki ni kansuru shōryōteki kōsa," *Shigaku zasshi,* 62, no. 11 (November 1953): 12–13.

45. Iwao, "Shih-ch'i shi-chi Jih-pen-jen chih Tai-wan," p. 137.

46. Wills, *Pepper, Guns, and Parleys,* pp. 154–157.

47. The English sources give a particularly vivid sense of these days; Paske-Smith, *Western Barbarians in Japan and Formosa,* pp. 108–122.

48. This is intriguing in view of Liu's relative autonomy within the Cheng Ching regime, the reports of Ch'ing negotiations with him, and the excellent evidence that he fought hard in the Pescadores. I suspect that if he had beaten off the Ch'ing fleet he would have seized power on Taiwan, installed his own Cheng puppet, and possibly led the remaining forces on an invasion of Vietnam or Manila. I develop this hypothesis in *Toward the Canton System.*

49. John E. Wills, Jr., *Embassies and Illusions: Dutch and Portuguese Envoys to K'ang-hsi, 1666–1687* (Cambridge: Council on East Asian Studies, Harvard University, 1984), pp. 148, 151.

50. Shepherd, *Statecraft and Political Economy,* p. 106; Fu Lo-shu, *A Documentary Chronicle of Sino-Western Relations (1644–1820)* (Tucson: University of Arizona Press, 1966), vol. 1, pp. 60–61.

5

The Island Frontier of the Ch'ing, 1684–1780

John R. Shepherd

The Mazu Temple in Lukang.

Establishing Ch'ing Rule

Shih Lang, the victorious Ch'ing admiral, moved quickly to consolidate his control over Taiwan. The peaceful surrender of the Ch'eng-kung regime meant that there was no organized resistance to the Ch'ing takeover. The new government did, nevertheless, have to expend considerable effort rounding up unruly remnant soldiers and Cheng deserters.[1]

Shih Lang's immediate task was to preserve civil order. Shortly after his landing on the island in the fall of 1683, he met with representatives of the Chinese inhabitants and the aborigine tribes and assured them that Taiwan's entering the empire meant that all of Taiwan's people would be considered loyal subjects whom the government would protect and pacify. Shih acted to maintain the discipline of his troops in order to minimize points of friction between the occupying forces and the local population. Shih forbade government troops to occupy people's homesteads; commerce and agriculture were to continue "at the people's convenience" with no interference in the local markets. Military rations were imported to avoid overburdening the local supplies, and commandeering supplies at cheaper prices was forbidden. In addition, a tax holiday to celebrate Taiwan's peaceful return to the empire was declared. All these measures were to ensure a smooth transition to the new order.

Officials at court in Peking had originally intended, once the rebel Cheng regime was defeated, to abandon Taiwan and evacuate its Chinese population to the mainland. Accordingly, Cheng military forces were either sent back to their home communities or incorporated into Manchu armies. In all, forty thousand soldiers were repatriated. Many soldiers and refugees, who had been driven by the civil wars from the mainland and had had a difficult life under the hard-pressed Cheng regime, eagerly returned to their mainland homes.

The civilian population was also under pressure to leave. The Ch'ing coastal regulations of 1683 decreed that anyone sojourning in Taiwan who had neither wife nor livelihood must return home to Fukien. Those with wives and property and desiring to remain were required to register with the local officials. By the ninth month of 1684 Shih Lang estimated that nearly half the total Chinese population had already left the island. Tax quotas for cash and grain had to be substantially reduced (the per-capita burden remained high). Taiwan's Chinese population must have fallen below eighty thousand at this time, since its maximum under Cheng is estimated at only one hundred and twenty thousand.

Shih Lang vigorously opposed abandoning Taiwan, a prize he had fought many long years to gain. In late 1683 several high officials met at Foochow to debate the course of Ch'ing policy on Taiwan. Shih Lang argued that Taiwan was too important strategically and economically for it not to be incorporated into the empire and that governing the new territory need not burden the national treasury. Shih pointed out the dangers to coastal security were Taiwan to fall into the hands of a hostile power. Moreover, if Taiwan were under Ch'ing control, the garrisons along the southeastern coast (and the attendant expenditures) could be reduced; indeed some of these troops could be used to garrison Taiwan, thereby reducing the expense of administering the new territory. Shih named sulfur (a strategic item) and deer hides as some of the valuable products that made Taiwan worth keeping or at least worth keeping out of others' hands. Shih also pointed out that the complete evacuation of Taiwan's Chinese population would take years and would serve only to create masses of vagrants. Cheng remnants hiding among aborigines in the mountains could never be entirely cleared out—to abandon Taiwan to them would turn it into a pirates' lair.[2]

Shih Lang's arguments in favor of incorporating the island into the empire prevailed, and in the fourth month of 1684 Taiwan was made a prefecture of Fukien province, and land and marine forces were assigned to garrison Taiwan and the P'eng-hu islands (Pescadores). At the same time the prohibition on maritime trade, instituted to embargo the Cheng forces, was lifted, giving Fukien's fishermen and merchants access to the seas, including Taiwan, and allowing Fukien's farmers to return to their coastal villages. In adopting these policies, the government hoped to foster an economic recovery along the southeastern coast that would stabilize its social order and generate taxes and customs revenues (from foreign trade) that would ease the court's own fiscal problems. Maritime commerce therefore gravitated back to Amoy as Taiwan lost the entrepôt functions it had under the Dutch and Chengs when maritime trade (e.g., with Japan) had been outlawed by mainland governments.

In the case of Taiwan, however, the court imposed a partial quarantine, as it was determined to prevent the island from again becoming a staging ground for rebellion. Rather than actively foster colonization by Chinese farmers the government sought to limit the further spread of settlement in Taiwan. The court feared that Han immigration to Taiwan would create a potentially rebellious population in areas beyond its effective control; it also saw expanding Han settlement as an intrusion on aborigine villages that would upset the ethnic status quo on the island. Quarantine policies had the effect of sheltering the indigenous tribes, but the government's priority was to preserve control at the lowest cost, not to defend aborigine societies against the frontiersmen. Disturbances and aborigine revolts in Taiwan were nearly always attributed to the misdeeds of Chinese. Perpetuation of the status quo was seen as the key to the maintenance of order and effective control over this strategically important periphery.

The government thought that it could ensure its control over the island indirectly by regulating immigration, preventing the migration of families (to keep the immigrants, mostly single males, dependent on access to the mainland), and restricting exports of rice (to guarantee that food shortages would not be a source of disturbances). Direct control over the island was to be exercised by a military garrison and a civil administration concentrated in the southwest core around the prefectural capital of Tainan (neither the military nor the civil bureaucracy reached the northern third of the western plain). This was all the government presence that the tax revenues of the underpopulated island and financially strapped Fukien could support.

A sketch of the initial structure of the Ch'ing civil and military administration of Taiwan will set the stage. The highest-ranking civil official in Taiwan was the Taiwan–Amoy military administrative intendant. The intendant had the power to move troops and oversaw communications between the ports of Tainan and Amoy through the coastal defense subprefects stationed in each port.

For purposes of territorial administration, Taiwan was organized as a prefecture of Fukien province and headed by a prefect. The Taiwan prefect was subordinate to the intendant, the governor of Fukien, and the governor-general of Chekiang and Fukien. Subordinate to the prefect were magistrates of three counties, Chu-lo county covering the northern plain, T'ai-wan county, covering the most heavily settled areas around Tainan, and Feng-shan county, covering the plains south of Tainan. The Ch'ing disbanded the Cheng armies and replaced them in Taiwan with garrison forces totaling ten thousand land and marine troops, headed by a brigade general. These soldiers were rotated every three years from armies in Fukien. Both the civil and military administrations were concentrated in the Tainan core. A few scattered military outposts reached as far north as Chang-hua but none extended beyond the Ta-chia river.

Ch'ing Taxation and Administration of the Aborigines

The repatriation of much of the Chinese population of Taiwan at the beginning of Ch'ing rule and the imposition of quarantine policies that restricted new immigration meant that aborigine society and trade were left relatively undisturbed by the accession of the new regime. Indeed, the pressure of expanding Chinese population on aborigine hunting territories diminished. The Dutch and the Chengs had suppressed intervillage warfare and head-hunting among the plains aborigines and imposed overarching systems of administration and taxation on the villages. The Ch'ing had no desire to disturb the status quo by creating a new administrative and tax apparatus; it simply adopted the Cheng system of administering the plains aborigine villages and continued the Cheng practice of imposing both a head tax and corvée on the aborigine tribes. Tax farming of aborigine villages and monopoly merchant control of the deer trade continued to structure the interaction of government, Chinese, and aborigines well into the early eighteenth century.[3]

The Chinese designated tribes that had submitted to Chinese authority and paid taxes as "ripened" or "civilized" aborigines *(shu-fan)*. These peoples inhabited the western coastal plains, in contrast to "raw" or "uncivilized" aborigines *(sheng-fan)* who inhabited the mountains and lived outside Ch'ing control. The plains tribes were grouped into thirty-eight tax-paying units, thirty-four in Chu-lo county to the north, four in Feng-shan county to the south, plus eight tribes in Feng-shan who paid taxes in grain.

The Chinese tax farmer paid the tribal tax on behalf of an aborigine settlement. In return he acquired a trade monopoly on both buying aborigine produce from and selling trade goods to that settlement. Farming taxes to private merchants was advantageous for the state because it guaranteed the payment of the tax quota at the same time it eliminated the expense of administering a tax collection system in the villages. The monopoly merchant system, however, concentrated great power in the tax farmer and his subordinates, who mediated between the state and the weakly organized and unsophisticated aborigines. Such power was often abused, as it had been in Dutch and Cheng times. Yu Yung-ho, who traveled throughout Chu-lo on a trip to obtain sulfur in Tan-shui (Tam-sui) in 1697 comments as follows:

> The Chengs extracted heavy labor service and taxes from the barbarians [aborigines], and our dynasty continues this practice. . . . In each administrative district a wealthy person is made responsible for the village revenues. These men are called "village tax farmers" [literally, village merchants, or *she-shang*]. The village tax farmer in turn appoints interpreters and foremen who are sent to live in the villages, and who record and check up on every jot and tittle [grown or brought in by hunting] of all the barbarians. . . . They make a profit from the sale of both of these things after paying their taxes.
>
> But these interpreters and foremen take advantage of the simple-mindedness of the barbarians and never tire of fleecing them, looking on whatever they have as no different from their own property. In connection with the activities of daily life, great and small, all of the barbarians—men, women, and children—have to serve in their homes without a day of respite. Moreover, they take the barbarian women as their wives and concubines. Whatever is demanded of them they must comply; if they make a mistake they must take a flogging. And yet the barbarians do not hate them greatly.[4]

Officials in Taiwan became concerned about corrupt practices in the administration of the aborigine tribes because of the disturbances they might cause and because they interfered with the government's ability to farm the taxes.

In addition to the tribal revenue tax exacted in kind or silver, the Ch'ing administration required the natives to provide corvée labor service. Like tax farming, corvée reduced the state's administrative expenses, was subject to similar abuses, and was the source of frequent troubles. Aborigines were required to render many different kinds of services, including bearing mandarins in sedan chairs, delivering official documents, and supplying oxcarts to transport lumber for ship building. Aborigines also served as porters for the troops rotated from Fukien every three years. Labor duties were assigned by the tribal merchants and interpreters, who rarely observed any distinction between the levy of government corvée and the extortion of personal service.

The extortions and abuses of the tax farmers and interpreters often reached unbearable levels. In a few instances the oppression exercised by the tribal bullies met with violent resistance. Two plains aborigine revolts occurred in

1699, both in northern Taiwan, and led to calls for reform of the tax farming system. The large-scale aborigine revolt of 1731 and 1732, discussed below, demonstrates that the early reform attempts often made little headway, especially in the area of corvée exactions, where the government was itself the prime source of abuse.

Quarantine and Restrictions on Immigration

The court, persuaded primarily by considerations of maritime security, decided in 1684 to keep Taiwan. But instead of adopting a policy of actively opening the Taiwan frontier, the court imposed a partial quarantine on the island. The court's primary motive remained its fear that pirates, Cheng remnants, and rebels might make Taiwan into an antigovernment base. This led to the numerous restrictions on mainland communications and the immigration of Chinese settlers adopted in 1684.[5]

Discouraging permanent settlement by outlawing the migration of families meant that only single males could legally make the crossing to Taiwan. This gave rise to a population of migrant laborers and sojourners crossing for the spring planting and returning to their mainland homes after the fall harvest. This served Ch'ing policy by creating a population of male laborers dependent on the government for access to their families on the mainland. Filial obligations to parents and the duty to maintain ancestral sacrifices reinforced this dependence. The government could avenge wayward behavior on the hard-to-control Taiwan frontier by holding families on the mainland responsible. This guaranteed that the migrants remained law-abiding.

These attempts to quarantine Taiwan and to prevent permanent settlement resemble the policies the Ch'ing applied to some other frontiers of new settlement. The Ch'ing government sought to limit the migration of Han Chinese settlers into areas occupied by non-Han peoples where the Chinese were sure to upset the ethnic status quo. Thus in Manchuria and Inner Mongolia, as in Taiwan, the Ch'ing tolerated the seasonal migration of male farm laborers, but prohibited the migration of families and women in order to prevent the disruption that would come with permanent settlement by Han Chinese.[6] Ch'ing frontier quarantine policies, however, were difficult to enforce and in the Taiwan case were opposed by many officials, who saw them as the source of much of the unsettled state of Taiwanese society.

By the end of the reign of the K'ang-hsi emperor (1662–1722), the pressure of a growing population was undermining the restrictions on immigration. Sparsely populated Taiwan lay opposite the southeastern coast, which had now recovered from the devastation of the coastal evacuation policy and was well on its way to becoming one of eighteenth-century China's most densely populated rice-deficit regions. Migrants to Taiwan came from southeastern coast prefectures that had the worst man/land ratios: Chang-chou and Ch'uan-chou in Fukien were the home of Hokkien immigrants, and Hui-chou and Ch'ao-chou in Kuangtung province were the home of Hakka immigrants.[7] And the heavy demand for rice on the southeast coast meant that those who took up farming in Taiwan could get high prices for their grain. These demographic and economic facts subverted attempts to enforce the restrictions on immigration. Furthermore, Ch'ing coastal authorities had difficulty patroling the Fukien and Taiwan coasts, where numerous landing points made it easy for immigrants to escape official detection and official squeeze. It seems clear that by 1718 Taiwan's population more than exceeded its Cheng period high point and that areas of concentrated Chinese settlement had spread beyond the old Tainan core, to both the north and south.

The prohibition on the immigration of wives and families led to the growth of a volatile, bachelor-dominated society in Taiwan that was prone to brawling and rebellion. The predominance of bachelor sojourners was common on Chinese frontiers and in overseas migration and was not unique to Taiwan.[8] That government policy barred these men, even when they became established property owners, from bringing over wives and relatives to join them, did, however, exacerbate conditions in Taiwan. The immigration restrictions prevented the growth of a rooted and more stable population of families. Attempts to tighten enforcement of limits on immigration after 1717 may have helped fuel the antigovernment resentment that burst forth in the Chu Yi-kuei rebellion.[9]

The Chu Yi-kuei Rebellion of 1721

The Chu Yi-kuei rebellion of 1721 demonstrated the volatility of frontier society and the fragility of Ch'ing rule in Taiwan and forced the government to reevaluate its policies toward its island prefecture.[10] In 1721 Feng-shan county was under the rule of a magistrate, Wang Chen, whose harsh methods of tax collection had already alienated the populace. His son's indiscriminate use of extortion in an attempt to round up bandits had further antagonized the law-abiding population.

Chu Yi-kuei, thirty-three years old in 1721, and a native of Chang-chou prefecture in Fukien, had arrived in Taiwan in 1713. Chu had taken up raising ducks in the Feng-shan area south of Tainan. In the third month of 1721, Chu and several confederates met in Feng-shan to plan an uprising. Chu appears to have emerged as leader of this newly formed rebel band in part simply because he bore the surname of the deposed Ming ruling house. Chu's rebel comrades judged that this would be of use in gathering followers under the banner of Ming loyalism.

On the night of April 19 Chu and a group of between fifty and eighty rebels attacked a military outpost at Kang-shan (south of Tainan) and robbed it of its weapons. Two days later this band conducted a successful raid on another outpost. Upon hearing news of these exploits, the Hakka outlaw leader Tu Chunying came forth to ally his own bandit group with Chu's rebel band.

On the twenty-first the government mobilized its troops and called up plains aborigine porters and auxiliaries. Although the outbreak was still small in scale and containable, several government missteps in the following days caused the revolt to spread and escalate. Chief among these was a careless attempt to incite plains aborigine auxiliaries against the rebels by offering bounties for rebel heads. When overzealous plains aborigines torched houses and killed innocent civilians instead, panic spread among the populace. It was then easy for the rebels to spread fear of the government troops and win support in Chinese villages. Over the next few days the rebels defeated government troops in several skirmishes and forced them to withdraw from Feng-shan and return to Tainan. Tu Chun-ying's bandit forces then launched attacks on the Feng-shan county seat.

News of these defeats caused panic among the officials in Tainan, who began putting their families aboard ships to flee the island. On the thirtieth the rebel forces approached Tainan but were dealt an initial defeat by government troops. On the May 1, rebels "by the ten thousands" congregated outside Tainan and the forces of Chu Yi-kuei and Tu Chun-ying launched a united attack. The Ch'ing brigade general was assassinated, and ferocious battles resulted in heavy casualties for both sides. The government troops appear to have been badly outnumbered despite their superior weapons. Sensing defeat, the military and civil officers commandeered all available shipping and fled to the Pescadores and Fukien.

The rebels then easily occupied Tainan, the prefectural capital. Tu Chun-ying set up his headquarters in the brigade general's yamen, and Chu Yi-kuei set up his in the intendant's yamen. Within a few days the Chu-lo county seat to the north also fell into the rebels' hands, leaving only the Tan-shui–Keelung area under Ch'ing control. On May 3, Chu Yi-kuei was declared king, and official ranks and titles were bestowed on the various rebel leaders.

Thus Ch'ing rule in Taiwan had collapsed within less than two weeks. A bungled government response had allowed a small outbreak to escalate into a major rebellion. Rivalry between Chu Yi-kuei and Tu Chun-ying soon began to undermine rebel unity, however. In the ensuing weeks, communal tensions increased as additional clashes led to the polarization of the Hakka and Hokkien settlers. In Feng-shan the Hakka villages organized a self-defense corps. A large pitched battle between the Hokkien rebels and the Hakka self-defense corps was in progress in southern Feng-shan when the Ch'ing reconquest began in the middle of the sixth month.

By the beginning of the sixth month, the government had assembled an armada of six hundred ships, six thousand sailors, and twelve thousand soldiers in Amoy and the Pescadores. The first wave landed outside Tainan on June 16 and quickly gained control of the port of An-p'ing; the Ch'ing forces made heavy use of cannon to defeat rebel counterattacks, and within a week the prefectural capital was once again in Ch'ing hands. Chu Yi-kuei's resistance collapsed and within a few weeks he was betrayed and taken prisoner. Tu Chun-ying, who had fled to the mountains, surrendered on September 10. The large Ch'ing armies dispersed rebel forces and rounded up the remnants. They were assisted by the

Hakka self-defense corps, now styled "loyalists," in Feng-shan, and by plains aborigines, who served as guides to troops clearing out bandits from mountain hideaways.

Ch'ing rule in Taiwan was restored in 1721 almost as quickly as it had been lost, but only after a sizable loss of life and expenditure of revenues. The sudden collapse of government demonstrated that the official administration had failed to build ties to Taiwan's frontier society that could be counted on to impede the spread of outbreaks and shore up government control. To critics like Lan Ting-yuan, the restrictive immigration policy only exacerbated the problem of creating a stable social order in Taiwan that would have vested interests in preserving government control.

Colonization Policy Debates in the Post-Rebellion Period

After the Chu Yi-kuei rebellion, Lan Ting-yuan became an outspoken critic of conservative quarantine policies toward Taiwan. Lan had come from Fukien to Taiwan in 1721 in the company of the imperial forces (under his cousin's command) that suppressed the Chu Yi-kuei rebellion. The rebellion's rapid spread among Taiwan's immigrant Han population reawakened fears that Taiwan might become a rebel base that could threaten the southeastern coast. In the wake of the rebellion and on into the Yung-cheng emperor's reign (1723–1735), many of the old policies concerning Taiwan were reconsidered and new ones proposed. Lan Ting-yuan, an advocate of aggressive colonization policy, was one of the most prolific participants in these debates.[11]

In 1683 the Ch'ing court had been impressed more by the burdens than the benefits of the incorporation of Taiwan into the empire. The court, afraid that Taiwan might again become a rebel base, imposed a partial quarantine on the island. Policies of quarantine, strictly regulating migration and trade between the island and the mainland, were adopted to prevent disruptions of the status quo on Taiwan. The court judged that indirect control, exercised by quarantining the island, would be a less expensive and more cost-effective means of preventing disturbance on the frontier.

Quarantine and the maintenance of the status quo were the hallmarks of early Ch'ing policy toward Taiwan; the spread of Han settlement and the extension of the government's presence were simply not envisaged. By the end of the K'ang-hsi emperor's reign, the recovery of the southeastern coast, the growth of its population, and the expansion of its commerce and foreign trade were subverting the quarantine of Taiwan.[12] Migrants from the crowded southeastern coast were flocking to Taiwan to take advantage of its unopened fields and the high prices Taiwan's sugar and rice fetched in mainland markets. These developments were leading to the growth of an unstable settler society and upsetting the ethnic status quo on the Taiwan frontier. The Chu Yi-kuei rebellion demonstrated how serious the threat to government control had grown.

The government's first response to these developments was to tighten enforcement of the quarantine policies and the restrictions on immigration. Attempts were made to quarantine aborigine territories by drawing a "raw aborigine" boundary and to limit the spread of Han settlement in Taiwan to areas under effective government control (see below). But several statesmen, the most outspoken of whom was Lan Ting-yuan, argued for a reversal of the quarantine policies and the adoption of a procolonization course as the best way to ensure control over Taiwan. These officials argued that government control was best maintained directly by intensifying the civil and military presence so that it could crush both Han and aborigine sources of disturbance and by filling up open frontier spaces with Chinese agricultural settlers. To help finance the governmental presence, land tax revenue could be collected from areas newly reclaimed by immigrant Chinese families, who were the allies, not the enemies, of government control.

To observers like Lan Ting-yuan, the restrictions on bringing wives and families had perpetuated a population of rootless vagrants without family ties. Lan argued that migrants wishing to farm in Taiwan should be allowed to take families with them and those already in Taiwan should be allowed to return home to bring their families over. It was those without families who should be barred from crossing and the vagrants who should be sent back. Once all settlers had families, the sources of rebellion would be eradicated.

The government moved more cautiously than Lan, but largely in the directions he and his fellow procolonization advocates supported. In the first year of his reign, the Yung-cheng emperor approved a plan to subdivide Chu-lo county by adding Chang-hua county and Tan-shui subprefecture. This increased the presence of the civil administration on Taiwan's northern frontier. However, no expansion of the already large and expensive military presence was ordered at this time.

Throughout the Yung-cheng era, the quarantine policies were abandoned piece by piece and procolonization ones put in their place. Beginning in 1725 Taiwan's growing rice surpluses were designated for export to Fukien garrisons and for famine relief sales on the rice-deficient southeastern coast. Aborigine tribes were encouraged to rent their lands to Han so that "both might benefit and the treasury be filled." Cadastral surveys in 1728 enrolled large amounts of land on the tax registers, especially in the territory of the newly established Chang-hua county, which was badly in need of a tax base. In 1731 land tax rates were lowered to encourage voluntary registration of land; the new policy, unlike that of the K'ang-hsi years, looked to the continued expansion of reclaimed land and growing land tax rolls, rather than high tax rates, to fill the tax quotas. Also in 1731 the court added several submagistrates to its civil administration. But at the end of the year, excessive imposition of corvée on civilized aborigines ordered to build yamens in the north brought on the large-scale Ta-chia-hsi tribal revolt.

The Ta-chia-hsi and Wu Fu-sheng Revolts of 1731–32
and Their Aftermath

The most serious plains aborigine revolt to challenge Ch'ing authority in Taiwan's history began in the twelfth month of 1731. Taiwan's local gazetteers simply state that a revolt broke out at this time in the plains aborigine village of Ta-chia-hsi, under the leadership of one Lin Wu-li. Ta-chia-hsi was a plains aborigine settlement located on the coastal plain of present-day Taichung county, north of the Ta-chia river. Palace memorials make clear that excessive imposition of corvée and ill treatment of the aborigines by officials, yamen underlings, and soldiers were basic causes of the revolt.[13]

Early in 1731 as part of the procolonization policy of extending direct government control onto the frontier, it was decided to give full fiscal and administrative power to the Tan-shui subprefecture, which had been created in 1723, and to create a number of new subdistrict magistracies. This meant that yamen offices had to be built to house the new officials. The Tan-shui subprefect, Chang Chung-hung, ordered the local tribes to supply labor for the construction. The increased official presence meant increased official extortion, and the tribes were soon complaining that yamen runners were sleeping with aborigine women and that government soldiers were commandeering aborigine food supplies. Aborigine complaints went unheeded.

Subprefect Chang had ordered aborigine laborers from Ta-chia-hsi to supply large logs (for pillars) from forests in the nearby mountains and aborigine women to drive out the carts bearing the lumber. When the women refused, the interpreters beat them with rattan strips. Unable to bear this treatment any longer, braves from Ta-chia-hsi and the neighboring village of Ta-chia-tung surrounded subprefect Chang in his offices, killed some of his subordinates, and set the yamen on fire. Chang escaped this attack by fleeing south to the county seat of Chang-hua. This left unprotected many settlers in the vicinity, who were then killed and had their homes burned down by the aborigines.

In the next weeks Ta-chia-hsi was joined in revolt by two more neighboring villages. Ch'ing troops engaged the aborigines on several occasions but were unable to defeat them. The government reinforced its northern garrisons, enlisted the aid of loyal aborigines, and pressed the attack. By the third month of 1732, many of the rebel tribes, who had retreated into the mountains, were reported to be surrendering.

The government had responded to its early defeats at the hands of the aborigines by moving northward troops usually stationed in the south. Taking advantage of the government's difficulty, a group of Han rebels, including some remnants of the Chu Yi-kuei rebellion, raised the flag of rebellion in Feng-shan county in the south. Led by one Wu Fu-sheng, they attacked several government outposts. But within ten days, by the early part of the fourth month of 1732, the commander Wang Chun had crushed these Han rebels.

Things next took a turn for the worse in the north. Official crimes and arrogance alienated hitherto loyal aborigines and forced them to join the rebellion. In the fifth month of 1732, nearly two thousand aborigines surrounded Chang-hua city, devastated the area around it, and slaughtered the soldiers stationed at two nearby military posts. Chang-hua city escaped being taken only because of the timely arrival of troop reinforcements and several hundred Hakka braves from the south (who had earlier proved their effectiveness in the victory over Chu Yi-kuei in 1721).

In the sixth month of 1732, Governor-General Hao Yu-lin was forced to dispatch to Taiwan several thousand soldiers from Fukien's garrisons. News that mainland reinforcements were arriving frightened some rebel aborigines into submitting, while others prepared for an onslaught by building defensive stockades. Commander Wang Chun took charge of the campaign, gradually swept the rebels from the plain, and by the eighth month of 1732 had the remnants surrounded in the mountains.

The dual threat posed to Ch'ing authority by the revolts of aborigines and Han in 1732 left a strong impression on Governor-General Hao. In 1733 he ordered a reorganization of the military in Taiwan, boosting its overall strength by several thousands. Of this number, 1,280 soldiers, the largest of the troop increases, were stationed on the northern route, more than doubling its original strength. This effected a significant shift in the balance of military power on the northern frontier. To have attempted an extension of the civil administration without a concurrent strengthening of the military was one of the fundamental errors of the government's control strategy in 1731.

This double rebellion, rather than forcing the government to retreat from its new procolonization and expansionist strategy, was taken as proof of the failure of the old policies. To pay for the military reinforcements, continued expansion of reclamation would be necessary to generate additional land tax revenues.

To those like Lan Ting-yuan, these revolts were added proof that the old immigration and quarantine policies were a failure. Vagrant Han in the south and the near absence of taxpaying Han in the north weakened the government's ability to maintain control. So when, in 1732, the Kuangtung Governor Omida, who had invited Lan to be his secretary, petitioned to allow families to cross to Taiwan, the emperor's councilors (including Ortai, famed for aggressive colonization policies in Southwest China) found Omida's arguments sound. Omida proposed that those with property and a livelihood in Taiwan could apply to the local authorities to allow their families to move to Taiwan. This proposal was adopted by the emperor in 1732.

The period from 1732 to 1740 was the first in which families could legally join settlers in Taiwan and it appears that many took advantage of the change in policy. In 1743 it was reported that Taiwan's population had increased by several thousands since the lifting of the ban. By the end of the Yung-cheng reign nearly all the quarantine policies had been abandoned. In their place was a strategy of extending direct control over the frontier through the civil and, belatedly, the military administrations, financed by revenue from taxes on land newly reclaimed by Chinese settlers.

By the beginning of the Ch'ien-lung reign (1736–95), the costs of the procolonization policies were beginning to loom large in the guise of a burgeoning and unruly Chinese population and continued aborigine disturbances. These problems arose in spite of the fact that an expanded civil and military presence and tax base had recently been put in place. That many of the procolonization policies had already been tried deflated the arguments counseling continuation of the procolonization course; so when policy reversals were proposed the new court was receptive. Governor-General Hao Yu-lin ordered a halt to the further reclamation of aborigine land in 1738, and in 1739 he sought an end, after a one-year grace period, to the legal immigration of families. In 1741 government rice export quotas were reduced, and in 1744 land tax rates were raised. But the revived quarantine policies had now to operate in an environment transformed since the Yung-cheng years by a large influx of Han Chinese farmers and the expansion of frontier settlement. Nor was the government any more successful than it had been in the late K'ang-hsi years at stopping illegal immigration and reclamation. In 1746 another survey of aborigine lands had to be ordered, the 1738 ban on their reclamation reasserted, and new punishments set to deal with violations. The revived quarantine policies had to be repeatedly adapted and compromised to deal with the reality of continued immigration and the spread of Han Chinese settlement throughout the remaining Ch'ien-lung years. We review below developments in the plains aborigine and Han settler segments of Taiwan's frontier society.

The Role of the Plains Aborigines

Following the Ta-chia-hsi revolt of 1731–32, the government took steps to strengthen the cultural and educational foundations of Ch'ing authority among the civilized aborigines. In 1734 the Taiwan intendant proposed that instructors be appointed to the tribes in every county to educate aborigine youth and that county directors of study conduct seasonal examinations in these schools. A total of forty-seven aborigine schools were founded, the great majority located in villages that were also major aborigine tax-paying units.[14]

In 1737 the tribal tax was changed into a head tax figured at the same rate as for Han Chinese, which had been lowered the year before to two-tenths of a tael per head. The 1737 reform reduced the official tribal tax quotas by more than 80 percent. The Ch'ien-lung emperor's stated purpose in adopting this reform was to remove inequalities in taxation among the tribes and to tax them at a rate equal to that levied on his Han subjects. He thereby sought to demonstrate that he harbored no prejudice and considered the aborigines, like the Han, his loyal subjects.

The substantial reduction of aborigine taxes in 1737 was in one sense the ultimate solution to the state's inability to create a tax collection system that was not subject to official corruption and interpreter abuse. It also reflects shifts in the fiscal structure of government in Taiwan, as the reclamation of new farms added land to the tax registers and revenues to the treasury and reduced the fiscal significance of taxes on aborigines.

The large reduction in the aborigine head tax in 1737 marks the end of a phase in the history of the plains aborigines of Taiwan's west coast that transcends three regimes. From the imposition of Dutch rule, through the Cheng era down to the early decades of Ch'ing administration, the deerskin trade, and the extraction of revenue from that trade, whether by hunting licenses, trading monopolies, or head taxes, structured the relations of plains aborigine hunter-horticulturalists to Chinese traders and governmental authority. The system lasted until the growth of the Chinese population and the spread of Chinese farming in the eighteenth century, combined with overhunting, eroded the plains aborigine economies and transformed the fiscal basis of Ch'ing rule.

Expanding reclamation and agricultural colonization put tremendous pressure on the livelihoods of Taiwan's plains aborigine hunter-horticulturalists. Yet the plains aborigine villages were not displaced by Han agricultural colonization, nor were they forced to migrate into the mountains. The ability of the plains aborigines to remain on the plains and adapt to the transformation of the frontier depended on the government's willingness to recognize and enforce plains aborigine claims to land. The Ch'ing government took numerous measures to guarantee aborigine livelihoods by managing the allocation of rights in land on the expanding frontier. The government took these measures because the plains aborigines were both tax-paying subjects and valued sources of loyalist militia. At first the government had viewed expanding Han settlement as a threat to the ethnic status quo on the frontier and pursued quarantine policies to limit the disruptive effects of agricultural settlement. Later, as the government found it impossible to impede the flow of immigrants to the frontier, it adopted increasingly accommodative policies that sought to reconcile the competing interests of Han settlers and plains aborigines over land.

Land policies fluctuated in conjunction with the other pro- and anticolonization policies. In general, procolonization advocates supported policies giving settlers expanded access to tribal territories and reducing the extent of aborigine claims, while advocates of quarantine favored limiting Han settlement to restricted areas and recognizing a greater range of aborigine claims over frontier land. The Ch'ing state used its authority to allocate rights and duties with respect to land to manage the relations between Han settlers and the plains aborigines while at the same time pursuing its own revenue and security goals.

By the first decades of the eighteenth century, the population and regional economy of the southeastern coast had recovered from the devastation of the anti-Cheng campaigns and the policy of coastal removal. Chinese farmers from the crowded coastal prefectures began pouring into Taiwan to take advantage of strong mainland demand and high prices for rice and sugar produced in Taiwan. By this time the deer herds, on which aborigine livelihoods and taxpaying depended, had been seriously overhunted. As the expanding Chinese population converted deer fields into farmland, disputes began to arise as Chinese encroached on aborigine lands. This put pressure on Ch'ing officialdom to formulate policies governing aborigine land rights.

In Taiwan state authorities recognized two broad categories of frontier land, tribal land and government-owned wasteland. Under Chinese law, all land not under cultivation was generally considered to be subject to government ownership. But just as the government recognized the ownership claims of Chinese when they paid land taxes, so did the government recognize tribal land ownership when the aborigines paid their taxes. Accordingly, the Ch'ing state came to recognize tribal ownership over large amounts of uncultivated land that served as aborigine hunting grounds and pasture.

To reclaim government wasteland, settlers and land developers could petition the government for patents according to an established procedure. To reclaim tribal land, settlers had to come to terms with the aborigine claimants. Because the Ch'ing recognized tribal ownership of hunting grounds, a large amount of the land that Han immigrants desired to open was subject to prior ownership claims. But some settlers simply squatted on land, defying both tribe and government (though sometimes aided by colluding officials) to remove them. The government explicitly condemned and sought to prohibit such abuses of aborigine land rights because the government feared they would lead to Han–aborigine conflict and frontier disorder. In 1704 the Taiwan intendant decreed that settlers seeking to contract privately for land with aborigine tribes must also request official permission; approval of such contracts would only be granted after an investigation was made by county officials to ensure that aborigine claims were respected.

One early method of acquiring aborigine land that received explicit official sanction (it had the added advantage of guaranteeing state revenues) required a settler to assume the head tax burden of a tribe in return for rights in land. This method derives directly from the monopoly merchant system of farming aborigine taxes. As the herds were depleted and as land-hungry Chinese immigrants pushed the agricultural frontier forward (one or the other came first in different localities), tribal livelihoods based on deer hunting were disrupted, but their tax obligations remained the same. By assuming responsibility for the tax obligations of the aborigines, Han could acquire land rights in tribal territories.

Measures to ensure order and to protect aborigine land rights took a new direction in response to the Chu Yi-kuei rebellion in 1721. In the wake of the rebellion, Governor-General Manpao ordered the construction of an islandwide set of boundary trenches ("earth-oxen") to be built in a north–south direction, paralleling the mountain foothills. This cordon was intended to keep Han settlers (and escaping outlaws) out of the mountains and to keep raw aborigines from coming out of the mountains to take heads. Reclamation beyond this boundary was forbidden. The quarantine policies were thereby extended to limit expansion of Chinese settlement on the frontier.

Lan Ting-yuan strongly opposed Manpao's extension of the protectionist quarantine approach to the frontier. Lan denounced the new boundary policy that removed settlers behind a government patroled boundary, arguing that it would further disrupt an already unsettled society, that an artificial boundary could not prevent trouble from arising in the quarantined areas, and that instead unreclaimed land should be opened and tax revenue thereby increased. Lan also had procolonization views on tribal land rights.

Lan proposed to give the aborigines a year to reclaim land, after which they would lose all rights to land left unopened, which would then be open to Han settlement. Lan knew that giving deer hunters one year to open farmland and adopt agriculture would not preserve aborigine livelihoods. His analysis of the state of Taiwan's society required encouraging Han settlement, reclamation, and the expansion of taxable acreage, and he gave little thought to either the cost to the aborigines or the dangers of aborigine revolt. But even Lan approved the common practice whereby settlers paid taxes on behalf of aborigines in return for rights to reclaim land. Lan's proposal to eliminate aborigine title was not adopted by the government. In the following years many officials expressed the fear that civilized aborigines pressed too hard and too fast by encroaching Han settlement would revolt and join the raw aborigines in the mountains. Official policy on aborigine land claims, therefore, moved more cautiously than Lan had advocated.

In 1724 the emperor, some say in response to Lan's advocacy, ordered the following regulation entered into the Ch'ing institutes *(hui tien)*: "Order the local officials to investigate all aborigine deer fields left as waste that are reclaimable. Each tribe may rent *[tzu]* these fields to settlers for cultivation. Enter them on the tax registers."[15] This new regulation gave the first official approval to private rental agreements between tribes and settlers, reducing the need to use the rubric of "assuming the aborigine revenue tax" to justify these arrangements, and opening the way for greater use of "large-rent" arrangements in which reclaiming Han tenants paid aborigine tribes a ground rent for access to land. The government intended to tax the tribal lands whose lease to settlers it was now approving. By taxing newly reclaimed tribal lands, the government could raise the revenues needed to pay for its expanded administration (Chang-hua county and Tan-shui *t'ing* were created in 1723) and the military grain export quotas set the same year.

In sum, the thrust of the 1724 decree was to give Han settlers access to tribal land on condition that they pay rents to aborigine tribes and land taxes to the state. The discussions leading to the 1724 decree aimed to arrive at allocations of rights and duties with respect to land that balanced the government's goals of regulating Han competition for land, preserving aborigine livelihoods, increasing revenues from land taxes, and maintaining peace on the frontier.

The procolonization and proreclamation policies had their costs in the increasing frequency of conflicts involving settlers and aborigines, and repeated violation of aborigine boundaries. Under these conditions land disputes and enforcement of the boundary policy demanded the constant attention of officials.

Concern about the uncontrolled expansion of Han settlement mounted in the early Ch'ien-lung years. Officials reported that many rootless troublemakers were taking advantage of the relaxation of restrictions on migration and posing a threat to local order, and that unlicensed reclamation of aborigine land was causing friction between Han and aborigines. In 1738 the Governor-General Hao Yu-lin called for clarification of the boundaries between areas cultivated by aborigines and Han. Hao ordered a land survey and required that land contracts between Han and aborigines be presented for official inspection before the land could be registered. Land opened without such contractual agreements was to be returned to aborigine ownership, and future encroachment on aborigine land was forbidden.

For the next twenty-five years, the growing settler population exerted continuous pressure on aborigine lands and on Ch'ing policies designed to protect aborigine land rights. Clarifications of the boundaries between Han and aborigine land had to be made repeatedly. Squatters were ordered evicted, but those who had privately contracted with the tribes were often allowed to stay as long as they paid aborigine rents. Because it was militarily unable to evict large numbers of frontiersmen and financially unable to resettle them, the Ch'ing state was forced to acquiesce in most Han reclamation, even though it was technically illegal. The government merely drew new boundary lines that it declared to be permanent and tried to enforce the payment of rents to aborigines. These lines were extensions of and additions to Manpao's original "earth-oxen" trench. Many officials doubted the wisdom of trying to restrict reclamation, as had Lan Ting-yuan, both because they were anxious to fill tax quotas and because they were unimpressed by the threat of strife between settlers and aborigines.

In 1767, an order was promulgated allowing aborigines to recruit tenants to reclaim tribal lands and to collect rents from them, following the model of Han land developers and large-rent holders. In 1768 aborigine lands rented to Han farmers were made tax-exempt. Ch'ing authorities finally realized the futility of trying to stop Han reclamation and recognized that the tribes needed the rental income more than they needed land depleted of deer herds, which they themselves were unable to reclaim or farm profitably. Under these conditions the aborigine large-rent system accommodated both groups.

After the 1760s the salience of disputes over plains aborigine land markedly declined. Other problems came to the fore—"raw aborigine" head-hunting raids and, most threatening to Ch'ing authority, communal strife among Chinese immigrant groups. Because they had a role to play in the solution of both these problems, plains aborigines were able to maintain their position. Civilized aborigines living in the mountain foothills were familiar with the mountain trails and the raw aborigine tribes that lived in the interior. Their knowledge of the mountain areas made them invaluable when the government wanted to punish a tribe for a head-taking raid or to apprehend a Chinese bandit or rebel taking refuge in the mountains. Aborigine hunting also gave plains aborigine braves skills as archers and marksmen that made them an effective fighting force. As a non-Han ethnic group, plains aborigine militia could be counted on to remain loyal to the Ch'ing during the frequent outbreaks of Han communal strife. After the Lin Shuang-wen rebellion of 1786–87, their martial role was institutionalized with the founding of the *fan-t'un,* or aborigine military colonies along the mountain foothills.

Thus plains aborigine utility as a military force loyal to the state (and fear of their potential for revolt), their status as taxpayers, ambivalence toward the immigration of Chinese settlers who disrupted the status quo but contributed to land tax revenues, and a Confucian concern to preserve the livelihoods of subject peoples all motivated the Ch'ing state to arbitrate relations between Chinese immigrant farmers and civilized aborigines. The goal of the Ch'ing state was to keep the competition between settlers and aborigines from disrupting its control of a strategic periphery of the empire and imposing additional costs that Taiwan's inadequate revenues did little to defray. Aborigine taxpaying established, in the government's eyes, their claim to rights in land. The government's attempts to restrain the immigrants led it to adapt the institution of split ownership rights to Taiwan's frontier conditions. Han settlers seeking to reclaim tribal lands were required to respect the tribes' prior claims by paying an aborigine large-rent.

Income from aborigine large-rents was critical to the survival of the plains tribes. The destruction of the deer herds, caused by both overhunting and the spread of farming, eliminated the hunting sector of the aboriginal economy. Aborigine hunters only gradually, and unenthusiastically, adopted intensive agriculture. In this difficult period of adjustment aborigine large-rents provided a critical margin to tribal livelihoods. But the challenge posed by the spread of Chinese settlement was only partially economic, and culture contact and intermarriage brought more dislocation and change in plains aborigine lives.[16]

The Growth of Han Settler Society

During the eighteenth century, Taiwan's population increased rapidly, especially in the period from 1732 to 1740, when families were first allowed to immigrate legally to Taiwan. In 1738 Governor-General Hao Yu-lin, upset by increasing disorder and conflict on the frontier, called for clarification of the boundaries between areas cultivated by aborigines and Han and an end to further reclamation of aborigine lands. Hao Yu-lin then convinced the emperor to put an end to the legal migration of families to Taiwan in 1740. Thus the major procolonization policies of the late Yung-cheng years were reversed and the old philosophy of control through quarantine was revived.[17]

The end of legal migration did not, however, mean the end of illegal migration, which continued at a steady pace, much to the consternation of officials deputed to bring it to an end. It was too late to turn back the clock. The Chinese population had grown substantially in the years of open migration and now included a large number of females, making possible a rapid rate of growth compounded by continued immigration.

Whatever its policy, the Ch'ing court had to work through officials who had private goals that were as often satisfied by subverting official policy by extorting bribes as by carrying that policy out. And it had to enforce its policy against a populace determined to escape poverty in its overpopulated home prefectures on the southeastern coast. Migrants who had immediate interests in earning livelihoods and raising families took little regard of official proclamations and preferred to avoid official contact. These people are referred to in official decrees as "secret crossers"; the Ch'ing state simply could not bring their movement to a halt.

Few statistics document the actual rates of immigration to Taiwan. Thus it is difficult to gauge the impact of fluctuating official policies (impeding or facilitating) or the push and pull of changing social conditions (whether on the southeastern coast or in Taiwan itself) on the numbers of migrants crossing to Taiwan during any period. We have noted the few impressionistic observations recorded by officials who were struck by rapid population growth. The local gazetteers reflect this increase in their listings of village settlements and market towns, which show large increases in the frontier regions of Chang-hua and Tan-shui. The number of villages recorded in Chang-hua's territory increased from one in 1717 to 110 in 1740 and 132 in 1768. The number of villages recorded in the territory of Tan-shui subprefecture went from zero in 1717 to 35 by 1740 and 132 by 1768. The village lists also give a crude measure of the impact of the spread of Chinese settlement on aborigine villages. In 1717 only eight of the seventy-six northern plains aborigine villages were also sites of Han settlements. By 1740 thirty, and by 1768 forty-five, sites accommodated both aborigines and Han.

We can also note the expansion of registered farmland and the spreading area of colonization in Taiwan itself as evidence of population growth. The population figures reported in Table 5.1 indicate substantial increases over the fifty thousand plains aborigines and the fewer than eighty thousand Han who remained in Taiwan after 1684, the first year of Ch'ing rule. The large population increases, the bulk of which resulted from illegal immigration, testify to the ultimate failure of the policy of quarantine.

The increasing amounts of land entered on the tax registers reflect the spread of Han reclamation (and government tax collectors). Registered areas grew fastest in the frontier areas beyond the old core area around Tainan. The gains in Chang-hua to the north were especially impressive.

The easy availability of open land that could be reclaimed to produce rice surpluses, as well as sugar cane, in close proximity to the rice-deficient southeastern coast (whose growing population was causing its demand for rice to

Table 5.1

Growth of Population and Land Area Registered for Taxation, 1684–1905

Year	Population estimate (Han and plains aborigines only)	Land area registered for taxation in *chia*
1684	130,000	18,454
1700	187,000	—
1710	—	30,110
1735	415,000	50,517
1756	660,147	—
1762	—	63,045
1777	839,803	—
1824	1,328,069	—
1893–95	2,545,731	361,417
1903—5	2,973,280	534,157

Source: Shepherd 1993: 161–62, 169. The *chia* is equal to 0.97 hectares.

grow) was Taiwan's major attraction to the commercially oriented farmers who risked migrating to its shores. The rice and sugar crops commanded good prices and reliable profits for the island's farmers. The profits from export sales, in turn, financed a steady pace of investment in irrigation works and the expansion of more productive irrigated acreage.

The outlook for Taiwan's rice production was so good that after 1725 the government itself decided to make regular shipments to mainland Fukien of portions of Taiwan's tax rice (100,000 *shih* of unhusked rice), and officially purchased rice, for relief and to provision troops and their dependents. Previously Taiwan tax rice had supplied only troops stationed in Taiwan and the Pescadores, and surpluses had collected in government granaries, because officials feared any rice shortage would destabilize Ch'ing control of the island's populace. But harvests had grown substantially since the days when Shih Lang first arrived and had to import his troops' provisions. These newly authorized government exports helped relieve pressure on rice-short southern Fukien, where the Ch'ing garrisoned a large military force. These amounts were increased several times in the next years. In its efforts to ensure that rice harvests would be adequate for these needs, the government itself acquired a vested interest in policies that encouraged the reclamation of new farmlands, for example, by approving the renting of aborigine lands and lowering land taxes on newly opened land.

Price data compiled by Ng Chin-keong and Wang Yeh-chien show that between 1723 and 1756 rice prices rose generally and that prices in Ch'uan-chou (Taiwan's major market) remained above those in Taiwan.[18] Rising prices and the higher prices in Ch'uan-chou made rice farming and exporting profitable in Taiwan.

Thus from the early years of Ch'ing rule, Taiwan developed an important role as grain supplier to the chronically rice-deficient Fukien coast, in addition to its role as outlet for Fukien's burgeoning population. Ng's study of the Amoy trading network shows that Taiwan's rice and sugar exports constituted a large proportion of the cargoes carried in the Amoy coastal trade and played a critical role in the development of the regional economy of the southeastern coast in the early eighteenth century.[19] That a rice and sugar export economy emerged on Taiwan despite the government's attempts to restrict the cross-strait trade, prohibit family immigration, and limit the reclamation of aborigine lands testifies to the powerful economic stimuli at work in the densely populated but productive southeastern coast. No group in the arena of southeastern coast policy formation had the interest or the power to sustain enforcement of the quarantine policies against these economic pressures and opportunities.

As settlement intensified, Taiwan's frontier society did not become more peaceful, as Lan Ting-yuan had predicted. Rather, instances of large-scale subethnic strife appear to have become more frequent. Government police actions against gangsters sparked conflicts that escalated into communal strife when one subethnic group gave refuge to its outlaw compatriots and the other subethnic group took the side of the government to do in their rivals. These affrays, sometimes induced and sometimes merely exploited by opportunistic elements in the population, and unchecked by ineffective government peacekeeping, polarized Han society into hostile blocs of settlers united primarily by common provenance.

If we are to understand the patterns of Han frontier community organization, we need to consider the special characteristics of the migration and settlement process, and how certain of these characteristics contributed to the emergence of a society easily polarized into hostile subethnic blocs.

Most migration began as a sojourning strategy and only evolved over time into a permanent relocation of families to Taiwan. When male family members (traveling in groups of friends and kin) left home in search of economic opportunity, they retained important rights in and obligations to their families at home. Those who were married left their wives behind to serve the husband's parents and care for children. But most of the initial migrants were unmarried young men. This preponderance of unattached males, fond of gambling and brawling, helped destabilize frontier society.[20]

A key characteristic of the migration to Taiwan was the tendency for social ties to reinforce, rather than cross-cut, native place ties and subethnicity. Migrants left their home districts in small groups of kin and fellow villagers. In Taiwan they tended to locate among and associate with other migrants from home. Chain migration reinforced this pattern. Among their fellows, migrants formed voluntary associations such as brotherhoods and worship groups that rendered mutual aid and provided fellowship and common security.[21] Larger communities coalesced around temples dedicated to patron gods identified with their home communities. Larger groups tended to identify with home counties and prefectures, such as Chang-chou and Ch'uan-chou among the Hokkien, and with province and speech group, as among the Hakka. Social networks therefore followed primarily lines of common origin, and migrants relied on common provenance to identify which strangers could be trusted. Settlers were suspicious of neighbors who were immigrants from other locales, and misunderstandings were frequent between groups speaking different dialects and worshiping different patron deities. Social relations did form and could be quite cordial across the lines of common provenance and speech group, but the tendency was for such cross-cutting ties to be more casual, superficial, and contextually specific.

The migrants to Taiwan also brought with them traditions of violence and self-defense. The communities of China's southeastern coast are famous for their feuding clans and lineages, and the turbulent history of the dynastic interregnum on the coast in the seventeenth century no doubt reinforced local traditions of violence. Migrants arriving in Taiwan knew how to defend themselves if conditions required, and how to employ violence to obtain advantage. Combine this with large numbers of unattached males, fond of gambling and brawling, and the presence of a criminal and vagrant element from the coast, and it is not hard to explain the frequency of violent episodes on the frontier. The effect of these characteristics of migration to Taiwan was to lead to the emergence of a society that was easily polarized into hostile subethnic blocs.

Lamley notes that Taiwan entered a severe phase of subethnic strife in the late eighteenth century, a phase that lasted from 1782 to 1862.[22] Lamley speculates that growing population and intensifying competition for land and other resources helped fuel intensified subethnic strife. Whether or not population pressure was the cause, it certainly contributed to the "magnitude" of the conflicts. The key to the intensification of subethnic strife in this period is the overall decline in the effectiveness of government social control and the militarization of the social structure that occurred throughout China in this same 1782–1862 period.[23] When both the government and local leadership proved incapable of containing outbreaks, they turned into epidemics.[24]

The importance of common provenance to immigrant social organization, legal and extralegal, and the mutual suspicion between competing groups is testified to repeatedly by the frequency with which subethnic feuds broke out in the eighteenth century. The government frequently found it to its advantage to exploit subethnic divisions among the settlers. Loyalist militia recruited from the Hakka villages of Feng-shan were crucial to its victories over Chu Yi-kuei (a native of Fukien's Chang-chou) in 1721 and over the dual revolts of Wu Fu-sheng (also a Chang-chou native) and the Ta-chia-hsi aborigines in 1731–32. Hakka loyalists also played an important role in the defeat of the Lin Shuang-wen rebellion. The government also played on Ch'uan-chou vs. Chang-chou divisions in recruiting militia in Hokkien communities. Plains aborigine auxiliaries, as noted above, were also reliable allies of the government in putting down Han communal disturbances.

The government had to find means to manage and contain, as well as exploit, communal divisions, if social order was to be maintained. The appearance of official impartiality was important to winning the trust of competing groups. But the government's success in doing so was declining. A series of impeachments and an uncontained outbreak of communal strife in 1782 point to a low ebb in the effectiveness of Taiwan's administration. These serious disturbances set the stage for the disastrous Lin Shuang-wen rebellion in 1786.

Notes

1. More detailed treatment of the events treated in this section along with references to sources can be found in Shepherd 1993, chaps. 5 and 6.

2. Several sources give accounts of the policy debate over the future of Taiwan: Shih Lang 1958: 59–62; Chuang Chin-te 1964: 1; KHSL: 131; Fu Lo-shu 1966: vol. 1, 60–61.

3. For more detailed treatment of the subjects treated in this section and references, see Shepherd 1993, chap. 5.

4. Thompson 1964: 195–196.

5. For a detailed treatment of the subject of this section and references, see Shepherd 1993, chap. 6.

6. Lattimore 1934: 80; Serruys 1981: 496; Lee 1970: 184.

7. Viraphol 1977: 74, 76; Fu Lo-Shu 1966: vol. 1, 193.

8. Ho Ping-ti 1959: 152; Purcell 1965: 36.

9. Wills 1979: 232–233.

10. This summary account of the Chu Yi-kuei rebellion is drawn primarily from Lan Ting-yuan (1958: 1–8ff.), and secondarily from Huang Shu-ching (1957: 85ff.), the revised Feng-shan gazetteer (CHFSHC: 272ff.), and the veritable records (KHSL: 174). The Chu Yi-kuei rebellion figures heavily in Ming restorationist and Heaven and Earth Society (Tien ti hui) fictions (see Croizier 1977: 66–67). For more a detailed treatment and references, see Shepherd 1993, chap. 6.

11. See Lan Ting-yuan 1958. For a fuller treatment of the subjects discussed in this section, see Shepherd 1993, chaps. 5, 6, and 7.

12. Ng Chin-keong (1983) gives a detailed account of the recovery of south Fukien's economy and coastal trade after 1683, and Leonard (1984: 71ff.), Blussé (1986: 115ff.), and Viraphol (1977) trace the recovery of Fukien's trade with Southeast Asia.

13. For a more detailed treatment of the subject of this section, see Shepherd 1993, chap. 5.

14. For a more detailed treatment of the subjects of this section, see Shepherd 1993, chaps. 5, 9, and 10.

15. Yung-cheng Hui-tien 1733 (YC 11) 27: 25a–b.

16. For a fuller treatment of the transformations in plains aborigine societies, see Shepherd 1993, chap. 11.

17. For a fuller treatment of the subjects of this section, see Shepherd 1993, chaps. 6, 7, 8, and 10.

18. Ng Chin-keong 1983: App. A; Wang Yeh-chien 1986: 100.

19. Ng Chin-keong 1983: 217.

20. On sojourning strategies see Skinner 1976. On frontier society see Meskill 1979: 32; Lamley 1981: 297; and Hsu Wen-hsiung 1980: 88.

21. In an important article, Pasternak (1969) refutes Freedman's frontier hypothesis, pointing out that migration to the frontier inhibited, rather than stimulated, lineage growth, and fostered voluntary associations on non-agnatic bases of shared experience and provenance. A more relevant comparison to Taiwan comes from Freedman's work on immigrant associations in Singapore (1979: 61–83).

22. Lamley 1981: 303–4, also Hsu Wen-hsiung 1980: 94; this also fits Meskill's "strongman era," 1979: 87–89, 258–262.

23. Kuhn 1970.

24. On the sociological dynamics of how specific disputes escalate into general hostility, and social networks polarize (regardless of whether the disputes have anything to do with "ethnicity"), see James S. Coleman's 1957 classic, *Community Conflict.*

References

Blussé, Leonard. 1986. *Strange Company: Chinese Settlers, Mestizo Women and the Dutch in VOC Batavia.* Verhandelingen, 122. Leiden: Koninklijk Instituut voor Taal-, Land- en Volenkunde.

Ch'ing Sheng-tsu shih lu hsuan chi (KHSL) [Selections from the Veritable Records of the K'ang-hsi reign]. TW, no. 165.

Ch'ung hsiu Feng-shan hsien chih (CHFSHC) (Feng-shan county gazetteer, revised). 1764. Ed. Wang Ying-tseng. TW, no. 146.

Chuang Chin-te. 1964. "Ch'ing ch'u yen chin yen hai jen min t'ou tu lai T'ai shih mo" [A history of early Ch'ing prohibitions on crossing to Taiwan]. Parts 1 and 2. *T'ai-wan wen hsien,* 15, no. 3: 1–20; no. 4: 40–62.

Coleman, James S. 1957. *Community Conflict.* New York: Free Press.

Croizier, Ralph C. 1977. *Koxinga and Chinese Nationalism: History, Myth, and the Hero.* Cambridge: East Asian Research Center, Harvard University.

Freedman, Maurice. 1979. *The Study of Chinese Society.* Ed. G.W. Skinner. Stanford: Stanford University Press.

Fu Lo-shu. 1966. *A Documentary Chronicle of Sino-Western Relations.* 2 vols. Tucson: University of Arizona Press.

Ho Ping-ti. 1959. *Studies on the Population of China, 1368–1953.* Cambridge: Harvard University Press.

Hsu Wen-hsiung. 1980. "Frontier Social Organization and Social Disorder in Ch'ing Taiwan." In *China's Island Frontier: Studies in the Historical Geography of Taiwan,* ed. Ronald G. Knapp, pp. 87–105. Honolulu: University Press of Hawaii.

Huang Shu-ching. 1736/1957. *T'ai hai shih ch'a lu* [A tour of duty in the Taiwan sea]. TW, no. 4.

KHSL. Ch'ing sheng-tsu shih lu hsüan chi [Selections from the veritable records of the K'ang-hsi reign]. TW, no. 165.

Kuhn, Philip A. 1970. Rebellion and Its Enemies in Late Imperial China: Militarization and Social Structure, 1796–1864. Cambridge: Harvard University Press.

Lamley, Harry. 1981. "Subethnic Rivalry in the Ch'ing Period." In *The Anthropology of Taiwanese Society,* ed. E.M. Ahern and H. Gates, pp. 282–318. Stanford: Stanford University Press.

Lan Ting-yuan. 1732/1958. *P'ing T'ai chi lueh* [History of the pacification of Taiwan]. TW, no. 14.

Lattimore, Owen. 1934. *The Mongols of Manchuria.* New York: John Day .

Lee, Robert H.G. 1970. *The Manchurian Frontier in Ch'ing History.* Cambridge: Harvard University Press.

Leonard, Jane Kate. 1984. *Wei Yuan and China's Rediscovery of the Maritime World.* Cambridge: Council on East Asian Studies, Harvard University.

Meskill, Johanna M. 1979. *A Chinese Pioneer Family: The Lins of Wu-feng, Taiwan, 1729–1895.* Princeton: Princeton University Press.

Ng Chin-keong. 1983. *Trade and Society: The Amoy Network on the China Coast, 1683–1735.* Singapore: Singapore University Press.

Pasternak, Burton. 1969. "The Role of the Frontier in Chinese Lineage Development." *Journal of Asian Studies,* 28: 551–561.

Purcell, Victor W. 1965. *The Chinese in Southeast Asia.* London: Oxford University Press.

Serruys, Henry. 1981. "A Study of Chinese Penetration into Caqar Territory in the Eighteenth Century." *Monumenta Serica,* 35: 485–544.

Shepherd, John Robert. 1993. *Statecraft and Political Economy on the Taiwan Frontier, 1600–1800.* Stanford: Stanford University Press.

Shih Lang. 1685/1958. *Ching hai chi shih* [Record of pacifying the seas]. TW, no. 13.

Skinner, G.W. 1976. "Mobility Strategies in Late Imperial China: A Regional Systems Analysis." In *Regional Analysis,* vol. 1, *Economic Systems,* ed. Carol Smith, pp. 327–364. New York: Academic Press.

T'ai-wan wen hsien ts'ung k'an (TW) [Literary collectanea on Taiwan]. 1957–72.309 titles. Ed. T'ai-wan yin hang ching chi yen chiu shih. Taipei: T'ai-wan yin hang.

Thompson, Laurence. 1964. "The Earliest Chinese Eyewitness Accounts of the Formosan Aborigines." *Monumenta Serica,* 23: 163–204.

Viraphol, Sarasin. 1977. Tribute and Profit: Sino-Siamese Trade, 1652–1853. Cambridge: Council on East Asian Studies, Harvard University.

Wang Yeh-chien. 1986. "Food Supply in Eighteenth-Century Fukien." *Late Imperial China,* 7, no. 2: 80–117.

Wills, John E., Jr. 1979. "Maritime China from Wang Chih to Shih Lang: Themes in Peripheral History." In *From Ming to Ch'ing,* ed. Jonathan Spence and John Wills, pp. 203–238. New Haven: Yale University Press.

Wong Young-tsu. 1983. "Security and Warfare on the China Coast: The Taiwan Question in the Seventeenth Century." *Monumenta Serica,* 35: 111–196.

6

From Landlords to Local Strongmen

The Transformation of Local Elites in Mid-Ch'ing Taiwan, 1780–1862

Chen Chiukun

Rooftops in the town of Sanhsia.

From a Frontier to a Settled Society

The early development of Taiwan during the Ch'ing dynasty took place approximately from 1680 to 1770 and is generally referred to as the "pioneering stage" in the island's history. During that period, the Ch'ing government headquartered its administrative organs in the prefecture city (*fu-ch'eng*) of Tainan and gradually established a bureaucratic system of both civilian and military control. The Ch'ing also adopted policies for organizing and colonizing the P'ing-p'u aborigine tribes in the western region of the island. At the same time, the Ch'ing gradually converted to private property the royal lands and agricultural properties that had been established under the control of Cheng Ch'eng-kung (Koxinga) after his conquest of the island from 1662 to 1683. Under the new system, landowners had full property rights over their land with effective control over management and production decisions and with full tax obligations. As a result, many wealthy merchants from the coastal areas of the mainland in Fukien and Kuangtung provinces rushed to the island to explore and develop the vast open grasslands on the island to seek new opportunities for becoming wealthy. Some applied to local officials to acquire the requisite documents granting them the right to develop and acquire ownership over large tracts of land. Others leased land from the aborigines, which granted them cultivation rights, or they simply laid claim to underdeveloped, barren land. After securing their new properties, many of these homesteading property owners returned to their home villages and towns on the mainland to hire neighbors, relatives, and friends to return with them to Taiwan and assist in the opening up and development of their land.

According to local regulations on Taiwan, homesteaders were required to supervise their tenant farmers and to pay tax to the government based on the amount of land opened up and put under cultivation. Tenant farmers were also required to develop a certain amount of the land within a specified period of time and were under obligation to pay rent to the owner on a seasonal basis. Homesteaders were granted permanent ownership rights over the land while tenants were given permanent cultivation rights, that is, permanent leasing rights.

In addition, the Ch'ing government determined that aboriginal landlords enjoyed the same rights as their Han counterparts. Han settlers were also prohibited from intruding on the lands and territories of the island's non-Han population. To get around this restriction, however, many Han immigrants negotiated tenancy agreements with the aborigine landowners that produced a system of aboriginal–Han landlord–tenant relations. Basically, as private ownership was legally established for these lands, landlords—both Han and aborigine—were encouraged to monitor the agricultural production and rent payments of their tenants, a system that, to a considerable extent, helped to strengthen the social order in rural Taiwan.

Translated and edited by Nancy Yang Liu (Columbia University) and Lawrence R. Sullivan (Adelphi University).

Until the 1720s, as a result of increased great demand on the mainland for the rice and caned sugar produced on Taiwan, many wealthy merchants and landlords formed partnerships as a way to pool capital for construction of large-scale irrigation and water control systems. This, in effect, brought about an agricultural revolution on the island that, by the mid-eighteenth century, led to the opening up of vast tracts of irrigated land for rice and sugarcane production by tenant farmers. This system led to a situation in which, before 1800, Taiwan supplied the mainland with 500,000 *tan* [1 *tan* = 50 kilograms] of rice annually, thereby dramatically increasing rice supplies in China's southeast coastal regions, which reduced inflationary pressure on food staples on the mainland. In addition, Taiwan also exported approximately 600,000 *tan* of sugarcane to northern China, Japan, and Southeast Asia, earning large sums of Mexican silver dollars. These huge sales of caned sugar and rice meant that, by the mid-eighteenth century, Taiwan had developed from a remote frontier island into a vibrant new grain market in Southeast Asia.[1]

Many historians have characterized the period from the 1780s to the 1860s as the "intermediate stage" in the development of Taiwan that occurred before the opening of its ports to foreign trade.[2] Overall during this period, Taiwan was distinguished by several characteristics, beginning with the formation of its landlord class. Even though the homesteaders and aboriginal proprietors retained cultivation rights, these groups did not themselves directly engage in agricultural production. Instead, the general practice was to lease these rights to tenant farmers and others in return for rents in kind. In subsequent years, many of the tenant farmers who had secured permanent rights subleased surplus lands to other tenants, from which they, in turn, collected rent in kind, usually in the form of grain. These tenant farmers were referred to as "estate masters," or "farm managers" who enjoyed management rights over agricultural lands, which they often subleased to secondary tenants. Under such an arrangement, land rights were divided between two parties: the proprietor who retained ownership rights over the land and the "farm manager" who exercised management rights, which entitled him to collect rents in cash or kind and to buy and sell these rights. And, of course, the farm manager had to pay rent to the landowners. In general, proprietors were referred to as the "primary lease holder" and the farm manager as the "secondary lease holder." Under this system of "dual ownership of land," proprietors and farm managers dominated Taiwan's agricultural production and distribution. In addition, since most proprietors did not reside on their lands, they became absentee landlords who did not directly supervise their tenant farmers. In contrast, most farm managers lived on the land for extended periods and thereby became intimately familiar with the agricultural economy of their lands, including the production decisions of the tenant farmers. In addition, they also participated in local activities involving religious temples and village security measures. This was why the influence of the farm manager in the rural areas was much greater than that of the proprietors. After the end of the eighteenth century, therefore, most people referred to the farm managers, rather than the proprietors, as the "landlord class."

A second major characteristic of the island during the "intermediate stage" was the surge of immigration from the mainland. According to census data, immigrants into Taiwan numbered 600,147 in 1756, 839,800 in 1777, 912,000 in 1782, and 1,786,883 in 1824.[3] During these earliest stages of settlement, new-comers constituted fully half the total population, and from 1782 to 1811 they made up two-thirds of the island's population. Most immigrants to Taiwan left the mainland because of increasing population pressure and the growing shortage of land, which had severely taxed people's capacity to make a living. This was particularly the case following the uprising on Taiwan led by Lin Shuang-wen in 1786, which led the Ch'ing government to lift its restrictions on immigration to the island by individuals whose relatives had already emigrated there.[4] The im-pact of these immigrants on the island was quite profound. On the one hand, most were young single males whose devotion to hard labor contributed substan-tially to the development of the agricultural base on the island. It was their diligent work that led to the extension of wet-rice paddy agriculture to relatively remote areas of Taiwan and substantially enhanced the sustainable development of island agriculture. On the other hand, since the opening up of new lands on the island could not keep up with the increasing numbers of immigrants, more and more people went landless and without work and as a result became part of a growing army of wanderers. Some in this group joined secret societies, which often became embroiled in riots and uprisings that increasingly threatened the stability of rural areas on the island.

Scholars who have examined official documents and materials have come up with a rough calculation of the number of uprisings and civil disturbances in Taiwan during this period. From 1684 to 1895, 159 major incidents of civil disturbances rocked Taiwan, including 74 armed clashes and 65 uprisings led by wanderers.[5] During the 120 years from 1768 to 1887, approximately 57 armed clashes occurred, 47 of which broke out from 1768 to 1860. In other words, most disturbances and uprisings occurred during the mid-Ch'ing era, when Tai-wan was undergoing very rapid social and economic transformation.[6] The rea-sons for these various outbreaks were quite complex. One was the pervasive corruption of local Ch'ing bureaucrats and the general backwardness of Ch'ing soldiers stationed on the island, which often led to incidents that engendered popular outrage. Another reason was that most of the immigrants to the island came from different regions on the mainland and were unable to agree on a workable distribution of water rights and other resources, over which they fre-quently fought. Before 1780, most of these conflicts broke out in areas inhabited by immigrants from Fukien and Kuangtung. After 1800, such conflicts were concentrated in territories inhabited by immigrants from the Chang-chou and Ch'uan-chou regions in Fukien province and in areas where immigrants from Fukien and Kuangtung resided in close proximity. Usually, the secret societies set up by wanderers often benefited from these clashes as they were able to expand their network of social influence through all sorts of means. Until around 1840, most of the clashes and uprisings occurred primarily among residents from

Chang-chou and Ch'uan-chou, led by individuals from wealthy landlord families who had resided on the island for two to three generations. Not only did these individuals own huge tracts of land, but they also were backed by local powerful religious organizations and could mobilize large numbers of tenant farmers as militia. Generally speaking, the major goal of such clashes was to gain control over land resources and water rights. But by far the most important reason was to use these forces to maintain and enlarge the power of the landlords at the local level in a situation in which Ch'ing officials could not effectively protect the property rights of landlords.[7]

In light of these facts, the purpose of this chapter is to discuss the transformation of the rural landlord families and the local elites during the period when Taiwan society was converted from a frontier region to a settled society. First, the formation of the landlord class will be discussed and, then, the social and political background of the emergent local elites. Here it is argued that the Ch'ing civil and military bureaucratic system on the island failed to adjust to the increased demands on administrative management created by the rapid transformation and development of Taiwanese rural society. This failure, in effect, fostered an increasing reliance on social connections among people from the same clan, while armed clashes broke out as these same groups sought to defend themselves and also tried to expand their areas of influence and control. Until 1860, most landlord families settled down in the countryside where they devoted considerable energy to building up local armed militia and to setting up clan organizations in the traditional fashion. By 1860, most landlords had assumed the characteristics associated with a local strongman in response to the general failure of the Ch'ing bureaucracy to provide for local security and protection. Several prominent landlord families even managed to rely on their extensive local connections to be appointed to semiofficial posts in exchange for assisting the Ch'ing in suppressing local uprisings.

The Formation of the Landlord Class in Rural Taiwan

The origins of the landlord class in Taiwan during the Ch'ing dynasty are very complex. In the early stages of class formation, landlords were composed of three groups: civil and military officials; homesteaders from the mainland; and the aboriginal tribes. Subsequently, in order to prevent civil and military officials from gaining a monopoly over the land, the Ch'ing dynasty decreed that all land be under private ownership. Hence, from the mid-eighteenth century onward, a system of private ownership emerged in which homesteaders from the mainland and aborigines comprised the majority of the landlord class. However, since, as was pointed out above, there was great reliance on tenants to farm the land, this rather simple ownership system was quickly transformed. During the initial period of settlement, homesteaders and aboriginal landowners did not engage directly in actual farm work but, instead, leased out the land and then collected rents, part of which they paid out as tax. The tenant farmers, in contrast, devoted themselves wholeheartedly to pooling the capital and applying the labor necessary to convert large swaths of barren territory into arable land. In return, they were ultimately granted permanent tenancy rights, which meant that proprietors could not increase rents or terminate their leases. In areas where tenants lived and worked the land, they often subleased surplus lands to other farmers and collected their own rents. In addition, tenant farmers also had the right to sell their leasing rights or even to pawn the land. These rights meant that permanent tenant farmers, in effect, enjoyed landlord status while the proprietors were prevented from interfering in their management decisions. This turned the ownership rights of the proprietors into a "lease deed" in which their rights were restricted to collecting rent on an annual basis. The farm managers, in effect, exercised full management rights including the sale or transfer of land on their own. In general, the practice on Taiwan was to consider rents paid to the landlord as the "primary rent" (*ta-tzu*), which amounted to about 10 to 15 percent of the farmer's annual harvest. Rent paid to the farm manager was known as the "secondary rent" (*hsiao-tzu*) and constituted about 50 percent of the cultivator's output.

Before the late eighteenth century, the asking price for land underwent constant increases as the number of immigrants to the island generally outstripped the available land. This effectively created a system of "dual or multiple ownership of land." Not only were ownership rights over a single piece of property divided between the proprietor and the farm manager, but in some cases the farm manager also pawned his rights.[8] This was because many investors believed that the profits earned by the farm manager were greater than that of the proprietor, and for that reason they invested considerable capital to buy the cultivation rights from the farm manager or the proprietor.

Some of these investors directly engaged in agricultural production, but most simply took the cultivation rights as a kind of commercial investment that yielded yearly rents. Their estimate of the value of cultivation rights derived not from the actual size of the plots but, rather, from the amount of annual rent guaranteed by the lease. In this sense, land rights no longer referred so much to actual ownership of property as to what became known as a "commercial lease." Moreover, since the secondary lease offered a much greater return than the primary lease, and, considering that the farm manager often resided on the land where he could directly monitor the work of the tenants, the farm manager (the secondary leasing agent) had more effective control of the farmland in terms of production and distribution than did the proprietor (the primary leasing agent). As a result, the former was able to gain greater social and economic benefits.

From the 1780s onward, many resident secondary leasing agents replaced the absentee primary leasing agents as the managerial class and major source of rural capital and loans, effectively making them the dominant social class in the countryside. Whenever primary leasing agents were in need of cash they would pawn their ownership rights to rich peasants (that is, the farm managers). Thus, the relationship between the proprietor and their tenant farm managers emerged into one of leaser and banker. As a result, the ownership rights of proprietors, particularly among the aborigines, gradually slipped into the hands of the farm managers.

Following the uprising on Taiwan led by Lin Shuang-wen in the fifty-third year of the Ch'ien-lung era, the Ch'ing government sent a scholar official by the name of A-kui to the island to investigate the social and economic conditions that had fostered the uprising. Properties owned by people who had joined the uprising were confiscated by the government. In his report prepared for the emperor, A-kui described the situation on the island in which primary leasing agents were the de jure landlords and secondary leasing agents the de facto landlords. He also noted that the annual rents collected by proprietors ranged from six to eight *tan* for every *chia* [approximately eleven *mu*] of rice paddy while the secondary leasing agents collected up to 10 *tan* per *chia* in rent. Thus, the total value of primary and secondary leasing agents and the respective social and economic status of the two groups were, in effect, contrary to expectations. This phenomenon, it should be pointed out, became even more prevalent in the early nineteenth century. In the thirteenth year of the Tao-kuang emperor (1833), a Ch'ing official named Ch'en Sheng-shao provided the following explanation as to why the leasing rights of the primary leasing agent had become relatively less valuable in comparison to those of the secondary leasing agent.

> Farm managers collect the largest rents because they control the flesh and bone of the land while the homesteaders collect relatively small rents because they merely control the skin of the land. Why is it that rents paid to the primary leasing agent are relatively small and those paid to the secondary leasing agent are relatively large? With a rent of around 8 *tan* on an [average] piece of land and 4 *tan* on the dwelling, very little profit is earned by the primary leasing agent. This small return reflects several conditions: the lack of a formal or written agreement between the parties; the view on the part of tenants that the secondary leasing agent is the real landlord; and the fact that the proprietor cannot arbitrarily change tenants. As for the secondary leasing agent, he collects upwards of 20 to 30 *tan* on the land. No agreement is signed with tenants who simply receive a receipt based on rent paid in kind in an amount determined by the farm manager. While farm managers often resist paying the primary leasing agent, this does not occur with the secondary leasing agent. This is why the value of the latter's stake is considered greater.

These observations by Ch'en Sheng-shao reflect the fact that farm managers had two weapons at their disposal: First, they held one-year leases with their tenants, and once the lease had expired, they were completely free to take on new tenants; second, farm managers were also in a position to directly monitor the work of their tenants and to collect up to 50 percent of their harvest as rent. This in effect meant that the farm manager could direct the work of their tenants and also usually collect more sizable rents. By comparison, the proprietor was only able to collect the fixed rate of 8 *tan* while they were also obligated to pay a relatively fixed amount of taxes on their property, which significantly reduced their return on the land, especially in comparison to the return enjoyed by farm managers. In addition, most proprietors chose to live in towns and urban areas, where they could enjoy a better life-style but where they also were more subject to meeting their tax obligations. This effectively isolated them from rural life and agricultural work, which caused most landowners to be generally ignorant of both the location and size of their holdings. This led to increasing reliance by proprietors on agents who were sent into the countryside to collect rent where they often encountered resistance from both the farm manager and the tenant farmers. Once conflict broke out, the primary leasing agent and the farm manager became mortal enemies locked in constant conflict. In a recent study by Wang Shi-ch'ing and Stevan Harrell of local elites in the Shu-lin area of the Taipei basin, the authors noted that farm managers effectively replaced the proprietors as the dominant class in the countryside. During the period when the Shu-lin area was attacked by the Japanese in 1895, these authors also noted that proprietors generally sided with Lin Pen-yuan and the Japanese in repelling attacks by the locals, who had organized a so-called righteous army composed of farm managers and tenant farmers who led the opposition against the Japanese.[9] Overall, this historical evidence indicates that the secondary leasing agents enjoyed a rather intimate relationship with their tenant farmers and that they, rather than the primary leasing agents or proprietors, constituted the real local elite.

The Political and Social Background of Emergent Local Elites

During the early era of Ch'ing rule in Taiwan, the basic policy of the government was to maintain the stability of the existing social order. In general, this entire policy relied heavily on military rule. Security for the island was the responsibility of a brigade-general who headed a number of different military units, including coastal security units and naval forces stationed in Fukien. In the 1730s, 12,670 regular soldiers (and at times upward to 14,000) were sent to the island for duty from their regular base in Fukien. These troops were rotated every three years and were stationed in several areas, including the seat of Ch'ing administration in Tainan prefecture city and other local government sites, plus at river mouths and critical seaports. Overall, the number of soldiers stationed in these areas was greater than generally found in comparable areas on the mainland. Since the population and income on Taiwan were insufficient to support this large force, the Ch'ing government was forced to transfer resources from Fukien and Chekiang in order to make up the difference. And given that Taiwan was a primary supplier of rice to mainland markets and an important strategic island, the Ch'ing was willing to maintain a significant military presence despite its high costs.[10] From this distribution of troops, it is evident that their primary purpose was to protect the offices of the various prefecture and county governments and to prevent illegal immigration into the island. Most troops stationed at river mouths amounted, however, to only a few squads and were thus generally unable to provide adequate security for the life and property of the many tenant farmers.

As for the civil administration, the highest-ranking official was the inspector, who exercised jurisdiction over both Taiwan and Amoy prefectures. In 1727, the official title of this position was changed (a common practice during the Ch'ing) along with its jurisdiction, which from that point onward covered Taiwan and the P'eng-hu archipelago. Because of the relatively remote location of Taiwan and the complex and diverse origins of its population, along with the constant threat of local uprisings, the Ch'ing government exercised great caution in selecting its highest-ranking official posted on the island, who was an intendant of a circuit. In principle, qualifications for this post included substantial administrative experience and exemplary moral conduct. The intendant of a circuit was under the direct jurisdiction of both the Fukien governor and the governor-general of Fukien and Che-kiang. During the initial period of Ch'ing rule, the intendant was in charge of the administrative work on the island including local tax collection, though he lacked the authority to report to the emperor directly. After the suppression of the Lin Shuang-wen uprising in 1788, however, the Ch'ing government felt it necessary to learn more about conditions on Taiwan and so allowed officials at the rank of intendant and brigade-general to report directly to the emperor so as to avoid any delay in deploying local military forces in the event of another uprising. At the same time, the Ch'ing government also altered the structure of the civil and military administration. On the one hand, it granted more power to the intendant, giving him the authority to supervise and monitor military and political affairs; on the other, the emperor also gave the brigade-general more authority over judicial and administrative matters. In addition, in order to effectively monitor Taiwan's affairs, the Ch'ing government also ordered the commanding general and governor-general of Fukien and Chekiang to make annual inspection tours of Taiwan to ensure the most effective allocation and deployment of military forces.[11]

Under the jurisdiction of the intendant, there were two important administrative positions: the civil prefect and the coastal defense subprefect. The civil prefect was in charge of collecting land and property taxes and adjudicating criminal cases among residents. The coastal defense subprefect was primarily responsible for the supervision of ports and docks and coastal shipping and also for preventing mainland residents from slipping into the island as illegal immigrants. The civil prefect, in turn, was in charge of three counties, T'ai-wan, Feng-shan, and Chu-lo, which included offices set up to assist the county in gathering social and economic information and to assist in apprehending thieves. Since the term of office for Ch'ing officials was limited to three years, they were forbidden to bring along their wives or other family members. The most important matters, therefore, ended up being taken care of by local officials. Unfortunately, the level of education and training among these local officials was often

lacking, leading them to misuse their power and exploit both the immigrant settlers from the mainland and the aborigines. The result was widespread antigovernment riots and uprisings such as in 1723, when Chu Yi-kuei reacted to unbearable
exploitation by local officials by leading an uprising. After this incident, the
Ch'ing government responded by punishing corrupt officials while it also realized
that some local government offices had become so bureaucratic that they were
unable to manage the vast rural areas in the central and northern part of the island
effectively. It was for this reason that an administrative change was effected in
which Chu-lo county was broken up into Chang-hua county and Tan-shui subprefecture, which assumed jurisdiction over the entire region north of Ta-chia-hsi.
In 1776, despite the fact that the majority of the P'ing-p'u aborigines had become
very "Hanified," they still became deeply involved in disputes with the Han over
land rights and other such conflicts. To deal with this situation two subprefecture
offices were established in Tainan and Lu-kang with the authority to oversee
public security work, to manage the buying and selling of land, and to deal with
the various problems created by the loss of aboriginal land rights to the Han.[12]
The establishment of these subprefectures meant, in effect, that the P'ing-p'u
aborigines had been effectively integrated into the social and political system of
the Han and had been brought under the umbrella of the rural security system. In
1787 following the Lin Shuang-wen incident, the Ch'ing government changed the
name of Chu-lo county to Chia-yi county. And in 1812, following the takeover of
northeast Taiwan by armed Han people and after a number of villages had been
built, the Ch'ing government set up the Hamalan subprefecture to manage agricultural affairs for both the P'ing-p'u aborigines and the Han. From then until the
1870s, after the Taipei basin became the center of tea, camphor, and sugarcane
production for international trade, the Ch'ing government set up Taipei prefecture
along with three additional counties, Hsin-chu, Tan-shui, and Ii-lan. These various
administrative changes reflected a major shift in the political and economic center
of power on the island from Tainan to Taipei.

This expansion of the civil and military offices indicated that the Ch'ing
government had generally resisted any local administrative reorganization until
after population growth had become so great that it brought about serious social
conflicts. The same pattern was also evident on the mainland where the Ch'ing
resorted to administrative reorganizations as a way to restrict the growth of the
bureaucratic system.[13] However, since Taiwan was a more mobile and unsettled
society and generally lacked the system of village elders and clan organization
prevalent on the mainland, whenever conflicts arose on Taiwan, it was up to the
local landlords, farm managers, and aboriginal leaders to solve these problems
and resolve local disputes. This, in fact, is the reason that the local elite emphasized building up their own private militia. Further, since many of the bureaucratic officials and soldiers sent over from the mainland often abused their power
by collecting illegal taxes and skimming off profits, the local population had no
alternative but to gather in secret and form organizations along ethnic or geo-

graphic lines to protect their property rights and living standards from bureaucratic parasiticism. These self-defense groups and organizations followed the practices of more traditional clan organizations by becoming involved in social conflicts that often posed a major threat to the rural social order.

In 1721, a Taiwan resident of Fukienese ancestry named Chu Yi-kuei mobilized the people of southern Taiwan and started a major uprising in which local officials were killed and many villages plundered. In the beginning of the uprising, Chu basically succeeded in uniting the population of Fukienese and Kuangtungnese to oppose the Ch'ing. Later, however, internecine disputes split Chu's forces into two groups that did their own killing and looting. Such divisions among Fukienese and Kuangtungnese in this uprising effectively sowed the seeds of disputes between these two groups that would fester for many years to come.[14]

In 1782, Chia-yi and Chang-hua prefectures experienced large-scale social disorders between people of Chang-chou and Ch'uan-chou backgrounds. The roots of this disorder lay in a dispute over gambling debts that had broken out between two villages composed of people from Chang-chou and Ch'uan-chou. The conflict spread when both villages sought allies from their kin in nearby areas. Local headmen in some areas used the conflict as an opportunity to expand their economic interests and to carry out acts of revenge over old vendettas. The conflict was further intensified by the mobilization of unemployed wanderers from nearby areas. Local officials meanwhile were basically helpless in their attempts to mediate the conflict, which eventually expanded to a few dozen villages. During the period of the greatest strife, several thousand villagers from numerous clans were brought into the fray by local leaders who organized their followers into militia units along the lines of common language or surname. More than four hundred villages were burned to the ground and several thousand people killed while many residents of nearby areas were forced to flee.[15] Some turned to their clan groups and leaders for help, while other tenant farmers picked up and moved to areas composed of people from the same ancestral background where they hoped to create some sort of collective defensive network.

In 1786, a member of the Lin family of Wu-feng named Lin Shuang-wen set up an organization called the Heaven and Earth Society (T'ien-ti hui) under the slogan of killing officials and fanning disorder. This turned into an uprising that eventually involved several tens of thousands of participants and lasted for over a year, making it the largest such conflict in the history of the island. Following suppression of the uprising, local officials collected information indicating that as many as 70 percent of the participants were unemployed wanderers. Further examination, however, revealed that many of the "rioters" actually owned considerable amounts of land, "as much as 3,500 *chia,* or more than 33,000 *mu.*"[16] Such evidence indicated that, although a substantial portion of the "rioters" were unemployed wanderers, landowners and farm managers were also involved, usually as leaders. Furthermore, it was generally believed by the Ch'ing government that the uprising had resulted from the commingling of residents from Chang-chou and Ch'uan-chou in Fukien with people from Kuangtung between whom there were constant conflicts over land and water rights. In response, the Ch'ing ordered the local commander, Fu K'ang-an, to resettle people out of the island's central regions so that locals from these separate areas would now live apart and conflicts could be reduced.[17] This decision led to substantial changes in the village system at the hands of officials. At the same time, several local strong-men were afforded the opportunity to rebuild villages destroyed in the conflict, while residents from the same ancestral homelands or of the same surname were able to create their own local militia forces. After the outbreak of the uprising led by Tai Ch'ao-ch'un from 1862 to 1865 (discussed below), the government fi-nally realized that most local leaders in this and other such conflicts were local strongmen who had organized secret societies and other such organizations. Tai Ch'ao-ch'un and Lin Jih-ch'eng, leaders of the uprising, were, in fact, from wealthy landlord families dating back several generations who had also served as leaders of local militia. Yet another participant was a man named Ch'en Nung, who was also from a family of considerable wealth and who had provided food and other such supplies to the thousands of participants in the uprising.

Leaders of various organizations involved in the conflict were also from influential landlord families. Before the outbreak of the conflict they had organ-ized various secret societies devoted to venerating the local goddess Ma-tsu, which they used as an opportunity to expand their power for eventual conflicts with others over land and water rights. Once an uprising was threatened, this led to the assimilation and militarization of local organizations as various villages joined together, usually in groups composed of people with the same surname or language group. This was done to protect themselves from outside attack or to launch their own attacks against any and all opponents. Local strongmen with considerable landholdings also formed their own more powerful groups com-posed of relatives, friends, and tenants.

Although local officials of the Ch'ing could not halt the formation of these local organizations and groups and were helpless in stopping the outbreak of conflicts over land and water rights, they did adopt policies aimed at ensuring a kind of balance of power among these local forces and at eradicating the social conditions that fostered major uprisings. For instance, after the 1830s, some local officials, such as Yao Ying, demanded that local commercial organizations and rich farmers donate money to assist the many homeless wanderers with food and shelter and to provide them with some work to reduce their inclination to be-come involved in uprisings. In 1831, an official in Tan-shui by the name of Lo Yun realized that the local military forces at his disposal were woefully inade-quate and so decreed the "Four Rules of Decorum" and the "Eight Forbiddens," which effectively committed local leaders and clan heads to maintaining local social order. He also decreed as a guiding principle of punishment for any offender that "involvement by any family member means punishment for all." From 1847 to 1854, Hsu Tsung-kan was the intendant of the circuit in Taiwan who attempted to persuade the local governor to set up organizations to apprehend thieves and to provide for local self-defense. According to a study of local security organizations in northern Taiwan during the nineteenth century by Mark Allee, local officials were often so short of staff that they were unable to manage the affairs of the villages and instead recruited local leaders to serve as managers or trustees to help mediate local problems. Many of these local leaders were not, in fact, local strongmen but, rather, elderly people or prestigious local leaders. In ordinary times, they assembled residents at local temples to announce government decrees or to assist in mediating local conflicts. This made it possible for government orders to be promulgated despite the shortage of local officials. In this way, various local groups were recruited to become part of the bureaucracy.[18] As it was the powerful landlord families whom local officials tried to entice into service, we must therefore analyze the process by which this class of local elites was formed.

The Transformation of the Landlord Class: From Landlords to Local Strongmen

During the early period of the Ch'ing dynasty, the majority of immigrants to Taiwan settled in rural communities among people of the same ancestral or geographical background. As time passed, many of the landowning farmers organized themselves into clan groups to protect their property rights and to pool their capital. These groups were generally set up in the name of a common ancestor and were known as clan "cooperatives." Members of these organizations who were generally from the same ancestral area, signed an agreement delineating their various rights and obligations governing entry and withdrawal from the cooperative.[19] On the one hand, such organizations united villagers in collective self-defense in the unstable environment of rural Taiwan. On the other, these groups pooled clan capital and labor for investment in large-scale irrigation and water control systems that benefited agricultural development and production. In the early nineteenth century, when the landlord class had become firmly established and had already accumulated substantial amounts of property, they began to set up consanguineous organizations, based on common geographical background, as well as intervillage ancestral and spiritual worship groups. Many landlord families, after having engaged in agriculture for two or three generations, also set up family clan organs commonly known as "share groups." The primary function of these groups was to honor the "pioneering generation" of ancestors who had come to Taiwan in the early years. Before the family patriarch divided up clan property, a parcel of land was set aside to support ancestral worship. Rent collected from these lands was to be used primarily by later generations to carry on ancestor worship, and thus the property could not be sold. Chuang Ying-chang and Ch'en Lien-tung have studied the history and development of the various clans in the Miao-li area of northern Taiwan during the eighteenth and nineteenth centuries. They found that, after 1790, residents there established clan organizations based on consanguineous ties. In the 1850s, many landlord families also adopted the practice of maintaining clan lineage records.[20] Properties devoted to ancestor worship and to the various clan organizations both symbolized the localization (*pen-t'u-hua*) of landlord families. They were also important landmarks in the social transformation of Taiwan from an unstable, immigrant society to a more stable, settled one.[21]

Moreover, as a response to the threat of conflicts between people of different ancestral backgrounds, new villages and residential areas were built, consisting of people from the same clan or language group, or of the same religion. They too engaged in common defense and protection against outside enemies, at times including the Ch'ing government. For instance, in 1832, Chang Ping, a resident originally from Chang-chou, Fukien province, led a resistance to Ch'ing officials by farmers and residents around the town of Chia-yi who opposed the shipment of rice out of the area. This incident stemmed from a particularly devastating drought that had afflicted the rural areas of central and southern Taiwan, which by substantially cutting into the rice harvest convinced villagers that they had to hold on to their product. Yet, once corrupt local officials were bribed by shady merchants and traders to ship out rice surreptitiously, a full-scale rice riot quickly ensued. In the beginning, Chang Ping only wanted to lead the villagers to resist corrupt local officials. Later, however, with growing tensions between the Fukienese and Kuangtungnese, the conflict expanded from an anti-Ch'ing action into a general anti-Kuangtungese movement. In the end, as more and more migrants and drifters joined the fray, the movement turned into an old-fashioned fight between Fukienese and Kuangtungese that engulfed the entire island. But once the conflict died down, significant changes were effected in residential areas and general living patterns that gradually brought about greater commingling and mutual assimilation among more and more people. On the one hand, powerful families emerged as local armed strongmen; on the other, temples and places of worship that were formerly restricted to people of the same ancestral and geographical background were expanded incorporating entire villages and instilling a set of common beliefs and identities among immigrants from different backgrounds. For example, the Three Mountain King Sect (Sanshan Kuowang) had been traditionally confined to Kuangtung immigrants. But with the growing assimilation among the local population, people of both Fukienese and Kuangtungnese ancestry joined in revering this spirit despite their previous conflicts and tensions.[22] Common places of religious worship, in effect, emerged as local civic bodies that brought together residents from a single village or several neighboring villages who were already involved in agricultural production or used the same irrigation and water control system. In towns with agricultural business and commerce, public temples and shrines were also established devoted to worshiping a common god or spirit according to the tradition of "separating the incense."[23] In ordinary times, these places of worship served to develop closer emotional bonds among the villagers as they gathered together to revere the local spirits and engage in other religious activities. But when incidents or other occurrences demanded their attention, the temple then was a public forum where residents could hold meetings and discuss the situation.

Based on available research, by the early nineteenth century many influential landlord families on Taiwan began to accumulate substantial wealth. They built shrines and temples and purchased land to support ancestral worship. They also frequently purchased official ranks (the lowest being the imperial rank of *chiensheng*) as a quick way to bolster their family's social status. Ts'ai Yuan-chie's study of two of the most influential landlord families in the central and northern regions of rural Taiwan—the Ch'ens of T'ou-fen and the Lins of T'ao-yuan—revealed many similarities in their paths to local leadership. The first member of the Ch'en family, a man by the name of Ch'en Feng-ch'iu (1761–?), came to Taiwan in 1774 and engaged in agricultural work for many years. Not until the age of forty was he able to save enough money to get married. His eldest son received some education but also did not get married until the age of thirty-nine because of the generally impoverished conditions of the family. Thus it was not until the third generation that Ch'un-lung (1834–1903) was able to purchase a lease on agricultural land and collect rent. It was also at this time that the family became involved in the sugarcane processing and wholesale grain businesses from which they made a sizable fortune and gradually became a influential local landlord family. By 1871, the third-generation Ch'en had purchased a *chien-sheng* imperial title and in 1892 he became the temple headman and local leader.

Another example of an influential landlord family were the Lins from Lan-chu town in T'ao-yuan county. Originally tenant farmers, they gradually moved up the socioeconomic ladder and became the wealthiest family in the area. Their ancestor, Lin Wen-chin, had come to Taiwan in 1745 and worked for thirty years as a tenant farmer. By 1775, he had saved enough money to buy 19 *chia* of land, which he divided up and leased to other tenants in return for rent. Lin T'ien-ts'ih (1806–1878) of the third generation expanded the family's operations from agriculture into the cloth dyeing business and the rice trade. The family reportedly collected one thousand *tan* of rent per year, which propelled them into the position of local leadership. In addition to donating money in exchange for an imperial title, the Lin family also built a mansion in 1873 to symbolize their growing social status.[24] In short, both the Chens and the Lins spent two or three generations at hard work in agriculture, in addition to becoming involved in the rice retail and cloth dyeing business, before they could achieve their wealth and high social status. In so doing, they were able to accumulate the funds necessary to set up their own clan organization. In a similar manner, in the nineteenth century two influential families in Hsin-chu town—the Chengs and Lins—also worked for two or three generations to accumulate the wealth necessary to purchase imperial titles and to expand their social influence through marriage arrangements. In this way, they were gradually able to assume the status of country gentry.[25] In all, these examples demonstrate that, for local influential families to climb up the social ladder and achieve leadership positions in local society, they not only had to accumulate wealth but also had to expand their social status and reputation, especially through calculated marriage arrangements. This helped them establish extensive political and social influence and acquire long-term reputation and respect.

Many of the influential families also used the opportunity afforded by the government's suppression of local uprisings and riots to win military awards and merit. For instance, following the quelling of the 1786 Lin Shuang-wen uprising on Taiwan, sixty-seven influential family leaders won official recognition and received military citations. Among the sixty-seven, forty were representatives from low-level gentry families at the *wu-sheng* or provincial (*chu-jen*) rank and the other twenty-seven were common citizens. In 1790, fifty-six people received awards after the Ch'en Chou-ch'uan uprising was suppressed, thirty-nine of whom were local leaders who had never before received official honor or rank. In 1862, following the Tai Ch'ao-ch'un incident, although only ten representatives from influential families received awards, even fewer commoners received such recognition, numbering only six.[26] All this demonstrates that, by becoming involved with government efforts to suppress local uprisings, many influential families were able to use their clan power to set up local militia for self-defense and to protect their families.

However, not all landlord families were able to become local strongmen by building up their own militia. In fact, the majority of local leaders were merely representatives of landlord families with no such power at their disposal. In most cases, they simply donated money in return for low-ranking imperial titles while they generally avoided establishing their own armed militia. The experience of the Lins of Wu-feng with their personal militia was instructive in this regard since they had been punished by the government for misusing their forces despite their considerable social and political influence. In order to analyze the multifaceted situation of the local elite structure on Taiwan, we therefore examine three separate examples of prominent families on the island. They are the Chang family of the Taipei basin area, the P'an family of the P'ing-p'u aborigine tribe in central Taiwan, and the Lins of Wu-feng. These three families lived in separate areas of central and northern Taiwan and made a fortune from agricultural work. The Chang family came to Taiwan relatively early and were a typical example of a family with considerable entrepreneurial spirit. The P'ans were a leading family in the Pazeh tribe. In the eighteenth and nineteenth centuries, they established a cooperative relationship with the government on the strength of their personal military power and strategic calculations, from which they gained considerable landholdings that were then leased out. As for the Lins of Wu-feng, they were a prime example of a landlord family that in the nineteenth century had emerged as local strongmen. By leasing out their extensive landholdings, the Lins made a fortune, which they used to set up and lead a local militia made up of people from several villages. In subsequent years, the Lin family was awarded by the government for their effort in helping to suppress local uprisings. In this way they managed to enter the bureaucratic system and also became the most powerful family in central Taiwan.

The Chang Land-Owning Family of the Taipei Basin

The Chang family was originally from Chin-chiang county, Ch'uan-chou, Fukien province. In 1702, Chang Shih-hsiang (1673–1732) cheated on his application for the civil service exam by claiming to be from Hui'an county. After he was reported to the authorities, Chang decided to cross the strait and seek out new opportunities on Taiwan. Initially, Chang Shih-hsiang continued to seek personal fame while at the same time he invested in the land reclamation business and helped to open new lands in the Yun-lin area of southern Taiwan. Around 1720, through an introduction from an acquaintance, Chang leased a substantial amount of uncultivated grasslands from the Mao-erh-kan tribe of the P'ing-p'u aborigines and as "farm manager" hired tenant farmers to develop the land. Relying on the practice of "Han management of aboriginal property," Chang established his management rights over the land, from which he earned considerable wealth and capital. Later, Chang's sons and grandsons used these gains to invest in various irrigation and water control projects. In 1735, Chang's eldest son, Chang Fang-kao (1698–1764), constructed the "Ta-yu-chen" water control system, which opened up hundreds of *chia* of farmland to irrigation. On average, one *chia* of land generally yielded two *tan* of rice. The success of these land development measures and water control projects enabled the Chang family to accumulate large amounts of wealth in a rather short period of time and to become local strongmen.

In 1751, the fourth son of Chang Shih-hsiang, Chang Fang-ta (1715–1764), used the gains from the family business in central Taiwan to invest in the Hsin-chuang plain near the upper reaches of the Tan-shui river in the Taipei area. He also established a reclamation company called Chang-wu-wen along with two other men named Wu Lo and Mao Shao-wen. Through this partnership, the three jointly invested and managed their landholdings. In 1755, the Mao family asked to withdraw from the partnership because of the lack of funds, leaving Chang and Wu to continue to manage the remaining lands on a share basis. Ultimately, Chang formed his own Chang-pi-jung company while Wu set up the Wu-chi-sheng company. From that point onward, the two families managed their landholdings and tenants separately.[27]

On the basis of the experience of these three families in setting up and then abolishing a management partnership, one can learn a great deal about the entrepreneurial spirit of the landlord class in its early formation. In order to establish control over large tracts of land, they each invested considerable funds through a partnership-type organization. The primary purpose of such a company was to earn profits and collect rents through the leasing of land. In other words, they invested primarily for the purpose of collecting rent but without bringing about major improvements in agricultural technology and production methods. For that reason, they generally allowed the original tenants to continue to cultivate the land and to maintain a steady level of rent payment. On the one hand, such a leasing system encouraged their tenants to invest to improve the productivity of the land over the long term. On the other, the landlords avoided spending great amounts of their own money in search of new tenants. Such a tenant-leasing system that commingled the management of capital investment and protection of tenant rights guaranteed the security of rural land rights while also promoting land and agricultural development. In fact, one can argue that this was one of the primary reasons for the rapid development of agriculture on Taiwan.

At the same time that Chang Fang-ta expanded his agricultural business, Chang Fang-kao started his land business in a nearby village known as Hsing-chih (later renamed Hsin village). In 1753, he established his own Chang-kuan-fu agricultural settlement and purchased cultivation rights on a large piece of grassland from the P'ing-p'u aborigines. Both parties agreed that the Chang family would pay rent to the aborigines on a regular basis in return for the right to hire tenants or transfer cultivation rights. In accord with common practice, these rights granted to Chang conferred on him the status of "landlord." The rights of the aborigines were limited to collecting rent as they were prevented from interfering in the management of the farm, even though the tribe retained the superficial status of landlord. Once he gained cultivation rights, Chang hired more than fifty tenant farmers and opened up more than 130 *chia* of land. With one *chia* yielding on average 8 *tan* of crops, the family collected 1,000 *tan* of rent a year, which back then constituted a huge fortune.[28]

Besides developing land and collecting rent, Chang also invested huge sums in developing irrigation networks and water control projects. In 1757, the Changs established a partnership with the Wu family to build a water control project in Fu-an-chen about eight *li* in length. However, during the summer two years after its construction, a huge rain storm virtually destroyed the entire project turning more than 200 *chia* of land into a swamp almost overnight. Even more unfortunate was that before this project was even completed, a homesteading family named Liu living in a nearby area received the rights from the local government authority to build their own water control–irrigation system on Chang family property. Two years later, the Lius successfully constructed their own Wan-an-p'o hydro dam with a capacity to irrigate up to 300 *chia* of farmland. The Chang family sued on several occasions over the Liu family's intrusion onto their land, but were ignored. It was not until 1764 when the eldest son of Chang Fang-kao, Chang Yuen-jen, successfully passed the provincial scholar (*chu-jen*) exam that the Chang family was able to force the local government to deal with the case. The result was that in 1765 the Chang and Liu families signed an agreement in which the Liu family would pay the Changs 600 *tan* a year in water rent (*shui-*

tzu) as compensation for using Chang family land. The Chang family, in turn, allowed the Liu's dam to remain in place. At the same time, the two families agreed to share the available water resources to irrigate their lands.

From this experience, one can tell that, by the eighteenth century, partnerships were widely employed by the landlord class as a way of investing in the development of agricultural land. On the one hand, they leased land from the aborigines thereby gaining management rights over the land. This, in fact, was the method the Chang family used to acquire the right to the manage lands, which yielded them considerable wealth. On the other, landlords such as the Chang family subleased their cultivation rights to other tenant farmers. Landlord families also invested heavily in irrigation and water control systems evidently in the belief that relying on rich water resources ensured continuous growth in the productivity of the land. Since control over water resources effectively guaranteed continued control over rent collection, many wealthy landlord families invested huge sums in water projects. However, the disastrous experience of the Chang family described above also made it apparent that construction of such projects was very risky.

Another important factor in the rise of the Chang family was their reliance on a relative who had achieved the official provincial rank of *chu-jen* in the Ch'ing bureaucracy. Although at the lower rung of the official hierarchy—since he was far from the center of political power—his position still carried great weight in the local rural power structure. This, in fact, is why many wealthy landlord families encouraged their family members to pass the scholar-official exams or to donate money in exchange for an imperial title.

The P'an Land-Owning Family of the Anli Tribe of the P'ing-p'u Aborigines

The P'ing-p'u are an aboriginal tribe living in the plains area along the coast of Taiwan. After the island was taken over by the Ch'ing, the government divided the aboriginal tribes into two groups: those in category one were known as "civilized aborigines" (*shu-fan*), that is, aborigines who accepted the authority of the Ch'ing and who willingly paid taxes based on the number of people per household; those in the other category were referred to as "uncivilized aborigines" (*sheng-fan*), tribes that refused to accept the authority of the Ch'ing. According to Ch'ing practice, before their naturalization, the *shu-fan* donated land to the Ch'ing court and in return received land on which they could hunt and make a living. Since this group was willing to pay taxes to the Ch'ing government and exhibited considerable bravery in traveling over long distances, the Ch'ing recruited them to deliver government documents across great distances and to assist its military forces in suppressing local uprisings. In return, the Ch'ing adopted policies to protect aborigine rights including prohibitions against any Han from occupying aboriginal land. However, from the beginning of the eighteenth century onward, many *shu-fan* enticed Han settlers into their home-lands to help in reclaiming and converting barren land into cropland. This prac-tice of "Han management of aboriginal property" was a way to circumvent official regulations, which had prohibited the Han from occupying aboriginal farmland. In pursuing this surreptitious course, the aborigines were able to retain control over their land rights while also collecting rent or lease fees. This ap-proach was beneficial to both the Han and the aborigines and was especially popular in the western aboriginal regions of the island. Throughout the Ch'ing dynasty, quite a few tribes used this method to develop large amounts of land, which ultimately resulted in the formation of an aboriginal landlord class.[29] The P'an landlord family discussed below was, in fact, the most outstanding example of such an aboriginal landlord class.

The Anli tribe belonged to the Pazeh branch and was referred to as the Pazeh people. The P'ing-p'u consisted of four large tribes: the Anli, P'u-tz'u-li, Alishi, and Wuniulan. Since the Anli tribe had for many years led the other tribes, it was generally considered the representative of them all. During the mid-eighteenth century, when the Anli tribe was at the height of its influence and power, it controlled considerable land rights in the northeast region of the central Taiwan basin and the hilly region between Ta-chia-hsi and Tien-hsi. The Anli were also the largest tribe among the P'ing-p'u aborigines.[30]

As early as 1699, the Anli people accepted the authority of the Ch'ing by helping government forces to suppress the anti-Ch'ing uprising among the T'un-hsiao tribe in the north-central region of Taiwan. Later, in Chu-lo county (subse-quently renamed Chia-yi county), the district magistrate (*chih-hsien*), Chou Chung-hsuen, realized that many Han had moved into and taken control of the grasslands north of Ta-tu-hsi and Ta-chia-hsi, creating a situation in which the Han "lived among the *fan,* married *fan* women, and adopted *fan* children." In order to stave off conflict and any acts of revenge between the aborigines and the Han, Chou put the local leader of the Anli tribe by the name of A-mo in charge of all P'ing-p'u affairs in the central region of the island. Then in 1716, the former provincial governor of Fukien province, Sha Mu-ha, conducted an in-spection tour of Taiwan after which he suggested to the governor-general of Fukien and Kuangtung, Chue Lo-man-pao (a Manchu), that the Anli people be naturalized. The Anli were therefore recognized as *shu-fan* and submitted as tax 50 hides of deer (equivalent to 12 *liang* of silver). At the same time, A-mo recommended that a Han man by the name of Chang Ta-ching (1690–1773), who was of Kuangtungnese origin and spoke the aboriginal language, be put in charge of the general affairs of the aborigines.

Around 1710, the Anli tribe consisted of 422 households, totaling 3,300 peo-ple. (Based on the Han household registration system, the average number per household was eight people.) Their life-style involved slash-and-burn agriculture along with fishing, and they were generally unaware of the Han method of wet-rice production. However, after being naturalized, they applied for permission from the government to engage in the long-term cultivation of the land. In 1732, the Anli tribe obeyed official demands to send their forces to assist the Ch'ing in suppressing an uprising among the Ta-chia-hsi tribe. Following this action, once the government had declared as "traitorous property" all the holdings on the grasslands of those tribes that had been involved in the uprising, ownership of these territories in the northeast area of the central Taiwan basin was transferred to the Anli. Later, with the assistance of Chang Ta-ching, the Anli began large-scale wet-rice production.

Chang Ta-ching was originally from Ta-p'u county, Kuangtung province, and in 1711 crossed the strait to Taiwan, where he became involved in agriculture. In 1716, he gained the trust of the Anli by providing them with medicine. Later, as noted above, he was chosen to take charge of Anli affairs because of his fluency in the tribal language. He was put in charge of their financial dealings and also handled official Ch'ing documents and decrees directed to the Anli. In 1732, after the Anli had acquired land from the Ch'ing government, Chang helped the newly appointed native headman by the name of Tun-tzu (a grandson of the general headman A-mo) in opening up and developing the grasslands. On the one hand, Chang encouraged a great number of friends from his hometown on the mainland to invest in and develop barren land along the lines of "Han management of aboriginal property." On the other, in order to speed up the process of turning dry land into wet-rice paddies to increase production, Chang recommended that the six wealthy families of Lu-kang (generally known as the "six-family enterprise") sign an agreement with the Anli tribe that "divided up land in exchange for water" and committed both sides to joint investment in water irrigation projects. In line with this agreement, the Anli turned over large tracts of land to these wealthy families in exchange for capital and the necessary technology to build an irrigation system. Relying on the strategy of "Han management of aboriginal property" and "dividing up land in exchange for water," the Anli grasslands were successfully converted into rice paddy and sugarcane fields from which the Anli collected a fixed amount of rent every year. It was these benefits from land rights that enabled the Anli people in the eighteenth century to accumulate substantial wealth, making them the most power aboriginal landlords in central Taiwan.[31]

Based on the traditions of the Anli tribe, all the lands of the various tribes were subject to the authority of the "tribal headman." In 1747, since the tribal headman at that time had become old and infirm, Tun-tzu was invited to take charge of the tribe's landed properties, which he divided into two categories— "common" and "private commercial" land—as a way to facilitate land management. Common lands were put under the control of the native family patriarch, who oversaw development of these lands and collected rents that were used to support the affairs of the entire tribe. The private commercial land was made the responsibility of individual households. But if any member wanted to transfer or sell their land rights, this required the approval of the native family patriarch of the tribe for the transfer or sale to be effected.

Tun-tzu used the method of "Han management of aboriginal property" to manage the common lands. Based on Ch'ing records from the year 1770, there were 290 *chia* of common lands, from which 4,600 *tan* of rent was collected annually. The private commercial lands belonging to Tun-tzu also yielded about 4,000 *tan* of annual rent, on which he relied to accumulate the wealth necessary to follow the traditional gentry landlord's life-style of cultivating a broad social network. In ordinary times, he used part of the profit from the rent collected on the common lands to buy gifts for civil officials and to provide donations to the government to assist it in suppressing uprisings. In addition, Tun-tzu often supported the construction of local temples in villages and various communities and participated in religious activities. He also developed the hobby of growing orchids and even went so far as to hire a gardener from the mainland to cultivate them. In 1758, at the suggestion of Ch'ing officials, he adopted "P'an" as his surname. As was apparent from his approach to agricultural management and his social-cultural activities, Tun-tzu had become very sinified and had also established himself as an influential landlord family.

Before Tun-tzu passed away, he made out a will that divided his property into two parts. The P'an family common lands, which yielded about 1,700 *tan* per year, were devoted to venerating the family's ancestors and paying for family-related expenses. The other parcels of land were bequeathed to the children and grandchildren of his two wives. Each family received rental property worth 4,500 *tan*. Also, Tun-tzu's titles as headman, director, and others were also inherited by his two sons. His eldest son, P'an Shih-wan, was not only put in charge of the Anli common lands but was also temporarily appointed as director. In 1786, during the Lin Shuang-wen uprising, P'an Shih-wan led his militia to assist the Ch'ing suppression of the rebels and was awarded a class six decoration. The second son, P'an Shih-hsing (1761–1818), also purchased an imperial title for himself in 1786 and titles for his two sons in 1811 and 1814. The practice of donating money in exchange for an imperial title indicates that, before the early nineteenth century, the P'an family maintained its ownership of substantial amounts of property while also taking full advantage of the purchase of imperial titles to maintain the social status of the family.

During the third generation of the P'an family, however, its social situation rapidly deteriorated along with the rest of the P'ing-p'u aborigines. The eldest son of P'an Shih-wan, P'an Chin-wen (1766–?), was, in fact, the real son of a Han family who had been adopted by the P'ans and was in a position to inherit P'an family property. From 1796 to 1803, he was appointed the headman of the Anli tribe. Unfortunately, P'an Chin-wen began to spend money wildly and was perpetually in debt and could make a living only by pawning family property. An extravagant life-style was also the culprit in driving P'an Ch'un-wen (1781–?), a son from P'an Shih-hsing's second wife who was of pure Anli lineage, deep into debt. By the 1820s, the heirs of the P'an family had thus lost much of their land to Han bankers, something that also occurred with the majority of P'ing-p'u aboriginal landlords. The result was that, by pawning off their land rights, the people were gradually reduced to poverty.

The Lin Family of Wu-feng

Since Johanna Meskill published her 1979 work on the Lin family, academics have generally considered the Lins as the typical example of how a border area landlord had become a member of the urban gentry during the Ch'ing dynasty.[32] Indeed, the Lin family was not only an important family from Fukien that had come to Taiwan and opened up lands and earned enormous wealth, it also controlled a very large militia comprising the family's tenant farmers. In the 1850s, the Lin family donated money to the Ch'ing while the family militia assisted Ch'ing troops in suppressing the forces of the T'ai-p'ing Heavenly Kingdom on the mainland. As a result, the Lin family was promoted to the position of provincial commander-in-chief in charge of land forces. Indeed, the primary reason the Lin family was able to develop from a wealthy farming family into urban gentry was that Taiwan was far from the center of Ch'ing control, which made it possible for powerful families like the Lins to establish their militia forces.

In recent years, Huang Fusan has examined more original data and materials on Lin family history, providing us with a somewhat better understanding of the twists and turns in the rise and fall of the Lin family. The success story of the Lin family began with the founding father, Lin Shih (1729–1788), who came to Taiwan in 1746 and opened up agricultural lands near the central mountain region. As with most early homesteaders, Lin Shih acquired grasslands from the aborigines and then returned to his hometown on the mainland to hire friends and relatives to assist in developing and establishing a community in which the Lins were the primary members. Once they became wealthy enough, the Lins got involved in the rice trade and rural loans. Together, their various investments yielded as much as 10,000 *tan* in profits every year.[33]

Unfortunately, as a result of the uprising led by Lin Shuang-wen, a member of the Lin clan, the Lins were almost completely destroyed. Living in the same community near Ta-li-fa, Lin Shuang-wen had called on Lin Shih for assistance. In 1786, as the leader of the Heaven and Earth Alliance, Lin Shuang-wen joined with other secret societies such as the T'ien-ti [untranslatable, characters different from Heaven and Earth Society—Eds.] and the Thunder Alliance (Lei kung hui), and became involved in armed conflicts. Later, to avoid being arrested by local officials, Lin sparked an uprising and took over the county seat of Chang-hua. In 1788, however, Lin was captured and killed and had all his properties, many linked to the Lin family, confiscated by officials. Since Lin Shih was considered a relative of a traitor, he was imprisoned and more than 400 *chia* of his farmland was confiscated, causing great suffering for the entire Lin family. Eventually, he decided to move to Wu-feng and start all over again in making his fortune.

The second-generation Lin, Lin Chia-yin (1782–1839), after considerable effort, was very successful in reestablishing the family. Making good use of the mountainous environment around Wu-feng, he purchased cultivation rights from the aborigines and hired tenant farmers to cultivate the fields. Also, seeing the increasing number of Han in the area who were in need of timber to build houses and of charcoal for cooking and heating, Lin started a thriving timber and charcoal business, which made him a huge fortune. According to Huang Fusan's research, Lin Chia-yin's investment in farmland and his timber/charcoal business yielded 4,000 *tan* of profit every year, which enabled the Lin family once again to assume the status of influential landlord.

The first two generations of the Lin family not only accumulated large sums of wealth and established an influential family-clan network, but also recruited their tenant farmers into their personal militia. As the leader of the Lin family during the third generation, Lin Ting-pang had learned martial arts as a youth and was frequently involved in fights in town. Later, he took charge of training the family militia and handling the mediation of family and clan conflicts over such matters as money and marriage. At that point, Lin Ting-pang's living situation had become quite different from that of his ancestors. The Lin family lived in a densely populated area with quite a few influential family clans among whom there were all kinds of conflicts over property rights and water resources. For instance, Lin Ma-sheng of Ts'ao-hu village was very powerful and he himself was the head of a local militia and a VIP in the local community. Lin Chia-yin's family was not as powerful and influential as Lin Ma-sheng's. Moreover, since Lin Chia-yin lived close to the mountains, some of his tenants traveled into the mountain region surreptitiously to cut timber, which the aborigines deeply resented since it disrupted their hunting. Given their situation, the Lin family, like other farmers, learned martial arts and carried farm tools, knives, and guns as weapons. Once an incident occurred, they would gather together and rush to confront the enemy. In 1850, a member of Lin Ting-pang's clan was suspected of raping a housemaid of Lin Ma-sheng's, which provoked a huge fight between the two families in which Lin Ting-pang was killed by one of Lin Ma-sheng's bodyguards. Since the murder involved two influential clans, local officials took considerable time to solve the case. Ultimately, the Lins spent large sums of money to bring the suit all the way to the central yamen in Peking, a process that took seven years.

The fortunes of the Lin family improved during the fourth generation of Lin Wen-ch'a (1828–1864). At the time of Lin Ting-pang's death, Lin Wen-ch'a was already twenty-three years old. During his youth, Lin Wen-ch'a had enjoyed playing with guns and knives and admired the historical heroes Kuan Yu and Yueh Fei. Lin himself was famous for being a born fighter and so after his father was killed, Lin Wen-ch'a planned to lead the whole family in an act of revenge. Prevented from taking action by his mother, Lin planned his revenge in secret. In 1851, he led two hundred family militia and killed the guard who had murdered his father. Just to ensure that Lin Wen-ch'a's family would not carry out more revenge, Lin Ma-sheng reported the incident to the Taiwan prefect and even to the Fukien inspector and the Fukien–Chekiang governor-general, which ultimately led to Lin Wen-ch'a's becoming wanted by the police.

During the period of conflict between Lin Ma-sheng and Lin Wen-ch'a, many uprisings broke out in Taiwan while at the same time the coastal areas of Fukien were threatened by T'ai-p'ing forces. In 1853, when Lin Mu of Feng-shan county learned that T'ai-p'ing troops had captured the city of Nanking, he called together the local heads in Chang-hua and Chia-yi and organized an uprising. It was said that from Tainan prefecture to Feng-shan county, tens of thousands of households joined in the uprising while the number of Ch'ing soldiers stationed in the prefect city was no more than three thousand. Although the uprising lasted for only four months or so, it revealed the weakness and corruption of security in Taiwan. Earlier, Hsu Tsung-kan, who was the Taiwan intendant of the circuit from 1847 to 1854, pointed out that there were too many uprisings and conflicts occurring on the island. Since the government could not rely on its troops to effectively maintain order, Hsu was left with no choice but to encourage local influential family clans to train village residents to assist official troops in suppressing local uprisings and conflicts. In 1853, a large number of property owners in Fukien had formed the "Small Sword Society" (Hsiao tao hui) to oppose attempts by tenant farmers to avoid paying rent. Once the two sides began killing each other, the Small Sword Society launched an attack on the yamen and killed local government officials and for a while occupied Amoy as its base. Later, after being encircled by government troops and broken up, some members of this secret society escaped to Taiwan, where they attempted to occupy port cities and towns. Ch'ing troops stationed in Taiwan were obviously unable to put down their rebellion, and so someone recommended that Lin Wen-ch'a take control of the situation. In this way, he could finally make up for his earlier crimes against the Ch'ing. Lin Wen-ch'a did a good job, launching a successful counterattack against the Small Sword Society. In return, Lin and his militia were awarded a class six decoration, which opened the door for his family to enter the formal bureaucracy. Later, Lin Wen-ch'a donated a considerable sum of money to support government forces and was appointed by officials to head the Ch'ing's mobile forces.

As a result of Lin Wen-ch'a's outstanding performance, the officials gained trust in him, and, given that the situation in Taiwan had not yet stabilized, he was ordered to go to Fukien and Chekiang provinces to assist the Ch'ing government in its effort to suppress the T'ai-p'ings. From 1859 to 1863, Lin Wen-ch'a led three thousand soldiers known as the "brave heroes of Taiwan" in winning a number of victories, which resulted in his eventually being promoted to several positions including commander-in-chief of Fukien troops, the highest position ever attained by a Taiwanese during the Ch'ing dynasty. This position also ensured that he became an influential landlord and country gentry.

During the period when Lin Wen-ch'a fought battles on the mainland, a large-scale uprising led by Tai Ch'ao-ch'un broke out in Lin's hometown in Taiwan (1862–1865). The Tai Ch'ao-ch'un family was a prominent clan in central Taiwan with three generations as renowned and wealthy landowners and with prominent positions in the military defense system for northern Taiwan. Before the uprising, his elder brother, Tai Wan-sheng, had joined with other wealthy landlords in forming secret societies similar to the Land God Society (T'u ti kung hui) and the Eight Diagrams Society (Pa kua hui). The purpose of these societies was to protect property and water rights and to resist rival clans. Tai Wan-sheng himself organized the Heaven and Earth Society to train militia. Many landlords and wealthy households thought that since the government troops were unable to provide armed protection of their cultivation rights and personal safety they had no choice but to join Tai's organization. It was said that, at the height of its influence, ten thousand or so people were members of the organization while Tai Wan-sheng became the leader of all the local strongmen.[34]

As Tai Wan-sheng was gradually enhancing his power, several members (of his organization) abused their position and caused local disturbances. For this reason, in 1862 the government moved to outlaw the activities of the Heaven and Earth Society. In response, Tai Wan-sheng organized the local strongmen to kill local government officials in a large-scale uprising that spread throughout central Taiwan. In 1863, Lin Wen-ch'a learned that his hometown of Wu-feng was under attack by rebels, so he returned to Taiwan to suppress the uprising. Soon, Tai Wan-sheng was caught and killed, but the other societies continued to fight to the end and the uprising was not put down until 1865.

After the Tai Wan-sheng incident ended, the Lin Wen-ch'a family inventoried and seized the property of local strongmen who had participated in the uprising. According to estimates by Huang Fusan, from 1864 to 1865 the property of the Lin family increased dramatically as it purchased large chunks of these lands at cut-rate prices. Over the years, the Lin family built mansions and ancestral temples as a way to increase the family's social status and prominence. The Lin family also expanded its marital ties in an attempt to combine with local strongmen to build up their regional power. In addition, the Lins also donated huge sums of money to local temples and ultimately became the primary leader of the Ma-tsu Society.[35] In short, by the 1860s, the Lin family had emerged as the representative of the local elites who, by virtue of their landholdings, had become the most powerful groups in Taiwan.

Conclusion

This chapter focuses on three representative examples of landlord families that assumed the role of local elites in Taiwan during the Ch'ing dynasty: the Chang family of Taipei, the P'an family in central Taiwan, and the Lin family of Wu-feng. The Changs represented the entrepreneurial type of landlord, who came to Taiwan to open up and develop land in the early eighteenth century. The P'ans were an example of a family that in the eighteenth century moved from the position of P'ing-p'u tribal leader to become a large-scale property owner by engaging in the extensive leasing of land while also accepting the authority of the Ch'ing government. In addition, they readily adjusted to and became involved in the commercial economy of the Han. The Lin family of Wu-feng demonstrated how, beginning in the eighteenth century and extending into the nineteenth, a landlord family emerged as local strongmen. The common feature among the three landlord families was that they benefited from the multifaceted and flexible property rights system on Taiwan while also investing in land development and the leasing of agricultural land from which they collected rents and accumulated huge sums of wealth. They also traded their property rights in exchange for capital that was used for other types of investment. The same approach to land use was also apparent in southern Fukien province and the Pearl river delta of Kuangtung at different stages of the Ming and Ch'ing dynasties.[36] But after the immigrants came to Taiwan, they substantially modified their original concept of property rights. In the early period, all landlords directed their efforts at gaining cultivation rights over the land and hiring on tenants to work the fields as the way to gradually accumulate their wealth. At the same time that they established a landlord–tenant relationship, however, the phenomenon appeared of dividing up the structure of land ownership. That is, the landlords maintained their land-owning status while the tenants who had developed the land became the de facto landlords with management rights. After the end of the eighteenth century, a major influx of immigrants from the mainland promoted the speedy growth of the tenant market and also stimulated the commercialization of property rights. During that era, many landlord families traded their tenant rights and collecting small rents from other tenants to earn huge profits. The landlords described in this article were all land-leasing landlords, but not owners who were actually involved in the direct management of their farmland.

At the beginning of the nineteenth century, the local elites proliferated along with the increase in population and the growth of villages and towns. Although landlord families were the leading members of the rural communities, in the towns and villages, however, leading positions in the temples and public safety organizations were held by rich merchants and local landlords. This role of the merchant class in the towns and villages is, however, beyond the scope of this chapter. By examining the rural landlord class, we can tell that, after settling in Taiwan, they used any means to establish cooperative relationships with the local Ch'ing bureaucracy. For instance, the Chang family became wealthy by investing in property rights and constructing irrigation and water control systems. Chang family members also exhibited an entrepreneurial spirit and hence were aware of the importance of establishing cordial relations with the bureaucracy from which they gained fame and status for family members. Later, a member of the Changs successfully passed the scholar-official exam and was able to play a vital role in resolving disputes with other families and successfully protecting the Chang family property. The history of the P'an and Lin families also demonstrated how they frequently employed their own armed militia to assist the Ch'ing government in putting down uprisings for which they won various orders of merit and were able to expand their property holdings and family power. The fact that most landlord families and local strongmen were not formal members of the bureaucracy with imperial title, as was the case with mainland gentry, indicates that until the mid-nineteenth century local elites in Taiwan retained their flare for independent action and individual acts of bravery and did not focus solely on gaining fame and fortune.[37]

Some scholars argue that, from the 1860s onward, the opening up of Taiwan's ports to the outside world produced the phenomenon known as the "interiorization" of rural social organization, religion, and the culture of local elites. On the one hand, the Ch'ing government feared that foreign forces intended to invade Taiwan and so it sent highly capable officials to the island to build its defenses and to engage in social education while it also encouraged local elites to enter the bureaucracy. On the other hand, the opening up of ports promoted the production and export of tea, camphor, and sugarcane, all of which by the 1870s brought about remarkable changes in the economic structure of the entire island. The previous agricultural economy centered on rice and sugarcane produced solely for the mainland market was transformed into a highly commercial agriculture that supplied products primarily to the world market. In this new environment, many new landlords and merchants, after establishing a stable economic basis, intentionally weakened the social network and power structure of the local strongmen. In its place there emerged the traditional town gentry with interest in building ancestral temples, maintaining family histories, donating funds to schools, and gaining fame and status for family members and relatives to enter the bureaucracy.[38] Indeed, the cultural tendency of the elite class of Taiwan formed an interesting contrast with the gentry class on the mainland, where available research indicates that during and after the T'ai-p'ing rebellion (1850–1870) the social structure of the mainland elite became more and more militarized, while the gentry class responded to the weaker central power of the Ch'ing government by forming its own militia and becoming local strongmen with control over substantial territory.[39] In sum, this and other historical phenomena indicate that further analysis is needed of the salient transformations in the elite structure on Taiwan during the 1860–90 period.

Notes

1. Ch'en Ch'iu-k'un, "The Development of Taiwan in the First Half of the Eighteenth Century," in *Journal of Chinese Cultural Renaissance* 8, no. 12 (1975), pp. 60–66; Yang Guo-zhen,"The Development of agrarian Taiwan in the Early Qing Period," *Journal of Taiwan Research*, no. 13 (1983), pp. 1–23; Chen Kongli, *An Outline of Taiwan History* (Beijing: Jiu-chou Publishing Co., 1996), 153–155.

2. Harry Lamley, "Subethnic Rivalry in the Ch'ing Period," in *The Anthropology of*

Taiwanese Society, ed. Emily Ahern and Hill Gates (Stanford: Stanford University Press, 1981), 303–305.

3. John Shepherd, *Statecraft and Political Economy on the Taiwan Frontier, 1600–1800* (Stanford: Stanford University Press, 1993), 161.

4. Teng Kongchao, "Impact of Qing Dynasty Restrictions Surreptitious Immigration and Visitation by Relatives from Coastal Regions of the Mainland Across the Straits to Taiwan," in *Ten Years of Taiwan Studies* (Taipei: Poyuan Publications, 1991), 345–370.

5. Hsu Hsueh-chi, *Chinese Military Camps on Taiwan During the Ch'ing Dynasty* (Taipei: Modern History Research Institute, 1987), 109; Chen Kongli, *An Outline of Taiwan History*, 235–238.

6. Lamley, "Subethnic Rivalry in the Ch'ing Period," 304–305; Chen Kongli, *Social Studies of Immigrants to Taiwan During the Ch'ing Dynasty* (Xiamen: Xiamen University Press, 1990), 261–262; Liu Ni-ling, *Research Study of Demographic Changes on Taiwan During the Ch'ing Dynasty* (Taipei: History Research Institute, National Teacher's University of Taiwan, 1983), 109–120.

7. Hsu Wen-hsiung, "Frontier Social Organization and Social Disorder in Ch'ing Taiwan," in *China's Island Frontier: Studies in the Historical Geography of Taiwan,* ed. Ronald G. Knapp (Honolulu: University of Hawaii Press, 1980), 87–105; Liu Ni-ling, *Research Study of Demographic Changes,* 289–290; Lin Weisheng. "Origins of Parochial Conflicts on Taiwan During the Ch'ing Dynasty," in *Collection of Research Papers on Taiwan History*, pt. 1, comp. Chang Yanhui et al. (Taipei: Yushan Publishing House, 1986), 263–288.

8. Yang Guo-zhen, (1988), *Studies of Land Contract Documents in the Ming-Qing Period* (Fukien: Ren-min Publishing Co., 1988), 113–122.

9. Wang Shih-ching, "The Lin Pen-yuan Leasing Business and the Anti-Japanese Resistance of Hsing Yi-wei of Wu-pei," *Taiwan Archives*, 38, no. 4 (1987); Stevan Harrell, "From Xiedou to Yijun: The Decline of Ethnicity in Northern Taiwan," *Late Imperial China*, 11, no. 1 (1990): 99–127.

10. Shepherd, *Statecraft and Political Economy*, 191–198.

11. Hsu Hsueh-chi, *Chinese Military Camps on Taiwan.*

12. Ch'en Ch'iu-k'un, *Aboriginal Property Rights on Taiwan During the Qing Dynasty: Transformation of the Land Under Bureaucratic Rule, Han Tenancy, and Anli Tribal [Ownership], 1700–1895* (Taipei: Modern History Research Institute, Academica Sinica, 1994), 115–119.

13. Susan Naquin and Evelyn Rawski, *China in the Eighteenth Century* (New Haven: Yale University Press, 1987), 225–228

14. Liu Ni-ling, *Research Study of Demographic Changes,* 186–188.

15. Lin Weisheng, "Origins of Parochial Conflicts on Taiwan During the Ch'ing Dynasty"; David Ownby, "The Ethnic Feud in Qing Taiwan: What Is this Violence Business, Anyway? An Interpretation of the 1782 Zhang-Quan Xiedou," in *Late Imperial China* 11, no. 1 (1990), pp. 75–98. 1990.

16. Liu Ni-ling, *Research Study of Demographic Changes*, 282–283, 325.

17. Cheng Zhenghan, et al., ed., *Materials for Economic History in Qing Veritable Records (Shih-lu): Agriculture Section*, vol. 2 (Beijing: Beijing University Press, 1989) p. 56.

18. Mark Allee, *Law and Local Society in Late Imperial China: Northern Taiwan in the Ninteenth Century* (Stanford: Stanford University Press, 1994), 256–259.

19. Chuang Ying-chang, "Issues of Lineage Development in Taiwanese Society," in *Journal of the Institute of Ethnology*, Academia Sinica, 36 (1975), pp. 121–126.

20. Chuang Ying-chang and Ch'en Lien-t'ung, "Lineage and Social Development of Tou-feng in Northern Taiwan," in *The First Symposium on History and Chinese Social*

Change, Taipei: The Sun Yat-sen Insitute for Social Sciences and Philosophy, 1982, pp. 361–367; Cheng Zhenghan et al., ed. *The Qing Archives on Economic History: Agricultural Section*, vol. 2 (Beijing: Beijing University Press, 1989), 199–226.

21. Ibid.

22. Chen Chunsheng. "The Three Mountain King Sect and Taiwan Immigrant Society," *Collection of Research Studies on Minority Society*, vol. 80 (Taipei: Academica Sinica, 1995), 61–113.

23. Lin Mei-jung, "From Reverence to Belief: The Geographical Formation and Development of Taiwan Folk Society," in *Chinese Maritime Development History Research Papers*, pt. 3 (Taipei: Academia Sinica, Chungshan Social Science Research Institute, 1988), 95–125.

24. Tsai yun-chieh, "The structure of Immigrant Society in Ch'ing Taiwan," in *Society and Cultural Change in Taiwan*. Taipei: Institute of Ethnology, Academia Sinica, 1986, pp. 45–68.

25. Huang Chaochin, *Prosperous Families and Territorial Society of the Zhuzhan Area During the Qing Dynasty with a Focus on the Zheng and Lin Families* (Taipei: National History Archives, 1985), 131–141.

26. Liu Ni-ling. *Research Study of Demographic Changes*, 321–325.

27. Yin Ch'ang-yi. "The History of the Chang Shih-hsing Family Case Study of an Immigrant Family to Taiwan During the Early Period of the Ch'ing Dynasty, 1702–1983" (Taipei: Chang Shih-hsing Family History Research Committee, 1983), 121–138.

28. Ibid., 128–134.

29. Ch'en Ch'iu-k'un, "Minority Policies and Traditional Aboriginal Property Rights on Taiwan During the Early Ch'ing Dynasty, 1690–1766," *A Collection of Papers on the Early Stages of Modern Chinese History* (Taipei: Modern History Research Institute, Academica Sinica, 1989), 1023–1038.

30. For more on the history of the Anli tribe, see Ch'en Ch'iu-k'un, *Aboriginal Property Rights on Taiwan During the Ch'ing Dynasty: Transformation of the Land Under Bureaucratic Rule, Han Tenancy, and An-li Tribal Ownership, 1700–1895* (Taipei: Modern History Research Institute, Academica Sinica, 1994).

31. Chen Kongli, *An Outline of Taiwan History* (Beijing: Jiu-chou Publishing Co., 1996), 153–155.

32. Johanna Meskill, *A Chinese Pioneer Family: The Lins of Wu-feng, Taiwan, 1729–1985* (Princeton: Princeton University Press, 1979); Joseph Esherick and Mary Rankin, *Elites in Late Imperial China* (Berkeley: University of California Press, 1990), 13–24.

33. Huang Fu-san, *The Rise of the Lin Family of Wu-feng: From Crossing the Straits to Opening the Land, 1729–1864* (Taipei: Independent Evening Post, 1987), 58–65.

34. Liu Ni-ling, *Research Study of Demographic Changes*, 288.

35. Huang Fu-sun, *The Downfall of the Lin Family of Wu-feng, 1861–1885* (Taipei: Independent Evening Post, 1992), pp. 57–71, 85–86.

36. Chen Chenhan et al., ed., *The Qing Archives on Economic History*, 199–226; Helen Siu and David Faure, *Down to Earth: The Territorial Bond in South China* (Stanford: Stanford University Press, 1996), 4–11, 209–222.

37. Chen Chunsheng. "The Three Mountain King Sect and Taiwan Immigrant Society," 61–113.

38. Li Kuo-chi, "Social Transformation During the Ch'ing Dynasty," *China Scholar's Journal*, 5, no. 2 (1978): 589–592; Chen Kangli, *Social Studies of Immigrants to Taiwan During the Qing Dynasty*. Xiamen: Xiamen University Press, 1990), 53–56.

39. Phillip Kuhn, *Rebellion and Its Enemies in Late Imperial China* (Cambridge: Harvard University Press, 1970); Esherick and Rankin, *Elites in Late Imperial China*, 13–24.

7

From Treaty Ports
to Provincial Status, 1860–1894

Robert Gardella

Presbyterian Chapel at the Tainan Seminary in Tainan.
(Photo by M. Rubinstein)

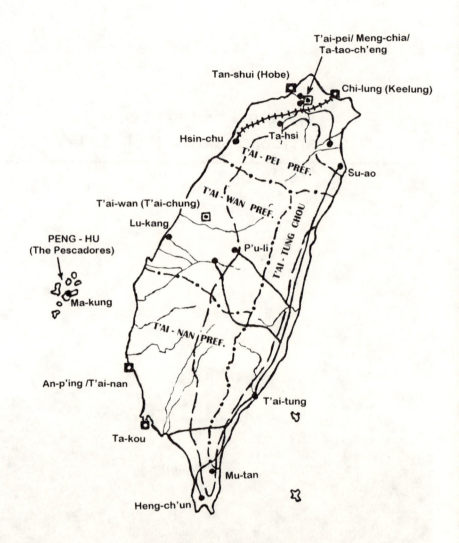

T'ai-pei/ Meng-chia/
Ta-tao-ch'eng

Tan-shui (Hobe)

Chi-lung (Keelung)

Hsin-chu

Ta-hsi

Su-ao

T'AI - PEI PREF.

T'ai-wan (T'ai-chung)

T'AI - WAN PREF.

Lu-kang

PENG - HU
(The Pescadores)

P'u-li

T'AI - TUNG CHOU

Ma-kung

T'AI - NAN PREF.

An-p'ing /T'ai-nan

T'ai-tung

Ta-kou

Mu-tan

Heng-ch'un

LATE CH' ING T'AI-WAN (1885-95)

—.—.— prefectural boundary   ╫╫╫ railroad   ▣ treaty port

—— —— aboriginal boundary   —— road   ◙ capital

● other city / town / village

(Source: adapted from Li Kuo-ch'i, <u>Chung-kuo hsien-tai hua...</u> T'ai-pei, 1982)

A single theme dominated Taiwan's history from 1860–1894, distinguishing the late nineteenth century from a preceding era in which changes were for the most part indigenously generated, and the half-century of Japanese colonial domination to follow. That theme—or predicament, at least in the eyes of Ch'ing authorities—was the greatly intensified involvement of the island in the political, economic, and cultural cross-currents sweeping Pacific Asia in the second half of the nineteenth century. For the first time since the seventeenth century, large sectors of Taiwan's agrarian economy became closely meshed with the market mechanisms of international commerce. Tea, camphor, and sugar exports flourished after the opening, at opposite ends of the island, of treaty ports legitimated by the Peking round of Sino-foreign settlements in 1860. Again, for the first time since the late 1600s, Taiwan emerged as one of China's pressing "national security" concerns. Large-scale foreign military interventions punctuated this period on three occasions, vividly exposing Taiwan's vulnerable status within the late Ch'ing empire. In 1874 the Japanese launched a punitive expedition in southern Taiwan, an imperialist probe that threatened to bring about war between Japan and China. In 1884–85 French naval and land forces blockaded the island and assaulted Keelung (Chilung), Tan-shui (Tam-sui), and the P'eng-hu islands (Pescadores). Japanese military occupation, although vigorously contested by popular insurrections, followed Taiwan's cession to that country in 1895. In each of these cases, conflicts that arose essentially over other issues in other territorial settings came to involve this no longer "solitary island" on the margins of the East and South China Seas.[1]

While they were always few in number, Western merchants, Christian missionaries, and civil and military officials were far from insignificant in the turbulent history of these years. They were harbingers, and at times catalysts, of rapid and often unsettling changes occurring in various aspects of life in late nineteenth-century Taiwan. The swift expansion of commodity production for the global market, the intensified exploitation of forested highlands that exacerbated Han–aboriginal conflict, the reintroduction of Christianity and its cultural concomitants (especially Western medicine and education), and the pressing need to reconstitute Ch'ing authority in the face of foreign challenges all reflected the direct or indirect influence of outsiders.

Taiwan's officials, local strongmen and landlords, merchants, farmers, and workers on the whole profited, albeit far from equally, from trade-induced economic expansion. The symbolic and substantive center of the island's wealth and power, if not its higher culture, dramatically shifted from southwestern coasts and fertile plains centered upon venerable Tainan (the new designation of the former prefectural capital of T'ai-wan-fu) to the northern hills and river valleys encompassing Taipei, the raw new provincial capital. Local elite culture came more and more to resemble its counterparts on the mainland, as political power based on uncouth wealth and undisguised coercion perceptibly gave way to cultivated scholar-gentry styles of life and norms of leadership.

Three of nineteenth-century China's most capable and innovative administrators—Shen Pao-chen, Ting Jih-ch'ang, and Liu Ming-ch'uan—presided over the most dynamic period in the entire checkered history of Ch'ing rule in Taiwan. Loosely encoded under the term "self-strengthening," their various programs commonly strove to enhance Taiwan's domestic stability and external security. Administrative reshufflings and reorganization culminated in the formal attainment of provincial status in 1885. Vigorous efforts were made to enhance Taiwan's shaky revenue base through fiscal rationalization, extend its settled frontiers via Han Chinese colonization and aboriginal "pacification," and introduce strategically significant elements of Western technology and techniques (i.e., military hardware, a railroad, indigenous steamship services, modern mining, telegraphic links to the mainland, a modern postal service). Striking as they appear in the late Ch'ing context, these innovations and reforms were simply unequal to the larger task of ensuring Taiwan's political fate in the jungle of fin de siècle East Asian power politics.

The Opening of Taiwan: The Initial Phase (1860–1874)

One way of assessing Taiwan's geopolitical status in the last half of the nineteenth century envisages the island standing "at the interface between the traditional Chinese world order and the modern capitalist world system."[2] The expression "capitalist world system" refers to Immanuel Wallerstein's concentric ring conceptualization of modern world history centered on a modern European "core," which directly dominates the political economy of an inner belt of "semiperipheral" states and gradually subordinates a distant penumbra of less important "peripheral" states. More specifically, the theory sets late nineteenth-century China on the periphery of a core of dynamic, expansive Western states. Since China's sovereignty was diminished after two rounds of spectacularly unsuccessful wars with European powers, post-1860 Taiwan ipso facto entered an era marked by political deterioration and foreign exploitation of the island's natural and human resources.[3]

Another, less deterministic, perspective—one more nuanced and more convincing to the present writer—argues, in contrast, that signs of economic growth and political regeneration were more apparent over the 1860–94 period as a whole. The capacity of Taiwan's populace, or at least the Han Chinese majority of it, to respond rapidly and creatively to new opportunities and challenges outweighed the adverse aspects of opening a few small ports to foreign trade and residence.[4] In view of Taiwan's obvious locational vulnerability and comparatively small size, one might also recall that the treaty system itself, along with the assertiveness of Ch'ing authorities (not to mention the island's Han and aboriginal inhabitants) served to ward off outrageous forms of foreign intervention before 1895. Taiwan was not like Borneo or Singapore. No enterprising Western soldiers of fortune successfully established a tropical kingdom or founded an imperial city-state on Taiwan. Consider the clear-cut failure of a colonization scheme concocted by a German opium and camphor trader, James Milisch, and his British partner, James Horn, in 1868–69. Although the two adventurers got to the point of actually fortifying an outpost in a remote coastal valley near Su-ao in northeast Taiwan, Ch'ing authorities successfully pressured the British and Prussian governments to disavow the illicit project and its expatriate sponsors.[5]

Consuls, Merchants, and Missionaries: Some Sketches

In 1860, Tan-shui (also known as Ho-pei) and An-p'ing, two of the principal seaports on Taiwan's western coastline, were formally "opened" by the Treaty of Peking. The settlement was negotiated amidst the humiliating Anglo-French occupation of the Ch'ing capital, climaxing two years of renewed warfare after the inconclusive Tientsin treaty negotiations of 1858. By opportunistically extending their treaty rights to include adjacent settlements, foreigners quickly established a southerly presence at T'ai-wan-fu (next to An-p'ing) and Ta-kou (the site of modern Kao-hsiung), as well as at Keelung in the northeast. The same elastic diplomacy also enabled Westerners to reside at two Tan-shui river ports—time-honored Meng-chia, where they were decidedly unwelcome, and rapidly emerging Ta-t'ao-ch'eng, where their trade was actively solicited.[6]

The very rapid growth of Taiwan's outbound commerce in tea, camphor, and sugar was balanced largely by imports of foreign silver and foreign opium. The number of Westerners who pursued such trades during the first decade and a half after 1860, indeed the number of resident foreigners of any description, was unimpressive. Arriving at Ta-kou in May 1866, a visiting British naturalist depicted a European community consisting of a British vice-consul, one or two British merchants, a commissioner of the Imperial Maritime Customs, and a pair of "medical gentlemen." At Meng-chia, the same traveler encountered a single European inhabitant, the shady German trader Milisch mentioned above.[7] By comparison, at least forty-six Western merchant ships (the majority of them British) were wrecked off Taiwan's poorly charted, still-unlighted coasts from 1861 to 1874. It is reasonably safe to say that more foreigners were unwittingly stranded on the island during these early years than actually chose to dwell there.[8]

While the United States neglected to establish consular representation on Taiwan, choosing instead to economize by maintaining its consulate in Amoy, Great Britain's weightier range of interests were consistently if not always intelligently represented on the island after 1861. The British consular presence, in fact, was tantamount to *all* Western diplomatic representation on Taiwan between 1861 and 1895, since resident British officials personified the interests of half-a-dozen other foreign powers, including the United States (after 1875).[9]

This is not to say very much. Assignments on Taiwan were regarded by British civil servants as hardship posts, accompanied by high mortality rates because of tropical fevers and rugged living conditions. An officer who had failed in his duties elsewhere might anticipate a demotion to Ta-kou or Tan-shui. This had some unfortunate consequences for Sino-Western relations, most notably in the case of John Gibson (a vice-consul recently downgraded from Hankow to Taiwan) in 1868–69.[10] Antimissionary incidents, combined with a prolonged dispute (over British traders' right to export camphor without regard to current local monopoly regulations), led to a nasty personal confrontation between Gibson and Ta-kou's circuit intendant in mid-1868. Backing up threats of force with actual coercion, Gibson called in a small-scale naval attack to seize and hold An-p'ing until British grievances were satisfied. Gibson's wild correspondence and rash behavior in this so-called Camphor War awakened second thoughts among British diplomats in Peking and London. They had no desire to sanction swashbuckling activities by unstable subordinates that threatened the status quo. Cashiered from Her Majesty's Service in disgrace in mid-1869, Gibson died soon thereafter in Amoy, broken and impoverished.[11]

While Gibson lost what remained of his diplomatic career in Taiwan, John Dodd made his commercial fortune there. Arriving in northern Taiwan in 1864, this bold, pugnacious British merchant quickly established himself as a leading entrepreneur during the rapid emergence of the export tea trade. Dodd was exploring camphor forests in 1865 when he came across cinnamon trees and tall tea bushes. Finding the startup costs of a cinnamon trade too high, Dodd turned his attention to tea, as he proudly related some years later:

> On making inquiries I found that between Kelung and Banka [Keelung and Meng-chia], and to the south-west of the latter town, small patches of tea were cultivated in the gardens of farmers, but that it was grown principally for home consumption. All the tea I could get I bought up, and finding that it fetched a good price in Macao, I at once made loans to the farmers, through my compradore, for the purpose of extending the cultivation, and also imported slips of the tea plant from Amoy. I then started firing on a small scale at Banka, and after-wards took larger premises at Twa-tu-tia [Ta-t'ao ch'eng]. In the course of three or four years, Formosan teas acquired a reputation in America . . . and the exports increased by bounds year after year.[12]

Dodd here refers to his "compradore"—the term for a Chinese middleman employed by a Western trading firm. Li Ch'un-sheng served Dodd in that key capacity for a number of years. Born into a poor family in Amoy, Li eventually went into business on his own and became a wealthy tea and camphor exporter.[13] As regards his tea-processing business in Meng-chia and Ta-t'ao-ch'eng, Dodd apparently needed all the help he could get. In 1868 two of his Western employees were attacked and almost murdered by an angry crowd in Meng-chia as they tried to gain possession of a rented warehouse. The result was the dispatch of a British gunboat at the request of Tan-shui's acting British consul (a U.S. gunboat's coincidental arrival enhanced the pressure), and collection of damages and apologies from Ch'ing authorities literally on the spot.[14] The tables were turned on Dodd in an analogous property dispute in 1886, however. When Dodd and his employees brutally pressed a disputed claim to some Ta-t'ao-ch'eng property by roughing up, then threatening the life of, a senior Chinese official, the British consulate rejected his claim and apologized for his actions. Anything but a diplomat, this "fussy" and "obstinate" merchant did very well by Taiwan, accumulating a small fortune (more than 10,000 pounds sterling) by the time he died back home in 1907.[15]

The prospect of saving souls rather than silver attracted both Catholic and Protestant missionaries to the island after 1860, where their protracted efforts frequently met with less than cordial receptions. Perhaps the most influential Christian missionary in late nineteenth-century Taiwan was the Canadian Presbyterian George Mackay. Here he describes his uncomfortable early sojourns in Bang-kah (Meng-chia)—"the Gibraltar of heathenism in North Formosa," as he colorfully phrased it—in 1875:

> The citizens of Bang-kah, old and young, are daily toiling for money, money—cash, cash. They are materialistic, superstitious dollar-seekers. At every visit, when passing through their streets, we are maligned, jeered at, and abused. Hundreds of children run ahead, yelling with derisive shouts; others follow, pelting us with orange-peel, mud, and rotten eggs.[16]

By 1893 Mackay was being paraded through Meng-chia's streets in a sedan chair as an honored member of the community, and a small Christian congregation could routinely worship without harassment.[17] The change in popular attitudes reflected adroit leadership and a sustained, multifaceted effort to root Presbyterianism in Taiwanese soil after a lapse of two centuries.

Reformed Protestants nonetheless did not have Taiwan all to themselves as a mission field. A small delegation of Dominicans dispatched from the Philippines in the 1860s sought Roman Catholic converts in Keelung, Ta-kou, and T'ai-wan-fu. Apparently marked by public indifference and the hostility of local officials, their efforts had little success among Han Chinese, yet some converts were made among the plains aboriginal villagers of southern Taiwan.[18]

Murray Rubinstein's research on the mission history of that period reveals that British and Canadian Presbyterian pioneers actively promoted an indigenous church, one that closely identified with local communities and delivered social services as well as the gospel. Historically favoring independent, self-supporting congregations, Presbyterians laid great stress upon translating the Bible and evangelical tracts into the Southern Min dialect (the lingua franca of Taiwan) and training an indigenous clergy. The British mission in southern Taiwan dated from the mid-1860s, with the Canadians (and George Mackay) arriving in the far north in the early 1870s.[19]

Mackay established Western-style schools for boys and girls in Tan-shui and capped his educational initiatives by founding a seminary there known as Oxford College. His evangelical energies also led to the establishment of some sixty chapels in northern Taiwan by 1895.[20] British Presbyterians brought the practice of Western medicine to southern Taiwan in the mid-1860s, yet it was Mackay and his colleagues in the north who made the most lasting impression in this respect. When his Tan-shui clinic began operation in 1880, it treated 1,346 new patients during the course of the year; in 1890, merely a decade later, that total had nearly tripled to 3,696. The foundations of modern medical science and a basis for training indigenous practitioners of it were clearly in place on Taiwan by the end of the century.[21]

The effort to harvest souls for Christianity in late nineteenth-century Taiwan could be as prosaic as practicing amateur dentistry—witness George Mackay's description in 1895:

> Our usual custom in touring through the country is to take our stand in an open space, often on the stone steps of a temple, and, after singing a hymn or two, proceed to extract teeth, and then preach the message of the gospel. The sufferer usually stands while the operation is being performed, and the tooth, when removed, is laid on his hand. To keep the tooth would be to awaken suspicions regarding us in the Chinese mind. Several of the students are experts with the forceps, and we have frequently extracted a hundred teeth in less than an hour. I have myself, since 1873, extracted over twenty-one thousand, and the students and preachers have extracted nearly half that number.[22]

Chewing betel nut, a habit that Taiwanese share with several other Southeast Asian peoples, probably contributed to the high incidence of dental woes. Mackay's shrewd practice of returning extracted teeth to their rightful owners served to allay fears of black magic or sorcery—a persistent slander against missionaries at the time.[23] Far more teeth were pulled than conversions made in these grass-roots exhibitions of Western oral hygiene. In 1895 there were still only a few thousand Han and aboriginal Christians among a population of around 2.5 million.[24] Yet the long-term influence of Mackay and his colleagues, as indicated earlier, far exceeded that suggested by any head count of converts.

Commodities for the World Market: The Tea, Camphor, and Sugar Trades

The outstanding feature of Taiwan's economic history from 1860 to 1894 was the rapid growth of major commodity trades oriented to international markets—a scenario that, as fate would have it, had an even more decisive impact on the island's development a century later. Ramon Myers aptly sums up the situation as follows: "Prior to 1858 population growth, settlement of new land, and slowly expanding commerce determined Taiwan's economic growth. After 1858 new trade opportunities encouraged more specialization and greater production in agriculture for export."[25] Myers's view is more apt than Samuel Ho's dismissal of late Ch'ing Taiwan as "a closed, self-sufficient economy," one supposedly "incapable of responding in a sustained manner to the stimulus of external trade."[26] In basic functional terms, Taiwan's economy proved quite capable of facilitating the mobilization of land and labor to support substantial commodity trades. Not surprisingly, considering the island's long experience as a commercial backwater, what was lacking were sources of trading capital and overseas market connections.

Indigenous financial support as well as suitable transport and marketing services capable of handling international trade were notable by their absence. Mid-nineteenth-century Taiwan had a basic credit system geared to providing loans for local agriculture and commerce—landlord and merchant households with funds to spare were the principal sources of loans, and land was a common form of collateral. Overseas transport by and large meant coastal shipping to and from the mainland in local watercraft.[27] Foreign commercial firms, banks, and merchant vessels arrived to provide these essential services, not out of altruism but because there was money to be made in dealing with Taiwan.

In the reproachful judgment of a number of modern Chinese historians, Taiwan thereby sank to the lowly status of an economic dependency or "semicolony" of Western commercial capitalism.[28] On balance this appraisal is not very convincing, although it may well reflect valid concern about the way the island came to be integrated into the world marketplace and what effects that had on its inhabitants. Foreign commerce did carry some unfortunate consequences for Taiwan—chief among them an increased consumption of imported opium and heightened Sino-aboriginal conflicts—yet it is misleading to argue that it negatively affected Taiwan as a whole. There is considerable evidence that would suggest the opposite was the case.

Exports of rice and sugar to the China mainland were the staples of Taiwan's external trade before 1860. Table 7.1 indicates the continued significance of the sugar trade, and the sharp decline of rice exports because of rising local demand. Above all, the figures point up the volatile state of the camphor industry and the astonishing growth of the tea trade in value terms from the 1860s to the 1890s.

During the same period, Taiwan's imports consisted of consumer goods, with opium being the single largest imported item in value terms. Samuel Ho notes that opium accounted for 45–75 percent of all imports over these three decades. When Japanese colonial authorities conducted a survey in 1901, they discovered that 152,044 people (fully 5 percent of the island's population) were opium smokers. Foreign cotton and woolen textiles, the second most popular category of goods in demand, constituted some 12–16 percent of the remaining imports. The most hopeful trend in an import trade dominated by drug trafficking was the growing diversification of imported products, which, as Samuel Ho remarks, "perhaps reflected the increased prosperity brought about by the expanding foreign trade."[29] Opium made up 72.6 percent of all imports by value in 1868–70,

Table 7.1

Major Exports as a Percentage of Value of Total Exports, 1868–1894 (annual averages)

	1868–70	1871–75	1876–80	1881–85	1886–90	1891–96
Camphor	8.4	3.3	2.3	0.8	0.9	9.1
Sugar	59.6	60.7	46.9	36.4	26.9	25.6
Tea	9.4	26.6	46.1	58.7	66.6	58.4
Rice	9.8	2.3	0.1	—	—	0.2
Other	12.8	7.1	4.6	4.1	5.6	6.7
Total	100.0	100.0	100.0	100.0	100.0	100.0

Source: Adapted from Samuel P.S. Ho, *Economic Development of Taiwan, 1860–1970* (New Haven: Yale University Press, 1978), p. 14, Table 2.2.

but only 43.5 percent in 1891–96; during the same period "miscellaneous" imports rose from 8.9 to 38.6 percent of the total.[30]

The Camphor Trade

The manufacture of camphor was really a homespun form of economic forestry rather than a type of agricultural industry akin to tea or sugar production. Like tea growing, however, camphor making forced the pace of exploitation of the densely wooded uplands of northern and central Taiwan, which in turn provoked incessant Sino-aboriginal clashes. Between 1881 and 1890, for example, camphor exports often came to a standstill because of such armed conflict. The product for which Hakka hillmen and other Chinese literally risked their heads was obtained by felling stately camphor trees and reducing them to large heaps of wood chips. Whitish camphor crystals were then extracted from the chips by a crude but effective distillation apparatus set up on the spot. The rights to fell camphor trees in a given area were customarily negotiated with resident aboriginal tribes, but these niceties were often disregarded and the natives defrauded. If camphor gatherers tended to cut corners, they themselves often owed money to native and foreign merchants. The upshot of these loans was that merchants gained exclusive rights to the producers' hard-earned output.[31]

Between 1863 and 1868, camphor purchases and sales in Taiwan were under an official monopoly, which in practice meant that the trade was contracted out to Chinese merchants. The set purchase price for a picul (133.3 lbs.) of the substance was $6, and the selling price to foreign exporters was $16; local authorities and the contracting merchants shared the $10 difference. At Hong Kong the camphor usually sold for $18, leaving a scant $2 per picul profit for aggrieved Western traders. The 1868 "Camphor War" suppressed the monopoly.

With middlemen eliminated, slightly more went to the producers ($7.50 per picul), exporters' profits soared, and aggrieved Ch'ing officials lost some $60,000 in annual revenues. The trade was stagnating by the late 1880s, however, when chemical research in the West came to its rescue. Camphor suddenly became a hot commodity on the world market, while profits and government revenues rose to unprecedented heights.[32]

Traditionally employed simply as a medicinal ingredient and aromatic, camphor became an important component in the industrial production of celluloid (used in making film and a primitive type of plastic). More ominously, it was essential to the manufacture of smokeless gunpowder for new types of Western ordnance, including the machine gun, repeating rifle, and rapid-fire artillery. Smokeless powder did not obscure battlefields, reveal hidden gun positions, or foul weapons as much as conventional gunpowder.[33] In the early 1890s, Taiwan was the source of at least two-thirds of the world's camphor supply; its export price rose to $30–36 per picul during that period (average annual sales exceeded 4 million lbs. at that time). By levying high taxes on camphor stills (an effort to resuscitate the camphor monopoly having failed), revenue-starved provincial officials absorbed about half of these proceeds and producers about a third (some $10 per picul).[34]

Tea—The "Green Gold" of Taiwan

Although some tea was grown on Taiwan and marketed in mainland China well before the 1860s, opening of trade with the West made tea into the island's "green gold."[35] It became Taiwan's most valuable export during the latter half of the nineteenth century, as Americans in particular acquired a taste for "Formosa oolong" (*wu-lung*) tea (see Table 7.1). Unlike the camphor industry, which involved scattered groups of woodsmen and dealers operating in rugged mountainous areas, tea growing, processing, and trading came to include a large part of a settled population widely spread over the uplands, plateaus, and valleys of the northern third of Taiwan. Sugar production offers a more appropriate comparison with tea, but besides being spatially confined to the plains of southwest Taiwan, it actually decreased in importance during the late 1800s (note Table 7.1).

John Dodd's firm attracted rivals, facing competition from branches of four other British tea processing and packing firms in the early 1870s. After buying crudely fired tea from growers in the hinterland, foreign merchants refired it at their own premises in Ta-t'ao-ch'eng (tea processing required two stages—the first to ready fresh tea leaves for local marketing, the second to prepare the final product). The firing rooms contained from fifty to three hundred stoves, with adjacent warehouses for tea storage. Oolong tea leaves were piled into baskets above the stoves, slowly roasted over charcoal fires, and then carefully packed into sturdy lead-lined wooden chests.[36]

Early twentieth-century tea pickers in Taiwan. *(Photo: S. Naquin/S.Cochran)*

Enterprising local and mainland Chinese merchants recognized opportunity for themselves in these Western initiatives. By the mid-1870s, they had assumed full control of tea manufacturing (thirty-nine Chinese firms were so engaged in 1876, all but six of them owned by Taiwanese and Amoyese interests). Western business enterprises henceforth largely confined themselves to the purely commercial end of the business—a far from negligible role, as it involved financing the trade, buying tea, and dispatching it overseas from Tan-shui via the intermediary port of Amoy.[37]

Taiwan's tea trade relied upon the capitalization of foreign and mainland Chinese banks. Agencies or branches of major Western exchange banks, especially the Hongkong and Shanghai Bank's Amoy branch, extended loans to foreign exporters and several types of native banks. These funds were relent directly (or indirectly, using mainland Chinese brokerage firms called *ma-chen-kuan* or "merchant houses") to the native tea reprocessors, who in turn used most of the capital to buy crude tea from and extend credit to local cultivators. The rapid expansion of the island's tea production could not have occurred in the absence of this pyramid of sustained credit relationships.[38]

Two patterns of tea cultivation became prevalent in northern Taiwan. Many villages combined small-scale family-owned tea plots and rice paddies, but the

T'ao-y'uan plateau featured large-scale tea estates rented out to tenant farmers. The largest owner of tea lands on the island in the late 1800s (and Taiwan's single wealthiest family) were the Lins of Pan-ch'iao. Along with other great familial and corporate landowners, the Pan-ch'iao Lins drew income from renting their properties under a flexible, sophisticated contractual system of land tenure. Written contracts as commonly used stipulated the terms of tenancy with considerable precision. They were on that account largely self-enforcing (although contract disputes were also adjudicated by local magistrates).[39] As an example, see this 1881 version of a long-term or "perpetual" tea cultivation contract from the Tan-shui area between a corporate Chinese religious association (chi-ssu kung-yeh) and a tenant farmer:

> A perpetual contract for tea cultivation. The managers of the Ch'ün Fu Ssu, Huang Szu-ch'ang and Hu Ho-an and others, last year purchased a plot of paddy land. . . . In the eastern part of this property there are three pieces of land. At present the tea cultivating tenant, Tseng Ho-ch'ang, has come to raise tea on these three pieces of land. Having clarified the boundaries of this land, it is rented to Tseng, who is to supply the tea plants, the capital, and undertake the cultivation and the construction of a fence. When the tea is planted, the tenant is to pay a rent of six silver dollars per each ten thousand tea bushes per year. When this is paid to the managers, a receipt will be given as evidence of payment. The tenant is not allowed to pay less than the stipulated amount of rent . . . and must cultivate said land and not allow it to go to waste. From the winter of this year [1881] when the tea is planted to the summer of 1885, an estimation of the number of plants is to be made; when this is determined, payment in full is to be made by the middle of the fifth month without delay. If there is a delay, then this cultivation contract for tea will be voided. This agreement between landlord and cultivator allows of no other interpretation; the annual rent payment is to be born by the cultivator. If this tea land reverts to wasteland and the plants fail to flourish, then the three pieces of land [including all improvements made by the tenant] will revert to the Ch'ün Fu Ssu manager's control; the tenant will not question this . . . Fearing that word of mouth is insufficient, we have set down this contract for the perpetual cultivation of tea in two identical copies, one for each party [i.e., the tenant and the landlord] . . . (signed by the tenant, two land managers, a witness and a scribe, May/June, 1881).[40]

Many of these contracts open with the self-evident declaration that tenants are planting tea with the confidence of making profits. These expectations were usually born out in late nineteenth-century Taiwan. Thanks largely to the large American demand for oolong rather than smaller markets for *pao-chung* or other Taiwan teas, annual exports from Tan-shui increased a hundredfold from the mid-1860s to the late 1880s (from 185,000 lbs. to 18–20,000,000 lbs.). The average price of tea per picul at Tan-shui rose from U.S.$9.00 in the late 1860s to about $43.00 by the mid- to late 1890s.[41] In retrospect, Formosa tea offered an initial demonstration of Taiwan's subsequent capacity to realize rapid gains from international trade.

Sugar Production: Patterns and Problems

During the 1860s and 1870s sugar was Taiwan's most valuable export (see Table 7.1). Ten to 12 percent of this trade consisted of refined white sugar, with the bulk of it being unrefined or crude brown sugar. Brown sugar was both easier and less costly to produce than white, but yielded commensurately lower returns.[42] Northern China, the lower Yangtze region, and Japan were the steadiest consumers of Taiwanese sugar in the second half of the century. Until the mid-1880s, it was also competitive in the Australian, British, and American markets.[43] More than 100 million *chin* (about 132 million lbs.) of sugar were exported at that time from An-p'ing, Tainan, and Ta-kou, the ports adjacent to the extensive cane fields of southern Taiwan.[44] Taiwan's sugar trade nevertheless failed to match the expansion of the tea and camphor trades. While Taiwan maintained a near-monopoly in both oolong tea and camphor production, it faced strong price and quality competition in third-country markets from suppliers of both beet and cane sugar.

There were no vast sugar plantations to speak of on Taiwan. Sugarcane was grown just as tea was—on a relatively small-scale basis by individual farm families. Monetary advances by merchants were commonplace in the crop-financing agreements of rural sugar producers just as they were among tea growers.[45] Here the production technologies of the two commodities sharply diverge. Unlike tea-farming households who made crude tea, cane growers could not manufacture sugar on an individual household basis. Even brown sugar processing required relatively large investments of fixed capital, including millstones and stone rollers, mill tools, and draft animals (oxen) for motive power. These were supplied either by private sugar mills (*kung-chia-pu*) or cooperative mills (*niu-kua-pu*), with the latter alternative the most popular one by far in the late 1800s.[46]

Private mills were corporate bodies that enrolled small groups of investors. They banded together to finance the establishment and operation of a sugar mill, lending cash to growers to secure a supply of cane, hiring seasonal processing workers, marketing the output, and sharing profits on the basis of their individual investments. Cooperative mills, as the term itself suggests, operated as service organizations for their membership, which was itself determined by shareholdings known as "oxen-stock." Shareholders provided their quota of oxen and capital to maintain the mill and pay its workers, in return for which the mill would exclusively process members' cane. Unlike the private mills, the cooperatives neither bought raw cane nor sold processed sugar on the open market.[47]

Regardless of these organizational differences, Taiwan's sugar producers by the turn of the century were crippled by a legacy of backward technology and a preindustrial production organization. Sugar production around the globe experienced a technological revolution, which made processing operations increasingly efficient and engendered major economies of scale. At the end of the century, falling world market prices for refined sugar had driven Taiwanese crude sugar from its last strongholds in mainland China. Old-style, small-scale private and cooperative sugar manufacture effectively ceased, as Japanese colonial authorities scripted a radically new chapter in this industry's long history.[48]

Aspects of Social Change in the Late Nineteenth Century

Boisterous and often violent festivals for lonely or hungry ghosts, the lumpenproletariat of Chinese folk religion, became very popular in cities and towns throughout northern Taiwan in the late nineteenth century. Mounds of foodstuffs were lavishly displayed at these feasts in order to pacify ne'er-do-well spirits. The hapless ghosts were promptly and rudely "robbed" by their real life counterparts—the mobs of famished beggars, tramps, and criminals who invariably descended upon the scene. Robert Weller's documentation and analysis of these episodes suggests their deeper socioeconomic significance—growing commercialization, migration, and economic instability prompted northern Taiwan's local elites to propitiate a marginal and growing "ghostly" underclass of vagrants and day laborers.[49]

Whether responding in spiritual or secular forms, Taiwanese society could hardly remain unaffected by the course of changes marking the island's final years under Ch'ing administration. Three of the most consequential processes are briefly outlined here: population shifts and growing urbanization, forms of inter- and intraethnic social conflict, and evidence of the cultural and political redefinition of Taiwan's social elite.

Population Shifts and Urbanization

The most dramatic indicator of the economic and social transformation Taiwan was experiencing in the mid- to late nineteenth century was the pronounced shift in the island's population distribution. Taking Li Kuo-ch'i's figures as a reasonable approximation, in 1811 some 70 percent of the island's Han population of about 1,944,000 resided in southern Taiwan, with only 17 percent inhabiting central Taiwan, and 13 percent northern Taiwan. In 1893, when a total of 2,545,000 Han settlers was recorded, fully 30 percent lived in the north (meaning Taipei prefecture), 27 percent in central Taiwan (T'ai-wan prefecture), and only 43 percent in the south (Tainan prefecture).[50] Lured by undeveloped land, exploitable natural resources, and emerging commercial opportunities, migrants from across the strait as well as from southern Taiwan steadily tilted the island's demographic balance.

Several overlapping microanalyses of this phenomenon have focused upon Hai-shan, a region of rugged hills and narrow valleys southwest of modern urban Taipei. As documented by Stevan Harrell, Arthur Wolf and Chieh-shan Huang, and P. Steven Sangren, Hai-shan experienced very rapid population growth and mushrooming local urbanization in the second half of the nineteenth century.

The townships (*chen*) of Shu-lin and San-hsia went from a combined total of 9,600 to 20,000 residents between 1841 and 1895.[51] With over 20,000 camphor stills, Ta-hsi by 1870 had emerged as the camphor marketing center of northern Taiwan and was also a growing center for the tea trade.[52]

The mountainous areas surrounding San-hsia and other Hai-shan towns rapidly filled up with Han settlers and their tea fields in the 1870s and 1880s, this despite fierce resistance from Atayal aborigines who contested every Chinese encroachment.[53] Not coincidentally, many new immigrants to Hai-shan (and adjacent areas in and around the Taipei basin) hailed from the famed tea-growing region of An-ch'i *hsien* in southeast Fukien. So many An-ch'i settlers flocked to northern Taiwan in the 1800s that one in ten Taiwanese traces ancestors to that locality.[54]

Taiwan's principal urban centers, in traditional order of importance, consisted of T'ai-nan (modern Tainan), Lu-kang, and Meng-chia. By the end of the nineteenth century (1898), Tainan had become a treaty port and was still the island's largest city with 47,283 inhabitants, but Meng-chia (with 23,767 people) had been eclipsed by Ta-t'ao-ch'eng (population 31,533), the tea-trading center of the Taipei basin.[55] Ta-t'ao-ch'eng was only a small village in 1853, when it welcomed an influx of Chang-chou and Ch'uan-chou people—the latter seeking refuge from Meng-chia's subethnic strife.

Tea-processing and -packing businesses drew up to 20,000 day laborers—many of them women and children—to this commercial mecca with its paved streets, foreign consulates, and Chinese and foreign trading firms. During the last twenty years of Ch'ing rule, both Ta-t'ao-ch'eng and Meng-chia became the riverfront economic axis of the emerging provincial capital city of Taipei.[56]

Tan-shui's development as the principal treaty port of northern Taiwan was determined by its site at the mouth of the river serving as a gateway to the tea and camphor trades of the Taipei basin. With only 1,200 inhabitants in 1829, Tan-shui in 1895 registered a population of 6,148 and had become a focal point of the foreign diplomatic and missionary presence in the north.[57] Even by 1895 it was being overtaken by Keelung, which had a larger population (9,500) clustered around a far better natural harbor. By the end of the century, Keelung was developing as an outlet for nearby coal and gold mining industries and a modern transport and communications hub.[58] Some twenty other urban centers (standard and intermediate-level marketing towns, in G. William Skinner's terminology) in northern and central Taiwan including Miao-li, Hsin-chu, Kuan-hsi, Tou-liu, Hsin-p'u, Chu-tung, and P'u-li also experienced substantial growth related to the expansion of camphor and tea exports or mining operations.[59]

Forms of Social Conflict

Taiwan's reputation for local turbulence and endemic violence was never really in jeopardy during the late nineteenth century. There were significant variations in the forms of social conflict if not in the basic fact of its recurrence, however. Whether as a prefecture or a province, the island lacked a strong administration that was both fiscally and organizationally equipped to ensure social order from day to day and place to place (the high price of that insurance, as it turned out, was the imposition of Japanese colonialism). Ch'ing authorities in fact put themselves in a paradoxical position. While striving to curb the social dissonance accompanying economic expansion and openness to the wider world among the Han populace, officials pursued aggressive policies toward the aborigines, which involved a continual high level of armed conflict.

There is as yet no scholarly consensus on the issue of whether the opening of Taiwan diminished or promoted social conflict in the three decades after 1860. Lin Man-houng has contended that expanded economic opportunities and an increased need for cooperation among Taiwan's Chinese inhabitants reduced the incidence of Han subethnic strife. The development of the tea and camphor trades conferred locational advantages upon settlers from Chang-chou and the Hakka in northern Taiwan, serving to balance the scales against previously dominant Ch'uan-chou residents. Whether of Hakka, Chang-chou, or Ch'uan-chou origins, Han settlers all benefited by exploiting Taiwan's upland frontier regions.[60]

Lin's argument continues to be persuasive, having been reiterated and reworked by local historians such as Chang Ming-hsiung. Chang discerns a diminished sense of parochialism and communal identity among Han Chinese that accompanied the growth of foreign commerce. Associated with this, unfortunately, were wider gaps between the island's social classes: an increasingly wealthy elite of great landlords, powerful families, merchants, and compradors; a middling stratum of yeoman farmers, urban shopkeepers, and other professionals (i.e., teachers, Taoist clergy), and a lower class including tenant farmers, petty traders, and common laborers. A Japanese survey of Meng-chia in 1899–1901 gave substance to these disparities, finding that wealthy households had annual incomes ten times greater than those of middling households, who in turn had twenty times the income of the poor.[61]

Latent tension between classes, as Weller argues in connection with the hungry ghost festivals, may well have been ameliorated by community rituals. In more concrete and personalized terms, open social discord in northern Taiwan is well documented in Mark Allee's analysis of Ch'ing legal cases from the Tan-Hsin Archives. A boundary dispute involving tea land between a corporate joint partnership and four adjacent villages dragged on from 1882 to 1888. Complicated by a murder and sabotage (crop destruction), it exemplifies the potential for violence as rapidly extended cash cropping provoked disputes over still weakly delimited property rights.[62] Another quarrel between a local strongman entrepreneur and an official trying to tax and regulate the camphor trade lasted from 1887 to 1895. In this case, aborigines were prepared to press their grievances in court against the official (a deceitful *likin [li-chin]* tax collector), rather than take up arms.[63]

Such trust in regularized judicial procedures was hardly universal, especially when Sino-aboriginal conflicts were involved. A legacy of mistrust was kindled by mutual atrocities and vendettas. The Presbyterian missionary William Campbell reported the following ghastly example in his memoir *Sketches from Formosa*:

> I saw a party of armed savages returning through Po-li-sia. . . . A stout lad was trudging wearily after them carrying some sort of a bundle dangling down behind him. On reaching the hut, where they were to pass the night, I got a closer look of the little fellow, and found that the bundle he was carrying consisted of two freshly-cut Chinamen's heads which he had fastened by the queues held over his shoulder. . . . He threw the two heads on the ground, made a pillow of them by coiling the hair on the top, and was fast asleep in a minute or two.[64]

Reciprocity on the Chinese side included gory official beheadings of "wild" aborigines in public places, followed by crowd behavior, as in this account by George L. Mackay, showing that Han Chinese could still regard indigenes as menu items and medicinal ingredients rather than fellow human beings: "Scores were there on purpose to get parts of the body for food and medicine . . . the heart is eaten, flesh taken off in strips, and bones boiled to a jelly and preserved as a specific for malarial fever."[65] Several dozen official military expeditions were launched against the Atayal, Ami, Paiwan, and Tsou tribes between 1875 and 1895. They evince a key shift in Ch'ing frontier policy, now aggressive and expansive rather than cautious and defensive—thus a prime factor in exacerbating interethnic hostility in the final decades of imperial Chinese rule on Taiwan.[66]

Redefining Taiwan's Social Elite

The process by which Taiwan's social elite redefined itself was of course a protracted one, as Chen Qiukun illustrates in Chapter 6. Extensive landholdings, control of irrigation systems, and dominant local military power had long been ingredients of rustic prestige and effective social control, judging from Johanna Meskill's superb family history of the Lins of Wu-feng. Scholarship, gentry status based upon degree-holding, and a cultivated upper-class life-style struggled to establish themselves in this rugged and often insecure environment.[67] Nonetheless, as in other frontier regions of the empire in the late nineteenth century (in Kueichou and Hsinkiang provinces, for example), Taiwan's local elites were steadily undergoing a process of "gentrification." In Taiwan as elsewhere, elites adroitly used both local and extralocal resources and opportunities to enhance their power and prosperity, and translated these into the "symbolic capital" of Chinese high culture.[68]

Scholars are in general agreement that Taiwan was becoming a more "Confucianized" as well as a wealthier society as the nineteenth century wore on. Quoting the proverb "First [comes] prosperity, and then a knowledge of the rites" (*Fu erh hou chih li-mi*), Lin Man-houng notes the founding of fourteen new Confucian academies (*shu-yuan*) between 1860 and 1893, only twenty-three having been established during the entire period from 1683 to 1860.[69] Li Kuo-ch'i points out the quickening tempo of gentry elite formation. Taiwan generated 343 degree holders from 1862 to 1894—over a third of the island's total output produced since 1688—with 104 of these winning higher degrees.[70] Harry Lamley cites the rapid growth of both the scholar and student segment of Taiwan's population, but also cautions that, as late as 1895, there were still barely 350 higher-degree holders and 5,000 lower-degree holders amidst some 2.5 million Han inhabitants.[71] The value of a given degree status was of course relative to one's location in China—holding the lowest degree (*sheng-yuan*) in underdeveloped Taiwan carried more prestige than it would have in more refined areas such as Kiangsu or Chekiang.[72] Both the Lins of Pan-ch'iao and the (unrelated) Lins of Wu-feng added to familial prestige in this way in the mid- to late nineteenth century.[73]

The two Lin families exhibited another common strategy for enhancing local elite status: the use of official patronage and administrative roles to further their local wealth and power.[74] With their reputation badly tarnished and their funds depleted by a protracted litigation crisis, the Wu-feng Lins recouped both in the mid- to late 1880s under Governor Liu Ming-ch'uan's auspices. Lin Ch'ao-tung's private militia of five hundred fought well against the French invaders of Keelung in 1884–85, was placed on the Ch'ing payroll, and participated in three consecutive aboriginal "pacification" operations from 1885 to 1887. Although militarily inconclusive, these campaigns brought new camphor forests into the hands of the Wu-feng Lins, since Lin Ch'ao-tung headed the mid-Taiwan branch of the official "Pacification and Reclamation Bureau" that made these uplands safer for economic exploitation. Along with extensive landholdings concentrated in central Taiwan (Meskill records holdings of 5,720 acres and 4,000 tenants on Lin rent rolls), the Wu-feng Lins dominated camphor production in that area by the 1890s. They had turned both foreign trade and foreign aggression to their own good account.[75]

The Pan-ch'iao Lins were no less proficient, becoming the richest and most powerful family in late Ch'ing northern Taiwan. Lin Wei-yuan, as the dominant figure in the family during this period, became Liu Ming-ch'uan's righthand man in the north. He headed the pan-Taiwan Pacification and Reclamation Bureau, supervising efforts to resettle poor Fukien cultivators in upland locations like Hai-shan, as well as punitive expeditions against recalcitrant aborigines. These managerial operations made the Pan-ch'iao Lins the largest landlords in northern Taiwan; much of this tenanted land was soon planted to tea. Holding strong commercial interests and property in Ta-t'ao-ch'eng, the Lins then capitalized on both the production and marketing aspects of the booming tea trade.[76]

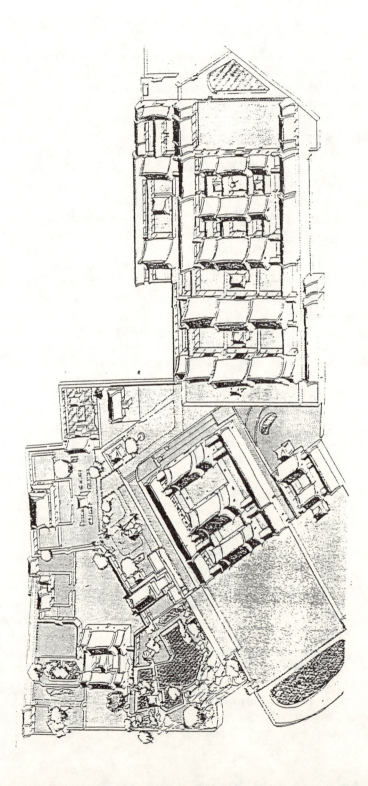

Lin House Blueprint

Both the Wu-feng and Pan-ch'iao Lins translated their wealth into conspicuous philanthropic activities and even more tangible symbols of their local preeminence—vast, elaborate mansion residences. The Wu-feng Lins financed road repairs, small ferries, and constructed small bamboo bridges in their bailiwick. Covering more than two acres of ground, their mansion complex had virtually been imported from the mainland, along with the artisans who labored over its well over two hundred rooms.[77]

Lin Wei-yuan established the Pan-ch'iao Lins as the island's greatest philanthropists by generous support for public disaster relief and dike work on the mainland, and the family played a leading role in supporting the construction of the walled city of Taipei as the new provincial capital.[78]

The Lin mansion at Pan-ch'iao, in its newly restored form, remains the best-known expression of the splendor of Taiwan's late Ch'ing elite families. It consists of an original compound, plus three courtyards built in 1853, and five new courtyards and an intricate garden added (at an estimated cost of half a million taels) from 1888 to 1893. As Ron Knapp puts it, "a hierarchy of privacy evolved as the fortunes of the Lin family developed."[79] In sum, the Wu-feng and Pan-ch'iao Lins were undoubtedly among the most visible examples—but decidedly not the only ones—of rising elite family fortunes linked to the growing commercial and political opportunities arising in the late nineteenth century.[80]

Strategic Imperatives and the Making of a Province

In late November 1871, four ships carrying sixty-six mariners from the Liu-ch'iu (Ryukyu) islands were shipwrecked on the extreme southern coast of Taiwan during a typhoon. The area was inhabited by Paiwan aborigines, who apparently took the seamen for local enemies and proceeded to massacre fifty-four of them near the village of Mu-tan.[81] The Mu-tan incident looms large in the history of late Ch'ing Taiwan, as it precipitated a tangled crisis in Sino-Japanese relations. Involved at one and the same time were the issues of sovereignty over the Liu-ch'ius (Were the victims really Japanese nationals?), de facto as well as de jure political control over the rugged eastern half of Taiwan (Were the Mu-tan aborigines actually Ch'ing subjects?), and the strategic security of the island itself (Could China effectively administer and defend Taiwan?).[82]

Over the next three years Japanese diplomats fenced with the Ch'ing over all these issues, asserting that, since Japanese citizens of the Liu-ch'ius had been murdered in territory that China claimed but did not actually administer, Japan was within its rights in seeking retribution. Peking's rebuttal was reasoned but unavailing—Japan had no cause whatever to meddle in the Mu-tan affair. The Liu-ch'ius were not Japanese territory but a Chinese tributary state, while Ch'ing policy in Taiwan precluded responsibility for aboriginal behavior beyond the effective reach of Chinese administration.[83]

In the spring of 1874, the Japanese government launched a large-scale punitive expedition to Taiwan consisting of three ships and 3,600 men. While failing to fulfill its ostensible objective of humbling the aborigines, the mission succeeded in bringing China and Japan close to open war.[84] A diplomatic rather than a military resolution of the crisis was achieved; by most accounts it was a humiliation for China, which found itself compensating Japan for invading Taiwan. A half a million taels in indemnities was forwarded to Tokyo, along with an implicit Chinese acknowledgment of Japanese sovereignty over the Liu-ch'iu archipelago (annexed in 1879 as Okinawa prefecture).[85]

The Ch'ing empire responded in 1874–75 on both national and local levels with an uncharacteristic urgency. It conducted the first serious nationwide policy debate on the content and goals of China's "self-strengthening" efforts (the strategic, limited modernization initiatives undertaken in several provinces since the 1860s).[86] More importantly for Taiwan itself, Ch'ing administrators initiated a vigorous, multifaceted "self-strengthening" program, which has since been termed "the first constructive policy the Qing court ever really evidenced in regard to the internal affairs of the island."[87] The concluding portion of this chapter addresses the central components of this program, as well as the three Ch'ing administrators most closely associated with it—Shen Pao-chen, Ting Jih-ch'ang, and, above all others, Liu Ming-ch'uan.

Shen Pao-chen and Ting Jih-ch'ang: The Initial Phases of Self-Strengthening, 1874–1878

Shen Pao-chen's duties as director of the Foochow Navy Yard, China's first modern naval defense project, took on added dimensions from mid-1874 to mid-1875. Given the emergency appointment of imperial commissioner, Shen was assigned the formidable task of bolstering Taiwan's defenses in anticipation of Japan's assault. In immediate terms, Shen redeployed troops, ships, and munitions from the mainland to the island in case Sino-Japanese negotiations failed.[88] A longer range view of Taiwan's security requirements was clearly in order. In framing one, Shen relied upon the firsthand perceptions of Luo Ta-ch'un, a trusted military subordinate, as well as his own experience.[89] Despite his brief tenure on Taiwan, Shen Pao-chen established a framework of policy parameters, which his successors elaborated over the next two decades.[90]

Technological modernization was to play a conspicuous role in the Ch'ing self-strengthening agenda on the island. Shen's own contributions here were modest. Between 1867 and 1875 he promoted the initial development of coal mining in the vicinity of Keelung using Western operational methods, the objective being to supply the Foochow Navy Yard's fuel requirements. Conscious of frequent communications gaps between Taiwan and the mainland, Shen advocated a telegraphic cable link between Amoy and T'ai-wan-fu in 1874.[91] Both these projects would eventually yield limited results, but Shen's real priorities appear more imperial than technological—to bring Taiwan's underdeveloped central mountain belts under Han Chinese settlement and control those aborigines who stood in the way by suasion if possible, or coercion if necessary.[92]

John Shepherd observes that the late nineteenth-century self-strengtheners' aggressive program of "opening the mountains and pacifying the aborigines" (*k'ai-shan fu-fan*) constituted a clear departure from the time-honored, passive (but cost-effective) Ch'ing policy of quarantining Taiwan's unsubmissive upland tribes. By the late 1800s Taiwan had become strategically more vulnerable as well as economically more significant. This justified both the assertion of formal imperial control over the island's rugged central and eastern regions and the development of sufficient indigenous fiscal resources to sustain this effort. An indication of this new resolve occurred in 1875, thanks to Shen Pao-chen's prodding. Taiwan's administration was tightened, now divided into the two prefectures of T'ai-wan and T'ai-pei (the latter given jurisdiction over the increasingly important northern third of the island), which presided over eight counties and four subprefectures.[93]

To Shen Pao-chen, "opening up the mountains" signified a well-planned program of Han Chinese immigration and settlement. This included recruiting cultivators, clearing virgin forests and burning off grasslands, building roads, founding villages, and establishing the rudiments of civil administration and military security. "Pacifying the aborigines" involved much more than situating Ch'ing garrisons among them or sending punitive expeditions against them. Introducing "proper" Chinese cultural values, modes of dress, language, and commodities, while stamping out "improper" native customs such as vendetta killings and wearing scanty attire would steadily acculturate and thus civilize the upland tribes.[94]

Shen served on Taiwan scarcely long enough to initiate his complex agenda (in mid-1875 he was re-assigned to the mainland). Between 1874 and 1875 a total of 307.5 miles (859 Chinese *li*) of roads were extended from the lowlands into three sectors—northern, central, and southern—of the mountain ranges. Varying in width from ten feet in the plains to seven feet in the mountains, the routes were punctuated by occasional military outposts.[95] Heng-ch'un at the extreme southern tip of the island and T'ai-tung on the southeastern coast were designated as primary centers of the "pacification" and immigration programs. The establishment of public schools (*yi-hsueh*) to tutor the aborigines, their introduction to Chinese-style economic life, and the settlement of Han colonists from Fukien and Kuangtung among them were key aspects of Shen's program. Notwithstanding these initial colonization efforts, few mainland Chinese farmers volunteered to become state-subsidized pioneers on the southern Taiwan frontier.[96]

As governor of Fukien, Ting Jih-ch'ang assumed responsibility for Taiwan's administration from late 1875 to mid-1878. In 1876 he made a thorough inspection tour of the island. A year later, Ting put forth a set of projects that embraced many refinements and modifications but in general outline resembled those of

Shen Pao-chen. Ting's aboriginal policy took the form of a listing of twenty-one regulations in the spring of 1877. The gist of these express a preference that the upland natives should be culturally and economically seduced rather than militarily repressed. Locally managed gentry bureaus were supposed to function as paternalistic missionaries, introducing Han Chinese schooling, medicine, and farming practices, while curbing Chinese exploitation of the aborigines. Only a very limited area of the island was affected by this program, specifically P'u-li in the central mountains and the Heng-ch'un area.[97]

In his concern with soil types, water supplies, and potential varieties of economic crops, Ting's approach to Han agricultural colonization was more schematic and decidedly more market-oriented than Shen's original proposals. Ting's commercial bias toward exploiting the uplands, including mining as well as farming activities, is clear from the following statement:

> From cultivating fields and cutting trees the profits are slight and slow. From opening mines and planting tea profits are large and quick. [If] profits are great, naturally many people will come without being recruited, [and if] the population is numerous, naturally the land under cultivation will be extended. A group of fifteen [households?] thus becomes a village; a group of villages thus becomes a city.[98]

Notwithstanding Ting's preference for volunteers rather than officially recruited settlers, two thousand Han colonists from eastern Kuangtung arrived in 1877 to populate the countryside near Hua-lien. A smaller influx of mainland migrants also relocated in the vicinities of T'ai-tung and Heng-ch'un at this time.[99]

Ting Jih-ch'ang's most notable contribution to the island's technological development was his ambitious 1876–77 scheme to construct a railway from Keelung to Heng-ch'un. The strategic desirability of such a route (particularly for rapid transfers of troops along the entire length of the vulnerable western coast) was more than offset by the impracticability of financing it. Although Ting became the earliest proponent of railroad building on Taiwan, his 350-mile-long line with an estimated cost of 2 million taels would remain a fantasy until the early twentieth century.[100]

Like Shen Pao-chen, Ting Jih-ch'ang served for only a brief term as Taiwan's chief magistrate. No fewer than six individuals succeeded Ting over as many years (from 1878 to 1884), indicative of certain long-standing, fundamental problems in late Ch'ing administration. The relentless turnover of personnel at the highest level, combined with widespread corruption, poor morale, continued fiscal weakness, and administrative dependency upon Fukien, frustrated or at least constrained reform initiatives. As in 1874, an international crisis was required—in this case, the Sino-French War of 1884–85—to compel the Ch'ing to "reinvent" Taiwan's administrative system.[101]

Taiwan Becomes a Province: The Governorship
of Liu Ming-ch'uan (1884–1891) and Its Aftermath

Liu Ming-ch'uan arrived in Taiwan in July 1884. The governor-to-be (as of October 1884) faced the immediate threat of an invasion by combined French naval and land forces.[102] Low in morale and lax in preparedness, Taiwan's garrison of 16,500 faced an opponent far inferior in numbers, but far superior in war materiel and training. The struggle occupied almost an entire year, from August 1884 to July 1885. Except for the anticlimactic French seizure of the Pescadores at the end of the war, hostilities were confined to the far north of Taiwan. Frequent sharp clashes as well as protracted engagements with Chinese regular and militia forces followed French landings outside Keelung and Tan-shui. A half-year French naval blockade impeded, but did not halt, the island's vital overseas commerce. While Taiwan was only one theater in a wider war centered upon Vietnam, the French sought to capture the treaty ports and coal mines in the north. These might then, as strategy dictated, be held for ransom in the form of indemnities and the security of future customs and mining revenues.[103]

After an initial repulse, French expeditionary forces made a successful assault on Keelung and occupied the port in October 1884. Thanks to dogged Chinese resistance, disease, and foul weather, the enemy was never able to penetrate farther inland than the rugged hill country surrounding the city. Liu Ming-ch'uan was roundly denounced at court for failing to dislodge the French from Keelung during the subsequent course of the war, but he apparently lacked sufficient troops and weaponry to do so. An attack on Tan-shui (which also took place in October 1884), did vindicate Taiwan's defenders, as it resulted in an abject French defeat.[104]

In the fall of 1884, the overconfident invaders thus found themselves stalemated. As one authoritative analysis of the entire Sino-French conflict notes, "Only on Taiwan were the Chinese forces able to hold their own man-for-man against the French."[105] When the war ended in June 1885, Liu Ming-ch'uan's credentials as the island's savior were hardly in doubt. He soon reconstructed and re-armed the fortifications guarding Taiwan's principal seaports, but in the aftermath of the crisis, Liu determined that self-strengthening required much more—a "thorough reorganization of the entire island," as Samuel Chu states. This daunting task would occupy the next half-dozen years of Liu's life and constitute the final phase of Taiwan's maturation within the Ch'ing empire.[106]

The cornerstone of this "thorough reorganization" was the achievement of provincial status—an acknowledgment of Taiwan's administrative parity with the mainland provinces, as well as the fiscal solvency to back this up. Liu at first opposed such a move, perhaps feeling that it was premature and might simply complicate the handling of more urgent civil and military tasks. In any event, the island's intricate transition from prefecture to province proceeded at a cautious pace under Liu. The court authorized the change in 1885, but took until 1887 to

Table 7.2

Annual Revenue Income of Taiwan, 1888–1894 (in taels)

	Amount	Percent
Maritime customs and ship tonnage duties	996,069	22.6
Li-chin (likin) taxes (on tea, opium, and miscellaneous goods)	665,640	15.1
Ti-ting (land and poll taxes)	512,969	11.7
Commercial Bureau (steamship and railway income)	400,000	9.1
Coal Mine Bureau	400,000	9.1
Camphor Trade Profits	400,000	9.1
Subvention from Fukien province	440,000	10.0
All other revenue sources	588,649	13.3
Total:	4,403,327	100.0

Source: Adapted from Li Kuo-ch'i, *Chung-kuo hsien-tai-hua te ch'ü yen-chiu: Min-Che-T'ai ti-ch'u, 1860–1916* (Regional study of China's modernization: The Fukien, Chekiang, and Taiwan region, 1860–1916) (Nan-kang: Institute for Modern History, Academia Sinica, 1982), p. 400.

create the procedures and laws to put it into place. Hsinkiang's gradual separation from Kansu province after 1884 furnished a model, inasmuch as close financial and administrative ties between Taiwan and Fukien were continued during a prolonged rite of passage.[107]

For five years Fukien provided Taiwan with a critical yearly subsidy of 440,000 taels, amounting to 10 percent of the island's annual revenue during the transition era (see Table 7.2). Liu was simultaneously designated as governor of Fukien and governor of Taiwan, although the Min–Che governor-general, based in Foochow, was now vested with primary responsibility for mainland affairs.[108] As the map reveals, Taiwan's administrative network was also intensified to suit the island's new status. There were now three prefectures instead of two, plus an independent department to govern the isolated eastern coast; the number of counties and subprefectures rose from eight to eleven and four to six, respectively.[109]

Liu Ming-ch'uan immediately became very unpopular in southern Taiwan, however, and remained so for the rest of his term in office. Moving against widespread bureaucratic corruption in 1885, he impeached Liu Ao, Taiwan's popular circuit intendant (*tao-t'ai*). Formerly the highest-ranking Ch'ing official on the island, Liu Ao was an able man with wide support among the local elite in the south despite a reputation for venality.[110] Having ousted a potential rival from office, Liu ostentatiously shifted the location of the new provincial capital from historic Tainan to the rustic site of present-day Taichung. During the construction phase of this new capital city of T'ai-wan-fu, Taipei was built up as both a prefectural capital and the island's temporary provincial capital. Taipei's "temporary" status, of course, eventually became permanent (thanks to a deci-sion in 1893 by Shao Yu-lien, Liu Ming-ch'uan's successor, to cancel plans for T'ai-wan-fu).[111]

The local elites of northern Taiwan, above all the Lins of Pan-ch'iao, basked in this northward shift of power and the benefits associated with Liu Ming-ch'uan's self-strengthening program. Their counterparts in southern Taiwan, dis-advantaged by declining political influence, and paying the costs rather than reaping the rewards of Liu's modernization efforts, were of another temper. This unfortunate regional polarization became clear in Liu's major campaign to re-form Taiwan's inadequate taxation system.[112]

The financial needs of the new province were partially met by the temporary subvention from Fukien, and by the court's allowing Liu to utilize all the exten-sive maritime customs and *li-chin* revenues collected on Taiwan. As Table 7.2 illustrates, however, these three sources combined satisfied a little less than half of the province's yearly revenue needs. Solidifying the fiscal basis upon which Taiwan's self-strengthening rested meant raising considerably more income than in the past from land and commercial taxation. Liu approached this problem with characteristic energy and aggressiveness, provoking antipathy from Chinese and foreigners alike. He strove to increase the government's "take" of growing profits from foreign trade, but his signal achievement was to preside over the only major cadastral survey and land tax reform ever conducted in late Ch'ing China.[113]

Liu's efforts to increase *li-chin* revenues from sugar exports, reinstitute an official monopoly of camphor exports, and raise *li-chin* taxes upon goods im-ported on foreign ships met with the predictable opposition of British and other foreign merchants. The results were mixed, in that Liu was forced by foreign diplomatic pressure to reduce his original *li-chin* levies and disavow his monop-oly scheme, while revenues from various forms of commercial taxation (and official enterprises related to trade, such as coal mines and steamship lines) became an essential fixture in the province's annual budget (see Table 7.2).[114]

Land tax reform required Liu to cut through the Gordian knot of Taiwan's multitiered land tenure systems, a historical tangle of tenural rights intermingled with fiscal liabilities and iniquities. The complexities of the *ta-tzu/hsiao-tzu* (big rent, small rent) system meant that a cadastral reform survey (*liang-t'ien ch'ing-fu*) became an essential element in land tax reform. The entire process extended over three and a half years, from June 1886 to January 1890. Two general survey bureaus were set up in Taipei and Tainan and subbureaus in each county. Local gentry were obliged to assist the teams of official land surveyors and assessors in their work, which was to be guided by the need to establish fair and uniform standards of tax assessment and fiscal obligations.[115]

Informed by new sets of *pao-chia* (collective responsibility) reports for each locality, the cadastral survey field teams measured and graded each piece of land according to a scale of tax liability (for example, a *chia* of top-grade paddy field, equivalent to 11 *mu*, was assessed 2.46 silver taels at the high end of the scale).

Tax liability in turn served as a basis for issuing new land deeds. In this entire process, *hsiao-tzu* households rather than *ta-tzu* patent holders now became direct taxpayers as well as the actual proprietors on the land. As compensation for their new tax burdens, the state reduced *hsiao-tzu* payments to *ta-tzu* households by 40 percent, another step closer to the latters' gradual elimination as a significant factor in landed property holding on Taiwan.[116]

While local landholders in northern Taiwan generally cooperated in the reform process, the same could not be said of the central and southern sectors of the island. Here Liu was operating far from his power base, and here he met sharp resistance. Local *ta-tzu* interests, who (unlike their northern counterparts) had invested much more in developing their holdings, were particularly aggrieved by Liu's policies. In 1888, an armed uprising broke out, affecting the area from Chang-hua to Feng-shan counties and culminating in a siege of Chang-hua city itself. The revolt was crushed, but it demonstrated anew Liu's political vulnerability outside of the north and even forced him to make tax concessions to the southern *ta-tzu* holders.[117] The receipts resulting from the land tax reform fell short of Liu Ming-ch'uan's expectations, but still constituted a sizable gain in income. Table 7.2 reveals that land and poll taxes combined realized slightly over 500,000 taels per year, less than the 674,000 taels Liu had anticipated but far greater than the presurvey total of 183,000 taels.[118] This added income from land taxes, commercial levies, official enterprises, and the like was certainly matched by Liu's added expenditures in pursuit of his self-strengthening goals. The comments below touch upon two critical and problematic components of that program—Liu's aboriginal policy and his technical modernization ventures.

There was no fundamental discrepancy between Liu's approach toward the upland tribes and the program initiated by Shen Pao-chen and Ting Jih-ch'ang under the designation of *k'ai-shan fu-fan*. While recognizing from the first the importance of this issue for Taiwan's immediate security and future development, Liu was not particularly innovative in handling it.[119] Given a continuous official tenure lasting almost seven years, Liu certainly was in a stronger position to implement the civil and military components of his program than either of his predecessors. By all accounts he did so, but made little headway in either sinicizing the mountain aborigines or overcoming their determined resistance through force of arms.

Taiwan was divided into three zones under Liu's system of aboriginal control: a mountain zone north of P'u-li, a mountain zone south of P'u-li and north of Heng-ch'un, and a coastal zone extending from Heng-ch'un to T'ai-tung. Headquartered in the town of Ta-hsi (Ta-k'o-k'an) south of Taipei, a general pacification and reclamation bureau (*fu-k'en-chu*) supervised eight local bureaus and eighteen branch offices.[120] Along the lines of Liu Ming-ch'uan's other projects, local elites and officials collaborated in managing this network (as noted earlier, Lin Wei-yuan headed the general bureau, and Lin Ch'ao-tung ran the mid-island bureau). The diverse activities of the bureaus ran from educating aborigines in vernacular Chinese (either Hokkien or Mandarin), tutoring them in the Confucian classics, introducing Chinese medicine, and inculcating Chinese farming practices, social customs, standards of dress, and coiffeurs (for males, this naturally meant shaving one's head and wearing the queue). Establishing and manning Ch'ing military outposts in the midst of aboriginal territory, building roads serving both civil and military needs, and encouraging settlements of armed Chinese colonists completed the fundamental agenda.[121]

In reporting to the court, Liu often spoke confidently of the submission of the mountain tribes and the opening of vast tracts of untamed wilderness for tea and grain cultivation and camphor production. In 1887, for example, he boasted that 88,000 aborigines had shaved their heads and become good subjects of the empire; several hundred thousand *mu* of virgin uplands thus became available for development.[122] Yet the aborigines' apparent "submission" time and again waned as quickly as their hair grew back. In view of the more than forty military expeditions Liu felt compelled to launch against the aborigines from 1884 to 1891, the court came to discount his exaggerated claims of success.[123]

Numerous punitive campaigns were launched against the Atayal and Ami tribes of the northern mountains in particular, but prolonged conflict was hardly restricted to that area.[124] Ch'ing forces were repeatedly ambushed by aboriginal guerrilla fighters who made good use of rifles as well as blades and spears. Han troops struggled to capture well-fortified and tenaciously defended tribal villages. In these bitter engagements, with Liu on several occasions personally in command, several thousand Chinese troops employed modern as well as old-style military hardware, including cannon, rockets, fire bombs, land mines, and even machine guns and ironclad warships.[125] The end result of these clashes must be accounted a costly failure, both in terms of Chinese casualty rates (from disease as well as battles) and the diversion of scarce resources that might have been used more productively. According to one estimate, of some 17,500 Ch'ing soldiers stationed on Taiwan under Liu's command, fully a third were killed or disabled in his incessant struggles with the island's native tribes.[126]

Liu Ming-ch'uan's record of technological innovation during his governorship is both impressive and instructive—impressive in the variety of innovations he enthusiastically promoted, and instructive in that the most important of them yielded disappointing results. The list of novelties included (but was not limited to) electric lighting and jinrikshas for Taipei's streets, machinery for lumbering, coal mining, sugar refining, and brick making, modern cannon and rifles plus an arsenal to re-equip Ch'ing troops, and a much improved communications infrastructure comprising a railway, cable and telegraph lines, a local steamship service, roads, harbors, and an up-to-date postal service.[127] The present account cannot offer comprehensive coverage of these diverse activities. It sums up four technical projects that were the centerpiece of Liu's self-strengthening program—modern coal mining, a steamship line, cable and telegraphic services, and Taiwan's first railway system.[128]

Throughout his term as governor, Liu tried to revive coal-mining operations in the hinterland of Keelung, an industry that he himself was compelled to destroy in 1884 to deny coal to French warships. By 1888 the Keelung mines had been completely taken over by the government and were again producing at the rate of 100 tons per day. Mining operations were unfortunately also losing some 3,000 to 4,000 taels per month because of difficulties in shipping and marketing the coal, as well as managerial problems compounded by the exhaustion of accessible coal seams. Convinced that an influx of foreign capital and expertise was needed to develop new mines, Liu courted foreign business interests in 1889–90. He was never able to strike the bargain he desired with potential Western investors, however. Strenuously objecting to Western control of Taiwan's coal resources as too high a price to pay even for modernization, the court forced Liu to suspend his protracted negotiations.[129]

The Sino-French War again confirmed Taiwan's maritime vulnerability, as well as the desirability of establishing a commercial shipping service under local Chinese control. Liu's attempts to do just this between 1885 and 1890 were repeatedly frustrated by intrabureaucratic wrangling, and the loss of shipping tonnage in several mishaps at sea. Li Hung-chang's patronage of the well-entrenched China Merchants Steam Navigation Company ensured that Liu's fledgling Formosan Trading Company (Shang-wu chu) faced powerful domestic as well as foreign competition. With scarcely half a dozen vessels in its fleet, the company lost three to shipwrecks from 1886 to 1889, and the remaining ones operated on an irregular, unprofitable basis.[130]

Greater success in improving Taiwan's communications was achieved in 1886–88 with the construction of a telegraph line from Tainan to Tan-shui and Keelung, and the laying of a cable linking Foochow and Tan-shui. In both cases, Liu secured the prompt cooperation of foreign firms (a German concern provided the telegraph equipment, and Jardine Matheson & Co. arranged for the construction of a cable-laying ship). Unfortunately, while the cross-strait cable provided reliable service, maintaining an overland telegraph system proved more difficult. For natural causes as well as because of chronic vandalism, the system rarely operated for more than a week at a time.[131]

In 1887 Liu Ming-ch'uan memorialized Peking that a railway parallel to Taiwan's western coast could alleviate the problem of troop movements, ease the transport obstructions posed by several local rivers, and serve as a lifeline for the new provincial administration. His ideas on the subject were not dissimilar to Ting Jih-ch'ang's, including his ambition to construct a railroad stretching from Keelung to Tainan. Work on the project, Ch'ing China's most extensive railway-building project up to that time, actually began in 1887, but only the Keelung to Taipei portion of the route had been completed when Liu departed from office in 1891. His successor, Shao Yu-lien, extended the line to Hsin-chu, two-thirds of the way short of its planned destination, and there railway building on Taiwan ceased until the Japanese colonial era.[132]

Construction of the twenty miles of track through the hilly country between Keelung and Taipei was plagued by difficulties. Not the least of these was the habitual lack of cooperation between Liu's foreign engineering advisers in overall charge of the project, and the Ch'ing commander of the soldier-laborers doing the actual work. No fewer than five foreign engineers—a German and four Englishmen—served in succession, which helps to account for muddles such as the failure of two tunnel excavating crews working toward each other to meet in the middle.[133] With the arduous tunneling and track laying completed, the day-to-day operation of the railway came as something of an afterthought. As it turned out, the railway line had been poorly constructed and required a thorough overhaul, the rolling stock consisted of small cars that carried too few passengers and not enough cargo, and the management of the system left much to be desired.[134] The last-named problem was evident to James W. Davidson, a U.S. consular official who inspected the line in 1895, soon after Taiwan's cession to Japan:

> The Chinese in charge of the stations along the line actually worked in opposition to one another. They conducted the business on the principle of personal enhancement, and only paid as much of the funds collected as they thought necessary to enable them to retain their positions. . . . There was absolutely no uniformity in rates, and this system naturally became so unsatisfactory and unreliable that but little freight was entrusted to the tender mercies of the employees of the Formosan Imperial Railway.[135]

The fate of the railway can serve as a metaphor for Liu Ming-ch'uan's self-strengthening program as a whole—begun with the best of hopes and the broadest objectives, but somewhat tarnished in execution and ultimately diminished in impact. Scholarly evaluation of Liu's multifaceted career in late Ch'ing Taiwan has by no means ceased, but it seems clear that his reach exceeded his grasp.[136] By attempting to do so much so soon, Liu courted frustration and failure within a late Ch'ing administrative order that was still relatively sluggish and financially weak. His modernization efforts were regionally biased toward northern Taiwan and lacked coordination. At key junctures, as in his handling of mining policy and costly aboriginal campaigns, Liu even aroused the court itself against him.[137] Yet Liu Ming-ch'uan nonetheless remains the most energetic, engaging official persona in the island's nineteenth-century history. His failures are evident enough, but they ought not offset an impressive list of tangible achievements, including a successful defense of Taiwan versus a determined Western adversary, far-reaching fiscal reforms, and the inauguration of a particularly vigorous mode of Ch'ing administration willing to engage challenging problems. Shao Yu-lien, following in Liu's footsteps as governor from 1891 to 1894, thus symbolized an all but complete reversal. Shao's term in office was notable chiefly for relentless fiscal retrenchment and administrative contraction that, in William Speidel's words, "undermined all of Liu's efforts."[138]

In brief, with the approval of Peking, Shao Yu-lien dismantled Liu's scaffolding of numerous administrative bureaus and also terminated key projects, including the railway and the construction of a new centrally located provincial capital.[139] After Liu's bold, and at times rash activism, Taiwan's relapse into administrative lethargy may have seemed a necessary respite. It would certainly be a brief one. By the time Shao left office in the fall of 1894, Ch'ing China and Meiji Japan were already at war, with Taiwan's long-term future already at stake.

Notes

1. Edwin A. Winckler, "Mass Political Incorporation 1500–1800," in *Contending Approaches to the Political Economy of Taiwan*, ed. Winckler and Susan Greenhalgh (Armonk, NY: M.E. Sharpe, 1988), p. 47.

2. Edwin A. Winckler and Susan Greenhalgh, "Analytical Issues and Historical Episodes" in *Contending Approaches to the Political Economy of Taiwan*, p. 8.

3. Ibid.

4. See Lin Man-houng, "Mao-yi yu Ch'ing-mou T'ai-wan te Ch'ing-chi she-hui pien-ch'ien 1860–1895" [Trade and economic and social change in late Ch'ing Taiwan], *Shih-huo yueh-k'an*, 9, no. 4 (July 1979): 18–31; and Ramon H. Myers, "Taiwan Under Ch'ing Imperial Rule, 1684–1895: The Traditional Economy," *Journal of the Institute of Chinese Studies of the Chinese University of Hong Kong*, 5, no. 2 (December 1972): 373–409.

5. Chan Lien, "Taiwan in China's External Relations, 1683–1874," in *Taiwan in Modern Times*, ed. Paul K.T. Sih (New York: St. John's University Press, 1973), pp. 121–125.

6. Ibid., pp. 106–113; Sophia Su-fei Yen, *Taiwan in China's Foreign Relations, 1836–1874* (Hamden, CT: Shoestring Press, 1965), chaps. 4 and 5; Kuo T'ing-yi, *T'ai-wan shih-shih kai-shuo* [An outline history of Taiwan] (T'ai-pei: Cheng-chung shu-chu, 1954), p. 151.

7. George W. Carrington, *Foreigners in Formosa* (San Francisco: Chinese Materials Center, 1977), pp. 118–121.

8. James W. Davidson, *The Island of Formosa, Past and Present* (London: Macmillan, 1903), pp. 180–182, 216–217.

9. Chan, "External Relations," pp. 111–113; P.D. Coates, *The China Consuls: British Consular Officers, 1843–1943* (New York: Oxford University Press, 1988), pp. 162–163,

10. Coates, *China Consuls*, pp. 268, 319 ff.

11. Ibid., pp. 324–326; Carrington, *Foreigners*, pp. 229–241; and Chan, "External Relations," pp. 129–134.

12. John Dodd, "Formosa," *Scottish Geographical Magazine*, 10 (November 1895): 569.

13. See Robert Gardella, *Harvesting Mountains: Fujian and the China Tea Trade, 1757–1937* (Berkeley: University of California Press, 1994), pp. 64–65.

14. Carrington, *Foreigners*, pp. 221–222; Coates, *China Consuls*, p. 334.

15. Coates, *China Consuls*, pp. 334–335.

16. George Leslie Mackay, *From Far Formosa: The Island, Its People and Missions*, 4th. ed. (New York: Fleming H. Revell, 1900), p. 164.

17. Ibid., pp. 170–171.

18. Carrington, *Foreigners*, pp. 247–252.

19. Murray A. Rubinstein, "Mission of Faith, Burden of Witness: The Presbyterian

Church in the Evolution of Modern Taiwan, 1865–1989," *American Asian Review*, 9, no. 2 (summer 1991): 70–73; see also Hollington K. Tong, *Christianity in Taiwan: A History* (Taipei: *China Post*, 1961), pp. 21– 51.

20. Rubinstein, "Mission of Faith," p. 73; Tong, *Christianity*, p. 46.

21. Chou Tsung-hsien, "Ch'ing-mou Chi-tu-chiao hsuan-chiao-shih tui T'ai-wan yi-liao te kung-hsien" [The Christian missionaries' contribution to medical treatment in Taiwan during the late Ch'ing era], *T'ai-wan wen-hsien*, 35, no. 3 (September 1984): 1–10; Tong, *Christianity*, pp. 23, 28–29, 37–40, and 49.

22. Mackay, *From Far Formosa*, pp. 315–316.

23. Tong, *Christianity*, pp. 26–27, 47–48.

24. This is, at least, the number of converts suggested in Tong, *Christianity*, pp. 33, 40, and 44; the total population is derived from John Shepherd, *Statecraft and Political Economy on the Taiwan Frontier, 1600–1800* (Stanford: Stanford University Press, 1993), pp. 160–161.

25. Myers, "The Traditional Economy," p. 373.

26. See Samuel P.S. Ho, *Economic Development of Taiwan, 1860* (New Haven: Yale University Press, 1978), pp. 3 and 16.

27. Wang Shih-ch'ing, "Shih-chiu shih-chi chung-yeh T'ai-wan pei-pu nung-ts'un chin-jung chih yen-chiu—yi Hsing-chih-pao yin-chu hsiao-tsu-hu Kuang-chi wei li" [A study on rural money circulation in the northern part of Taiwan during the mid-nineteenth century—a case study of the Kuang-chi of Hsing-chih-pao], *T'ai-wan wen-hsien*, 39, no. 2 (June 1988): 1; Li Ziji, "Lun waiguo shangye ziben dui Taiwan maoyi de kongzhi (1860–1894)" [On the control of Taiwan foreign trade by foreign commercial capital (1860–1894)], in *Ch'ingdai Taiwanshi yanjiu* (Research on Taiwan history during the Ch'ing dynasty), ed. Chen Zaizheng, Kong Li, and Deng Kongzhao (Xiamen: Xiamen University Press, 1986), pp. 446–447.

28. Li, "Lun waiguo shangye," p. 449; Li Kuo-ch'i, *Chung-kuo hsien-tai-hua te ch'ü-yu yen-chiu: Min-Che-T'ai ti-ch'u, 1860–1916* [Regional study of China's modernization: The Fukien, Chekiang, and Taiwan region, 1860–1916] (Nan-kang: Institute for Modern History, Academia Sinica, 1982), p. 357; Huang Fucai, *Taiwan shangye shi* [A history of Taiwan's commerce] (Nanchang: Jiangxi People's Publishing House, 1990), pp. 189–204.

29. Ho, *Economic Development*, p. 15.

30. Ibid., p. 15, table 2.3.

31. Davidson, *Island of Formosa*, pp. 397–420; Li, *Chung-kuo hsien-tai-hua*, pp. 355–356.

32. Li, *Chung-kuo hsien-tai-hua*, pp. 355–356; Li, "Lun waiguo shangye," pp. 441–442.

33. Davidson, *Island of Formosa*, pp. 405–407; Theodore Ropp, *War in the Modern World* (New York: Macmillan, 1962), p. 215.

34. Li, "Lun waiguo shangye," pp. 441–442; Li, *Chung-kuo hsien-tai-hua*, pp. 356–357; Davidson, *Island of Formosa*, p. 407; and Myers, "The Traditional Economy," p. 378, table 8.

35. The term (a Chinese expression) is manifest in the excellent study by Dan M. Etherington and Keith Forster, *Green Gold: The Political Economy of China's Post-1949 Tea Industry* (Hong Kong: Oxford University Press, 1993).

36. Gardella, *Harvesting Mountains*, p. 65.

37. Ibid., p. 65.

38. Ibid., pp. 65–67.

39. Ibid., pp. 78–81; see also Mark A. Allee, *Law and Local Society in Late Imperial China: Northern Taiwan in the Nineteenth Century* (Stanford: Stanford University Press, 1994), chaps. 4 and 5.

40. Wang Shih-ch'ing, ed., *T'ai-wan kung-ssu tsang ku-wen-shu ying-pen* [Copies of Taiwanese historical documents in private holdings], series 2, n.d, Fu Ssu-nien Library, Academia Sinica, Nan-kang, Taiwan, document no. 02–05–09–208.

41. Ho, *Economic Development*, p. 21; Gardella, *Harvesting Mountains*, p. 64, table 10 and p. 82.

42. Ho, *Economic Development*, p. 14, table 2.2; Christopher M. Isett, "Sugar Manufacture and the Agrarian Economy of Nineteenth Century Taiwan," *Modern China,* 21, no. 2 (April 1995): 243–244.

43. Li, "Lun waiguo shangye," pp. 438–439; Lin, "Mao-yi yu Ch'ing-mou T'ai-wan," pp. 18–19.

44. Myers, "The Traditional Economy," p. 387.

45. See C. Daniels, "The Handicraft Scale Sugar Industry and Merchant Capital in South Taiwan, 1870–1895," *Toyo gakuho,* 64, nos. 3–4: 65–102.

46. Isett, "Sugar Manufacture," pp. 244–251.

47. Ibid., pp. 244–250.

48. Ibid., pp. 252–255; note also Chih-ming Ka, *Japanese Colonialism in Taiwan: Land Tenure, Development, and Dependency in Colonial Taiwan, 1895–1945* (Boulder: Westview, 1995).

49. Robert P. Weller, *Unities and Diversities in Chinese Religion* (Seattle: University of Washington Press, 1987), pp. 74–81.

50. Li, *Chung-kuo hsien-tai-hua*, pp. 470–472.

51. Arthur P. Wolf and Chieh-shan Huang, *Marriage and Adoption in China 1845–1945* (Stanford: Stanford University Press, 1980), p. 37.

52. Stevan Harrell, *Ploughshare Village: Culture and Context in Taiwan* (Seattle: University of Washington Press, 1982), p. 21; P. Steven Sangren, "Social Space and the Periodization of Economic History: A Case from Taiwan," *Comparative Studies in Society and History*, 27, no. 3 (July 1985): 540–541.

53. Harrell, *Ploughshare Village*, pp. 23–26; Sangren, "Social Space," pp. 540–542; Wolf and Huang, *Marriage and Adoption*, pp. 39–40.

54. Wolf and Huang, *Marriage and Adoption*, p. 38; Pai Ch'ang-ch'uan, "Wei T'ai-ch'a hsun-ken—t'an An-ch'i yu T'ai-wan-jen ho Hua-ch'iao te hsueh-li kuan-hsi" [Investigating the roots of Taiwan tea—A discussion of An-ch'i, Taiwanese and the Hua-ch'iao kinship], *T'ai-pei wen-hsien*, 65 (September 1983): 167 ff.

55. See Chang Ming-hsiung, "Wan Ch'ing shih-ch'i T'ai-wan t'ung-shang k'ou-an te k'ai-fang yu she-hui Ch'ing-chi te pien-ch'ien" [The opening of treaty ports and socioeconomic change in late Ch'ing Taiwan], *T'ai-wan wen-hsien,* 42, nos. 3–4 (September–December 1991): 9–10.

56. Wen Chen-hua, "Tan-shui k'ai-kang yu Ta-tao-ch'eng chung-hsin te hsing-ch'eng" [The opening of Tan-shui port and the rise of Ta-tao-ch'eng center], *Li-shih hsueh-pao,* 6 (May 1978): 1–15; Harry J. Lamley, "The Formation of Cities: Initiative and Motivation in Building Three Walled Cities in Taiwan" in *The City in Late Imperial China*, ed. G. William Skinner (Stanford: Stanford University Press, 1977), pp. 168–173 and 180.

57. Chang Tao-chang, "T'ai-wan Tan-shui chih li-shih yu mao-yi" [The history and trade of Tan-shui, Taiwan], *T'ai-wan Ch'ing-chi shih,* 10 (1966): 163–168; see also the exhaustive coverage in Tai Pao-ts'un, "Ch'ing-chi Tan-shui k'ai-kang chih yen-chiu" [Research on the history of the opening of Tan-shui port in the Ch'ing], *T'ai-pei wen-hsien,* 66 (December 1983): 127–317.

58. Li, *Chung-kuo hsien-tai hua*, p. 475.

59. Lin, "Mao-yi yu Ch'ing-mou T'ai-wan," p. 26; Chang Chia-ming, "Nung ch'an-p'in wai-mao yu ch'eng-chen fan-hsing—yi Ch'ing-mou T'ai-wan pei-pu ti-ch'u te fa-

chan wei lieh" [The relationship between the exportation of agricultural products and the rise of cities—using the development of late Ch'ing northern Taiwan as an example], *Tung-hai ta-hsueh li-shih hsueh-pao,* 7 (1985): 169–187.

60. Lin, "Mao-yi yu Ch'ing-mou T'ai-wan," pp. 26–27.

61. Chang, "Wan-Ch'ing shih-ch'i," pp. 12–14.

62. Allee, *Law and Local Society,* pp. 100–117.

63. Ibid., pp. 117–130.

64. Rev. W. Campbell, *Sketches from Formosa* (London: Marshall Brothers, 1915), p. 120.

65. Mackay, *From Far Formosa,* p. 276.

66. Gudula Linck-Kesting, *Ein Kapitel chinesischer Grenz-geschichte: Han und Nicht-han im Taiwan der Ch'ing-Zeit: 1683–1895* [A chapter in Chinese border history: Han and Non-Han in Ch'ing Taiwan: 1683–1895] (Wiesbaden: Steiner, 1979), pp. 265–268. The writer is grateful to Professor Jack Wills for bringing this work to his attention.

67. See Johanna M. Meskill, *A Chinese Pioneer Family: The Lins of Wu-feng, Taiwan 1729–1895* (Princeton: Princeton University Press, 1979).

68. See Joseph W. Esherick and Mary B. Rankin, "Introduction," p. 24, and "Concluding Remarks," pp. 313–315 and 327, in *Chinese Local Elites and Patterns of Dominance,* ed. Esherick and Rankin (Berkeley: University of California Press, 1990).

69. Lin, "Mao-yi yu Ch'ing-mou," p. 29.

70. Li, *Chung-kuo hsien-tai hua,* pp. 569–570.

71. Harry J. Lamley, "The Taiwan Literati and Early Japanese Rule, 1895–1915" (Ph.D. dissertation, University of Washington, 1964), pp. 8–13.

72. Esherick and Rankin, "Concluding Remarks," p. 306.

73. Meskill, *Chinese Pioneer Family,* pp. 200–201; and Li, *Chung-kuo hsien-tai hua,* pp. 571–572.

74. Meskill, *Chinese Pioneer Family,* pp. 251–252; Li, *Chung-kuo hsien-tai hua,* p. 191; and Huang Fu-san, "The Character of Gentry Power in Ch'ing Taiwan: A View from the Expansion of Wealth of the Lin Family of Wufeng," *Taiwan Studies,* 1 , no. 1 (spring 1995).

75. Meskill, *Chinese Pioneer Family,* pp. 179–191 and 233–241.

76. See Li, *Chung-kuo hsien-tai hua,* pp. 191–193; Wolf and Huang, *Marriage and Adoption,* p. 40; Gardella, *Harvesting Mountains,* p. 79; Lamley, "Formation of Cities," p. 199; and William M. Speidel, "Liu Ming-ch'uan in Taiwan, 1884–1891" (Ph.D. dissertation, Yale University, 1967), p. 135.

77. Meskill, *Chinese Pioneer Family,* pp. 208 and 216–219; note also Harry J. Lamley, "The Taiwan Literati and Early Japanese Rule, 1895–1915: A Study of Their Reactions to the Japanese Occupation and Subsequent Responses to Colonial Rule and Modernization" (Ph.D. dissertation, University of Washington, 1964), p. 126.

78. Lamley, "Formation of Cities," p. 199.

79. See Ronald G. Knapp, *China's Traditional Rural Architecture: A Cultural Geography of the Common House* (Honolulu: University of Hawaii Press, 1986), p. 95; Kyoko Ishikure, "The Lins of Pan-ch'iao," *Blaisdell Institute Journal,* 9 (1974): 50–53; and Lamley, "Taiwan Literati," p. 126.

80. Chang, "Wan-Ch'ing shih-ch'i," pp. 12 and 14. As Chang notes, among the island's other elite families at the time were the Chengs of Hsin-chu, who owed their fortunes to camphor, the Ch'ens of Ta-kao (Kao-hsiung), who owed theirs to sugar, and the comprador-merchant Li Ch'un-sheng and his kin.

81. The episode is summarized in Feng Tso-min, *T'ai-wan shih pai-chiang* [A hundred lectures in Taiwan history] (Taipei: Ch'eng-wen, 1970), pp. 92–95.

82. See the full account in Yen, *China's Foreign Relations,* pp. 125–305; also note

Leonard Gordon, "Japan's Abortive Colonial Venture in Taiwan, 1874," *Journal of Modern History*, 37, no. 1 (March 1965): 171–185; and Edwin Pak-wah Leung, "Li Hung-chang and the Liu-ch'iu (Ryukyu) Controversy, 1871–1881," in *Li Hung-chang and China's Early Modernization*, ed. Samuel C. Chu and Kwang-Ch'ing Liu (Armonk, NY: M.E. Sharpe, 1994), pp. 162–175.

83. See Immanuel C.Y. Hsu, "Late Ch'ing Foreign Relations, 1866–1905," in *The Cambridge History of China,* vol. 11, *Late Ch'ing, 1800–1911,* pt. 2, ed. John K. Fairbank and Kwang-Ch'ing Liu (Cambridge: Cambridge University Press, 1980), pp. 86–87.

84. John L. Rawlinson, "China's Failure to Coordinate Her Modern Fleets in the Late Nineteenth Century," in *Approaches to Modern Chinese History,* ed. Albert Feuerwerker, Rhoads Murphey, and Mary C. Wright (Berkeley: University of California Press, 1967), pp. 114–115.

85. Yen, *China's Foreign Relations*, pp. 302–303, stands virtually alone in seeing the episode as a Chinese political and diplomatic triumph; the pessimistic consensus view is expressed in Hsu, "Late Ch'ing Foreign Relations," pp. 87–88.

86. See David Pong, "The Vocabulary of Change: Reformist Ideas of the 1860's and 1870's," in *Ideal and Reality: Social and Political Change in Modern China 1860–1949*, ed. Pong and Edmund S.K. Fung (Lanham: University Press of America, 1985), pp. 49–51.

87. Lamley, "Taiwan Literati," p. 37.

88. David Pong, *Shen Pao-chen and China's Modernization in the Nineteenth Century* (Cambridge: Cambridge University Press, 1994), pp. 291–293.

89. See Luo Ta-ch'un, *Luo Ch'ing-shan T'ai-wan k'ai-shan jih-chi* [The diary of Luo Ta-ch'un on the opening up of Taiwan], edited with an introduction by David Pong (Taipei: 1972).

90. Li, *Chung-kuo hsien-tai hua*, pp. 176–177.

91. Pong, *Shen Pao-chen*, pp. 284–289 and 293–295.

92. See Shepherd, *Statecraft and Political Economy*, pp. 360 and 408.

93. Ibid., p. 360; see also Ramon H. Myers, "Taiwan Under Ch'ing Imperial Rule, 1684–1895: The Traditional Order," *Journal of the Institute of Chinese Studies of the Chinese University of Hong Kong,* 4, no. 2 (1971): 497.

94. Li, *Chung-kuo hsien-tai hua*, pp. 169–170.

95. Ibid., pp. 171 and 177.

96. Ibid., pp. 172–174.

97. Ibid., pp. 177–180.

98. Ibid., p. 181, citing Ting Jih-ch'ang, *Fu Min tsou-kao, chuan* 3; and Lu Shih-ch'ang, *Ting Jih-ch'ang yu tzu-ch'iang yun-tung* [Ting Jih-ch'ang and the self-strengthening movement] (Taipei: Institute of Modern History, Academia Sinica, 1972), pp. 292 ff.

99. Li, *Chung-kuo hsien-tai hua*, p. 181.

100. Ibid., pp. 325–326.

101. See Chang Shih-hsieh, *Wan-Ch'ing chih T'ai cheng-tse* [Late Ch'ing policy toward Taiwan] (Taipei: n.p., 1978), pp. 216–218; and Li, *Chung-kuo hsien-tai hua*, pp. 183–187. The writer is grateful to David Pong for the reference to Chang Shih-hsieh's work.

102. Samuel Chu, "Liu Ming-ch'uan and Modernization of Taiwan," *Journal of Asian Studies,* 23, no. 1 (November 1963): 38.

103. Speidel, "Liu Ming-ch'uan," pp. 42–45. The French side of the Taiwan campaign is thoroughly covered in E. Garnot, *L'Expédition française de Formose, 1884–1885* [The French expedition to Formosa, 1884–1885] (Paris: Librairie Ch. Delagrave, 1894); on the blockade (and its implications in international law), see Ernest Ragot, *Le Blocus de*

l'Isle de Formose [The blockade of the island of Formosa], (thèse doctorale, Université de Paris, Faculté de Droit; Paris: Imprimerie A. Mellottée, 1903).

104. Speidel, "Liu Ming-ch'uan," pp. 44–48; see also Davidson, *Island of Formosa*, pp. 219–242, for a journalistic overview of the course of the war.

105. Kwang-Ch'ing Liu and Richard J. Smith, "The Military Challenge: The North-west and the Coast," in Fairbank and Liu, ed., *Cambridge History of China*, vol. 11, p. 252.

106. Chu, "Liu Ming-ch'uan," pp. 38–39.

107. William M. Speidel, "The Administrative and Fiscal Reforms of Liu Ming-ch'uan in Taiwan, 184–1891: Foundation for Self-strengthening," *Journal of Asian Studies,* 35, no. 3 (May 1976): 446–448; Li, *Chung-kuo hsien-tai hua*, p. 193.

108. Speidel, "Administrative and Fiscal Reforms," p. 447; Li, *Chung-kuo hsien-tai hua*, pp. 193–194.

109. Speidel, "Administrative and Fiscal Reforms," p. 447 n28; Myers, "The Traditional Order," pp. 496–497.

110. Speidel, "Administrative and Fiscal Reforms," pp. 446–447; Lamley, "Taiwan Literati," pp. 42–43 and 116–119.

111. Speidel, "Administrative and Fiscal Reforms," p. 447; Lamley, "Formation of Cities," pp. 196–202.

112. Speidel, "Liu Ming-ch'uan," pp. 127–129; Lamley, "Taiwan Literati," pp. 120–124.

113. Speidel, "Administrative and Fiscal Reforms," pp. 452–456.

114. Ibid., pp. 454–456.

115. Li, *Chung-kuo hsien-tai hua*, pp. 397–398; Speidel, "Administrative Reforms," pp. 452–453.

116. See Speidel, "Liu Ming-ch'uan," pp. 222–235; idem, "Administrative and Fiscal Reforms," p. 453.

117. Speidel, "Administrative and Fiscal Reforms," pp. 453–454; Speidel, "Liu Ming-ch'uan," pp. 230–231.

118. Speidel, "Administrative and Fiscal Reforms," p. 453.

119. Liu, *Chung-kuo hsien-tai hua*, pp. 189–190; Speidel, "Liu Ming-ch'uan," pp. 275–276.

120. Liu, *Chung-kuo hsien-tai hua*, p. 190; Speidel, "Administrative and Fiscal Reforms," p. 457.

121. Li, *Chung-kuo hsien-tai hua*, pp. 190–191; Speidel, "Liu Ming-ch'uan," pp. 277–288.

122. Speidel, "Liu Ming-ch'uan," p. 282.

123. Speidel, "Administrative and Fiscal Reforms," pp. 457–458.

124. Linck-Kesting, *Ein Kapitel chinesischer Grenzgeschichte*, pp. 266–268.

125. Speidel, "Liu Ming-ch'uan," pp. 289–303.

126. Ibid., p. 294 ff.

127. See Speidel, "Administrative and Fiscal Reforms," p. 442; Davidson, *Island of Formosa*, pp. 346–352; and Liu, *Chung-kuo hsien-tai hua*, pp. 312–334.

128. See Chu, "Liu Ming-ch'uan and Modernization of Taiwan," 37–53.

129. Ibid., pp. 40–42; Liu, *Chung-kuo hsien-tai hua*, pp. 312–324.

130. Chu, "Liu Ming-ch'uan and Modernization," pp. 42–46.

131. Ibid., pp. 47–48.

132. Liu, *Chung-kuo hsien-tai hua*, pp. 327–329; ibid., pp. 48–49 and 51.

133. Chu, "Liu Ming-ch'uan and Modernization," pp. 49–50; Davidson, *Island of Formosa*, pp. 248–250.

134. Liu, *Chung-kuo hsien-tai hua*, pp. 330–331; Davidson, *Island of Formosa*, p. 251 n1.

135. Davidson, *Island of Formosa*, pp. 251–252 n1.

136. Contrasting perspectives on Liu's accomplishments are readily apparent in Chu, "Liu Ming-ch'uan and Modernization," which presents a generally positive view of his technological innovations, and Speidel, "Administrative and Fiscal Reforms," which stresses the limitations of his administrative reforms. For an example of the continued interest in Liu in the People's Republic, see the twenty-odd essays in Hsiao K'o-fei, Chung Ch'ung, and Hsu Tse-hao, comp., *Liu Mingquan zai Taiwan* [Liu Ming-ch'uan on Taiwan] (Shanghai: Shanghai shehui kexue yuan, 1987). The writer is grateful to David Pong for reference to this work.

137. Speidel, "Liu Ming-ch'uan," pp. 397–402.

138. Ibid., p. 383.

139. Ibid., pp. 383–384.

8

Taiwan Under Japanese Rule, 1895–1945

The Vicissitudes of Colonialism

Harry J. Lamley

The Presidential Office Building in Taipei.

Taiwan, including the P'eng-hu islands (Pescadores), was ceded to Japan in 1895 at the conclusion of the Sino-Japanese War of 1894–95. This sudden act ushered in a fifty-one-year period of colonial rule in Taiwan that is now undergoing a major reassessment. Until recently, appraisals of the Japanese period generally reflected two contrary frames of reference: a positive perspective highlighting the achievements brought about under a colonial regime, and an anti-imperialist orientation featuring harsh Japanese rule and the hardships suffered by the island's subject population.[1] Sinophiles and exponents of Chinese nationalism subscribed to the latter view in keeping with their anti-Japanese sentiment. This led to a highly biased historiography by which resistance to colonial rule was emphasized and constructive measures were often slighted or ignored. In postcolonial Taiwan, after the colony's retrocession to China in 1945, the Japanese period tended to be discredited as a dark age or as a mere cipher wedged between Taiwan's late Ch'ing and Nationalist eras, when Chinese mainlander governance prevailed.

Currently, more constructive assessments of the colonial past are emerging in Taiwan in line with the democratization process under way there. Taiwanese scholars are now able to research the hitherto sensitive Japanese period, and many have come to accept the colonial legacy as an intrinsic part of their island heritage and an important factor in Taiwan's modern development. Nevertheless, colonialism and imperialism still seem reprehensible to the Taiwanese, and there is a lingering concern as to the dire effects of Japan's late wartime efforts and the abrupt Japanese unconditional surrender in August 1945.

Befitting an updated history of Taiwan, this chapter reflects more the current Taiwanese perspective of the colonial past. This view allows for a broader frame of temporal and spatial reference. The Japanese period is envisioned as an integral part of Taiwan's modern age, for throughout a longer continuum, extending from the Opium War (1839–42) to the present, the island has remained under foreign threat or outside domination, and its inhabitants have been continually exposed to modern Western and Asian influences. Moreover, colonial Taiwan is perceived within a larger Asian-Pacific context, not merely as a secluded island colony linked to metropolitan Japan.[2] As discussed below, Taiwan became involved in new patterns of overseas relationships and the Taiwanese, as Japanese subjects, derived a separate status and identity vis-à-vis mainland China and the expanding Japanese empire. This current perspective, with its sharper focus on the Taiwanese people, also admits a more complete and in-depth representation of their colonial experience.

In accordance with the Taiwanese perspective, the main theme in this chapter relates to the vicissitudes—that is, the sudden or unexpected changes, opportunities, setbacks, and hardships—the Taiwanese encountered as a result of Japanese rule. This theme serves to highlight the Taiwanese colonial experience, although essentially within a Japanese context, for major changes in circumstance or fortune experienced by the Taiwanese were invariably brought about under Japanese domination and by means beyond their immediate control. Therefore, the Japanese presence is emphasized throughout the chapter, as are colonizer–colonized relationships between the metropolitan Japanese (*naichijin*) residents and the subordinate islander (*hontōjin*) inhabitants.

The organization of this chapter is suggestive of the constant Japanese presence. Each of the following sections, beginning with the annexation and military takeover of Taiwan in 1895–97, and ending with the 1937–45 wartime period, denotes a distinct time frame set off by Japanese policies and actions. As colonizers, the Japanese seized the initiative and imposed measures designed for their immediate advantage or for long-term benefits to the home country. The Taiwanese, as a result, generally adjusted to or reacted against Japanese controlled situations, a responsive condition universal among subject populations enthralled by modern colonialism.

Annexation and Armed Resistance (1895–1897)

Japan's annexation of Taiwan was not the result of long-range planning. Instead, this action came about by way of strategy adopted during the war with China and diplomacy carried out in the spring of 1895. Prime Minister Itō Hirobumi's "southern strategy," supportive of Japanese navy designs, paved the way for the occupation of the P'eng-hu islands in late March as a prelude to the takeover of Taiwan. Soon thereafter, while peace negotiations were still in progress, Itō and Mutsu Munemitsu, his minister of foreign affairs, stipulated that both Taiwan and P'eng-hu were to be ceded by imperial China.[3] Li Hung-chang, China's chief diplomat, was forced to accede to these conditions as well as to other Japanese demands, and the Treaty of Shimonoseki was signed on April 17, then duly ratified by the Ch'ing court on May 8.[4] The formal transference of Taiwan and P'eng-hu took place on shipboard offshore the Keelung (Chi-lung) coast on June 2. This formality was conducted by Li's adopted son, Li Ching-fang, and Admiral Kabayama Sukenori, a staunch advocate of annexation, whom Itō had appointed as governor-general of Taiwan.[5]

The acquisition of Taiwan marked an historic occasion for Meiji Japan. An island province and its inhabitants had been wrested from Ch'ing China, and the status of a colonial power achieved. Moreover, extraterritoriality privileges in China (along with a large indemnity) had been gained as an outcome of a war highlighted by impressive military and naval victories. In East Asia, at least, Japan now seemed to have almost gained parity with the Western powers that it would continue to emulate, boasting modern armaments and overseas empires.[6]

The annexation of Taiwan was also based on practical considerations of benefit to Japan. The large and productive island could furnish provisions and raw materials for Japan's expanding economy and become a ready market for Japanese goods. Taiwan's strategic location was deemed advantageous as well. As envisioned by the navy, the island would form a southern bastion of defense from which to safeguard southernmost Japan and also serve as a base for Japan's expansion southward by way of southern China and southeastern Asia. These considerations turned out to be accurate forecasts of the major roles Taiwan would play in Japan's quest for power, wealth, and greater empire.[7]

At the time, however, Meiji Japan was hardly prepared to enter upon its first colonial venture. That country had only begun to modernize, and the Meiji constitution had been in effect for less than six years. Even Japan's own "unequal" treaties with the Western powers were still being negotiated. The sudden acquisition of an overseas colony represented another unprecedented development that challenged Meiji leaders. Hence it is not surprising that they expressed uncertainty as to how Taiwan and its inhabitants were to relate to the Japanese home country. In Tokyo, members of the hastily organized Taiwan Affairs Bureau, headed by Itō, debated the merits of two conflicting proposals: the French assimilationist convention by which colonial Taiwan might be fused with metropolitan Japan and the Taiwanese readily assimilated; and the British model whereby the new island colony would be governed separately and its people allowed, by and large, to retain their own culture and society.[8]

The resistance initially encountered by the Japanese in Taiwan made political integration by constitutional means appear unrealistic. Eventually, in March 1896, Kabayama requested additional authority so that he could exert more complete control over the new colony. In response to his petition, the Imperial Diet enacted the controversial "Law 63," which authorized the Taiwan governor-general to issue executive ordinances (*ritsurei*) having the same effect as Japanese law.[9] This extraordinary measure granted almost supreme legislative power to the governor-general and made colonial rule in Taiwan seem more in keeping with the British system of separate governance. Meanwhile, pacification efforts about the island, coupled with the disdain the Japanese newcomers generally exhibited toward the inhabitants, forestalled the prospects of readily assimilating the Taiwanese.

Nonetheless, assimilation (*dōka*) remained a key issue in Taiwan under Japanese rule and was often a declared policy of the governor-general. In this colonial context, assimilation conveyed the idea that the *naichijin* were the bearers of a superior culture to be imparted to the *hontōjin*. Thus the concept connoted a one-sided response on the part of the Taiwanese, who, in effect, were expected to give up not only many of their customs and usages but, ultimately, their Chinese heritage as well. Yet there was an element of humanitarianism in all such ethnocentric dictates since assimilation, as a doctrine, was linked with the familiar admonition of "impartiality and equal favor" (*isshi dōjin*) for all Japanese subjects, attributed to the Meiji emperor. Under this alleged mandate his majesty's concern for his subjects not only seemed to promise equal treatment for the Taiwanese but was further construed to mean that, as assimilated subjects, they would share the benefits of "civilization and enlightenment" associated with modern progress in common with the *naichijin*.[10]

Governor-General Kabayama expressed similar benevolent sentiments after he arrived in Taiwan. He used the *"isshi dōjin"* adage in several of his early proclamations, including one announcing the inauguration of his government in Taipei (Taihoku) on June 17.[11] Assimilation also seemed plausible to a number of the educated elite in Japan because of the commonly held conviction that the Han Taiwanese shared cultural and racial affinities with the Japanese people. The proximity of Taiwan to Japan likewise promoted some to favor a merger of that island territory with the home country.[12]

However, disagreement concerning the prospects of Taiwan and its people under colonial rule continued to prevail among the Meiji leadership. This added to the problems and confusion Kabayama and his immediate successors faced in Taiwan, for many administrative decisions were initially made in Tokyo and reflected political dissension there rather than consensus as to how affairs in the colony were to be managed. Meanwhile, the colonial authorities and Japanese military encountered armed resistance throughout much of Taiwan: almost five months of sustained warfare in opposition to the military takeover, then sporadic local partisan attacks until 1902. Throughout the 1895–97 period, the first three governors-general relied mainly on military means in conjunction with local pacification efforts. The results were disappointing. Segments of the population remained unruly, and the colonization of Taiwan proved a costly venture. Later on, a Japanese observer referred to this three-year period as an "age of mistakes and failures."[13]

It was the island inhabitants, though, who suffered the most from the chaos initiated by the sudden cession and military takeover. Signs of unrest became evident in late March 1895, when P'eng-hu was seized. Disorder and panic ensued over the next several months as rumors of the impending cession of Taiwan spread and were subsequently confirmed. Tension about the island increased after an imperial edict, issued from Peking on May 20, ordered all Ch'ing officials to vacate their island posts and return to China. Amid the outcry that Taiwan had been abandoned by the Ch'ing court, frenzied mobs appeared in Taipei, the capital. There the governor's yamen was gutted by fire, the arsenal looted, and the nearby powder mill demolished shortly before Japanese troops reached the city on June 7.[14]

Further destruction and widespread misery accompanied the five-month war and its aftermath. Walled cities were damaged, and entire villages razed. Epidemics of cholera and typhus raged in war-torn localities while endemic diseases, especially malaria, affected both the general population and the Japanese military. Meanwhile, tension continued to prevail. Townspeople and villagers remained apprehensive of the intrusion of all outside forces, no matter whether Japanese or those of the resistance. Long-standing ethnic animosities flared up as well. Villages near the reaches of the Central Range feared attacks from hostile mountain tribes. Elsewhere, rancor resurfaced among segments of the Han Taiwanese population, most notably between Hakka and Hokkien (southern Min–speaking) elements.[15]

The war of resistance had broken out soon after units of the Imperial Guards staged the first Japanese landings at a secluded coastal area southeast of Keelung. This occurred on May 29, five days before the formal transference of Taiwan took place offshore in the same vicinity. By then, the Japanese were well aware that a military occupation of the island was necessary, for Kabayama had already been denied access to Tan-shui (Tam-sui) harbor by heavy bombardment from shore batteries. Thereafter, armed resistance continued, mainly directed from Taipei at first and then from the two prefectural centers and various of the county seats to the south, until Tainan city surrendered on October 21.[16]

A variety of resistance forces participated in this five-month war. In the north, remnant Ch'ing units from the mainland, together with ill-trained Kuangtung irregulars, briefly faced the well-disciplined Japanese advance. Following the loss of Taipei on June 7, armed resistance was offered mostly by local volunteers, including militia bodies and partisan bands. However, in the far south a small Black Flag force from southern China, led by Liu Yung-fu, a hero of the 1884–85 Sino-French War, also hindered Japanese landings and helped delay the occupation of Kao-hsiung (Takao) and, ultimately, Tainan. Throughout the war various resistance leaders capitalized on the defenses and military reforms developed in Taiwan as part of the late Ch'ing self-strengthening effort. They also made use of troops and arms dispatched from China until late in May.[17]

Although input from China was involved, this organized resistance to the military takeover amounted to a separate conflict apart from the Sino-Japanese War that had just ended. The Ch'ing court took pains not to become involved, fearing Japanese reprisals as well as setbacks in negotiations over the retrocession of the Liao-tung peninsula in North China.[18] Nevertheless, widespread indignation over the cession of Taiwan and the popular demand for retaliation against Japan made it difficult for China to sever its relations with its former island province so abruptly. After the May 20 edict, Governor T'ang Ching-sung and his aides in Taipei took advantage of the unstable situation and endeavored to carry on anti-Japanese resistance under an island regime, labeled the "Taiwan Republic." T'ang still professed to be a loyal Ch'ing servitor, however. The desperate act of forming a "republic" (*min-chu-kuo*), he alleged, was to delay the Japanese occupation so that one or another of the Western powers (France, in particular) might be prompted to come to the defense of Taiwan or be induced to take possession of the island in lieu of Japan.

Under the guise of a republic T'ang also sought to demonstrate a semblance of popular support by means of petitions and a "parliament." Given the chaotic conditions in Taipei by late May, though, T'ang was unable to control the military forces at his disposal, much less command the support of the troubled populace. Hence the Taiwan Republic, established amid a festive atmosphere at the capital on May 25, vanished from the northern Taiwan scene some twelve days later when T'ang and his aides secretly crossed over to the mainland shortly before Japanese troops entered Taipei.[19]

Soon thereafter, vestiges of the Taiwan Republic appeared in the south when, in June, Liu Yung-fu formed a temporary government at the old Tainan prefectural center. Liu, however, refused to accept the seals of the presidency (as T'ang had previously done). Instead, he imposed a makeshift type of military dictatorship based on a blood-pledge compact he entered into with representatives of the local elite. Eventually, around mid-October, Liu and his entourage similarly escaped to the mainland while Japanese forces were closing in on Tainan, and the Taiwan Republic disappeared forever as a guise for ad hoc island governance.[20]

Upon the surrender of Tainan, Governor-General Kabayama declared that Taiwan had been pacified.[21] His proclamation was premature, though, because the Japanese soon encountered further armed resistance, initially from Hakka villagers in the southernmost counties. Then the first of a prolonged series of local partisan attacks broke out near the end of the year, and the Japanese pacification efforts continued. Over the next seven years, partisan bands, dubbed "local bandits" or "rebels" by the Japanese, were active throughout Taiwan in or near cities and towns as well as in villages and remote mountainous areas.[22]

The partisan leaders ranged from prominent inhabitants to outcasts and criminal elements, all of whom espoused a strong xenophobic sentiment current among the local population. They staged guerrilla raids on Japanese installations, such as police stations and guard posts, but bandit types also centered their attacks on towns and villages, where the inhabitants were caught between the onslaught of these predators and the Japanese military and police. The Japanese reprisals were often more brutal, as demonstrated by the infamous "Yun-lin massacre" in June 1896, when some six thousand Taiwanese were slain.[23]

In an attempt to expedite his pacification efforts the third governor-general, Lieutenant General Nogi Maresuke, implemented a triple-guard system in June 1897. Under this plan, army units, assisted by military police, were dispatched to highland regions to confront major partisan gatherings and unruly mountain tribes; military and civil police forces were assigned to lowland areas where there was still active resistance; and the civil police undertook to safeguard more orderly rural and urban localities.[24] This system was not very successful during the twelve-month period that it was in effect. Various Japanese units failed to work in unison and often were unable to distinguish between submissive and unruly components of the population, despite Nogi's strategy of enticing the partisans to surrender. Hence many anxious Taiwanese continued to sympathize or even cooperate with local partisans.

Casualty figures further suggest why the Japanese forces still encountered so many terrified townspeople and villagers over the next few years. Estimates indicate that, from 1898 to the early part of the Kodama reign in 1902, some 12,000 more "bandit-rebels" were slain: a total of about twice as many inhabitants as those who died in battle during the 1895 war of resistance.[25] The postwar pacification efforts were costly to the Japanese as well. Soldiers, military porters, and policemen continued to die from disease and wounds in addition to the 5,300 who had been killed or wounded and the 27,000 more hospitalized as a result of the 1895 war.[26]

In all, only a small percentage of the island population actively participated in the war and subsequent partisan resistance. Most responded to the military occupation and uncertain prospects under Japanese rule in other ways. Many Taiwanese assumed a submissive demeanor or exhibited forms of passive withdrawal. A few even collaborated with the Japanese from early on. But given the general fear and panic, many fled to the hills and mountains, while more sought to cross over to the mainland. There was a heavy exodus of Taiwanese to China in 1895 and a steady stream of departures thereafter, for in exercising an option contained in the Treaty of Shimonoseki, Meiji Japan allowed the registered inhabitants a choice: to return to China by May 8, 1897 (two years after the treaty's ratification), and remain Ch'ing subjects, or stay in Taiwan (or return there by that deadline) and become Japanese citizens.[27] Altogether, more than 6,400 people, or about 23 percent of the total population, are estimated to have departed for China during this two-year period, not counting those who made secretive crossings.[28]

Among the Taiwanese who undertook channel crossings were people of wealth and eminence. Most of the upper gentry, including portions of their families, left the island during these two years.[29] Upon their departure, the elite structure throughout the settled portion of Taiwan began to change. It soon appeared that the remaining gentry—who by virtue of their degrees, titles, and classical education had enjoyed high status and privileges under Ch'ing rule—would suffer a serious decline under Japanese governance. Their group had already begun to experience an acute identity crisis as a result of their "abandonment" by the Ch'ing court.

The gentry-holdover dilemma, brought about by the sudden change of rule, was generally shared, at least in part, by the Han Taiwanese at large. No longer Ch'ing subjects, they nonetheless remained ethnic Chinese with ancestral and cultural ties to areas of southern Fukien and eastern Kuangtung. During the occupation, these strong attachments fostered xenophobic feelings of defiance, yet failed to produce an effective ideology of resistance. By 1895, there had not yet emerged a vital form of Chinese nationalism that might have brought about a more united stand against the Japanese takeover. Moreover, Taiwan's elevated standing as a separate province of China, attained in 1887, had not engendered any widespread type of popular support for the 1895 war. After the partisan resistance set in, the lack of a common unifying political sentiment was even more apparent. Local partisans expressed their xenophobic feelings in a variety of ways ranging from lingering outcries for self-rule to archaic Ming loyalist pronouncements.[30] Meanwhile, Taiwan and its inhabitants grew more and more detached from China as a consequence of the 1895 cession, the subsequent occupation and, finally, the 1897 deadline signifying that the Taiwanese were no longer of Chinese registry or nationality.

Colonial Reform and Taiwanese Accommodation (1898–1915)

Colonial rule in Taiwan gained a new lease on life when the fourth governor-general, General Kodama Gentarō, assumed office in 1898. Most of the policy-making and supervision, heretofore conducted in Tokyo, was then placed under his authority. Kodama soon restricted the power of the military in Taiwan and, in turn, delegated jurisdiction over domestic affairs to his chief of civil administration, Gotō Shimpei. This enabled the Taiwan governor-general to operate on a more consolidated basis and allowed Gotō considerable leeway in formulating plans and policies for the island colony during the Kodama reign (1898–1906).[31]

Gotō launched a variety of projects that laid the foundation for extensive economic development and modernization in Taiwan. The harbor at Keelung (Kirin) was improved and work continued on the trunk railway line connecting that northern port with nearby Taipei (Taihoku) and the southern seaport of Kao-hsiung, a project begun in the late Ch'ing and completed in 1908. More pushcart (*daisha*) trackage was also laid, and road building continued at a relatively rapid pace. By the time Gotō left office in 1906, primary and secondary roads had been extended three times over their 1899 length. Postal and telegraph facilities were likewise expanded, the first modern newspapers established, and telephone services introduced at the turn of the century. Soon thereafter, Taiwan's initial hydroelectric generating plant was constructed to serve Keelung and the administrative center at Taipei. In order to further modernize the economy, accounting and banking systems were introduced, along with Japanese corporate enterprises. Moreover, the Bank of Taiwan, founded in 1899, was assigned the duty of issuing silver (and later gold-backed) currency. A year later, a uniform system of weights and measures was established as well.[32]

Greater efforts were also made to harness Taiwan's economy to that of metropolitan Japan. Major exports, including rice, sugar, and camphor, were diverted to the home country, and Japanese shipping lines came to monopolize commercial and passenger service with the colony. After 1902, the largest percentage of Taiwan's export–import trade was conducted with Japan rather than with the Chinese mainland as before. Meanwhile, Western firms operating in Taiwan were soon squeezed out of most overseas trade, except for those engaged in tea exports. Consequently, few European and American merchants remained in the colony after the turn of the century.[33]

Above all, Gotō's civil administration sought to make Taiwan an agricultural appendage of Japan. In accordance with the long-range program for the development of commercial agriculture devised by Nitobe Inazō, who had been sent earlier from Japan to research forestry and subtropical agriculture, more land was placed under cultivation and several large irrigation projects were initiated to increase rice and sugarcane production in the central and southern coastal plains. Gotō figured prominently in the rise of Taiwan's modern sugar industry by promoting scientific farming, attracting investments, and providing subsidies to Japanese sugar producers.[34]

The costs of introducing economic reforms, as well as a modern-type infrastructure and technology, were high. Hence the Kodama regime adopted a policy of deficit financing in order to carry out many of its ambitious projects. Both Kodama and Gotō had to call upon the home government for funds and capitalization. They also sought out private Japanese and Taiwanese investors and urged the inhabitants at large to contribute through a postal savings system. At the same time, considerable revenue was raised from new excise taxes following the creation of opium, salt, camphor, and tobacco monopolies in the colony.[35] A land-tenure reform brought about much larger tax revenues as well after an extensive land investigation project, beginning in 1898, was completed in 1901. As a result of this investigation, a larger amount of untaxed "hidden land" was registered, and more landowners were placed on the tax rolls when the incidence of tax payment was shifted from the "large-rentholder households" (*ta-tzu hu*), whose claim to the land was redeemed in marketable bonds, to the former "small rentholders" (*hsiao-tzu hu*).[36] These measures, together with additional revenue generated through commercial and industrial taxes, made the governor-general less dependent on annual subsidies allotted by the Imperial Diet. By 1905, Taiwan no longer required such direct budgetary support from the home government, despite continuous heavy expenditures for new and ongoing projects.[37]

Gotō, who had received Western medical training, also introduced a series of reform measures pertaining to public health and sanitation. As a result of their widespread application and strict enforcement, marked improvements in the control of cholera, smallpox, and bubonic plague came about by 1905. Furthermore, Gotō established a public hospital and medical college in Taipei and helped to found charity hospitals and treatment centers about the island.[38] These advances in health standards and medical services, together with the gradual rise in prosperity, were reflected in higher rates of natural increase among the inhabitants by the second decade of Japanese rule. The first full census of the colony's population, carried out in 1905, indicates that the Han Taiwanese then numbered 2,890,485, only a slight increase over the 1900 estimate of 2,650,000. In contrast, by 1943, the subject population had more than doubled these early counts to a total of 5,962,000, a figure that also included more than two hundred thousand aboriginal inhabitants.[39]

Coupled with Gotō's concern for the well-being of the colonial inhabitants were his educational reforms. His administration established a system of elementary common schools (*kōgakkō*) and phased out the few Japanese-language schools created for Taiwanese youths during the Kabayama reign. The common schools not only offered instruction in Japanese language and culture, but also training in classical Chinese and Confucian ethics as well as in practical subjects, including science. In addition, an elementary school for girls continued to operate and, in 1899, three normal schools were opened. However, these various government schools served only a small percentage of the Taiwanese school-age population, while well over half the resident Japanese children attended separate primary schools (*shōgakkō*). Furthermore, few Taiwanese were admitted to the secondary level or had a chance to enter the medical college.[40] In part because of the limited access to government sponsored education, another segment of young inhabitants continued to enroll in the types of private schools that had been operating since the Ch'ing period. Most boys attended Chinese schools (*shobō* or *shu-fang*) offering more traditional learning, while a lesser number of males and females received training at the handful of religious schools, most notably those run by Dominican and Presbyterian missions.[41]

Discrimination with respect to educational opportunities seemed a suitable colonial policy to Gotō. He deemed it imprudent to provide universal education for the subject population since full assimilation of the Han Taiwanese appeared unlikely in the near future. Furthermore, schooling for aboriginal children of the remote mountain tribes was as yet only a projected venture. On the other hand, Gotō fostered elementary education, featuring both moral and scientific training, for those Taiwanese students whose families could afford such schooling. He also enabled the brightest to advance in the fields of teaching and medicine. He envisioned that, through a selective admissions process, there would emerge a generation of upright and enlightened Taiwanese leaders responsive to reform and modernization. For this reason Gotō opposed what he considered the outmoded *shobō* training, which, he believed, impeded progress and mainly perpetuated empty learning.[42]

Despite the accomplishments initiated by the Kodama regime, the early period of colonial rule remained a turbulent one. Partisan disturbances persisted, and almost twelve thousand more "bandit-rebels" were killed in battle or executed between 1898 and mid-1902.[43] After the partisans had been quelled, a series of local uprisings flared up, a phenomenon indicative of a new phase of Taiwanese armed resistance. The succeeding regime of General Sakuma Samata (1905–15), the fifth governor-general, witnessed at least six such insurrections from 1907 to 1915. These resulted in more casualties among the inhabitants and more than eight hundred executions.[44]

Meanwhile, the mountain tribes remained restive and prone to attack guard posts and raid nearby settlements. In order to bring about peace and stability within Taiwan's rugged interior, Gotō imposed a boundary encircling the high country, a huge area that was designated as a reservation for the various tribes.[45] The peaceful seclusion he sought to maintain was disrupted in 1911, however, by Sakuma and his chief of civil administration, Uchida Kakichi, who arranged for a large military force to open up Taiwan's mountainous reserve so as to gain access to its prime timber resources. Over a two-year span (1913–14), a bitter "subjugation" campaign ensued, involving even an aerial attack and naval bombardments from off the eastern seacoast. By 1915, many aboriginal villages had been destroyed and lives lost, especially among the Atayal and Bunun people, who offered the fiercest resistance.[46]

The year 1915 marked the end of a twenty-year period of armed resistance against Japanese authority. Notwithstanding the fact that disturbances continued well after their tenure in office, Kodama and Gotō are credited with having devised a successful pacification strategy by which such turbulence was eventually eliminated. Soon after assuming office, Kodama abolished Nogi's triple-guard system and relieved the army from primary responsibility for police affairs. Instead, the civil police were authorized to maintain order and take action against partisan and aboriginal incursions, while the military police were held in readiness for emergency use.[47] The civil police force, under Gotō's supervision, was then enlarged and assigned to rural and urban posts throughout the colony. Because of the shortage of trained Japanese policemen, a sizable number of Taiwanese were added to the force after the junior grade of assistant patrolman was instituted in 1899. Meanwhile, a separate force of specially trained mountain police, also composed of both Japanese and Taiwanese patrolmen, was posted at guard stations along or within the aboriginal reservation boundary.[48]

In their efforts to subdue unruly partisan and aboriginal bands, the colonial authorities had also to enlist the support of local forces. These consisted mainly of "able-bodied" militia *(sōteidan,* or *chuang-ting t'uan)* drawn from *hokō (pao-chia)* units among the Han Taiwanese population, and *aiyuū (ai-yung)* guards, composed of armed bodies of Taiwanese and acculturated aborigines, that had operated since the late Ch'ing to provide protection from mountain aborigine forays. Gotō relied heavily on the *sōteidan* to help combat partisan guerrilla onslaughts. Later on, Sakuma made use of "able-bodied" militia contingents in actions against insurgents and during the "subjugation" campaign he and Uchida waged against the mountain tribes. In the meantime, the *aiyū* guards were used during the Kodama and Sakuma reigns to contain and then cordon off the mountain people as a five-hundred-mile guard-line *(aiyūsen)* was constructed around their territory.[49]

It is noteworthy that both of these auxiliary forces were brought under direct Japanese control in 1903. In the case of the "able-bodied" militia corps, this happened when the *pao-chia* bureaus and branches, established by local Taiwanese managers with Gotō's approval in 1898, were abolished and a reconstructed *hokō* system was formed under the jurisdiction of the civil police. Thereafter, until 1943 when it was disbanded, the *sōteidan* functioned as an appendage of the police system.[50] Similarly, the private *aiyū* bands were absorbed as government-directed units and eventually, along with the mountain police, assigned to an aboriginal affairs office.[51] After armed resistance had been crushed, the colonial authorities clearly endeavored to maintain full control over all community and private paramilitary bodies.

The prolonged resistance, in fact, made the Japanese extremely security-minded with regard to their first overseas colony and its subject population. The

Taiwan governor-general retained full authority over the military and naval command assigned to the colony; whereas virtually all civil affairs came under the purview of the police after Gotō revamped his head office, the Civil Administration Bureau, and centralized its police system. At about the same time, two major reorganizations of the local government, implemented in 1898 and 1901, enabled the police force to become an integral part of colonial administration on the district and subdistrict levels and to establish an islandwide network of local stations and substations.[52] Security matters and daily governance were thus combined in the hands of widespread, though relatively small, bodies of police sergeants and patrolmen functioning within a well-structured police system.

Colonial rule in Taiwan was patriarchal in nature by virtue of the supreme power vested in the governor-general. Since that high official remained aloof from the inhabitants as a rule, it was the local police who most often personified an authoritarian or even draconian type of colonial regime.[53] Their constant vigilance and harsh exactions, along with their active involvement in a multitude of duties and services extending well beyond those relating to law and order, became familiar features of civil authority. The commanding influence exercised by local patrolmen was most often apparent in village areas. There, besides attending to vexatious security and tax matters, they enforced regulations pertaining to agriculture, hygiene and sanitation, and a variety of other matters. They also intruded into private households during their investigations and pried into the conduct and personal affairs of the residents.[54]

In order to maintain such tight control over the Taiwanese population, the civil police made steady use of town and village headmen between 1897 and 1909, then ward or section chiefs (*kuchō*) until 1920. Moreover, they co-opted members of various community associations (merchant, agricultural, and the like) to do their bidding.[55] Above all, the police made able use of the *hokō* system after it came under their direct authority in 1903. According to Hui-yu Caroline Ts'ai, the *hokō* system was the "key factor" that enabled the colonial administration to exercise effective control over the Taiwanese inhabitants without further increasing the size of the police force.[56]

Current research has revealed more about the nature of the colonial *hokō* system in Taiwan. This was basically a reconstructed version of the Ch'ing *pao-chia* system of mutual household surveillance that had lasted into the Japanese period. The *hokō* system, too, featured a two-level structure consisting of *ho (pao)* and smaller *kō (chia)* household groupings. These units operated under the informal leadership of unpaid *ho* and *kō* heads (*hosei* and *kōchō*) nominally selected by the household heads within each grouping. The constituent households were held mutually responsible for the actions and obligations of their respective members as well as for carrying out duties and services assigned by the police.[57] The local police (including Taiwanese patrolmen), on the other hand, exercised close supervision over the inhabitants by virtue of their contacts with the *ho* and *kō* heads, the pressure they brought to bear on the household heads, and their frequent incursions into *hokō* communities and households. Furthermore, local police stations maintained constant surveillance over the Taiwanese inhabitants by means of updated household registries based primarily on registers kept by the *hosei* and, eventually, *hokō* clerks (*shoki*).[58]

Although the *hokō* (including the *sōteidan* militia) functioned under strict police authority, the *hokō* communities seem to have enjoyed a measure of self-government, at least according to the colonial authorities. Each unit abided by a *hokō* compact (*kiyaku*) allegedly drawn up by household representatives at its inception, and *ho* assemblies met annually to "elect" *hokō* heads when necessary and to negotiate the household fees to be assessed during a given year. In reality, however, the compacts were based on procedures determined beforehand by the authorities. Also, the selection of *ho* and *kō* heads was controlled by the police, and the annual household fee assessments likewise required local police supervision and approval.[59] Hence, instead of promoting self-government, the *hokō* compacts really served as basic covenants by which tight control over the Taiwanese was enforced and legitimized. In effect, each household was bound to a *hokō* constituency, and every registered Taiwanese inhabitant obligated to his or her designated household and to the household head, who most often was the senior male member.

The *hokō* system served as an auxiliary arm of the civil police force from 1903 on. Therefore, as time passed, the *hosei* and *kōchō* became more involved in the many services performed by the police. Already the *pao* heads, enrolled under the *pao-chia* bureaus, had participated in the 1898–1903 land-tenure investigation along with the local police.[60] Thereafter, the *hosei* engaged in a much wider range of large-scale undertakings initiated by the colonial authorities, but carried out by *hokō* units or contingents under police supervision. These included malaria prevention campaigns and projects requiring conscripted labor for the construction of roads, buildings, and other public works.[61] Such massive undertakings helped foster allied *hokō* offices managed by paid *hokō* clerks. These offices were more uniformly established throughout the colony soon after ward or section jurisdictions were created in 1909. They administered to extensive *ho*-unit complexes within the police precincts, where the clerks also supplemented ward or section-level administration handled mainly by the police.[62] The widespread distribution of these offices, located in or nearby police stations and substations, indicates that the *hokō* system had become an integral part of the local police network well before 1915.

The *hokō* system was burdensome to the Taiwanese. From early on, *hokō* labor service proved especially onerous when large contingents of villagers were conscripted for lengthy intervals to construct "*hokō* roads."[63] Thereafter, the "*hokōmin*" designation, ascribed to all registered Taiwanese inhabitants—men and women, the young and old—continued to be repugnant to most. Not only were the Taiwanese exposed to oppressive colonial measures and police brutality, but they were assessed household fees and subjected to fines and corporal punishment for petty violations.[64] In effect, the *hokō* system was highly discriminatory in nature. Only the Han Taiwanese (together with Ami and other acculturated aborigine households) were required to be registered under the system; Japanese and foreign residents, along with the mountain tribes, were exempt. Nevertheless, despite the resentment and occasional outcries from more outspoken Taiwanese, there does not appear to have been any well-organized local opposition to the *hokō* system per se.

This is understandable, for the system required the Taiwanese to be submissive in their dealings with the colonial authorities and police. It also enabled the police to keep tabs on criminals and unruly sorts and, in fact, to bring an end to the collective violence (banditry and communal feuds) that had long plagued Taiwanese society. From the perspective of the Japanese officials the *hokō* system was beneficial as well because it not only helped them introduce reform measures but allowed them to mobilize a sizable body of compliant local elites. By 1905, the combined number of *hosei* and *kōchō,* together with the *sōteidan* chiefs and deputy-chiefs, totaled around 58,000, or about 5 percent of the Taiwanese population.[65] This number comprised the greater proportion of the native elite that served the Japanese in both formal and informal capacities. Such a select group also included government schoolteachers, junior grade patrolmen, and minor officials in the bureaucracy, as well as supernumeraries and clerks attached to colonial offices.

The need to maintain a substantial native elite was apparent to the colonial authorities, for Taiwan remained an "occupation colony" in which a small minority of *naichijin* prevailed over a much larger subject population. In 1905, for example, the Japanese residents (exclusive of the military) numbered only 57,335, fewer than the *hokō* functionaries in service at the time.[66] Although this resident population increased nearly fivefold in size by 1935, the Japanese presence in Taiwan was still minimal except in a few major cities. Hence, from the outset of Japanese rule, the authorities constantly had to rely on the services of compliant local servitors in order to control and manage the colony.

The initial group of Taiwanese servitors consisted of a marginal set of collaborators, along with local spokesmen, who cooperated with the Japanese mainly to protect their neighborhoods and villages from armed conflict. Among the latter type were merchants and gentry holdovers who managed bureaus (*pao-liang chu*) to protect law-abiding inhabitants and, subsequently, the *pao-chia* bureaus and branches. Some of these managers were appointed to minor posts later on or else served as *hokō* functionaries, as did other inhabitants who had been *pao* and *chia* heads.[67] Meanwhile, as part of an appeasement plan complementary to his pacification policy, Governor-General Nogi began, in 1897, to bestow "gentlemen's" (*shinshō*) awards on Taiwanese deemed outstanding because of their wealth, social status, or community service. Kodama and Sakuma made further use of this award system to induce many more reputable and ambitious sorts to render unswerving support to their regimes. By this means, there came into being a formal body of local elites subject to regulation and close supervision by the colonial authorities.[68]

Kodama and Gotō expanded upon Nogi's appeasement plan in other ways as well. In particular, they initially made a concerted effort to cultivate a larger range of gentry holdovers besides the relatively few who held informal appointments or had been awarded *shinshō* medals. Between 1898 and the end of 1900, Kodama also made rare personal appearances in four major cities to honor the family elders of such local elites. His imperial-like bearing at these ceremonial occasions made a favorable impression not only on the Taiwan literati but also on the general populace.[69] In March 1900, Kodama further endeavored to mollify and enlist the support of the gentry holdovers by staging an elaborate conference for a select number of them. There, in a conciliatory manner, he called upon his guests, as traditional scholars, to engage in the cultural transformation taking place under his administration. Gotō, in turn, urged the gentry holdovers to help promote the "new learning" being introduced in Taiwan by his government schools and heralded this learning—a fusion of Chinese neo-Confucian doctrine with Meiji-style education—as the foundation for cultural advancement in the colony.

The Taiwan gentry holdovers, however, were not a very cohesive group. The conference participants were impressed by the material improvements they beheld during guided tours of the Taipei area, but otherwise reacted differently to the speeches and proposals made at the eight-day affair. In particular, many had mixed feelings about modernization and cultural change, especially as advanced by the government schools. Those supportive of the old *shobō* schooling, in fact, seemed resentful of Gotō's design to fuse traditional Chinese training with more modern Japanese instruction.

Kodama and Gotō must have been disconcerted by such resentment and the lack of accord among their distinguished guests. For this 1900 Yōbunkai conference, convened purportedly to "uplift culture" (*yōbun,* or *yang-wen*), marked the last time that their administration endeavored to solicit support from the remnant scholar-gentry group on essentially an islandwide basis. Although Gotō made good use of the gentry participants as native informants in preparation for the investigation of local customs and usages his office conducted the following year, the colonial authorities now realized that they would have to rely more fully on the growing body of *shinshō* elites under their control to help advance their plans and undertakings.[70]

The varied responses evidenced by the Yōbunkai participants reflected the anxiety experienced by the Taiwanese under more orderly conditions after the turn of the century. Cultural change and reform had brought about insecurity and even adversity to many. Classically educated literati often remained unemployed, for example, because they lacked competence in the Japanese language required for government service and positions in colonial enterprises. More inhabitants became apprehensive when public campaigns were conducted against the "bad customs" deemed most prevalent among their people.[71] Extensive reforms mandated by the colonial authorities also fostered widespread uncertainty and resentment. For instance, the 1901–5 land-tenure reform, together with the three-year land investigation that preceded it, had an unsettling effect among the large rentholders as well as alarmed bystanders in the countryside.[72]

Again, anxiety and resentment were induced by discriminatory colonial measures. These pertained to a wide range of matters, including education, intermarriage with Japanese, and requirements that Taiwanese firms acquire Japanese business partners.[73] Many such measures were based on colonial ordinances (ritsurei) authorized by the governor-general. Among the harshest were the 1898 Bandit Punishment Ordinance, which in practice was applied only to the Taiwanese, and the 1904 Fine and Flogging Ordinance that related specifically to Taiwanese offenders. The latter law was abolished in 1921, but the notorious bandit punishment law, although never applied after 1916, remained in effect throughout the rest of the Japanese period.[74] However, the 1898 Hokō Ordinance, which lasted until 1945, fostered more continuous hardship and long-standing resentment among several generations of island inhabitants. Indeed, well-informed Taiwanese came to regard the hokō system and their hokōmin identity as hallmarks of servitude and inequality universal to modern colonialism.

The profound economic change brought about under Japanese rule also created widespread concern. Already by 1905, a much heavier per-capita tax burden had been imposed on the subject population as a consequence of Gotō's many costly projects.[75] Other sensitive issues developed as Taiwan was incorporated into Japan's capitalist economy, and agricultural production was basically commoditized by allotting a large proportion of the cultivated land to sugarcane and rice production, primarily for export to Japan. These developments affected prices, wages, and profits, often adversely in the case of Taiwanese farmers, laborers, and entrepreneurs—all of whom had little or no control over market conditions.[76] Such adversities became apparent early on with respect to Taiwan's modernized sugar industry. Taiwanese sugarcane producers, engaged in small family farming of the type enhanced by the land-tenure reform, had to deal primarily with large Japanese sugar companies. As these Japanese enterprises gained more control over the industry, in part because of the preferential treatment they received from the colonial government, the small farmers operated at more of a disadvantage. Some even had to part with their lands. Meanwhile, most Taiwanese sugar mill owners soon lost out to highly capitalized Japanese interests.[77]

Elements of the Taiwanese population also became discontented because of the political influences emanating from China. The spread of reform and revolutionary movements there, together with the rise of Chinese nationalism, attracted considerable attention in Taiwan. A few Taiwanese also managed to witness the new and radical trends on the mainland, along with the overthrow of the Ch'ing dynasty in 1911–12 and its aftermath. Moreover, several Chinese activist leaders paid brief visits to Taiwan, including the revolutionary Sun Yat-sen in 1900 and the proponent of constitutional reform, Liang Ch'i-ch'ao, in 1911.[78] At the same time, some disgruntled Taiwanese took advantage of the anti-Japanese sentiment prevailing in the colony to incite disturbances. Several of the major insurrections that occurred during the 1907–15 period were sparked by such types. The Lo Fu-hsing uprising in 1913, for example, was instigated by a Miao-li Hakka of the Hsin-chu (Shinchiku) district, who had become inspired by Sun Yat-sen's doctrine while sojourning in Kuangtung. As a result of concerted efforts by Lo and other local insurgents, some fifty to sixty thousand restless Taiwanese were marshaled for action within a few months.[79]

Taiwanese living in the security of cities and the larger towns, however, had begun to accommodate themselves to colonial rule and foreign or modern ways. In fact, a Western observer claimed (in 1909) that the urban dwellers were "fast becoming Japanned." They rode bicycles, made use of modern innovations like the telephone and public post offices, and were starting to wear wooden *getas,* the conventional Japanese footwear. He also noted that the Taiwanese language was being "marvelously altered and enriched" by new expressions derived from combinations of Japanese and foreign words. The hairstyles and attire displayed by young Taiwanese males also reflected a degree of accommodation by that portion of the urban population. Although some still wore the traditional Chinese queue, others had short haircuts and appeared in Western dress but with the prominent cuffs and collars popular among the Japanese.[80]

It was during this period that a younger generation of educated Taiwanese was beginning to participate in community affairs. Born and raised near the end of Ch'ing rule in Taiwan, its members had received some or most of their schooling under Japanese governance. They were often the most susceptible to modernization and change. Many became active in local reform societies formed for the purpose of stamping out the "bad customs" identified by the colonial authorities: most notably, footbinding among Hokkien women, and queue wearing by adult Taiwanese males.[81] This educated generation was especially concerned about the need for modern educational facilities for their areas and the discrimination they and their offspring faced in regard to matriculation in the few government schools. As a consequence, more Taiwanese commenced to enter primary and secondary schools in Japan. In the mid-island area of Taichung (Taichū) local leaders also began campaigning for the inauguration of the Taichū Middle School, despite the reluctance of Japanese officials to authorize this first middle school for Taiwanese males.[82]

The Taichū school controversy called attention to local dissatisfaction with the unwarranted discrimination and abuse evidenced by the Sakuma regime. Prominent Japanese in Tokyo, in turn, became alarmed by reports of brutal conduct by the Taiwan authorities for, after the outbreak of World War I in 1914, Japan desired to present a liberal image to its Western allies as well as a benevolent one to those Asian colonies under European and American rule.[83] Expressions of indignation from both the home country and Taiwan soon led to what proved to be an anomalous event in the island colony—an active, though brief, assimilation movement of liberal pretensions involving joint Japanese and Taiwanese participation.

The 1914 Taiwan assimilation movement was led by Itagaki Taisuke, a venerable politician and statesman living in retirement in Japan. Itagaki had been attracted to the cause of assimilation not only because of his egalitarian views and strong predilection to bolster Japanese national interests abroad but also in response to personal appeals made by distraught visitors from Taiwan. The latter included two idealistic Japanese proponents of assimilation serving in minor colonial posts and a pair of influential Taiwanese spokesmen of the renowned Wu-feng Lin family, Lin Hsien-t'ang and his cousin, who had helped to initiate the Taichū school project. Through such contacts, Itagaki and a small group of Japanese adventurers were able to solicit contributions from wealthy Taiwanese and draw up plans for an islandwide movement.[84] Between the two brief trips Itagaki made to Taiwan in 1914, he also garnered written endorsements from an impressive array of public figures in Japan, some of whom still professed the assimilationist notion that Taiwan should eventually be fused with metropolitan Japan.[85]

In December during his second trip, Itagaki formally inaugurated an assimilation society, the Taiwan Dōkakai, to advance his movement. The results were impressive at first. Crowds gathered wherever he appeared, and within a week or so the society attracted a membership of more than three thousand Taiwanese from communities about the island, as well as forty-five resident Japanese. Enthusiastic Taiwanese at these public gatherings seemed to fancy the idea of "becoming Japanese" so as to gain equal treatment with the resident *naichijin* and acquire the full constitutional rights enjoyed by Japanese citizens in the home country. Among this following were many of the younger generation of educated Taiwanese, including some who had received *shinshō* awards.[86]

Since Itagaki was an eminent figure in Japan, the colonial authorities allowed his movement to continue without interference. Following his final departure late in the month, however, the Taiwan Dōkakai came under relentless attack by the colonial establishment: the officials and police, government-run newspapers, and powerful groups among the Japanese residents. Its leaders were arrested and some well-known Taiwanese members detained or harassed. Finally, in late January 1915, Governor-General Sakuma disbanded the society some three months before his own recall, and the assimilation movement was brought to an end.[87] Thus under a notoriously harsh colonial regime this threat to the hegemony, which the resident *naichijin* had exerted over the native *hontōjin* for almost twenty years, was promptly removed, at least all but in memory.

Colonial Governance and Peacetime Experiences (1915–1936)

New influences from metropolitan Japan and abroad had an impact on colonial rule in Taiwan from 1915 through 1936. The severe Twenty-one Demands, which Japan attempted to impose on China early in 1915, alarmed the security-minded colonial authorities at the outset, for they feared anti-Japanese reprisals from aroused elements of the Han Taiwanese population. Other influences stemming from the World War I period also led the Japanese to be more circumspect in their dealings with the Taiwanese. These included the Wilsonian principle of self-determination, which seemed to promise autonomy, if not independence, to colonized peoples throughout the world, and the May Fourth movement in China, which helped to foster radical trends and a sense of nationalism among Taiwanese intellectuals. Meanwhile, the growth of "Taishō democracy" in Japan had a moderating influence on many of the harsher aspects of colonial governance. This effect became more apparent after Premier Hara Kei instituted party government in Japan and, in 1919, selected Den Kenjirō as Taiwan's first civilian governor-general. After the Japanese conquest of Manchuria in 1931, however, the moderate influences emanating from the home country began to give way to militaristic ones and, amid a growing ultranationalist mood, Japan prepared its colonies to render military support for eventual wartime endeavors.

At the outset of this eventful period the harsh rule in Taiwan did not immediately lessen after Sakuma was recalled. Over the latter part of 1915 his successor, General Andō Sadayoshi, ruthlessly quelled the final two major uprisings staged by local insurgents, again with heavy casualties.[88] Nevertheless, the Andō regime endeavored to resolve conflicts between the security forces and law courts that had developed during the Sakuma reign, primarily through the efforts of Shimomura Hiroshi, the new chief of civil administration. Shimomura, a Western-trained legal specialist and an avowed exponent of liberalism, continued to play a conciliatory role in Taiwan's colonial affairs under the next two governors-general, General Akashi Motojirō (June 1918–October 1919) and Den Kenjirō (October 1919–September 1923).[89] Signs of moderation in colonial governance were also reflected by the assimilation policies these two head officials promoted in the belief that the assimilation of the Taiwanese was essential; otherwise, Japan ultimately risked losing its hold on the colony.[90]

Although Akashi and Den shared a strong belief in the need for assimilation, they differed markedly with regard to their assimilationist outlooks and agendas. Akashi advanced a limited form of assimilation whereby a certain number of Taiwanese would be Japanized, but not in a complete sense. He favored segregation in the colony so as to maintain the status quo between the dominant Japanese residents and the subordinate colonial inhabitants. Unlike Itagaki, Akashi envisioned assimilation not as a means to bring about equality for the Taiwanese but, rather, as a way by which Taiwanese with suitable training could be integrated into Taiwan's growing economy and be made more susceptible to Japanese national interests. Akashi's education rescript of 1919 evidenced his restricted version of assimilation as it applied to administrative policy. His rescript continued to enforce strict segregation between Japanese and Taiwanese students by welding the government schools for Taiwanese into a single, coordinated system, yet one that offered the Taiwanese better educational advantages, especially in the field of vocational training.[91]

Den, on the other hand, promoted a much broader version of assimilation when, on assuming office, he announced that the Japanization of Taiwan and the assimilation of the Taiwanese people were to be his major goals. In this respect, Den followed Hara Kei, who had been an early proponent of fusion and integration for Taiwan and its inhabitants at the outset of Japanese rule.[92] Subsequently, Den attempted to overcome discriminatory colonial practices, which, he felt, obstructed the assimilation process. This led him to replace Akashi's education rescript, featuring segregation, with his own 1922 rescript that inaugurated an integrated school system in the colony. Under this decree all government schools became accessible to both Taiwanese and Japanese students. Admission to the common and primary schools was to be based on each student's background in spoken Japanese instead of on ethnic or racial distinctions.[93]

Den recognized that education played a crucial role in the assimilation process and, like Akashi, insisted that Taiwanese had to be trained properly in order to become Japanese. Den, however, proposed to assimilate the entire Taiwanese population, not merely that portion receiving education in government schools. Therefore, he declared that acculturation (*kyōka*) must be extended well beyond the instruction offered through formal schooling. In the hands of the colonial authorities, *kyōka* amounted to a form of political and cultural indoctrination whereby Taiwanese of all ages were to be imbued with the sacred Japanese spirit and inspired to change their life-style and learn Japanese, the national language.[94] These elements of indoctrination remained among the cardinal assimilationist objectives proclaimed by the colonial government for the rest of the Japanese period.

Nevertheless, the eight civilian governors-general, who succeeded Den in consecutive reigns until September 1936, related to the issue of assimilation in different ways. Their varied responses reflected not only their personal convictions and experiences in colonial service but also the tension between the ideals of assimilation and the compulsion to maintain Japanese supremacy that had resurfaced in the colony as a result of the conflicting policies, involving segregation or integration, invoked by Akashi and Den.[95]

Meanwhile, the authority of the Taiwan governor-general had diminished somewhat by the time Den Kenjirō became the eighth incumbent in 1919. Factional and party politics in Japan, along with the entrenched interests of bureaucrats and other influential residents in the colony, had an offsetting effect on the pronouncements of that chief executive. When civilians were appointed to that high office as a result of reforms initiated by the home government, the post lost a degree of formal power as well. At the beginning of Den's reign, his office was no longer entrusted with the command of the Taiwan garrison. Instead, direct authority was shifted to a new post, that of a commander-in-chief designated to head the garrison's army and naval staff. This duplication of supreme military authority in the colony continued until 1944, when the commander of the Taiwan garrison became concurrently the last governor-general.[96]

Moreover, the extraordinary legislative power enjoyed by the Taiwan governor-general since the 1896 enactment of Law 63 was reduced. Law 3, enacted by the Diet in 1921 to replace Law 31 (a 1906 revision of Law 63), allowed for a wider application of homeland law (*naichihō*) to Taiwan. Consequently, from 1922 to 1945, many more Diet statutes were extended to the colony, while fewer *ritsurei* were issued by Den and subsequent governors-general, or continued in effect from the previous reigns.[97]

In the meantime the Taiwan governors-general were gradually brought under closer supervision of the home government in Tokyo. Earlier, they had been mainly subject to the surveillance of the premier and the bureaus he headed although, as high officials of the *shin'nin* rank, they were ultimately responsible to the emperor for the outcome of their colonial policies and administrations. Under the party government of Hara Kei, though, Den and his immediate civilian successors were also held more fully accountable to the various ministries and the Diet. Eventually, in 1929, the office of the Taiwan governor-general was placed under the direction of the newly created Ministry of Colonial Affairs in an attempt to centralize control over Japan's colonies and, finally, after 1942, under the jurisdiction of the Home Ministry in a further effort to bring about a more integrated colonial empire.[98] These post-1919 developments, including the Law 3 enactment, suggest that as the supervisory power of the home government increased and the authority of the governor-general was reduced by reform, Taiwan's political integration with metropolitan Japan became more feasible and more in keeping with the assimilationist ideal of an eventual merger and the "extension of the Japanese homeland" (*naichi enchō*) to the island colony.[99]

Within the colony, however, the Taiwan governor-general still wielded considerable power. He maintained firm control over his subordinates heading the civil bureaucracy and police and authority to formulate and implement colonial policies as he saw fit. The system of self-government (*chihō jichi*), introduced to the colony after 1920, failed to diminish his executive power. The few Taiwanese elites and Japanese residents added to the consultative council (*hyōgikai*) within the government-general were his own appointments. Hence this part-time assembly remained merely an advisory body. Neither did the reduction of his extraordinary legislative power deter the Taiwan governor-general from shaping the contents of the colonial law. He continued to issue *ritsurei* when Japanese laws needed to be altered, so as to fit the special conditions in the colony or when appropriate Diet statutes were lacking. His use of executive ordinances and decrees (*furei*) also enabled him to regulate the colonial courts. Since the governor-general also approved the appointment of all judges and public prosecutors in Taiwan, he in fact retained full control over the colonial judiciary.[100]

Therefore, in a Japanese colony not bound by the Meiji constitution, the Taiwan governor-general continued to reign like a virtual sovereign. Officials at the lower levels of government were held responsible for carrying out his orders and policies and, through an efficient chain of command that reached down to the local authorities and police, his centralized authority was made to impinge on the Taiwanese and, by 1915, the mountain tribes as well. The governor-general maintained close surveillance over the Japanese residents, too. This was done primarily by urban neighborhood leaders and the mayors, for this civilian population, which numbered over 270,000 by 1935, was concentrated mainly in the nine major cities.[101]

His office maintained even stricter supervision over the foreign resident population, composed largely of Westerners and sojourners of Chinese registry. From early on, the few Western merchants were permitted to trade only in the six principal ports of Taiwan, and their businesses were subjected to further restrictions. Foreign missionaries, together with their churches and schools, also remained under his scrutiny. The several Presbyterian and Dominican secondary and higher-level schools were constantly investigated and tended to be regulated in a discriminatory manner as private schools, compared to the favored government schools—a practice that dated back to the Gotō era. Tighter control was placed over missionary establishments after 1931, when ultranationalistic influences began to pervade the colonial regime in Taiwan.[102]

In the meantime, the Taiwan governor-general kept watch over the influx of mainland Chinese, whose numbers grew decade by decade and eventually peaked at more than 60,000 in 1936.[103] This group, consisting chiefly of laborers from Fukien and Kuangtung, merited close security, for some of its organized members engaged in demonstrations and strikes in the cities. Moreover, the colonial authorities feared that these sojourners would spread Chinese nationalistic sentiment among the Taiwanese inhabitants. The governor-general attempted to control this Chinese immigrant population by various means, including its enrollment in the *hokō* system along with the Han Taiwanese. Eventually, in 1931, a compromise was worked out whereby the alien Chinese residents were registered, instead, in an overseas Chinese association, the Chung-hua Hui-kuan, that functioned under the auspices of the consul-general of the Republic of China stationed in Taipei.[104]

The Taiwan governor-general also continued to exert considerable influence in southern coastal China and portions of Southeast Asia. After Kodama failed to launch an assault on Fukien, as planned in 1900, none of his successors attempted to initiate further military actions overseas. Nonetheless, that high colonial post has been described as the "claws and teeth" of Japanese imperialism because of the aggressive economic and political operations it directed toward these nearby Asian regions.[105] In coastal Fukien and Kuangtung, such actions involved the advancement of Japanese interests and investments, including those of the Taiwan Bank and its overseas branches, as well as the control and protection of resident Taiwanese of Japanese registry designated as *sekimin*. As sizable Taiwanese communities developed in Amoy, Foochow, and Swatow, the office of the Taiwan governor-general increased its efforts to supervise the *sekimin* and to provide "cultural advancement" for their communities by sponsoring special schools, hospitals, and newspapers.[106]

The Taiwan governor-general worked closely with the Japanese consuls posted in these Chinese treaty ports in conjunction with its operations there. Hence there developed a close rapport that resulted in a series of annual consular conferences hosted by the governor-general in Taipei, beginning in 1915 and lasting through the early 1920s. These were held to deal with matters relating to Taiwan and South China and were attended by Japanese consuls stationed in Canton and Hong Kong as well, and even (in 1923) by those serving in the distant southwestern province of Yunnan, a gateway to the Southeast Asian interior.[107]

The Taiwan governor-general conducted similar types of operations in the Philippines and other Southeast Asian areas where Taiwanese tended to trade. There his office worked closely with the local Japanese consulates in a joint effort to maintain surveillance over the overseas Taiwanese, or *kyōmin*. The governor-general also contributed in other ways to the Japanese penetration of Southeast Asia in terms of economic gain and preparation for future military conquests. Since Taiwan was still regarded as a base for Japan's southward expansion, it was especially fitting that the various governors-general sponsored surveys of the resources and economic potential of portions of Southeast Asia, the South Seas (Nan'yō), and South China, as Akashi endeavored to do when he added a foreign affairs research section to his office in 1919.[108] Others followed suit in such overseas investigations until, by the outbreak of the Pacific War in 1941, the Taiwan governor-general had amassed a first-rate research collection relating to these regions.[109]

Meanwhile, under the civilian governors-general, colonial rule in Taiwan was modified somewhat during the 1920s. Direct police involvement in local administration was curtailed in urban areas, and elements of self-government were introduced on various levels. Moreover, the colonial law codes were revamped. Most of the harsher punishments ordained by *ritsurei* enactments were (or already had been) abolished or suspended, and the Japanese Code of Criminal Procedure of 1922 became effective in the colony by 1924. A year earlier, most provisions of Japan's civil and commercial law codes became applicable in Taiwan.[110] Such significant changes in governance reflected not only moderate influences emanating from Taishō Japan but also accommodation by the colonial authorities to economic and social development in Taiwan and, in general, to the more orderly conditions there. For with the exception of the brief Wushe (Musha) incident of 1930, when aroused Atayal tribesmen killed and injured some three hundred and fifty Japanese, armed resistance to colonial authority had ceased.[111] Local administration continued to be strict, however, and not all modifications in governance had liberal overtones. Special criminal statutes, relating to public order and peace preservation, were introduced from Japan, for example.[112] These severe enactments also included governmental responses to the peaceful resistance developed in the colony: in particular, to the new modes of protest staged by leaders among the younger generation of Taiwanese.

Important modifications in civil administration ensued upon the final reorganization of local government in 1920. The western and northern portions of Taiwan were then divided into five provinces (*shū*) and the less-populated parts of the east coast into two subprovincial jurisdictions, or *chō*. A third such jurisdiction (the Hōkotō-chō) was established in P'eng-hu in 1926. (See map on next page.) Two subadministrative levels were formed under the provinces: namely, midlevel municipalities (*shi*) and counties (*gun*), and lower-level townships (*gai*) and villages (*shō*). The *chō,* in contrast, had branch *(chō)* offices and were further subdivided into townships and sections (*ku*) at the lowest level.[113]

Under this three-tier system of local government, a certain amount of decentralization occurred as more authority was delegated to the ranking officials in charge of these various jurisdictions. Such developments were evident in the governance of the municipalities (eventually nine in number) headed by mayors. These civil officials functioned under the direct supervision of the provincial governors, while the police were detached from the municipal administrations. Yet, despite Den's general aim to separate civil administration from the police, such a division failed to materialize in the county jurisdictions. Hence in the subcounty townships and administrative villages (as well as in the *chō* townships and sections)—that is, in predominantly rural areas where the bulk of the Taiwanese population lived—police involvement in local affairs continued to be pervasive until the end of Japanese colonial rule.[114]

The 1920 governmental reorganization also enabled the *hokō* system to assume an important coordinating function at the county level in conjunction with the joint type of police and civil administration. Subsequently, county *hokō* associations, consisting of allied *hokō* and *sōteidan* functionaries, were formed as liaison bodies. Meanwhile, the township and village structure allowed the allied *hokō* offices to play a greater role in countryside administration. Not only did the *hokō* clerks become engaged in an increasing number of local matters involving the colonial authorities and police, but their offices came to operate as virtual community centers rivaling in some respects the role long played by community temples in Taiwan.[115]

This latter development occurred, as Hui-yu Caroline Ts'ai indicates, when new townships and village administrative boundaries replaced those of the old settlements and thereby helped to bring about the decline of "natural villages."[116] In the process rural communities were often split among several local jurisdictions, and their household units assigned to different *hokō* offices operating within separate police zones. Such jurisdictional adjustments contributed to the formation of communities more closely attuned to institutions introduced or co-opted by the colonial government, such as school districts and agricultural cooperatives, in addition to the spread of allied *hokō* offices centrally located in or nearby police stations and substations.[117]

Taiwan: Adminstrative Divisions, 1920–1945 (showing the colony's five provinces [shū] and three subprovincial jurisdictions [chō], including Bōkotō, estab. 1926)

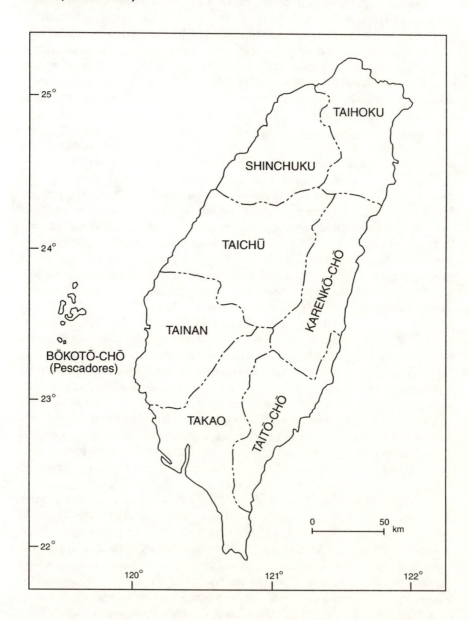

The 1920 reforms also introduced a system of local self-government by which councils were created at the lower levels of government. Between 1920 and 1935, these councils functioned merely as advisory bodies, and their members were appointed by the colonial authorities. After further self-government measures were introduced in 1935, the provincial and municipal councils were granted decision-making powers, and half their members were elected either by the lower councils within their jurisdictions, as in the case of the provincial councils, or by qualified voters in the municipal elections. Such a limited form of self-rule enabled a few Taiwanese elites (together with leading Japanese residents) to participate marginally in colonial governance and more of the registered population to vote in public elections.[118] However, during the 1920s more spirited elections were held at times for *hosei,* zone heads, and board members serving occupational associations, at least in the cities and towns where there briefly emerged a "popular" form of local politics.[119]

On the other hand, a much larger portion of the Taiwanese population was obliged to participate in government-sponsored associations designed to bring about extensive cultural and social change deemed essential to the assimilation process. Around 1915, the colonial authorities had already begun to pre-empt societies and movements devoted to the reform of "vile customs and social practices" organized by Taiwanese leaders. This happened in the case of the antifootbinding and queue-cutting campaigns that had been launched by local reformers around the turn of the century.[120] Following the education rescripts of 1919 and 1922, various officials urged that more such reform societies be formed so that moral and social instruction, as well as Japanese language training, might be extended beyond the classroom. Indoctrination, as prescribed by Den Kenjirō, was also emphasized. During the early 1930s political training was intensified, while the number of local reform associations increased and became more highly regulated.

The Taiwanese historian Wang Shih-ch'ing has described how a local assimilationist venture that began in his home area of Shu-lin (near Taipei city) in 1914 ultimately developed into a regimented, colonywide movement by 1937. Initially, a Shu-lin reformer founded a Common Customs Society (T'ung-feng hui) in support of Itagaki's assimilation movement. Two years later, nearby society branches were established with the encouragement of the governor-general and the police. The society continued to expand and then, in 1925, experienced phenomenal growth when the T'ung-feng hui was organized throughout Taipei at the provincial and county levels with closely regulated chapters in the cities, towns, and villages. Operating under these society chapters were affiliated associations for male household heads, their wives, and youths (male and female). This structure was extended throughout the colony after the Taiwan Youth Corps was established by the government in 1930, and the local youth associations were incorporated in that organization. By 1931, the "T'ung-feng hui" title appears to have been dropped, and the new designation, "United Instructional

[Kyōka] Association," suggests that colonial assimilationist measures now entailed a massive amount of indoctrination among the Taiwanese population at large.[121]

Finally, in 1936, the entire associational structure was merged with a newly formed *buraku* (village community) system and managed by the Buraku shinhōkai (Village Community Promotion Association). The *buraku* system, similar to the *hokō* system, was based on household membership and had liaison agents on government levels extending from the provinces and *chō* down to the townships, administrative villages, and sections. However, the *buraku* units were formally attached to the civil administration instead of to the police.[122]

Thus, by 1937, most Taiwanese were enrolled in two complementary control systems as well as in subsidiary adult and youth organizations. From the local Taiwanese perspective, the distinctions between the *hokō* communities and those of the *buraku* must have been blurred. Indeed, there is evidence that *hosei* and *hokō* clerks performed *buraku* services as well.[123] To the colonial authorities, however, there were distinct differences, including the fact that the *hokō* system had long nurtured segregated localities where the Taiwanese speech and local Chinese customs were preserved. The *buraku* system, through Buraku shinhōkai management and local supervision by reform-minded civil administrators, was supposed to perform a more integrative function throughout the colony, in keeping with Japanese assimilationist objectives.

The Japanese also planned for the assimilation of the aboriginal inhabitants, but primarily through schooling. Well over a fourth of this native population, totaling over two hundred thousand by 1935, lived in designated villages scattered in the hills and lowlands, where some of the children attended elementary and even secondary schools.[124] Yet the large majority were members of the mountain tribes and continued to dwell within the guarded reserves in Taiwan's rugged interior. Special police, assigned to posts there, served as teachers as well as doctors, counselors, and, above all, disciplinarians. The education they imparted to the mountain children consisted of moral and social training, schooling in practical subjects related mainly to agriculture and trade, and instruction in the Japanese language and national spirit. The latter form of instruction was not only crucial to the Japanization process but also important because for the first time members of the diverse mountain tribes were able to share a common idiom and national sentiment. In general, this elementary type of schooling better enabled the colonial government to control and domesticate the mountain people, especially after they were forced to move from remote habitants to settlements nearby the police stations and outposts.[125]

The Taiwan colonial government also endeavored to educate and indoctrinate members of the Taiwanese communities in southern China, primarily through schools and newspapers funded by the Bank of Taiwan. However, assimilation was not a major objective with respect to these overseas sojourners (*kyōmin*). In fact, the governor-general, together with the Japanese consuls stationed in the treaty ports, sought to preserve their *sekimin* status as a distinct body of resident Japanese nationals. Accordingly, the Taiwanese *sekimin* enjoyed extraterritorial privileges under Japanese consular jurisdiction. They also gained other benefits under Japan's protection and by virtue of their Chinese descent.[126] Their communities within the treaty port concessions also derived a measure of representation in the public assemblies (*kōkai*) maintained by the Japanese consulates for their resident citizens.[127] Such gestures of self-government, though, were offset by the constant vigilance the consuls and Taiwan authorities maintained over the *sekimin* and their businesses, as well as by the various forms of discrimination these resident Taiwanese still experienced at the hands of the Japanese while abroad.

Taiwanese overseas settlements were essentially business communities. In China these communities consisted mainly of merchants and shopkeepers, along with their staffs and family members. The *sekimin* settlements were initially limited to the treaty ports near the ancestral areas of most Han Taiwanese: that is, Amoy and Foochow in coastal Fukien, and Swatow in eastern Kuangtung. In 1907, only 335 Taiwanese of Japanese registry were recorded in these three treaty ports. Their numbers there increased appreciably during World War I and, by 1936, totaled around 12,900. In all three ports the Taiwanese outnumbered the Japanese residents.[128] After 1931, some merchants began to relocate in Shanghai until almost seven hundred registered Taiwanese resided in the International Settlement in the mid-1930s. Taiwanese businessmen had also started to trade in Manchuria by 1926, and a Taiwanese community emerged in Dairen (Ta-lien) after the Mukden Incident of 1931. The northward advance of Taiwanese entrepreneurs was sparked by the increased Japanese commercial and military activity in Shanghai and Manchuria, and was further stimulated by new Japanese shipping services introduced between Taiwan and the ports at Shanghai and Dairen. After 1932, more Taiwanese business connections developed in Manchukuo, by way of Dairen, chiefly because of the continuing Japanese presence there and the expanding market for Taiwan tea.[129]

In Fukien and Kuangtung the *sekimin* identity at times proved to be ambiguous and detrimental to the community residents. A few of the Taiwanese émigrés, among the many who fled to these two coastal provinces in 1895, became prominent entrepreneurs in the local treaty ports. There they associated with the Japanese consuls and colonial agents much like the *sekimin* did, but without having attained Japanese registry. Members of the wealthy Pan-ch'iao and Wu-feng Lin families, with established residences in Amoy and Foochow, were prime examples.[130] On the other hand, some opportunistic local Chinese managed to acquire Japanese registry so that they might gain extraterritorial privileges by virtue of the *sekimin* designation. Eventually, too, a sizable group of Taiwanese *ronin* operated within the treaty-port communities. These thugs became notorious for their dealings in narcotics, prostitution, and organized crime, and cast a bad light on the other residents and their *sekimin* identity.[131]

Transgressions committed by the *ronin* further aroused Chinese ill will against their Taiwanese "brethren," since the local inhabitants had already come to resent the privileges and protection the resident Taiwanese received as Japanese citizens. As a result of this general animosity, Taiwanese shops and establishments frequently became targets of abuse, especially during anti-Japanese boycotts and demonstrations.[132] In order not to be associated with the *sekimin* stigma, as well as to avoid Japanese surveillance, many Taiwanese students and intellectuals stayed away from the treaty-port communities while in China and attempted to pass as Chinese nationals. During the wartime period, the Taiwanese stationed in China, as members of Japanese labor and military units, also remained detached from these communities and did not share the *sekimin* identity due to their service in the imperial armed forces and assignments to military or occupied areas apart from the treaty ports.

Meanwhile, Taiwanese continued to reside in metropolitan Japan under different circumstances than those they encountered in China as foreign nationals or in Taiwan as colonial subjects. In Japan they were regarded as citizens and neither placed under the supervision of Japanese consuls nor required to hold passports or visas. As Japanese citizens, they were also accorded equal status, at least in a formal sense, and did not suffer the blatant discrimination that they experienced as *hokōmin* in their colony. Taiwanese residents, in effect, were able to live more freely in the cities of Japan, where they congregated, and to associate with Japanese in a less restrained manner. As a consequence, Taiwanese students and long-term residents there adapted to Japanese ways more readily than their counterparts in Taiwan and elsewhere.[133] Nevertheless, assimilation, leading ostensibly to full Japanization, was rare even among those who settled in Japan. Well-acculturated Taiwanese, on the contrary, seem to have become acutely aware of their own distinctive traits and island background while living in Japan, and some evidenced strong feelings of being a different people and of a separate nationality.

Before the turn of the century few Taiwanese colonials ventured to Japan, except for several Christian medical students and a handful of *shinshō* sightseers. The Taiwanese essentially began to "discover" their new home country during the Osaka Exhibition of 1903, when some five hundred local elites toured the exhibition and made side trips to Tokyo under joint governmental and private sponsorship.[134] Thereafter, a steady flow of Taiwanese travelers reached Japan by way of the Japanese steamship lines serving the colony, while students from Taiwan began to increase appreciably after 1915. By 1922, at least 2,400 Taiwanese students were reportedly enrolled in educational institutions in metropolitan Japan. This number expanded to almost seven thousand in 1942.[135] However, these official figures did not include all the Taiwanese students attending various public and private institutions in Tokyo and other Japanese cities. Neither did the published reports indicate the graduates and professionally trained Taiwanese who continued to reside in Japan. Altogether, this larger student and ex-student grouping, together with merchants and wealthy individuals who took up long-term or permanent residency, comprised a Taiwan population in metropolitan Japan that well exceeded the official counts. Around 1945, the total number of Taiwanese living there may have grown to between twenty and thirty thousand.[136]

Much of this resident population was concentrated in Tokyo, where a greater number of schools and institutions of higher learning were located. Educational opportunities there continued to attract many Taiwanese because of the limited access to schooling and the even fewer chances to receive advanced education or specialized training in the colony. Within Tokyo's cosmopolitan environment, a new Taiwanese intelligentsia was spawned. Composed of students and intellectuals, as well as professionals and members of the educated elite from the colony, this group was influenced by modern ideas and trends current not only in Japan but in China and the West. In 1920, leaders among the Taiwanese intelligentsia began to establish associations and publish periodicals. Through such means they soon became leading spokesmen of the Taiwanese community in Japan. More significantly, they fostered political and cultural movements extending from the metropole to the colony.

These movements initially flourished in the liberal climate of the postwar era after the inception of the New People's Society (Shinminaki) in March 1920. Founded by a group of Taiwanese students in Tokyo with the support of Lin Hsien-t'ang and other wealthy individuals, the society soon attracted a following in Japan and Taiwan by publishing a monthly magazine, the *Formosan Youth* (Taiwan seinen).[137] The first several issues featured articles on political, economic, and social issues. Over the next several years, language and literary concerns also became standard topics. Thereafter, the *Formosan Youth,* under various names and in different formats, continued to promote reform and peaceful resistance to colonial rule and to be heralded as the prime mouthpiece of the Taiwanese.[138] In addition, the magazine and its successor publications endeavored to introduce deep-rooted cultural and social change to Taiwan, much like the influential periodical *New Youth* (Hsin Ch'ing-nien) had done during the New Culture and May Fourth movements in China.

With this motive in mind the backers of the *Formosan Youth* changed the name of their magazine to the *Taiwan People's Journal* (Taiwan mimpō) so as to attract a wider reading audience. The Taiwanese readership further expanded a few years later when they were permitted to shift the site of their publication from Tokyo to Taiwan and the *Journal* was transformed from a weekly to a daily newspaper. The change of location, accomplished by 1927, signified that the center of Taiwanese activism had gravitated more to the colony.[139]

Already, though, the more highly vocal Taiwan Cultural Association (Taiwan bunka kyōkai) had been operating in the colony since 1921. Organized primarily by Chiang Wei-shui, a Taipei physician and an admirer of Sun Yat-sen, the Cultural Association nonetheless disavowed any political goal other than to advance the Taiwanese culture. Yet it supported Taiwanese political movements calling for home rule and the establishment of a Taiwan parliament and has been considered "the one organization most responsible for the development of Formosan nationalism."[140] In Taiwan, the association maintained close contacts with the island's educational institutions and their graduates and attracted wide support by way of public lectures. Its leaders also expounded strains of cultural nationalism in articles published in the *Taiwan People's Journal.*[141]

The Taiwan Cultural Association helped to launch a new mode of Taiwanese drama. Performances in the colony now reflected recent developments in Chinese and Japanese theatrical production as well as the influence of political and social change and the Western impact in East Asia. Generally, though, audiences tended to distinguish contemporary plays from traditional drama more in terms of the modern themes portrayed rather than changes in dramatic or stage techniques.[142] After 1920, the study of Taiwanese folklore and modern styles of music and dance was also advanced by the association.

Over roughly the same period, literary and feminist movements spread among the Taiwanese students and intellectuals in Japan and the colony. Again, the *Formosan Youth* and *Taiwan People's Journal* played an important role in these developments. These publications were especially well suited to help launch the literature movement, for they featured both Chinese- and Japanese-language sections.[143] This enabled Taiwanese writers to introduce the popular style of *pai-hua* (vernacular) already in use in China or else to compose in Japanese and adhere more to the current Japanese literary fashions. After 1930, various literary circles and their short-lived journals appeared in Taiwan and carried on the creative efforts and translation work fostered by the new literature movement during its early phase. For several years a Taiwanese vernacular movement also strove to replace classical Chinese, *pai-hua* Mandarin, and Japanese with a written equivalent of the local southern Fukien dialect.[144]

The new literature movement peaked in 1934. By that time Japanese literary standards and styles prevailed, for the younger generation of Taiwanese writers were generally more proficient in the Japanese language by virtue of their educational background.[145] Nevertheless, the new literature helped to create a more distinctive Taiwanese cultural identity: a modern one, tinctured with nationalistic overtones, that set off Taiwanese intellectuals and the island homeland they represented from their Japanese and Chinese counterparts in the colonial and East Asian setting.

The Taiwanese feminist movement developed around 1920 as well and figured in the cultural and intellectual ferment of the period. Modern feminist issues had already become of concern to Taiwanese (mostly males) studying abroad in China and metropolitan Japan. Women's movements flourishing in these countries further influenced feminist activities in the colony. Between 1920 and 1932 more widespread interest in the Taiwanese movement was aroused through spirited articles calling attention to the major problems that impeded female emancipation in the colony: namely, old-style marriages, unequal economic and educational opportunities for women, and the lack of suffrage rights.[146] Local support was also derived from lectures and other activities sponsored by the Taiwan Cultural Association and, subsequently, through alliances with the Taiwan Farmers' Union (Taiwan nōmin kumiai) and the Taiwanese Communist Party during the heyday of radical Taiwanese politics in the late 1920s and early 1930s.[147] Basically, though, the Taiwanese feminist movement remained a middle-class campaign that relied on the active participation of educated Taiwanese women and, in particular, female teachers employed in schools throughout the colony.[148]

Meanwhile, the first of a series of Taiwanese-inspired political movements developed on the founding of the New People's Society in 1920. In that year the possibility of full assimilation and fusion with metropolitan Japan became unacceptable to most of the new intelligentsia after the unpopular Law 63 was again extended by the Imperial Diet, but this time for an indefinite period. In protest, the leaders of the New People's Society rejected the options of integration with Japan or restoration to China then being debated and, instead, opted to advance home rule by establishing a parliament in Taiwan.[149] They reckoned that, through enactments by an elected colonial legislature, not only could the Meiji constitution and Japanese laws be made to prevail in Taiwan but Taiwanese customs and other worthwhile attributes of the native culture might also be preserved. In effect, moderate Taiwanese spokesmen, while professing loyalty to Japan, now ventured to demand a separate and more equal standing for their people, culture, and island homeland within the Japanese empire.

The Japanese residents in Taiwan, however, strongly objected to a popularly elected legislative body in which their representatives would be vastly outnumbered by those of the Taiwanese. Governor-General Den Kenjirō, despite his liberal inclinations, thus was compelled to oppose the Taiwanese demand for a colonial parliament. Thereafter, other governors-general reacted negatively too, as did Japanese officials in Tokyo, including the prime minister, who in 1926 suggested as an alternative that the Taiwanese might be granted representation in the Imperial Diet.[150] In addition to opposition from powerful officials the proponents of a Taiwan parliament faced coercive pressures in the colony. For this reason some members of the New People's Society were reluctant to engage in political affairs. Eventually, in 1923, the more active leaders created a new organization, the League for the Establishment of a Taiwan Parliament (Taiwan gikai kisei dōmeikai) to head their movement.[151]

Their movement lasted for fifteen years and, annually between 1921 and 1934, Taiwanese supporters submitted petitions to the Diet requesting favorable legislation. The 1926 petition bore almost two thousand signatures, indicating widespread support for the movement from among educated Taiwanese as well as less-literate community leaders and *hokō* heads and even illiterate individuals in the colony.[152] Yet the movement failed to achieve its goal since none of the petitions gained a hearing on the floor of the Diet.[153] Finally, when faced with mounting ultranationalist pressures in Japan and Taiwan, Lin Hsien-t'ang and other key members of the league dissolved their organization in 1934, and the sustained Taiwanese effort to gain home rule virtually ended.

By then, the league was regarded as a relatively conservative element in Taiwanese politics. Disgruntled leaders, along with younger Taiwanese activists, had turned to more radical designs in their ongoing confrontation with Japanese colonialism and efforts to resolve pressing economic problems in Taiwan. During the mid-1920s, a number of militants became active in farm and labor disputes. Some espoused Marxism, and a few joined the small, short-lived Taiwanese Communist Party.[154] In 1927, the Taiwan Cultural Association, which had supported the league and its movement for a parliament, came under the control of such radical members, causing the moderate leaders to withdraw from the league and organize the Taiwan Popular Party (Taiwan minshūtō). The moderate platform of this new party called for local autonomy in the context of self-government and popular elections based on universal suffrage. On the other hand, radical party members helped to organize a labor union federation. Their involvement in strikes and political demonstrations reflecting Chinese Nationalist influences, together with their strident call for a united front of workers and peasants, led the colonial government to close down the party in 1931.[155]

Meanwhile, moderate members, fearful of police retaliation for such radical conduct, had withdrawn from the Popular Party during the previous year. Their leaders, in turn, created a more conservative organization, the Taiwan Federation for Local Autonomy (Taiwan chihōjichi renmei) for the sole acclaimed purpose of improving the existing system of colonial self-government. After 1931, the federation was the only Taiwanese political organization registered in the colony.[156] It claimed to represent the entire Taiwanese people and focused attention on some of the sensitive issues of colonial governance, such as the *hokō* system and the restricted form of self-government introduced to Taiwan after 1920. However, the federation failed to gain universal suffrage for the Taiwanese, even in the municipal elections held in 1935 when the long-awaited local autonomy reform was introduced with few of the democratic innovations that had been anticipated. Hence, according to Edward Ti-te Chen, self-government in the colony remained "in essence, a rigged system in favor of Japanese residents."[157] Subsequently, in September 1936, the new governor-general, Kobayashi Seizō, advised even this conservative and largely discredited Taiwanese organization to disband, which it did voluntarily in August 1937, following the outbreak of war with China.[158]

In retrospect, it is remarkable that Taiwanese cultural and political movements should have grown so radical in the late 1920s and early 1930s, when Japanese rule at home and in the colonies was becoming more repressive and ultranationalistic in tone. Noteworthy, too, was the determination of the new Taiwan governor-general to put an end to the islandwide Federation for Local Autonomy, which had attempted to advance self-government and universal suffrage, essentially under a Taiwanese label, until the eve of the wartime period.

The Wartime Period (1937–1945)

The wartime period for Japan began in July 1937, after the Marco Polo Bridge incident in North China gave rise to an undeclared war with China, styled the "Sino-Japanese Conflict." Taiwan's war period, though, may be said to have begun ten months earlier in September 1936, when Admiral Kobayashi Seizō became the colony's seventeenth governor-general. Kobayashi's appointment ostensibly extended the sequence of civilian governors-general in Taiwan, for the admiral was on the navy's retired list.[159] Nonetheless, Kobayashi functioned very much as a militarist from the outset of his reign by implementing three basic policies by which Taiwan was to be industrialized and its people "imperialized," in preparation for a full-scale Japanese war effort, and the island colony to become a springboard for Japan's "southward advance" *(nanshin)* into southern China and Southeast Asia. His *nanshin* policy resembled southern expansionist schemes entertained previously by Meiji proponents favoring the Japanese navy,[160] except that, in 1936, "southward advance" had been adopted as part of a national policy to balance off the Japanese army's designs for the domination of Northeast Asia with the navy's plans for southern conquests. In this official context Kobayashi's appointment reflected the navy's consolidation of its authority in Taiwan as a base for future actions in Southeast Asia.[161]

Military events during Kobayashi's four-year reign (1936–40) indicate the positive effects of his *nanshin* policy. Taiwan served as a major staging area for the conquest of Canton in late 1938, and for the naval occupation of Hainan island in February 1939.[162] By 1940, the main Fukien ports and the entire Taiwan strait were controlled by the Japanese navy, and the way had been cleared for the invasion of Southeast Asia through the South China Sea. A full year before this major incursion began, Kobayashi was replaced by Admiral Hasegawa Kiyoshi, who was on active duty and involved in strategic planning for a military advance southward.[163]

Admiral Hasegawa's appointment, in late 1940, came at a time when Japanese leaders realized that it would probably be necessary to seize the American, British, and Dutch colonies in Southeast Asia in order to secure oil and other vital wartime resources. Accordingly, the vision of a "Greater East Asia Co-Prosperity Sphere" (Dai Tōa kyōeiken) was heralded in Tokyo in an effort to legitimize Japan's penetration southward and territorial expansion elsewhere.[164] Moreover, both services were now in agreement that war with the United States and Britain seemed inevitable. A joint planning and logistical center was established in Taiwan, and the colony subsequently assumed an important role in Japan's southern military ventures after the bombing of Pearl Harbor, Hawaii, on December 7, 1941, which sparked the Pacific War.[165]

Hasegawa's tenure as governor-general (November 1940 to December 1944) lasted until the final eight months of the Pacific War. At the outset of this "decisive conflict" *(kessen)*, Taiwan served primarily as a launching center for

Japanese air and naval attacks on Luzon until the surrender of the Philippines in May 1942.[166] Then the colony functioned as a rear staging area for more distant military conquests that reached Burma and the borders of India by the end of that year. In 1943, however, the tide of war began to turn against Japan, and Taiwan suffered as a consequence. Concern over the serious damage inflicted on Japanese shipping by Allied submarines eventually led Hasegawa to propose that Taiwan become self-sufficient and prepare for the loss of sea contact with Japan proper. In addition, the colony began to experience massive U.S. air raids on its industries, ports, and military installations during the latter part of 1944.[167] Taiwan faced mounting shortages and a decline in morale among the colonial population by the time Hasegawa was relieved of office at the end of that year and Andō Rikichi became the nineteenth and last governor-general.

General Andō was serving as the commander of the Taiwan military garrison at the time of his appointment.[168] As governor-general, he retained command over the garrison and reigned as the supreme military authority in the colony, as had the earlier Taiwan governors-general before Den Kenjirō assumed office in 1919. Andō also relied on a deputy civil administrator to handle domestic affairs, much like other governors-general had done since the Kodama-Gotō era, including the two wartime incumbents who preceded him.[169] The Andō administration engaged in what may be termed a holding operation for, by 1945, Taiwan was virtually an isolated colony in Japan's diminishing wartime empire. Preparations were made for a long siege, and the entire population readied to defend Taiwan at all costs from an anticipated invasion.[170] Despite the desperate situation, made worse by more U.S. air strikes, Andō maintained order and tight discipline in the colony until the emperor's decision to surrender unconditionally to the Allied powers was announced on August 14. Ten weeks later, on October 25, 1945, General Andō signed documents "restoring" Taiwan and P'eng-hu to Nationalist China.[171]

While *nanshin* directly involved Taiwan in Japan's expansionist designs, the other two policies introduced by Governor-General Kobayashi also had a lasting impact on the colony and its people during the wartime period. Industrialization entailed the development of Taiwan's economy and infrastructure for Japan's military needs. Basically, heavy industry was to be introduced in key areas where vital raw materials from Southeast Asia were to be processed, then shipped to industrial centers in metropolitan Japan. Imperialization *(kōminka),* on the other hand, called for the complete Japanization of the colonial population, in particular, the Han Taiwanese. As dictated by the *kōminka* movement that Kobayashi set in motion, Taiwan's inhabitants were to be transformed into imperial subjects *(kōmin)* fully loyal to the emperor and at one with Japan's national polity, or *kokutai.* Neither policy was essentially new to the colony by the time of Kobayashi's appointment. Japan had already begun to plan for an industrial base in Taiwan, and broad assimilationist policies had been advanced by colonial officials since the 1920s. During the wartime period, though, the two policies were implemented in a more intense manner by the government-general and local authorities, and also through the initiative of Japan's leaders in Tokyo as the home government sought to integrate the inner *(naichi)* colonies with metropolitan Japan.[172]

Official planning for the industrialization of Taiwan, in preparation for war, commenced at a major Taipei conference held in 1935. There blueprints were produced for new industries that would process bauxite, iron ore, crude oil, and rubber from Malaya and the East Indies. More seaports and electrical generating facilities were also called for to accommodate the upsurge of heavy industry.[173] This conference was followed up, in 1938, by the formation of a commission in Taipei to bring about rapid industrialization about the island. The commission advanced further plans for electrification and transportation as well as for up-grading Taiwan's prime industries, including mining.[174] A number of notable accomplishments resulted from such planning. Massive hydroelectric installations were constructed and new harbors created. Modern industrial complexes were then formed at seaports where water transportation and abundant power were available, as highlighted by the large Japan Aluminum Company plants that began operating at Hua-lien and Kao-hsiung in 1940.[175]

The creation of a wartime industrial base represented Taiwan's final stage of economic development as a Japanese colony. Initially, during the first three decades of colonial rule, sugar and rice production had been emphasized and Taiwan viewed as an agricultural appendage of metropolitan Japan.[176] The industrial sector remained very small. By the mid-1920s light industry began to make substantial gains, especially in food processing, because of the rise in agricultural productivity and the greater availability of investment capital. Only a few large, modern industrial firms existed, however, and most of them were Japanese sugar companies. In contrast, many of the numerous small enterprises (mainly food processing, handicraft, and other local industries) now tended to be owned and operated by Taiwanese.[177] Heavy industry, introduced during war, brought on an advance in modern technology, as signified by the greater number of large plants with power-driven machinery. Yet differences in economic opportunity continued to prevail between the largest favored companies, under Japanese ownership and management, and small firms in the hands of Taiwanese investors. Under this colonial arrangement, heavy wartime industry was capitalized by Japanese investment derived from banking and credit institutions in the colony and business interests in Japan, including *zaibatsu* (conglomerates).[178]

Industrial growth, paralleled by other wartime needs, brought about a much larger work force in Taiwan's nonagricultural sector. In 1935, somewhat over 68,000 workers were employed in 7,000 factories (mostly of small size). By mid-1943, the number of skilled laborers in manufacturing plants increased to around 147,000, while the total male and female workers employed in the nonagricultural sector (also including mining, transportation, communications, and services) rose to some 214,000. An additional civilian work force of this magnitude became engaged in construction and military-related employment.[179] The increase in specialized openings in many fields led to the hiring of Taiwanese laborers and lower-level managers for positions that had previously been allotted to trained Japanese residents.[180] Industrial and military needs had other consequences as well. The urban population grew when villagers were drawn to factory jobs in cities. Enrollments in elementary and vocational schools also peaked, partly because of the greater demand for skilled labor.[181]

The wartime demand for labor led to a variety of efforts to mobilize the Taiwanese for productive services. In 1939, the governor-general established a labor cooperative association to coordinate its mobilization efforts and, in April 1940, created a Patriotic Youth Corps (Hōkoku seinentai) to secure voluntary labor for the construction of new plants and industrial sites.[182] Meanwhile, the hokō system continued to supply village conscripts for social service campaigns. Already throughout the early 1930s, such campaigns had involved sizable segments of the rural population in plague prevention and sanitation drives as well as in additional road and bridge construction. After 1937, the use of hokō labor increased when wastelands were reclaimed and construction of military airports and defense installations was undertaken.[183]

A more complete mobilization plan was introduced early in 1941, after Hasegawa Kiyoshi took over as governor-general. Hasegawa proposed to mobilize Taiwan's labor force and material resources under a controlled economy so that industrial output could be augmented and domestic consumption restricted.[184] He also sought to advance public services so that the colony's entire population and governing structure would be involved in the war effort. In keeping with these objectives, the Imperial Subjects' Public Service Association, or Kōmin hōkōkai, was founded in April, in commemoration of Japan's 2,600th anniversary and unbroken imperial line.[185] This patriotic colonial organization was designed to guide the kōminka movement and to garner the support of Taiwan's population of nearly 6 million for the impending "decisive conflict" with the Allied powers. Under Hasegawa's direction the Kōmin hōkōkai also responded to the home government's call for tighter control over the economy and social life of the colonies.

The Kōmin hōkōkai was the most extensive organization formed in Taiwan during the war. The association functioned at each level of formal government, while within the townships it maintained urban ward units (kukai) and rural village units (burakukai). Also fundamental to the association's local operations were its many public service teams (hokōhan), each corresponding to a kō, or neighborhood grouping of about ten families. These teams increased in number as the association reached more remote areas and totaled 70,380 by April 1944.[186] The Kōmin hōkōkai incorporated Japanese residents in its memberships as well. In several cities with large naichijin neighborhoods, Japanese civilians were assigned to separate block units (chōkai).[187] Thus the association fostered segregation in some major urban centers, despite the strong assimilationist bent of the *kōminka* movement and contrary to the fact that Taiwanese leaders were co-opted within its structure at all levels, as had happened to an extent in the *buraku* system managed by the Buraku shinhōkai.

The overall structure of the Kōmin hōkōkai, in terms of its offices and units, roughly paralleled those of the *buraku* and *hokō* systems. Consequently, the association's operations often appeared ill defined when it interacted with the two systems. In particular, there was a great deal of overlap in personnel. The same ranking officials served as officers or chief administrators at each formal level, while *hokō* clerks and heads also were involved in the informal operations. Nonetheless, the Kōmin hōkōkai performed in a distinctive manner. As a wartime appendage to colonial governance, it functioned without close attachments to the well-entrenched civil police force, in marked contrast to the *hokō* system. Most significantly, its operations at the local level spread well beyond its public service teams and jurisdictional units, for the association penetrated into schools, factories, occupational associations, and the many societies formed to promote the war effort.[188]

In effect, the Kōmin hōkōkai created informal networks within and between local communities. This enabled the colonial authorities, along with association leaders and public service teams, to reach adult and youthful Taiwanese at their job sites and places of study and training, as well as within their own ethnic neighborhoods. The association was instrumental in increasing the tempo of wartime indoctrination and propaganda, as evinced by the many patriotic demonstrations and donation drives that ensued during the early 1940s. The colony's carefully monitored newspapers and radio broadcasting further helped to muster Taiwanese support of the war effort, as did the activities of the Youth and Young Women's Corps.[189] Meanwhile, the workings of the *buraku* and *hokō* systems, in conjunction with the activities of the Kōmin hōkōkai, enabled the colonial authorities to regiment more fully the inhabitants within their households and neighborhood or village units. Clearly, wartime rule in Taiwan took on a totalitarian cast, especially when one takes into account other major control mechanisms then in effect: namely, strict household registry, constant surveillance by the police and special security agents, and the presence of local paramilitary units along with the large Japanese military contingents stationed in the colony.

Over the last months of war, Governor-General Andō made further use of such controls when he ordered the entire civilian population—Japanese, Taiwanese, and aborigine—to carry on a united, last-ditch defensive effort. Then, in June 1945, a new "volunteer corps" *(giyūtai)* was established with rural and urban branches throughout Taiwan. Although termed a voluntary service organization, the Taiwan Giyūtai law introduced compulsory military conscription to the colony for both men and women. In anticipation of its enactment, the *hokō* system was abolished on June 17, and the Kōmin hōkōkai soon thereafter, when *giyūtai* squads were formed to bolster Taiwan's defenses and to engage in vital public labor.[190] Thus Japanese rule also assumed a much more militaristic guise in Taiwan before its conclusion there in August.

Crucial to wartime rule in the colony was the imperialization, or *kōminka,* policy introduced by Governor-General Kobayashi. Only as fully assimilated subjects, it was reckoned, could Taiwan's inhabitants be expected to become committed, both in mind and spirit, to Japan's war effort and nationalistic aspirations. The "Japanization" of the mountain tribes was regarded as a relatively easy undertaking because of their lack of ethnic unity and the effective police instruction to which they were already subjected. The rapid imperialization of the much larger Han Taiwanese population was a more complex project and called for stricter procedures than those employed in conjunction with "liberal" assimilationist policies of the past.[191]

Kōminka policy embraced a number of government-sponsored assimilationist programs and reforms. These were implemented through colonial directives and staged mainly through a series of campaigns and local drives during the war. In effect, such sustained imperialization efforts constituted a highly regulated movement guided centrally by the governors-general. Kobayashi's first *kōminka* measures were introduced in April 1937, when the Chinese-language sections of the colony's newspapers were abolished and classical Chinese was removed from the elementary school curriculum.[192] These measures foreshadowed a national language *(kokugo)* program, initiated later that year, which discouraged the use of Chinese and reportedly increased the percentage of Japanese speakers among the Taiwanese population from some 37 percent in 1937 to 51 percent in 1940. However, the fluency of many of the adults, after only a minimum of language instruction, is doubtful. Even members of some model "national language" families *(kokugo katei),* designated from among well-educated Taiwanese households, were hardly conversant in Japanese.[193]

In order to imperialize the Taiwanese more thoroughly the Kobayashi regime launched a name-changing *(kaiseimei)* campaign early in 1940. This *kōminka* program involved replacing Chinese names with Japanese ones as a means to detach the Han Taiwanese from their descent groups and ancestral areas in China. Publicly, however, the government heralded name changing as an opportunity for colonial inhabitants to demonstrate that they were devoted subjects and "true Japanese." The bestowal of full Japanese names was acclaimed a great honor and carried out on a selective basis among approved Taiwanese households, as was the case with "national language" family conferrals. Name-changing procedures were rigorous and required formal application by household heads on behalf of their respective family members and then official investigation of the Japanese names chosen. Although less stringent regulations were announced in 1944, only about 7 percent of the Taiwanese had adopted Japanese names by the time the war ended.[194] A version of the *kaiseimei* campaign was conducted among the aboriginal population as well. In all, a higher percentage of these non-Han inhabitants appears to have complied with modified name-changing procedures under more lenient requirements.[195]

The most effective campaigns launched during the *kōminka* movement, as indicated by the widespread positive response, involved recruitment for military service. Before 1937, colonial subjects had not been allowed to serve in the Japanese armed forces. As the war in China spread, however, Taiwan authorities began to recruit porters and interpreters for short-term enlistments with units operating in the Yangtze river and southern coastal regions. Women were also enlisted to serve as wartime nursing assistants. The early recruitment drives for these essentially civilian assignments attracted many applicants among young people. After an army volunteer system was established in Taiwan in 1942, several hundred thousand more Taiwanese and aborigine youths applied for regular military service during each recruitment campaign, despite the relatively small annual quotas. Nearly as many volunteered for active duty in the Japanese navy when a similar naval program (also with restricted quotas) was introduced the following year. The positive response to military recruitment continued after general conscription was implemented in the colony in April 1945. By the end of the war, the number of inhabitants recruited for military duty totaled 207,183, including 80,433 servicemen, and 126,750 civilian employees.[196]

The military recruitment campaigns and drives amounted to a special wartime project. Active participation by the Youth and Young Women's Corps had a strong impact, as did the patriotic appeals directed at young people. They were told that the highest honor for Japanese subjects was to fight and die for the emperor and that military service was one of their "three great obligations" *(sandai gimu)* as citizens, the other two being compulsory education and taxpaying.[197] Military service, though, was not made compulsory in Taiwan until 1945. Hence recruitment depended mainly on persuasion and incentives, fostered by the colonial government and its informal structures, as well as by pressures exerted within the family and community or at school and among youthful peer groups. In this respect, military recruitment resembled such other major *kōminka* activities as national language family conferrals and the name-changing campaign: recruitment was also conducted on a voluntary, rather than a mandatory, basis as a rule, and the end result—military duty by avowedly loyal and patriotic colonial subjects—was also viewed as an essential part of the Japanization process.

The *kōminka* movement had a harsher cast as well. From the outset Governor-General Kobayashi and his subordinates undertook to root out characteristics of the Taiwanese culture declared to be "un-Japanese" or otherwise objectionable and, whenever possible, to replace them with Japanese ways. Previously, the colonial authorities had tolerated or even sought to preserve many of the Chinese traditions and practices deeply ingrained in Taiwanese society. Now, suddenly, such overtures to cultural accommodation were cast aside, and overbearing *kōminka* reforms imposed instead.

The most drastic of these reforms related to Kobayashi's efforts to force the Japanese state religion, Shintoism, upon the Taiwanese. He advised the inhabitants to show reverence to Shinto shrines *(jinja)* and to maintain domestic altars *(kamidana)* in their households, where they were expected to worship paper amulets *(taima)* sent from the sacred Ise shrine in Japan. Regulations specified how the *kamidana* were to be arranged, including instructions that the shrine shelf, set up to accommodate the Ise amulets in each household, was to be situated in the place where family and ancestral tablets, together with Chinese deities, were venerated.[198] Kobayashi also advanced the construction of more Shinto shrines in the colony in a vain attempt to undercut or eliminate the traditional Chinese religions practiced in Taiwanese communities. This led some local officials to order that religious idols and artifacts be removed from native temples and that these edifices themselves be demolished. Such "temple reorganization" measures caused great consternation among the inhabitants and were deemed too severe by officials in Tokyo.[199] Governor-General Hasegawa soon discontinued the wholesale destruction of Taiwanese temples. Nevertheless, as Wan-yao Chou notes, the official pressure on the Taiwanese to revere Shinto shrines, and even to worship the Japanese imperial palace from afar, became more intense as such rituals were practiced on a more massive scale.[200]

Meanwhile, other *kōminka* reforms were directed at Taiwanese customs and practices. Efforts were made to have marriages arranged in the Japanese manner and Shinto wedding ceremonies performed at shrines. Japanese-style funeral services and burial practices were encouraged as well, including cremation for purposes of sanitation and land conservation. Moreover, traditional Taiwanese operas and puppet plays were banned, as were fireworks and the burning of gold and silver paper foil at temples. The daily Taiwanese life-style was directly affected by measures that discouraged the wearing of Chinese attire in public, betel-nut chewing, and noisy commotions.[201] Altogether, such *kōminka* reforms, including those calling for the common use of Japanese speech and name changing, impinged on Taiwanese households throughout the colony.

The *kōminka* movement appears to have been generally unsuccessful in the long run. Few Taiwanese were transformed into "true Japanese" by way of the imperialization process, and local resentment was stirred by harsh and demanding *kōminka* measures. Above all, it was simply not feasible to assimilate fully such a large colonial population, especially in only a few years. The results of the wartime imperialization process can be better gauged, however, when "Japanization" is construed more realistically as a way by which the Taiwanese were to be rapidly acculturated rather than completely assimilated. In this respect, *kōminka* indoctrination efforts seem to have been relatively effective under controlled conditions.

On the whole, the Taiwanese and aborigine inhabitants performed well as imperial subjects, or *kōmin*. The Taiwanese complied with wartime demands entailing hardships and personal sacrifice on their part. Some individuals and families evidenced extreme forms of patriotism, and a few intellectuals were swayed to write "*kōminka*" literature on behalf of Japan's war effort.[202] By early 1945, even the middle-aged and elderly prepared to fight to the bitter end in response to Governor-General Andō's biddings. There were very few hostile incidents staged by the Taiwanese or the mountain tribes during the war period. Furthermore, the Taiwanese and aboriginal people served faithfully in the Japanese armed forces as a rule. Most were volunteers who had been selected for duty on the basis of their professed patriotism and dedication to the emperor and nation. Although many were civilian employees and did not bear arms, those assigned to combat units in Southeast Asia and the South Pacific during the Pacific War reportedly fought bravely. Altogether, such regular-duty servicemen native to Taiwan numbered 61,591 and were deployed as far away as Rabaul, in New Britain, and the Solomon Islands.[203]

Colonial military enlistments in Taiwan were derived from among the younger generation of inhabitants whose formative years roughly spanned the wartime period. This generation of adolescents and young adults also contributed to the domestic war effort as a low-paid or voluntary labor force and by their continuous involvement in "spiritual mobilization" activities spurred by the *kōminka* movement and the Kōmin hōkōkai.[204] Among the Taiwanese, this younger generation rendered more active public service as a rule than did the senior generations in good measure because of the more extensive public school training its members received at an early age. The number of Taiwanese boys and girls who gained at least an elementary education increased at a steady rate between 1937 and 1945. By 1944, nearly three out of every four children were enrolled in primary schools after attendance had been made compulsory the previous year.[205]

Attempts were made to indoctrinate these young Taiwanese students more thoroughly during the war period than had been done in the past. They were still taught about the divine origin of Japan's imperial rulers and the superiority of the Japanese race. In addition, though, they were subjected to propaganda about Japan's wartime mission and urged to assist in the development of the new order being created by the Japanese military. School conditions also enabled Taiwanese youngsters to allot more time to Japanese studies. Eventually, in 1941, Taiwanese and Japanese primary schools in the colony were unified under a single public system, and a standard curriculum was adopted so that education offered there might keep pace with that provided in elementary schools throughout the home country.[206] Hence many of the younger Taiwanese generation became functionally literate in Japanese and more familiar with the Japanese culture than were their parents and elders. Moreover, wartime needs served to bring Taiwanese students into closer contact with their teachers and Japanese classmates, especially after 1942, when public service brigades were made mandatory for both students and staff at all levels of education in Taiwan.[207]

This wartime schooling and indoctrination amounted to an intense acculturation program of the *kyōka* variety and had a lasting effect on many young Taiwanese men and women. Although not fully Japanese, they could relate to being imperial subjects and accept, or readily subscribe to, the *kōminka* movement and *kōmin* identity. Their early schooling also helps account for the many who volunteered for military duty with such a fanatical display of patriotism: When submitting enlistment applications, these young people attached strongly worded "desires written in [their own] blood" *(kessho shigan)* by which they pleaded for the honor of serving in the military.[208] This practice began in 1937, when Taiwanese first applied for positions as military porters. By the time army and navy volunteer systems were established in Taiwan during the early 1940s, "blood pleading" had become widespread among Taiwanese and aboriginal male applicants. Even young women sent in blood pleas with their applications for nursing assistant appointments.[209]

Once assigned to military duty, members of this younger generation accommodated to the wartime political culture. In their service units they were not subject to colonial *hokō* controls and no longer suffered the inferior *hokōmin* identity. Instead, as loyal *kōmin,* they could feel more on a par with the ethnic Japanese. Moreover, when dispatched overseas in military or civilian capacities, they came into contact with less "Japanized" colonials from elsewhere, as well as with unacculturated inhabitants of Japan's newly acquired territories. Under these circumstances, some members, along with older Taiwanese, came to believe that they and their people, and indeed Taiwan itself, deserved an equal or even an exalted standing within Japan's wartime empire by virtue of the degree of Japanization that the Taiwanese had undergone.

In Taiwan, though, the great majority of Taiwanese hardly entertained such visionary notions of the future under Japanese rule. Many still harbored opposition sentiments embodying Taiwanese or Chinese nationalistic ideals. Another fifty thousand by 1945 were serving the colonial government in various capacities and could be expected to uphold the style of Japanese hegemonic rule that had long prevailed in Taiwan.[210] Meanwhile, the Taiwanese inhabitants, by and large, had really no other recourse during the war period than to remain loyal and obedient, so tight was the security and so restrained were their leaders. The moderate and radical spokesmen of the past were now in custody or else had been co-opted within the structures of the Buraku shinhōkai and Kōmin hōkōkai. The Taiwanese people even lacked a means to express their opinions and grievances in the press. There were no longer any independently managed newspapers in the colony, such as the *Taiwan People's Journal,* which had previously served as their mouthpiece. The wartime successor to its sequel, the *Taiwan New People's Journal* (1930–32), was but an organ of the Kōmin hōkōkai and lasted only from 1941 to 1944.[211]

The Taiwanese *sekimin* residing in China also endured tighter Japanese wartime control. Even before 1937, their community schools in Amoy, Foochow, and Swatow had been obliged to train students along lines set by the public school system in Japan so that young overseas Taiwanese might resemble ethnic Japanese and prove to be loyal and patriotic subjects. Subsequently, some of these second-generation *sekimin* were placed in Japanese military units operating in the region. The Taiwanese could not but comply with such assignments, so dependent were they on Japan's protection and the successful outcome of aggressive Japanese policies and military ventures. *Sekimin* patriotism was demonstrated when the major establishments in the Amoy settlement dutifully flew Japanese flags after war with China broke out in July 1937.[212]

During the war, the Taiwanese *sekimin* experienced great tension. They had to remain loyal to Japan, or at least seem to do so within the confines of their business communities, yet at the same time they incurred rebuke from local Chinese inhabitants harboring strong anti-Japanese sentiments. They were also blamed for the pernicious activities of *ronin* members, who worked closely with Japanese agents and the occupation forces. Everywhere in China, it seemed, the Taiwanese were regarded as spies or Chinese traitors *(Han-chien)*.[213] The larger *sekimin* settlements in southern coastal China were continually caught up in such strife. There the Taiwanese had to obey the dictates of Japanese consuls and naval officers, as well as conform to directives issued from the Foreign Ministry in Tokyo. As a consequence, *sekimin* communities in Fukien suffered considerable loss of life and property damage over the first two years of the war, when a Kuangtung army division, and then the provincial governor and local Chinese authorities, endeavored to clear out the Taiwanese from Amoy, Foochow, and other seaport areas of the province.[214]

Despite these setbacks, the *sekimin* population appears to have increased on the mainland over the wartime period. Some 80 to 90 percent of the estimated one hundred thousand Taiwanese civilians residing there, before 1945, consisted of such registered Japanese subjects concentrated mainly in Canton, Hong Kong, and the older coastal settlements of Fukien and eastern Kuangtung. Taiwanese *sekimin* also conducted business in occupied areas of the lower Yangtze and North China, including Shanghai and Peking, as well as in Manchukuo.[215] The smaller segment of Taiwanese residents were students, intellectuals, or merchants, who had elected to remain or seek refuge in China during or before the war. Around a thousand of these belonged to various Chinese Nationalist organizations in the unoccupied areas, and many were active in the anti-Japanese resistance.[216] After the late 1943 announcement of the Cairo Declaration, in which the Allied powers demanded the complete restoration of all Chinese territories lost to Japan (including Taiwan and P'eng-hu), more Taiwanese became directly involved in Kuomintang politics. A few of their representatives visited the Nationalist wartime capital in Chungking and urged that Taiwan again be made a separate province of China after its retrocession.[217] By then, other Taiwanese involved in the resistance movement had already begun to declare that their people were actually devoted Chinese brethren, rather than traitors and Japanese lackeys, in an effort to improve the tarnished Taiwanese image that had long been ascribed to the *sekimin* residents.[218]

The Cairo Declaration, though, does not appear to have had an impact on Taiwan's wartime population, and few inhabitants may have learned of its announcement in 1943. Nevertheless, the colonial authorities continued to make concessions to the Taiwanese so that the latter might be induced to render further support of the war effort under the worsening conditions. Already, in 1940, the Taiwan governor-general had introduced additional self-government reforms in an attempt to appease or co-opt more of the local elite and native activists. As a result, nearly half the council members at the municipal, county, and township levels were elected, rather than appointed, and the township councils came to have entirely Taiwanese memberships, as did most of the village councils.[219] Subsequently, the colonial and home governments endeavored to provide better treatment to natives serving in colonial bureaucracies. Hence Taiwanese functionaries received salary increases and special wartime benefits. Taiwanese were also allowed to hold posts in Japanese-occupied areas of Southeast Asia. While serving as overseas officials, they were accorded equal treatment with ethnic Japanese.[220]

Again, in 1945, major concessions were made to the Taiwanese and Koreans by the hard pressed imperial government. An enactment passed by the Diet on March 21 stipulated that a designated number of representatives from each of their colonies was to be elected to the Diet's lower house (five from Taiwan and twenty-three from Korea). The elections were to be held in their respective colonies and conducted in accordance with the limited franchise granted to qualified male adults.[221] Then two days later, an imperial rescript called for the appointment of a few notable Taiwanese and Koreans to the upper house (three and seven members, respectively). Selections were made on April 3, but because of the critical military situation, a special session of the Imperial Diet was not convened as scheduled, nor were Diet elections ever held in Taiwan for representatives in the lower house over the last few months of the war.[222]

These 1945 concessions seemed to indicate that wartime leaders in Tokyo were still endeavoring to integrate the *naichi* colonies with metropolitan Japan. However, they raised questions about the future status of Taiwan under Japanese rule. Would Taiwan remain a colony, or would it perhaps become a prefecture? This latter alternative appeared feasible not only to ardent assimilationists, who had long proposed that Taiwan and its inhabitants be fused with the home country, but also to those who might yet favor home rule. Lin Hsien-t'ang was one of the three Taiwanese appointed to the House of Peers, and there was speculation that an elected prefectural assembly would be forthcoming in Taiwan so that the prime goal of the Taiwanese home rule movement—gaining a separate and more equal standing for Taiwan and its people—could be achieved.[223] Aside from such speculations, though, these late wartime concessions demonstrated Japan's determination to retain possession of Taiwan, its oldest colony, even as the Japanese empire was disintegrating.

Hence the sudden news of Japan's unconditional surrender in August 1945 shocked virtually the entire island population. The *naichijin* and local inhabitants alike were stunned to learn that the "decisive war" had ended so abruptly and that Taiwan would soon pass out of Japanese hands. Colonial officials and the military were also taken by surprise. One group of young officers threatened to stage a revolt, so strong was their belief that the emperor had not broadcast the surrender of his own volition.[224] At the same time, a few vengeful Taiwanese reviled Japanese residents and policemen in the street and even assaulted their own kind, including *hosei* and "imperialized gentlemen" *(goyō shinshi)* who had collaborated with the colonial authorities.[225]

Meanwhile, Taiwanese overseas were troubled by the war's sudden end. In China, the *sekimin* came under attack, as did those on military duty. On Hainan island, where the largest contingent of Taiwan servicemen was stationed, many were slain by Chinese troops or else perished from disease and starvation before the survivors managed to make unheralded returns to Taiwan. Instances of suffering and suicide among Taiwanese servicemen and nurses posted elsewhere in China, as well as in the Pacific and Southeast Asian sectors, were also reported when war veterans from these far-flung areas began to be repatriated, but again without fanfare or tokens of honor.[226]

Despite such incidents and alarming reports from abroad, the Andō regime maintained order in the colony. During the subsequent weeks, most of the population refrained from further acts of violence, and the Taiwanese people more eagerly anticipated the inauguration of Chinese rule over their island homeland. Then they had time to reflect on the negative aspects of colonial governance, particularly during the war. Consequently, huge numbers of enthusiastic Taiwanese turned out to greet the Chinese Nationalist forces as they started to arrive by ship in mid-October. Soon thereafter, on October 25, widespread public celebrations were held when Taiwan and P'eng-hu were formally retroceded to China in accordance with the terms of the Cairo Declaration and the 1945 Potsdam Proclamation that had been drawn up by the major Allied powers: the United States, Great Britain, and the Soviet Union. By virtue of these wartime pronouncements and General Andō's signature, it appeared that Japan's island colony had been shifted to the side of the victorious Allies as well as "restored" to Nationalist China. Clearly, Taiwan and its people were about to enter a new, postcolonial era.

However, the vicissitudes of colonialism were such that the Taiwanese never had control over their own destiny. In 1895, Taiwan had suddenly been ceded to Japan, much to the consternation of the inhabitants, and painful years of resistance and accommodation had ensued. Thereafter, the Taiwanese were not granted home rule and allowed only a limited measure of self-government. They were not allotted representation in the Diet before March 1945, nor were they appointed to high office in the imperial government.[227] Subsequently, as an outcome of another international war, their colony was retroceded to China in an equally abrupt manner. This time the transference of rule again occurred without a semblance of self-determination by the Taiwanese people or their leaders. The inhabitants were not even given a chance to indicate their preferences for citizenship, as had been done in 1895, despite the fact that most had loyally supported

Japan's war effort and had suffered wartime deprivations and casualties, although to a lesser extent than in 1895.[228] As a consequence, the Taiwanese once more came to be governed by "outsiders"—only this time they would be dominated by the Kuomintang and mainlander Chinese instead of by Japanese colonial authorities and *naichijin* residents.

Notes

1. From the beginning of the colonial period, Western observers tended to adhere to a positive, pro-Japanese perspective and to comment favorably on the order, the effective administration, and the modernization and economic progress brought about under Japanese rule. For example, see James W. Davidson, *The Island of Formosa Past and Present* (London and New York: Macmillan, 1903). Post-1945 studies by most Western scholars have likewise commended the material accomplishments by the Japanese and noted Japan's success in managing Taiwan's resources for its own interests, as does George W. Barclay, *Colonial Development and Population in Taiwan* (Princeton: Princeton University Press, 1954), pp. 6–8.

2. These perceptions have developed from a Taiwanese historiography that emphasizes Taiwan's own discrete identity and unique past. Many Taiwanese scholars now maintain that Taiwan's history should no longer be studied from either a China-centered perspective or a dominant Japanese orientation. The new Taiwanese "historiography" has recently been set forth in a major article: Chang Yen-hsien, "T'ai-wan shih yen-chiu te hsin ching-shen" [The new spirit of Taiwan historical research], *T'ai-wan shih-liao yen-chiu*, no. 1 (February 1993): 78–86.

3. Edward I-te Chen, "Japan's Decision to Annex Taiwan: A Study of Itō-Mutsu Diplomacy, 1894–95," *Journal of Asian Studies*, 37, no. 1 (November 1977): 66–67.

4. Leonard H.D. Gordon, "The Cession of Taiwan—A Second Look," *Pacific Historical Review*, 44, no. 4 (November 1976): 558–559.

5. A detailed account of the transference of Taiwan, translated from the *Japan Mail*, is contained in Davidson, *The Island of Formosa*, pp. 293–295.

6. Marius B. Jansen, "The Meiji State: 1868–1912," in *Modern East Asia: Essays in Interpretation*, ed. James B. Crowley (New York: Harcourt, Brace and World, 1970), p. 115.

7. Chen, "Japan's Decision to Annex Taiwan," pp. 71–72, argues that Itō and Mutsu wanted Japan to gain equality with the Western powers. Japan's decision to annex Taiwan was not based on any long-range design for future aggression.

8. Edward I-te Chen, "The Attempt to Integrate the Empire: Legal Perspectives," in *The Japanese Colonial Empire, 1895–1945*, ed. Ramon H. Myers and Mark R. Peattie (Princeton: Princeton University Press, 1984), pp. 248–250.

9. Ibid., p. 251. For a discussion of the legal, constitutional, and colonial policy issues relating to "Law 63" and its successive revisions (Law 31 in 1906, and Law 3 in 1921), see Tay-sheng Wang, "Legal Reform in Taiwan Under Japanese Colonial Rule (1895–1945): The Reception of Western Law" (Ph.D. dissertation, University of Washington, 1992), pp. 90–101.

10. The concept of assimilation and its implications under Japanese colonial rule until 1920 is treated in Mark R. Peattie, "Japanese Attitudes Toward Colonialism, 1895–1945," in *The Japanese Colonial Empire*, pp. 96–104.

11. Hung Ch'iu-fen, "T'ai-wan pao-chia ho 'sheng-huo kai-shan' yun-tung" [The Taiwan *pao-chia* and the movement "to improve living conditions," 1937–1945], *Shih-lien tsa-chih*, 19 (December 1991): 70.

12. Strong sentiments with regard to the assimilation of the Taiwanese and the merger of Taiwan were still expressed in Japan by supporters of Itagaki's Taiwan assimilation movement during 1914–15. Personal testimonies are included in "Taiwan dōkakai ni okeru meishi no shoka" [Sentiments of celebrities in regard to the Taiwan assimilation society], comp., Hamaguchi Yūkichi (unpublished draft, January 1919).

13. Yosaburo Takekoshi, *Japanese Rule in Formosa* (London: Longmans, Green, 1907), p. 18.

14. Harry J. Lamley, "The 1895 Taiwan War of Resistance: Local Chinese Efforts Against a Foreign Power," in *Taiwan: Studies in Chinese Local History,* ed. Leonard H.D. Gordon (New York: Columbia University Press, 1970), p. 24; Davidson, *The Island of Formosa,* pp. 301–304, 311–312.

15. Lamley, pp. 28, 56–67.

16. Ibid., pp. 23, 39–55; Gordon, "The Cession of Taiwan," p. 562.

17. Lamley, pp. 31–46.

18. Ibid., pp. 56–61.

19. For a description of the Taiwan Republic and Governor T'ang's role, see Harry J. Lamley, "The 1895 Taiwan Republic: A Significant Episode in Modern Chinese History," *Journal of Asian Studies,* 27, no. 4 (August 1968): 739–754.

20. Ibid., pp. 754–758; Davidson, *The Island of Formosa,* pp. 362–364.

21. Kabayama's proclamation, dated October 27, 1895, was addressed to the inhabitants of T'ainan. *Nisshin-eki Taiwan shi* [History of Taiwan in the Sino-Japanese War], comp., Wakumoto Otokuchi (Taihoku: Taiwan nichi shimpō, 1930), pp. 177–178. Later, on November 18, the governor-general issued a more formal pacification announcement. Sugiyama Seiken, *Taiwan rekidai sōtoko no chiseki* [Administrative record of Taiwan's successive governors-general] (Tokyo: 1922), p. 27.

22. A detailed study of the partisan resistance over these seven years is one by Weng Chia-in (Angkaim), *T'ai-wan Han-jen wu-chuang k'ang-Jih shih yen-chiu* [Taiwanese armed resistance under the early Japanese rule (1895–1902)] (Taipei: National Taiwan University, 1986). According to Weng, pp. 92–93, from the end of 1895 through 1902 there were attacks on fifty-four Japanese installations and ninety-four incidents staged by partisans.

23. Ibid., p. 95.

24. Huang Chao-t'ang, *Taiwan sōtokufu,* Chinese translation by Huang Ying-che (Taipei: Tzu-yu shih-tai, 1989), pp. 78–79.

25. Ibid., p. 93. Davidson, *The Island of Formosa,* p. 365, estimates that the number of Taiwanese killed in 1895 may have totaled 6,760.

26. Davidson, *The Island of Formosa,* p. 364.

27. Wu Wen-hsing, *Jih-chū shih-ch'i T'ai-wan she-hui ling-tao chieh-ts'eng chih yen-chiu* [Study of the elite stratum of Taiwanese society during the Japanese period] (Taipei: Cheng-chung shu-chu, 1992), pp. 27–33.

28. Ibid., p. 31.

29. Among them were prominent gentry leaders, such as Ch'iu Feng-chia, Lin Wei-yuan, and Lin Ch'ao-tung of the powerful Wu-feng Lin family, who had offered support to Governor T'ang and his resistance effort.

30. Weng Chia-in, *T'ai-wan Han-jen wu-chuang,* pp. 135–169. The author also discusses the incipient Chinese nationalism that developed in China and Taiwan as a consequence of the Sino-Japanese War and Ch'ing defeat, as well as local religion that helped inspire Taiwanese resistance.

31. Kodama remained in Taiwan for only several years until around 1900, and during subsequent intervals to 1906. Therefore, the actual governance of the colony often rested in Gotō's hands. Huang Chao-t'ang, *Taiwan sōtokufu,* pp. 82–83.

32. Ibid., pp. 87–93; Chang Han-yu and Ramon H. Myers, "Japanese Colonial Development Policy in Taiwan, 1895–1906: A Case of Bureaucratic Entrepreneurship," *Journal of Asian Studies,* 22, no. 4 (August 1963): 441–442. Light push cart railway lines were introduced in Taiwan in 1895, soon after the Japanese takeover. "In most cases daisha routes preceded steam railroad lines and improved roads," according to Ronald G. Knapp, "Push Car Railways and Taiwan's Development," in *China's Island Frontier: Studies in the Historical Geography of Taiwan,* ed. Ronald G. Knapp (Honolulu: University Press of Hawaii, 1980), p. 209.

33. Davidson, *The Island of Formosa,* pp. 633–644, 624–626; Lin Man-houng, *Ssu-pai nien lai te liang-an fen-ho: i-ke ching-mao shih te hui-ku* [Analysis and synthesis of four hundred years on both sides of the strait: A retrospection of economic-trade history] (Taipei: Tzu-li wan-pao, 1994), pp. 32–33.

34. Chang and Myers, "Japanese Colonial Development Policy," pp. 443–446; Davidson, *The Island of Formosa,* pp. 452–455. The long-range effects of the Japanese colonial strategy to make Taiwan an agricultural appendage of Japan, vis-à-vis sugar and rice production, is discussed in Samuel P.S. Ho, *Economic Development of Taiwan, 1860–1970* (New Haven: Yale University Press, 1978), pp. 29–32. Mainly by means of sugar and rice exports to Japan, along with finished products and services imported or purchased from Japan, an "export surplus" was created and in part reinvested to increase Taiwan's productive capacity. Taiwan's controlled trade with Japan, based on the colony's exports of its major agricultural products (except rice) and natural resources (camphor, in particular), has recently been interpreted more in terms of the expulsion of foreign capital and the penetration of Japanese capital, along with the subordination of Taiwanese merchants who had shared in this export trade during the late Ch'ing. Chih-ming Ka, *Japanese Colonialism in Taiwan: Land Tenure, Development, and Dependency, 1895–1945* (Boulder: Westview, 1995), pp. 65–69.

35. Chang and Myers, "Japanese Colonial Development Policy," p. 446; Chih-ming Ka, *Japanese Colonialism in Taiwan,* pp. 50–54.

36. Ka, *Japanese Colonialism in Taiwan,* pp. 58–62.

37. Chang and Myers, "Japanese Colonial Development Policy," p. 446; Ka, *Japanese Colonialism in Taiwan,* pp. 54–56.

38. George H. Kerr, *Formosa: Licensed Revolution and the Home Rule Movement, 1895–1945* (Honolulu: University Press of Hawaii, 1974), pp. 80–84.

39. Barclay, *Colonial Development,* p. 16, table 3, for the 1905 count of the Han Taiwanese only; p. 13, table 2, for the 1943 estimate of the entire subject population, including the aborigines. Kerr, *Formosa,* p. 73, cites a June 4, 1900, figure for the Han Taiwanese.

40. For an account of elementary common schools and other schooling administered by Gotō, see E. Patricia Tsurumi, *Japanese Colonial Education in Taiwan, 1895–1945* (Cambridge: Harvard University Press, 1977), pp. 18–44.

41. Ibid., pp. 34–38.

42. Ibid., pp. 38–43.

43. See note 25.

44. Some authors only list six major insurrections. However, Weng Chia in *T'ai-wan Han-jen wu-chuang,* pp. 144–146, lists thirteen cases of armed resistance against the Japanese during the 1907–15 period.

45. Kerr, *Formosa,* pp. 79–80.

46. Ibid., pp. 102–105; Huang Chao-t'ang, *Taiwan sōtokufu,* pp. 101–102.

47. Huang, *Taiwan sōtokufu,* pp. 57–58.

48. Ching-chih Chen, "Police and Community Control Systems in the Empire," in *The Japanese Colonial Empire,* p. 215. By 1901, the civil police system had assumed its

permanent form under Japanese colonial rule and, according to Chen, some 920 police substations existed about the island.

49. For an account of the *aiyū* guards and their background, see ibid., pp. 216–220. For the *sōteidan* refer to Hui-yu Caroline Ts'ai, "One Kind of Control: The *hokō* System in Taiwan Under Japanese Rule, 1895–1945" (Ph.D. dissertation, Columbia University, 1990), pp. 74–82. Kerr, *Formosa*, p. 102, refers to Sakuma's use of the *sōteidan* in his campaign, but under the title of "auxiliary Youth Corps."

50. The development of the *hokō* system and its *sōteidan* militia by 1903 is described in Hung Ch'iu-fen, "Jih-chu shih-ch'i T'ai-wan te pao-chia chih-tu (1895–1903)" [Taiwan's *pao-chia* system during the early Japanese period], *Chin-tai shih yen-chiu chi-k'an,* 21 (June 1992): 439–471. For the inception of the *sōteidan,* see p. 469. In 1943, it was incorporated in the wartime Civilian Guards. Ts'ai, "One Kind of Control," p. 65.

51. Ching-chih Chen, "Police and Community Control Systems," pp. 218–219.

52. Takekoshi, *Japanese Rule in Formosa,* pp. 18–19; Chen, "Police and Community Control Systems," pp. 216–217.

53. Takekoshi, *Japanese Rule in Formosa,* p. 147. The powers of the Taiwan governor-general, as of 1905, are listed on pp. 22–23.

54. Ibid., pp. 147–149. The civil police also exercised strict supervision over the registered inhabitants in the towns as well as in the Taiwanese neighborhoods within cities. In such urban communities they enforced ordinances and codes, and promoted campaigns endorsed by the colonial government.

55. Ts'ai, "One Kind of Control," pp. 168–169. For the network of "occupational associations" developed under the Gotō administration, see Kerr, *Formosa,* pp. 62–64.

56. Ts'ai, "One Kind of Control," pp. 46–47.

57. The duties and responsibilities of *hokō* heads are discussed in ibid., pp. 102–106.

58. Ts'ai Hui-yu (Caroline), "Jih-chih shih-tai T'ai-wan pao-chia shu-chi ch'u-t'an, 1911–1945" [Notes on Hokō Secretaryship in Taiwan under Japanese Rule, 1911–1945], *T'ai-wan shih yen-chiu,* 1, no. 2 (December 1994): 9–11. The household registers maintained by the colonial police, however, continued more detailed information about Taiwanese households than did the registries kept by the *hosei* and *hokō* clerks. For a description of the household registers compiled by the police (some of which have been preserved), see Arthur P. Wolf and Chieh-shan Huang, *Marriage and Adoption in China, 1845–1945* (Stanford: Stanford University Press, 1980), pp. 16–33.

59. The early *hokō* compacts and regulations are described in Hung, "T'ai-wan te pai-chia chih-tu (1895–1903)," pp. 450–452; and Ts'ai, "One Kind of Control," pp. 87–102.

60. Ts'ai, "One Kind of Control," pp. 61–62.

61. The "operational functions" of *hokō* and *sōteidan* units also related to local security and campaigns against opium smoking. Ibid., pp. 102–26, 151–56. By 1919, according to Ts'ai, "the *hokō* system was used to assist in virtually every important aspect of colonial administration." Ibid., p. 163.

62. Ibid., pp. 228–234.

63. So-called *hokō* roads were usually the fourth-grade local feed routes. Ibid., p. 338. *Hokō* laborers were also conscripted for more extensive bridge and highway projects as well as to maintain railway lines. Ibid., pp. 336–342.

64. Such Taiwanese protests, along with Japanese arguments favoring the *hokō* system, are set forth in Ide Kiwata, *Jih-chu hsia chih T'ai cheng* [Taiwan government under Japanese rule], translation of the 1936 Japanese edition by Kuo Hui (Taipei: T'ai-wan sheng wen-hsien wei-yuan-hui, 1956), pp. 962–964.

65. This total of 58,000 is derived from Ts'ai, "One Kind of Control," p. 67, table 1.2,

and represents about 5 percent of the Taiwanese population in 1905, as indicated in Barclay, *Colonial Development*, p. 16, table 3.

66. Barclay, *Colonial Development*, p. 16, table 3. Mark R. Peattie has noted that within the Japanese colonial empire most of the territories "were essentially occupation colonies where a minority of Japanese colonials existed amid a sea of indigenous peoples." See his "Introduction" in *The Japanese Colonial Empire*, p. 11.

67. Harry J. Lamley, "The Yōbunkai of 1900: An Episode in the Transformation of the Taiwan Elite During the Early Japanese Period," in *Jih-chu shih-ch'i T'ai-wan shih kuo-ch'i hsueh-shu yen-t'ao-hui lun-wen chi* [hereafter, cited as *1992 Conference Volume*], comp. National Taiwan University, Department of History (Taipei, 1993), pp. 121–124. More details on Taiwanese elites who early became compliant colonial servitors are found in Wu Wen-hsing, *Jih-chū shih-ch'i T'ai-wan*, pp. 53–65.

68. Lamley, "The Yōbunkai of 1900," pp. 125, 129–132; Wu Wen-hsing, *Jih-chū shih-ch'i T'ai-wan*, pp. 63–75.

69. Lamley, "The Yōbunkai of 1900," pp. 128–129.

70. Ibid., pp. 132–142.

71. These campaigns focused mainly on queue wearing by adult males, footbinding among the womenfolk, the use of opium, and allegedly superstitious practices.

72. Kerr, *Formosa*, pp. 86–88.

73. Marriages with Taiwanese were prohibited by law before 1932. Barclay, *Colonial Development*, p. 16 n12 and p. 214. The formation of pure native-owned joint-stock companies was also illegal. Chih-ming Ka, *Japanese Colonialism*, p. 80.

74. Tay-sheng Wang, "Legal Reform in Taiwan," pp. 116–118; 133, 139.

75. This tax burden was heavier than that imposed on the people of Japan or that incurred under Ch'ing rule. Chih-ming Ka, *Japanese Colonialism*, p. 54; Takekoshi, *Japanese Rule in Formosa*, p. 136.

76. Chih-ming Ka, *Japanese Colonialism*, pp. 62–74.

77. Ibid., pp. 74–82.

78. Kerr, *Formosa*, pp. 47–48, 108. Liang Ch'i-ch'ao had visited the Wu-feng Lin family. Harry J. Lamley, "Assimilation Efforts in Colonial Taiwan: The Fate of the 1914 Movement," *Monumenta Serica*, 29 (1970–71): 510–511.

79. Kerr, *Formosa*, pp. 106–107; T'ai-wan shih-chi yen-chiu hui, comp., *T'ai-wan ts'ung-t'an* [Collected chats about Taiwan] (Taipei: Yu-shih wen-hua, 1977), pp. 476–478.

80. Rev. D. Ferguson, "Formosan Chinese," *Chinese Recorder and Missionary Journal*, 40, no. 9 (September 1909): 494–496.

81. For a detailed account of the anti-footbinding and queue-cutting movements, see Wu Wen-hsing, "Jih-chu shih-ch'i T'ai-wan te fang-tsu tuan-fa yun-tung" [Taiwan's anti-footbinding and queue-cutting movements during the Japanese period], in *T'ai-wan she-hui yu wen-hua pien-ch'ien*, comp., Ch'u Hai-yuan and Chang Ying-hua (Taipei, Institute of Ethnography, Academia Sinica, 1986), vol. 1, pp. 69–108. These popular movements lasted until 1915, when the colonial authorities began to enforce *hokō* regulations against these practices.

82. Tsurumi, *Japanese Colonial Education*, pp. 65–66, 68–71.

83. Kerr, *Formosa*, pp. 105–6.

84. Lamley, "Assimilation Efforts," pp. 507–511.

85. See note 12.

86. Lamley, "Assimilation Efforts," pp. 512–514.

87. Ibid., pp. 514–516. See also the account by Tsurumi, *Japanese Colonial Education*, pp. 66–71, who associates Itagaki's assimilation movement more closely with the campaign in support of the Taichū Middle School.

88. Huang Chao-t'ang, *Taiwan sōtokufu,* p. 107.
89. Kerr, *Formosa,* p. 115; Huang Chao-t'ang, *Taiwan sōtokufu,* p. 108.
90. Tsurumi, *Japanese Colonial Education,* pp. 83–84, 91.
F91. Ibid., pp. 84–90.
92. Ibid., pp. 92–93.
93. However, because of opposition by Japanese authorities, integration was limited on the elementary school level, and Den's 1922 rescript only brought about "completely integrated schools from the secondary level up." Ibid., pp. 94–99. Also, according to Tsurumi, *Japanese Colonial Education,* pp. 102–103, integration through Den's educational reform "actually reduced the number of Taiwanese who received higher training in the colony" due to the stiff competition from Japanese.
94. Ibid., pp. 93, 146.
95. Ibid., p. 107.
96. Edward I-te Chen, "Japanese Colonialism in Korea and Formosa: A Comparison of the Systems of Political Control," *Harvard Journal of Asiatic Studies,* 30 (1970): 135–136.
97. Tay-sheng Wang, "Legal Reform in Taiwan," pp. 98–108.
98. Chen, "Japanese Colonialism in Korea and Formosa," p. 133.
99. Ibid., p. 157. See also Peattie, "Japanese Attitudes," pp. 102, 124. Subsequently, after the governors-general of Korea and Taiwan, as well as the governor of Karafuto, were brought under the control of the Minister of Home Affairs in 1943, a substantially integrated colonial empire was created. Then all three colonies were under the direct governance of Tokyo in a manner almost similar to the way prefectural government in Japan operated under central authority. Edward I-te Chen, "The Attempt to Integrate the Empire: Legal Perspectives," in *The Japanese Colonial Empire,* pp. 264–265.
100. Chen, "Japanese Colonialism in Korea and Formosa," pp. 139–140.
101. Barclay, *Colonial Development,* p. 16, table 3, and 116–120.
102. Wang Shih-ch'ing, "Jih-chu shih-ch'i T'ai-wan wai-shih jih-chih" [Chronicle of Taiwan's foreign affairs during the Japanese period], pt. 1, *T'ai-wan wen-hsien,* 12, no. 2 (June 1960): 264; Tsurumi, *Japanese Colonial Education,* pp. 35, 124–125. For post-1931 control of the Presbyterian missions, see Murray A. Rubinstein, "Mission of Faith, Burden of Witness: The Presbyterian Church in the Evolution of Modern Taiwan, 1865–1989," *American Asian Review,* 9, no. 2 (summer 1991): 78–80.
103. Wu Wen-hsing, *Jih-chu shih-ch'i tsai T'ai "Hua-ch'iao" yen-chiu* [A Study of the *"Hua-ch'iao"* in Taiwan during the Japanese occupation] (Taipei: Taiwan hsueh-sheng shu-chu, 1991), pp. 151–153, and p. 52, table 3.
104. Ibid., pp. 64–65. The Taipei Chinese consulate-general, in fact, was established in 1931, superseding the Chung-hua hui-kuan of the Republican period that was founded in 1923. Hsu Hsueh-chi, "Jih-chu shih-ch'i te Chung-hua Min-kuo T'ai-pei tsung-ling-shih-kuan" [The Taipei Consulate-General of the Republic of China during the Japanese period, 1921–1927], in *1992 Conference Volume,* pp. 509, 513.
105. Wang Shih-ch'ing, "Jih-chu shih-ch't T'ai-wan," pt. 1, p. 237.
106. Ibid., pt. 1, p. 247: pt. 2, *T'ai-wan wen-hsien,* 12, no. 2 (June 1961): 106–109. For a more detailed account of the Taiwanese *sekimin* in Fujian, see Tai Kuo-hui, "Jih-pen te chih-min-ti chih-p'ei yu T'ai-wan chi-min" [Japan's colonial management and the Taiwan *chi-min (sekimin)*], trans. Hung Wei-jen, in *T'ai-wan te chih-min-ti shang-hen,* comp. Wang Hsiao-po (Taipei: P'a-mi-erh shu-tien, 1985), pp. 239–269.
107. Wang Shih-ch'ing, *T'ai-wan wen-hsien,* pp. 108–109, 111.
108. Ibid., p. 109.
109. This collection was housed in the Government-General Library, founded in

1914. Its holdings are revealed in that library's catalogues, especially those relating to South China and Southeast Asia issued in 1938 and 1943, respectively. Chang Wei-tung, "Jih-chu shih-ch'i T'ai-wan Tsung-tu-fu T'u-shu-kuan kuan-shih" [History of the Taiwan Government-General Library during the Japanese occupation] (unpublished paper presented at the Conference on Taiwan Historical Research and the Archives of the Taiwan Branch Library of the National Central Library, Taipei, October 21–22, 1993), p. 17.

110. Tay-sheng Wang, "Legal Reform in Taiwan," pp. 134–135.

111. Kerr, *Formosa,* pp. 151–154; Huang Chao-t'ang, *Taiwan sōtokufu,* pp. 131–134. According to Huang (p. 133), almost five hundred members of the mountain tribes were slain in reprisal over the next few months following this incident.

112. Tay-sheng Wang, "Legal Reform in Taiwan," pp. 134–135.

113. Chen, "Japanese Colonialism in Korea and Formosa," pp. 141 and 142, table 3; Ts'ai, "One Kind of Control," pp. 167–169, and 171, figure 4.1.

114. Ching-chih Chen, "Police and Community Control Systems," pp. 217–218. According to Chen: "Until 1945 the police system remained highly centralized and widely dispersed in the countryside, with awesome authority to manage and to intervene in the life of the Chinese [Taiwanese]" (p. 218).

115. Ts'ai, "One Kind of Control," pp. 175–177, 232–233.

116. Ibid., p. 176. Such boundary shifts usually occurred when "large-district" administrative villages, formed after the 1920 reform, caused previous administrative divisions to merge under larger demarcations. Ibid., pp. 176–177. In line with the formation of the "large-district" system, *hokō* associations (*hokō kyōkai*) began to be established on the county level. Subsequently, during the wartime period, *hokō* federations developed at the prefectural level as well. Ibid., pp. 235–236.

117. Of course, other factors also fostered community change and development: namely, advances in communication and transportation, economic growth, and the burgeoning Taiwanese population.

118. Chen, "Japanese Colonialism in Korea and Formosa," pp. 149–155.

119. Ts'ai, "One Kind of Control," pp. 183–192. Spirited *hosei* elections were held even a few years earlier in a few cities after allied *hokō* offices were allowed to sell opium permits. Ibid., pp. 265–275.

120. See note 81.

121. Wang Shih-ch'ing, "Huang-min-hua yun-tung chien te T'ai-wan she-hui sheng-hua kai-shan yun-tung" [The movement of social living improvement before "imperialization" (*kōminka*) in Taiwan: The case of Haishan area (1914–1937)], *Ssu yu yen,* 29, no. 4 (December 1991), pp. 1–13.

122. Ibid., pp. 16–18: Ts'ai, "One Kind of Control," pp. 454–456.

123. Ts'ai Hui-yu (Caroline), "Pao-cheng, pao-chia shu-chi, chieh-chuang i-ch'ang—k'u-shu li-shih (san)" [*Pao-cheng (hosei), pao-chia (hokō)* secretaries, town and village substations—oral history] (3), *T'ai-wan feng-wu,* 45, no. 4 (December 1995): 100.

124. Barclay, *Colonial Development,* p. 16, table 3, cites the aborigine count in 1935 as 270,674. Not until the 1930s were they brought fully within the scope of the census. In 1934, the total number dwelling in aboriginal districts was estimated to be 148,472. Hideo Naito, *A Record of Taiwan's Progress, 1936–37 Edition* (Tokyo: Kokusai Nippon Kyokai), p. 60.

125. Kerr, *Formosa,* pp. 165–167; *A Record of Taiwan's Progress, 1936–37 Edition,* pp. 62–63.

126. For a discussion of the Taiwanese *sekimin* status and its derivation, see Tai Kuo-hui, "Jih-pen te chih-min-ti chih-p'ei," pp. 242–249.

127. Mark R. Peattie, "Japanese Treaty Port Settlements in China, 1895–1937," in *The Japanese Informal Empire in China, 1895–1937,* ed. Peter Duus, Ramon H. Myers, and Mark R. Peattie (Princeton: Princeton University Press, 1989), p. 191 and n31. Reference

to the Taiwan public assembly in Fuzhou is found in Ch'en San-ching, Hsu Hsueh-chi, interviewers, *Lin Heng-tao hsien-sheng fang-wen chi-lu* [The reminiscences of Mr. Lin Heng-tao] (Taipei: Institute of Modern History, Academia Sinica, 1992), pp. 49–50.

128. Lin Man-houng, *Ssu-pai nien lai te liang-an fen-ho,* pp. 70–71.

129. Ibid., pp. 65–66, 69, 71.

130. Ibid., pp. 126–131; Ch'en San-ching et al., pp. 49–51. The activities of Lin Ch'ao-tung, senior head of the wealthy Fu-feng Lin family, after his crossing to Fujian in 1895, are described in Huang Fu-san, "Jih-pen ling T'ai yu Wu-feng Lin chia chih ssu-ying—i Lin Ch'ao-tung wei chung-hsin" [Japanese control of Taiwan and the responses of the Wu-feng Lin family—with focus on Lin Ch'ao-tung], in *1992 Conference Volume,* pp. 93–99.

131. Tai Kuo-hui, "Jih-pen te chih-min-ti chih-p'ei," pp. 255–256, 266.

132. Ibid., pp. 256–257, 262–264. Liang Hua-hung, "Jih-chu shih-tai T'ai-wan chi-min ts'ai Min sheng te huo-tung chi ch'u-ching" [Actions and circumstances of the Taiwan *chi-min (sekimin)* in Fujian province during Japanese times], in *1992 Conference Volume,* pp. 479–485, also deals with the wartime period.

133. For example, note the experiences of Ch'en I-sung, who went to Japan as a young student in 1920. Wu Chun-ying, recorder, "Ch'en I-sung hui-i lu" (Reminiscences of Ch'en I-sung), pt. 1, *T'ai-wan wen-i,* 19 (October 1993): 110–165.

134. *Taiwan kyōkukai zasshi,* 18 (September 25, 1903): 21 (*han-wen*); *Taiwan kyōkai kaipō,* 52 (January 20, 1903): 57 (*han-wen*).

135. Tsurumi, *Japanese Colonial Education,* pp. 126–127; p. 128, table 12.

136. There seems to have been no accurate count. My estimate is based on Mendel's statement: "Most of the approximately 25,000 Formosans living in Japan during the 1960's had migrated before 1945 for economic reasons." Douglas Mendel, *The Politics of Formosan Nationalism* (Berkeley: University of California Press, 1970), p. 147.

137. Ts'ai P'ei-huo et al., comp., *T'ai-wan min-tsu yun-tung shih* [History of the Taiwanese national movement] (Taipei: *Tzu-li wan-pao,* 1983, 3d printing), pp. 545–546.

138. Shao-hsing Chen, "Diffusion and Acceptance of Modern Western Artistic and Intellectual Expression in Taiwan," *Studia Taiwanica,* 2 (summer 1957): 3. The *Formosan Youth* was renamed "*Taiwan*" in 1922. After the demise of the New People's Society in 1923, the magazine was changed into a fortnightly, entitled *Taiwan People's Journal,* and then, as a daily newspaper, retitled the *Taiwan New People's Journal,* from 1930 to 1932 over the last two years of its existence. Hsuang Hsiu-cheng, "*T'ai-wan min-pao*" *yu chin-tai T'ai-wan min-tsu yun-tung* [The *Taiwan min-pao* and the modern Taiwan national movement] (Changhua: Hsien-tai ch'ao, 1987), pp. 1, 7–19.

139. Shao-hsing Chen, "Diffusion and Acceptance," p. 3.

140. Edward I-te Chen, "Formosan Political Movements Under Japanese Colonial Rule, 1914–1937," *Journal of Asian Studies,* 31, no. 3 (May 1972): 489.

141. Ts'ai P'ei-huo et al., *T'ai-wan min-tsu yun-tung shih,* pp. 289–308.

142. Ch'iu K'un-liang, *Chiu-chu yu hsin-chu: Jih-chih shih-ch'i T'ai-wan hsi-chu chih yen-chiu* [Old drama and new drama: Study of Taiwanese plays during the period of Japanese rule, 1895–1945] (Taipei: *Tzu-li wan-pao,* 1992), pp. 289, 301–302.

143. Most periodicals and newspapers, catering to Taiwanese readers in the colony before 1937, were divided into Chinese and Japanese sections. These portions were of equal length in the *Formosan Youth* and *Taiwan* magazines, while the *Taiwan People's Journal* and its sequel were published about two-thirds in Chinese. Huang Hsiu-cheng, pp. 14–29.

144. Douglas L. Fix, "Advancing on Tokyo: The New Literature Movement, 1930–1937," in *1992 Conference Volume,* pp. 270–271. For an extensive review of the Taiwanese new literature movement during the 1920–37 period, see Hsu Chu-ya, *Jih-chu*

shih-ch'i T'ai-wan hsiao-shuo yen-chiu [Research on the Taiwanese novel during the Japanese period] (Taipei: Wen shih che, 1995), pp. 52–108.

145. Fix, "Advancing on Tokyo," pp. 276–277.

146. Yang Ts'ui, *Jih-chu shih-ch'i T'ai-wan fu-nu chieh-fang yun-tung—i "T'ai-wan min-pai" wei fen-hsi ch'ang-yu (1920–1932)* [The Taiwanese women's liberation movement under Japanese rule—with the *Taiwan mim-pō* as a basis of analysis, 1920–1932] (Taipei: Shih-pao wen-hua, 1993), pp. 181–218.

147. Ibid., pp. 319–380. By this time issues of gender and class had become intertwined.

148. Tsurumi, *Japanese Colonial Education,* pp. 222–223. For a detailed study of female Taiwanese teachers in the common schools, and their increase in numbers to 457 (including teacher substitutes) in 1925 (totaling, in all, 15,126 from 1903 to 1943), see Yu Chien-ming, "Jih-chu shih-ch'i kung hsueh-hsiao te T'ai-chi nu chiao-shih" [Common school female teachers of Taiwanese registry during the Japanese period], in *1992 Conference Volume,* especially pp. 572–573, and p. 574, chart 1.

149. Chen, "Formosan Political Movements," pp. 481–483.

150. Ibid., pp. 486–487, 488–489.

151. Ibid., pp. 483–484. For a listing of the League's regulations, see Ts'ai P'ei-huo et al., *T'ai-wan min-tsu yun-tung shih,* pp. 203–204.

152. Chen, "Formosan Political Movements," p. 485, tables I and II, lists the number of signatures on each of the fifteen petitions, and indicates the divisions in educational background of 17,262 persons whose names appeared on one or more of these petitions.

153. Nonetheless, the league had managed to attract much more widespread sympathy for the movement, both in Japan and Taiwan, after some of the leaders were arrested by the colonial police in 1923. In the ensuing trials the league and its objectives were ultimately judged to be legal and not in violation of the constitution. Detailed accounts of this incident and its implications are found in Ts'ai P'ei-huo et al., *T'ai-wan min-tsu yun-tung shih,* pp. 201–244; and Chou Wan-yao, *Jih-chu shih-tai te T'ai-wan i-hui she-chih ch'ing-yuan yun-tung* [The petition movement for the establishment of a Taiwan parliament during the Japanese period] (Taipei: Tzu-li wan pao, 1989), pp. 81–89.

154. For accounts of the sugar and tea farmers' disputes, along with those of strikes and labor movements, again with involvement by radical Taiwanese intellectuals and youth, see Lien Wen-ch'ing, *T'ai-wan cheng-chih yun-tung shih* [A history of Taiwan political movements], ed. Chang Yen-hsien and Weng Chia-in (Taipei: Tao-hsiang, 1988), pp. 128–139, 250–257. Even before 1927, the Taiwan Culture Association was active in organizing farmers' unions and helped in the formation of the islandwide Taiwan Farmers' Union in 1926. Chen, "Formosan Political Movements," p. 491. The Taiwanese Communist Party was created in Shanghai in 1928. Although influenced by the Communist movement in China, the Taiwanese party operated as a branch of the Japanese Communist Party. Ibid., p. 478 n2. An account of the Taiwanese Communist movement is found in Lien Wen-ch'ing, *T'ai-wan cheng-chih yun-tung shih,* pp. 213–220, followed by a briefer description of Taiwanese anarchism (pp. 221–223). The history of the Taiwanese Communist Party, until it was abolished in April 1932, is presented in Lu Hsiu-i, *Jih-chu shih-tai T'ai-wan Kung-chan-tang shih (1928–1932)* [A history of the Taiwan Communist Party during the Japanese period, 1928–32] (Taipei: Ch'ien-wei, 1992, 3d printing).

155. Chen, "Formosan Political Movements," pp. 492–493. Chen notes that the Popular Party helped organize several labor unions and a labor union federation (formed in 1928) into which twenty-nine unions were merged. For longer accounts of the Taiwan Popular Party, see Ts'ai P'ei-huo et al., *T'ai-wan min-tsu yun-tung shih,* pp. 355–443; and Lien Wen-ch'ing, *T'ai-wan cheng-chih yun-tung shih,* pp. 225–257.

156. The politicized Taiwan Culture Association was suppressed in 1931 (as was the Popular Party). Ts'ai P'ei-huo et al., *T'ai-wan min-tsu yun-tung shih*, p. 353. A description of the Federation and its activities is in ibid., pp. 444–491.

157. Chen, "Formosan Political Movements," p. 494.

158. Ibid., pp. 494–495.

159. Kerr, *Formosa*, p. 175.

160. Besides Meiji leaders and naval spokesmen, several of the early Taiwan governors-general urged that Japanese military strikes be launched from the colony. The second governor-general, General Katsura Tarō, pressed for a southward strike on Luzon in 1896. Then, in 1900, Katsura and Kodama Gentarō planned for a cross-channel operation to launch troops to coastal Fukien. Moreover, the "Kodama Report" of 1901 allegedly called for attacks on French Indochina. Ibid., pp. 42–49. Kobayashi's three policies are cited in Wan-yao Chou, "The *Kōminka* Movement in Taiwan and Korea: Comparisons and Interpretations," in *The Japanese Wartime Empire, 1931–1945*, ed. Peter Duus, Ramon H. Myers, and Mark R. Peattie (Princeton: Princeton University Press, 1996), p. 44.

161. Mark R. Peattie, "*Nanshin:* The 'Southward Advance,' 1931–1941, as a Prelude to the Japanese Occupation of Southeast Asia," in *The Japanese Wartime Empire*, p. 216. The national military policy referred to is the "Outline of National Policy," drawn up in April 1936 and as modified in August of that year. Ibid., pp. 214–216.

162. Ibid., p. 217; Kerr, *Formosa*, pp. 190–191, 202.

163. For the circumstances concerning Kobayashi's replacement, see Huang Chao-t'ang, *Taiwan sōtokufu*, pp. 172–173; Kerr, *Formosa*, pp. 200–201.

164. This vision was so named by the new foreign minister in early August 1940. Peter Duus, "Introduction/Japan's Wartime Empire: Problems and Issues," in *The Japanese Wartime Empire*, p. xxii.

165. Peattie, "*Nanshin*," p. 223; Kerr, *Formosa*, p. 207ff.

166. Kerr, *Formosa*, pp. 211–214.

167. Ibid., pp. 221–222, 228–229.

168. Actually, by this time the Taiwan garrison had been expanded to become the Tenth Military District (*hōmen*). Huang Chao-t'ang, *Taiwan sōtokufu*, p. 175.

169. In general, Taiwan's three wartime governors-general have been rated better than their civil administrators, especially in the case of Morioka Jirō, who squandered funds during the Kobayashi reign. Ibid., p. 166.

170. An American invasion of Taiwan, planned by the U.S. Navy for February 1945, was abandoned and Okinawa was subsequently invaded instead. Kerr, *Formosa*, pp. 227–228.

171. Ibid., pp. 228–230, 232–234.

172. Chen, "The Attempt to Integrate the Empire," pp. 241–242, 265. Edward Chen notes that in the late 1930s two contrasting terms were introduced in the official Japanese colonist vocabulary: "*gaichi,* referring to all colonies, and *naichi,* meaning metropolitan Japan." Taiwan, Korea, and, eventually, Karafuto were placed under the control of the Ministry of Home Affairs since the legal integration of these three colonies with metropolitan Japan had been completed, at least in appearance.

173. Kerr, *Formosa*, pp. 173–174.

174. Lai Tse-han, Ramon H. Myers, and Wei Wou, *A Tragic Beginning: The Taiwan Uprising of February 28, 1947* (Stanford: Stanford University Press, 1991), p. 40.

175. Kerr, *Formosa*, pp. 173–174, 215; Ho, *Economic Development of Taiwan*, pp. 74–75.

176. According to Samuel Ho, the colonial government and the Japanese capitalists did little to diversify Taiwan's economy, so fixed were they "on the image of Taiwan as

an agricultural appendage to Japan" (*Economic Development of Taiwan,* p. 73).

177. Until 1924, Taiwanese were not allowed to organize or operate corporate businesses without Japanese partners or participation. Ibid., p. 38. A brief account of the food processing and other private industries operating in the colony is in ibid., pp. 71–73.

178. Ibid., pp. 86–87.

179. These figures and estimates are taken from Lai et al., *A Tragic Beginning,* pp. 38–39.

180. On the basis of a 1943 survey of male workers employed by industrial establishments with more than thirty workers, Samuel Ho maintains that "it was [still] the Japanese who provided the skills and know-how" for the operation of most of Taiwan's large industrial and business enterprises (*Economic Development of Taiwan,* p. 81). The hiring of Taiwanese for skilled positions continued over the wartime period despite an increase of the *naichijin* population until at least 1943. The Japanese community in Taiwan had grown to 312,386 by 1940. Barclay, *Colonial Development,* p. 16.

181. Lai et al., *A Tragic Beginning,* p. 41. Barclay, *Colonial Development,* p. 116, table 24, indicates impressive gains in the Taiwanese populations of nine major cities from 1930 to 1940.

182. Lai et al., *A Tragic Beginning,* pp. 39–40.

183. For a more complete account of social service projects involving *hokō* labor, see Ts'ai, "One Kind of Control," pp. 426–437.

184. Lai et al., *A Tragic Beginning,* p. 28.

185. This colonial association served as an extension of the Imperial Rule Assistance Association (Taisei yokusan-kai) founded in metropolitan Japan the previous year to strengthen allegiance to the emperor in his wartime role. The general organization of the imperial rule association was duplicated in Korea and Karafuto, as well as in Taiwan. Wan-yao Chou, "The *Kōminka* Movement: Taiwan Under Wartime Japan, 1937–1945" (Ph.D. dissertation, Yale University, 1991), pp. 48–49; Ts'ai, "One Kind of Control," pp. 452–454.

186. Chou, "The *Kōminka* Movement," pp. 50–51. For more details, see Ts'ai, "One Kind of Control," pp. 454–469.

187. Ibid., pp. 457–458.

188. Ibid., p. 457. Wan-yao Chou notes that the Kōmin hōkōkai has been described as "being like the big rope . . . of a net holding together all of the net's more than six million joints . . . , each of which was constituted by one individual of the population and each one of which was interconnected" ("The *Kōminka* Movement," p. 53).

189. For reference to the wartime activities of the Youth Corps and Young Women's Corps, see ibid., p. 53. Radio broadcasting began on a trial basis in Taiwan in 1925, and regular broadcasts commenced in 1928 under the Post and Telecommunication Section of the Taiwan government-general.

190. Lai et al., *A Tragic Beginning,* pp. 37–38; Huang Chao-t'ang, *Taiwan sōtokufu,* p. 190.

191. Wartime *kōminka* policy also did not allow for conciliatory assimilationist measures that seemed primarily to benefit components of the colonial population, as happened in 1932, for example, when registered marriages between Japanese and Taiwanese were legalized. See note 73.

192. Chou, "The *Kōminka* Movement," pp. 44, 49. A Japanization movement was formally designated in Korea under a different name in October 1937. Ibid., p. 42.

193. The colonial authorities had long maintained that speaking *kokugo* was a major prerequisite for "becoming Japanese." Before 1937, they had already set up extensive language study and outreach programs in Taiwan. For the percentages of Japanese speakers among the Taiwanese population, also see ibid., pp. 52 and 54. A more detailed study

of the national language program and national language families, including accounts of Taiwanese who mastered the Japanese language, is in ibid., pp. 55–100.

194. Ibid., p. 57. A more complete study of the name-changing campaign is in Chou's "Renaming Oneself a True Japanese: One Aspect of the *Kōminka* Movement, 1940–1945, in *1992 Conference Volume,* pp. 155–212.

195. Chou, "Remaining Oneself," pp. 193–195.

196. Of this total, 30,304 died in service. Chou, "The *Kōminka* Movement," p. 65. These figures, as well as those of the enlistments through the army and navy volunteer systems, are cited in Chou's more recent article, "Jih-pen tsai T'ai chun-shih tung-yuan yu T'ai-wan-jen ti hai-wai ts'an-chan ching-yen" [Japan's military mobilization and the Taiwanese overseas war experiences, 1937–1945], *T'ai-wan shih yen-chiu,* 2, no. 1 (June 1995): 93–96.

197. Chou, "The *Kōminka* Movement," p. 65.

198. The Shinto "reforms" imposed by the Japanese are dealt with in Chou, "The *Kōminka* Movement," pp. 40–43. Other Taiwanese scholars have also addressed the issue of household altars and Shinto shrines. See, for example, Ts'ai Chin-t'ang, "Jih-chu mo-ch'i T'ai-wan-jen tsung-chiao hsin-yang pien-ch'ien: i 'chia-t'ing cheng-t'ing' wei chung-hsin" [Changes of Taiwanese religion and faith in the late Japanese period: as centered on the 'domestic ancestral hall'], *Ssu yu yen,* 29, no. 4 (December 1991): 65–83.

199. Ts'ai Chin-t'ang emphasizes that the Taiwan government-general tended to take a more moderate stand with regard to religious reforms than did the local officials (ibid., pp. 79–80). According to Chou, thirty-eight out of the sixty-eight *jinja* in Taiwan were built between 1937 and 1945 ("The *Kōminka* Movement," p. 45). The Taiwan Grand Shrine was located in present-day Yuan-shan, in Taipei.

200. Chou, "The *Kōminka* Movement," p. 43.

201. Ibid., pp. 44–46. Here Chou lists other "unsound" Taiwanese social customs of which the Japanese disapproved, as well as a sample of reform proposals set forth in one town (p. 46 n76).

202. Recently, Taiwanese and Japanese specialists on Taiwan's colonial literature have discovered several Taiwanese authors of "*kōminka*" short stories published in the early 1940s. Lin Jui-ming, "Sao-tung ti ling-hun—chueh-chan shih-ch'i ti T'ai-wan tso-chia yu huang-min wen-hsueh" [Troubled souls—Taiwanese writers and *kōmin* literature of the decisive war period], in *1992 Conference Volume,* pp. 443–461.

203. Chou, "Jih-pen tsai T'ai chun-shih tung-yuan," Abstract (p. 26). In this article the author lists the many areas and places in China, Southeast Asia, and the South Pacific where Taiwanese served on overseas military duty throughout the 1937–45 period.

204. Youthful involvement in wartime "spiritual mobilization" may best be ascertained by the many Youth Corps and Young Women's Corps activities.

205. Lai et al., *A Tragic Beginning,* p. 34.

206. Ibid., pp. 33–34.

207. Tsurumi, *Japanese Colonial Education,* pp. 129–130.

208. Chou, "Jih-pen tsai T'ai chun-shih tung yuan," p. 93. Chou translates *kessho* as "blood plea" in her dissertation and in her essay in *The Japanese Wartime Empire.*

209. Chou, "The *Kōminka* Movement," pp. 63–65, 66. By the early 1940s, more than fervent wartime patriotism appears to have motivated the younger generation to volunteer for military service on a massive scale and to write blood pleas so frequently. Chou suggests that a degree of cynicism may have been involved. Even fake applications could be submitted without much fear of detection, for there were so many applicants for such a relatively small number of openings. Ibid., p. 64.

210. This figure is cited in Lai et al., *A Tragic Beginning,* p. 22.

211. Ts'ai P'ei-huo et al., *T'ai-wan min-tsu yun-tung shih,* pp. 569–570; Huang Hsiu-

cheng, pp. 22–23. This wartime newspaper was renamed the *Kōnan nippō*.

212. Liang Hua-hung, "Jih-chu shih-tai T'ai-wan," pp. 474, 481.

213. Ibid., pp. 482, 483.

214. At the outset of the war the local Japanese consuls directed the *sekimin* to actively support the Japanese military, but soon urged them to return to Taiwan after the Kwangtung troops and the governor began to take action against the Taiwanese residents. The latter were unable to leave, and many were arrested and killed. *Sekimin* residing in Chang-chou and Ch'uan-chou, the ancestral areas of most Taiwanese, were also apprehended and sent to areas in the interior where many were confined and perished. Ibid., pp. 481–482.

215. J. Bruce Jacobs, "Taiwanese and the Chinese Nationalists, 1937–1945: The Origins of Taiwan's 'Half-Mountain People,' " *Modern China,* 16, no. 1 (January 1990): 85. Traces of Taiwanese residents in wartime Peking may be found in records of two Taiwan guilds (*hui-kuan*) established there late in the nineteenth century. Both were managed by a Fukien guild until 1937, when they began to be operated by native Taiwanese. Hu Chunhuan and Bai Hequn, *Beijing de huiguan* [Peking's guilds] (Beijing: Zhongguo jingji chubanshe, 1994), pp. 110–111.

216. Jacobs, "Taiwanese and the Chinese Nationalists," p. 86.

217. Ibid., p. 105; George H. Kerr, *Formosa Betrayed* (Boston: Houghton Mifflin, 1965), pp. 46–47. Kerr suggests that these Taiwanese representatives were members of a loose association of six expatriate groups, formed in 1943.

218. Liang Hua-hung, "Jih-chu shih-tai T'ai-wan," pp. 483–484.

219. Lai et al., *A Tragic Beginning,* pp. 187–188.

220. Huang Chao-t'ang, *Taiwan sōtokufu,* pp. 187–188.

221. The male voters had to be at least twenty-five years old and affluent enough to pay a direct state tax of fifteen Japanese yen or more. Ibid., pp. 188–189.

222. Ibid., pp. 189–190.

223. George Kerr alludes to this sort of home-rule speculation, but in an inaccurate manner: "In a dramatic bid for support, it was announced that the island would no longer be considered a colony, [and] that general elections would be held in 1945 to establish a Prefectural Assembly" (*Formosa,* pp. 229–230).

224. Ibid., p. 233.

225. There are now many published oral history sources that indicate such Taiwanese behavior at the end of the colonial period. See, for example, Ch'en San-ching, Hsu Hsueh-chi, interviewers, *Lin Heng-tao hsien-sheng fang-wen chi-lu.*

226. Chou, "Jih-pen tsai T'ai chun-shih tung-yuan," pp. 121–123.

227. The successful Taiwanese collaborator Ku Hsien-jung had been appointed to the House of Peers in 1934, however. Ku served in a nominal capacity until his death in 1936. Huang Chao-t'ang, *Taiwan sōtokufu,* p. 189.

228. George Kerr estimates that only a few hundred Taiwanese died in the bombing raids, but "some thousands had died because of the breakdown in public health and medical services" (*Formosa,* p. 230). Kerr does not mention the more than thirty thousand who perished while on military duty. See note 196 and Huang Chao-t'ang, *Taiwan sōtokufu,* p. 253, table 14. Most homefront casualties were caused by diseases that began to spread at a rapid rate in the colony during the war period when many inhabitants suffered from overwork and malnutrition (Ho, *Economic Development of Taiwan,* p. 98). See also Barclay, *Colonial Development and Population in Taiwan,* pp. 133–139, for a discussion of public health and the risks of death in Taiwan.

9

Taiwanese New Literature and the Colonial Context

A Historical Survey

Sung-sheng Yvonne Chang

The National Palace Museum

Whereas most literary practices in Taiwan until the 1920s carried on the classical Chinese tradition, a new strand of modern Taiwanese literature emerged in the early 1920s in a process commonly referred to as the Taiwanese New Literature movement (T'ai-wan hsin wen-hsueh yun-tung).[1] Compared to its counterpart, Modern (vernacular) Chinese Literature, Taiwanese New Literature displayed two distinctive features that seem to universally characterize colonial cultural products: multilinguisity and political impact. In addition to works in Chinese, many of the literary products of this movement—especially in the later stage—were written in Japanese. There was also a viable Taiwanese language movement (T'ai-wan hua-wen yun-tung) in the early 1930s, advocating the use of a new written language based on spoken Taiwanese, which is a version of the southern Min dialect used by the majority of the population in Taiwan. Moreover, from the beginning, Taiwanese New Literature was an integral part of a new phase of sociopolitical resistance by the Taiwanese people to the Japanese colonial rule. In the 1920s, the Taiwanese intelligentsia, revolving around the Taiwanese Cultural Association (T'ai-wan wen-hua hsieh-hui) (1921–31), launched a large-scale cultural reform program with a political agenda, which replaced the futile and often brutally suppressed armed revolts in the first two decades of the Japanese period. Key figures of the early stage of the movement, such as Lai Ho (1894–1943), frequently regarded as the "father of Taiwanese New Literature," Chen Hsu-ku (1896–1965), and Ts'ai Ch'iu-t'ung (b. 1900), were also active members of the Cultural Association, participating in its well-known islandwide lecture tours. Unsurprisingly, their literary works contained a strong nationalistic component. Even after 1931, when a harsh crackdown by the colonial government put an end to the lively resistance activities of the previous decade, the New Literature, nourished by the sociopolitical movements of the 1920s, continued to grow among the increasingly bilingual intellectual class in Taiwan. The legacy of resistance to colonialism also persisted, in either overt or covert forms, until the very end of the Japanese period.

However, the broadly defined political nature of the Taiwanese New Literature refers not only to explicit criticism of the colonizers, in works by such undaunted anti-imperialist fighters as Lai Ho and Yang K'ui (1906–1985), but also to the cultural hybridity in later works of the Taiwanese New Literature movement written in Japanese. That tongue, as the colonizer's language, is by definition a political product and thus is shaped by an unjust power relationship. The first generation of writers of the Taiwanese New Literature, even though most of them were born after the Japanese takeover, still exhibited characteristically Chinese cultural and artistic outlooks; but the second generation of Taiwanese New Literature writers exhibited a notable shift. This shift, the overall increase in the degree of hybridity in Taiwanese culture in the second half of the Japanese period, can be explained by changes in the colonizer's governing policies.

Beginning in 1918–19, the Japanese adopted an effective assimilation policy (*nei-ti yen-ch'ang chu-yi,* or the principle of treating Taiwan as an extension of

Japan proper), which moved from high-handed police control and differential treatment of the Taiwanese to more enlightened civil governance, emphasis on education, and cultivation of a more congenial relationship between Japanese and Taiwanese. As the new colonial condition steadily took shape and Japanese-language education became more effectively implemented, more students in the colony went to study in Japan. Those among them who enrolled in college literary departments and had contact with famous Japanese writers later played influential roles in Taiwan's literary scene. An even more drastic change was that, during the last phase of the Japanese period (1937–45), as Japan declared war on China, the colonial government mobilized great social resources to enforce an intensified Japanization program, including a ban on Chinese-language publications.

The hybrid nature of the colonial literature should not be regarded with embarrassment, as it often has been by narrow-minded nationalists, but, rather, as a true testimony to collective atrocities done by one culture to another in the period of imperialist expansion. A state comprising Han settlers since the seventeenth century and a province of the Manchu-governed China since 1885, Taiwan in the early part of the twentieth-century was incorporated by Japan into a different geopolitical and economic system and as a result experienced the initial stages of modernization because of its East Asian colonizer, which had itself recently modernized based on the Western model. The kind of society produced in Taiwan by this process was inevitably of a hybrid nature, with modern and traditional institutions of different ethnic origins coexisting side by side. What makes it even more complicated is Taiwan's strategic position in Japan's imperialist project and its capacity to serve as a base for Japan's further advancement in South China and Southeast Asia. For this reason, it allegedly received relatively benign treatment from the Japanese—as compared to Japan's other colonies, such as Korea—which considerably mitigated the hostility between the colonizer and the colonized. The colonial condition in Taiwan is thus a product of the extremely intricate political and cultural negotiations between the colonial government and the local elite, and between the elite and the more disadvantaged classes in a capitalist economy, for whom the progressive intellectuals served as spokesmen. Because writers of Taiwanese New Literature overlap considerably with the last group, their work offers rich materials for general studies of colonialism, which have until now largely overlooked the East Asian experience.

Viewed from another perspective, the fact that such fine Taiwanese writers of the later period as Chang Wen-huan (1909–1978), Lu Ho-jo (1914–1950), Yang K'ui, and Lung Ying-tsung (b. 1911) achieved their distinctive art under the influence of Western artistic trends through Japanese literary institutions exemplified the frequently convoluted trajectory of cross-cultural literary influences. And this is by no means a purely artistic phenomenon: Appropriation of Western literary codes constitutes a crucial part of the larger Westernization program undertaken by East Asian intellectuals in the past century and a half. Whereas an individual government's official policies toward the West vary, as a pervasive intellectual discourse, the Westernization program invariably promotes the assimilation of Western cultural products as a means of self-strengthening, that is, of equipping oneself for the Western-dominated modern world. Thus bilingual intellectuals with access to knowledge of a foreign culture, while endowed with useful personal capital, also unwittingly play a part in the country's publicly conceived nationalist project.

From the point of view of cultural studies, this nationalist project operates with a negative logic: Its potency rests precisely in its ability to challenge, by virtue of its reformist or oppositional discourse, the dominant culture in the native context. Thus such literary trends as Realism before World War II and Modernism after the War, with their specific—emancipatory, revolutionary, or liberalizing—ideologies, have served, for several East Asian countries, as powerful alternative intellectual discourses vis-à-vis the dominant cultures. The Taiwanese colonial intellectuals' involvement in this cross-national East Asian movement, because of their peculiar environment—the facts that the dominant culture in Taiwan was a mixture of Chinese and Japanese elements and that the particular form of their nationalism was increasingly plagued with a sense of indeterminacy (Chinese or Taiwanese?)—constitutes an exceptional case that demands better understanding.

Early Stage of the Taiwanese New Literature Movement: Three Debates

As stated earlier, the Taiwanese New Literature movement began as part of a larger cultural reform movement during the 1920s. A brief introduction of this cultural movement, sometime called Taiwanese New Culture movement (T'ai-wan hsin wen-hua yun-tung) may be in order. The first events of this movement took place in 1920, when some Taiwanese expatriates in Tokyo organized the New People Association (Hsin-min hui), followed by a student-based Taiwanese Youth Association (T'ai-wan ch'ing-nien hui). The two organizations published a journal called *Taiwan Youth* (T'ai-wan ch'ing-nien) to propagate progressive ideas and voice opinions about the current state of affairs in Taiwan. The zeal for cultural reform soon spread to the island itself and was carried on by the Taiwanese Cultural Association. There were significant parallels between the Taiwanese New Culture movement and China's May Fourth movement (wu-ssu yun-tung).[2] First of all, intellectuals in both societies, faced with the imperative to modernize, identified the cultural sediments of the neo-Confucianist moralism and the feudalist social orders as the reactionary forces that obstruct progress. Inspired by democratic ideas of modern Western society, both groups had come to associate the "old" with the conservative mentality of the gentry class and the "new" with ways of the "modern citizen"—to be transformed through popular education and cultural enlightenment. The idea of social Darwinism, which equates rejuvenation of national culture with survival of the people, adds to the urgency of the task of cultural reform as a means of national self-preservation. In addition, the new intellectuals of both societies were acted upon by the dynamics of progressive discourses on national emancipation and socialist revolution in years after World War I. Such currents of thought created an imaginary alliance among the "weak and oppressed" nations in the world and provided a powerful rationale for nationalistic resistance by victims of imperialist aggression, as obviously China and Taiwan both were. Thus a patriotic discourse combining and constantly negotiating the two components of sociocultural modernization (cultural enlightenment) and anti-imperialism (national salvation, anticolonialism) was developed in the 1920s and shared by the new intellectuals in both China and Taiwan.

Although the first two issues of the journal *Taiwanese Youth* contained articles on the topics of language reform and the need for contemporary Taiwanese literature to rejuvenate itself, it was not until the heated New Versus Old Literary debate (*hsin-chiu wen-hsueh lun-chan*), which began with Chang Wo-chun's attack on traditional poets in 1924 and lasted until 1926, that the Taiwanese New Literature movement was formally launched.[3] During the debate, new literary concepts—mainly those focusing on the advantage of adopting vernacular Chinese as a new literary medium and the social function of literature in the modern age—were introduced, criticized, and defended. Traditional poets were castigated for using literature to achieve social gains and political favor, and their literary style was criticized as hackneyed and insincere. Advocates of New Literature, on the other hand, were branded as shallow and ignorant charlatans, and their literary views were seen as ungrounded in solid learning. The result was a visible division in the cultural field. As in the case of many literary debates in modern times, the pumped-up antagonism between opposite sides of the participants precluded a meaningful exchange of ideas, and there was very little theoretically sound defense on the ground of aesthetics. Rather, the debate performed an important ritualistic function: After the debate, traditional literary activities were increasingly confined to poetry clubs that continued to thrive but with limited social reach, while New Literature was legitimized as a powerful social institution. Through this institution, the new intellectuals denounced their Chinese cultural heritage—in part by making traditional men of letters and their world views into scapegoats—and endorsed a vision of "modern civilization." The denunciation and the vision constituted the major component of Taiwanese New Literature for at least a decade.

If the two New Culture movements in China and Taiwan were analogous but separate, the relationship between the Chinese and Taiwanese New Literature movements, as constituting parts of the former, was actually much closer. At the initial stage, terms of literary reform in the Taiwanese New Literature movement nearly copied those of its slightly earlier Chinese counterpart (1917–25). When Chang Wo-chun wrote the polemical essays that triggered the Old Versus New

Literary debate, he was a student at Peking Normal University. During the debate, the major tenets of the May Fourth literary revolution, such as Hu Shih's "principle of eight don'ts" (*pa-pu chu-yi*) from his "Preliminary Suggestions for a Literary Reform" (Wen-hsueh kai-liang ch'u-yi) were introduced with slight modifications. Even the harsh way Chang Wo-chun castigated the traditional poets is immediately reminiscent of the radical Chinese reformist Ch'en Tu-hsiu. Furthermore, throughout the decade of the 1920s, creative works by Chinese New Literature writers, such as Lu Hsun, Hu Shih, Kuo Mo-jo, Ping Hsin, Wang Lu-yen, and Ling Shu-hua, were reprinted in Taiwanese journals and undoubtedly served as literary models.

However, within a decade, this dependent relationship began to change. Apparently, during this time the deepening of Japanese colonization had begun to structurally transform the society of Taiwan and veered it further away from China. Consciousness of this new reality among the Taiwanese intellectuals manifested itself in two consecutive literary debates in 1931–32: the Nativist Literary debate (*hsiang-t'u wen-hsueh lun-chan*) and the Taiwanese Language debate (*T'ai-wan hua wen lun-chan*), which represented a turning point in the Taiwanese New Literature movement.

The Nativist Literary debate testified to the prominent leftist influence on Taiwan's literary scene. The literary program proposed by its chief advocate, Huang Shih-hui—suggesting that writers target their creative works at the working class—was clearly modeled after the leftist concept of proletarian literature. And the split of the Taiwanese Cultural Association in 1927 was primarily a result of disagreement between the nationalist right wing and the socialist left wing over resistance strategies. After the split, the Association was controlled by the left-wing members, led by Lien Wen-ch'ing and Wang Min-ch'uan. The more moderate members formed the Taiwanese People's Party (T'ai-wan min-tsung tang) and continued to fight for greater constitutional rights for the Taiwanese people. Yet the political climate in the colony was so disillusioning that even the Taiwanese People's Party later displayed a leftward leaning tendency and in 1931 was forced to dissolve by the colonial government.

This phenomenon can be attributed in part to the popularity of various strands of leftist thought around the world at the time. More important, it should be seen as a consequence of the rapid social transition Taiwan underwent in the 1920s. At its initial stage, the Taiwanese New Culture movement focused on cultural enlightenment to address the society's internal needs to modernize; the main targets of its attack were old Chinese customs and the lingering social ills of feudalism. As Taiwan proceeded along the course of modernization, however, new types of social problems arose. The worldwide economic depression in the early 1930s made typical social problems of a capitalist society, such as unemployment and class exploitation, even more manifest, which necessarily contributed to the thriving of socialist ideology in Taiwan and, subsequently, the rise of hard-core nativism.

Primarily concerned with internal social problems and conflicts between classes, leftist intellectuals called for a Taiwan-centered literature. Aside from a class-oriented literary view, Huang Shih-hui also was known for forcefully arguing that Taiwanese writers should write in their own language and write about things in their own homeland. Considered by historians to be following the direction of "self-improvement based on one province (Taiwan)" (*yi-tao kai-liang chu-yi*), advocates of Nativist Literature clearly envisioned a "Taiwanese consciousness" as something to be distinguished from the more inclusive "Chinese consciousness," or ethnic Han consciousness.

This Taiwanese consciousness was precisely the core spirit of Kuo Ch'iu-sheng's campaign for Taiwanese language the following year. The Taiwanese language debate, with the literary journal *Nan-yin* as its major forum, revealed the anxieties and ambivalent feelings of a colonized people in their attempts to develop a national language. As an effort to assert the Taiwanese subjectivity, the movement also, even by implication, functioned to sever the Taiwanese intellectuals' emotional ties to China. Primarily, the movement called attention to the fact that early advocates of the Taiwanese New Literature had followed the Chinese model of the May Fourth movement too closely. They had thus unwittingly mistaken the latter's problematics and strategies for their own, without giving proper attention to the objective circumstances of Taiwan.

To facilitate popular education in a country with an extremely high illiteracy rate, advocates of the May Fourth movement proposed to replace the difficult, obsolete classical Chinese language with modern Chinese vernacular as the official written language. The basic theoretical assumption was that, since there would be a close correspondence between the spoken and written versions of modern Chinese, as reflected in the famous slogan "*wo-shou hsieh wo-hsin*" (My hand writes down whatever my mouth utters), the efforts required to become literate in Chinese would be greatly lessened. In reality, however, a standard Chinese vernacular was yet to be popularized within the country; people from different regions still predominantly used dialects for daily communication; and some Chinese dialects are mutually unintelligible. There was, to be sure, a considerable disparity between the standard Chinese vernacular and the southern Min dialect used by the majority of Taiwanese. Moreover, as Taiwan had already been politically separated from China for more than two decades, its people had many fewer channels for learning the standard Chinese vernacular through public institutions such as education, publications, or a state bureaucracy.

Nevertheless, early advocates of the Taiwanese New Literature movement still favored the adoption of Chinese vernacular as the medium for Taiwanese New Literature. The fact that this position was uncontested at the time shows that by then the ethnic-cultural identity of Taiwanese intellectuals was still predominantly Chinese. One popular argument they espoused was that, since most of the Taiwanese gentry class members were still tutored in the written language of classical Chinese in their childhood, minimal additional efforts would be needed to enable them to use the Chinese vernacular as a literary medium. The advantage of this was that it would facilitate the circulation of Taiwanese literary works in the larger Chinese community, which shows that Chinese recognition was still regarded as significant symbolic capital by Taiwanese intellectuals. In practice, however, despite the good will among most Taiwanese New Literature writers, the disadvantages were by no means negligible. It is said that Lai Ho had to write his works in classical Chinese first, then translate them into the Chinese vernacular, and finally revise them with the more lifelike Taiwanese colloquialisms. Yang Shou-yu (1905–1959), a writer well versed in the Chinese vernacular style, regularly had to rewrite the works submitted for publication when he served as the editor for the literary section of the *Taiwanese People's Newspaper* (T'ai-wan min-pao). Such a cumbersome and laborious process works against the fundamental principle of realistic literary writing, which explains why the kind of re-evaluation offered by the Taiwanese Language movement was well received even by Lai Ho, whose cultural identity was ostensibly Chinese.

Without political enforcement, however, the goals of the Taiwanese language movement were very difficult to realize. The fact that many words in the Taiwanese spoken language do not have corresponding Chinese characters made the development of a new writing system an enormous undertaking, beyond the reach of private groups. It is said that Lai Ho, after extensively using the Taiwanese language in writing his short story "A Comrade's Letter of Criticism" (Yi-ko t'ung-chih te p'i-hsin) (1935), was so frustrated with the experiment that he completely stopped writing fiction in the New Literature style. The colonial government, unsurprisingly, tried to cripple such a nationalistically motivated project, seeing it as an obstacle to the implementation of Japanese as the official language in Taiwan. The Taiwanese language debate thus reveals a typical dilemma facing colonized people: Because the project to develop a new national language based on the native tongue was conceived mainly as a linguistic strategy of resistance and as a means of asserting one's own identity, it did not receive the political support required for its success. Despite the failure, the Taiwanese language movement must be regarded as a significant turning point in the Taiwanese New Literature movement. After 1931 there was a marked decline in the number of works by Chinese New Literature writers reprinted in Taiwanese journals. From this point on, the development of Taiwanese New Literature began to consciously depart from the Chinese model and embark on a path of its own.

Maturity and Growth: Two Generations of Writers

The crackdown on leftist organizations and the general suppression of sociopolitical movements in 1931 ironically heralded a period of maturation and growth for Taiwanese New Literature, which began in the mid-1920s as part of the cultural reform, anticolonial social movement. In the following decade, various literary organizations were formed and new literary journals mushroomed. Having passed its initial, experimental stage, the new literary form, particularly in technical respects, made impressive progress during this period. Whereas the first generation of Taiwanese New Literature writers continued to be productive, a group of young talents also joined the ranks. There was, however, a notable gap between the two generations of Taiwanese New Literature writers in terms of cultural outlook, aesthetic preference, and vocational orientation. This apparent disjuncture in the relatively brief history of Taiwanese New Literature is noteworthy, as it points to a rapidly changing cultural landscape in the second half of Taiwan's Japanese period.

It has been argued that, by the time the New Literature movement began, the cultural identity of Taiwanese intellectuals was still predominantly Chinese—despite the fact that Taiwan had already been a Japanese colony for more than two decades. Members of an ordinary Taiwanese gentry family were still sufficiently exposed to the Chinese cultural tradition, as children were still sent to private tutorial classes, or *shu-fang*—the number of which decreased sharply in the late 1910s—to study classical Chinese. Most of the first generation of Taiwanese New Literature writers, as members of the traditional gentry class, were well versed in classical Chinese and competent in traditional Chinese poetry writing, a practice to which some of them reverted after Chinese publications were banned in 1937. The fact that there were no substantial changes in the ethnic content of cultural production is attributable to the particular colonial policies applied to Taiwan during the first two decades of Japanese rule. Acknowledging that the colony had a separate history of its own, the Japanese were primarily concerned with maintaining social stability, rather than culturally assimilating the Taiwanese people. The cultural upbringing and imagination of Taiwanese writers whose formative years took place during the first half of the Japanese period were therefore not fundamentally transformed by colonial rule, even though most of them also were trained in Japanese and received a modern education. Lai Ho, for example, went to a modern-style medical school and knew the Japanese language well, but he never used it in his creative writing. More important, as evinced in both his writing and the role he played in the literary community, he was in many ways an exemplary traditional Chinese intellectual.

Significantly influenced by the May Fourth movement and its reformist ideology, this generation of Taiwanese writers primarily played a historical role as new intellectuals in a premodern society struggling to break away from the past and to usher in progressive social visions. The past, however, was still very much with them. It can be easily demonstrated that, compared to their younger followers, this generation of Taiwanese writers carried over a considerable cultural legacy from the Chinese tradition in their works in the New Literature style. The fact that many of their works were concerned with criticism of the "spiritual ills" of Taiwanese society directly reflects the moralist world view of neo-Confucianism and the traditional intellectuals' value system. The formal quality of literary works by writers of this generation also displays a transitional character. The omniscient narrative point of view and episodic plot structure were obvious traits inherited from Chinese vernacular fiction. Although the modern short story, the novel, and free verse were essentially forms imported from the West, this generation of Taiwanese writers' assimilation of Western literary techniques and artistic conceptions was largely superficial.

The situation, however, was very different among writers born later (Yang K'ui was born in 1906; Ch'en Huo-ch'uan, 1908; Weng Nao, 1908; Chang Wen-huan, 1909; Lung Ying-tsung, 1911; Lu Ho-jo, 1914; and Wang Ch'ang-hsiung, 1916). During those writers' formative years, the colonial cultural institutions were increasingly consolidated, and there was consequently a marked decrease in the value of Chinese learning as cultural capital. Overall, unlike their immediate predecessors, the generation of Taiwanese writers active in the 1930s and 1940s did not have a solid background in traditional Chinese learning and demonstrated a more hybrid cultural identity. (As the scholar Hsu Chun-ya pointed out, the use of Japanese language in literary creation gradually increased after 1933, and, by 1936 and 1937, there were very few works written in Chinese.) At the same time, rapid social change is the norm in twentieth-century non-Western countries, and Japanese colonization accelerated Taiwan's modernization even further. The gap between the social visions of the two generations of writers was even more remarkable, as the younger writers were raised in a more modern society than that of their predecessors. The following example illustrates this point: Several critics have pointed out that Lai Ho seemed to be obsessed with the abusive power of laws and regulations enforced by the colonial government and its agents. These critics often justified Lai Ho's criticism by noting that police control was notoriously harsh in Taiwan during the Japanese period. Nevertheless, judging from many passages in Lai Ho's fiction in which he meditated on the demarcation line between justice and law from various philosophical points of view, one gets the impression that his ideals and frame of reference still derived from a premodern, Confucianist world view. The fact that younger writers tended to present both the evil and the benign sides of the law indicates that these writers held a more realistic view of the modern judicial system, in spite of discriminatory colonial practices. The different attitudes toward this particular issue demonstrates that in many ways the two generations of Taiwanese writers perceived differently how individuals related to the society at large.

Another significant factor is that the younger writers were oriented to the literary profession in an entirely different manner from Lai Ho's generation. The 1930s saw the emergence of a new cohort of writers who had studied in Japan, a group that constituted the majority of second-generation Taiwanese New Literature writers. While in Japan, these aspiring young Taiwanese writers found themselves on the periphery of an entirely different cultural system, and many of them began earnestly to seek membership in the Japanese literary institutions. They enrolled in university literary classes, attended salons revolving around famous writers, and, above all, joined literary contests, which seemed to be an effective way of earning recognition from the "center," or mainstream Japanese literary circles (often referred to as *chung-yang wen-t'an*). Yang K'ui, Lu Ho-jo, and Lung Ying-tsung were winners of literary prizes in the mid-1930s. Because Japanese assimilation of the West surpassed that of Chinese in the same period, the Taiwanese writers' knowledge of Japanese enabled them to gain a closer grasp of Western artistic concepts and, more important, of the kind of vocational vision that artists in a modern society often take for granted. As they came to perceive themselves as professional artists, with technical expertise and individual aesthetic vision, it is less conceivable that they would ever become such spiritual leaders as Lu Hsun or Lai Ho, whose status as major writers derived from personal charisma and outstanding moral character as well as literary talent.

Apparently, the younger writers enjoyed access to a wide range of literary models, mainly from the West, as shown by the remarkable diversity of their works in terms of both artistic mode and ideological outlook. To give a few examples: Yang K'ui adhered to the more orthodox leftism and dedicated his literary works to humanitarian criticisms of class exploitation, imperialism, and general evils in a capitalist society. Chang Wen-huan's approach is more humanistic in a liberal vein. His interest in the mystic power of the individual's inner self, projected onto nature, resulted in some well-crafted lyrical pieces. Lu Ho-jo successfully emulated naturalism, offering realistic portraits of Taiwan's degenerate gentry class through "typical characters." Lung Ying-tsung's works showed influences of symbolism, delicately aesthetic, with touches of decadence and agonistic impulses.

It is perhaps ironic that, whereas early advocates of the Taiwanese New Literature movement insisted on using vernacular Chinese to ensure a place in the Chinese literary world, two out of three Taiwanese stories first collected in anthologies published in China—"The Newspaper Man" (Sung-pao fu) by Yang K'ui; "The Oxcart" (Niu-ch'e), by Lu Ho-jo; and another Chinese-language story by Yang Hua (1900–1936), "The Ill-fated" (Po-ming)—were translated from Japanese. The high reputation these two stories enjoyed clearly derived from the fact that they had won prizes in literary contests sponsored by important Japanese magazines. Furthermore, Hu Feng, the editor of the Chinese collections in which these stories were published, *Mountain Spirit: Short Stories from Korea and Taiwan* (Shan-ling: Ch'ao-hsien T'ai-wan tuan-p'ien hsiao-shuo chi) and *Anthology of Stories from Weak and Small Nations in the World* (Shih-chieh jo-hsiao min-tzu hsiao-shuo hsuan), was a renowned leftist literary theorist. The fact that Hu selected Yang and Lu's stories in recognition of their anti-imperialist spirit points to an extremely complex relationship between the Taiwanese authors and their Japanese colonizer, who simultaneously played the roles of the oppressor and the bestower of cultural prestige. Such facts eloquently speak to the profoundly ambivalent cultural positions in which the second-generation Taiwanese New Literature writers found themselves in the 1930s.

The War Period and the End of an Era

After the Sino-Japanese war broke out in 1937, the colonial government in Taiwan started an intensive Japanization program and banned the Chinese-language sections in newspapers and magazines. The impact of the harsh reality of war was not, however, fully felt until 1941, when Japan bombed Pearl Harbor and touched off the Pacific War. The year 1937, for example, still saw the publication of a literary magazine *Wind and Moon* (Feng-yueh pao, the only Chinese-language magazine of this period), which featured popular types of literati writings, such as pulp romance, familiar essays, and occasional pieces of traditional scholarship, and enjoyed wide circulation. A literary organization consisting mainly of Japanese writers also published in 1940 an aesthetically oriented journal, *Literary Taiwan.* With the escalation of the Pacific War, however, the Japanese stepped up their war campaign efforts and actively began to mobilize people in the colony to make a contribution to the "Greater East Asian War" (ta Tung-ya chan-cheng). Between 1941 and 1943, *Literary Taiwan* chimed in with the colonial government's call for arms and published such stories as "The Volunteer Soldier" (Chih-yuen ping), by Chou Chin-po (b. 1920), "The Way" (Tao), by Ch'en Huo-ch'uan (b. 1908), and other unabashedly propagandistic poems and plays. Several well-known second-generation writers of Taiwanese New Literature, disapproving of both the political stance and artistic orientation of *Literary Taiwan,* formed their own literary organization and began to publish *Taiwanese Literature* in 1941. Before the two journals were forced to merge by the government under the new name *Taiwanese Literature and Art* (T'ai-wan wen-yi) in 1944, *Taiwanese Literature* published perhaps the most important works of the second-generation of writers of the Taiwanese New Literature: "Capon" (Yen-chi) and "Night Monkeys" (Yeh-yuen), by Chang Wen-huan; "Wealth, Offspring, and Longevity" (Ts'ai-tzu shou), "Peace for the Entire Family" (Ho-chia p'ing-an), and "Guava" (Shih-liu), by Lu Ho-jo; "A Village Without Doctors" (Wu yi ts'un), by Yang K'ui; and "Rapid Torrents" (Pen-liu), by Wang Ch'ang-hsiung.

The contention between *Literary Taiwan* and *Taiwanese Literature* from 1941 to 1943 represented a significant turn of events, as second-generation Taiwanese New Literature writers began to directly confront oppressive relationships within the colonial structure. For these writers, who had been partially nourished by Japanese culture in their formative years and held various degrees of allegiance to it, this experience was at the same time disillusioning and educating. Above all, it became clear to them that artistic approaches were not ideologically neutral. One thing that the Taiwanese writers objected to was *Literary Taiwan*'s Japan-centered, typically colonialist point of view, which treated Taiwan as an exotic "foreign" place, to be romanticized for the connoisseurship of readers in Japan. To the Taiwanese writers, such a literary approach was obviously complicitous in the colonial government's effort to implicate culture in political domination, by diverting people from sociopolitical concerns. Having been exposed to discriminatory and conflictual relationships between Japanese and Taiwanese artists, these writers must have been awakened to their own colonial status. Such realizations are undoubtedly behind the tactics used by writers of *Taiwanese Literature* in their endeavors to resist colonialism. As opposed to the exquisite aestheticism and romanticism of *Literary Taiwan,* writers of *Taiwanese Literature* privileged realism. Aside from works directly informed by leftist ideology, such as those by Yang K'ui, some writers of the *Taiwanese Literature* group consciously shifted to more detailed depictions of local customs, rural life, and folk traditions of Chinese/Taiwanese origin in order to register their resentment of the Japanization program.

The nationalistic orientation of *Taiwanese Literature,* however, failed to attract some of the ardent writers of an even younger generation, such as Yeh Shih-t'ao (b. 1925) and Chou Chin-po, who published in *Literary Taiwan* and expressed either aestheticism or political loyalty to the colonizer. Yeh wrote the controversial essay "Shit, Realism" (Fen hsieh-shih chu-yi), which provoked a heated response from colleagues at *Taiwanese Literature.* It was not until the next epoch that some of this younger generation of writers, too, began to reflect deeply upon the complicated issues surrounding colonial identity.

The unusually convoluted trajectory traveled by Taiwanese New Literature writers may also be illuminated by a brief examination of their intriguingly different attitudes toward the issue of modernity. The first-generation writers' embrace of modernity as an advanced stage of civilization was expressed in largely vacant terms, for essentially they had no real experience of a truly modern society. Most of the second generation, pressured by wartime literary policies, engaged in indirect resistance by asserting nativism, with the effect of notably decreasing their criticism of traditional, feudalist traits of the Taiwanese society. However, if some of them consciously denigrated modern urban civilization, symbolically represented by the Japanese metropolis, still others took exactly the opposite stance. In works of the younger writer Chou Chin-po, who opted to side with progress, a prominent theme was the urgency to modernize in view of the obvious benefits that modernity could bring to the Taiwanese people. Because Japan was equated with civilization, they ardently supported Japanization, albeit not without doubts from time to time.

In artistic terms, the modern literary form of the Taiwanese New Literature significantly departed from the classical Chinese tradition, but its evolution abruptly ended at the conclusion of World War II, when Taiwan was returned to China. Several years later, the Nationalists, having lost mainland China to the Communists in the civil war, retreated to the island and started an entirely new era. The drastic changes such historical events brought to the society of Taiwan caused most of the Taiwanese New Literature writers to halt their creative activities. Much artistic potential was therefore never developed to its fullest extent, and the movement ended before any genuinely masterful works of art appeared.

The legacy of the Taiwanese New Literature movement was suppressed in the postwar years, as the dominant culture was now constituted by the mainland Chinese tradition. But there were still significant works written and published, and the exploration of colonial identity continued to be the dominant concern of works written by writers directly nourished by the Taiwanese New Literature of the Japanese period, such as *The Orphan of Asia* (Ya-hsi-ya ku-erh), by Wu Cho-liu (1900–1976); "The Oleander Flowers" (Chia-chu-t'ao), by Chung Li-ho; *Trilogy of Taiwanese,* by Chung Chao-cheng; *The Man Who Rolls on the Ground* (Kun-ti lang), by Chang Wen-huan; and later works by Yeh Shih-t'ao. Whereas the majority of writers directly nourished by the Taiwanese New Literary Movement were marginal to the society's cultural production and reproduction in the martial law period, those still alive have played a crucial role in the "nativization," or *pen-t'u-hua,* movement of the past two decades.

Notes

1. Chuang Shu-chih, *T'ai-wan hsin wen-hsueh kuan-nien te meng-ya yu shih-chien* [Early developments of the concept of New Literature in Taiwan's Japanese period] (Taipei: Mai-t'ien ch'u-pan you-hsien kung-ssu, 1994), 22–29.

2. The following are some recently published studies on Taiwanese literature of the Japanese period: Hsu Chun-ya, *Jih-chu shih-ch'i T'ai-wan hsiao-shuo yen-chiu* [A study of Taiwanese fiction of the Japanese period] (Taipei: Wen-shih-che ch'u-pan she, 1995); Huang Ying-che, ed., *T'ai-wan wen-hsueh yan-chiu tsai jih-pen* [Studies of Taiwanese literature in Japan], trans. T'u Ts'ui-hua (Taipei: Ch'ien-wei ch'u-pan she, 1994); Kawahara Akira, "T'ai-wan hsin wen-hsueh yun-tung te chan-k'ai" [The unraveling of the Taiwanese New Literature Movement], trans. Yeh Shih-t'ao, *Wen-hsueh T'ai-wan,* no. 1 (1991): 217–245, 238–271; and no. 3 (1992): 225–264; Lin Heng-che and Chang Heng-hao, eds., *Fu-huo te ch'un-hsiang: T'ai-wan san-shih nien-tai tso-chia lieh-chuan* [Portraits of the resurrected: on Taiwanese writers of the 1930s] (Taipei: Ch'ien-wei ch'u-pan she, 1994); Liang Ming-hsiung, *Jih-chu shih-ch'i T'ai-wan hsin-wen-hsueh yun-tung yen-chiu* [A study of the Taiwanese New Literary Movement in the Japanese period] (Taipei: Wen-shih-che, 1996); Lin Jui-ming, *T'ai-wan wen-hsueh te li-shih k'ao-ch'a* [A historical examination of Taiwanese literature] (Taipei: Yun-ch'en wen-hua, 1996]; and Lin Jui-ming, *T'ai-wan wen-hsueh yu shih-tai ching-shen: Lai Ho yen-chiu lun chi* [Taiwanese literature and the spirit of its time: studies of Lai Ho] (Taipei: Yun-ch'en wen-hua, 1993).

3. The modern Chinese literary tradition was established in the so-called New Literary Movement (*hsin wen-hsueh yun-tung*) or vernacular literary movement (*pai-hua wen yun-tung*) between 1917 and 1919. During the following decades, literature written in the modern Chinese vernacular (*pai-hua*) and heavily influenced by Western literary forms has replaced the traditional literary forms, which use the literary language (*wen-yen*), to become the mainstream of modern Chinese literature.

10

Between Assimilation and Independence

Taiwanese Political Aspirations
Under Nationalist Chinese Rule, 1945–1948

Steven Phillips

The Chiang Kaishek Memorial Hall in Taipei.

Japan's fifty years of colonial rule over Taiwan ended on October 25, 1945. At a brief ceremony in Taipei, the island returned to China, then governed by Chiang Kai-shek's Nationalist Party.[1] The simple transfer of sovereignty accomplished in a single day, however, belies the complexity and contradictions of the 1945 to 1948 period, which blended a troubled decolonization with an abortive reintegration into China.[2] Even after 1945 the colonial experience remained an important factor in determining the course and content of political activity on Taiwan.[3] The Taiwanese relied upon their collective memory of Japanese rule to create frameworks for evaluating and interacting with the Nationalist government.[4] They also invoked positive aspects of the colonial experience, such as economic development, in order to justify their criticism of the state. The colonial legacy, however, was a double-edged sword. Taiwanese had to legitimize their political activity by proving that they had become loyal citizens of China who had not been "Japanized" by collaboration with their former overlords.[5]

Reintegration of Taiwan into China, which had ruled the island from the late 1600s until 1895, was no simpler than decolonization.[6] Although the mainland, sometimes called the motherland *(tsu-kuo),* was the source of most of the island's population, the legacy of Japanese rule assured that reintegration was marked by ambiguity, then conflict. Furthermore, both Taiwan and mainland China had changed so much between 1895 and 1945—politically, socially, and economically—that the retrocession was less the restoration of historical ties than the attempt to forge an entirely new relationship.[7] Because of their limited knowledge of Taiwan, well-justified animosity toward all things Japanese, and the pressures of reconstruction and civil war on the mainland, the Nationalists sought tight control over the economic and political life of the island. The central government delegated this responsibility to a provincial administration staffed almost exclusively with mainlanders. As they had during the colonial era, the Taiwanese attempted to maximize the island's autonomy within a larger political entity, in this case, the Republic of China.[8] The islanders' call for reform under the broad heading of self-government represented a middle ground between independence and complete assimilation into the Nationalist polity and a troubled China.[9]

Decolonization and reintegration began with the interregnum, two months of uncertainty between Japan's surrender in mid-August 1945 and the formal Nationalist takeover in late October. From late 1945 through mid-1946 the Nationalists attempted to solidify their control over the island, causing considerable hardship and increasing tensions between the provincial administration and the local population. The Taiwanese, even as they broke with their past in the process of decolonization, consciously and unconsciously recalled Japanese rule as they navigated their way through this extraordinarily difficult period. Islanders wrestled with two interrelated problems: Where did they fit in the nation of China? What was their place in the Nationalist state? To many, China appeared chaotic and backward—a potential drain on the island's resources and a threat to its stability. The Nationalist state failed to meet many standards of acceptable governance that the Taiwanese had formed under the previous regime. Increasingly, they saw the mainland government and its representatives on the island as new, yet less competent, colonial rulers. Reintegration became, to many of them, recolonization. Taiwanese criticism of the state mirrored calls for expanded provincial autonomy.[10]

In early 1947, simmering tensions between state and society exploded in what became known as the February 28 incident.[11] Taiwanese quickly took control of the island from an ill-prepared provincial administration. Although the elite did not lead the uprising, they used this opportunity to demand a larger role in governing the island and controlling its resources. After a week of tense negotiations, military reinforcements arrived from the mainland, crushing all opposition and massacring thousands of the island's inhabitants. The process of decolonization made a quantum leap forward as those who had invoked the memory of the Japanese era to justify political reform were killed or cowed into silence. After the incident, the state dominated debate over Taiwan's place in China and the Nationalist polity. Subsequent changes in the political and economic spheres came from and through the regime, not as a result of requests from the Taiwanese themselves. The high point of reintegration was 1948. By the end of that year, the collapsing Nationalist regime had begun to retreat to the island. Communist victory and U.S. support for Chiang's regime assured that, by mid-1950, Taiwan was isolated more completely from the mainland than at any time under Japanese rule.

Creating an Ambiguous Colonial Legacy

An understanding of Taiwanese political activity after the retrocession must begin with the colonial era. After a devastating defeat in the first Sino-Japanese war, China's beleaguered Ch'ing dynasty ceded Taiwan to Japan.[12] The Japanese quickly crushed armed resistance as the inhabitants of the island were poorly armed and led, and divided among themselves. The Taiwanese had little prospect of rejoining the mainland until World War II drew to a close fifty years later. Considering the whirlwind of anti-Ch'ing revolution, imperialist pressure, warlord struggles, civil war, and finally Japan's outright invasion of the mainland, however, the island enjoyed relative peace and order. Taiwan's colonial masters also made major improvements in areas such as sanitation and education. The Japanese unified measurements and currency; created postal, banking, and telegraph systems; built infrastructure including harbors, railroads, and power plants; and developed industry in areas such as sugar, aluminum, cement, iron, chemicals, textiles, and lumber.[13] The Taiwanese paid a huge price for this progress: life in a brutal police state, second-class citizenship, economic exploitation, and constant uncertainty over their place in the world. In particular, many Taiwanese viewed their island as "Asia's Orphan" *(Ya-hsi-ya te ku-erh),* a place cast off by China and accorded second-class status by Japan.[14]

The colonial administration set the stage for Taiwanese political movements and demands—experiences that would influence events profoundly after 1945. Law 63 established the framework for Japanese rule by giving a series of military governors-general *(sōtoku)* broad powers over the military, administrative, legislative, and judicial organs on the island, with only limited interference from Tokyo.[15] In 1918, the first of a string of civilian bureaucrats held governor-generalship, symbolizing the slight liberalization of colonial policies in Taishō-era Japan. After 1937, only military officers held this post as the island mobilized for Japan's war effort. The Taiwanese directed much of their political activity toward curbing the power of the governor-general and the bureaucracy under him.

Japanese education and economic policies fostered a Taiwanese elite.[16] Imperialism required a compliant local elite to work in the middle and lower levels of business and industrial enterprises, hospitals, schools, and the colonial police force and bureaucracy. The island's elite, born during the last years of Ch'ing rule or the first decades of colonial rule, would eventually mold the memory of the Japanese era as part of its own political activities, especially the drive for local autonomy, after 1945.[17] The education system sought to build a loyal population with technical skills to support the colonial economy.[18] Primary school enrollment of Taiwanese increased from 21 percent of males and 4 percent of females in 1917 to 81 percent and 61 percent, respectively, by 1943.[19] Instruction above the high school level often meant travel to Japan and was available only to a select group of relatively wealthy and extremely hardworking youth from the families of landlords, businessmen, or professionals. In 1922, 2,400 Taiwanese were studying in Japan; by 1942 this increased to 7,000.[20] The two most important fields were medicine and education—the Japanese discouraged the study of topics they feared likely to lead to political activity such as history or literature.[21] The Japanese also established the first modern institutions of higher education on the island. Taipei Normal School trained thousands of the island's teachers, and Taipei Imperial University grew from 20 Taiwanese students in the 1930s to about 170 by 1944.[22] The colonial bureaucracy and economy provided these educated youth with careers. The island served not only as a market and source of agricultural products and raw materials for Japan but also as the base for the empire's expansion into South China and Southeast Asia.

In a pattern common to colonies, the very people who obtained education, wealth, and status under the Japanese led movements resisting that regime. Calls for reform developed mainly as a reaction to the autocratic powers of the colonial administration under civilian and military governors-general, beginning with opposition to Law 63. From the 1910s through the 1930s, the Taiwanese elite formed a variety of political organizations.23 The drive for greater self-government at all levels of the administrative system became a common theme of this activity. First, they sought to increase the island's autonomy vis-à-vis Japan and the governor-general. Second, the Taiwanese advocated expanding their influence at the city, district, and town levels. Responding to requests for increased self-government by the Taiwanese and the currents of Taishō Democracy in Japan, in 1920 Governor-General Den Kenjiro reorganized the local administration and created assemblies at the city, district, street, and neighborhood level.[24] He also established an islandwide body called the Taiwan Governor-General's Consultative Assembly *(Taiwan Sōtokufu Hyōgikai)* in 1921.[25] These reforms were cosmetic, as the governor-general selected the assembly members (most were prominent Japanese residents or officials) and participants could only question officials—they lacked decision-making power or control over local budgets and administration. Taiwanese criticized these measures as "false," "half," or "in name only."[26]

The first half of the 1930s marked the high point of Taiwanese agitation for self-government under Japanese rule. A group of prominent islanders formed the Taiwan League for Local Self-Government *(Taiwan Chihō Jichi Renmei)* in 1930.[27] The leaders and members of this movement took a middle position—they dared not attempt and probably did not desire to overthrow Japanese rule, but they did seek greater influence over the island's affairs. Voicing themes that became common in disputes between the Nationalist state and the Taiwanese after 1945, indigenous political leaders emphasized that they were best able to manage the internal affairs of the island—they *should* have a greater role—and that their economic development and education levels warranted such measures—they *could* take on this responsibility.

In 1935, based primarily upon confidence in their tight control over the island, the Japanese reformed the assemblies to permit Taiwanese and Japanese residents of the island to elect half the members (assuming that the governor-general allowed them to be candidates). The powers of these bodies, however, remained limited to interpellation of colonial officials, and they could be dissolved at any time by the governor-general. Under an increasingly oppressive atmosphere as Japan marched toward war with China and then the Western powers, the Taiwanese had fewer opportunities to press their demands. By the time full-scale war broke out on the mainland in August 1937, even the most moderate political organizations were banned. The drive for greater self-government would resurface in political discourse after 1945.

To mobilize the Taiwanese for their war effort, the Japanese relied upon effective police repression of dissent, an education system designed to promote loyalty, and a record of providing limited material progress and relative stability.[28] Based upon a compliant local population and Taiwan's location, the island became a key staging and supply area for military operations in southern China and Southeast Asia. The colonial government's propaganda sought Taiwanese support on two levels. Among the bulk of the population—farmers and laborers—the Japanese emphasized loyalty to the emperor, pan-Asianism, and the benefits of the Greater East Asia Coprosperity Sphere. After the Diet passed the National General Mobilization Law in 1938, many Taiwanese were drafted to work in military-related industries, often in Japan. More than 200,000 young draftees served in the Imperial Army or Navy during the war, mainly in Southeast Asia. More than thirty thousand Taiwanese died; the balance returned safely to the island in 1946, swelling the ranks of unemployed.[29] At the elite level, the governor-general focused his attention on the interests of individual local leaders by providing status, such as political posts, and the promise of greater equality with Japanese residents and officials on the island.[30] Most Taiwanese supported the war effort as loyal, albeit second-class, members of the empire. Others retreated from political activity. A few openly opposed their colonial masters or felt the pull of Chinese ancestry and fled to areas of the mainland not occupied by the Japanese. No significant armed resistance movement or sabotage of the war effort occurred on the island itself.

Across the Taiwan strait, the expansion of the Sino-Japanese conflict into a broader war including the Western powers raised Chinese hopes of recovering Taiwan. At the Cairo Conference of November 1943, U.S. president Franklin Roosevelt, Generalissimo Chiang, and British prime minister Winston Churchill stated their intention of returning Taiwan to China after the war. Simultaneously, the Nationalist government stepped up its efforts to prepare for the restoration of Chinese sovereignty over the island.[31] In April 1944, Chiang established the Taiwan Investigation Committee within the Central Statistical Bureau. Chiang named Ch'en Yi, former chairman of Fukien province (directly across the Taiwan straits from the island), to head the committee. Cooperation with Taiwanese who had moved to the mainland became an important facet of postwar planning as about a thousand islanders joined Nationalist government or party organizations, many in the wartime capital of Chungking.[32] These Taiwanese became known as "half-mountain people" *(pan-shan-jen).*[33] They served as an important link between the island and the central government when they returned to Taiwan after the retrocession.[34] Many of them, however, were torn between loyalty to their native place and to the Nationalist state, which had provided them with status and careers.

On August 15, 1945, the Taiwanese dutifully turned on their radios—they had been told by Japanese officials to expect an important announcement. They strained to hear the Showa emperor announce that the time had come to "endure the unendurable." After fifty years, the empire had collapsed; the Taiwanese were no longer second-class citizens of Japan—but would they be first-class citizens of China? The colonial era left the Taiwanese with a dual legacy. As the Taiwanese would emphasize after the retrocession, their standard of living, level of education, and sanitary conditions all exceeded those of the mainland, even Manchuria (part of China under Japanese control since 1931).[35] Due to a well-enforced system of compulsory education, there were few under age forty who could not read Japanese. The island was more advanced economically and industrially and had avoided the chaos of warlords, civil war, and invasion that had plagued the mainland during the previous decades. In this context, most Taiwanese became loyal subjects of the empire and eager participants in modernization.

They also took advantage of the opportunity for limited political activity in local assemblies. Another aspect of the legacy, however, was a negative one. The Taiwanese endured second-class citizenship, systematic discrimination, frustrated political aims, an economic order developed solely for Japan's benefit, and wartime deprivation. They had struggled to reform Japanese rule, symbolized by the governor-general system, through a variety of political movements designed to expand self-government. The contradictions of the colonial experience set the stage for the difficult processes of decolonization and reintegration.

Nationalist Rule Established

Upon hearing of Japan's surrender, the Taiwanese reacted initially with elation, for it marked the end of U.S. bombing and the return of sons serving in the military. This joy, however, was tempered by uncertainty. The island was rife with rumors of Nationalist intentions, Taiwanese cliques, and foreign plots.[36] For example, the diaries of colonial-era doctor and political activist Wu Hsin-jung referred repeatedly to the feelings of unease *(pu an)* in himself and his compatriots.[37] The "problem" of the colonial legacy became apparent even before the arrival of the new government. The son of a traditional Chinese scholar who became a doctor and advocate of self-government under Japanese rule, Han Shih-ch'uan reported on the events in T'ainan, an important city on the southwest coast of the island. He divided his fellow citizens into four groups. First, some people who had helped the Japanese rule *(wei hu tso ch'ang)*—"aid to an evildoer") suddenly became ardent Chinese patriots. Second, others with a conscience stayed indoors because they were ashamed of their past collaboration with the Japanese. Third were those loyal to China who had opposed Japan. They eagerly sought to use the opportunity to grasp political power. Last were the masses who went wild with joy and released fifty years of accumulated hatred toward the Japanese.[38]

As the initial shock and confusion of Japan's defeat wore off, some Taiwanese took the initiative in decolonization and reintegration. These men had become leaders to the people of the island based upon their economic power, positions in prominent families, and roles in political movements during the Japanese era. They would be the ones who attempted to shape the relationship between state and society after the retrocession. The Taiwanese organized themselves to preserve public order, taking this task over from the Japanese, and to prepare for the arrival of the Nationalist government. Political leader, landlord, and businessman Lin Hsien-t'ang and other well-known figures in central Taiwan offered to cooperate with the Japanese to maintain stability during this time of uncertainty.[39] This exemplified the collaborative relationship between wealthy Taiwanese and their colonizers, an issue that would become extremely sensitive in the years to come. These men worked closely with local youth, many with Japanese military training, to keep order as the colonial police had little enthusiasm for the endeavor.[40] This cooperation also highlighted a gap between the elite and their fellow islanders. While many poor Taiwanese might have benefited from the breakdown of law and order, the elite had property, businesses, and social status to protect—chaos was not in their class interests.

The Taiwanese realized that their collaboration with the Japanese colonial empire would be an extraordinarily sensitive issue in their relationship with the mainlander-dominated Nationalist state. As they turned their attention to building ties with the new regime, the Taiwanese almost uniformly offered public professions of loyalty to the ideal of a reuniting with China under Chiang Kai-shek's regime.[41] To take the initiative on reintegration, prominent Taiwanese formed the Preparatory Committee to Welcome the National Government. Participants included Lin, Yeh Jung-chung, and others who were simultaneously cooperating with the Japanese to maintain order. They organized activities to show their support for new government (such as distributing Nationalist flags and banners), met newly arrived mainland officials, and traveled to Nanking to meet with leaders in the central government. Smaller versions of this committee were established in communities throughout the island.

The Nationalists established their administration in this atmosphere of Taiwanese public support and private reservations. Chiang Kai-shek's government sought tight control of Taiwan to promote decolonization and advance reintegration by erasing Japanese influence and bringing the island under the economic, political, and cultural sway of China. While the Nationalists were suspicious of the Taiwanese because of their long collaboration with the Japanese, they hoped to exploit the island's wealth and industrial base for the mainland's postwar reconstruction and struggle against the Communists. Toward this end, in August 1945 the Nationalists established an administrative system unlike that of any other province in China—the Taiwan Provincial Administrative Executive Office (T'ai-wan-sheng hsing-cheng chang-kuan kung-shu). Ch'en Yi became administrator *(hsing-cheng chang-kuan)* and commander of the Taiwan Garrison.[42] Ch'en, working through the Executive Office, had direct control over the administrative, military, judicial, and regulatory organs on the island. Although not intentionally modeled after Law 63, this system's similarities to the colonial regime laid the base for conflict with the Taiwanese after the retrocession.

Nationalist rule of Taiwan during the latter half of the 1940s was a failure.[43] State policies involving important issues such as the disposition of Japanese assets and economic reconstruction, cultural reintegration and language, and participation in political activity all led to disputes with the island's people. Because the Taiwanese came to see few major differences between Japanese and mainland Chinese economic and political systems and goals, they transferred their ambiguity toward the colonial experience to their relationship with the Nationalist government. Although both regimes were seen as exploitative, the new government was deemed particularly deficient in important areas such as honesty, competence, predictability, and efficiency.

After Ch'en Yi formally took power as administrator on October 25, the Nationalists began to wrestle with the problems of postwar Taiwan. In the economic sphere, the island faced two difficult transitions: from the Japanese to the Chinese orbit, and from wartime mobilization to peacetime reconstruction.[44] The Nationalists inherited an industrial infrastructure worn down from the demands of Japan's war effort and American bombing.[45] The most devastated areas included harbors, housing in coastal cities, sugar refineries, and communication or transportation facilities. Work on repairs ceased in August 1945 as Japanese technical experts and managers began to return home and spare parts for equipment became difficult to obtain.[46] Agricultural production declined because of the lack of labor and fertilizer.[47] In this context, any government would have had a difficult time managing the island's economy. The state magnified these problems by attempting to link Taiwan to the mainland even as the latter struggled, then failed, to recover from the war. The Nationalists placed colonial-era enterprises and monopolies under state control, confiscated Japanese private property, and established trade bureaus to manage commerce between the island and the mainland or the outside world.

Ch'en Yi molded the general strategies set in Chungking to fit his own ideas on the need for government domination of Taiwan's economy.[48] He emphasized Sun Yat-sen's ideas of placing national capital over private investment.[49] Since the nation and government belonged to the people, he reasoned, state enterprises were inherently good. Administrator Ch'en tied support of his policies to patriotism, leaving the Taiwanese little room for dissent. He attacked those who opposed his economic measures, stressing that such critics held the "traditional ideology of the gentry." He asked, "The government should not make money, but merchants should? How can you say this? The money the government earns is for the benefit of the people, but the money earned by merchants goes into private pockets."[50] This uncompromising attitude laid the base for conflict with Taiwanese businessmen.

The new regime's efforts to increase its control over all facets of the economy collided with the drive by wealthy Taiwanese to expand their enterprises into areas formerly controlled by Japanese firms or the colonial government.[51] Businessmen large and small could neither compete with state firms nor trade freely with either old markets (Japan and its former colonies) or new (the mainland). In August 1946, U.S. officials reported that "economic paralysis has set in, attributed primarily to the policy of creating semi-official companies against which private enterprise cannot successfully compete."[52] Extortion by undisciplined soldiers and officials from the mainland, bad management, and corruption magnified problems stemming from government policies.[53] Taiwanese saw corruption as particularly troublesome, as they came to recall fondly that they had learned the importance of the rule of law under the strict—yet predictable—police state run by the Japanese.[54]

In the competition between Taiwanese and mainlanders to control colonial-era assets, the disposition of Japanese private property, especially homes, became a contentious issue. Ownership was often unclear because many Japanese had sold their homes at bargain prices at the end of the war; Taiwanese simply occupied other dwellings. In the eyes of most islanders, much of this property had been confiscated by the colonial government or sold to Japanese enterprises at unfair prices over the previous fifty years and was thus rightfully theirs. According to Nationalist law, however, all Japanese property now belonged to the government.[55] Corruption complicated this issue as some mainlanders took advantage of their power and positions to take property that may have belonged to Taiwanese. The colonial legacy became part of this conflict. One Taiwanese observed later, "When a Chinese with some influence wanted a particular property, he had only to accuse a Formosan of being a collaborationist during the past fifty years of Japanese sovereignty."[56] For the next few years, islanders attempted to obtain property that they believed was their own through largely unsuccessful lawsuits and petitions.

For most Taiwanese, living conditions worsened after the retrocession. In the central part of the island, people talked of "three hopes." First there existed hope *(hsi-wang)* from the time of Japan's surrender through the arrival of the Nationalist administration two months later. Next was lost hope *(shih-wang)* that resulted from the performance of the new government. Finally came *chueh-wang* (hopelessness) as the people felt that "the future was black."[57] The most serious problems were inflation and unemployment. Although the island had its own currency, as had been the case during the colonial era, it was tied to a government that did not and could not make Taiwan's welfare a high priority. Ch'en Yi's attempt to insulate Taiwan from the ravages of inflation on the mainland failed and prices rose according to the changing value of the central government's currency *(fa-pi)* and perceptions of Nationalist China's stability.[58] Unemployment resulted from the lack of industrial recovery, magnified by the demobilization of many youth who had served as laborers or soldiers for the Japanese. State monopolies on goods such as tobacco, alcohol, salt, and matches proved unable to meet the needs of consumers. Grain and housing shortages also harmed most Taiwanese. Government attempts to control grain prices and sales proved ineffective. Hoarding and profiteering by businessmen and officials—both Taiwanese and mainlanders—magnified these difficulties.[59] Finally, public health and sanitation declined. For example, a cholera epidemic hit southern Taiwan during the summer of 1946, the incidence of malaria and leprosy increased, and bubonic plague reappeared for the first time since 1919.[60]

Policies concerning culture and language formed another problematic aspect of decolonization and reintegration. The government sought to eradicate Japanese influence and sinicize the Taiwanese through a process of cultural reconstruction *(wen-hua ch'ung-chien).*[61] Toward this end, Administrator Ch'en used organizations like the Three Principles of the People Youth Corps and the Taiwan Office of Translation and Compilation. The latter was headed by an associate of Ch'en named Hsu Shou-t'ang who thought that Taiwan needed its own

May Fourth movement to sweep away the influence of Japanese colonialism and feudal thinking.[62] Hsu promoted the writings of Lu Hsun, an icon of China's youth and one of the leading authors of the mainland's New Culture movement.[63] This program presents an excellent case study of Nationalist efforts at decolonization and reintegration in the cultural sphere. First, the program failed because of limited interest in Lu Hsun. Many Taiwanese gave cultural change a much lower priority than economic recovery. Second, some who read Lu Hsun's work interpreted it as a critique of the mainland and its culture. Thus it served as much to turn Taiwanese intellectuals against China and its representatives, the Nationalist government, as it did to build ties.[64] Finally, the Taiwanese received mixed messages from the state. Hsu's work to spread the thought of Lu Hsun conflicted with much of the Nationalist Party's (Kuomintang) official ideology, which emphasized Sun Yat-sen's Three Principles of the People, and attacked Lu as a Communist sympathizer.[65]

Linguistic differences resulting from colonial rule became a point of conflict between the Taiwanese and the new administration. Over fifty years spoken Japanese had come to replace the common Chinese dialects (Taiwanese, or *T'ai-yu,* and Hakka, or *K'e-chia hua)* among the better educated.[66] In response, the Nationalists struggled to spread the use of Mandarin Chinese *(kuo-yu),* literally "national language"), the officially sanctioned dialect of the mainland government. In April 1946, the government established a committee for the promotion of *kuo-yu.* While most Taiwanese enthusiastically studied their new language—whether out of patriotism, drive for profit in the China market, release of curiosity stifled by the Japanese, or simple self-interest is difficult to say—there were several problems with the government's approach. The state vastly overestimated the speed at which Taiwanese could learn *kuo-yu* well enough to discuss political issues (the fastest process) and read or write official materials (the slowest). This proved especially troublesome for those seeking positions in the provincial administration. Even in the Provincial Consultative Assembly (T'ai-wan-sheng ts'an-i-hui) meetings of 1946, translation was required as so few representatives could speak "standard Mandarin" *(piao-chun kuo-yu).*[67] Also, many newly arrived mainlanders could not speak understandable *kuo-yu*—they brought with them the plethora of dialects that existed in China. Finally, language competence became a symbol of one's "Chinese-ness" and the use of Japanese turned into a "political problem."[68] The inability to speak, read, and write the official language suggested a lack of patriotism and backwardness to mainland Chinese.[69] Taiwanese became especially upset when the ability to communicate in Mandarin became a symbol of political and educational development required for the implementation of self-government.[70] Nevertheless, the government moved ahead with its attempts to restrict the use of Japanese. On the first anniversary of the retrocession, periodicals using the colonial language were banned.

Conflicts over policies concerning economic reconstruction and cultural reintegration created the context for Taiwanese political activity. The retrocession appeared to present an unprecedented opportunity for participation in public life, which had been severely restricted by the Japanese. Through factions, the media, appointed posts, and elected assemblies, the Taiwanese endeavored to increase their role in governing the island. Factions were a way of distributing political power and controlling resources through personal relationships. These relationships had grown out of shared experiences (such as education or military service), place of birth, ideology, or a combination of the three. At the national level, Chiang Kai-shek deliberately promoted factions to protect his own power by keeping potential rivals divided and off-balance. For example, Ch'en Yi, part of the Political Science Clique, was in constant conflict with the C-C Clique while in Fukien and Taiwan.[71] Administrator Ch'en had his own underlings who, in turn, formed factions.[72]

Politically active Taiwanese divided themselves into three groups: half-mountain *(pan-shan)*, Taichung, and Ah Hai.[73] Each had its own subfactions. The relationships and rivalries between cliques were extraordinarily complex. During the early 1940s the Nationalists had begun working with some Taiwanese, the "half-mountain people *(pan-shan-jen)*," in preparation for the retrocession. This uneasy alliance continued after the war. These men often joined mainland factions and had their own rivalries as well. After the retrocession, half-mountain clique members brought other Taiwanese into their circle. In the eyes of many Taiwanese who never ventured off the island, however, the strength of *pan-shan-jen* ties to the Nationalist government reduced their legitimacy as representatives of the island's interests. The Taichung clique consisted of men such as Lin Hsien-t'ang, Yang Chao-chia, Yeh Jung-chung, and others with relatively high social standing in Japanese-era Taiwan.[74] Many had been involved in social and political activity during the colonial period such as the movements to abolish Law 63 and to establish an islandwide assembly. After the retrocession, they sought to take what they believed to be their rightful place as political leaders of the island. Administrator Ch'en opposed this faction because it contained many merchants or landlords who fought his economic policies. The Ah Hai clique tended to represent the youthful elite of Taiwan. Some had been strident anti-Japanese activists who spent time in jail while others had actively collaborated with their colonizers. They shared a strong antipathy toward the half-mountain clique and antagonized Ch'en with their harsh criticism of his rule. Mainlanders disdained some of those in the Ah Hai clique for their past subservience to the Japanese.

The media became the most visible avenue for the Taiwanese to attempt to influence the state. For two reasons, immediately after the retrocession the press enjoyed greater freedom than at any time before the lifting of martial law in 1987. First, the Nationalists had difficulty manipulating the media any more effectively than they controlled prices, promoted the use of Mandarin Chinese, or implemented any other policy. Second, the depth of Taiwanese discontent did not become clear until well into 1946. Nationalist officials did not immediately seek to control all print media—they seemed genuinely surprised at the criticism they received.[75] By mid-1946, however, the limits of Ch'en Yi's tolerance became increasingly clear, as reporters and editors were harassed, sued, or arrested.[76] For example, Wang T'ien-teng, newspaper publisher, member of the Provincial Consultative Assembly, and part of the Ah Hai clique, was arrested for "undermining public confidence in authority."[77] Wang's difficulties were part of an attack on *Jen-min tao-pao,* one of the newspapers most openly critical of the provincial government.[78] Shortly after the paper had ceased publishing, the highest court on Taiwan announced that the case against him was being dropped for lack of evidence.[79]

Official posts represented another part of political activity. The mainlanders' near-monopoly over important positions in the provincial administration, including state enterprises and monopoly bureaus, antagonized the Taiwanese. Here, too, the colonial legacy played an important role. To many Nationalists, islanders lacked the qualifications for holding these posts because of their lack of Chinese-language ability and administrative experience, as well as their previous collaboration with the Japanese.[80] Only three of the first twenty-three county magistrates posts or mayorships, and one of the twenty-one highest posts in the provincial government, were delegated to Taiwanese.[81] Islanders made up only a small portion of midlevel officials in the various departments. Opportunities for employment (and influence) at all levels declined after the war as the bureaucracy shrunk from 85,000 persons (including Japanese and Taiwanese) in 1944 to 44,000 in 1946. The Nationalists sent about 28,000 officials to the island. In the end, about 36,000 Taiwanese lost their jobs in the change of administrations.[82] Not only the quantity but also the quality of mainland officials became a contentious issue. Incompetence, corruption, and nepotism were rampant. Another problem was that, as had been the case during the colonial era, a salary differential existed between the Taiwanese and officials sent by the central government.[83]

Representative assemblies became a key aspect of political life. The Taiwanese were eager to participate in governing the island, as they had been during the colonial era, and the Nationalists' willingness to create assemblies held great promise. The first registration of candidates occurred in February 1946. At the lowest level, 36,966 candidates vied for 7,771 posts on village and town councils. They, in turn, elected 523 district or city representatives in March and April. These representatives then elected thirty provincial assemblymen. Reflecting the continuity of personnel between the Japanese and Nationalist eras, of 1,180 candidates for the Provincial Consultative Assembly in 1946, 400 had been involved in assemblies at various levels during the Japanese era, which had fewer positions.[84] The limited powers of the local and provincial bodies, however, left the Taiwanese dissatisfied. Assemblies at all levels were little more than advisory and consultation *(tzu-hsun)* organs. At the same time, these bodies provided a forum for the political elite to express their increasingly critical views of the government.[85]

The Colonial Legacy and Self-Government

In debates carried out through factions, the press, and representative assemblies, the Taiwanese linked the colonial legacy with their immediate concerns over Nationalist misrule. Perceptions of the provincial administration's corruption and ineptitude, defined by standards derived from the experience of Japanese rule, motivated a drive for reform. The goal of that reform—greater self-government—represented a return to a political movement from the pre-retrocession era. Colonial rule, however, was also a historical burden. Only by showing that they had not been "tainted" by Japanese influence could the Taiwanese justify their participation in political activity or criticism of the government. Since the Treaty of Shimonoseki had been signed in 1895, many Taiwanese faced the dilemma of reconciling pride in their Chinese cultural background with the reality of Japanese military power, institutional efficiency, and economic modernization.[86] After 1945 the conflict between admiration of Japanese material progress and Chinese ancestry became a major point of contention between the Nationalist state, which presented itself as synonymous with China, and the Taiwanese. Even some mainlanders became aware of this problem. For example, Chekiang-born Chou Hsien-wen outlined the problem of the colonial legacy in an essay examining the island's history. According to Chou, some observers claimed that Taiwan was more advanced than the mainland because of developments between 1895 and 1945. Others responded that the colonial legacy required complete reform of the island. He concluded that Taiwan's special characteristics, based on its fifty-year experience under foreign control, were not the sole cause of its problems—the island must unite with the mainland while avoiding its defects.[87] Chou did not provide specifics on how to resolve the contradiction of uniting and avoiding defects, which goes to the heart of the Taiwanese conflict with the mainland-based Nationalist government.

The colonial legacy proved inescapable for those discussing the island's place in the Nationalist China. For example, editorials in a newspaper run by the provincial government, *T'ai-wan hsin-sheng-pao,* credited the Japanese with raising education levels and promoting economic development on the island. At the same time, it stressed that the culture of Taiwan, while not low by world standards, did not equal the motherland's *(pu-ju tsu-kuo).* Increased contact with the mainland was advocated as a solution.[88] Another editorial stressed Taiwan's advances in education, industry, agriculture, and transportation under the Japanese. The island was compared to the Szechwan province of old, a land of plenty *(t'ien-fu).* The editorial concluded, however, that Taiwan was now in good hands under Administrator Ch'en Yi's able leadership.[89] In this context, the Taiwanese were to continue to follow, not lead, in the island's development. For the most part, though, the government did not discuss Japanese influence as much as wield it as a political weapon. In light of Nationalist control of Taiwan, the term "Chinese" often meant little more than acceptance of Chiang Kai-shek's rule.

Many mainlanders portrayed the Taiwanese as disloyal to China because of their Japanization *(Jih-pen-hua),* often put in terms of "slavization" *(nu-hua)* at the hands of their colonial masters. They complained that Taiwanese knew little of the mainland or its culture, or worse, disdained China. Islanders were also viewed as exclusionary of mainlanders.[90]

The Taiwanese vigorously rejected the charge that they had been incurably infected by Japanese education or culture because this would delegitimize their participation in politics. Emphasizing Taiwanese resistance to colonial rule formed a key part of this effort. At the end of the war, Li Wan-chu, who worked with the Nationalist government on the mainland in activities opposing the Japanese, emphasized that the Taiwanese had not been Japanized by their colonial experience. He complained that mainlanders did not understand that the Taiwanese had preserved the Chinese race's superior tradition and withstood attempts at assimilation by the Japanese.[91] An editorial in the newspaper *Min-pao* claimed that the mainlanders' frequent use of the terms "slavization" or "slaves" when discussing the Taiwanese represented the sort of insult that caused the island's people to turn against outsiders. Mainlanders did not realize that the Taiwanese had attempted to resist colonial rule as much as possible, particularly by opposing the governor-general system.[92]

Sung Fei-ju serves as an interesting case study in changing Taiwanese attitudes toward the colonial legacy. Sung fled to the mainland during Japanese rule and returned in 1946 as vice-chief of the Education Office in the provincial government, a post he held despite his leftist views. He wrote occasionally for *Jen-min tao-pao,* a newspaper frequently critical of both the provincial administration and the central government. In early 1946, he claimed that Taiwan had missed fifty years of global progress as well as specific advances on the mainland such as the May Fourth movement. Sung described the culture of the island as a complicated mixture of Japanese slave education and the precolonial Han orthodoxy.[93] The Taiwanese, because of Japanese rule, lacked the notion of ruling themselves and required a lengthy education. Sung urged Taiwanese to cultivate themselves to be worldly and think about more than their families' or the island's affairs.[94] Based on his increasing disaffection with the provincial administration, by mid-1946 Sung's position shifted as he emphasized Taiwanese resistance to colonial rule. He wrote that the results of Japan's *kōminka* program had already been completely overturned.[95] Sung explained that the Japanese attempt to educate the Taiwanese had only awakened resistance and that this led to more than twenty years (1920s to 1945) of opposing "slavization" through activities such as the movement to obtain an islandwide assembly.[96] By showing a history of resistance to Japanese rule, Sung was attempting to legitimize a larger Taiwanese role in governing the island.

The Taiwanese used a variety of rhetorical tactics to explain their vital role in forging the island's future. For example, essayists often used the image of a family to describe China. An editorial in *Hsin T'ai-wan,* a magazine published by Taiwanese in North China after Japan's surrender, portrayed islanders as a younger brother separated from his loved ones for fifty years.[97] His experience of slavery made him love the family even more than his parents did. Since the parents have sent an older brother to rule, however, some conflict is inevitable. Peace and renewal required that the family sometimes listen to the younger brother.[98] Other materials were more blunt. An anonymous article in *Hsin T'ai-wan* stated that the Japanese knew the value of the island as a "treasure house." It also warned that although the Taiwanese were not seeking independence from the mainland, the island could become an entirely self-sufficient nation.[99] This represented a challenge to the Nationalists to manage Taiwan's resources as efficiently as the Japanese had done.

Other Taiwanese appropriated the theme of colonialism to promote their political agendas vis-à-vis the Nationalist government. Some people even reached back to Ch'ing rule of China—another instance of imperialism—and compared it to Japan's domination of the island. Poet and democracy activist Wang Pai-yuan's essay in *Cheng-ching-pao* stressed that the Taiwanese did not absorb Japanese thinking any more than Ch'ing rule poisoned the minds of mainland Chinese. Taiwan was very orderly, he claimed, and should be easier to rule than other recovered areas. Thus, the island possessed optimal conditions for modern democratic development. Wang decried that some mainlanders treated Taiwan as a colony.[100] The theme of Taiwan as a Chinese colony became a common one in 1946. For example, an editorial in *Jen-min tao-pao* frankly stated that prejudices between Taiwanese and mainlanders prevented their mutual progress. Although they were all Chinese ("sons of the Yellow Emperor"), many of those from outside the province felt superior and looked upon Taiwan in the same manner as the British treated India.[101]

To many Taiwanese, the new regime compared unfavorably to the old. Dissatisfaction became especially clear in the realms of preserving public order and preventing corruption, areas of particular importance to the island's elite, who had substantial assets to protect and who dealt frequently with government officials. Taiwanese joked about "Passing the Five Tzu Imperial Exam" *(wu tzu teng-k'e)*. This indicated the five things newly arrived mainland officials craved: gold, automobiles, rank, homes, and women.[102] Wang T'ien-teng wrote, "The good people of Taiwan still do not dare hope for real governance under the Three Principles of the People, they only hope for a little rule of law. . . . [They also] hope that the system of not daring to disrespect the rule of law [that existed] under Japanese imperialism can continue."[103] Ch'en Feng-yuan, successful businessman under both Japanese and Nationalist rule, said that the term denoting the mainland's takeover *(chieh-shou)* was replaced by a homonym meaning to plunder. He complained that corrupt officials monopolized Japanese assets and that public security had declined.[104]

The Nationalists' initial concerns over hostile Taiwanese attitudes were realized. Islanders connected the failures of the state, as represented by the provincial government, to a broader critique of the nation of China. Some members of the elite saw the mainland as feudal, even as the island had advanced to the industrial age during Japanese rule. Specifically, nepotism, which was rampant in the provincial administration, was portrayed as a remnant from a stage of development through which the island had passed. Taiwanese depicted corruption as part of the mainland's defective political culture.[105] To others, the Nationalist ideology, San Min Chu-I (Three Principles of the People), had become *ts'an-min chu-i* (Cruel person-ism).[106] The views of average Taiwanese were even more blunt. Some said that the dogs (the Japanese) had left, but the pigs (mainland Chinese) had come. Pigs in this case emphasized the greedy and uncultured nature that many Taiwanese saw in mainlanders.[107] By mid-1946, newspapers reported brawls between mainlanders and Taiwanese as living conditions worsened and tensions rose.[108]

Among the elite, concerns over Nationalist misrule drove calls for change. The Japanese legacy not only determined the type of reform sought—greater autonomy from the central government—but also served to justify it. Hsieh Nan-kuang, a leftist who had worked with the Nationalists on the mainland, attempted to synthesize Nationalist political ideology and Taiwan's colonial experience. He used one aspect of Sun Yat-sen's Three Principles of the People, democracy, as a foil to present his case. The Taiwanese, he wrote, were prepared for a high level of self-government and democracy because of their high education levels and experience with political organizing during the Japanese era. Hsieh added a plea for mainlanders to understand Taiwanese political aspirations, which had been frustrated under colonial rule. The Nationalists were urged to show that they were different from the Japanese.[109] Others shared Hsieh's focus on the colonial legacy as a key factor in post-retrocession politics. One of the most prominent Taiwanese of the immediate postwar era was Nationalist official Ch'iu Nien-t'ai.[110] Based on Ch'iu's analysis, Taiwan was suitable for a high level of self-government and could become a model province for two reasons: political legitimacy based upon resistance to colonial rule, and material progress that stemmed from Japanese investment. First, the Taiwanese could not be considered disloyal to China since the Middle Kingdom had cast them out in the Treaty of Shimonoseki. Further, during the Japanese era, the Taiwanese formed many organizations for expressing the popular will and resisting their colonizers. Second, colonial rule had some positive results. The island's well-developed industry, agriculture, and transportation deserved special protection by the government.[111]

Despite a wide range of emphases, the ambiguity of the retrocession disappeared in 1946 as Taiwanese sought to reconcile their vision of the island's future with the reality of reintegration into a chaotic China. For example, Li Ch'un-ch'ing, a frequent contributor to *T'ai-wan p'ing-lun,* wrote an essay on Chinese rule of Taiwan.[112] While clearly rejecting independence, he urged islanders to avoid the whirlpool of party struggles on the mainland and called for Taiwan to become a model province of local self-government.[113] Some politically active islanders moved toward advocating looser ties with the increasingly chaotic mainland. Lin Hsien-t'ang stressed that Taiwanese could do nothing to affect the growing conflict between the Nationalists and Communists. He suggested that self-government through a confederation of provinces *(lien-sheng tzu-chih)* would be the most effective system to govern China. This had the advantage of letting people select and be ruled by their own provincial representatives. He and others took pains to stress that they did not seek to exclude those from outside the province.[114] Like many others grappling with this problem, however, Lin was unclear on how to resolve this apparent contradiction.

The limited powers of the representative assemblies did not meet Taiwanese expectations of self-government. The first and second sessions of the Provincial Consultative Assembly did, however, become a forum where the Taiwanese called for greater influence over the island's administration. Assembly members requested elections for mayors and district heads (appointed posts at that time) as well as expanded powers for assemblies at all levels—town, district, city, and provincial. One representative raised the issue of Taiwan's material progress during the colonial era, asking the head of the Civil Administration Department, "According to Sun Yat-sen's teachings, the order of each province's implementation of local self-government depends upon the conditions in each location. This province is more advanced than others, so why cannot Taiwan carry it out first?" Kao-hsiung's Kuo Kuo-chi, whose anti-Japanese activities and arrest during the 1930s first brought him into the public eye, stressed the middle ground of self-government that many of his peers were seeking. He charted a course between independence and complete assimilation by attempting to illustrate how self-government was part of building a better China: "The Taiwanese advocate ruling themselves. Because Taiwan is part of the territory of China, and the Taiwanese love their nation and their native place, self-government and self-strengthening are natural requests and logical hopes." Like many other politically active Taiwanese, however, Kuo had to confront the negative aspects of the Japanese legacy. Even as he advocated self-government, he was careful to invoke the memory of Taiwanese resistance against colonial rule, stressing that they had not been turned into slaves of the Japanese.[115]

By the end of 1946, the Taiwanese knew what they wanted and why. Nationalist misrule provided the Taiwanese with a motive to request reform. The Japanese-era experiences of economic development and political activism became justifications for change through expanded self-government. The problem lay in opportunity—how to increase autonomy at the provincial and local levels.

The February 28 Incident: Failed Reintegration

The February 28 incident epitomized the collision between decolonization and reintegration. The drive for self-government linked these two complicated processes. Taiwanese concerns, amorphous at the time of the retrocession, then increasingly specific and linked to criticism of Nationalist policies in 1946, finally exploded in concrete antistate action in early 1947. Islanders briefly overthrew the provincial administration and attempted to change their relationship with the central government. The incident represented the high point of Taiwanese demands for self-government. The Nationalists reacted brutally, crushing the island's elite as a political force capable of operating outside the mainlander-dominated state or the Kuomintang.

A series of crises on the mainland and on Taiwan formed the context for the incident. On January 6, U.S. General George Marshall abandoned his mediation efforts between the Nationalists and the Communists and returned to Washington. The mainland was soon embroiled in full-scale civil war.[116] Student unrest throughout early 1947 presented another pressing problem for the Nanking government.[117] Political instability spurred inflation. These problems diverted the central government's attention from increasing tensions on the island. Taiwan's currency, which was tied to the mainland's finances, depreciated rapidly. The government lost control of the economy—when it was willing and able to enforce price controls on commodities such as rice, shortages resulted. When it did not control prices, inflation soared. On February 14, Taipei's rice market closed briefly because of a riot as citizens struggled to buy ever-smaller amounts of rice at increasing prices.[118] The problems of reintegration—inflation, grain shortages, corruption, lack of military discipline, unemployment, industrial collapse, and cultural conflict—led to simmering discontent in the towns and cities of Taiwan.[119]

On the evening of February 27, six officers from the Monopoly Bureau attempted to arrest a woman selling cigarettes illegally in Taipei.[120] A policeman struck the woman, an angry crowd gathered, and violence broke out after an officer fired into the crowd, killing a bystander. The uprising soon spread to many of the island's urban centers as Taiwanese and government forces battled for control of public infrastructure such as buildings, railroad stations, and police stations. Some Taiwanese brutally attacked any mainlander that they could find. In many cities, officials and police sought safety together in local military outposts.[121] Youth who had received Japanese military training re-formed their old units when taking power in many of the island's cities—singing wartime songs, wearing their uniforms, and sporting swords. This served to justify the suspicions of mainlanders that the Taiwanese had been "Japanized" by their colonial experience.

Although few of the elite participated in the initial uprising or anticipated that the Nationalists would so quickly lose control, they suddenly found themselves negotiating between the state and Taiwanese society. The Taipei City Council hurriedly organized a committee to bring calm to the city and seek punishment of the policemen responsible for the conflict. At this time, these representatives limited themselves to discussing problems stemming directly from the incident itself. The committee members wanted policemen and soldiers to return to their barracks, an end to indiscriminate shooting on the streets, the release of those arrested, compensation for damage or injury, and the restoration of communications.[122] Administrator Ch'en Yi appeared to respond positively and promised to punish anyone in the police force guilty of crimes. The organization in Taipei was duplicated throughout the large towns and cities of the island. These groups often cooperated with local youth in order to maintain public order, much as the elite had done immediately following the Japanese surrender.[123] In addition to taking over the functions of the police force, the network of committees attempted to restore communication and transportation—in many ways replacing the government.

During the first days of March, the immediate opportunity presented by the incident and long-term trends of advocating self-government merged, as the Taipei committee expanded both in membership and goals. It grew into an organization made up of prominent Taiwanese from all levels of assemblies on the island—district, city, and provincial—as well as representatives elected to the National Assembly. What became known as the February 28 Incident Settlement committee also included prominent Taiwanese from other walks of life. Officials from the provincial government participated in the first few meetings. The committee became the focal point for negotiations with the state. Its representatives met with Ch'en during the first days of March, each time moving further toward urging fundamental political reforms under the rubric of self-government.[124] Many of their demands were similar to those articulated during the Japanese-era or in the post-retrocession press and Provincial Consultative Assembly. Although some political leaders, particularly *pan-shan-jen,* attempted to moderate Taiwanese demands, passions ran high. By March 4, government officials participating in the Settlement committee were no longer welcome.

During the first week of March, events spun out of control. After a disorderly public meeting, on March 6 the Settlement committee drafted a set of requests known as the Thirty-two Demands. The committee members called for reforms including the election of mayors and district magistrates, greater Taiwanese representation in the provincial administration (including government bureaus, courts, and police), abolition of the trade and monopoly bureaus, and that Taiwanese not be drafted to fight in the mainland's civil war. In a chaotic meeting the next day, ten additional far-reaching demands were added, such as the abolition of the Administrator's Office and Garrison Command and greater Taiwanese control over the military forces on the island.[125] When provincial assemblyman and head of propaganda for the Settlement committee Wang T'ien-teng, chairman of the Provincial Consultative Assembly Huang Ch'ao-ch'in, and other prominent Taiwanese presented the demands to Ch'en Yi on February 7, the administrator became visibly angry. Many members of the committee realized that they had overstepped themselves and feared that military reinforcements were en route from the mainland. The next day they repudiated much of the previous day's statement, especially the sections that called for Taiwanese control over the police or military. They also admitted that the demands had not been discussed thoroughly and that the government had met their initial requests for police restraint. The Taiwanese themselves were divided on what course of action to follow. Although most of the committee emphasized that order had been restored and that they did not wish to expand the incident, a few prominent Taiwanese called for armed struggle against the Nationalists.[126]

The state answered the challenge presented by the Taiwanese takeover and political demands with force. On March 8, Nationalist reinforcements from the mainland arrived in the northern port city of Keelung (Chi-lung), then in the southern port of Kao-hsiung. The troops reasserted the government's control by indiscriminately shooting anyone on the streets. Ch'en declared martial law throughout the island and announced that the committee was illegal, stating that it had become part of a revolt. With few exceptions, resistance quickly collapsed—Taiwanese were poorly armed and lacked a unified command. Furthermore, most islanders never sought a pitched battle with mainland forces because their goals were essentially reformist, not revolutionary. Nevertheless the state targeted prominent Taiwanese for arrest or execution. By March 13, even as the island returned to Nationalist control, the government embarked upon a movement to "exterminate traitors" *(su chien)*—rounding up Taiwanese who may have offended anyone in the government. This was accompanied by the "clearing of the villages" *(ch'ing hsiang)* campaign, where troops and police hunted down those involved in the incident who had fled the cities.[127] Now, the state moved ahead with decolonization at gunpoint. Ch'en Yi outlawed Japanese-language materials and phonograph records and ordered the confiscation of Japanese military uniforms, flags, and other items from the colonial era.[128] As soldiers spread terror through the island, they crushed the Taiwanese as a political force that could advocate change outside the Nationalist state or Kuomintang party structure.

Even today, there exists a heated debate over the incident and its aftermath.[129] When were the troops ordered to the island? How many people were killed? Some scholars have deemed Taiwanese political demands for self-government essentially irrelevant, claiming that the Nationalists had decided to send troops from the mainland—which Ch'en Yi had promised not to do—as early as February 2.[130] Ch'en was still talking with the Taiwanese even as the first troops arrived in Keelung. Another theory is that agents from Ch'en Yi or the central government infiltrated the Settlement committee meetings and agitated for the strident demands in order to justify a crackdown later.[131] Such conspiratorial theories attribute greater cohesion and coordination to the Nationalists than actually existed. Perhaps the Nationalists saw the February 28 committee and its activities as a rebellion that became an opportunity to crush opposition on the island. Officials on Taiwan first ignored the crisis, then exaggerated it, in order to cover up their own inability to prevent the conflict or reach compromise with the Taiwanese.[132]

Estimates of the number killed range from ridiculously low (500) to high (100,000). Those who have closer ties to the Nationalist government provide lower figures for the dead and injured, while supporters of Taiwan independence insist on higher numbers. One common estimate is 10,000 killed and 30,000 wounded.[133] The most detailed English-language account of the incident provides a figure of 8,000 dead.[134] Although knowing whether 5,000, 10,000, or more died is important for understanding the scope of this massacre, it is also worth asking who was killed and what impact this had upon later political activity. Many of those who criticized the state and promoted self-government after the retrocession died, fled, or were frightened into silence.[135] For example, Wang T'ien-teng, a vocal critic of the provincial administration and advocate of greater autonomy, was taken away by police, doused with gasoline, and burned to death. Those arrested included Kuo Kuo-chi, a provincial assemblyman who strongly advocated expanded self-government. All together, two members (of thirty) of the Provincial Consultative Assembly were killed and five others arrested, while four members of the Taipei City Council died and seven were jailed.[136]

Now, the state alone defined the Japanese legacy, which it placed at the core of evaluations of the February 28 incident. Yang Liang-kung, head of the Supervisory Yuan for Fukien and Taiwan, reported on the incident for the central government. According to him, two important causes of this uprising were Taiwanese misunderstanding of the motherland (China) and the poisonous Japanese legacy.[137] Yang focused blame on criminals, youth with Japanese military training, students, Japanese who remained on the island, and Communists. He also pointed to "evil politicians" and former members of Japan's Imperial Loyalty groups—a clear reference to many members of the Taiwanese political elite.[138] Yang's interpretation represented an extension of the perceptions many mainlanders had of Taiwanese before the incident. Editorials stated that those who had called for more democracy in early March 1947 were despicable traitors acting purely in their own interests. They also warned that some evil conspirators remained hidden.[139] This interpretation of the February 28 incident reminded the Taiwanese that their Japanese-era experience represented a liability and that their political standing and personal safety were tenuous.

The February 28 incident was a watershed in the island's modern political history. It marked the defeat of the Taiwanese attempt to implement concrete policies—under the broad heading of self-government—that reflected their ambiguity toward mainland China and its representative, the Nationalist government. The process of decolonization essentially came to a close in early March 1947 as many of the Taiwanese most likely to use the Japanese era as a basis for evaluating the Nationalists or promoting self-government were killed or cowed into silence. Now, the state dominated debate over the colonial legacy and thus prevented its application as a justification for political reform.

Post–February 28: Reform, Repression, and Retreat

Self-government as the Taiwanese had envisioned it was dead. The Nationalist state now managed political debate and change from the top down, with little concern for the requests of the Taiwanese. Government policies became relatively easy to implement since few people dared voice open opposition. Criticism of the state in the press became muted, as outspoken Taiwanese had disappeared and the most independent publications were banned or forced out of business. Emphasizing a pattern that would define the relationship between the government and the Taiwanese until the 1980s, the islanders' political aspirations were largely ignored or suppressed while economic development received a great deal of attention.

The state did carry out several minor reforms in response to the incident and resulting U.S. unease over Nationalist misrule. On April 22, 1947, the Nanking government announced that Taiwan would have a regular provincial government under Governor Wei Tao-ming. Ch'en Yi was recalled to the mainland to take a post in Chekiang.[140] Upon his arrival in May, Wei announced four policies: (1) to lift martial law, (2) to conclude the "clearing villages" campaign, (3) to remove controls over communications, and (4) to implement currency reform to limit inflation.[141] The Taiwanese, minus the most vocal advocates of self-government, held slightly more posts in the provincial government and state-controlled enterprises.[142] Also, a Provincial committee was created to provide advice on the administration of the island. Seven of fifteen committee members were Taiwanese.[143] This body, however, had little formal power or informal influence over the state. The Nationalists acted to gain support in two other areas. The Taiwanese enjoyed better health care through the Taiwan Provincial Health Department. No cases of plague or cholera were reported after 1948 because of compulsory vaccinations, effective quarantines, and improved sanitation.[144] Wei also relaxed slightly the written policy on speaking or publishing in Japanese. The colonial language, however, remained closely tied to political issues.[145]

The state focused on economic development even as it quashed Taiwanese political aspirations. Wei stated that one principle of his administration would be to move Taiwan "from stability to prosperity." In mid-1948, a *Kung-lun-pao* editorial said that, especially when compared to the situation on the mainland, Taiwan enjoyed stability *(an-ting)*. Concerning prosperity *(fan-jung)*, however, there had been only slight progress over the previous year.[146] Although most of the problems that led to the February 28 incident awaited resolution, Taiwanese criticism was muted and requests for change were made with much less force than before. For example, the Taiwanese remained concerned over the role of mainlanders and the government in the island's economy. They complained that, through various "mysterious reasons" *(mo ming ch'i miao)*, the government sold the island's products at low prices to mainland buyers. They also urged that, other than mining companies with direct military importance, public enterprises be privatized.[147] Some progress was noted in increasing Taiwanese investment in the match and chemical industries, but printing enterprises had been sold to mainlanders.[148] On the other hand, the vice-chair of the Provincial Consultative Assembly, Li Wan-chu, one of the most prominent non-Kuomintang political figures, pointed out that the Taiwanese lacked the capital to purchase these state enterprises. Thus, selling major companies like the Taiwan Sugar Corporation could only increase the economic influence of outsiders.[149]

One newspaper editorial hinted at the new political environment after the February 28 incident, writing that the dispute over the disposition of Japanese property had changed from a hot war *(jeh chan)* to a cold war *(leng chan)*. Although less was said in public, people still submitted requests for assistance in recovering property to the city and provincial assemblies, while a special committee established to sort out these claims made little progress.[150] The issue came to closure, though not in the way Taiwanese would have wished. In early December 1948, the Taiwan High Court upheld an earlier ruling by a Tainan court invalidating all transfers of Japanese property made after August 15, 1945.[151] This meant that much of the property sold by the Japanese to Taiwanese at the end of the war belonged to the state.

The government carried out a variety of measures to consolidate its control and make clear the limits of acceptable political discourse. These policies included nationwide acts like the declaration of Temporary Provisions for Mobilization for the Period of Suppressing Rebellion, as well as tighter controls over movement to and from Taiwan, and the implementation of household registration and identification cards.[152] Police carried out arrests in February 1948 to prevent protests marking the February 28 incident.[153] To keep students under control, the government placed mainland Chinese in leadership positions at Taiwan's universities.[154] Reflecting the pressures of all-out civil war on the mainland, communism joined Japanization as the primary enemies of the state. For example, in December Governor Wei announced that criticism of the Nationalists was prompted by the Communists and Taiwan independence activists, most of whom had fled to Japan.[155] An editorial entitled "Opposing the Government and Commenting on Politics" defined the scope of tolerable debate. "Opposing" threatened the existence of the nation's people (as defined by the government) and was equated with support for the Communists or that which benefited them. "Commenting" pointed out errors of the government and was done in the interest of the people.[156] The police and military determined the difference between commenting and opposing.

The bloody aftermath of the February 28 incident made clear the penalties for running afoul of the Nationalists—the Taiwanese were now much more cautious in their political activity. Although occasional violence between mainlanders and islanders occurred, organized resistance or revolts approaching the scale of early 1947 did not recur. In the Provincial Consultative Assembly, the political elite avoided issues that could antagonize the state. In July 1948, an editorial stated euphemistically that, in order to be taken seriously, members had to avoid empty talk and raising issues that were impossible to resolve.[157] Now, the Taiwanese focused on individual officials and their actions, not the administrative structure or self-government. For example, members of the Provincial Consultative Assembly attacked the head of the Transportation Bureau, Ch'en Ch'ing-wen, and his subordinates in the Railroad Bureau, saying he fostered an atmosphere of corruption and exclusion of Taiwanese "one hundred times worse than the plague."[158] The solution offered, however, was the removal of a few officials, not systematic change.

In the clearest sign of state confidence in its control—reflecting the decline of Japanese influence and success at government-controlled reintegration—the provincial government began to move forward with its own program for local self-government in 1948. The state set the agenda and limits on these discussions by rejecting provincial self-government (changing the relationship between Taiwan and the central government) while promoting its version of local self-government at the city, town, or district level.[159] The state made clear that self-government outside its own program was synonymous with seeking independence from China.[160] The press, now more tightly controlled by the authorities, emphasized that the state-sponsored self-government in no way sought to weaken the island's links to the mainland government—completely the opposite of the vision held by Taiwanese.[161] The process started with meetings sponsored by the Civil Administration Office to train cadres in the Nationalist program of local self-government.[162] In early July 1948, the Taiwan Provincial Local Self-Government Association was created under government auspices. Chaired by the head of the Civil Administration Office, it included leading members of the Kuomintang and government officials, as well as the commander of the Taiwan Garrison. The state placed this activity in the context of a broader program of "citizenship training" for the Taiwanese and the newly promulgated constitution for the Republic of China.[163] The Japanese legacy was no longer a justification for self-government. Now the Taiwanese would have to earn the state's version of local self-government by assimilating into the Nationalist Chinese political order.

Even as the government consolidated its domination over political reform and debate, conditions on Taiwan worsened because of the Nationalists' military, administrative, and financial collapse on the mainland.[164] More than thirty-one thousand refugees per week fled to Taiwan during November 1948. This increased to approximately five thousand people, mostly troops and officials, arriving each day by New Year's Day 1949.[165] The evacuation continued through 1950. As the Nationalists began to flee the mainland, Taiwanese complained that "Taiwan was number three" *(T'ai-wan ti san)*—the island became the third most desirable destination for mainlanders: They claimed that the wealthiest and most influential refugees moved to the United States, and others with money went to Hong Kong.[166] Refugees from the mainland exacerbated crime, unemployment, and food and housing shortages. Rampant inflation, sparked by the mainland's civil war, devastated Taiwan. It was an atmosphere of "spending money as soon as one possesses it" *(yu ch'ien ch'u ch'ien)* as mainlanders flooded the island with increasingly useless currency.[167] As early as July, Nationalist authorities had strengthened regulations against hoarding grain.[168] Even the Nationalist press had to admit that chaos on the mainland led to "panic purchases" of food in the early fall of 1948.[169]

Increasingly, the Republic of China and Taiwan province overlapped. By late 1948, it was becoming clear that the island would be one of the last redoubts of the Nationalists. As a result, fewer Taiwanese resources were sacrificed for the mainland struggle. The government stopped exporting food and other commodities from the island on October 27, thus easing shortages and relieving inflation. Also, the ridiculously low prices mandated by the central government were widely ignored, thus giving merchants an incentive to sell goods.[170] Chiang, planning his retreat and ever mindful of potential rivals, moved to strengthen his hold over Taiwan by replacing Wei with a long-time ally.[171] The central government announced the appointment of Ch'en Ch'eng as governor on December 30, 1948.[172] Based on Ch'en's slogan of "the people are on top, the people's livelihood comes first" *(jen-min chih shang, min-sheng ti yi),* local self-government and economic reconstruction were to be top priorities.[173] In reality, local self-government was a sham. The system finally implemented in 1950 and 1951 mandated new assemblies at the provincial level and below. These bodies had little power and lacked control over government administration or budgets.

Conclusion

After the retrocession, the Taiwanese had hoped that local self-government—a position between formal independence and complete assimilation—would enable them to move successfully through the processes of decolonization and reintegration. Growing dissatisfaction with Nationalist rule strengthened the Taiwanese people's emphasis upon maximizing their autonomy within a larger political entity, reinvigorating the most important political movement of the colonial era. When urbanites briefly wrested control of Taiwan from the provincial administration in early 1947, the elite used the opportunity to pursue its long-term political agenda. This attempt to reconcile the Japanese legacy of seeking self-government with the reality of Nationalist rule failed disastrously. After the February 28 incident, the state controlled not only the pace and scope of reforms to the island's administration, it even dominated how those changes were discussed. By 1948, the Nationalists had redefined local self-government in their own interests. The eventual implementation of limited reform in the early 1950s reflected the Nationalists' confidence in their ability to prevent dissent and engage in state building from the top down.

The 1945–48 period taught a harsh lesson to the Taiwanese elite. They learned to focus on local issues, not national-level policies or systematic change to the provincial administration. In particular, after the February 28 incident discussion of topics such as weakening Taiwan's ties to the central government or the positive aspects of Japanese colonial rule (a justification for demanding reform) became dangerous. For example, the fate of Wang T'ien-teng served as a warning to the elite. Through the press and Provincial Consultative Assembly, he strongly criticized the state and advocated expanded self-government, often comparing aspects of the new regime unfavorably with the old. Wang became too visible a challenge because of his role in the February 28 Incident Settlement committee and was killed in early March 1947.

Taiwanese power vis-à-vis the mainlander-dominated government was weakened not only by oppression but also by divisions among the island's elite. Some Taiwanese, particularly half-mountain people, generally avoided the topic of the Japanese legacy and did not strongly advocate expanded local self-government. These men often built upon their pre-1945 relationship with the Nationalists. For example, Huang Ch'ao-ch'in was a success in the Nationalist state, party, and economy. He served as chairman of the Provincial Consultative Assembly for more than twenty years and steadily moved up the Nationalist Party hierarchy. Huang also held important posts in several banks and state enterprises. His success can be attributed in part to the fact that he clearly placed national (or Nationalist) prerogatives ahead of provincial ones. His views of Taiwan's relationship with the mainland and local self-government closely matched the state's. During his long tenure in the provincial-level body, he did little to expand the powers of that body vis-à-vis the central government. This is not to suggest that a relatively powerful figure such as Huang lacked any constituency or legitimacy among the Taiwanese. However, he focused on the distribution of benefits from the state, not on issues involving systematic change such as self-government.

A few islanders, such as Li Wan-chu and Kuo Kuo-chi, managed to remain active in politics outside the Nationalist party and state structures. Although Li held the posts of vice-chair of the Provincial Consultative Assembly, then representative to the National Assembly, his actual influence over concrete policies was limited. His main venues for advocating change were the small (and powerless) China Youth Party and newspapers such as *Kung-lun-pao*. During his tenure at this newspaper he generally placed his criticism of the Nationalist government and calls for reform in the context of anticommunism and the future of China. Li's political activity became as much part of a broader movement led by prodemocracy liberals from mainland as it was specifically Taiwanese. Kuo Kuo-chi relied upon his immense popularity in Kao-hsiung, a major city in southern Taiwan, for his political influence. He spent his career in the Provincial Consultative Assembly, carefully attempting to represent what he believed were the Taiwanese people's interests, without incurring the wrath of the government. His arrest and harassment at the hands of the Japanese served to "protect" Kuo after the retrocession—whatever his political positions, mainlanders could not accuse him of collaboration, much less "Japanization."

Japan became home for a community of Taiwanese who found that they could not live under Chiang's government. To these people, the burdens of reconciling Taiwan's colonial experience with the immediate problems of Nationalist rule made remaining on the island untenable. Some agitated for the island's perma-

nent independence from China and the overthrow of the Nationalist regime. For
example, immediately after the retrocession, Liao Wen-yi (Thomas Liao) did not
call for independence, but he did stress the need for Taiwan to remain insulated
from the chaos of the mainland's civil war. Nationalist misrule and personal
setbacks, however, pushed him toward a more radical position.[174] After moving
to Tokyo, Liao became among the most visible leaders of the independence
movement.

Some moderate Taiwanese who had advocated self-government, such as Lin
Hsien-t'ang, dropped out of politics. During the Japanese era, he embodied the
ambivalent relationship between the Taiwanese and their colonizers. Although
reconciled to living under colonial rule, Lin did not attempt to assimilate culturally into the empire—he did not learn Japanese, as many of the elite had. He was
a leader in political movements designed to increase the Taiwanese voice in
governing the island. At the same time, Lin participated in the self-government
institutions created by the governor-general and was even named to the Japanese
House of Peers. After Japan's surrender, Lin led activities welcoming the new
government and was soon elected to the provincial and national assemblies. He
had been eager to work with the Nationalist government, but soon became discouraged and retreated from public life. Lin's economic success and relatively
cooperative relationship with the Japanese raised mainlanders' suspicions. In
1946 Lin was briefly listed as a traitor by the Nationalist government. Further,
the elected assemblies in which he participated proved to have little influence
over the government. By the late 1940s his image became that of an elder
statesman—generally venerated but powerless when compared to half-mountain
Taiwanese or mainlanders. Finally, the promise of rent reduction and land reform
threatened his economic well-being. In 1949 Lin emigrated to Japan, ostensibly
for medical treatment, and died there in 1955.[175]

The state had cleared a path for innovative policies to promote development
that is today characterized as an "economic miracle." Few prominent Taiwanese
would dare oppose measures such as rent reduction and land reform, even if they
did not think that it was in their best economic interests.[176] In the political realm
the Nationalists blocked any change in the relationship between the state and
Taiwanese society. Restrictions on civil society grew in scope and severity as
Chiang Kai-shek and the remnants of his defeated army retreated to the island,
beginning a "White Terror" in 1949.[177] Thousands of Taiwanese and recently
arrived mainlanders were killed, arrested, or intimidated for their alleged ties to
the Communists. The Korean War and resulting U.S. support for Chiang's regime was the final step in solidifying the relationship between the Taiwanese and
the Nationalist Chinese government, creating a pattern that would exist largely
unchanged for almost forty years. Although mainlanders represented a minority
on the island, the Nationalist government had no fear of overthrow by the Taiwanese. It was not until the 1980s that the Taiwanese could safely advocate a
political agenda of their own. Economic development and resulting social

change enlarged a middle class that increasingly pressured the state for democratic reform. Also, Taiwanese gradually came to dominate the Nationalist Party and government from the inside—thus making both institutions more amenable to the interests of the island's people.

Notes

1. The Nationalist government (Kuo-min cheng-fu) established the Republic of China (Chung-hua min-kuo). Almost all important figures in the government were members of the Nationalist Party (Kuomintang).

2. The recent work done by scholars on Taiwan is invaluable, and this chapter reflects their contributions. Because of the sensitivity of this era, historians on Taiwan published little about the immediate postwar period until political reform began in the late 1980s. After the Nationalist government lifted martial law in 1987, wide-ranging reforms included the relaxation of controls over the press, speech, assembly, and political opposition. A subsequent series of elections led to the replacement of legislators and National Assembly members (most of whom had been elected on the mainland in the late 1940s). In late 1994, elections were to elect the provincial governor and mayors of the two largest cities (Taipei and Kao-hsiung) and, in March 1996, the president. The most visible manifestation of the new political and academic environments was the creation of the Institute of Taiwan History within the Academia Sinica, the premier research institution in the Republic of China. Other new organizations devoted to researching the island's history include the Taiwan Materials Center at the Taiwan Provincial Branch of the National Central Library and the Wu San-lien Foundation's Taiwan Historical Materials Center. The research commission created under the auspices of the central government to study the February 28 incident also serves as an example of a more open attitude by the government. Several interesting overviews of recent trends in the historiography of Taiwan are in the *Free China Review*, 42, no. 3 (March 1992) and 44, no. 2 (February 1994). For an excellent Chinese-language discussion of the changing nature of Taiwan historiography and its connection to the political environment, see Chang Yen-hsien, "T'ai-wan-shih yen-chiu te hsin ching-shen" [The new spirit of Taiwanese historical research], *T'ai-wan shih-liao yen-chiu*, 1 (February 1993): 76–86.

3. Although their experiences in the Japanese empire varied widely, the people of Taiwan, Korea, the Philippines, Vietnam, Burma, British Malaya, the Dutch East Indies, and large parts of mainland China all faced difficult transitions after World War II. In the case of Taiwan, the length of Japan's rule (a half-century) made its process of decolonization far more problematic. In much of East and Southeast Asia, the collapse of the Japanese empire marked the beginning of a new (and successful) stage of long-running struggles against Western imperialism. In other cases, civil war or agrarian revolutionary movements ensued. For brief overviews of Japanese colonialism and its aftermath in Asia, see Franz Ansprenger, *The Dissolution of the Colonial Empires* (New York: Routledge, 1989); Raymond F. Betts, *Uncertain Dimensions: Western Overseas Empires in the Twentieth Century* (Minneapolis: University of Minnesota Press, 1985); and David Joel Steinberg, ed., *In Search of Southeast Asia,* rev. ed. (Honolulu: University of Hawaii Press, 1987).

4. In many ways, the history of the Taiwanese relationship with the state during the immediate postwar period represents an examination of collective memory and how it shaped—both consciously and unconsciously—political activity. This chapter focuses on the collective memory formed by the Taiwanese political elite. As Patrick Hutton wrote, "Collective memory is an elaborate network of social mores, values, and ideals that marks

out the dimensions of our imaginations according to the attitudes of the social groups to which we relate. It is through the interconnections among these shared images that the social frameworks (*cadres sociaux*) of our collective memory are formed, and it is within such settings that individual memories must be situated if they are to survive" (*History as an Art of Memory* [Hanover, NH: University Press of New England, 1993], 78). One of the premier historians of memory, Maurice Halbwachs, wrote that "collective frameworks are . . . precisely the instruments used by the collective memory to reconstruct an image of the past which is an accord, with the predominant thoughts of the society" (*On Collective Memory*, trans. and ed. Lewis A. Coser [Chicago: University of Chicago Press, 1992], 40).

5. "Taiwanese" are Han Chinese who had emigrated to Taiwan before 1945. Most had come from provinces along the southeastern coast of the mainland during the Ch'ing dynasty (1644–1911) but before the Japanese occupation in 1895. Taiwan is sometimes called Formosa, which is Portuguese for "beautiful." Although this term has become less popular in recent years, the Taiwanese are also known as Formosans. Traditionally, the Taiwanese have been divided into two main groups, Hokkien and Hakka. The southern Min people from Fukien are often called Hokkien or *Fu-lao* (Old Fukienese). They constitute about 85 percent of the Taiwanese population. They can be subdivided into two groups named for the areas of Fukien from which many immigrated to Taiwan: Chang-chou and Ch'uan-chou. The coastal cities of Hsia-men (Amoy) and Foochow were also important sources of migrants to Taiwan. The smaller group is the Hakka, also called *K'e-chia-jen* or *Yueh-min* (Yueh is a traditional term for Kuangtung). These people came from the highlands of Kuangtung (often Ch'ao-chou prefecture). "Mainlanders" are Chinese who came to the island after 1945, the majority arriving between late 1948 and mid-1950 as the Nationalist government faced defeat at the hands of the Chinese Communists. The other two groups are the aborigines (*yuan-chu-min*), who comprise about 2 percent of the population. They are not Han Chinese, but are most closely related to the island peoples of Southeast Asia.

6. As one of the last parts of China settled and brought into the Middle Kingdom, the island was more weakly tied to the central government and dominant Confucian culture than other areas populated by Han peoples. Taiwan's historical ties to the mainland are a source of great academic debate on Taiwan today.

7. October 25, Retrocession Day, is an official holiday on Taiwan. The term retrocession (*kuang-fu*) has strong political implications. It stresses the restoration of Chinese sovereignty over lands temporarily taken away by foreigners. Thus, *kuang-fu* presupposes the legitimacy of the Nationalist government's rule over Taiwan. Others use the term *chieh-shou*, which means "to receive" or "to take over" and lacks the emphasis on political legitimacy. This paper uses retrocession because it is still the most commonly understood term.

8. In particular, two scholars on Taiwan have explored the continuity of political aspirations before and after 1945. Cheng Mu-hsin (Cheng Tzu), *T'ai-wan i-hui cheng-chih ssu-shih-nien* [Forty years of Taiwan assembly politics] (Taipei: Tzu-li wan-pao wen-hua ch'u-pan-she, 1987); and Li Hsiao-feng, *T'ai-wan chan-hou ch'u-ch'i te min-i tai-piao* [Representatives of the popular will in immediate postwar Taiwan] (Taipei: Tzu-li wan-pao ch'u-pan-she, 1993).

9. Some supporters of Taiwanese independence (*T'ai-tu*) go to great lengths to show a long-term drive for permanent and formal separation from the mainland. Although a few Taiwanese did seek independence immediately after the war, their influence was more limited than these authors claim. Examples of this approach include Peng Ming-min, *A Taste of Freedom: Memoirs of a Formosan Independence Leader* (New York: Holt, Rinehart and Winston, 1972); and Shih Ming, *T'ai-wan-jen ssu-pai-nien shih* [A Four-hundred-year history of the Taiwanese] (Taipei: n. p.). Shih Ming's massive history of

Taiwan emphasizes that the Nationalists were imperialists no different from the Dutch, the Manchus of the Ch'ing era, or the Japanese. Li Hsiao-feng, however, has researched the life histories of ten independence activists and makes a convincing case that this movement really began in the late 1940s. Although their understanding of the island's long-term history was important, he emphasized that leaders of the movement were motivated by specific grievances against the Nationalist government that arose after the retrocession. Li Hsiao-feng, "Kuo-chia jen-t'ung te chuan-hsiang: i chan-hou T'ai-wan fan-tui jen-shih te shih ke ke-an wei li" [The shift of national identity: Ten postwar Taiwanese as case studies], in *Jen-t'ung yu kuo-chia: Chin-tai Chung-Hsi li-shih te pi-chiao* (Nan-kang: Chung-yang yen-chiu-yuan chin-tai-shih-suo, 1994), 323–362.

10. One failed alternative to the reformist program of self-government was radical social and political revolution led by a communist party. The Chinese Communist Party has claimed that it played an active role in leading a revolutionary struggle on Taiwan immediately after the retrocession. In reality, while some leftists or supporters of communism were present at that time, they did not have a major influence. Communism never took root because of Japan's effective repression coupled with its ability to provide the colony some measure of material progress and stability, thus limiting support for radical change. However, a small communist movement did exist on the island. The radicalization of some Taiwanese students in Japan or the mainland during the 1920s was key to the creation of the Taiwanese Communist Party (TCP). The TCP, organized in Shanghai in 1928, was to be a branch of the Japanese Communist Party (JCP) but "seek guidance from the CCP (Chinese Communist Party)." The Taiwanese party was constantly torn between the CCP, the JCP, and Taiwanese nationalist factions. In 1930, the TCP was put under the control of the CCP because of the JCP's weakness. The Japanese proved very effective in arresting TCP members on the island, and the party almost completely disappeared after 1937. After World War II Communists on Taiwan remained weak and factionalized. The most detailed English-language articles on the TCP are Frank Hsiao, "A Political History of the Taiwanese Communist Party, 1928–1931," *Journal of Asian Studies*, 42, no. 2 (March 1983): 269–289; and Lawrence Sullivan, "The Chinese Communist Party and the Status of Taiwan, 1928–1943," *Pacific Affairs*, 52, no. 3 (1979): 446–467. The most detailed Chinese-language account is Lu Hsui-yi, *Jih-chu shih-tai T'ai-wan kung-ch'an-tang shih, 1928–1932* [A history of the Taiwan Communist Party during the Japanese era, 1928–1932] (Taipei: Ch'ien-wei ch'u-pan-she, 1989). Many mainland books attempt to put the Communist Party in the center of conflict between the Taiwanese and Nationalist China. For example, see Wu Yuan, ed., *Taiwan de guoqu he xianzai* [Taiwan's past and present] (Beijing: Tongyu duwu chubanshe, 1954); Li Zhifu, *Taiwan renmin geming douzheng jianshi* [A brief history of the Taiwanese people's revolutionary struggle] (Guangzhou: Huanan renmin chubanshe, 1955); and Su Hsin, *Wei-kui te T'ai-kung tou-hun: Su Hsin tzu-chuan yu wen-chi* [The Taiwanese Communist spirit who will not return: The autobiography and writings of Su Hsin) (Taipei: Shih-pao wen-hua ch'u-pan ch'i-yeh yu-hsien kung-ssu, 1993).

11. Another sensitive issue is how to refer to the events of early 1947—incident? popular uprising? rebellion? massacre? Each term implies a political agenda. For the purposes of this chapter, "incident," a relatively neutral term, is used. For more information on this topic, see the translator's introduction in Yang I-chou, *2–28 min-pien: T'ai-wan yu Chiang Chieh-shih* [The February 28 popular uprising: Taiwan and Chiang Kai-shek], trans. from the Japanese by Chang Liang-tse (Taipei: Ch'ien-wei ch'u-pan she, 1991), 13–16.

12. Under the Ch'ing dynasty (1644–1911), China was ruled by a minority people who originally came from an area today called Manchuria or Northeast China (*Dongbei*).

13. For an overview of Taiwan's development, see Samuel P.S. Ho, *Economic Devel-*

opment of Taiwan, 1860–1970 (New Haven: Yale University Press, 1978). The same author places the island's experience in a comparative perspective in "Colonialism and Development: Korea, Taiwan, and Kwantung," in *The Japanese Colonial Empire, 1895– 1945*, ed. Ramon H. Myers and Mark R. Peattie (Princeton: Princeton University Press, 1984). Trends of economic growth and development were not entirely absent during the late Ch'ing period. As is the case with studies of the mainland, a lively academic debate exists over the genesis of modernization on the island. A comprehensive overview of Taiwan's economic and political development during the late Ch'ing is in Li Kuo-ch'i, *Chung-kuo hsien-tai-hua te ch'u-yu yen-chiu: Min-Che-T'ai ti-ch'u, 1860–1916* [Modernization in China: A regional study of the Fukien, Chekiang, and Taiwan region, 1860– 1916] (Nan-kang: Chung-yang yen-chiu-yuan chin-tai-shih yen-chiu-suo, 1982). For the best review of theories explaining Taiwan's economic development, see Sung Kuang-yu, "Li-shih wen-hua lun te t'i-ch'u" [Presenting theories of history and culture], in T'ai-wan ching-yen: Li-shih ching-chi p'ien, ed. Sung Kuang-yu (Taipei: Tung-hai ta-hsueh, 1993), 1–65. The author posits that the commercial culture and trade networks that existed on Taiwan since large-scale migration to the island in the 1600s were the keys to the island's economic development.

14. The stories and reminiscences of Wu Cho-liu are important source material for understanding Taiwan's experience of oppression, material progress, and ambiguity under both Japanese and Nationalist rule. See Wu Chuo-liu, *Ya-hsi-ya te ku-erh* [Asia's orphan] (Taipei: Ts'ao-ken ch'u-pan shih-yeh yu-hsien kung-ssu, 1995); *Wu-hua-kuo: T'ai-wan ch'i-shih-nien te hui-hsiang* [The fig: Looking back at Taiwan over seventy years] (Taipei: Ch'ien-feng ch'u-pan-she, 1993); and *T'ai-wan lien-ch'iao: T'ai-wan te li-shih chien-cheng* [Taiwan forsythia: Witness to Taiwan's history] (Taipei: Ch'ien-feng ch'u-pan-she, 1988).

15. The original law was replaced by Law 31 in 1907. In 1921, this became Order No. 3. The powers of the governor-general changed relatively little over fifty years and "Law 63" became the term used most frequently for this system. For an overview of Japanese colonial policies, see Huang Chao-t'ang, *T'ai-wan tsung-tu-fu*, trans. from the Japanese by Huang Ying-che [The Taiwan governor-general's office] (Taipei: Ch'ien-wei ch'u-pan-she, 1994).

16. The focus for much of this chapter is the Taiwan provincial elite. This group could also be called a "subelite" as they held a position below the national elite under both Japanese and Nationalist rule. They represent a political elite, but not necessarily a governing or positional elite. In other words, although they were involved in political activity and attempted to play a role in shaping government policies, they did not necessarily hold formal elected or appointed posts. Their role as middlemen between Taiwanese society and a central government was based upon their leading positions in social networks on the island—thus displaying the characteristics of a functional elite. They typically worked as doctors, reporters, teachers, managers in trade or light industry, or landlords. Most had education above the high school level. Their political activity focused on issues at an islandwide level, not that of a single city or district. Some Taiwanese did travel to the mainland and made their careers with the Nationalist government. Upon their return to the island in 1945, they too became part of the political elite. Unlike other Taiwanese, however, their influence depended less upon their role in society (a functional elite) than upon formal state posts (a positional elite). Ch'en Ming-t'ung, in his examination of provincial assembly candidates, explains that the elite's influence stemmed from its power to control the distribution of resources. Resources include the personal (political power, social authority, and personal resources) and the nonpersonal (natural resources, capital, and financial resources). Ch'en Ming-t'ung, "Wei-ch'uan cheng-t'i hsia T'ai-wan ti-fang cheng-chih ching-ying te liu-tung (1945–1986): Sheng-ts'an-i-hui-yuan chi sheng-i-hui-

yuan liu-tung te fen-hsi" [Fluidity of the Taiwanese elite under authoritarian rule (1945–1986): An analysis of fluidity of Taiwan provincial assembly members] (Ph.D. dissertation, National Taiwan University, 1990). For more information on the issue of elite definition, see William A. Welsh, *Leaders and Elites* (New York: Macmillan, 1977).

17. For overviews of elite formation under the Japanese, see Wu Wen-hsing, *Jih-chu shih-ch'i T'ai-wan she-hui ling-tao chieh-ts'eng chih yen-chiu* [Research into the Taiwanese elite of the Japanese era] (Taipei: Cheng Chung shu-chu, 1992); and Chen Ching-chih, "The Impact of Japanese Colonial Rule on the Taiwanese Elite," *Journal of Asian History*, 22, no. 1 (1988): 25–51.

18. See Patricia Tsurumi, *Japanese Colonial Education in Taiwan* (Cambridge: Harvard University Press, 1977); and Patricia Tsurumi, "Colonial Education in Korea and Taiwan," in Myers and Peattie, eds., *The Japanese Colonial Empire*, 275–311.

19. Paul K.C. Liu, "Economic Development and Population in Taiwan Since 1894: An Overview," in *Essays on the Population of Taiwan* (Taipei: Academia Sinica Population Papers, 1973), 11.

20. Tsurumi, "Colonial Education," 92.

21. Tsurumi, *Japanese Colonial Education,* 255.

22. The majority of the students, however, were the children of Japanese residents of the island. Today, this institution is National Taiwan University.

23. Organizations created by the Taiwanese to further their interests under colonial rule included the Taiwan Cultural Society, the New Taiwan Alliance, the Taiwan Assembly Petition Movement, and the Taiwan Masses Party. For detailed information on Japanese-era political activity, see Ts'ai P'ei-huo et al., *T'ai-wan min-tsu yun-tung-shih* [A history of the Taiwanese national movement] (Taipei: Tzu-li wan-pao wen-hua ch'u-pan-she, 1971); Lien Wen-liao, *T'ai-wan cheng-chih yun-tung-shih* [A history of Taiwanese political movements], ed. Chang Yan-hsien and Weng Chia-in (Taipei: Tao-hsiang ch'u-pan-she, 1988); Chou Wan-yao, *Jih-chu shih-tai te T'ai-wan i-hui she-chih ch'ing-yuan yun-tung* [The Taiwan Assembly petition movement of the Japanese era] (Taipei: Tzu-li wan-pao wen-hua ch'u-pan-she, 1989); and Wu, *Taiwan she-hui ling-tao chieh-ts'eng*. In English see George Kerr, *Formosa: Licensed Revolution and the Home Rule Movement, 1895–1945* (Honolulu: University Press of Hawaii, 1974); and Edward Chen, "Formosan Political Movements Under Japanese Colonial Rule, 1914–1937," *Journal of Asian Studies*, 31, no. 3 (May 1972): 477–497.

24. Taishō democracy refers to the period after the accession of the Taishō emperor in 1912, when political parties and the Diet (National Assembly) were relatively powerful in comparison to the military, the Privy Council, and the *genrō* (elder statesmen from the Meiji era). This period was marked by greater demands for public participation in politics.

25. An earlier islandwide group had been made up solely of Japanese officials. It was somewhat analagous to a cabinet.

26. Primary source material on the drive for self-government includes Yang Chao-chia, "Tai-wan ti-fang tzu-chih chih-tu" [Taiwan's system of local self-government], in *T'ai-wan ti-fang tzu-chih wen-t'i* [Problems in Taiwan's local self-government] (Tokyo: Shinminsha, 1928); and numerous articles and editorials in magazines and newspapers published by the Taiwanese including *Taiwan, Taiwan minpō*, and *Taiwan shinminpō* (*T'ai-wan min-pao* and *T'ai-wan hsin-min-pao* in Chinese).

27. As would be the case after 1945, the Taiwanese often used the adjective "local" (Chinese: *ti-fang;* Japanese: *chihō*) to describe the type of self-government they sought. To islanders, "local" included greater autonomy at the islandwide level and below.

28. For details on Japanese wartime mobilization, see Lai Tse-han, Ramon Myers, and Wei Wou, *A Tragic Beginning: The Taiwan Uprising of February 28, 1947* (Stanford: Stanford University Press, 1991), 26–49; and Huang, *T'ai-wan tsung-tu-fu*, 182–193.

29. Huang, *Taiwan tsung-tu-fu,* 253. For information on the Taiwanese role in the Japanese military, see "Programs and Personnel of Japan on Formosa: Extracts from Short Wave Radio, Tokyo and Affiliated Stations from December 1941 to March 15, 1944," OSS/Honolulu, April 19, 1944, "U.S. Military Intelligence on Japan (1918–1941)," University Publications of America microfilm; and "Certain Aspects of the Formosan–Japanese Relationship," Allied Translator and Interpreter Section, South West Pacific Area Research Report 223, March 31, 1945, "U.S. Military Translations of Japanese Broadcasts and Documents," CIS *microfilm.*

30. When the Japanese faced defeat at the hands of the Allies, they held out the promise of increased local autonomy in order to buttress Taiwanese support. In 1945, the Japanese announced plans for equal salaries and treatment for Taiwanese and Japanese officials on the island. The government in Tokyo also selected three Taiwanese for membership in the House of Peers and announced plans for Taiwanese representation in the Diet. The same defeat on the battlefield that spurred these measures, however, prevented their implementation.

31. For the most detailed account of the planning and implementation of Nationalist policies regarding the takeover of Taiwan, see Cheng Tzu, *Chan-hou T'ai-wan te chieh-shou yu ch'ung-chien: T'ai-wan hsien-tai-shih yen-chiu lun-chi* [The takeover and reconstruction of postwar Taiwan: A collection of essays on modern Taiwanese history] (Taipei: Hsin-hua t'u-shu, 1994).

32. J. Bruce Jacobs estimates that during the early 1940s one hundred thousand Taiwanese lived in China. Most lived in Japanese-occupied areas as merchants, soldiers, students, and low-level officials in the occupying administration. These Taiwanese appeared to have few emotional or political ties to China. J. Bruce Jacobs, "Taiwanese and the Chinese Nationalists, 1937–1945: The Origins of Taiwan's 'Half-Mountain People,' " *Modern China,* 16, no. 1 (January 1990): 89–118. Between 1940 and 1942, six groups of Taiwanese on the mainland allied to form the Taiwanese Revolutionist League, a loose coalition under Kuomintang auspices. Presaging future conflicts between the Taiwanese and the Nationalist government, the league was held together by anti-Japanese sentiment, not a single plan for postwar Taiwan. "Taiwanese Revolutionary Movements," "Taiwanese Independence Movements, 1683–1956," National Archives, Department of State Records, RG 59, Office of Intelligence Research, August 8, 1956, IR 7203, 6.

33. Many of these men fled because of conflicts with the Japanese. The term half-mountain people (*pan-shan-jen*) comes from the fact that Taiwanese referred to the mainland as the "Tang mountains" (*T'ang shan*). Mainlanders were often called "*Ah shan.*" ("Ah" is a prefix to a term of address.) The term *pan-shan-jen* was not merely descriptive; it was often a normative judgment of the suspect loyalties of Taiwanese with close ties to the Nationalists.

34. In order to emphasize the ties between their government and the Taiwanese, the Nationalists have stressed that many Taiwanese fled to the mainland and actively worked with the Chungking government. For example, see Chang Jui-ch'eng, ed., *T'ai-chi chih-shih tsai tsu-kuo te fu-T'ai nu-li* [Taiwanese fighters' endeavor on the motherland to recover Taiwan] (Taipei: Kuomintang tang-shih-hui ch'u-pan-she, 1990); and Chang Jui-ch'eng, ed., *K'ang-chan shih-ch'i shou-fu T'ai-wan chih chung-yao yen-lun* [Selected important documents on recovering Taiwan] (Taipei: Kuomintang tang-shih-hui ch'u-pan-she, 1990).

35. Some scholars suggest that Taiwan underwent its own Meiji Restoration under Japanese rule. Following the overthrow of the Tokugawa bakufu by court nobles and samurai, administration of Japan was returned to the emperor, who adopted the reign name of Meiji (Enlightened Rule) in 1869. The Restoration marked the beginning of a wide-ranging program of modernization led by the central government. Li Hsiao-feng,

Tao-yu hsin t'ai-chi: ts'ung chung-chan tao 2–28 [The island's new birthmark: From the end of the war to the February 28 incident] (Taipei: Tzu-li wan-pao wen-hua ch'u-pan-she, 1993), 80.

36. An important primary source that discusses the swirl of rumors and uncertainty of the interegnum is the diary of Ikeda Toshio, "Chan-pai hou jih-chi" [Diary after defeat in war], trans. Ryō Sogyōmi, *T'ai-wan wen-shu,* 85 (November 1983): 179–196. The complete Japanese version is available in Ikeda Toshio, "Haisen nikki" [Diary of defeat in war], *Taiwan Kingendaishi kenkyū,* 4 (1982): 59–108.

37. Wu Hsin-jung, *Wu Hsin-jung jih-chi: Chan hou* [The diaries of Wu Hsin-jung: Postwar] (Taipei: Yuan-ching ch'u-pan shih-yeh kung-ssu, 1981), 3–7.

38. Han Shih-ch'uan, *Liu-shih hui-i* [Memoirs of sixty years] (Tainan: Han Shih-ch'uan hsien-sheng shih-shih san-chou chi-nien chuan-chi pien-yin wei-yuan-hui, 1966), 63.

39. See Yeh Jung-chung, "T'ai-wan kuang-fu ch'ien-hou te hui-i" [Memories of Taiwan's retrocession] , in *T'ai-wan jen-wu ch'un-hsiang* [A portrait of Taiwanese], ed. Li Nan-heng and Yeh Yun-yun (Taipei: Shih-pao wen-hua ch'u-pan ch'i-yeh yu-hsien kung-ssu, 1995), 400–435. Yeh was an assistant and confidant to Lin Hsien-t'ang, and later became important in political and cultural circles in his own right after the retrocession.

40. Taiwanese had many reasons for disliking the police, both Japanese and Taiwanese, at the end of the war. In addition to enforcing criminal codes, police managed household registration, price controls, and sanitation regulations. They also monitored Taiwanese political activity—harassing and arresting those seen as a threat to the colonial administration.

41. Some seemed to accept wholeheartedly Taiwan's assimilation into Nationalist China. For example, Huang Ch'ao-ch'in, a Japanese- and American-educated half-mountain person who became mayor of Taipei, then chairman of the Provincial Assembly in 1946, clearly subordinated the island and its experience to the mainland. In his writings, he focused on his Chinese identity and accurately pointed out that the mainland had suffered the hardships of war far more than had Taiwan. In general, Taiwanese with looser ties to the mainland echoed allegiance to the ultimate goal of mainland rule, but did not stress the inequality of suffering. Huang Ch'ao-ch'in, "Tsai chien-kuo yun-tung chung T'ai-pei shih-min tui-yu tzu-yu chi shou-fa ying-yu chih jen-shih" [What Taipei citizens should know about freedom and respect for the law in the movement for national reconstruction], *T'ai-wan hsin-sheng-pao,* November 28, 1945, 1. On the other hand, there is ample evidence that a few Taiwanese sought the island's independence immediately after World War II. Most accounts focus on the activities of Ku Chen-fu. He and a few others with close ties to the Japanese attempted to cooperate with Japanese military officers to work for independence. Little came of their efforts, as the governor-general opposed this endeavor. Ku and others were arrested after the war. For a generally sympathetic account of Ku Chen-fu and his father, see Shen Tz'u-chia and Chang Chueh-ming, *Ku Chen-fu chuan* [Biography of Ku Chen-fu] (Taipei hsien: Shu-hua ch'u-pan shih-yeh yu-hsien kung-ssu, 1993).

42. "*Chang-kuan,*" translated here as administrator, is sometimes rendered "governor-general" (Chinese: *tzung-tu;* Japanese: *sōtoku*), the same term used for the top official on the island during the colonial era. Ch'en Yi's full title was T'ai-wan-sheng hsing-cheng chang-kuan (Taiwan province adminstrative executive).

43. Nationalist misrule was by no means confined to Taiwan. For an overview of the Nanking government's failure to obtain or hold support on the mainland after World War II, see Suzanne Pepper, *Civil War in China: The Political Struggle, 1945–1949 (*Berkeley: University of California Press, 1978).

44. "Chung–Mei ho-tzo ching-ying: T'ai-wan lu yeh" [Sino–American cooperative management: Aluminum in Taiwan], *Kung-lun-pao,* February 7, 1948, 2.

45. By 1945, the U.S. Navy and Army Air Corps were regularly bombing the island. The aerial assault focused primarily upon Taiwan's harbors, which contained ships and supplies vital for the Japanese war effort in Southeast Asia and China, but also targeted industrial targets such as sugar refineries and transportation links including railway stations and airfields.

46. At the end of the war, about 488,000 Japanese remained on the island: 322,000 civilians and 166,000 soldiers and sailors. Huang estimates that as many as 200,000 planned to stay on Taiwan for an indefinate period because of rice shortages and uncertainty about their future in Japan. By early 1946, however, they began to return home because of declining public order and orders from Governor-General Ch'en Yi. It was only in mid-1947 that the last Japanese technical experts returned to Japan. Huang, *T'aiwan tsung-tu-fu*, 254–257.

47. In 1946 poor weather was also a factor, as a major typhoon hit the island in September, reducing agricultural production and damaging industrial facilities.

48. Ch'en Yi and the Nanking government were in frequent conflict over the management of Taiwan and its resources. It is difficult to determine whether Ch'en's desire to limit the central government's influence was based upon his concern for the welfare of the Taiwanese or upon factional rivalries among top Nationalist leaders. For background on Ch'en's views of economic development, see Chang Fu-mei, "Ch'en Yi yu Fu-chien sheng-cheng (1934–1941)" [Ch'en Yi and the provincial government of Fukien (1934–1941)], in *2–28 Erh-erh-pa hsueh-shu yen-t'ao-hui lun-wen-chi* (Taipei: 2–28 Erh-erh-pa min-chien yen-chiu hsiao-tsu, 1991), 9–26.

49. Sun Yat-sen (1866–1925) was revered by the Chinese Nationalists and Communists alike. His political ideology, known as the Three Principles of the People (San-min chu-i) stressed nationalism, democracy, and people's livelihood (a program based primarily upon land reform and a large state role in the economy).

50. Ting Wen-chih, "Ch'en chang-kuan lun 'guan-liao tzu-pen'" [Administrator Ch'en discusses 'bureaucratic capital'], *Ho-p'ing jih-pao*, August 1, 1946, 2; and August 2, 1946, 3.

51. One American report stated: "Now that the Japanese are to be eliminated, the Formosans anticipate an opportunity to return to full control and ownership of their private businesses." "Conditions in Formosa," State Department Report, March 15, 1946, National Archives, State Department Records, Record Group 59, 894A.00/3–1546 (hereafter, cited as RG 59). See also "Report on Current Public Opinion in Formosa, November 23, 1945," RG 59, 894A.00/1–2846. William Kirby has examined Taiwan's retrocession from the perspective of the central government and the provincial economy. He writes: "Policies were pursued from a national agenda that was not one of 'plunder' but of planned nationalization and economic 'synchronization.' The policies may have been ill-conceived and the state industries ill-managed; and certainly from that perspective, 'nationalization' seemed much more like 'expropriation.' Given Taiwan's initial place in national economic planning, which was one of relatively low priority, it is likely that the Nationalist policies would result in a lowering of Taiwan's standard of living" ("Planning Postwar Taiwan: Industrial Policy and the Nationalist Takeover, 1943–1947," Harvard Studies on Taiwan, Papers of the Taiwan Studies Workshop, Volume 1 [1995], 297).

52. "Memorandum from Ralph Blake, U.S. Consul in Taipei, to J.L. Stuart, Ambassador to China," RG 59, 894A.00/8–1246. Possibly as an attempt by merchants to avoid Nationalist monopolies, export controls, and taxes, smuggling occurred among Taiwan, Japan, Okinawa, and the Philippines. This in fact represented a continuation of trade patterns from the Japanese era. Review of press reports in State Department files, RG 59, 894A.00/5–2146. See also "Ralph Blake, American Consul in Taipei, to the Ambassador to China, J.L. Stuart, October 31, 1946," RG 59, 894A.00/10–3146.

53. Li, *Tao-yu hsin t'ai-chi,* 48.

54. Ibid., 32–33.

55. A comprehensive collection of official decrees and other materials on the disposition of Japanese property can be found in Jiau Ho-fang, ed., *Cheng-fu chieh-shou T'ai-wan shih-liao ts'ung-p'ien* [Collection of data on the government's takeover of Taiwan] (Hsin-tien: Kuo-shih-kuan, 1990).

56. Peng, *A Taste of Freedom,* 54.

57. "Hsiao kan k'un" [Little Heaven and Earth], *Min-pao,* February 20, 1946, 2.

58. Li, "Tao-yu hsin t'ai-chi," 51–52. For details on economic reconstruction and inflation during this period, see Yin Nai-p'ing, "T'ai-wan kuang-fu i-lai te wu-chia wen-ting cheng-ts'e" [Policies for price stabilization since Taiwan's retrocession], *Chung-kuo hsien-tai chuan-t'i yen-chiu pao-kao,* 17 (1995): 330–376; and Yen Chen-hui, "T'ai-wan kuang-fu ch'u-ch'i te ching-chi ch'ung-chien ch'u-t'an" [A preliminary investigation of economic reconstruction immediately after Taiwan's retrocession], *Chung-kuo hsien-tai chuan-t'i yen-chiu pao-kao,* 17 (1995): 377–429.

59. For example, by early 1947, a desperate Kao-hsiung city government was blaming profiteers (*chien shang*) for hoarding grain. It also urged that the provincial government act quickly to distribute rice. "Yen-chung ch'u-ti t'un-chi chien shang" [Severely punish hoarding profiteers], *Kuo-sheng-pao,* January 31, 1947, 4.

60. "Conditions on Formosa," RG 59, 894A.00/3–1546. "Pen-shih tsuo fang-i tsung tung-yuan" [Yesterday city began general mobilization against epidemic], *Chung-hua jih-pao,* July 29, 1946, 3.

61. Huang Ying-chu, "Lu Hsun ssu-hsiang tsai T'ai-wan te ch'uan-po, 1945–49: She-lun chan-hou ch'u-ch'i T'ai-wan te wen-hua ch'ung-chien yu kuo-chia jen-t'ung," [The transmission of Lu Hsun's thought on Taiwan, 1945–49: A discussion of cultural reconstruction and national identification in immediate postwar Taiwan], in *Jen-t'ung yu kuo-chia: chin-tai chung-hsi li-shih te pi-chiao* (Nan-kang: Chung-yang yen-chiu-yuan chin-tai shih yen-chiu suo, 1994), 301–322.

62. The May Fourth movement began when the warlord government that controlled Peking accepted the humiliating Twenty-one Demands from the Japanese in 1919. Intellectuals, students, and others took to the streets to protest imperialism and warlord rule. Although quickly crushed by China's militarists, the movement was a key step in radicalizing youth, increasing resistance to imperialism, sparking a broad social and cultural critique of traditional China, and speeding the spread of politically motivated colloquial literature (New Culture movement).

63. During the 1920s some young Taiwanese became familar with the authors of the May Fourth era, including Lu Hsun. Understanding and readership of Lu Hsun was limited on Taiwan, however, and Chinese publications were forbidden by the Japanese after 1937.

64. Huang, "Lu Hsun ssu-hsiang," 304–317.

65. Hsu himself was criticized by other Kuomintang members who tied him to Lu Hsun's leftist ideology. After the February 28 incident, there was little discussion, much less state promotion, of Lu Hsun. His works were forbidden after 1950. Hsu himself was relieved of his post after Ch'en Yi left Taiwan in 1947. Huang, "Lu Hsun ssu-hsiang," 317–318.

66. For a comprehensive overview of the language policies of the Nationalist government on Taiwan during this period, see Hsu Hsueh-chi, "Taiwan kuang-fu ch'u-ch'i te yu-wen wen-t'i" [The language problem in immediate post-retrocession Taiwan], *Ssu yu yen,* 29, no. 4 (December 1991): 155–184.

67. This body had powers to advise and consult (the Nationalists often used the words

interpellate—*tzu-hsun*), but not legislate. The *ts'an-i-hui* should not be confused with a *ts'an-i-yuan*, a national-level legislative body usually translated as "senate."

68. Hsu "Yu-wen wen-t'i," 166–168.

69. Ibid., 173. For example, editorials in pro-Nationalist newspapers claimed that certain "beautiful young gentlemen" who persisted in using Japanese had a problem with their mentality (*hsin li*)—namely, that Japanese education had reduced their nationalist spirit. This was deemed a great disgrace to the Taiwanese. "Ta-chia tou chiang kuo-yu" [Everyone speak Chinese], *Chung-hua jih-pao*, October 2, 1946, 1.

70. Hsu "Yu-wen wen-t'i," 184.

71. Ch'en Ming-t'ung, "P'ai-hsi cheng-chih yu Ch'en Yi chih T'ai lun" [A discussion of political factions and Ch'en Yi's rule of Taiwan], in *Taiwan kuang-fu ch'u-ch'i li-shih,* ed. Lai Tse-han (Nan-kang: Chung-yang yen-chiu-yuan Chung Shan jen-wen she-hui k'o-hsueh yen-chiu-so, 1993), 353–355. See also Ch'en Ts'ui-lien, *P'ai-hsi tou-cheng yu ch'uan-mou cheng-chih: 2–28 pei-chu te ling-i mien-hsiang* [Factional struggles and power politics: The other face of the February 28 tragedy] (Taipei: Shih-pao wen-hua ch'u-pan-she, 1995). The Political Science Clique (also called the Political Study Clique) included many administrative or technical experts who had been educated in Japan or the United States. They gave less importance to anticommunist ideology and one-party rule than did the C-C Clique. The C-C Clique was named for its two most powerful members, brothers Ch'en Li-fu and Ch'en Kuo-fu. This clique represented a combination of Leninist organization, support from Chinese secret societies, violent anticommunism, and strong nationalism. Americans described (perhaps mistakenly) the Political Science Clique as "progressive" and "oriented toward Western democracies." This was true when Political Scientists were compared to other groups, such as the C-C Clique. Chiang Kai-shek was dependent upon the C-C Clique for control of the Nationalist Party.

72. Most of Ch'en's subordinates formed ties with him during his study in Japan or Germany, or during his tenure as chairman in Fukien province from 1934 to 1941.

73. *Ah hai*, meaning "one of the sea," contrasts with mainlanders—*ah shan* (mountain). See note 33 for a short explanation of *pan-shan-ren* and *ah shan.*

74. Taichung is a large city in central Taiwan.

75. Historian Lin Heng-tao states in his oral history: "Upon his arrival on Taiwan, Ch'en Yi supported a certain level of freedom of expression and permitted newspapers to reflect some practical questions." (Ch'en San-ching and Hsu Hsueh-chi, *Lin Heng-tao hsien-sheng fang-wen chi-lu* [A record of a visit with Mr. Lin Heng-tao] [Nan-kang: Chung-yang yen-chiu-yuan chin-shih yen-chiu-so, 1992], 75).

76. For example, a reporter for the *Ho-p'ing jih-pao* was arrested in late 1946, prompting some Taiwanese to demand guarantees for freedom of the press. Ch'en Yi responded that this freedom should be protected in accordance with law, but that he hoped that reporters would cooperate with provincial administration, spread government decrees, and build a new Taiwan. "Cheng-fu tzu-yu ho-fa pao-chang" [Government to guarantee accordance with the law], *Ho-p'ing jih-pao*, November 23, 1946, 3.

77. "Memorandum from Ralph Blake, U.S. consul in Taipei, to J.L. Stuart, ambassador to China," RG 59, 894A.00/1–3147.

78. This newspaper was one of the most important voices for Taiwanese outside the Nationalist ranks. It was published until government pressure and financial problems forced it to close in mid-1946.

79. "Wang T'ien-teng wen-tzu huo-an kao-fa-yuan hsuan-p'an wu tsui" [High court determines that no crime was committed in the Wang T'ien-teng case], *Kuo-sheng-pao,* January 31, 1947, 3. "Wang T'ien-teng an yu chuan-chi" [A turning point in the Wang T'ien-teng case], *Ho-p'ing jih-pao*, January 29, 1947, 3. Wang was not the only prominent Taiwanese harassed by the state. Chiang Wei-ch'uan, former president of the Taipei

Chamber of Commerce with ties to the C-C Clique, was sued for libel by the provincial government under Ch'en Yi. Chiang's ties to the mainland-based faction may also have been a factor in his being named as a conspirator in the wake of the February 28 incident. Ch'en, "P'ai-hsi cheng-chih," in Lai, ed., *Taiwan kuang-fu ch'u-ch'i*, 355–356.

80. Li, *Tao-yu hsin t'ai-chi*, 25–27.

81. They were Taipei mayor Yu Mi-chien, Hsin-chu magistrate Liu Ch'i-kuang, and Kao-hsiung mayor Hsieh Tung-min. Sung Fei-ju, a half-mountain person who disappeared during the February 28 incident, held the second most important post in the provincial government's Education Office.

82. Lai et al., *A Tragic Beginning*, 65.

83. *2–28 shih-chien wen-hsien chi-lu* [Historiographical records of the February 28 incident] (Taipei: T'ai-wan-sheng wen-hsien wei-yuan-hui, 2–28 shih-chien wen-hsien chi-lu chuan-an hsiao-tsu, 1991), 13–14.

84. Wu Nai-te and Ch'en Ming-t'ung, "Cheng-ch'uan chuan-i ho ch'ing-ying liu-tung: T'ai-wan ti-fang cheng-chih ch'ing-ying te li-shih hsing-ch'eng" [The transfer of political power and elite fluidity: The historical form of Taiwanese local political elite], in *T'ai-wan kuang-fu ch'u-ch'i li-shih, ed.* Lai Tse-han (Nan-kang: Chung-yang yen-chiu-yuan Chung Shan jen-wen she-hui k'o-hsueh yen-chiu-so, 1993), 318–323.

85. For more information on the workings and powers of the Provincial Assembly, see Li Hsiao-feng, *T'ai-wan chan-hou ch'u-ch'i te min-i tai-piao* [Representatives of the popular will in immediate postwar Taiwan] (Taipei: Tzu-li wan-pao ch'u-pan-she, 1993); and Cheng Tzu, *Chan-hou T'ai-wan i-hui yun-tung-shih chih yen-chiu: pen-t'u ching-ying yu i-hui cheng-chih* (1946–1951) [Research into the history of the postwar Taiwan Assembly movement: Native elites and representative politics (1946–1951)] (Taichung: Cheng Tzu, 1993).

86. "Since the late nineteenth century, many Chinese both hated Western imperialism and admired many Western ways. Similarly, a number of Taiwanese resented their status as colonial subjects while simultaneously appreciating many Japanese ways, liking many Japanese individuals, taking for granted the validity of many Japanese values and perspectives, and feeling superior to Chinese without these values" (Lai et al., *A Tragic Beginning*, 47).

87. Chou Hsien-wen, "Ju-ho k'an T'ai-wan?" [How should Taiwan be seen?], *T'ai-wan hsin-sheng-pao,* June 9, 1946, 1.

88. "Chien-she T'ai-wan hsin wen-hua" [Establishing Taiwan's new culture], *T'ai-wan hsin-sheng-pao*, November 6, 1945, 2. This publication was managed by Lee Wan-chu, a Tainan native who studied in France and Shanghai before moving to the mainland to work with the Nationalists. He was forced out of his post in 1947. He then began to publish *Kung-lun-pao*, one of the few newspapers on the island that took a relatively independent stance toward the government. Lee also served as an elected official and leader of the China Youth Party. Because he was not a member of the Kuomintang, his influence on policy was minimal.

89. "T'ai-wan te t'e-tien" [The particularities of Taiwan], *T'ai-wan hsin-sheng-pao*, July 5, 1946, 1.

90. Li, *Tao-yu hsin t'ai-chi*, 94–105. In particular, the Taiwanese interest in the activities of the Provincial Assembly and the strong views of some members were portrayed portrayed as extremist and exclusionary of those from outside the province. "Sheng ts'an-i-hui pi-mu" [Closing of the Taiwan Provincial Assembly], *Min-pao*, May 16, 1946, 1.

91. Lee Wan-chu, "T'ai-wan min-chung ping-mei yu Jih-pen-hua" [The Taiwanese masses certainly have not been Japanized], *Cheng-ching-pao*, 2, no. 3 (February 10, 1946): 4. This magazine was established in October 1945 under chief editor Su Hsin, an anti-Japanese activist and leftist labor organizer who had been jailed by the Japanese in

the 1930s. He eventually fled the Nationalist police for the mainland in the late 1940s. He also edited *Jen-min tao-pao* and other short-lived publications after the retrocession.

92. "T'ai-wan wei ch'ang 'nu-hua' " [Taiwan has not been enslaved], *Min-pao,* April 7, 1946, 1.

93. Sung Fei-ju, "Ju-ho kai-chin T'ai-wan wen-hua chiao-yu (shang)" [How to improve Taiwan's cultural education (part I)], *Jen-min tao-pao*, January 11, 1946, 1.

94. Sung Fei-ju, "Ju-ho kai-chin T'ai-wan wen-hua chiao-yu (hsia)" [How to improve Taiwan's cultural education (part II)], *Jen-min tao-pao*, January 12, 1946, 1.

95. *Kōminka* (Chinese: *huang min hua*) literally means "becoming a person of the emperor." It was a long-term colonial program to turn the Taiwanese into full citizens of Japan. On Taiwan, the program focused on the promotion of Japanese language and culture, as well as loyalty to the emperor.

96. Ting Wen-chih, "Fang Sung Fei-ju fu-ch'u-chang" [A visit with Vice Chief Sung Fei-ju], *Ho-p'ing jih-pao,* July 4, 1946, 2. Sung was executed in the wake of the February 28 incident.

97. Taiwanese who had lived in Japanese-occupied areas of the mainland had first-hand knowledge of the Nationalists' defects and greater affinity for the colonial administration. As a result, their criticism of the state's efforts at reintegration came earlier and was stated more forcefully than that of other Taiwanese. *Hsin T'ai-wan* (New Taiwan), a magazine published in early 1946 by Taiwanese stranded in North China, contained information about views of the mainland, Taiwan, and their relationship. Some of the more than 3,000 Taiwanese in North China at the end of World War II organized and wrote this journal. In addition to students, teachers, and businessmen, this figure included bureaucrats of the shattered Japanese colonial empire. Fang Hao, "Hung Yen-ch'iu hsien-sheng fang-wen-chi" [A record of an interview with Mr. Yen-ch'iu Hung], in *Chin-hsien-tai T'ai-wan k'ou-shu li-shih* [Modern Taiwan oral history] (Taipei: Lin Pen-yuan Chung-hua wen-hua chiao-yu chi-chin-hui, 1991), 8.

98. "Ch'uang-k'an tz'u" [Inaugural issue statement], *Hsin T'ai-wan 1* (February 15, 1946): 2.

99. Che Yeh (pseud.), "T'ai-wan-jen te hu-huan" [A Taiwanese call for help], *Hsin T'ai-wan* 1 (February 15, 1946): 6.

100. Wang Pai-yuan, "Kao wai-sheng-jen chu-kung" [To all mainland gentlemen], *Cheng-ching-pao* 2, no. 2 (January 25, 1946): 1–2.

101. "Wai-sheng-jen wen-t'i" [Problems with those from outside the province], *Jen-min tao-pao*, May 9, 1946, 1.

102. *2–28 shih-chien wen-hsien chi-lu*, 13–14.

103. Wang T'ien-teng, "Sheng-ts'an-i-ui te ch'ien-wan-yen" (Some words about the Provincial Assembly], *Hsin hsin* 6 (1946): 4.

104. Wang Shih-ching, "Ch'en Feng-yuan hsien-sheng fang-wen chi-lu" [A record of an interview with Ch'en Feng-yuan], in *Chin-hsien-tai T'ai-wan k'ou-shu li-shih* (Taipei: Lin Pen-yuan Chung-hua wen-hua chiao-yu chi-chin-hui, 1991), 161.

105. Li, *Tao-yu hsin t'ai-ch*i, 30–35.

106. Su Hsin, "Chu-i, chi-kou, jen-wu" [Isms, structures, and people], *Cheng-ching-pao* 2, no. 3 (February 10, 1946): 6.

107. Li, *Tao-yu hsin t'ai-chi*, 94–105.

108. "Su-ch'ing tou-ou chih feng" [Exterminate the trend of brawling], *Chung-hua jih-pao*, June 25, 1946, 1.

109. Hsieh Nan-kuang, "Kuang-ming p'u-chao hsia te T'ai-wan" [A Taiwan with a promising future shining down upon it], *Cheng-ching-pao* 1, no. 4 (November 25, 1945): 6–7.

110. He left the island with his family shortly after the Japanese occupation in

1895. Ch'iu built his political career in Kuangtung province, on the southeast coast of China. Ch'iu became a member of the Nationalist government's Control Yuan Committee and the Kuomintang Provincial Party Committee.

111. Ch'iu Nien-t'ai, "Jen-shih T'ai-wan fa-yang T'ai-wan" [Understanding and enhancing Taiwan], *T'ai-wan hsin-sheng-pao*, March 6, 1946, 2. Ch'iu reiterated these points in many of his interviews and writings. "Ch'an-ming T'ai-jen wu Han-chien" [Clarifying that Taiwanese are not traitors], *Jen-min tao-pao*, March 9, 1946, 2.

112. Li was a Taipei-born leftist who wrote for various newspapers in Shanghai. He returned to Taiwan at least once after the retrocession.

113. Li Ch'un-ch'ing, "Chung-kuo cheng-chih yu T'ai-wan" [Chinese politics and Taiwan], *T'ai-wan p'ing-lun*, 1, no. 1 (July 1, 1946): 4–5.

114. "Tui shih-chu fa-piao cheng-chien" [Expressing political views on the current situation], *T'ai-wan p'ing-lun*, 1, no. 3 (September 1, 1946): 6–9.

115. *T'ai-wan-sheng ts'an-i-hui ti-i-chieh ti-i-ts'u ta-hui t'e-chi* [Special record of the first session of the first Taiwan Provincial Assembly] (Taipei: T'ai-wan-sheng ts'an-i-hui mi-shu-ch'u, 1946); and *T'ai-wan-sheng ts'an-i-hui ti-i-chieh ti-erh-ts'u ta-hui t'e-chi* [Special record of the second session of the first Taiwan Provincial Assembly] (Taipei: T'ai-wan-sheng ts'an-i-hui mi-shu-ch'u, 1946).

116. On February 1, the Peking–Tientsin railway link was temporarily cut by the Red Army and on February 23, the Communists resumed their offensive along the Sungari river. The Nationalists later considered January 1947 the beginning of the Communists' "all-out rebellion." China Handbook Editorial Board, *China Handbook, 1950* (New York: Rockport Press, 1950), 189.

117. Student protests around the New Year, 1947, in Peking, Shanghai, and Nanking were sparked by the alledged rape of a Peking University student by two U.S. Marines. Youth broadened their activity to include criticism of the Nationalist government, which was closely tied to the Americans. *Handbook, 1950*, 122.

118. A crowd of four thousand marched to the nearby city government offices, holding banners saying: "Request the government restrain rice prices." "Mi-shang pi-men hang-shih wen-luan" [Rice market closes, market in disorder], *Ho-p'ing jih-pao*, February 14, 1947, 3.

119. Most of the activity connected to the February 28 incident was limited to the towns and cities of Taiwan. In the countryside, which had a smaller government presence, tensions were lower until Taiwanese scattered in the face of Nationalist reinforcements in early and mid-March 1947. Taiwanese scholar Li Hsiao-feng points out that in 1946 there were several small incidents similar to that which sparked the February 28 incident. These conflicts, however, occurred in rural areas and did not expand. Li, *Tao-yu hsin t'ai-chi*, 69–73.

120. Tobacco was one of the products taxed and controlled by a state monopoly.

121. Li, *Tao-yu hsin t'ai-chi*, 113–120, has a short description of the incident and its aftermath in various towns and cities on the island. See also Lai et al., *A Tragic Beginning*, 99–139.

122. Li, *Tao-yu hsin t'ai-chi*, 120–121. Leighton Stuart to President Chiang Kai-shek, April 18, 1947, "Memorandum on the Situation in Taiwan," reprinted in *United States Relations with China, with Special Reference to the Period 1944–1949* (Washington, DC: Department of State, 1949), 928.

123. Li, *Tao-yu hsin t'ai-chi*, 123.

124. For a more detailed account of self-government and the February 28 incident, see Teng K'ung-chao, "Ts'ung 2–28 shih-chien k'an min-chu yu ti-fang tzu-chih te yao-ch'iu" [Looking at demands for local self-government and democracy from the February 28 incident], *Tang-tai* 34 (February 1, 1989): 66–79; and Ch'en Fang-ming, "Chan-hou

ch'u-ch'i T'ai-wan tzu-chih yun-tung yu 2–28 shih-chien" [The immediate postwar movement for self-government and the February 28 incident], in *2–28 hsueh-shu yen-t'ao-hui lun-wen-chi* (Taipei: 2–28 min-chien yen-chiu hsiao-tsu, 1992), 141–166.

125. An English-language version of the demands is in Lai et al., *A Tragic Beginning*, 197–200.

126. Li, *Tao-yu hsin t'ai-chi*, 150–151.

127. Ibid., 180–185.

128. For an overview of the attempt to promote Mandarin Chinese in the wake of the incident, see Hsu, "Yu-wen wen-t'i," 176–182.

129. A "taxonomy" of political agendas and understandings of the history of the incident is provided by Hou K'un-hung, "2–28 shih-chien yu-kuan shih-liao yu yen-chiu chih fen-hsi" [An analysis of historical materials and research related to the February 28 incident], *Chung-kuo hsien-tai-shih chung-t'i yen-chiu pao-kao*, 16 (1994): 332–388. By far the most comprehensive history of the incident in English is Lai et al., *A Tragic Beginning*, though George Kerr (*Formosa Betrayed* [Boston: Houghton Mifflin, 1965]) and P'eng Ming-min (*A Taste of Freedom*) provide first-person accounts in the context of their support for the island's independence.

130. For a brief review of Ch'en Yi's meetings with various Taiwanese and his possible role in the massacre of early March 1947, see Li, *Tao-yu hsin t'ai-chi,* 129–137. Lai et al. posit that Chiang Kai-shek had decided to dispatch troops to the island on March 5. Lai et al., *A Tragic Beginning*, 142–151.

131. Li, *Tao-yu hsin t'ai-chi*, 153.

132. Wu Wen-hsing, "2–28 shih-chien ch'i-chien kuo-min cheng-fu te yin-ying yu chueh-ts'e chih t'an-t'ao" [An investigation of the nationalist government's reaction and policies during the February 28 incident], in Lai, ed. *T'ai-wan kuang-fu ch'u-ch'i*, 107–126.

133. Historian Li Hsiao-feng's estimate does not include those caught up in the "clearing villages" campaign, which lasted well after the incident and initial Nationalist crackdown. Li, *Tao-yu hsin t'ai-chi*, 189.

134. For a discussion of the various estimates of dead, wounded, and arrested, see Lai et al., *A Tragic Beginning*, 155–164. In May 1947, the Taiwan Garrison Command attempted to minimize the number of casualties, reporting as follows: military officers: 16 dead, 135 wounded, 3 missing; soldiers: 74 dead, 262 wounded, 37 missing; public employees: 64 dead, 1,351 wounded, 8 missing; citizens: 244 dead, 383 wounded, 24 missing. Most of the public employees harmed were Taiwanese. Thirty people were held as the most important criminals from the incident, including Provincial Assemblyman Kuo Kuo-chi. About 500 were arrested and charged with some sort of crime in connection with the incident. "2–28 shih-pien" [The February 28 incident], *Kuo-sheng-pao*, May 28, 1947, 3.

135. Lai, Myers, and Wu estimate that 4,000 of those killed were part of the elite. They define 5 percent of the island's population of 6.5 million as the elite. (*A Tragic Beginning*).

136. For a brief list and analysis of prominent islanders killed in the wake of the incident, see Li Hsiao-feng, *T'ai-wan chan-hou ch'u-ch'i*, 216–224.

137. According to Yang Liang-kung, other contributing factors included inflation and unemployment, improper government policies, some corrupt or incompetent officials, public opinion out of control because of new freedom of the press after fifty years of Japanese control, calls of evil politicians, Communists who wanted to use the uprising for their own agenda, weakness of local military, and letting rebels gain control of radio station. Chiang Yung-ching, Li Yun-han, and Hsu Shih-shen, *Yang Liang-kung hsien-sheng nien-pu* [The chronological bibliography of Yang Liang-kung] (Taipei: Lian-ching ch'u-pan shih-yeh kung-ssu, 1988), 393–399. Lai, Myers, and Wu, *A Tragic Beginning*,

stress that the shortage of Nationalist troops on the island was key to the spread of violence. They state that the provincial government could only call upon five thousand soldiers and eight thousand police to restore control (Lai et al., *A Tragic Beginning*, 65). There is little evidence to back up the Nationalist charge of Communist involvement in the uprising of February and March. Certainly, the Communists welcomed the uprising as it diverted Nationalist resources and provided a propaganda coup. In a few areas, though, the Communists did play an important role in rallying resistance to the Nationalists. Hsieh Hsueh-hung, a Communist, led armed resistance to the Nationalists in central Taiwan. U.S. State Department official George Kerr received a letter from an informant in Taichung mentioning the presence of Hsieh and her attempt to incite violence. The Communists claimed later that a people's government was created in Taichung on March 2, 1947, and that it organized a military force to fight Nationalists. Other alleged representatives of "Taiwan compatriots who participated in the 'February 28' Uprising" claimed that the Communists supplied support and instruction by radio. In March, Hsieh escaped to Hong Kong and formed the Taiwan Democratic Self-Government League. She later went to the People's Republic of China to lead the China Youth League and participate in the Chinese People's Political Consultative Conference. On Communist involvement in the February 28 incident, see "Ralph Black, American Consul in Taipei, to J.L. Stuart, Ambassador in China, February 14, 1947," RG 59, 894A.00/3–1447; Peng, *Memoirs*, 67; Kerr, *Formosa Betrayed*, 278; *Twenty-Sixth Anniversary*, 4, 22; Fred W. Riggs, *Formosa Under Chinese Nationalist Rule* (New York: Macmillan, 1952), 55.

138. Chiang Yung-ching et al., *Yang Liang-kung,* 400–402. Yang's analysis was in fact more moderate than that offered publicly by the Nationalists. For example, Nationalist publications combined the ideas of a poisonous Japanese legacy and a Communist menace, stating: "The recent riots in Taiwan were instigated by Taiwanese Communist members who had during the war been drafted by the Japanese to fight in the South Seas." General Pai Chung-hsi, minister of national defense, blamed the Communists as well as Japanese education, which "gave Taiwan Chinese the wrong idea about their own motherland, the government, the people, and the national army." See *An Infamous Riot: Story of Recent Mob Violence in Taiwan* (Taipei: Taiwan News Service, 1947), 13 and 27.

139. "T'ai-wan min-chu-hua te ch'ien-t'u" [The future of Taiwan's democratization], *Kuo-sheng-pao*, May 2, 1947, 1. Indictments of prominent Taiwanese for their involvement in the February 28 incident continued through the summer of 1947. "Kao-chien-ch'u t'i-ch'i kung-su" [Prosecutor's office submits indictments], *Ch'uan-min jih-pao*, September 15, 1947, 3.

140. In 1949 Ch'en was accused of conspiring with the Communists. He was arrested, brought to Taiwan, and executed in June 1950, much to the delight of many Taiwanese.

141. "Wei chu-hsi hsuan-pu ssu-hsiang chueh-ting" [Chairman Wei announces four decisions], *Chung-hua jih-pao*, May 17, 1947, 1.

142. For example, the chairman of the Provincial Assembly, Huang Ch'ao-ch'in, also become chairman of the First Commercial Bank in 1947.

143. For details on the makeup of the committee, see "Kenneth Krentz, American Consul in Taipei, to the Secretary of State, January 2, 1949," RG 59, 894A.00/1–249.

144. Frederick H. Chaffee, *Area Handbook for the Republic of China* (Washington, DC: Government Printing Office, 1969), 84–85.

145. "Pao-chih hui-fu Jih-wen-pan wen-t'i" [Problems of restoring the use of Japanese in newspapers], *Kuo-sheng-pao*, May 21, 1947, 1. Local officials often went beyond the provincial level regulations. For example, the schools in P'ing-tung county in southern Taiwan mandated a variety of increasing penalties for employees who used Japanese. Tests of ability to speak Mandarin Chinese were given to staff. "T'ui-hsing kuo-yu,

chin-yung Jih-yu, hsiao-yung fang-yen" [Promote Chinese, prohibit Japanese, reduce the use of dialects], *Kuo-sheng-pao*, May 19, 1947, 3.

146. "Tai-cheng i-nien chien-t'ao" [A review of Taiwan's administration over the past year], *Kung-lun-pao*, May 16, 1948, 2. See also "Wei Tao-ming t'an shih-cheng fang-chen" [Wei Tao-ming discusses present policies], *Chung-hua jih-pao*, May 13, 1947, 1.

147. "Taiwan ching-chi te chi-pen wen-t'i" [The basic problems of Taiwan's economy], *Kung-lun-pao*, May 8, 1948, 2.

148. "Pu ch'e-ti te k'ai-fang cheng-ts'e" [An incomplete open policy], *Kung-lun-pao*, December 24, 1947, 2.

149. "Hsien kei sheng ts'an-i-hui ssu-tz'u ta-hui," [For the fourth session of the Taiwan Provincial Assembly], *Kung-lun-pao*, December 1, 1947, 2.

150. "Jih-ch'an fang-she chi-tai ch'u-chih" [People anxiously awaiting handling of Japanese property], *Kung-lun-pao*, August 3, 1948, 3.

151. "T'ing-chih ch'uan-i ch'i-hsien pien-keng" [The time period for ending transfers is changed], *Kung-lun-pao*, December 14, 1948, 3.

152. Lin Te-lung, "Kuo-fu ch'ien-T'ai ch'ien-hou she-hui k'ung-chih chih li-ch'eng" [The process of social control before and after the retreat of the national government to Taiwan], *T'ai-wan shih-liao yen-chiu*, 3 (February 1994): 114–119.

153. Kerr, *Formosa Betrayed*, 349.

154. For example, mainland scholar Fu Ssu-nien became chancellor of National Taiwan University in 1948. He had been a member of the Legislative Yuan and a professor at National Peking University. Although he was often critical of the Nationalists and called for democratic reform, the regime seemed to find mainlanders preferable to Taiwanese in these positions.

155. Kerr, *Formosa Betrayed*, 348.

156. "'Fan-tui cheng-fu' yu 'p'i-p'ing cheng-chih'" [Opposing the government and commenting on politics], *Ch'uan-min jih-pao*, August 5, 1948, 1.

157. "Sheng ts'an-i-hui ti-wu tz'u ta-hui te shih-ming" [The mission of the fifth session of the Provincial Assembly], *Kung-lun-pao*, July 1, 1948, 2.

158. "Ti-pa tz'u hui k'ung-ch'i chin-chang" [Atmosphere of eighth meeting tense], *Kung-lun-pao*, July 9, 1948, 4.

159. "Shih ti-fang tzu-chih chen-ti" [Explaining the real meaning of local self-government], *Ho-p'ing jih-pao*, April 25, 1948, 3.

160. The state made clear the connection between provincial self-government and independence. For example, in June 1947, the indictment of five Taiwanese charged with war crimes and promotion of the island's independence used the terms independence (*tu-li*) and self-government (*tzu-chih*) interchangeably to describe their activities. The five were Hsu Ping, Chien Lang-shan (both of whom had been named to the Japanese House of Peers for their loyalty), Ku Chen-fu, Lin Hsiung-hsiang (named to the governor-general's Consultative Assembly), and Hsu K'un-ch'uan (special agent for the Japanese). They were indicted for "war crimes"—conspiring to make Taiwan independent in concert with Japanese military officers immediately after the surrender. "Yen-ch'ang kung-shan" [Extension granted in public trial], *Kuo-sheng-pao*, June 27, 1947, 3; and "T'ai-chi chan-tsei ch'i-su shu ch'uan-wen" [Taiwan war criminals: Complete text of the indictment], *Kuo-sheng-pao*, June 29, 1947, 3.

161. "Tzu-chih chueh fei t'o-i" [Self-government is absolutely not severing], *Ch'uan-min jih-pao*, April 25, 1948, 3.

162. For example, see "P'ei-chih ti-fang tzu-chih kan-pu" [Cultivate local self-government cadres], *Kung-lun-pao*, July 28, 1948, 3.

163. "Ti-fang tzu-chih hsieh-hui ch'eng-li" [Association for local self-government established], *Kung-lun-pao*, July 9, 1948, 3. "Sheng ti-fang tzu-chih hsieh-hui" [The

Provincial Self-government Association], *Ch'uan-min jih-pao*, July 25, 1948, 3. "Kuan-yu pen-sheng tzu-chih shih-fan-ch'u" [Concerning the province as a model self-government jurisdiction], *Ho-p'ing jih-pao*, April 27, 1948, 2.

164. For a description of the beginning of the Communists' military offensive in late 1948, see "The Ambassador in China (Stuart) to the Secretary of State, September 22, 1948," in *Foreign Relations of the United States: 1948,* vol. 7, *The Far East* (hereafter, cited as FRUS) (Washington, DC: Government Printing Office, 1974), 467.

165. Kerr, *Formosa Betrayed*, 366.

166. In reality, many of the refugees in Hong Kong were poor. The Taiwanese view, however, was based upon the perception of the relative wealth of migrants to each destination.

167. "Tsai t'an tang-ch'ien te wu-chia" [Again discussing current prices], *Kung-lun-pao*, June 30, 1948, 2.

168. "T'ang-chu chia-ch'iang liang-shih kuan-chih" [Strengthen grain controls], *Kung-lun-pao*, July 14, 1948, 3.

169. "Pen-shih fa-sheng mi-liang k'ung-huang" [Rice shortage occurs in city], *Kung-lun-pao*, October 6, 1948, 3.

170. "Memorandum from American Consul Kenneth Krentz to the Secretary of State, October 29, 1948," RG 59, 894A.00/10–2948.

171. In late November Wei, bitter over his conflicts with the crumbling central government, discussed with U.S. officials the possibility of breaking completely from the mainland. "The Consul General at Taipei (Krentz) to the Secretary of State, November 23, 1948," in *FRUS*, 1948, vol. 7, 601. One option in early December 1948 was that Wei and the U.S.-educated General Sun Li-jen would break free of the Nationalists and form an independent Taiwan. The State Department ordered officials in Taipei not to discuss this possibility with Wei. "Memorandum of Conversation with General Douglas MacArthur at Tokyo, December 7, 1948," RG 59, 894A.00/12–748; and "L.F. Craig, Taiwan Regional Office, Economic Cooperation Administration, to Chief of Mission, January 13, 1949," RG 59, 894A.00/1–1349.

172. Ch'en's experience was almost exclusively in the military sphere. He served as commander-in-chief of Chinese forces in Burma (1943–44), minister of war (1944–46), and chief of staff (1946–48) (*Handbook, 1950*, 735). His personal ties to Chiang Kai-shek and Chiang Ching-kuo were much closer than were Wei's. On the same day as Ch'en's appointment, U.S. officials in Nanking reported that Chiang Kai-shek's personal files were being secretly moved to Taiwan, indicating the generalissimo's eventual plans. "Memorandum from Ambassador Stuart to the Secretary of State, December 30, 1948," RG 59, 894A.00/12–3048.

173. "Kai-shan min-sheng shih shou-yao cheng-wu" [Improving the people's livelihood is the first task of the administration], *Kung-lun-pao,* December 31, 1948, 3.

174. See Li, "Kuo-chia jen-t'ung te chuan-hsiang," 323–362.

175. For a brief overview of Lin's postretrocession activities, see Chou, *Jih-chu shih-tai te T'ai-wan yi-hui*, 248–262.

176. For an overview of the impact of rent reduction and land reform upon the Taiwanese rural elite and farmers, see Hou K'un-hung, "Kuang-fu ch'u-ch'i T'ai-wan t'u-ti kai-ko yun-tung-chung te cheng-fu, ti-chu, yu t'ien-nung" [The state, landlords, and farmers in Taiwan's postretrocession land reform], *Chung-kuo hsien-tai-shih chuan-t'i yen-chiu pao-kao*, 17 (1994): 273–329.

177. For a fascinating overview of the white terror as well as a series of oral histories of Taiwanese and mainland refugees arrested in the late 1940s and early 1950s, see Ho Ching-t'ai, *Pai-se tang-an* [White archives] (Taipei: Shih-pao wen-hua ch'u-pan ch'i-yeh yu-hsien kung-ssu, 1991). See also Lan Po-chou, *Pai-se k'ung-pu* [The white terror] (Taipei: Yang-chih wen-hua, 1993).

11

A Bastion Created, A Regime Reformed, An Economy Reengineered, 1949–1970

Peter Chen-main Wang

A view of Keelung Harbor from Zhongzhen Park.

When the Nationalist government retreated to Taiwan in December 1949, its demise seemed imminent. Li Tsung-jen, the acting president, flew to New York seeking medical treatment for a gastric ulcer.[1] Most of the Nationalist armies were either lost on the battlefield or had surrendered to the Chinese Communists.[2] After repeated defeats, the remaining officials, soldiers, and members of the Nationalist Party (Kuomintang, or KMT) that made the journey across the Taiwan strait suffered from low morale. Internationally, the Republic of China (ROC) lost its position as one of the four great powers. Only Korea decided to transfer its embassy to Taiwan, while others either followed the Soviet Union in recognizing the People's Republic of China (PRC) or like the United States, waited until the dust settled before deciding which government to recognize. The following two decades might be considered the most trying period for Taiwan as the Nationalist government tried to rebuild its strength by laying the foundation for what would become the "Taiwan miracle."

The Nationalist Retreat and the Recreation of the ROC: 1949–1952

In late 1949 and early 1950, U.S. policy toward China was very clear. America would not get involved in the Chinese civil war, which seemed to be approaching a quick end. The U.S. State Department was even contemplating the right timing and occasion to recognize the newly founded People's Republic of China. Hence, no military aid was forthcoming, nor would the United States use its military power to defend Taiwan because its loss would not affect vital U.S. interests. Although the Nationalist troops scored several impressive victories on the offshore islands at that time, they were not enough to bring about any change in U.S. policy toward Taiwan.[3] Only after the outbreak of the Korean War on June 25, 1950, did President Harry Truman order the Seventh Fleet into the Taiwan strait to neutralize the conflict. A year later, economic and military aid from the United States to the Nationalist government resumed and a U.S. Military Assistance and Advisory Group was established in Taiwan. The change in U.S. policy toward Taiwan provided the latter with a chance to devote itself to internal reform.

Chiang Kai-shek, who remained head of the KMT, was asked by the Emergency Committee of the KMT and the Legislative Yuan to resume the presidency.[4] At his inaugural ceremony on March 1, 1950, Chiang frankly and publicly admitted full, personal responsibility for the fall of the mainland. Learning from the recent defeat, Chiang started to rebuild the party, the government, and the island.

Chiang first dealt with the problem of revitalizing the KMT. The KMT became the prime force for the reconstruction of Taiwan as well as for the consolidation of the Nationalist government's power in Taiwan. After several months of preparation, Chiang implemented his reform project by first appointing a Central

Reform Committee composed of sixteen faithful followers.[5] There were several reasons why he chose these younger cadres (their average age was forty-seven) for this project. Many senior KMT members who accompanied the government's exodus to Taiwan were responsible for the fall of the mainland and were involved with the many political cliques that had paralyzed the bureaucracy in the first place. The younger members were more energetic and hardworking, and those chosen were either former students or confidential cadres. The Standing Committee of the Central Executive Committee granted Chiang permission to invest this committee with the full authority to reform the party while temporarily suspending the power of the Central Executive Committee and the Central Supervisory Committee.

The Central Reform Committee soon drafted various reform plans on organization, discipline, ideological reindoctrination, and the removal of all evil practices among party members. As for the party organization, all party members who came to Taiwan had to reregister with various levels of the Reform Committee within a certain time and then were put into specified party branches according to their location and profession. Party branches were established everywhere, including local districts, governmental departments, and even central and local people's representative bodies. Then the KMT examined its members and purged those who had defected, were corrupt, or were incompetent. In addition to requiring its members to study party papers, the KMT re-educated some thirteen thousand cadres through the newly established Sun Yat-sen Institute on Policy Research and Development within three years.[6]

When the Central Reform Committee concluded its mission and returned its power to the Central Executive Committee at the Seventh Party Congress in October 1952, the Nationalist Party was totally different. Many senior cadres had lost power, and "bad elements" were purged or driven out of the party. Because improved communication was established between related party branches in various government departments, the government went about doing its business more efficiently. Through self-examination, self-criticism, cadre training, and the establishment of various party branches, the Nationalist Party became a party with strong leadership, concrete structure, tight discipline, high morale, common faith in shared doctrines, greater efficiency, and less corruption. Even the party enrollment increased 200 percent in these three years, and the percentage of Taiwanese members climbed as high as 57.12 percent of the total membership.[7]

In order to maintain the legitimacy of the government, Chiang Kai-shek retained the title and structure of the government as set out in the constitution. The government retained the structure of the central government while establishing a provincial government for Taiwan divided into sixteen counties and five municipalities. The central government would select the governor of provincial government. Beginning in the early 1950s, elections were held at the county, municipal, and provincial levels.[8] In other words, local people could participate in local and provincial politics through elections, but not at the national level.

As early as May 1948, the government had already implemented the Provisional Amendments for the Period of Mobilization of the Suppression of Communist Rebellion, which entrusted the president with almost unlimited power to deal with the emergency situation. Based on these provisional amendments, Chiang Kai-shek instituted martial law, which continued when he regained power in Taiwan. The provisional amendments made the Nationalist Party domestically unchallengeable as long as a state of civil war existed. The people could not form any new political parties or publish new newspapers. Those restrictions were not removed until the late 1980s.

Chiang's reform also extended to the top-heavy army and the internal security apparatus. In order to eliminate cliques and deadwood, Chiang ordered several hundred incompetent generals and colonels to retire, and their soldiers were reorganized into different units. Sun Li-jen, a Virginia Military Institute graduate and the commander-in-chief of the Chinese army, helped to retrain and make nearly two hundred thousand soldiers into elite troops. In 1950, the Ministry of Defense established a Political Affairs Department, headed by Chiang Ching-kuo (Chiang Kai-shek's son), for the purpose of supervising and extending political and psychological training to the armed forces. The political officer system, under the Political Affairs Department, became juxtaposed with the regular military command system to ensure the loyalty of the troops. Later, Chiang Kai-shek inaugurated the Academy for Political Officers in 1952 to supply political officers.

The government paid attention to the problem of student movements. In the 1940s, student movements had a disastrous effect on society and the government's ability to govern during the civil war period. Chiang Ching-kuo dealt with the problem by establishing the Chinese Anticommunist National Salvation Youth Corps in October 1952 to promote various youth activities on all college and university campuses. This popular Youth Corps, the only legal intercollegiate organization, indoctrinated students with patriotism and the Three Principles of the People while searching for any kind of seditious activity. It also recruited young talent for the party and the government. Because of Chiang Ching-kuo's connections and influence, the corps obtained many privileges and received full cooperation from various governmental offices, playing a major role in indoctrinating and entertaining students.

The Nationalist government's security apparatus was notorious for its motley character and its abuse of privilege. Each security office administered its own affairs without coordination and at times competed for power with others. To rectify this practice, Chiang Kai-shek founded a Political Activities Committee in 1949 to reorganize the security system. This committee was a secret organization and, from its second year on, registered all personnel in the security system.[9] With Chiang Ching-kuo as head, this inconspicuous office gradually took control of the entire security system.

Economic collapse was one of the major reasons for the Nationalist regime's "loss of China." Interesting enough, economic reform in Taiwan turned out to be the most dazzling and successful part of Nationalist rule. To deal with skyrocketing inflation and plummeting currency value, the provincial government of Taiwan introduced the New Taiwan (NT) dollar with an exchange rate of one NT dollar to 40,000 old Taiwan dollars in June 1949. In March 1950, the government also initiated a preferential interest rate to absorb the surplus money. The interest rate was initially 7 percent per month or 125 percent per year (if compounded) before being gradually lowered to 2 percent per month in November 1952.[10] The amount of money in circulation and the inflation rate soon declined. From having reached 3,000 percent in the first half of 1949, the inflation rate then dropped to 300 percent in 1950 and then to 8.8 percent after 1952.[11] In addition to stabilizing prices the government also persuaded the private sector to invest in national reconstruction.

At the end of World War II, the agrarian situation did not look good. Land rents were unfavorable for the tenant farmers and the distribution of land poor, with most of the land resting in the hands of a few landlords.[12] The government, with no connection with local landlords, implemented economic reform, which involved rent reduction, the sale of public land, and a Land-to-the-Tiller program. In April 1949, Ch'en Ch'eng, the governor of Taiwan province, oversaw the reduction of rent prices to a maximum of 37.5 percent of the annual yield of the main crops. The government based this figure on the assumption that the landlord and the tenant had an equal total annual yield after first deducting 25 percent of the yield for basic labor and agricultural investment of the tenants. The first reform aimed to rule out many old customs such as exploitation of the tenants while guaranteeing a reasonable rent for the landlords. The second part of the land reform, started in 1951, was the sale of the public land to tenant farmers. The government opened to landless farmers about 181,490 *chia* of public land—nearly a fifth of the arable land in Taiwan—which was acquired by the government from the Japanese nationals and the Japanese administration after the conclusion of World War II. The tenant farmers could buy 0.5 to 2 *chia* of paddy land and 1 to 4 *chia* of dry land priced at 2.5 times of the annual main crop yield per *chia* of cultivated land.

The most powerful impact of the land reform came after January 1953. After a careful evaluation of all available land in Taiwan, the government declared that each landlord could only retain for himself a maximum of 3 *chia* of medium-grade paddy land or 6 *chia* of medium-grade dry land, or the equivalent amount of paddy and dry land of superior or inferior quality.[13] Private land in excess of this amount was purchased by the government and resold to Taiwanese tillers at a price of 2.5 times the value of the main crops, against a market value of between 5 and 8 times. The landlords were reimbursed by the government with mostly (70 percent) land bonds in kind and stock shares (30 percent) from four government enterprises.

The government achieved tremendous results with its land reform. Many landless farmers benefited from this reform as 139,267 hectares of private farmland were transferred to 194,823 tenant families by the end of 1953. The leased land was reduced from 38.6 percent of total farmland to 15.2 percent while owner-farmer families increased from 36 percent in 1949 to 65 percent in 1952. The number of tenant families dropped from 39 percent to 11 percent.[14] This redistribution of the land promoted a more equitable distribution of the land as well as income. While working on their own land, farmers were more hardworking and hence received a better yield. Consequently, the average income of tenant farmers rose 81 percent from 1949 to 1952. Rice yields quickly surpassed prewar levels. This was achieved in 1952. The value of agricultural exports reached U.S.$114 million in 1952. Furthermore, the government successfully shifted landlord investments from the land to industry, which had a deep and broad influence on the future.

After the land reform, farmers' associations were organized everywhere to offer services and facilities, such as rural credit and savings, the sale and marketing of farm products, rural health and transportation services, and the promotion of rural industry. Since the government monopolized chemical fertilizers, the farmers could obtain fertilizer only from these farmers' associations through the rice–fertilizer barter system. The government therefore could control the supply of rice and make huge profits from this barter system. The success of the land reform and related rural programs must be attributed largely to the financial support and technical advice of the Sino-American Joint Commission on Rural Reconstruction (JCRR), which, based on the China Aid Act, was a joint effort to devise and monitor the various rural projects in Taiwan.

The United States resumed its military and economic aid to the Nationalist government when it established the U.S. Military Assistance and Advisory Group in Taiwan in 1951. From this time until 1964, the United States offered $1.5 billion in nonmilitary aid to Taiwan, about U.S.$100 million per year. Needless to say, the Nationalist government and Chiang Kai-shek were pleased with these developments. It is generally believed that the appointment to important positions of several liberals, such as Wu Kuo-chen as governor of Taiwan province and Sun Li-jen commander of the army, were intended as friendly gestures to attract the support of the United States.

Both the Communist threat and U.S. aid helped promote the legitimacy of the Nationalist rule in Taiwan. Furthermore, with more and more Nationalist troops moving onto the island and with the consolidation of the Nationalist Party as well as the security system, the Nationalist Party came to life again. Taiwanese people, while still remembering the bloody suppression of the "February 28 incident," had no outside power to appeal to and had no choice but to accommodate themselves to the Nationalist government. Like the owner-farmers, the Taiwanese now concentrated on making economic gains and improving their surroundings.

Creation of a New Socioeconomic Infrastructure: 1953–1960

With the conclusion of the Taiwan–U.S. Mutual Defense Treaty in December 1954, Taiwan's position was further secured and the United States at the same time was further dragged into the Chinese mire. With the cold war nearing its peak, Washington could not afford to lose the confidence of its allies and to become the target of the domestic anti-Communist sentiments by letting Taiwan fall into Communist hands. However, on the other hand, the United States did not want to start World War III over Taiwan. Thus the treaty served several positive purposes. It demonstrated, first, American determination to defend Taiwan and the P'eng-hu islands (Pescadores). Moreover, it put a "leash" on Chiang Kai-shek by preventing him from attempting to "recover the mainland" by force.[15] It also made Taiwan a fortified link in the U.S. containment policy and, finally, appeased the protests of the China Lobby.* Although the PRC had taken I-chiang-shan island and forced the withdrawal of Nationalist troops from Ta-chen island in early 1955, it failed to take the two most important offshore islands—Quemoy and Ma-tsu—by heavy bombardment in 1958. After that, no more military offensives were ever launched by either the ROC or the PRC. The stalemate across the Taiwan strait remains to the present. Looking at it from another angle, these two crises in the Taiwan strait made the Nationalist government more dependent on the United States and strengthened the need for martial law in Taiwan.

The United States also rendered its support to the Nationalist government in the international arena. After 1950, the Soviet Union began to challenge the Nationalist government's position as representative of China at the United Nations. At that time, most UN members opposed the PRC's involvement in the Korean War and maintained diplomatic relations with the Republic of China. With U.S. help, the ROC had no difficulty in using the strategy of "deferment resolution," that is, deferring a vote in the China question, to deal with this problem. However, with more and more nations becoming independent, the Republic of China gradually faced strong competition from the PRC in winning friendship and support from these new countries.[16]

The ROC government, therefore, could once again concentrate its energy and effort on domestic affairs. The Nationalist government dealt with the problem of legitimacy by relying on the central representative bodies of the people—the National Assembly, the Control Yuan, and the Legislative Yuan. According to the constitution, the National Assembly and Control Yuan were to hold elections every six years, and the Legislative Yuan would hold elections every three years.

---

*The lobby was an eclectic aggregation of politically conservative organizations and individuals who supported the interests of the ROC in the United States.

After 1951, Chiang Kai-shek extended the tenure of the delegates of the Legislative Yuan every year. Up to 1954, the tenure of the delegates of the other two branches of government also came to an end. At the request of the Executive Yuan, the Council of Grand Justice of the Judicial Yuan reviewed this matter and concluded that all delegates should remain in their positions because the ongoing civil war prevented elections over all China. This ruling perpetuated the status of those delegates and also made their delegation exist in name only because they could not represent the provinces or the groups in mainland China and seldom reflected the views of the local people. Chiang Kai-shek himself also faced the same problem because of the two-term restriction in the constitution. When he reached the end of his second term in 1960, the National Assembly passed a constitutional provision releasing him from this two-term restriction "during the period of Communist rebellion."

In order to keep local politics under control, the Nationalist Party also did its best to manipulate local elections. Two methods were used to check and control the local politicians. The first was the granting of government-dominated economic privileges to cooperative politicians. The ruling party exerted its influence through the issue of licenses in great profit-making businesses, such as banking, insurance, transportation, broadcasting, securities, and shipping. Only those who would cooperate with and listen to the government could receive such licenses. The second method was manipulating local elections. The Nationalist Party tried to avoid fractional domination of any area. Therefore, it often tried to foster two or more factions in the same area. The KMT permitted the factions to take turns at controlling the mayoralty or the city council through nomination. By using this strategy of playing one against another, the KMT could win cooperation from all factions. Not many local politicians could resist the temptation of wealth and power, and the KMT had long enjoyed its control of local politics.[17] The KMT ruled in Taiwan by suppressing the formation of any possible opposition forces. Whenever there was indication of opposition, the government would deal with it unrelentingly, as discussed below.

An important reason for the extraordinary success of Taiwan's economy was the recruitment of many highly trained professionals to take charge of economic planning and development of state-run industries. This economic elite was composed of economists and engineers. Many had studied abroad and thus had years of fieldwork experience. This young and well-educated group received the full authorization of the government to cooperate with the American aid officials in the design and promotion of economic development in Taiwan. Among them, Chung-yung Yin (K.Y. Yin) and Kuo-ting Li (K.T. Li) were the two most important and distinguished figures. Yin and Li were not economists, but held degrees in electric engineering and physics, respectively. They had diligently and incorruptibly devoted themselves to the construction of the nation for many long years. Based on their long-term fieldwork and understanding of the Chinese scene, they successfully accommodated Western economic theories to Taiwan. It was also because of their past experience in the West that they had no problem in communicating with American aid officers while working together to build up postwar Taiwan. Many of those who participated in economic planning and affairs, such as Yen Chia-kan, Sun Yun-hsuan, Tsiang Yen-shih, Wang Tso-yung, and Lee Teng-hui, later became important government officials.[18]

To what extent U.S. aid assisted and promoted economic development in Taiwan is still debated by scholars. However, the impact of U.S. aid should not be underestimated. Of the U.S.$100 million in nonmilitary aid that Taiwan received every year between 1951 and 1965, about two-thirds was spent on the development of infrastructure projects and human resources. During this time, U.S. economic aid constituted about 40 percent of capital formation in Taiwan. Most of the American assistance was spent on communications, electricity, and transportation, which were important for agricultural and industrial development. The U.S. human resources program included the dispatch of specialists to Taiwan to train technicians or offer study tours to Chinese people. American aid also led American businessmen to invest in Taiwan.[19] Many sources indicate that U.S. aid officials, through many joint programs, such as the JCRR and the Council on U.S. Aid, exerted a strong influence on the making and execution of economic policy in Taiwan.[20]

At that time, most daily necessities, raw materials, and industrial equipment came from abroad, while only a few items, such as rice and sugar, were exported. This trade imbalance led to a huge trade deficit, causing a serious shortage of foreign reserves.[21] Worsening this situation was the 3.6 percent population growth rate and the more than 5 percent unemployment rate in Taiwan in early 1950. The government therefore adopted an import-substitution industrialization strategy to develop labor-intensive light industry. Many measures were formulated to assist this strategy. For example, the average nominal tariff rate was 44.7 percent, while the rate for some items increased to 160 percent in order to protect infant industries. In July 1955, a system of rebates was created to return to the manufacturer the import duties of the goods for export purpose. In 1956, certain industrial categories, new companies, or old companies making new investments that would enlarge production by 30 percent were exempted from paying a business tax for three years.[22] The government decided to abolish its dual exchange rate system and devalued the exchange rate in the second half of the 1950s from NT$15.55 per U.S. dollar to NT$25 in 1955, NT$38 in 1958, and NT$40 in 1960.[23] Ever since then, the government has maintained a unified exchange rate. In 1954 and 1955, other favorable measures were also introduced to attract foreign or overseas Chinese investment.

At the suggestion of the U.S. Agency for International Development mission, the government established the Economic Stabilization Board in 1951 to review and coordinate trade, payments, and monetary and fiscal policies in the interests of stabilizing price levels. The board was enlarged to absorb other related institutions in July 1953 and started its first and second four-year Economic Development Plan in 1953 and 1957, respectively. The first four-year plan placed strong emphasis on the development of electricity, fertilizers, and textiles. The reason for these priorities was simple. Electricity was the basis for all other industries. Fertilizers and textiles were two major imported commodities; while the former was crucial for agriculture, the latter was a basic daily necessity.[24] The government left the development of the textile industry to private enterprise. The government provided textile manufacturers with funds to start production and with raw cotton provided by the United States. In the end, the government bought the production of these companies. The quick development of textile industry created many job opportunities and permitted textilers to profit. Until 1958, the amount of textile exports surpassed that of textile imports. Electric power offered by the Taiwan Electric Company expanded 2.56 times between 1952 and 1960. At the end of the first four-year plan, the industrial production index went up 154.7 percent, while Taiwan's income per person rose 40 percent. However, the plan failed to reach the goal of industrial and agricultural self-sufficiency or to pay the balance of international payments. In 1956, the trade deficit was U.S.$98 million.[25] The second four-year plan extended the original goal to the issues of employment and income inequality. The second plan also focused on heavy industry, national defense industry, advanced technology, and regional cooperation. Extending the economic and industrial goals to the domestic and international arena over the next several decades was justified.

Besides textile manufacturers, other entrepreneurs benefited indirectly from the government's land reform. After the government compensated landlords with stock shares from four government enterprises (Taiwan Cement, Taiwan Pulp and Paper, Taiwan Industry and Mining, and Taiwan Agricultural and Forestry), people interested in these industries bought stock shares from landlords, who had no interest in these enterprises. Because of the government's protective tariffs and other inducements, they, on the basis of former government enterprise, successfully earned huge profits in the fields of cement making, petrochemicals, plastics, and agricultural production.

Another important reason for the success of Taiwan's economy was the government's ability to maintain and raise the quality of human resources. Moving to Taiwan with the Nationalist government were a large number of migrants with a good education, technical skills, administrative ability, and entrepreneurial experience. They soon found positions at the various levels of the government and filled the vacuum left by the Japanese. Their specialty and loyalty also contributed to the consolidation of the Nationalist government in Taiwan. Once the Nationalist government became stable again, it made great efforts to promote education, which later produced high quality human resources able to contribute to the political, economic, and social development of the "Taiwan miracle." The number of higher education institutions jumped from four in 1952 to fifteen in 1960. There were 1,248 primary schools and 148 secondary schools in Taiwan in 1952. By 1960, the number of primary schools rose to 1,982 whereas secondary schools increased in number to 299. The effect of increasing the number of schools can be seen from statistics showing that the percentage of six-year-old children who were not able to attend school dropped from 42.1 percent in 1952 to 27.1 percent in 1960 and to 14.7 percent in 1970.[26]

The security apparatus was also further strengthened. The Materials Section under the Presidential Office was transformed into the National Security Bureau under the new National Defense Council in 1955. This new bureau, under Chiang Ching-kuo, coordinated all security agencies, including related offices in the Kuomintang, the Ministry of Defense, the Ministry of Foreign Affairs, the Ministry of the Interior, Taiwan Garrison Command, the military police, and the local police. This widespread and enhanced security system, which contributed to the consolidation of the Nationalist government in Taiwan, also became a useful instrument for suppressing dissidents. The security apparatus was constantly "cracking down" on alleged Communist conspiracies or subversive cases. In its determination to exterminate all Communist agents and influence in Taiwan, the government arrested, imprisoned, and executed thousands on insufficient or circumstantial evidence. The 1950s became known as the period of "white terror." People dared not criticize the government, make comments on current politics, or voice grievances to strangers.

The suppression of any conspiracies and dissidents was not limited to the local people. At this time, government and party officials, no matter what their position, could be easily persecuted or purged. Some liberals who did not agree with or conform to policy were kicked out of the government. Wu Kuo-chen, then the governor of Taiwan province, was the first case. Wu was not a member of Chiang Kai-shek's circle and often publicly criticized Chiang Ching-kuo's methods of suppressing so-called Communist insurgents. Wu was forced to leave Taiwan in 1953 and formally broke relations with the Nationalist government in 1954, when he held a press conference in New York to criticize Chiang and his government as "undemocratic," for making Taiwan into a "police state," and for making the people submit to "one-party rule."[27] In 1955, Sun Li-jen, who was commander of the army and personal chief of staff to Chiang Kai-shek, was implicated in a plot to overthrow the government after a former subordinate, Kuo T'ing-liang, voluntarily confessed to being a Communist agent. Sun was forced to resign for "negligence" and spent the rest of his life under house arrest. It is commonly believed that the fall of Sun was in fact related to displeasure with Chiang Ching-kuo for imposing the political official system on the army.[28]

Another famous case was the suppression of the *Free China Fortnightly*, a magazine published by Lei Chen and supported by a group of liberals including Hu Shih, Yin Hai-kuang, T'ao Po-ch'uan, Ch'en Ch'i-t'ien, and Fu Cheng. They were critical of the government's growing autocratic tendencies and the overextension of the party system because this undermined democratic politics. When Lei Chen and a few Taiwanese politicians tried to organize a China Democratic Party in 1960, Lei was arrested for employing a Communist agent. Lei was sentenced to ten years in prison, thus silencing and dispersing the famous *Free China Fortnightly* group. It is clear that no opposition force or liberal groups were allowed to play a role in politics in this period and no one dared to try again until the 1970s.

The Creation of the Taiwan Miracle: 1960s

In the late 1950s and early 1960s, both Taiwan and the international environment underwent significant changes. The domestic market was saturated and economic development slowed down. Because of the success of land reform, the agrarian population grew every year, reaching 4.8 million in 1958. Farmland, which had heretofore experienced little expansion, became divided into small parcels. On average, a farmer owned 0.18 hectares of farmland in 1958. Profit from agricultural production fell, and farmers gradually lost interest in putting more labor and investment into the land. On the other hand, although the government had already begun to promote industry, the industrial products of Taiwan were unable to find an international market. The export statistics for 1958 show that agricultural products made up 86 percent of all exports. The population grew at a rate of 3.6 percent between 1953 and 1958, totaling more than 10 million people in 1958.[29]

The change in the international environment also played a role in the transformation of Taiwan's economy. The United States, with strategic and economic considerations in mind, began to promote self-financing and the improvement of the investment climate in Taiwan in the late 1950s. In America's competition with the Soviet Union, Taiwan served as a model in contrast to the PRC. A U.S.-supported Taiwan demonstrated that an open society would prosper more in its economic development. Equally important were economic considerations. Because of growing labor costs in their domestic markets, American and Japanese enterprises went overseas to seek less expensive labor. Furthermore, when the major industrial countries moved toward more advanced technology, they left room for the developing countries to move in.[30] All these factors gave Taiwan a golden opportunity to change its economic course.

In late 1959, the Council for U.S. Aid, which took over the duty of economic planning and development after the dissolution of the Economic Stabilization Board in 1958, was advised by American officials to accelerate Taiwan's economic growth. The United States hoped to expand its aid to Taiwan in the next several years so that Taiwan could become independent and plan its economic development and thereby become an example for other recipients of U.S. aid.[31] Stimulated by a promise of additional U.S. aid and a draft reform plan, government officials worked out a comprehensive nineteen-point program of economic and financial reform in 1960. This reform sought to increase production, liberalize trade, encourage savings and private investment, fully utilize government production facilities, and hold military expenditures to the real 1960 level. American aid officials even promised to offer an additional loan of $20–30 million to encourage the ROC government to implement the program promptly.[32]

The government started an export-oriented strategy to accommodate itself to the domestic and international factors. The government promoted many economic reforms, such as liberalization of foreign exchange controls, an increase in the electricity rate, the adoption of a single foreign exchange rate, a reduction in the rate of effective protection, establishment of investment banking machinery, and setting up a stock market. The reactivation of the Central Bank of China in 1961 was carried out to stabilize the currency, promote production, and assist economic development. Two other banks, the Bank of China and the Bank of Communications, were also reactivated in 1960 to assist domestic industries and enterprises as well as to deal with matters of foreign exchange and international trade. The tendency toward an export-oriented economy could be seen from its third four-year plan for "accelerated economic development" from 1961 to 1964.

One of the most important economic reforms in this period was the enactment of the Statute for the Encouragement of Investment in September 1960. This statute successfully attracted funds from local and international investors and diverted them to industrial construction in Taiwan. The incentives of the statute included a five-year tax holiday to a productive enterprise conforming to the statute's criteria; a maximum business income tax rate of 18 percent; business tax exemption on machinery; and business tax exemption on all imported raw materials for exporting manufacturers.[33] In addition to these benefits, the government also promised to assist in the acquisition of plant sites for enterprises because the land reform regulations had created obstacles in the transaction of the industrial-use land.

In addition to export promotion, the other major economic strategy of the government was the encouragement of investment in labor-intensive industries, which did not require a great deal of capital or advanced technology. An abundant labor force became available as the agricultural sector's labor needs decreased. The rapid growth of labor-intensive industries not only created job opportunities for unskilled labor but also promoted more equitable income distribution. Textiles, plastic and rubber products, paper and paper products, and chemicals were among the government-promoted industries. Statistics reveal Taiwan's transformation from an agricultural economy to an industrial economy. Agriculture's share of the labor force declined from 52.1 percent in 1952 to 35 percent in 1971, while that of industry increased from 20.2 percent to 30 percent. However, in terms of the growth rate of the net domestic product (NDP), the industrial sector of the economy averaged 14.2 percent between 1953 and 1970 compared with 4.9 percent of the agricultural sector. In 1952, agriculture accounted for 35.9 percent of the NDP, but this figure dropped to 30.4 percent in 1959 and to 19.2 percent by 1970. Meanwhile, industry grew from 18 percent of NDP in 1952 to 25.7 percent in 1959 and to 32.5 percent in 1970.[34] Various statistics prove that Taiwan's economy moved progressively toward industrialization.

The economic planning and strategy of this period came into realization with the establishment of export processing zones. With the promulgation of the Statute for the Establishment and Management of the Export Processing Zones in 1965, the first zone was completed in Kao-hsiung harbor in December 1966. The administrators of the zone were authorized to process all import and export transactions, and this has greatly facilitated business for the investors. Furthermore, in addition to tax incentives, all import taxes were exempted if the material and manufacture were for export purposes. This zone, the first one in Asia, received an overwhelmingly favorable response locally and internationally, the latter mostly referring to American and Japanese investors. The goals of the Kao-hsiung Export Processing Zone—the investment of U.S.$1.8 million, annual exports totaling U.S.$7.2 million, and the employment of 1,500 people—were reached within two years.[35] The government then decided to establish two more export processing zones in Taichung, another harbor city. The establishment of these zones absorbed foreign investment, created job opportunities, assisted the training of laborers, promoted the development of industry, and increased exports from Taiwan. Export growth in this decade averaged 25 percent, rising from U.S.$174 million in 1960 to U.S.$1.56 billion in 1970—eightfold growth. Imports grew from U.S.$252 million to U.S.$1.52 billion, an average 20 percent growth rate.

Despite the cessation of American aid in 1964, Taiwan became the fastest-growing economy in the world because of the sound economic and industrial infrastructure and the Statute for the Encouragement of Investment. Between 1960 and 1970, the average annual growth rate of the gross national product (GNP) in Taiwan was 9.7 percent while that of per capita income was 6.6 percent. The growth of capital formation was more impressive. It rose from 20.1 percent of GNP in 1960 to 26.3 percent in 1970. The wealth of the people in Taiwan, as well as their confidence in their own economy, is also evident in the amount of domestic investment, of which 60 percent came from domestic savings in 1960 and 95 percent in 1970.

Another characteristic of the "Taiwan miracle" was the remarkable equalization of income distribution. Many scholars used the Gini coefficient, which compares the income share of the richest 20 percent with that of the poorest 20 percent, to show the degree of income distribution inequality. In 1953, the Gini coefficient for Taiwan was 0.558, similar to that of Mexico or Brazil, but by 1970 it fell to 0.321, better than the U.S. rate of 0.36.[36]

The rapid development of Taiwan's economy was closely related to improvement in the quality of human resources, which reflected the education policy of the government. The government spent about 13 percent of its budget on education from 1954 to 1968. While the nation became richer and more stable, the Nationalist government decided to increase the allocation for education. In 1968, it extended compulsory education from six years to nine years. The proportion of primary school graduates who went on to junior high school jumped from 51 percent in 1961 to 80 percent in 1971.

Despite the smooth economic developments, the ROC met with less success in international politics. At this time, the United Nations became a major battle-field for the ROC. With the rapid increase in UN membership in the 1960s, it became more and more difficult for the ROC to compete with the PRC in claiming to represent "China." A new strategy was devised to win friends over-seas. The ROC initiated the International Technical Cooperation Program in 1959 to offer its specialty—agricultural technology—to other countries. The first technical assistance team (agricultural mission) was sent out in 1961 and soon was in some forty countries in Africa, the Middle East, Southeast Asia, and Latin America. This strategy achieved some returns in the form of abundant diplomatic support for the ROC.[37] That same year, the United States and four other nations proposed and passed a resolution making the PRC's application to the United Nations an "Important Question" requiring approval by two-thirds of the General Assembly.[38] Despite the ups and downs of the fight at the United Nations, the ROC was able to keep its seat through the 1960s.

America's war in Vietnam had a mixed effect on U.S.-ROC relations. On the one hand, Taiwan had strategic and logistical value for U.S. forces operating in Southeast Asia. The U.S. Air Force used Ching Chuan Kang airfield for trans-porting, refueling, and airlift support for its aircraft. Taiwan also became a major station and resort for thousands of U.S. soldiers in this period. On the other hand, the Vietnam War played a major role in leading U.S. policymakers to seek a compromise or understanding with the PRC in order to get the United States out of the war. Many suggestions from inside and outside the administration had been raised in the 1960s about the establishment of relations with the PRC. Although the "Cultural Revolution," launched in 1966, had temporarily damp-ened any U.S. expectations in this matter, the Sino-Soviet split in 1969 and the emergence of the PRC as a nuclear power in 1963 had a lasting influence on U.S. policymakers. Faced with growing antiwar sentiment at home and hoping to have a peaceful and stable Asia, President Richard Nixon decided to seek im-proved relations with the PRC after he was elected in 1968. To show its good-will, the Nixon administration adopted some conciliatory measures toward the PRC, including the resumption of the Warsaw talks with the PRC, which had been put on hold for two years.[39]

Domestically, there were some new domestic political developments in Tai-wan in this period. Ever since the founding of the Taiwan Provincial Assembly in 1959, the people in Taiwan had an opportunity to participate in politics at the provincial level. Changes also occurred as more and more Taiwanese entered the upper echelons of government and the military. Because of suspension of politi-cal participation at the national level for two decades, many delegates in the three parliamentary representative bodies died off, leaving the government no choice but to hold supplementary elections after 1969. Although the supplemen-tary quota for the three parliaments was small at this time, these elections were quite significant in two ways. First, the old system and old representatives presenting the "legitimacy" of the government on Taiwan were doomed to be replaced as the time passed. Second, the elections for the representatives at both provincial and central levels permitted local KMT and non-KMT politicians a greater role in politics.

The Nationalist government, though enjoying its success in economic development, did not loosen its grip on domestic politics. The government crushed dissension in every way in society. One famous dissident was Dr. P'eng Ming-min. P'eng, then the chairman of the Department of Political Science at National Taiwan University, and two of his students (Hsieh Ts'ung-min and Wei T'ing-ch'ao) issued a "Self-Rescue Declaration of Taiwan" in September 1964. The declaration appealed to all people in Taiwan—both Taiwanese and mainlanders—to work together to establish a democratic country because Taiwan was in reality already independent of China. They were soon arrested. P'eng and Wei were sentenced to eight years in prison whereas Hsieh was to serve a ten-year term. Because of P'eng's distinguished status and the pressure of the U.S. government, he received amnesty in November 1964 and left for Sweden in 1970.

Literature, popular songs, and artistic activities were also under strict scrutiny by the authorities. No criticism of the established political culture was tolerated. Two popular writers, Li Ao and Kuo Yi-tung (pen name Po Yang), wrote satires on the politics of the time, the conservatism of the government, and the negative features of traditional Chinese culture. The magazine *Wen Hsing,* which carried Li Ao's articles, was closed for a year in December 1965 while Li Ao was sentenced in 1972 to ten years in prison for his involvement in P'eng Ming-min's case. The government accused Kuo Yi-tung of being a communist agent, and he too was sentenced to ten years in prison in 1968. Liberals of this period usually were cowed into silence or lived abroad in self-imposed exile.

In Retrospect

Throughout these two decades, consolidation, stability, and prosperity were major concerns of the Nationalist government. While the government was preoccupied by these concerns, it failed to consider other, much-needed basic political and cultural issues with serious implications for the future. A review of those negative aspects illustrates the other side of the "Taiwan miracle."

The obsession of "recovering the mainland" led the Nationalist government to spend much of its budget on military expenditures. To maintain its "legitimacy" as the sole representative of all of China, the Nationalist government diligently defended its international status and, with the help of the United States, was able to maintain its status in the United Nations. However, the enlargement of the UN and the changing attitude of the United States toward the PRC inevitably put the ROC on the periphery of American concerns in Asia.

The Nationalist Party became revitalized after its reform movement in the early 1950s. The party, through the extension of the branches, became all-pervasive in the society and in the government. No opposition force could be formed by the "freezing" of parliamentary representatives, by the operation of the security apparatus, and by the manipulation of local politics. In the government, because of the dual status of most high-ranking officials, there was no distinctive line between the party and the government. The Nationalist Party could receive privileged support from the government, and some government policies and measures were formulated in favor of the ruling party. The party–state ruling system became entrenched and undermined the progress of democratization in Taiwan.

After the outbreak of the Korean War, the United States played a major role in the economic development and defense of Taiwan. Using U.S. economic assistance as both an incentive and a threat, the U.S. government guided the ROC toward becoming an industrialized and modernized country. The ROC also proved itself to be a model U.S. aid recipient—it graduated from the aid program and experienced rapid economic growth thereafter. However, contrary to its later policy of pressuring Taiwan to improve its human rights record, the U.S. government did not exert any strong pressure on the Nationalist government on the issue of democratization in Taiwan.

Since the Nationalist leaders never identified themselves as a regime in Taiwan, they thus did not pay due respect to local people and local culture. Only Chinese culture and Mandarin were officially honored in school and in society. Except for the symbolic representation of several Taiwanese in the cabinet in these two decades, the Taiwanese people had little opportunity to share political power in the central government. However, with the accumulation of wealth and the formation of a middle class in Taiwan, people on Taiwan, both Taiwanese and mainlanders, would soon look for the opportunity of political participation and their own way for the future of Taiwan.

Notes

1. When President Chiang Kai-shek announced his retirement as president on January 21, 1949, Vice President Li Tsung-jen became acting president.

2. It is generally estimated that about six hundred thousand Nationalist soldiers withdrew from the mainland and some offshore islands to Taiwan.

3. Those victories were gained in Quemoy in October 1949, in Ten-pu island in November 1949, and Ta-tan island in July 1950.

4. The Emergency Committee, a twelve-member council, was organized in July 1949 to take over the function of the Central Political Council as a supreme policymaking organ in the party in order to deal with the crises of the time.

5. Twenty of the old comrades were entitled to an honorary Advisory Committee of the Central Reform Committee. For the KMT's reform in 1950–52, see Ch'in Hsiao-i, ed., *Chung-hua min-kuo cheng-chih fa-chan shih*, vol. 4 (Taipei: Chin-t'ai Chung-kuo ch'u-pan-she, 1985), pp. 1607–1664; Hsu Fu-ming, *Chung-kuo kuo-min-tang ti kai-tsao (1950–1952)* (Taipei: Cheng-chung shu-chu, 1986).

6. Ramon H. Myers and Linda Chao, "A New Kind of Party: The Kuomintang of

1949–1952," in *Proceedings of Centennial Symposium on Sun Yat-sen's Founding of the Kuomintang for Revolution*, vol. 4 (Taipei: Chin-t'ai Chung-kuo ch'u-pan-she, 1995), p. 32.

7. Wu Nai-teh, "The Politics of a Regime Patronage System: Mobilization and Control Within an Authoritarian Regime" (Ph.D. dissertation, University of Chicago, 1987), p. 66.

8. Beginning in 1951, the Provisional Provincial Assembly was elected by county and municipal assemblies. This practice continued until the establishment in 1959 of the Provincial Assembly, which would be chosen by direct election.

9. Operated under a newly founded office, the Materials Section under the Office of the President.

10. Shirley W.Y. Kuo, Gustav Ranis, and John C.H. Fei, *The Taiwan Success Story: Rapid Growth with Improved Distribution in the Republic of China, 1952–1979* (Boulder: Westview, 1981), p. 65. The government did not suspend the preferential interest savings deposits until the end of 1958.

11. Ibid., p. 64.

12. The land rent generally equaled 50 percent—and sometimes as much as 70 percent—of the total annual yield of the main crop. At that time, landlords with more than 5 *chia* (1 *chia* = 0.97 hectare or 2.4 acres) of private farmland owned more than 30 percent of total private farmland land and comprised only 4.6 percent of the farmers. Farmers with less than 0.5 *chia* of farmland owned only 5 percent of total private farmland and comprised more than 30 percent of the farmers.

13. T.H. Shen, *The Sino-American Joint Commission on Rural Reconstruction: Twenty Years of Cooperation for Agricultural Development* (Ithaca: Cornell University Press, 1970), p. 61.

14. Ch'in Hsiao-i, ed., *Chung-hua min-kuo ching-chi fa-chan shih*, vol. 3 (Taipei: Chin-t'ai Chung-kuo ch'u-pan-she, 1983), pp. 1026–1029; Han Lih-wu, *Free China on Taiwan* (Taipei: Huo Kuo, 1972), p. 100.

15. The ROC's agreement not to attack mainland China without prior consultation with its treaty partner, the United States, demonstrates that the Mutual Defense Treaty restricted Nationalist troops in their attack on mainland China. Furthermore, Chiang Kai-shek was forced to state publicly in 1958 that the ROC would not resort to force to reunify China.

16. The states maintaining diplomatic ties with the ROC and the PRC changed from 39 : 19 in 1953 to 53 : 36 in 1960.

17. On the KMT's control of local politics, see Ch'en Ming-t'ung, "T'ai-wan ti-ch'u cheng-chih ching-ying ti ts'an-hsuan hsing-wei," National Science Council research paper (ROC), 1989; Wu Nai-teh, "The Politics of a Regime Patronage System"; Ch'en Ming-t'ung, *P'ai-hsi cheng-chih yu T'ai-wan cheng-chih pian-ch'ien* (Taipei: Yueh-tan ch'u-pan-she, 1995), pp. 152–190.

18. For an analysis of these economic elites, see Alan P.L. Liu, *Phoenix and the Lame Lion: Modernization in Taiwan and Mainland China, 1950–1980* (Stanford: Hoover Institution, 1987), chap. 3.

19. The inflow of private capital to Taiwan totals about $30 million a year since 1956.

20. See Richard E. Barrett, "Autonomy and Diversity in the American State on Taiwan," in *Contending Approaches to the Political Economy of Taiwan*, ed. Edwin A. Winckler and Susan Greenhalgh (Armonk, NY: M.E. Sharpe, 1988); Thomas B. Gold, *State and Society in the Taiwan Miracle* (Armonk, NY: M.E. Sharpe, 1986), pp. 68–69.

21. The trade deficit in 1950–55 totaled U.S.$444 million.

22. P'eng Po-hsien, "Chan-hou T'ai-wan tsai-cheng chih fa-chan yu pian-ko," (paper presented at the T'ai-wan kuang-fu hou ching-chi fa-chan yen-t'ao-hui, 1995), p. 3.

23. Yin Nai-p'ing, "T'ai-wan kuang-fu i-lai ti wu-chia wen-ting cheng-ts'e," (paper presented at the T'ai-wan kuang-fu i-lai ti wu-chia wen-ting cheng-t'se, 1995), pp. 14–15.

24. Textile imports from Japan alone in 1949–51 totaled 90 million yards, not including from other areas. In 1951, textiles became the most imported item, totaling 17.29 percent of all imports. Japan also became the chief source of Taiwan's fertilizer imports, which totaled half a million tons a year.

25. Imports totaled U.S.$228 million and exports U.S.$130 million. For an evaluation of the first four-year plan, see Ch'in Hsiao-i, ed., *Chung-hua min-kuo ching-chi fa-chan shih*, vol. 3, pp. 1041–1043; Wang Tso-jung, *Wo-men ju-ho ch'uang-tsao lo ching-chi ch'i-chi* (Taipei: Shih-pao wen-hua, 1989), p. 26.

26. *Taiwan Statistical Data Book*, 1989.

27. Howard L. Boorman, ed., *Biographical Dictionary of Republican China* (New York: Columbia University Press, 1970), vol. 2, pp. 439–440; Ch'en Ming-t'ung, *P'ai-hsi cheng-chih yu T'ai-wan cheng-chih pian-ch'ien*, pp. 140–142.

28. Ibid., p. 167.

29. Wang Tso-jung, *Wo-men ju-ho ch'uang-tsao lo ching-chi ch'i-chi*, pp. 37–40.

30. See Edwin A. Winckler, "Mass Political Incorporation, 1500–2000," and Susan Greenhalgh, "Supranational Processes of Income Distribution," in Winckler and Greenhalgh, ed., *Contending Approaches to the Political Economy of Taiwan*.

31. Chien-kuo Pang, *The State and Economic Transformation: The Taiwan Case* (New York: Garland, 1992), pp. 180–185.

32. Neil H. Jacoby, *U.S. Aid to Taiwan: A Study of Foreign Aid, Self-Help, and Development* (New York: Praeger, 1966), pp. 134–135.

33. Kuo, Ranis, and Fei, *The Taiwan Success Story*, pp. 74–75.

34. *Taiwan Statistical Data Book*, 1982, p. 33.

35. Ko Chen-ou, *Chia-kung ch'u-kou-chu ti she-chih* (Taipei: Lien-ching, 1983), p. 21.

36. Kuo, Ranis, and Fei, *The Taiwan Success Story*, pp. 44, 92–93.

37. Yu San Wang, "Foundation of the Republic of China's Foreign Policy," in Yu San Wang, ed., *Foreign Policy of the Republic of China on Taiwan: An Unorthodox Approach* (New York: Praeger, 1990), pp. 5–7; Bi-rong Liu, "Continuity and Change in the ROC's Foreign Policy" (paper presented at the Conference on the Period of Transformation of Contemporary China, May 20–22, 1988), p. 5; Ralph N. Clough, *Island China* (Cambridge: Harvard University Press, 1978), p. 151.

38. Clough, *Island China*, p. 151.

39. Ibid., pp. 21–25.

12

Identity and Social Change in Taiwanese Religion

Robert P. Weller

Puppets on display at the Chiang Kaishek Memorial for a Folk Arts Festival.

Religion is thriving in Taiwan. Political candidates sometimes secure their promises by publicly beheading a cock, thus making their oath directly to the gods. New temples have popped up everywhere; many are unlicensed, but the government has problems closing them because no workers are willing to tear them down. When Wang Yong-ch'ing, one of Taiwan's largest industrialists, visited Mai-liao (Yun-lin county) in 1991 to head off local environmental protests against his proposed construction of a naphtha cracker, he went first to make offerings (and monetary gifts) to the leading local temples. Buddhist clergy often preach for hours on television, and movies about various gods and temples are frequent. These examples attest to the health of religion in Taiwan and to the ways in which it is embedded in everyday life.

Religion has both shaped and reflected Chinese society in Taiwan from its beginnings. Early settlers brought tablets commemorating their ancestors with them, and built Earth God temples (*Tho-te biou*) as soon as they settled into villages. Larger temples soon branched off from mother temples in Fukien and became organizing points for Taiwan's social groups, from the family to entire regions and subethnic groups. Temples helped mobilize people to battle aborigines and competing Chinese groups and later to fight the Japanese occupiers in 1895. Other kinds of temples commemorate the dead from those battles.

Much of this activity is not "religion" in the usual Western sense of the term. Most Taiwanese religious practice takes place without regard to formal church organization, trained clergy, or sacred texts. The term "religion" itself (*cong-kau*) was borrowed from the West (via Japan) within the past century.[1] Many rural Taiwanese who perform daily rituals thus describe themselves as having no religion; a few do not even recognize the term. They say they just "carry incense."[2] Taiwan's former frontier conditions encouraged this kind of decentralized religion, with no higher authority to impose an interpretation. There were also more formally "religious" traditions—Buddhism, Taoism, pietistic sects, and eventually a little Christianity—but even these were far from the centers of doctrinal and ritual power on the mainland.

The embeddedness of religious practice in Taiwanese daily life has linked it closely to changing notions of identity. The close ties among religion, kinship, and community have made temples and rituals an arena in which we can see historical changes in contending notions of self and society, especially in the absence of a higher religious authority that could attempt to impose a set interpretation. Religious practice has both shaped and been shaped by Taiwan's history and speaks especially clearly about ethnic identities over time, the changing nature of social marginality, and the current dilemmas of modernity.

This chapter has three broad sections. The first outlines the broad range of religious possibilities in China generally and Taiwan specifically. The focus is primarily on everyday religious practice, including some exploration of more formalized religious traditions and of the sectarian movements that have periodically been so important there. The second section briefly traces major religious and social changes over the past several centuries, and the third takes up two specific examples that help reveal the changing role of religion in Taiwanese life. The first is the annual ghost festival, whose performance speaks to changing ideas about marginality. The second includes a set of more or less Buddhist sects that have become prominent in Taiwan, especially the Compassion Merit Society, which has attracted millions of members in the past twenty years. The chapter concludes with some thoughts about one of the issues implicated by the arguments over "Taiwanese" identity so common in Taiwan today—the degree to which it is sensible to argue for a uniquely Taiwanese religion.

Religion, World View, and Identity

Taiwanese religion is conducted above all by families. Even major community rituals tend to take the family as their most fundamental unit. One worships at home or in a temple by burning incense as a minimal offering. There need be no congregations, no preachers to explain dogma, no priests to lead worship. This section begins with a discussion of this kind of daily religious practice—"popular religion," if this term is understood to include all classes of society. Taiwan also has priestly traditions in Buddhism and Taoism, discussed subsequently, along with other kinds of religious movements.

Daily Religious Practice

Most Taiwanese religious ritual involves spirits of the dead in one form or another. In its most obvious form in all Chinese societies, this involves the commemoration of ancestors (*gongma*) by male descendants and their wives. Worship of ancestors was not always universal in China, but had long been standard practice by the time Taiwan was first heavily settled by mainland immigrants in the seventeenth century. In theory Chinese families extended back in time for millennia and would continue on indefinitely in a line traced from fathers to sons. Ancestor worship was one of many media that made such a view meaningful; it commemorated the patriline in tablets on a prominent altar in the front room of the house (and sometimes in communal lineage halls) and required periodic worship.[3] Marriage ritual made many of the same points by physically removing the bride from her natal family, ritually purifying her as she crossed the threshold into her husband's house, and having her worship his ancestors as one of her first married acts.

In actual practice, things were considerably more complex. Areas of Taiwan that had been settled relatively late, especially when little land was available, often had to compromise patriliny to survive. In some villages it is not uncommon to see three or four different surnames commemorated on the same altar and to hear genealogies that accentuate ties through marriage. If it were not China, one would be tempted to say they were not patrilineal at all.[4] This can happen when husbands live with their wives' families and give some of their children their wives' surnames, but continue to worship their own ancestors.[5] It also happens when wives come carrying the tablets of their own ancestors, because no one else remains to worship them. Ancestral altars in some areas thus do not look at all patrilineal. These exceptions to patriliny were suppressed in better-endowed areas, where strong lineages developed; village lineage leaders banned such tablets to dark corners of dusty rooms. In areas without these strong patrilineal networks, however, ties of marriage provided crucial support systems, and people easily sacrificed the patrilineal consistency of their ancestral altars for the realities of their lives.[6] In the absence of a lineage elite, the only authorities to promote a more unified vision of ancestor worship were prescriptive texts on family rituals, which could easily be ignored.

The frontier history of Taiwan, where lines of authority were sometimes difficult to establish, encouraged this kind of broad variation even in ancestor worship, which most Chinese (and foreigners) consider a defining feature of their values. Clearer state authority was finally established only by the Japanese occupiers, who had a very different culture of the family in spite of a shared Confucian heritage. It is thus no surprise that marriage ritual also varied widely from the norms established in elite manuals of ritual propriety, with an undercurrent that challenged the clear transfer of the bride from her father to her husband that those books of family ritual promoted. Newly engaged brides, for example, engaged in a silent battle with their future mothers-in-law—as the mother-in-law tried to place a ring over the bride's finger, the younger woman bent the joint to keep the ring from going all the way on in a silent battle of the wills.[7] Eventually, mothers-in-law just gave up the fight. Taiwanese religion typically experienced such arguments between what we might call an "official" set of rituals, laid out in popularizing texts written by neo-Confucian elites and promoted by local gentry, and an unofficial array of possibilities realized in daily life.[8]

A similar dynamic occurs in the worship of gods (*sin*). Most gods are also the spirits of dead men and women, but unlike ancestors they are incorporated by social communities of various sorts. These communities range from geographically defined neighborhoods with their Earth Gods (*Tho-te Kong*) to township-sized regions with their own patron deities, who were often affiliated with the local settlers' place of origin on the mainland. Certain crafts had their own gods, and so did sworn brotherhoods.

Most Taiwanese temples have strong geographical ties, drawing their supporters from the area under their god's jurisdiction.[9] Important community temples usually unite their regions by collecting various fees to run rituals, through periodic tours of their territory (with the gods carried in sedan chairs, which are now often put in trucks), and most obviously and importantly by housing gods who are thought to promote the legitimate interests of the community and its households. Gods' ties to local symbolic and political power are clear. Temples resemble (but expand upon) magistrates' yamens, and one communicates with gods through various bureaucratic means, from written petitions to bribes.[10] Many gods dress as imperial bureaucrats, and their periodic tours through their territory resemble the ones magistrates used to make. Many of them have official titles granted by past emperors. The committees who run temples usually include local elites and often represent one of the community's major political factions.[11] Most gods are also said to represent upright moral values; they protect the legitimate interests of their communities, but will not help supplicants with shady needs.

Yet even gods have another side, hidden beneath the trappings of bureaucratic legitimacy and imperial blessing.[12] A great many are characters who are not at all like civil officials—women (like Ma Co or Koan Im), Buddhist or Taoist hermits and eccentrics (like Co Su Kong or Ji Gong), or warriors (Koan Kong or Siong-te Kong). Many also have origin stories that accentuate their challenges to more commonly accepted values. Nearly all the goddesses, for example, committed the most unfilial act of not having children, and many actively refused marriage.[13]

Both local elites and the state tried to clean gods up as they grew influential. The emperor could promote particular deities and temples by granting titles or by giving commemorative steles. Ma Co, originally a goddess of fishing areas on the Fukien coast, was eventually promoted to be Empress of Heaven, and she is commonly referred to by that title in the Hong Kong area. Yet only a few officially constructed temples to her in Taiwan use the formal title. Taiwan's many important temples to her, like Taiwanese in their common discussions of this goddess, continue to use her original local title—Ma Co, the Ancestral Mother.[14] Much like in ancestor worship, there was no centralized control over ritual in practice, in spite of imperial legal regulations about who could worship and how. Even local elite attempts at control over ritual could have little effect, as when the management at the Co Su Kong temple in San-hsia attempted to promote vegetarian offerings at a major ritual and was simply ignored.[15]

The extensive use of spirit mediums in Taiwan made attempts at control over interpretation even more difficult. Gods possess mediums all over Taiwan, usually speaking directly through the medium, but sometimes causing him (or occasionally her) to write characters. Some areas, especially in southern Taiwan, have troupes of mediums who cut themselves with swords or other exorcistic weapons. Mediums are especially difficult to control because the god speaks directly to the listeners. There is no place for intervening interpretive control because the god is right there.

Some dead spirits are never incorporated as ancestors or gods; they have neither regional nor kin communities to worship them. These are the ghosts (*kui*), who live a miserable existence and occasionally cause trouble for the living. They are the improper dead: people who died with no children to worship them, or violently, or far from home where no one knew them. Note that this also describes the beginnings of many gods. In a broad sense, ghosts are everyone else's ancestors and kin. Some of them eventually become incorporated as gods because they have shown themselves to be particularly efficacious and power-ful.[16] The rest are ignored unless they are said to make someone sick, or unless their unidentified bones are buried in a small ghost shrine at the battlefield where they died, on the shore where they washed up, or by the road where they were accidentally disinterred. In such cases the shrines receive annual worship and may also receive an occasional stick of incense from someone like a gambler or prostitute, whom most gods would not help in their line of work.

The very willingness of ghosts to grant immoral requests marks the low degree of officializing control over them. The extensive historical variation in the annual festival for the ghosts is discussed below. This variation reflects in part the inability of the various states that have governed Taiwan to control interpretation of the ritual in spite of many attempts. In part they also show how easily people could reinterpret their own rituals in the absence of any higher theological authority like Catholic priests. This was typical of Chinese religion in many areas, but Taiwan's history of weak control from Peking followed by fifty years of foreign occupation greatly encouraged it.

Very little of what is discussed here so far is uniquely Taiwanese. Most of the major gods branched off from temples on China's southeastern coast and served emigrants from particular areas on the mainland. Thus Ma Co, Kaizhang Shengwang, Co Su Kong, and many others are closely affiliated with emigrants from particular counties on the mainland, even when (like Ma Co) they have also attracted a more general following. Taiwan has also developed some gods of its own, most importantly the cult of Koxinga (Cheng Ch'eng-kung), but also in-cluding other historical figures.[17] Yet even these newer temples do not differ fundamentally from the kinds of gods and the modes of worship common on the southeastern coast of the mainland. As discussed below, however, the kinds of decentralized variation that Chinese religion in general allowed, and that Tai-wanese religion in particular encouraged, fostered significant and revealing changes over time.

Professional Religion

Even a quick summary of Buddhism or Taoism in China cannot be attempted here. Instead this section discusses the kinds of religious options that Buddhism and Taoism created for people in Taiwan and how they related to those traditions on the mainland. As might be expected from a relative frontier of China, the monastic traditions in Taiwan remained undeveloped. There were no Taoist monasteries at all on the island, and Taoists desiring official ordination had to travel to the mainland.

Taoists were trained anyway, of course, following typical patterns of trans-mission from father to son and master to disciple. Indeed, Taiwan developed its own minor branches of Taoism based on the traditions of different masters. All roughly followed the Cheng-yi school of Taoism (centered on Mount Lung-hu in

Kiangsi), but local priests emphasized instead local differences. In northern Taiwan, for example, the primary split was between followers of the Lau family school and the Lim family school.[18]

Unlike popular religious practice, however, Taoism had a core of texts that were transmitted over the generations and periodically renewed by those who did make the trip to Mount Lung-hu. Thus even in the absence of any effective central religious control, Taoism maintained a kind of unity that was less possible in popular practice. These priests and their texts were closely integrated into local communities. They had families and lived in ordinary neighborhoods. They earned an income by performing rituals locally, from minor cures to major rites of community renewal.

For most people, Taoists imply a kind of ritual escalation; they provide more powerful access to gods or control over dangerous spirits than people can manage on their own. This creates a great deal of ritual overlap, as both Taoists and laymen generally find themselves sharing those rituals that laymen cannot perform on their own. At the level of interpretation, however, the differences are very clear. Taoist ritual, for the Taoists themselves, is not simply an intensification of local god worship. Taoism erases the local emphasis that is so strong in community temples and in the stories of most gods. For the priests, local gods are simply minor functionaries in a vast bureaucracy of gods, in which the Taoist himself is empowered to approach the highest deities (the Three Pure, who are not worshiped at all by others) and to command armies of lower spirits. In the most important rituals, the Taoist uses meditational techniques to achieve a unity with the highest gods and ultimately with the primal force of the Tao itself.[19] Nearly all rituals that Taoists share with laymen have such multiple layers of interpretation.

Unlike Taoism, Buddhism in Taiwan did have monks and nuns who left their secular families for lives of monastic discipline. Yet Taiwan was never a major center of Buddhist learning until after 1949, when important clergy came to Taiwan with the retreating Nationalist government. Many of these top clergy worked closely with the state, which helped them establish new Buddhist schools and temples. Buddhism after 1949 thus experienced a kind of refocusing around these new institutions, in a way that Taoism never matched. The new institutionalization of Buddhism helped paved the way for the revival of the past two decades.

The Buddhist belief system also differed significantly from the others. For example, it collapsed distinctions among gods, humans, and all other kinds of beings by emphasizing how none of them had left the cycle of reincarnation.[20] Unlike Taoism, it also attempted to bring lay believers into the fold by gradually changing ritual practice and encouraging people to recite sutras. Taoists instead maintained their texts and techniques as trade secrets.

Partly as a result of this push from Buddhism, Taiwan has had lay Buddhist organizations from the beginning. These usually revolved around small Buddhist "vegetarian halls" (*ch'ai-t'ing*), often with no ordained clergy.[21] Many of their followers were women who took vegetarian vows, but remained living at home with their families. Such organizations continue, but have been overtaken recently by other kinds of lay Buddhist organizations, usually based on loyalty to a single member of the clergy and his or her organization.[22]

Sects

Like much of China, Taiwan also developed a range of sects with important religious content. These fell into two broad types in China as a whole—groups based on oaths of sworn brotherhood flourished first in the south, and groups with more Buddhist connections, often centered on worship of a goddess, spread down from the north. Taiwan was the origin of the Heaven and Earth Society (Ti'en ti hui), one of the most important of the sworn brotherhoods.[23] This group and others like it in Taiwan became best known as foci for rebellions. They offered a set of ties beyond kinship that could cement people together and thus provided one of the few nonlocal resources through which people could be mobilized.

Voluntary religious brotherhoods had long borrowed the languages of kinship and religion to unite groups. Oaths of loyalty were sworn in front of gods, and religious activities might be one of the most important group activities.[24] The Heaven and Earth Society wedded this tradition to Ming dynasty loyalism against the Ch'ing. Given Taiwan's long resistance to the Ch'ing, the island was a good breeding ground for such discontent. The oath itself became highly elaborated, and religious secrecy made for an effective organization. Heaven and Earth Society activities were not at all confined to opposing the Ch'ing; these organizations eventually developed into the triads best known as criminal groups in the Hong Kong area.[25] In Taiwan, even where they rebelled, they tended to merge into factions based on the usual Taiwanese distinctions between people from different places of origin.

The Buddhist-oriented sects are most closely associated with the White Lotus and similar rebellions in northern China. As Jordan and Overmyer have shown, however, most of these sects, most of the time, showed no inherent tendency to rebel.[26] Instead, these groups center on the worship of a deity, often the Eternal Venerable Mother (Wusheng Laomu), who was seen as a creator/mother figure for humanity, but who also drew heavily on Buddhist imagery of compassion and nurturance. They typically feature spirit writing sessions where deities from various traditions (typically Buddhism, Taoism, Confucianism, Christianity, and Islam) explain the syncretic unity of all religions or expand on morality and ethics, often via commentaries on classical Chinese texts like the Analects. These sects have become increasingly popular in Taiwan since 1945, although some of them were illegal (because of their reputation for rebellion on the mainland) until the 1980s. All these sects move away from the local particularism of most

Taiwanese daily worship. Shared belief unites followers, rather than shared place of residence or kinship. Both their voluntarism and their universalism are reminiscent of Protestant Christianity.

Religion, Daily Life, and Social Change

The danger of the kind of quick summary and classification of Taiwanese religion in the preceding section is that it loses sight of Taiwan's historical dynamism. Taiwanese religion has not been static precisely because it ties closely to issues of identity and daily life. Religious organization in Taiwan has close ties to local power, to the creation of self-understanding, and to notions of how the world itself works. A great deal is at stake in religion anywhere, and it should be no surprise that ritual and belief become subject to pressures from changing ways of life. Religions may present themselves as unchanging truths, but they are never so immobile in practice. This is especially true in a place like Taiwan, where the absence of a powerful clergy with interests in maintaining a religious status quo made for very minimal pressures to preserve an orthodoxy in religious ritual or interpretation. The cumulative result of this structure over several centuries of drastic change on both Taiwan and the mainland is a gradual drift in emphasis and interpretation, especially during the time—nearly a century—when the two places were politically isolated.

Aborigines and Immigrants

We know very little about religious interactions between Taiwan's aboriginal populations and early Chinese settlers from the mainland. Nevertheless, there is good reason to think that such interactions were not unusual. First, we do have one strong case for the reverse process—where Han religion powerfully influenced but did not overwhelm aboriginal religion. This occurred among the Siraya in southwestern Taiwan, for whom John Shepherd has documented a remarkable combination of borrowing, retention of earlier ideas, and reinterpretation of both Han and aboriginal practice.[27] Second, we know such exchanges influenced Han as well as other groups in internal frontiers outside Taiwan. In parts of central Kwangsi during the nineteenth century, for example, we know that Han (mostly Cantonese and Hakka) immigrants worshiped important Yao deities and drew on Yao traditions of healing.[28] Finally, there are a few hints about direct Han borrowings in Taiwan, often associating a kind of black magic with aborigines. Gary Seaman documents one of the clearest, in an association between a "black dog demon" cult and aborigines in a part of central Taiwan.[29]

At the very least, these hints imply a kind of association between marginal places and dangerous power, which is not unusual in China. Distant mountain peaks house important pilgrimage sites as well as internal frontiers with aboriginal populations. Both draw on an uncontrolled power at the edges of civilization.

It is not a coincidence that drawings of non-Chinese groups in old gazetteers often resemble drawings of ghosts in clothing (usually animal skins) and body shape (usually grotesque). This power can be incorporated into Chinese religion as a kind of dangerous magic. The extent to which this process actually occurred in Taiwan and the possibility of its long-term influence will not be clear without much more research.

Toward Geography

The close ties between religion and local social organization appear clearly in ritual activity. Local settlements everywhere in Taiwan usually began to worship the Earth God early in their history.[30] Daily worship in these small temples typically rotates among all the households of the area, and they are thus both symbols of community unity and active markers of membership. Building a new Earth God temple is generally a declaration of independence by a new social community.

Early settlers also established a wide variety of god-worshiping associations (*sin-bieng hoe*).[31] These were shareholding organizations that united groups of all kinds, including irrigation associations, trade groups, kinsmen, local defense arrangements, pilgrimage groups, rotating credit associations, and sworn brother-hoods. The diversity of these groups and the ease of establishing them helped create a pool of religious possibilities, whose specific organizations would wax and wane as social conditions changed. The "belief sphere" of these groups could change its scale, and even the membership criteria sometimes changed over time.[32] Lin Mei-jung, for example, shows how the Chang-hua Ma Co belief sphere became a combination of Hokkien from Chang-chou and Hokkienized Hakka, united against Hokkien from Ch'uan-chou.[33] Wang Shih-ch'ing has a permutation on this theme, with a combination of Chang-chou and Ch'uan-chou Hokkien against local Hakka represented through an Earth God temple.[34]

Some of these temples grew into major community temples with geographic bases of support. Most often these were temples to gods associated with the subethnic groups that settled each area, and they usually became prominent when they were associated with rising economic centers or served as defense organizations. Occasionally lineage or other temples also developed a more strictly geographic base over time. Indeed the general trend in Taiwan over time has been for temples and god associations to emphasize geography over other forms of community, although all kinds of temples continue to exist. This has been especially true since the nineteenth century, as ethnic feuding ended and the religious functions of defense and ethnic solidarity lost their importance. Throughout most of the twentieth century, place of residence has been the most important local organizing principle in religion. The major religious organizations in Shu-lin (in northern Taiwan), for example, generally began with lineage or subethnic roots in the late eighteenth and early nineteenth centuries. Only one still retains its ethnic character in this ethnically mixed community. All the others have developed broader community bases, and some have even changed temple loyalties to reflect place of residence over place of origin on the mainland.[35]

Taiwan has, however, become a much more mobile society in the past two decades. So far people have retained some loyalties to temples in their family's home town. Yet there has also been a clear increase in the popularity of religions with more universalistic deities instead of the insistently local community gods discussed here. The data are not yet clear enough to say that another major change in the social base of religion is occurring, but the current situation is suggestive.

As some temples grew into major community centers, they also developed ties to local politics. Temples control many local resources: an ability to organize the entire community, the right to tax, and sometimes significant financial resources (money from donations, or land in the Ch'ing dynasty). As one might expect, local elites were attracted both to the social and financial resources of large temples and to their symbolic claims of patronage for the community. Temples were (and are) often run by committees on which local elites are well represented. Many temples often choose an annual "incense pot head" (*lo-cu*) in a way that favors the wealthy. Temples have thus been natural centers for military actions (for example, against the Japanese arrival in 1895) or for factional politics.[36]

Japanese Repression and Taiwanese Creativity

The Japanese occupation that began in 1895 put enormous pressure on popular religious practice in Taiwan. Although Taiwan was not able to put up a powerful or unified challenge to the Japanese takeover of the island, there were many cases of local armed resistance. These often naturally centered on community temples, with their ability to draw residents together around the local elite. The Japanese destroyed many of these temples in reprisal.[37]

At first popular religion in general, however, was neither actively encouraged nor repressed.[38] Destroyed temples were reconstructed, although large and expensive reconstructions were not generally allowed, leading to pent-up demand for temple rebuilding after the Japanese left in 1945. Yet this relative laissez-faire attitude changed considerably during the 1930s. By this time a generation of young Taiwanese had been educated in Japanese, and the build-up to the war effort in Japan created further pressures for Japanization. This meant that the colonial government began to repress popular religion. The process peaked when local governments removed the god images from popular temples in a number of towns; Chung-li was the most infamous one. The finer images ended up in Japanese ethnological museums, while the rest were burned. This, the government announced, indicated the promotion of local gods to heaven as Shinto deities.[39]

The Japanese backed away from this policy of total repression almost immediately, but they did actively promote alternatives, especially Shinto and Japanese Buddhism (which was intended to unite their Asian empire). Shinto temple construction increased rapidly from the 1930s until Taiwan's retrocession to China after World War II. The township of San-hsia, for example, came under the administration of a regional Shinto shrine built in 1938.[40] Construction was just about to begin on a township-level Shinto shrine when the war ended in 1945, and all such plans came to an end. Ironically, the lumber already purchased for the construction of the shrine was put to the massive reconstruction of the local community temple, which began in 1947. An earlier incarnation of that temple had been destroyed by angry Japanese troops in 1895, after playing an important role in organizing an ambush of the invading troops.

In spite of all this, Taiwanese were able to continue worshiping in their own ways. The colonial government quickly backed away from drastic acts like burning god images; they apparently feared needless unrest. At the same time, people became very creative in learning how to maintain rituals that were being discouraged. For example, the annual ghost festival in the seventh lunar month had been the occasion for massive and sometimes riotous gatherings of people, where apparently rootless young men sometimes rampaged for offerings to the ghosts.[41]

The late Ch'ing government had made this illegal for obvious reasons, but was unable to enforce the law. By the 1920s, these rootless young men were gone, for both political and economic reasons. Yet many areas retained the ceremony with all its furor by turning it into an "athletic competition" between village teams striving to grab the best offerings from high towers.

Through a similar maneuver, offerings of fattened whole pigs at a local god's birthday celebration took on the veneer of an agricultural competition.[42] This allowed villagers to claim that force feeding pigs to be as huge as possible was an exercise in agricultural modernization rather than a wasteful superstition. Creative responses like these enabled people to insist that they were responding to government preferences, while at the same time retaining as much as possible of the festival life they valued.

Modernity and Religion

Theorists of modernity used to expect that the dominance of a successful capitalist economy would mean the inevitable secularization of religion toward a rationalized civil philosophy. Taiwan's rapid economic success in the past few decades has empirically disproved this hypothesis. The number of temples per capita has been increasing since the 1970s and has probably never been as high as it is now. Religious activity is hard to miss, and nearly everyone takes part in some form.

Taiwan was in many ways already a commodity-based economy in the nineteenth century, with many farmers selling tea, camphor, sugar, and rice to distant markets.[43] Under Japanese rule public education, transportation, and security were greatly improved, and many new scientific agricultural practices were introduced. Although they discouraged the growth of large Taiwanese entrepreneurs, the Japanese did a great deal to set up the postwar economic boom. As other chapters in this book show, the 1970s and 1980s in particular saw spectacular growth in personal incomes, so by the 1990s Taiwan could no longer be considered a developing country.

Popular religion has played an interesting role in debates over the importance of cultural causes of this success. On the one hand, some have argued that religion offered inappropriate values. Max Weber and others, for example, argued that the "enchanted garden" of China's religion discouraged the ascetic secular rationalization Weber emphasized for Europe. Religious practice also encouraged exactly the kinds of ascribed, particularistic ties of family and community that earlier modernization theorists believed stood in the way of development, and it emphasized a kind of feudal hierarchy of gods.[44] On the other hand, many authors argue that the traditional values of ancestor worship—filial piety, cooperation, and long-term security—foster petty entrepreneurs by encouraging hard work, valuing independence from others, and cushioning the risks of private enterprise.[45] Others have suggested that popular religion supports appropriate values like loyalty, strengthens the informal social networks critical for raising credit and dealing with related enterprises, and provides experience with shareholding corporations via god societies.[46]

Any conclusion that Taiwanese religion simply helped or simply hindered capitalist development would clearly be misleading. The variation that was always inherent in local religion gave it aspects that would have both positive and negative effects in a changed economic environment. These have mixed in new proportions as times have changed, but without altering the most basic ideas.

There was, for example, always an individualistic undercurrent, especially in ghost worship. The very definition of ghosts rests on their existence apart from any normal social ties: They are the unincorporated dead, part of no larger social group. One worships for personal gain, not for family or community. Ghosts' individualizing function contrasts with the community base of gods, and their faceless anonymity and insistence on keeping the terms of a bargain recalls the market in ways that political petitions and tribute payments to gods do not. The ghostly side of Chinese religion grew very rapidly in the 1980s, at the point when many Taiwanese for the first time had achieved some significant wealth, but when the market economy also appeared particularly threatening and capricious, with few productive outlets for capital.[47]

The most utilitarian side of Taiwanese religion also appears to have grown. Spirit medium cults, usually based in private altars, provide personal help with none of the communal functions of major temples. Such cults have greatly increased recently in Taiwan. The horde of different gods that has begun appearing on private spirit medium altars—as many as forty or fifty different images in recent years—reinforces the utilitarian functions of such cults.[48] With each deity having its own specialty, these temples can meet the needs of a wider variety of clients, just like a shop that expands its selection of wares. Not coincidentally, spirit medium shrines themselves are profit-oriented petty capitalist enterprises.

The clear rise of organized sectarian religion in the past few decades also relates to the changing social and economic systems. The best-known pietistic sect is the Way of Unity (Yi-kuan tao), which has perhaps half a million regular followers.[49] Many of the sects have strong business support, and anecdotal evidence suggests that a disproportionate number of businessmen are sectarians.[50] Membership appears to have grown rapidly just during the period of Taiwan's most rapid economic growth, but the statistics may be misleading because the Way of Unity was illegal until 1987.

These sects claim a particular talent for capitalism, even more than everyday religion. While they drop some of the symbolic bolstering of a commodity economy in popular religion, like paper spirit money, they insist on a thorough moral accounting of their followers' entire lives, much like the Calvinists whose relation to capitalism Max Weber discussed.[51] As Berling writes about an earlier sectarian text, followers seek "self-improvement through morally responsible activity, including work."[52] Converts in these sects try to accumulate enough merit to achieve individual salvation; merit accrues to individuals, not families.[53] Even personal spirit-writing revelations usually apply only to the individual involved, with no attempt to force revelations on others.[54]

Sectarians also heavily emphasize explicit, textually validated values, much like Protestants, but unlike most popular religious practice.[55] Many spirit-writing sessions produce commentaries on Confucian and Taoist classics, and these may be discussed in regular meetings that resemble a combination of Protestant preaching and Sunday school. Constant themes include conservative standards in Taiwan like filial piety, respect for authority, and keeping appropriate relations of hierarchy between men and women, seniors and juniors, parents and children. At the same time, the sects share the utilitarian concerns of popular practice; they stress health, economic success, and similar issues.[56]

Various more strictly Buddhist sects have also grown enormously during the past two decades. They share at least two important characteristics with the pietistic sects like Yi-kuan Tao, both of which could be described as characteristically modern. First, all these religious organizations appeal to universalizing deities that claim relevance to all humanity, not just to their local turf. This feature is congruent with the new mobility of the population in its new realm of action on the national and world stages. It is difficult to argue for direct cause and effect here, but there is clearly what Weber called an elective affinity between religion and this feature of modern society.

Second, both Buddhism and pietistic sects offer reinvigorated systems of values for people who feel that values are disappearing from the world. Unlike most popular practice, which typically keeps its mixed moral messages implicit in practice, these groups offer explicit and systematic values. The perception that modernity destroys older communitarian values is widespread. It has been documented from areas just undergoing a market transformation, but is just as typical of societies like the United States with its regular complaints about the loss of family values.[57] Periodic revivals of such apparently nonmodern values have been a feature of modernity from the beginning, ranging from the nineteenth-century (and current) religious movements to the Romantics.

None of this means that there has been any fundamental transformation in Taiwanese religion, at least not so far. The very amorphous quality of popular religious practice has allowed it to adjust easily to changing times. Had it ever achieved a truly systematic orthodoxy, this religion might have faced a crisis during Taiwan's centuries of constant transformation. Instead, there has been a regular reproportioning and reinterpretation of the complex elements that had always been there.

Two Examples

To make this discussion more concrete, let us expand on two cases that exemplify religion changing over time. The first is the ritual treatment of ghosts in temples and in the Universal Salvation (Pho To), the major annual rite held for their benefit. Ghosts over the past century have retained their position of marginality to the social system and its moralities. Within that framework, however, evolving interpretations of ghosts have grown along with changing social experience and are reflected in ritual performance and even the scale of temples to ghosts. The second case is lay Buddhism, where existing resources have also taken on new forms, especially in the past few decades. Most striking has been the growth of an enormous charitable Buddhist group, with 3 million members and an annual charity budget of more than U.S.$20 million.

Ghosts

It is typically very difficult to trace popular religious practice back very far because the elites who wrote most of the texts tended to downplay it. We know that ghosts were worshiped in small shrines (*iu-ieng kong biou*), typically raised where unidentified bones have accidentally been exhumed or where unidentified bodies are found (battlefields, shipwrecks). Such shrines were never large or famous, but received occasional worship to keep the ghosts from causing trouble. They were said to be popular among people with the kinds of immoral requests that community gods would not grant—involving gambling or prostitution, for instance. These little temples are still very common everywhere in Taiwan.

A few good descriptions survive of the annual ghost festival dating from the middle and end of the nineteenth century, however, as do some earlier scraps of information. The contrast between these descriptions and the performances that could be witnessed a century later is striking, even though the priests conducting the ritual come from the same traditions and use the same ritual texts as they ever did. At least in some areas, the performance in the late nineteenth century frequently turned violent. Massive crowds would gather for the culmination of the priestly rituals, when the head priest ritually transformed the massive amounts of food offerings into even more massive (but invisible) amounts that could feed all the gathered ghosts. The real food offerings were piled onto raised platforms topped with poles that rose dozens of feet into the air. Masses of unruly young toughs would fight each other trying to steal the food offerings and the flags at the tops of the poles. The offerings were thought to bring good luck, and there was a market for the flags. The event was always partially out of control, and sometimes deteriorated into a riot, even as late as the 1920s. One Japanese colonial account describes how the platform of offerings was filled with people, "pushing and screaming, and robbing each other. Some people were pushed down the platform. They say that with the ghosts' protection they will not be hurt, but in fact large numbers are always hurt and killed."[58]

In all likelihood these violent performances became widespread only in the nineteenth century, although there is no way to prove the assertion. Certainly brief earlier mentions of the ceremony in Taiwan and descriptions from Fukien do not describe it in these terms. I have argued elsewhere that the rioters themselves took on the role of ghosts—they were socially marginal people acting just like starving ghosts desperate for their offerings.[59] By the late nineteenth century, parts of Taiwan had recreated a level of frontier violence that had not been common for a century. This was largely the result of the new camphor trade, which brought single young Chinese men deep into Taiwan's mountains for the first time. The new trade caused several kinds of social disruption: It fostered renewed battles with aborigines whose safe mountain strongholds were now being threatened; it created large numbers of unattached young men; and it encouraged them to organize a black market trade in defiance of the government monopoly on camphor.[60] These young men appear to have been the heart of the violent form of the Universal Salvation.

The riotous scenes disappeared sometime in the 1920s. By the time I first saw the ceremony in the 1970s there was no hint of violence, and the food offerings were being placed on ordinary tables. Concentration had moved from theft of the food offerings to the point of the ceremony when the priests toss out grains of rice and coins for the ghosts. These are caught by the human audience in front of the priests and bring good fortune. The spectators jostled and elbowed to get the thrown offerings, in a way vaguely reminiscent of the riots of much earlier. Yet the participants were no longer rootless young men; they were now primarily the old reproducing ghostly behavior in front of the altar. This was not a fundamental rethinking of the nature of ghosts. The riots had died out largely because that particular kind of marginal person was gone—the Japanese had discouraged Taiwanese camphor production, and chemical substitutes had undermined the world market for natural camphor by the early twentieth century. By the 1970s, however, the old had become a new kind of marginal persons, often feeling abandoned by a younger generation over which they had lost earlier kinds of parental authority to arrange marriage or to control major economic resources like farmland.[61]

By the 1990s two further uses of the ceremony had turned up. First, there has been a nostalgic revival of the earlier form, where offerings are placed on raised altars and people compete to grab them (but without the riot at the end). The eastern city of I-lan has led the way in this, encouraged by the local government, which wants to play up its preservation of tradition in the hope of building a reputation among tourists.[62] The effectiveness of such a strategy again shows a facet of modernity in the search to rediscover the pleasures of an idealized and romanticized past.

The second modern elaboration of the ceremony has been more strictly political. The Taipei county government, which has been under the control of the political opposition, has twice sponsored its own Universal Salvation. In part this is an appeal to specifically Taiwanese tradition. It implies a critique of the Kuomintang (Nationalist Party) government, which had discouraged such large and expensive religious festivals until democratization made such policies unpopular. In part it also offered a chance to appeal to quite modern causes. It included, for example, a ceremony for the salvation of the "dead" Tam-sui (Tan-shui) river—both appealing to the environmental movement and criticizing the industrial policies of the national government. It remains to be seen, however, whether such purely political uses of the festival will achieve any long-lasting significance.

Ghost shrines themselves have undergone a startling elaboration, especially during the economic boom of the 1980s. Apparently for the first time in Taiwan's history, some of them have grown to be among the most popular temples in Taiwan. These include the graves of a Japanese period outlaw, of a soldier turned bank robber, and of seventeen unidentified dead bodies and a dog that floated ashore in northern Taiwan. Like any ghosts, these will grant all kinds of wishes, not limited by any accepted standards of morality. All of them defied the government in some way (the two outlaws in life, and the seventeen dead bodies through their shrine, which halted construction of a nuclear power reactor). All of them earned a reputation in the 1980s by helping people choose winning numbers in an illegal lottery that swept the island. More important, they appealed to an image of the market at a time when people had a lot of cash but little direction for productive investment—an image of a tooth-and-claw world where those who get ahead do it without regard for anyone else, and with a great deal of serendipitous luck.[63] Ghosts are the ideal vehicle for such a view of the world.

This series of changes shows how the interpretation of ghosts has evolved over many decades, but without ever fundamentally altering the useful idea of ghosts as the unincorporated dead. Precisely because no one is in a position to successfully impose an interpretation on popular religious practice (although there have been many attempts), it has thrived in a changing world by allowing people to reproportion the many discontinuous possibilities it always included.

Buddhists

The history of Taiwanese lay Buddhism remains to be written. Buddhism itself, of course, has as long a history in Taiwan as does Chinese settlement. Monks and nuns have always taken on lay followers, who in turn provided an important means of financial support to Buddhist temples. These lay Buddhists often took some vows, emphasizing vegetarianism as the pre-eminent symbol of dedication to the Buddha. The "vegetarian halls" of women who ran their own small temples without any formal clergy involvement were mentioned above. This kind of lay involvement was often ideal for women, who could become deeply involved with Buddhism in this way without threatening their filial duty through vows of chastity. A few would bear and raise children to adulthood and then take full vows as Buddhist nuns.

Buddhism's particular appeal rested largely on its differences from other religious possibilities in Taiwan. Buddhism's complex cosmology reduced ultimately to two kinds of beings: Buddhas and Bodhisattvas, who had transcended the wheel of reincarnation, and everything else, from insects to humans to gods, who still suffered rebirth.[64] This contained the potentially radical implication that all the divisions of daily life—rich and poor, city and country, man and woman, even god and human—were ultimately empty. The Confucian hierarchy is at least potentially undercut by such a cosmology. In addition, Buddhism held up the ideal of the Bodhisattva, who had transcended this world, but swore not to leave it for nirvana until all humanity had been saved. This ideal was embodied in the Bodhisattva Koan Im, who has always been one of Taiwan's most important deities.

Koan Im is invariably depicted as a woman in long robes in Taiwan, although historically s/he appeared as a male in early Chinese representations, and I have had nuns tell me that s/he is beyond gender distinctions. This fits the idea of loving nurturance associated with the Bodhisattva, and Koan Im is sometimes shown holding a baby. Both sides of Buddhism—the erasure of worldly distinctions of rank and the nurturing ideal—help to explain the particular popularity of Buddhism among women in Taiwan.

We know very little about the sociology of lay Buddhism before the Nationalist period in Taiwan, except that women appeared to be especially active. After 1945, however, and especially from the 1970s on, Buddhism has been increasingly influential in Taiwan. Well-known monks and nuns began to draw large crowds for lectures and now regularly preach on television. College students were attracted to the subtleties of Buddhist philosophy and especially to the mysteries of Tibetan Buddhism, which had not been an important tradition in Taiwan earlier. Tibetan Buddhism offers them both an interesting intellectual world and the same sense of mystery and power that made Buddhism attractive to Romantics and transcendentalists in the nineteenth-century West.[65]

Some Buddhist clergy and monasteries have also attracted immense followings beyond intellectuals. Only one is discussed here, the Buddhist Compassion Merit Society (Tz'u-chi kung-te hui). This group now claims about 20 percent of Taiwan's population as contributors. It runs a hospital and a medical school in eastern Taiwan, has a larger welfare budget than the city of Taipei, and now has branches across the world, including at least five in the United States (with a free clinic in Los Angeles). It was founded in 1966 by a nun, the Rev. Cheng-yen, and a handful of followers. Cheng-yen says she was inspired to social action by two experiences—an aboriginal woman's miscarriage after she did not have enough money to be admitted to a clinic, and a visit from some Christians who criticized Buddhism for not helping anyone.

The original group of followers contributed a few cents a day of their shopping money and did piecework (originally sewing shoes) to raise a little more money. This very modest income was dedicated to helping the poor, especially to medical help. The massive popularity of the group began in the 1980s, by the end of which they had millions of members and a large core group of avid devotees. Followers make financial contributions in any amount. Some give just a few dollars, but there are many who give tens of thousands (in U.S. dollars) each year. Mere "checkbook membership," however, is discouraged. Cheng-yen pressures all followers to spend time volunteering—visiting the sick, identifying and taking help to the poor, or recruiting new members. Many of the wealthiest followers endure a long waiting list to put in a stint as candy stripers at the hospital. Members also meet regularly, where they listen to testimonials from each other about how their lives have improved since joining, and then hear from Cheng-yen herself, either in person or on videotape.

Buddhist ritual and Buddhist philosophy play only a minor role. Followers are not expected to recite sutras at length or to repeat the name of a Bodhisattva over and over, nor is there much explication of Buddhist thought. Instead the emphasis is consistently on action in the world—the Bodhisattva ideal made concrete. When Cheng-yen cites sutras, it is almost always to illustrate this idea of action in daily life. Followers are expected to cut down on personal consumption, be frugal in the broader world (for instance, by promoting recycling), and help the poor through contributions and work. This worldly emphasis differentiates the Compassion Merit Society from most other Buddhist groups and from the pietistic sects like the Yi-kuan Tao, which concentrate on text and ritual.

The Compassion Merit Society stands out in addition for its strongly female membership. Perhaps 70 to 80 percent of the members in Taiwan are women, although no formal rules of membership hint at any bias against men. To an extent, men feel the brunt of the group's discipline more than women; there is a prohibition on alcohol that appeals greatly to wives unhappy with their husbands' drinking, but that takes away an important business tool from men.

More important, however, are surely the special opportunities that the group offers to the relatively wealthy housewives who make up the core membership. These are women who do not need to work for a living (and prefer not to) and who can hire people to perform household chores. This is a new circumstance for the great majority of these women—it is the direct product of Taiwan's economic success. Yet for many it also comes with a feeling of alienation—that their lives have no point.

Many members of the group talk about their dissatisfaction with lives of conspicuous consumption, about their lack of goals in life, and about problems in their families. The Compassion Merit Society offers them a new kind of orientation, based very clearly on these women's ideas about femininity and motherhood. It allows them to take the ideas of nurturance, support, and love that valorize their roles at home, and play them out on a worldwide stage. As one informant put it:

> I realized that I used to love too narrowly. I had only two children, whom I was killing with my possessive love. And I was never happy with this painful love. But now I have so many children. I see everyone I help as my own child. I have learned that we have to make our mother love into a world love. And we will live a *practical* life every day! We will be happy every day![66]

Here the Bodhisattva ideal is read broadly as a dedication to social service, with a special appeal to women and nurturance. In some ways, the Compassion Merit Society is another in the long line of popularizing Buddhist revivals in Chinese societies. Yet its secular concerns with charity and particular appeal to women also recall similar movements in the modernizing West, like the Women's Christian Temperance Union or various women's Christian charities that thrived in the nineteenth century among similar classes of women. Its emphasis on nonmarket economics through charity, on avoiding the market pressures for consumption, and on recreating moral values mark the movement off as a reaction to Taiwanese modernity as much as it is a continuation of Chinese Buddhism.

A Taiwanese Religion?

It is difficult to escape the question of identity in Taiwan. Democratization since the lifting of martial law in 1987, a changing balance of power among mainland refugees and native-born Taiwanese, and the continuing tension in relations across the Taiwan strait have combined to foster a great deal of introspection about what it means to be "Taiwanese." Religious practice has always been tied closely to changing identity in Taiwan, and it should be no surprise that religion forms an important part of current arguments.

Religion could potentially be used to support at least three kinds of identity:

as Chinese, as part of a southeastern Hokkien and Hakka culture area, or as uniquely Taiwanese. All three cases are made by various people in Taiwan, although the main line of division is between the national reading and the local Taiwanese reading. In fact, of course, these three interpretations are not mutually exclusive, although their political implications may be—it is easy to imagine Taiwan as a part of China again, or as an independent nation, but the road between is difficult to travel, as the current government can attest.

At one level, Taiwanese religious practice is clearly Chinese. Even its more idiosyncratic developments like the popularity of ghost temples or the rise of the Compassion Merit Society remain comprehensible to Chinese people anywhere. Ancestor worship is widely shared and probably varies less across the Taiwan strait than within the mainland. Many of the same gods are important to Chinese everywhere—Koan Kong, Koan Im, and others play similar roles everywhere. Structurally, the association of gods with local communities in a nested hierarchy of kitchen gods at home, earth gods in the village, and community gods beyond is also ubiquitous. So is the idea of ghosts as the unincorporated dead, marginal to social categories of kin and community.

The case for a specifically southeastern religion, or ethnically Hokkien or Hakka religious traditions, rests primarily on local gods shared across the Taiwan strait, and on the genetic relationships between temples. Most community temples in Taiwan can trace the incense in their pots back to mother temples in Fukien. They either brought incense directly from these temples or took it from Taiwanese temples with direct ties to the mainland. This transfer of incense brings spiritual efficacy to the daughter temple and also establishes a hierarchy of incense-giver over incense-taker. On the other hand, similar regional networks tie temples together all across China. The case for a regional religious tradition may grow as economic and social links are reestablished, but it does not carry much weight so far.

The argument for Taiwanese uniqueness has been much more important in Taiwan and does have an empirical basis. Many of the regionally based gods have evolved independently on Taiwan to an extent, so that people can point to differences between images now carved on Taiwan and in Fukien. More important, the inherent flexibility and interpretability of ritual have allowed uniquely Taiwanese creations to develop. The Taiwanese versions of ghost worship discussed here may share some basic meanings with ghost worship across China, but they have also developed a particularly Taiwanese constellation of evocations, from the wild performances of the frontier days to the associations with the market in the past decade. The Compassion Merit Society is similarly a part of Chinese Buddhism, but also the creation of Taiwan's specific experience with modernity. One could as easily develop other examples, like the pietistic sects or the growth of spirit mediums.

Such regional variations themselves necessarily typify religious practice in a place like China, where there were no powerful institutions that could impose a unified interpretation. Taiwan is unique, but so is Szechuan or Shensi. Two opposing processes have affected how different Taiwan is. On the one hand, extensive Chinese settlement began only three centuries ago in Taiwan. Many areas of the mainland have had millennia to develop local traditions. This would lead us to expect relatively little difference between Taiwan and Fukien. On the other hand, Taiwan has been effectively separate from the mainland for almost all of the past century, which was a period of extraordinarily rapid change on both sides of the strait. This has helped encourage more rapid religious transformation. The lack of major structural change in the religion should not disguise how much day-to-day interpretations have evolved over the past century in Taiwan and thus how much they must differ from the mainland.

The situation has become significantly more complex in the past few years as lines of communication between Fukien and Taiwan have again opened up. One early result of this is that community temples send delegations back to mother temples on the mainland to renew their spiritual authority by taking incense ash. This process itself is open to multiple readings. Superficially it recreates the authority of home temples on the mainland over their Taiwanese descendants, putting the heart of authenticity on the mainland and leaving Taiwan as the dependent. One could easily see this as an affirmation of official government policy favoring a reunification of the Chinese people or possibly as a step toward some kind of southern Min ethnic unity.

Yet such a reading is too facile. Few members of these delegations would admit to having such intentions. Their actions have more important implications within Taiwan itself: these trips establish direct ties to the home temple, and can thus constitute a declaration of independence from intermediate mother temples on Taiwan itself. Thus several Taiwanese temples to the An-ch'i county god Co Su Kong have long claimed to be the original offshoot of the home temple on the mainland, from which the others grew as secondary or tertiary developments. One trip back, however, makes these arguments moot, as each returning temple can now claim direct ties to the original fount of spiritual authority. This attempt at upward mobility within the Taiwanese hierarchy has been seen most clearly in Taiwan's most famous Ma Co temples. The temple in Ta-chia returned to the home temple on the mainland very early, after which it claimed to be the equal of the temple in Pei-kang, arguably Taiwan's most famous single temple. It stopped participating in the annual pilgrimage to Pei-kang because it would no longer admit to an inferior status.[67]

The situation often becomes more complex still as a result of these trips. Taiwanese sometimes see temples whose neglect and abuse since 1949, especially during the Cultural Revolution, leaves them in terrible condition. Some complain about the poor quality of the restorations compared to Taiwanese temples or about how truly fine god images are now carved only in Taiwan. Such complaints begin to move the center of authenticity from the mainland back to Taiwan. After all, some people argue, Taiwanese temples never broke the stream of incense the way mainland temples did. This argument also evokes broader sentiments that Taiwan is now somehow more genuinely Chinese than China after decades of Communist rule. Such feelings that the power relations have been reversed are strengthened when Taiwanese donate huge amounts of money to rebuild mainland temples, as well as when they make business investments.

These return trips thus make a complex case: Power and authenticity appear in the mainland temples through the very act of going on pilgrimages there, but also shift back to Taiwan as pilgrims become the main investors in those temples and their communities, and as they experience a loss of tradition on the mainland. The political message is just as messy. Popular religion generally has been the realm of Taiwanese, not mainlanders, and using religion as the cutting edge of contact across the strait is ironic for both governments. Yet while the celebration of these very localist deities strengthens specifically Taiwanese traditions within Taiwan, it also promotes a kind of de facto reunification in this realm.[68]

This is a rather unsettled note on which to conclude this chapter, but perhaps that is appropriate for a situation in flux. The ironies, ambiguities, and contradictions in religious flows between Taiwan and the mainland, and within Taiwan itself, result in part from the fluid possibilities of Taiwanese religious practice itself: the relative weakness of the monastic tradition, the frontier conditions, the long separation from the mainland, the speed of social change, and the lack of any effective institutional authority over interpretation.

Notes

1. All romanization is in southern Min dialect unless noted otherwise.
2. For a discussion of problems in how the term "religion" is used in surveys in Taiwan, see Chang Mao-kui and Lin Pen-hsuan, "Tsung-chiao te she-hui i-hsiang—i-ko chih-shih she-hui-hsueh te k'o-t'i" [The social image of religion—a problem in the sociology of knowledge] (a paper presented at the Conference on the Psychology and Behavior of the Chinese, Institute of Ethnology, Academia Sinica, Nan-kang, 1992).
3. Important studies of ancestral worship include Emily Ahern, *The Cult of the Dead in a Chinese Village* (Stanford: Stanford University Press, 1973); Hsieh Jih-chang and Ying-chang Chuang, eds., *The Chinese Family and Its Ritual Behavior* (Taipei: Institute of Ethnology, Academia Sinica, Monograph Series B, no. 15, 1985); David K. Jordan, *Gods, Ghosts, and Ancestors: The Folk Religion of a Taiwanese Village* (Berkeley: University of California Press, 1972); and Arthur P. Wolf, "Gods, Ghosts, and Ancestors," in *Religion and Ritual in Chinese Society*, ed. Wolf (Stanford: Stanford University Press, 1974), pp. 131–182.
4. See Stevan Harrell, *Ploughshare Village: Culture and Context in Taiwan* (Seattle: University of Washington Press, 1982), pp. 117–128; and Robert P. Weller, *Unities and Diversities in Chinese Religion* (Seattle: University of Washington Press, 1987), pp. 31–32.
5. Such uxorilocal marriages were extremely common in some parts of Taiwan, although they completely reverse standard patrilineal practice. See Arthur P. Wolf and Chieh-shan Huang, *Marriage and Adoption in China, 1845–1945* (Stanford: Stanford University Press, 1980), pp. 94–107.
6. On affinal ties, see Bernard Gallin, "Matrilateral and Affinal Relationships of a

Taiwanese Village," *American Anthropologist*, 62 (1960): 632–642; and Robert P. Weller, "Social Contradiction and Symbolic Resolution: Practical and Idealized Affines in Taiwan," *Ethnology*, 23 (1984): 249–260.

7. See Emily Ahern, "Affines and the Rituals of Kinship," in Wolf, ed., *Religion and Ritual in Chinese Society*, p. 283; Margery Wolf, *Women and the Family in Rural Taiwan* (Stanford: Stanford University Pres, 1972), p. 125; and Robert P. Weller, "Social Contradiction."

8. I borrow this language from Pierre Bourdieu, *Outline of a Theory of Practice* (Cambridge: Cambridge University Press, 1977), pp. 34–35; see also Patricia Buckley Ebrey, *Confucianism and Family Rituals in Imperial China: A Social History of Writing About Rites* (Princeton: Princeton University Press, 1991).

9. On the definitions of ritual communities and belief spheres, see Lin Meirong, "Chang-hua Ma-tsu te hsin-yang ch'uan" [The belief sphere of Chang-hua Ma-tsu], *Bulletin of the Institute of Ethnology, Academia Sinica*, 68 (1989): 41–104.

10. See Emily Martin Ahern, *Chinese Ritual and Politics* (New York: Cambridge University Press, 1981).

11. On factions generally, see Joseph Bosco, "Taiwan Factions: Guanxi, Patronage and the State in Local Politics," *Ethnology*, 31, no. 2 (1992): 157–183; and Tsai Ming-hui and Chang Mau-kuei, "Formation and Transformation of Local P'ai-hsi: A Case Study of Ho-k'ou Town," *Bulletin of the Institute of Ethnology, Academia Sinica*, 77 (1994): 125–156.

12. See Meir Shahar and Robert P. Weller, "Introduction: Gods and Society in China," in *Unruly Gods: Divinity and Society in China*, ed. Shahar and Weller (Honolulu: University of Hawaii Press, 1996), pp. 1–36.

13. See, for example, Brigitte Baptandier, "The Lady Linshui: How a Woman Became a Goddess," in Shahar and Weller, eds., *Unruly Gods*, pp. 105–149.

14. James L. Watson, "Standardizing the Gods: The Promotion of T'ien Hou ('Empress of Heaven') Along the South China Coast, 960–1960," in *Popular Culture in Late Imperial China*, ed. David Johnson, Andrew J. Nathan, and Evelyn S. Rawski (Berkeley: University of California Press, 1985), pp. 300–302.

15. Weller, *Unities and Diversities, pp. 56–59.*

16. See Yu Kuang-hong, "Making a Malefactor a Benefactor: Ghost Worship in Taiwan," *Bulletin of the Institute of Ethnology, Academia Sinica*, 70 (1990): 39–66.

17. I have even run across one temple dedicated to Chiang Kai-shek.

18. Some of the flavor of the rivalries comes across in Michael Saso, *Teachings of Master Chuang* (New Haven: Yale University Press, 1978), which reflects in part the feelings of one important local Taoist.

19. For sources on this aspect of Taoism, see Saso, *Teachings;* Kristofer Schipper, *Le Corps Taoïste (Paris: Fayard, 1982); and Liu Chih-wan, T'ai-pei shih Sung-shan ch'i-an chien-chiao chi-tien* [Great propitiatory rites of petition for benifexperience at Sung-shan, Taipei] (Nan-kang: Institute of Ethnology, Academia Sinica, 1967).

20. Weller, *Unities and Diversities*, pp. 113–115.

21. There is a limited literature on these vegetarian halls, including Marjorie Topley, "The Great Way of Former Heaven: A Group of Chinese Secret Religious Sects," *Bulletin of the School of Oriental and African Studies*, 26 (1963): 362–392; Seiichiro Suzuki, *Taiwan chiu-kuan hsi-su hsin-yang* [Old customs and traditional beliefs of Taiwan] (Taipei: Chong-wen, 1978 [1934]), pp. 38–40; and J.J.M. DeGroot,. *Sectarianism and Religious Persecution in China* (Taipei: Literature House, 1963 [1903], p. 170). These groups deserve further study in Taiwan.

22. I will not discuss imperial state religion here, although it certainly was practiced in the Ch'ing dynasty. See Stephan Feuchtwang, "School-Temple and City God," in *The*

City in Late Imperial China, ed. G. William Skinner (Stanford: Stanford University Press, 1977), pp. 581–608.

23. See Dian H. Murray, *The Origins of the Tiandihui: The Chinese Triads in Legend and History* (Stanford: Stanford University Press, 1994).

24. Steven Sangren, "Traditional Chinese Corporations: Beyond Kinship," *Journal of Asian Studies*, 43, no. 3 (1984): 391–415.

25. See Cai Shaoqing, *Zhongguo jindai huidang shi yanjiu* [Research into the history of Chinese secret societies] (Beijing: Zhonghua shuju, 1987).

26. David K. Jordan and Daniel L. Overmyer, *The Flying Phoenix: Aspects of Chinese Sectarianism in Taiwan* (Princeton: Princeton University Press, 1986).

27. John R. Shepherd, "Sinicized Siraya Worship of A-li-tsu," *Bulletin of the Institute of Ethnology, Academia Sinica,* 58 (1984): 1–81.

28. Robert P. Weller, *Resistance, Chaos and Control in China: Taiping Rebels, Taiwanese Ghosts and Tiananmen* (London: Macmillan, 1994), pp. 47–48.

29. Gary Seaman, *Temple Organization in a Chinese Village* (Taipei: Orient Cultural Service, Asian Folkore and Social Life Monographs, vol. 101, 1978), pp. 114, 117; Gary Seaman, "The Sexual Politics of Karmic Retribution," in *The Anthropology of Taiwanese Society*, ed. Emily Martin Ahern and Hill Gates (Stanford: Stanford University Press, 1981), pp. 392–394.

30. See Lin Mei-rong, "Chang-hua Ma-tsu," p. 95.

31. Sangren, "Traditional Chinese Corporations."

32. The term *belief sphere* is from Lin Mei-rong, "Chang-hua Ma-tsu."

33. Ibid., p. 98.

34. Wang Shih-ch'ing, "Religious Organization in the History of a Taiwanese Town," in Wolf, ed., *Religion and Ritual in Chinese Society,* p. 81.

35. Wang Shih-ch'ing, "Religious Organization," pp. 89–91.

36. Seaman, *Temple Organization;* Weller, *Unities and Diversities,* pp. 54–56.

37. See, for example, Wang T'ien-tsung, *San-hsia ti-ch'u Yi-wei k'ang-Jih shih-liao* [Historical materials on the Yi-wei resistance to Japan in the San-hsia area] (San-hsia: author, 1967).

38. It was widely studied by folklorists whose materials have still not been adequately analyzed.

39. T'ai-wan sheng wen-hsien wei-yuan-hui, comp., *T'ai-wan sheng t'ung-chih* [Complete gazetteer of Taiwan province] (Taipei: Chung-wen, 1980), pp. 292–295.

40. Governor-general of Taiwan, *Taiwan ni okero jinja oyobi shukyo* [Shinto shrines and religion in Taiwan] (Taihoku: Bunkyokyoku shakaika, 1939), p. 10.

41. This was the part of the ritual called "robbing the lonely ghosts." See Weller, *Unities and Diversities,* for more detail.

42. P. Steven Sangren, "A Chinese Marketing Community: A Historical Ethnography of Ta-ch'i, Taiwan" (Ph.D. dissertation, Stanford University, 1979), p. 131.

43. See Lin Man-houng, "Wan Ch'ing T'ai-wan te ch'a, t'ang chi chang-nao" [Tea, sugar and camphor in late Ch'ing Taiwan], *T'ai-pei wen-hsien* 38 (1976): 1–9; and Ka Chih-ming, "Jih-chu T'ai-wan nung-ts'un chih shang-pin-hua yu hsiao nung ching-chi chih hsing-ch'eng" [The commodification of agricultural production and the formation of family farming agriculture in colonial Taiwan (1895–1945)], *Bulletin of the Institute of Ethnology, Academia Sinica*, 68 (1989): 1–40.

44. See Max Weber, *The Religion of China: Confucianism and Taoism* (New York: Free Press, 1951); and Robert N. Bellah, "Epilogue: Religion and Progress in Modern Asia," in *Religion and Progress in Modern Asia*, ed. Bellah (New York: Free Press, 1965), pp. 168–229.

45. Stevan Harrell, "Why Do the Chinese Work So Hard?" *Modern China*, 11, no. 2

(1985): 203–226; Hsieh Jih-chang, "The Chinese Family Under the Impact of Modernization," in *Anthropological Studies of the Taiwan Area: Accomplishments and Prospects*, ed., Kwang-chih Chang, Kuang-chou Li, Arthur P. Wolf, and Alexander Chien-chung Yin (Taipei: National Taiwan University, 1989), pp. 273–284; Siu-lun Wong, "The Applicability of Asian Family Values to Other Sociocultural Settings," in *In Search of an East Asian Development Model*, ed. Peter L. Berger and Michael Hsin-huang Hsiao (New Brunswick, NJ: Transaction, 1988).

46. Bernard Gallin and Rita Gallin, "Socioeconomic Life in Rural Taiwan: Twenty Years of Development and Change," *Modern China*, 8 (1982): 236–237; Harrell, "Why Do the Chinese Work So Hard?"; Li Yih-yuan, "T'ai-wan Min-chien tsung-chiao te hsien-tai ch'u-shih" [The modern tendencies of Taiwan's popular religion], *Wen-hua de t'u-hsiang* [Image of culture], 2 (1992): 117–138; Yu Ying-shih, *Chung-kuo chin-shih tsung-chiao lun-li yu shang-jen ching-shen* [Modern Chinese religious ethics and business spirit] (Taipei: Lunching, 1987).

47. See Weller, *Resistance, Chaos and Control,* pp. 146–153.

48. See Li Yih-yuan, "T'ai-wan Min-chien tsung-chiao."

49. Official statistics in 1991 listed about 1.5 million members of such sects, but they fail to distinguish sects officially registered as branches of Buddhism or Taoism (Tz'u-hui t'ang is the most important) or people who still deny membership because Yi kuan tao had been illegal until 1987.

50. See "Shenmi jiaopai chongshi tianri" [A secret sect sees the light of day again], *Yazhou zhoukan*, August 5, 1990, pp. 28–39; Chao Ting-chun, "Yi kuan tao ts'ai-li shen pu k'o ts'e" [The immeasurable wealth of the Yi kuan tao], *Wealth Magazine*, 121 (April 1992): 131. Perhaps 90 percent of Taiwan's vegetarian restaurants, for example, are said to be run by sect members (Chao, "Yi kuan tao"). The most prominent business example is Chang Jung-fa, chairman of one of the world's largest container shipping companies.

51. Max Weber, *The Protestant Ethic and the Spirit of Capitalism* (New York: Scribner's, 1958).

52. Judith A. Berling, "Religion and Popular Culture: The Management of Moral Capital in 'The Romance of the Three Teachings,'" in Johnson, Nathan, and Rawski, eds., *Popular Culture in Late Imperial China*, p. 217. Some current sects practice a kind of moral accounting, like the T'ien-ti chiao, which keeps track of good deeds. Many sectarians emphasize appropriate worldly action to realize religious ideals.

53. See Joseph Bosco, "Yiguan Dao: 'Heterodoxy' and Popular Religion in Taiwan," in *The Other Taiwan, 1945 to the Present*, ed. Murray A. Rubinstein (Armonk, NY: M.E. Sharpe, 1994).

54. See Jordan and Overmyer, *The Flying Phoenix,* p. 273.

55. See ibid., pp. 276–280; Cheng Chih-ming, "Yu-chi lei luan-shu so hsien-shih chih tsung-chiao hsin ch'u-shih" [The new trend in religious worship as seen from biographical travels, memoirs], *Bulletin of the Institute of Ethnology, Academia Sinica*, 61 (1987): 105–127.

56. See Cheng, "Yu-chi lei"; Chiu Hei-yuan, *Min-chien hsin-yang yu ching-chi fa-chan* [Popular beliefs and economic development], Report to the Taiwan Provincial Government (n.p.: Taiwan sheng cheng-fu min-cheng t'ing, 1989).

57. For two examples, see Michael T. Taussig, *The Devil and Commodity Fetishism in South America* (Chapel Hill: University of North Carolina Press, 1980); and Ai-hwa Ong, *Spirits of Resistance and Capitalist Discipline: Factory Women in Malaysia* (Albany: State University of New York Press, 1987).

58. Suzuki, *T'ai-wan chiu-kuan,* p. 473.

59. Weller, *Unities and Diversities*, pp. 80–81.

60. See chapter 7 in this volume by Gardella for more information on the camphor trade.

61. I develop this argument in *Unities and Diversities*, pp. 82–85.

62. This is based on interviews with the I-lan county executive, Yu Hsi-k'un, and the former county executive, Ch'en Ting-nan, in August 1993.

63. See Weller, *Resistance, Chaos and Control*, pp. 148–152, for more detail on this argument.

64. This simplifies to an extent, but probably captures the understanding of most lay Buddhists in Taiwan.

65. Tibetan Buddhism is similarly popular among intellectuals and professionals in the United States, and for very similar reasons.

66. See Chien-Yu Julia Huang and Robert P. Weller, "Merit and Mothering: Women and Social Welfare in Taiwanese Buddhism" (unpublished paper, n.d.), for an elaboration of this argument. See also Lu Hwei-syin, "Women's Self-Growth Groups and Empowerment of the 'Uterine Family' in Taiwan," *Bulletin of the Institute of Ethnology, Academia Sinica*, 71 (1991): 29–62.

67. See Hsun Chang, "Incense-Offering and Obtaining the Magical Power of Qi: The Mazu (Heavenly Mother) Pilgrimage in Taiwan" (Ph.D. dissertation, University of California at Berkeley, 1993), pp. 203–205; Murray Rubinstein, "The Revival of the Mazu Cult and of Taiwanese Pilgrimage to Fujian," *Harvard Studies on Taiwan: Papers of the Taiwan Studies Workshop*, vol. 1 (Cambridge: Fairbank Center for East Asian Research at Harvard University), pp. 89–125.

68. For a very sensitive discussion of the implications of religious transactions between Taiwan and Fukien, see Steven Sangren, "Anthropology and Identity Politics in Taiwan: The Relevance of Local Religion" (paper presented at the Taiwan Studies Workshop, Fairbank Center for East Asian Research, Harvard University, 1995).

13

Taiwan's Socioeconomic Modernization, 1971–1996

Murray A. Rubinstein

Chengde Road in Taipei.

This chapter examines the large-scale economic and societal changes that have occurred in Taiwan since 1971, such as the development of a new, more activist middle class, and a new urban environment. These new forces and conditions generated sociopolitical pressures that forced the regime to reform itself and that changed the pace and nature of political change and democratization. The chapter begins with an examination of the development of the export-oriented industrial economy that transformed the face of the island, made it a major player in the world economy, and forced the pace of both social change and political evolution.[1] The discussion then turns to the multileveled and multifaceted societal evolution that gave birth to an educated, articulate, and politically conscious middle class that would use its new-found power to push for changes in Taiwan's political structure (examined in Chapter 15).[2] The conclusion explores the process of urbanization that changed the face of the Taiwanese landscape.

Economic Development

The first stage of Taiwan's dramatic economic transformation took place from the early 1950s to the early 1960s. Formal planning structures were put in place, and Chinese economic specialists, with input and advice from American advisers, developed an import-substitution industrialization strategy to prevent the outflow of capital and to lay the foundation for further development. During the first phase of import substitution, certain products with potential value as exports were produced. Processed agricultural goods, for example, led the way here. Sugar and rice became the island's major exports. However, another key product that was not a foodstuff had potential in the world market—textiles. By 1959 textile production had increased 50 percent over earlier levels and exports of textiles increased 500 percent. In 1960 textile production increased yet another 19 percent and exports of textiles increased 74 percent over the previous year. Over the course of the 1960s, textiles would become Taiwan's single-largest export product.[3]

Before going further, we must examine the changes in another important sector of the economy from the 1950s to the 1990s—the rural sector. While many people left the countryside, agriculture remained important. The land reform measures gave many farmers greater opportunity, and they took full advantage of it. Rice continued to be the major crop, but after the 1970s there was also considerable diversification as new methods and new crops were introduced.[4] American and Chinese agricultural specialists worked hard to bring these developments about, teaching the farming population the new methodologies and promoting the introduction of new strains and new crops. Increasingly, farming became more commercialized.[5] Furthermore, better methods of flood control opened new lands or those that were formerly dangerous to use—primarily the river beds of the major central and southern westward-flowing rivers—for cultivation. In real terms, over the course of the 1950s and 1960s, agricultural output increased. However, by the early 1970s the rate of increase had slowed down, and in 1975 one could see a decrease in the growth of farm crops and related products. The general decline continued into the 1980s.[6]

This decline forced some to move into new forms of agricultural production. One important new crop was flowers. While floriculture has been practiced on the island since the 1600s, only since the 1970s have Taiwanese steadily developed this industry. By 1990, 6,300 hectares were devoted to growing flowers. One good reason for this shift to flowers was that in 1990 a hectare of rice produced U.S.$3,000, a hectare of flowers produced U.S.$24,000. As a result the island has become a major exporter of a wide variety of flowers and other decorative plants, finding major markets in nearby Japan, the United States, Singapore, Hong Kong, and that most famous of flower-producing nations, the Netherlands (which controlled Taiwan during the early seventeenth century). Japan was the largest market for live flowers, while the United States bought dried flowers and potted plants. The Netherlands bought potted plants as well as young sprouts that could easily be raised in Dutch greenhouses. The Taiwanese flower industry competed with those in Southeast Asia, but those who observed the industry believed that it would continue to meet the challenges with new varieties and with products of high quality.[7] Certainly for the farmers, this new crop proved a boon and kept people on the farm with the hope of good salaries and continued expansion of production.

These changes, while important, could not stop the inevitable decline of the agricultural sector. While 13 percent of the work force was involved in agriculture in the early 1990s, agriculture accounted for only 4 percent of the gross national product. Furthermore that work force was aging. Adding to the pressure on those farmers who remained was the fact that agricultural land near major suburbs was needed for new highways, rapid transit systems, or new housing complexes. Given the straits in which farming families found themselves, the money offered by the government was too high to turn down. It was also increasingly clear to farmers that agriculture was no longer the fundamental sector in the national economy. They experienced a liberation of sorts and felt emancipated from their static way of life. Because of this, the very value system of the farmer was changing. And this is clearly reflected in the attitudes toward the land itself. Huang Chun-chieh, a historian of modern Taiwanese agriculture *and* the age of the Chou philosophers, puts it this way: "Land was no longer considered 'sacred' family property; rather, it became a 'secular' transferable commodity."[8]

The development of aquaculture provided rural areas with a much-needed boost. Those holding property in low-lying areas along the coast now found new opportunities. Fish ponds and the raising of carp and other seafood had long been a part of the rural economy, but, on Taiwan, the new technologies were brought to bear on this sector as well as on agriculture. In the fish ponds that dot the landscape near the sea are grown many different fish and shellfish. Milkfish, a staple in soups and congee (rice porridge) for centuries, are grown in brackish or freshwater ponds in the southern part of the island near Tainan. Eel (*man*), brought by the Japanese in the early 1950s, are raised in freshwater ponds and prepared roasted or smoked. Tilapia is another popular fish grown in brackish or freshwater ponds. Carp, the classic pond fish, continues to be popular, especially during the lunar new year, and is usually served braised or steamed. Mullet are raised only for their roe, which are dried and roasted. Grass shrimp are raised in brackish ponds in southern Taiwan and are prized as a delicacy, as are oysters. Finally, sea cucumber, a basic ingredient in many Chinese seafood dishes, are now being produced.[9] Over the course of the 1970s and 1980s, the industry made notable gains, in part because of the government's willingness to set up research institutes that worked with those involved in the aquaculture industry. However, the shift to the use of fish ponds has created problems as well, including salinization and a sinking of the land due to the drainage of water from the existing water table. Industrial pollution of the water sources is seen as another problem, one with no easy solution. Moreover, the industry reached a point in the 1990s at which it was suffering from its own success, with certain species flooding the market. The solution to this problem is shifting production to higher-quality types of fish, which can bring higher prices from the consumer. In this realm of rural life, Taiwanese are making use of the readily available resources of brackish water and the centuries' old skills of the fish pond farmer to sustain and increase this industry's growth.[10]

The government realized from the beginning that import substitution was not an end in itself but simply a starting point for a more sophisticated and more realistic economic strategy. From the mid-1950s to the end of that decade, certain measures were taken to move the economy to this second, more sophisticated stage of development. In 1958 came the implementation of a monetary exchange formula that created a more unified exchange scheme. A second step was taken in 1960, when a five-year tax holiday was declared for new ventures in certain types of manufacturing. The income tax was exempted for redistributable (reinvested) profit and was also reduced for proceeds gained through export. Interest rates were also raised on savings, which may have led to a dramatic jump in the percentage of funds being saved by households—from between 5 percent and 8 percent from 1952 to 1962 to 13 percent in 1963. Such additional funds provided industry with additional seed money. The final step in the implementation of the new economic strategy came in 1966, when export processing zones were set up. Such zones had streamlined administrations and support from the power utilities and were developed to foster the export manufacturing sector.[11]

Each of these decisions, as the architects of the new strategy such as K.T. Li and as economic analysts such as Wang Chi-hsien have informed us, were designed to redirect the economy and fit the Republic of China into a worldwide, Western-directed economic system. Taiwan now had increasingly well-educated workers (though these workers were still paid little relative to their Western contemporaries), power and transportation infrastructure, and security guaranteed by both an American military presence and the existence of a now well-trained and well-armed military force. It was considered one of the five best places to locate an export-oriented economy. The island *was* resource poor but did have both a skilled and unskilled labor force, a stable monetary system, and a regime that was in control of the labor force and had a say in the role of the private sector.

During this preparatory period, government planners working with officials at the U.S. Agency for International Development (AID) had decided to exploit the island's major resource—its people. Those officials who represented the regime to foreign investors—at this point both Westerners and Japanese—could also offer the foreign industrialists a host of incentives—special economic zones and other attractive perks. They could guarantee, for example, that if the goods these manufacturers produced were intended only for markets outside Taiwan, then that concern could be wholly foreign-owned. If, however, these firms involved themselves in Taiwan's domestic market, then Taiwanese would have to own 50 percent of the company and Taiwanese would have to supply a certain percentage of the components of the product that was being assembled and sold in the Republic of China. This became the situation in the 1970s and 1980s as the effects of economic growth were felt more and more by larger numbers of people on the island and as the demand for readily available, cheaper, and better-quality consumer goods became widespread. The jointly established Taiwanese–American or Taiwanese–Japanese assembly plants that were set up were the most striking examples of this second pattern of foreign industrial investment.[12]

During the 1960s and for many years thereafter, it was the electronics industry that was most attracted to Taiwan and saw its potential as a processing or assembly center. This industry was important in several ways. First, it was not in any way indigenous to the island—there had been no tradition of producing products at this technical level. Second, it was not developed, at least at first, to meet the needs of local consumers. Finally, it was an industry whose owners supplied everything it needed from outside the country except a hard-working and increasingly skilled work force. The decision of the Republic of China's technocrats, a decision made with the help of U.S. AID officials, proved correct. As Wang and others have shown, major electronics companies in the United States, the Netherlands, and Japan were attracted to the incentives offered by ROC officials. These companies produced products that were compositions of components or component modules. These could be shipped easily from suppliers in other nations or, later, from other areas on Taiwan because of their light weight. Furthermore, while the design, development, and processing of key components was both technology-intensive and capital-intensive, the actual assembly of components could be done by hand by a low-skilled labor force for low wages. When one combined the nature of the electronics industry as it stood at that point in the 1960s with the willingness of a government to set aside land for industrial development, tax rebates, and the extended tax holiday, one came up with a package deal that the major players found irresistible.[13]

The newly arrived firms found a low-cost, dedicated, and readily trained work force at their disposal, a work force that—given the totalitarian nature of the Taiwan government and that state's control of labor unions—was not then able to organize itself and confront potential exploitation at the hands of the foreign owners. From 1965 to 1970 alone, the new industries helped create new growth in the work force and, in turn, made possible a dramatic drop in unemployment rates.[14]

The rise in employment in the industrial sector meant that within a relatively short time wages were able to rise. This rise in wages was accompanied by a corresponding rise in productivity, for the various educational reforms, including the single most important change in the educational process—the increase in the number of years of free public schooling—was creating a better-trained and more skilled labor force that was able to cope with the more technical demands made upon it. Furthermore, as the export orientation spread to other industries, new actors, not just the large-scale international firms, began to enter the picture. As a result the industrial structure that had evolved began to change. Decentralization became an accepted pattern. Smaller-scale industrial firms began to produce more specialized goods in an increasingly fragmented system. This alternative structure, one that was open to low-level and small-scale entrepreneurs, took hold and coexisted with the large-scale and largely foreign-owned structure that had evolved in the mid-1960s. Westerners learned to play roles in this new system: members of small and midsized import/export firms from the West soon learned the advantages offered by the new system. One rather basic advantage was the lack of any need by the Westerners to build on-site factories and invest in the machinery needed to manufacture their products. Instead these Western businessmen would help establish or work with an often complex network of suppliers who would in turn be linked to even smaller-scale manufacturers further down the chain. One result of this could be seen by the early 1970s in the appearance of the home factories that many members of the lower middle class and the working class either ran or labored in.[15]

Perhaps the best example of this facet of the "Taiwan miracle," the term most used for the process of economic transformation, can be found in the development of the shoe industry, an industry whose heyday paralleled Chiang Ching-kuo's years in power. Ian Skoggard, an anthropologist, has examined this industry, which he sees as a paradigm of Taiwan's market-dependent (or market-driven) economy. Under this system Taiwanese-owned factories manufacture shoes (or other commodities), which are then sold under the brand name of a transnational or foreign retailing company. The advantage of this arrangement is that Taiwan's capital-short entrepreneurs, who are removed from affluent foreign markets, are able to industrialize relatively cheaply. However, this same system places upon the Taiwanese businessman the burden of fixed capital costs without the market share to protect that investment. There were other problems as well, for the Taiwanese economy was vulnerable to world recessions, oil embargoes, trade restrictions, changes in exchange rates, and competition from industrializing nations with lower costs of living and even cheaper labor. To deal with these problems, these entrepreneurs spread the risk of investment broadly and this, in turn, resulted in a landscape of small-scale, decentralized industries. In the end, because they had no leverage to influence the prices of either the raw materials or the finished shoes, and had to be content to exist either as price-takers between the large Taiwanese petrochemical manufacturers who supplied the plastics that were their basic raw materials and the foreign marketing companies, they could only realize a profit and maintain their viability through two measures—the hiring of women and the paying of piece wages.[16] Skoggard argues that, in the final analysis, even in this industry where the raw materials or semiprocessed materials are available from local sources, it is still labor—and low-cost labor—that fueled the shoe industry and this important segment of the manufacturing sector.[17]

If we examine Taiwan's manufactured exports for the 1980s, we can see that most of them were produced either by the large export processors or by the smaller-scale local entrepreneurs who were part of the multilevel export-oriented manufacturing system. During this period, manufactured exports grew 267 percent in value. The effect that this development had could readily be seen. While the population grew at 2 percent per year, the labor force increased 3.6 percent. This differential was caused by the steady decline in the number of people involved in agriculture. The agricultural sector continued to release more labor, and industry gained 8.1 percent per year. By 1980 agriculture employed 20 percent of the work force, industry 42 percent, manufacturing 33 percent, and services 38 percent. The export-oriented strategy had changed the demographic profile of the Taiwanese work force and the face of the physical landscape as well.

There are other indicators of the effectiveness of this strategy over this period that Wang considers its heyday. From 1971 to 1976, exports contributed 80 percent of manufacturing growth or 68 percent of total product growth. And the value increase of exports from 1971 to 1980 was 789 percent. This growth was more in terms of quantity of units produced than in actual unit value.

But what of the economy as whole? This growth, as impressive as it was, could not mask certain realities, realities that as early as the mid-1970s were, government planners believed, impediments to future expansion. The most basic reality was the "sheer inadequacy of the infrastructure." Under the pressures created by two decades of growth severe bottlenecks appeared in transportation facilities and in power supply.[18] On the surface, the power system was adequate, for it showed an 88 percent increase in the years from 1966 to 1971. However, this growth, which averaged about 13 percent a year over this span, still lagged behind the rising demand of the industrial sector. Their demand for power increased 20 percent per year, creating a shortfall of 7 percent. A second problem that faced the industrial sector was the growing demand for key inputs. Only in the textiles and petrochemical-based plants were these demands met. In other industries shortages of inputs—raw or semiprocessed materials—remained the norm.

What was called for was a set of coherent and multifaceted governmental policies and actions. Chiang Ching-kuo, now in full command of his nation, and his technocratic subordinates rose to the challenge and developed initiatives that paved the way for further socioeconomic growth in the late 1970s and in the 1980s. The "Ten Major Projects" was the regime's full-scale assault on the problems plaguing infrastructure. Chiang decided to invest U.S.$8 billion in ten critical large-scale projects.

Some of these projects were designed to improve transportation. The first was the construction of a north–south superhighway. The second was the construction of a new full-scale international airport. The third was development of two new port facilities. The fourth and the fifth involved improvements of the island's rail system.[19]

Other projects were intended to cater to the growing demand for electric power. The economic planners had concluded some years before that nuclear power was the solution and had constructed a reactor in northern Taiwan to meet the needs of the Taipei basin. The second major plant was constructed on the site overlooking the Half-Moon bay near the Kenting/Olanpi resorts in the southernmost part of the island. Development of expanded industrial capacity was included in the plan as well. Two new factories were begun. One was a modern integrated steel mill, and the other was a large shipbuilding plant.[20]

Funds for these projects came from changes in the income tax system. As a result of these changes, savings were channeled into public capital formation. The multiplier effect that was generated by the public investment and these changes in fiscal policy provided the funds for infrastructure development and jump-started an economy hurt by the rapid rise in post-1973 oil prices.[21]

The "Ten Major Projects" was but a first step, however. Because he anticipated further expansion of the economy, Chiang Ching-kuo wanted to have his nation ready. Thus the government allocated U.S.$23 billion for fourteen additional large-scale projects. By the end of the 1970s the government's investment in the nation's transportation system, power grid, and large-scale industrial facilities had risen more than five times. The results of this investment were ultimately very impressive, as these two indicators suggest: The length of the highways had more than doubled, and the supply of electricity produced had tripled. Cheng concluded, "The improvement of the infrastructure laid the foundation for the further economic advances of the 1980s."[22]

A second facet of Chiang's plan for economic improvement concerned the industrial sector. The technocrats that worked with Chiang were aware of the industrial sector's two major vulnerabilities—its reliance upon foreign supply of oil and foreign technology.

The oil crisis that came in the wake of the 1973 Yom Kippur War forced the planners to confront the fact that Taiwan, as a nation without its own supplies of oil, would be held captive by events thousands of miles away in the Middle East. They urged that the industries develop more efficient modes of production. They also decided to promote and support those industries that were characterized by "low energy consumption, high technological intensity, and high value added."[23] The industries were also defined as "strategic industries." These included the machine tool industry, the transportation equipment industry, the electronics industry, and finally, the computer/information industry.[24]

Of these strategic industries, it was the information/computer industry that proved the most significant. Some statistics demonstrate this. Between 1984 and 1988, the export value of Taiwan-manufactured hardware products increased more than five times, from U.S.$1 billion to U.S.$5.15 billion, and by early 1990 Taiwan had emerged as one of the world's largest exporters of personal computers.[25] The annual visitor to Taipei could see this transformation taking place over the course of these years by visits to Haglers Alley, near the Taipei post office, and the Kuang-hua Market, on Pa-te Road, under the Hsin-sheng Nan Road underpass. In the early 1980s one could see shops on Haglers Alley selling Apple clones and pirated software. However, as the decade went on PC clones became the norm and more sophisticated hardware and software became available.

The transformation of the Kuan-hua market also demonstrates the change. In the late 1970s the site was a two-story bazaar where one could buy cheap antiques, old books and magazines, and student paintings. It was a delightful and always busy site that one could enjoy walking through, searching the stalls at one's leisure. By the late 1980s and early 1990s, it had changed. While the bookshops were still there, hi-fi stores occupied each story, as did antique stores carrying very high-quality merchandise (from China), and stores that specialized in PCs, printers, peripherals, and software took up much of the floor space. This classic, old, enclosed urban market had become a computer supermarket.[26]

A third major facet of the new economic initiative concerned the promotion of research and development. In 1979 the regime enacted a statute governing the establishment and administration of science-based industrial parks. The first such industrial park set up was designed to house residential and commercial centers, research institutes and institutes of higher learning, and industrial laboratories. The idea was to provide the enterprises operating in the park with easy access to "a large pool of highly trained scientists and technicians as well as technical data and R-and-D facilities."[27]

The Hsin-chu Science-Based Industrial Park (SBIP) was developed over the course of the 1980s, and by 1990 had become recognized as one of the most advanced R and D centers in East Asia. One hundred thirteen high-tech firms had located there, with total revenues of NT$60 billion. The major firms were producers of computers and computer peripherals. There are also producers of integrated circuits, manufacturers of telecommunications equipment, automakers, producers of environmental biotechnology equipment and energy-related equipment. Tsinghua University, Taiwan's most prestigious technical university, is also located in the area. This center of research and high-tech industry located 45 miles down the freeway from Taipei is the ROC's Silicon Valley and is, in Cheng's view, "a model for many developing countries."[28]

The high-profile projects that President Chiang promoted over the course of the 1980s were followed by less-spectacular but equally important changes in the way the people of Taiwan did business. There were five facets of this process of fiscal/financial liberalization that were introduced as a way of aligning the island's economy to the changing world and domestic situation.

One change was spurred by the problem of Taiwan's trade surplus, a problem recognized by both the Nationalist government and nations like the United States that were Taiwan's largest trading partners. These nations believed that Taiwan's domestic markets had to be opened. Before the government officials began reviewing the system there were 8,848 items subject to such restrictions. When the review was concluded, the number had been reduced dramatically to 86. Many more commodities were now allowed in the Taiwanese market. Furthermore the duties on imported goods were reduced to 5.7 percent, a figure similar to that found in the major industrialized nations. Over the course of the 1990s, rates were cut further to 3.5 percent.

Government action of this sort was only one step that was taken. The regime went even further. It voluntarily assisted U.S. firms, helping them secure a larger share of the domestic market as a means of stimulating the sale of foreign exports in Taiwan. And the government conducted extensive market promotions on the island. These policies were aimed at shrinking the trade surplus as a means of reducing tensions between Taipei and Washington.[29]

A second major fiscal/economic reform involved exchange controls. Before 1987 the government had exercised very tight control on the amounts of foreign currency individuals could hold and on the amount of New Taiwan dollars they could exchange. After 1987 and the new policy on Taiwanese interaction with the mainland, the government had drastically loosened such restrictions. Taiwanese citizens were now permitted to make outward remittances of U.S.$5 million per person per year. There is a ceiling on inward remittances in order to "prevent hot money flocking into Taiwan for speculation." The new currency regulation had the desired effects: There was an increasing outflow of capital—more than U.S.$25 billion from 1988 to 1992.[30]

A third step involved export markets for Taiwanese goods. Cheng, Wang, and other economists thought that the Republic of China was vulnerable because of its trade relationship with the United States. In the year 1985, for example, 48 percent of Taiwan's exports went to the United States. The U.S. government took initiatives to stem the outflow of capital to Taiwan. One step was to force the appreciation of the New Taiwan Dollar, which, over time, "substantially reduced Taiwan's competitive power in the international market place."[31] The United States also decided to end Taiwan's most favored nation trade status.

These steps forced the government of the ROC to act. It began a program to diversify Taiwan's export markets. Trade was expanded with Western Europe and with Southeast Asia—and investment in Southeast Asia also became significant. It also tried to promote its goods with sophisticated marketing campaigns.[32] This new policy has succeeded: by the 1990s the percentage of Taiwanese exports to the United States dropped below 30 percent while exports to Hong Kong, Southeast Asia, and Western Europe sharply increased.[33]

A fourth and related economic reform was designed to transform the financial system. Economists on the island had long considered the system outdated and inefficient because of the Bank of China's monopolistic position and because of laws these experts and those working within the system considered obsolete. The regime took dramatic steps to deal with these problems. Government banks were privatized, private banks were established, and foreign banks were allowed to open up offices.[34] The result of these reforms was enhanced efficiency, greater cooperation, liberalization of the whole banking structure, and globalization of what had been a national and rather isolated system.[35]

A final step taken was the opening to the People's Republic of China. This step had political, economic, social, and cultural consequences. It is examined in more detail in Chapter 16 within the context of Taiwan's political evolution and its diplomatic initiatives of the 1980s and 1990s.

The multitude of changes examined here helped pave the way for the island's development in the 1990s, but more was needed. As Wang Chi-hsien has suggested, the very strategy of export-oriented development had to be reconsidered, a view echoed by Philip Liu.[36] The government of the ROC had to take a hard look at basic infrastructure needs. An expanded and modernized infrastructure would be needed in order to help stave off or lessen the impact of the doldrums and the downshifts that developing nations sometimes experienced.[37]

The regime, now led by Lee Teng-hui, a Taiwanese Presbyterian, did not stand still. Recognizing looming crisis in urban development and transportation and a rising tide of middle-class dissatisfaction with the very visible negative side affects of rapid and often unchecked development, it began to take a new series of steps and consider long-range development goals. In 1991 it began yet another major and very costly initiative—the Six-Year National Development Plan. The projects included in this plan were similar to the large-scale governmental projects of the earlier decades and were intended to improve the island's infrastructure. One major new plan was the Taipei rapid transit system. This system was designed to combine subways with elevated railways in Taipei and surface system that connected Taipei with nearby suburbs such as Tam-sui.[38] Another project was a high-speed rail system designed to connect Taipei with Kao-hsiung.[39] These plans and related projects were ambitious, but there were problems, such as land acquisition. The Taipei real estate market was booming, and prices for the land needed raised the cost of the project considerably.[40] Design flaws in the system as well as problems with the quality of construction also plagued the effort. Some also criticized the government and conservative firms involved in building the system for creating difficulties in the transfer of needed technologies.[41] Financing of so grand a scheme was also a problem.[42] Yet the work continued throughout the 1990s.

Infrastructure changes were only one piece of the "redevelopment" puzzle. A second important component were changes in the industrial sector itself. Recognizing this, the Executive Yuan in 1993 began an initiative designed to "boost private investment in manufacturing industries."[43] Another equally ambitious initiative began to take shape in the early 1990s. Recognizing that a PRC-held Hong Kong would no longer serve as the communications and financial/corporate hub of East Asia, Taiwanese officials and business leaders began to make the case for Taipei to play that crucial role.[44]

This discussion of the implementation of the new multilevel plans developed in the early 1990s suggests that the ROC government saw the need for flexibility and for basic shifts in the nature of the economy. It set in motion what is now an ongoing process of "maturation."

This section offers insight into the nature of the economic changes that have transformed Taiwanese life, but without exploring the human dimensions of this process of economic development. The next section addresses the question of the impact of this far-reaching economic/fiscal development upon Taiwan's landscape, Taiwan's society, and life-style and personal interaction of Taiwan's citizens.

Social Change

The economic transformation had direct and very visible effects upon the society of Taiwan between 1971 and 1996. Such changes were many and complex.

One set of changes took place in the educational system. This expansion of the basic system helped make possible changes in career path and occupation. The Nationalists built upon the base that the Presbyterian Church and the Japanese had constructed and upon their decades of experience running an educational system in those parts of China that they controlled.[45] After the late 1940s the authorities began to reshape the Taiwanese system so that it would conform to the system they had developed, with some success, on the Chinese mainland.[46] The authors of a booklet published by the Ministry of Education show us that the number of students and the number of schools increased steadily from 1950 to 1977. In 1950 there were 1,504 schools serving the needs of 1,054,927 students, figures that rose steadily: By 1961 the figures stood at 3,095 schools and 2,540,665 students. In 1968 the government expanded the system by extending the years of mandatory public education from six to nine. By 1971, six years after the implementation of the export-oriented economic plan, and three years after an increase in the number of years of mandatory education, there were

4,115 schools and 4,130,671 students.[47] These figures continued to increase over the next six years, and, in 1977, the final year cited in the booklet, there were 4,698 schools with 4,522,037 students.[48] The amount of funding for the school system and the increase in levels of funding from 1961 to 1977—the last year statistics were available to the authors—appears in another chart in the booklet, showing that in 1961 the expenditure for education was about NT$2 billion and that it rose steadily after that date until 1974, when it stood at NT$15 billion and then increased at a higher rate for the next three years to the 1977 level of NT$31 billion. By 1977 the percentage of GNP spent on education stood at about 4.5 percent, an increase of two percentage points over the proportion in the base year, 1961.

The basic educational system, as it existed in 1978, consisted of primary schools that the students throughout the island attended for six years. At that point students had the option of attending junior high schools. After 1968 these junior high schools were constructed all over the country. All students were able to attend these schools, even though they were not compulsory. There was also a system of special junior high schools—elite schools in Taipei, for example—that could be entered only by recommendation, using inside influence (*kuan-hsi*), or by finding housing nearby. The competition to get into such schools was fierce, for attending such schools better prepared the student for the high school exams and for survival in the elite high schools and in the universities.[49]

Members of both sexes attended these schools though males outnumbered females in the junior high schools during the 1960s. During that decade there were 22 percent more boys than girls in the system. After the 1968, with the expansion of the junior high school system, the gap narrowed and by the mid-1970s that gap stood at 10 percent.[50]

There was also a high school system in place after 1950. Of those students who had attended junior high school, 75 percent entered either the academic or the vocational high schools. Those who did not go to either entered the expanding job market. To be admitted to the high schools, students had to take competitive examinations, which often defined one's occupation and career path. The vast majority of these high schools were public, but the Presbyterian high school in Tainan continued to operate, educating students as it had for more than a century. The impact of Taiwan's industrialization could be seen in the development of the high school system in the 1970s. After 1971 the number of vocational high schools increased, and those schools already built were expanded. By mid-decade the number of students in such schools exceeded the number of those in the academic high schools. The new industries demanded more educated workers, and these schools provided them.[51]

High school students who wanted to attend college had one hurdle remaining—another comprehensive examination. By the mid-1970s about 30 percent of those who took these exams passed them. For those who did not get a sufficiently high grade to attend college or university on a full-time basis there were a number of options: night classes for part-time students and a system of junior colleges and normal colleges. Thus the real figure for those attending institutions of higher learning stood at 60 percent.

About half the students who passed the exam were admitted to one of the public universities that dotted the urban and suburban landscapes of the island. The usual procedure was to apply for entrance to a university and a department and then hope that one scored well enough to attend the school of one's choice. National Taiwan University (T'ai-ta) was first on the list of many students. Following Tai-ta were other institutions in Taipei or its nearby suburbs such as Taiwan Political Affairs University (Cheng-ta), Taiwan Normal University (Shih-ta), or other national universities located in major centers or in smaller cities in other parts of the island. These schools included National Central University (Chung-ta) at Chung-li on the west coast, Tsinghua University in the industrial city of Hsin-chu, Chung Hsing University in Taichung, Cheng-kung University (named after the great hero Cheng Ch'en-kung) in Tainan. The structure of these universities was uniform, with a president at the top and the different colleges within the university headed by various deans, the key figure being the dean of studies. In addition to the deans of the academic divisions—the colleges—there were also deans or administrators for the Office of General Affairs and the Office of the Dean of Discipline and Guidance. Decisions on personnel were made by administrators such as deans and departmental chairpersons and not by members of the faculty.[52] This lack of American-style collegiality was seen by some faculty as a major flaw in the system, a system usually depicted by critics as too totalitarian in nature. To that degree, the typical public university reflected the centralized Leninist state of which it was a part.

A system of private universities also developed during this period. By 1978 the number of students at these private universities nearly equaled the number at the public institutions. Students could apply to these when taking the comprehensive exam. Tung-hai University in Taichung was considered the best of these private institutions of higher learning. It was a university begun with help from the Christian Board of Higher Education in Asia and academics with Western church connections had served as faculty and administration during its early years. A second major private and church-related university is Fujen Catholic University. This is run by a number of Catholic orders from Europe and the United States and is a descendent of (or replacement for) the famous Fukien University that had existed on the mainland. This university, like Tung-hai, has graduate programs in various fields. A third major private university is Tamkang University. This is a privately owned facility with a large campus in Tamsui, a suburb of Taipei, and a smaller campus in a commercial/residential district in central Taipei.[53]

Although most universities provided graduate training, many college graduates wished to continue their studies at Japanese, European, or American centers of higher learning.[54] The Foundation for Scholarly Exchange, the Chinese-run agency that worked with the Fulbright Foundation, administered the Test of English as a Foreign Language and other exams that opened the way for these students and also provided services to help those applying for education in the United States find a program that matched their interests and abilities. The most talented of these students were also able to apply for Fulbright scholarships to study in the United States or apply for other similar scholarships. Lu Hsiu-lien was one such student who was given a scholarship donated by a Taiwanese entrepreneur that allowed her to go to the University of Illinois at Champagne/Urbana for a master of law degree.[55] This same agency served Western scholars doing research at centers on Taiwan or who were involved in scholarly exchange and were teaching in universities on the island.[56]

Many of the students who went abroad did not return, preferring to spend their lives teaching or working in the West. Their presence has greatly benefited the many educational institutions or private companies where they found a home. However, their home island did suffer and the problem of brain drain was one that government leaders such as K.T. Li were well aware of.[57]

Taiwan developed an educational system that met the needs of the first generation of those who lived through the economic miracle. The second generation was less well served by the system. By the 1990s, many educators and lay people, though recognizing that national system of education had served their nation well, began to argue that it needed to be changed.

The major area of concern was the system of entrance examinations to the high schools. William Lew and recent critics such as Huang Wu-hsiung found such exams problematic for several reasons. First, they were only objective (i.e., short answer) and not creative. Second, they were the sole yardstick for admission to the two higher levels of schools. Third, they were given only once a year, forcing students who failed to wait a full year before trying again.[58]

These critics also argued that teachers all too often arranged their material in such a way as to help students prepare for the examinations. Teaching itself was directed not to developing skills related to critical thinking but, rather, to providing the students with the specific forms of knowledge needed to pass the entrance exams. This methodology had, in turn, helped to create an educational system that was too formal and rigid and that stressed memorization and conformity. Critics argued that this discouraged both creative and critical thinking—and suggested, by implication, that the educational system did not met the needs of individuals growing up in a new and more democratic Taiwan.

The seventh Conference on Education in June 1994 demonstrated that the Ministry of Education had listened to the critics and the parents. The conference was attended by 450 individuals, including scholars, educators, educational administrators, members of the non–public education establishment, and students. Attendees came up with many proposals and suggestions, of which the government decided to accept and implement quite a few. Perhaps the most important was the decision to increase the number of high schools, allowing the junior high schools to offer both junior high school and high school courses. Both the academic and vocational curriculum would be introduced at these expanded facilities. Textbook possibilities were also expanded, and those produced privately could now be considered for classroom use. There were also proposals to legalize the alternative schools if such schools met formal standards determined by the ministry.[59] The ministry, for its part, agreed to implement these proposals over the course of the next two years.[60]

There was also criticism of the system of higher education that had developed on Taiwan. During the late 1980s the Ministry of Education began to revise the University Law, which spelled out both administrative and academic policies for the fifty-nine colleges and universities on the island. The draft of the new law then was submitted to the Legislative Yuan. Here it remained, the subject of lively debate and numerous revisions for the next seven years. The revised University Law was finally passed in January 1994.

The new law spelled out basic guidelines for the institutions of higher education, but did not set out specific regulations, as had the previous version of the law. There were guarantees for greater autonomy, and this, in turn, paved the way for a system that had greater freedom and the possibility of greater diversity.[61]

It was in the area of curriculum that the colleges first felt the impact of the new law and its support of the concept of self-governance. A department within a university or college could now set its own curriculum, pending approval of its own Curriculum Committee and related university or college councils. The ministry still retained the power to set certain general course requirements, but even these are broadly defined. Instead of being required to take certain courses, students could now take one course in each of four different fields. The content of such courses was liberalized as well. A literature course could now contain more modern Chinese novels, for example. The faculty at the universities only began to revise the curriculum after the passage of the act and thus the process of reform moved slowly as 1995 ended.[62]

Personnel decisions are a second area that has been changed by the new law. Presidents of the universities were chosen by the ministry, and these presidents then had the power to select the other administrators, deans, and departmental chairmen. Now all appointments, including that of the president, are chosen by school committees or, in the case of departmental chairmen, by the faculty of the departments.[63] The fourteen major schools can hire faculty independent of ministry influence. However, the other forty-five institutions can hire faculty but need ministry approval to do so.[64]

A third key area where the new autonomy was felt was in finance. In the mid-1990s the universities began moving toward financial autonomy.[65]

By the mid-1990s, reforms were being instituted at various levels of the nationwide educational system designed to allow it to change in order to meet the new challenges a developed Republic of China was beginning to face.

The process of economic modernization and the availability of higher levels of education and job training changed the nature of work on Taiwan as well as the career patterns for its citizens for many reasons. First, Taiwan, even after an effective program of land reform had been implemented, was being transformed from a largely rural and agricultural nation to an urbanized and industrialized one.[66] Second, the government had put in place an educational system able to train people for the new industrial and technical and professional work environments.[67] The new industries demanded better-educated workers and legions of technically trained specialists and managers. The government also needed qualified people to do the type of tasks a regime controlling a mixed economy needed to have done. Finally, an expanding educational system needed qualified teachers and, at the college/university/research institute level, scholars who could produce provocative works of high quality.

Although many people left the countryside, work on farms remained an occupation for some, thanks to a deep and abiding sense of tradition here. Nevertheless, as Huang pointed out, the general commercialization of society destroyed most romanticism about rural life and work. By the early 1990s, only 9.1 percent of the population were still farmers. The majority of these individuals farmed in traditional ways, growing rice and other staples, but others worked in the flower industry and in the other branches of commercial farming. Still others remaining in the rural areas saw that industry provided a means of supporting their farms. Thus, over the course of the 1970s a network of village-based small-scale industry developed.[68]

But this was not sufficient to sustain life in the countryside, and many more people left agriculture and the small villages in search of greater opportunity for themselves and their families in the towns and cities. There they found access to higher-quality educational facilities as well as greater access to jobs and careers in the industrial and the service sectors to which a better education would give them entrée.

The educational system opened the way for many individuals on the island, providing them with the skills needed to compete in the new occupational marketplace. There was a clear relationship between the highest level of education attained and the career path that one followed, as seen below.

Those with primary and junior high school training moved into the lower rungs of the structure. Some women who could find little else entered the work force as "hairdressers" in the barber shops that were found in these urban centers. The problem is that such shops double as centers of the sex industry, and thus many rather naive country women were drawn into the degrading flesh trade for which the island became famous. Many other women found work in the network of small factories or did piecework in the apartments set up as subassembly plants for the handicraft-related industries, the garment industry, or the shoe industry. Men found various forms of low-skilled industrial or service jobs.

After these men and women had saved enough capital, they too became entrepreneurs and ran their own assembly lines or networks of home-based factories. Others set up the noodle stands or snack stands that line the side streets of busy neighborhoods. Families often pooled their resources to set up enclosed restaurants serving a few simple-to-prepare dishes to the breakfast or lunchtime crowd in the alleys and side streets off Roosevelt Road, Hsin-I Road, or Nanching East Road.[69]

With higher levels of education and greater skills at hand, individuals could find employment in the factories that were developing in the industrial parks and the research parks near such cities as Hsin-chu and Taichung. The electronics industry and the computer industry needed individuals with education and vocational training. The government also served as a major employer for people who had graduated high school and had finished their military service. Public transportation was one such service-related area. Skilled workers were also needed in other facets of government services and were important in a society with a growing public infrastructure.[70]

Those with college and university degrees found even greater opportunity, depending on their specialization. The educational system needed qualified teachers, and teaching offered many a stable and rewarding career, and benefits that the private sector did not offer. Teaching was considered a prestigious occupation, made even more attractive by the various perks. However, until the new wave of 1990s reforms, teaching was often a frustratingly confined profession dominated by a large and authoritarian bureaucracy that could control one's life even in the classroom.[71] The growth of the high-tech industries made engineers and research scientists increasingly valuable, creating demand for graduates of Tsinghua, the engineering and technical university. The development of the research/industrial parks with their focus on research and manufacture of computers and peripherals, and the general development of the computer industry in urban centers, increased the demand for engineers and provided opportunities for professionals who wished to become their own bosses. The small-scale factory suited the vendors of manufacturing components for the expanding computer industry, and such factories and firms often became the homes to the newly trained engineer or the returned student with American or Japanese graduate degrees in hand.

In the 1990s new opportunities developed for those trained in finance and economics. The government was opening up the financial system and allowing foreign banks to enter the Taiwanese marketplace. Those with business-related degrees and with MBAs in hand from Taiwanese or Western institutions found new positions waiting for them. The U.S. training was of particular value, given the island's close ties to the United States and the size and power of the overseas Taiwanese communities that can now be found in such financial and commercial centers as Los Angeles and New York.

Academia and research institutes served as magnets for others as well. Many of the new American- and Japanese-trained Ph.D.s who returned to Taiwan were able to build careers in the public or private universities. Others found employment at the research institutes of Academia Sinica, which has centers for studies in the humanities, the social sciences, the pure natural sciences, and the applied sciences. The academy also houses libraries and other facilities that are conducive to scholarly pursuits and scholarly production. However, Academia Sinica is not an isolated, ivory tower environment. Many of the scholars had come out of the ranks of the universities or had served at institutes before they went to the West to do their Ph.D. work. And when they returned, many of these scholars taught at the university level even as they did their research in Nan-kang. Academia Sinica and the universities became important as places where many that Hill Gates has termed the "new middle class" would find their homes.

The opening of the educational system and the existence of a wider range of occupational choices for men and women created shifts in traditional patterns of gender definition and relations between the sexes. Between 1971 and 1995 there arose new opportunities for education, new patterns of employment, new perceptions of what constitutes the good life. The rising cost of living transformed the nature of sexual roles and sexual relations in Taiwan in ways that parallel what has taken place in the West.

Traditional concepts of sexual roles and sexual relations remained very much the norm as the 1970s began, though one could see a transitional set of ideas in place that looked ahead to a more modern and Westernized view of both.[72] The legislation related to marriage and rights within marriage reflected, in the opinion of feminist social critics writing during the 1970s and 1980s, the traditional patriarchal nature of these concepts of relationships and of rights within relationships. In the eyes of the law and in the attitude of most males, women were second-class citizens. Perceptions and attitudes toward women and their roles in society had changed since the Republican revolution of 1911, and women could now pursue an education from the elementary to the university level. But as the number of women in universities on Taiwan increased, even this hard-won gain was being threatened.

Yet there were social forces working to force changes in men's attitudes and, ultimately, in the way the citizens and the government of a male-dominated society treated women. One such change was the economic miracle that had forced people to change where they lived and increased both their living standards and their expectation of improvement in that living standard. Both adult members of a nuclear family often found that they had to work to maintain a life-style to which they had grown accustomed. This, in turn, forced changes in the way that people managed their households and assigned and performed household responsibilities.[73] These new tensions between husband and wife sometimes led to divorce, an action frowned upon and often avoided in more traditional times.[74]

Societal factors led to changes in sexual relationships, but ideology and the development of new modes of social consciousness played a part as well. The architect of this movement was Lu Hsiu-lien. In 1971 she wrote an article criticizing a plan for reducing the number of women allowed at the universities. She saw the plan as a direct attack on women by a patriarchal government. Her newspaper article struck a responsive chord, leading to invitations to become a speaker on college campuses and in other forums. She attracted support from among both women and men and began to initiate various programs, in addition to opening a coffeeshop, which served as a meeting ground for women, and a press that published feminist works. For the first five years of her feminist activity, she remained a government employee. However, after an operation to treat a cancerous thyroid and brief summer trip that took her to the West and to Japan, she gave up her position and worked full-time in the movement, setting up hotlines, writing, editing, and publishing new books related to feminism. This activity continued until 1977, when she received an offer to study at Harvard Law School as a visiting scholar. When she returned to Taiwan the next year she entered politics as a member of the *tang-wai* and thus entered a new stage in what would be a long and multifaceted career.

While Lu was a central figure during the early stage of the movement, other women did important work and some of them took over command of the movement in the late 1970s and in the years of social protest in the early 1980s. In the 1990s the movement continued to grow. Gender studies became a subject studied in the universities and a gender studies program was established at the College of Social Sciences at Tsinghua University in Hsin-chu, a program headed by the American-trained sociologist Chou Pi-erh. Conferences held at the university united feminist academicians and activists, thus broadening the reach of gender studies and maintaining links between theoreticians and scholars and those who engaged in the day-to-day work of defending women's rights and expanding women's consciousness.[75]

Such redefinition of roles and relationships forced the transformation of the traditional Chinese/Taiwanese family system and the creation of family structures better adapted to meet the needs of an industrialized and urbanized society. What had been in the 1890s a largely agrarian society dwelling in small villages or towns had been transformed, first by the Japanese and then by the Nationalists, into a society that was increasingly urban. In that older Taiwanese society, extended families and stem families were the norm. The new industrial, urbanized society had forced individuals to migrate to the cities and the surrounding urban suburbs and in doing so had changed the shape of the family. Now the nuclear family so common in the industrialized West was becoming the norm. Furthermore, as sexual roles changed, older views of male/female responsibilities in the home gave way to the realities of the two-breadwinner families. As the 1970s and 1980s progressed, there came about a gradual sharing of the roles, at least among the middle-class families of urban Taiwan. One might argue that the sharing of tasks had been a part of the social reality of the rural and urban poor, as Hill Gates suggests in her portraits of working-class people. The difference now was a growing sense that shared responsibility also implied sexual equality.[76]

Some have argued that feminism has not gained much ground in Taiwan and that women remain second-class citizens. However, Taiwanese who are either involved in the movement or observe and study it suggest that feminism on the island has developed along paths more suitable to the society that existed when the movement began and has made substantial gains in various sectors. Such gains are reflected in the role that women now play in the professions and in politics and in the number of self-help groups and support groups that exist as a women's network on the island.

But the transformation of the extended and stem families had marked social costs. Latch-key kids have increasingly become kids in trouble. A question many asked was, in the words of journalist Amy Lo,"Who's Supposed to Take Care of the Kids?"[77] The need to provide child care forced husbands and wives to redefine their roles within the family. From 1971 to 1995, juvenile delinquency became an increasingly serious problem, in part because of the lack of supervision and the difficulty working parents sometimes had meeting the needs of their children in a fast-paced urban environment. The grandparents, who, in earlier and less complex times, had taken care of the children while their offspring worked, all too often lived in the towns or the villages, to be visited at the lunar new year. Or they lived in other neighborhoods in cities that were more daunting and difficult to get around in. Social critics have also argued that the materialism now increasingly common in Taiwanese life created demands and expectations of its own, which were frustrated by the realities of a family's income. Television presented images that produced the Taiwanese version of cognitive dissidence—of expectations unfulfilled—and this led in some measure to social problems that the families and the authorities and the social engineers were forced to learn to cope with.[78]

The transformation of the family has had effects at the other end of the life cycle as well. Families in the dying traditional society would have cared for elderly parents. However, by the 1980s the parents were not usually living in the same home. The burden of care of the elderly now shifted from family to society. Changes in the lives of individuals and families led, in turn, to a transformation of the structure of the social classes and of interclass relationships. Complicating this process of class realignment was the reshaping of ethnic self-definition and the parallel restructuring of interethnic power relationships.

In her seminal essay on ethnicity and class structure in Taiwan, Hill Gates has suggested that by the late 1970s Taiwan society could be broken into five classes.[79] The lowest class in the hierarchy is the underclass or lumpen-proletariat, poverty stricken and living on the edge. This class includes aborigines, but the vast majority are from the Taiwanese- and Hakka-speaking majorities and from the second-generation mainlander families. The chronically unemployed and criminals, who are unproductive and parasitical, also belong to this class.

Above this class is the lower or working class, which comprises the great body of industrial workers, landless agricultural workers, sales people, peddlers, and small-town craftsmen. The lives of members of this class have been shaped by low and uncertain incomes, little access to education, no prestige, and very restricted access to political power.

Gates sees two distinct middle classes. The first she terms the "new middle class," which resembles the class of salarymen in Japan and the bureaucratic "new class" in some state capitalist societies described by Milovan Djilas. The heads of the new-middle-class households are employees of large bureaucratic organizations such as government institutions, schools, and large industrial corporations. Their principal income is in the form of salaries and fringe benefits that include housing, rice allowances, wholesale buying co-ops, and special insurance plans. Education is the key to obtaining such positions. The factors around which the members of the "new middle class" shape their plans for maintaining or improving their social status are education, long-term career commitment to a single institution, and, finally, individual achievement. "For people in this middle class, the maintenance and or improvement of their position depends in part upon the continued power of the institutions that employ them. Consequently, they develop loyalties to and identifications with these institutions. Thus, their perception of their class status—their class consciousness—helps set them apart from the lower class."[80]

The second middle class fits the description of the traditional middle class. Members of this second middle class have their own farms, retail or wholesale businesses, and small factories. A major segment of Taiwan's production comes from such small-scale enterprises, linked in complex webs to wholesalers and to markets on the island or beyond Taiwan. The vast majority of such nonfarm enterprises employ one to six individuals. Members of these firms make up the lower rungs of this second middle class. While their incomes may parallel those of individuals in the working class, their aspirations and self-perceptions are those of the class members above them who have been able to accumulate capital and expand their small-scale enterprises. Businesses with more than six employees—from seven to ninety-nine—are defined as middle-level enterprises. Such firms made up 13 percent of the Taiwanese businesses in 1974 and were capable of "sustaining a secure traditional middle class position for their owners' families."[81]

The key to success in the "traditional middle class" differs markedly from that for the "new middle class": It depends on the ability to take a small-scale enterprise and turn it into a medium- or mid-level enterprise or one that is even larger. The factors that make for upward mobility in this class are business experience, frugality, long hours of hard work, good contacts, and a reputation for reliability. Education and specialized skills of the type that are demanded in the new middle class are not important here. In fact, education is often seen as needlessly time-consuming, removing one family member from too small a pool of labor.[82]

It is in defining the nature of the two middle classes and the differences between them and in defining the road to elite or upper-class status that the question of ethnicity and its effects on Taiwanese life can be seen in clearest relief. As shown by many authors, ethnicity and multileveled ethnic conflict have been and continue to be ever-present realities in Taiwanese life. Gates argues, "The paths that lead through the traditional middle classes to the commercial elite and through the new middle class to the bureaucratic elite are quite distinct." Individuals Gates interviewed talked in terms of two roads. Commerce is seen by some (one may assume, of *wai-sheng jen* background) as a crooked road that is less valuable to society than the straight road—public service. The general feeling is that being Taiwanese helps one attain traditional middle-class status and more and that "being Taiwanese" implies that one has roots in family and in community and that this provides a solid reputation in business. Ties to local temples and participation in local rituals add to an individual's sense of belonging to a larger ethnic community and in turn help that individual in his career. One must demonstrate that one is part of the larger mutually supportive network of the local community before that community will support an individual or family.

To be a mainlander gives one different forms of access that allow one to pursue a career path through the institutions of government. Modern Taiwan has been a society ruled by recently arrived immigrants, immigrants who possessed the "legitimacy" to rule and the military power to back up that claim of legitimacy. The types of local networks that a Taiwanese individual can make use of are not available to a mainlander, nor are there local institutions that can also provide support. Rather, mainlanders had nuclear families. What larger networks a given family once had lay to the west, in the PRC. New networks in the government or in government-related industries were developed, and these provided the access that many needed. Furthermore, the nuclear family worked to the advantage of the upwardly mobile mainlander, for nuclear families were better at providing encouragement and support for that family's children. Parents were able to help their sons or daughters with their schoolwork in a class environment where education determined the career path and the success of the individual. One must add that the *wai-sheng jen* preference for the straight road reflects the millenia-old Chinese (read Confucian) bias that government service is the noble path and commerce is the ignoble one.[83]

One must add that the composition of both classes changed over the years as a result of the Taiwanization of the government, intermarriage, and modernization. In the mid-1990s a paradoxical situation developed in which the lines and fractures that separate the *wai-sheng jen* (people from outside the province) and the *pen-ti jen* (local people) are less defined even as the Taiwanese majority try to define themselves in terms of a distinctive regional ethnic culture.[84]

A few other observations must be made concerning these middle classes. Scholars and observers have seen that, over the course of the past twenty-five years, the new middle class and the traditional middle class have both become engines of social change. Members of each group have begun to express their opinions on the nature of life on Taiwan and on the need for an improvement in the general quality of life. But many—more perhaps from the better-educated "new middle class" than from the business-oriented "traditional middle class"— do more than observe the passing scene or make comments about conditions. These increasingly prosperous and well-trained and articulate individuals have begun to play roles in local and regional organizations that focus on problems and issues that range from cultural preservation to environmental change.[85] And some among them have moved in the gray area of the public sphere—that zone between voluntary activity and political action—that scholars have been focusing on in recent years. The nature of this middle-class activism in the public sphere is examined in more detail below.

Above the two middle classes is the upper class. The members of this class through public and private enterprise control the means of large-scale production as well as the legal means under which their own and smaller businesses operate.[86] Members of this class have sufficient wealth to obtain the goods and life-styles that they desire. They also have access to the best educational institutions, political power, and prestige. While the upper class was at one point mainly mainlander and Taipei-centered, this too has changed in an increasingly open and more socially, as well as politically, democratic society.

Let us return to the question of race and ethnicity and their impact upon the development of modern Taiwanese life. Taiwan is home to two different races, one of which is Austronesian. The aborigine groups who first inhabited the island are of this racial background. In 1985, the year that Hsieh Shih-chung used for statistics in his important article on the *yuan-chu-min* (indigenous people), there were 317,936 aborigines (to use the most common English term) divided into ten groups. A second and larger group are Han Chinese, usually categorized by linquistic/ethnic or, perhaps more correctly, subethnic groupings. Two of these distinct ethnic groups are descended from groups that came to Taiwan from areas along the South China coast before 1945. One group, the largest population on the island, consists of descendants of peoples who spoke southern Min dialect from the counties of southern Fukien. They speak what is usually called Taiwanese, a dialect resembling the Hokklo spoken in Ch'uen-chou county, Tun-gan county, An-hsi county, and Hsia-men county. The second of the pre-1945 ethnic groups is the Hakka (or K'o-chia), whose ancestors came from the northern counties of Kuangtung. These two groups taken together comprise the *pen-ti jen*. The third ethnic group is not, strictly speaking, an ethnic group at all. While usually referred to in the politically loaded parlance of the present day as *wai-sheng jen* this group is really a combination of various mainlander Han ethnic groups that share only the fact that they came to Taiwan after the retrocession of 1945. What they share is their adherence to Mandarin, or *kuoyu* (national language), as their common tongue and the fact that many came as part of the army or the KMT beareaucracy and thus came to the island as a ruling immigrant elite. One must also add that this is an "ethnic" elite that, for a variety of political and sociocultural reasons, saw a need to impose its "mainstream" greater tradition upon the Hakka and Hokklo/Taiwanese-speaking peoples who had wrested the island from aborigine control.

To a degree, the issue of ethnic differentiation and the resultant ethnic conflict among the Han groups were products of cultural imperialism. As detailed by Douglas Mendel,[87] this process, which one can call Mandarinization, was seen in the direct acts of repression in the late 1940s and can also be seen in the years from 1945 to 1970. During the 1970s and the 1980s, the policy of Mandarinization continued in various facets of Taiwan's educational/cultural life and in the religious realm as well. One of the major facets of cultural imperialism has been the suppression of the Taiwanese language and the teaching of Mandarin in the schools. The language of instruction was Mandarin, and the use of Taiwanese was suppressed. How far this effort went is described by the linguist Robert L. Cheng.[88] Cheng argues that the regime made no attempt to create a bilingual system of education but forced the island to accept one that used Mandarin only. He made a strong case for bilingualism, but no one was willing to listen in the heated political atmosphere the 1970s when the article was written. There were other forms of bias against Taiwanese culture and society as well. Taiwan's own history was barely mentioned in elementary and secondary textbooks: The China that lay across the Taiwan strait was what students learned about. And there was little concern for the preservation of major historical sites as urbanization swallowed up the countryside. The determined efforts of local groups in such cities as Lu-kang, San-hsia, Pan-ch'iao, and Tainan were needed to press authorities to preserve Taiwan's rich past as an island frontier.[89] Furthermore, a few journals dealt with Taiwanese history and culture, and some historians and anthropologists worked on Taiwan-related issues, the study of Taiwan was not a mainstream subject. Only in the 1980s did Taiwan-related issues become central in certain institutes at Academia Sinica and on university campuses. And only in the 1990s was a Taiwan Institute established at Academia Sinica. Since its founding, other universities on the island have held academic conferences, begun formal study of Taiwan and its development, and begun to publish scholarly journals.[90] The new Taiwanese consciousness is also reflected in the pages of the *Free China Review,* published by the Government Information Office. Since 1989, it has gradually included more articles about Taiwanese culture—literature, film, painting, and the performing arts—as well as about Taiwan studies and Taiwan's history.[91] It has also devoted much space to Taiwanese religion and to the culture of the Han and non-Han ethnic groups; one issue was devoted to the Hakka and another to the indigenous peoples.[92]

Cultural imperialism was also directed against the Presbyterian Church on Taiwan, a major voice for the cause of Taiwanese self-hood. The church leaders made their own public indictment of the regime and its human rights and ethnic policies in a journal called *Self-Determination,* which was published over the course of the 1970s and 1980s.[93]

Mandarinization and the suppression of Taiwanese culture is one aspect of the ethnic conflict. These policies and the mainlanders' systematic exclusion of the Taiwanese from participation in the running of their own country fueled antagonism and distrust. That sense of distrust still runs very deep. However, to address the tensions that existed, Chiang Ching-kuo and other more pragmatic KMT leaders began the process of Mandarinization of the party and the government even as they attempted to suppress the political expressions of Taiwanese identity during the 1970s and 1980s. They were faced with a simple reality—as each year went by the united China that the ROC hoped to reconstruct or recover was becoming an impractical dream. Furthermore, their sons and daughters, the children of the *wai-sheng jen,* had been born on Taiwan and considered themselves Taiwanese even if the majority did not accept them as such.

These various trends—Taiwanization and the acceptance of Taiwan as home as well as the obvious economic growth that had created a prosperous society for all its citizens—muddied the differences and reduced the tension between mainlander and Taiwanese, but only to a degree. The ethnic identity card was too valuable for many to give up. Many politicians in the Democratic Progressive Party (DPP) who had bitter memories of their conflicts with the state felt there was much to lose by forgiving and forgetting. The DPP chairman, Shih Mingteh, spent half his life in ROC prisons for various antistate activities and retained painful memories of his long years of incarceration.[94] Thus even as the real differences were fading, and as the government was opening the system up and allowing more and Taiwanese and Hakka dialects to be heard and was allowing Taiwanese culture and history to be studied and to be taught, the divisions between ethnic groups seemed to remain and become the subtext of a sometimes poisonous public discourse.

One ethnic/racial group remained on its own and out of the mainstream—the indigenous. Over the past two decades they have faced two enemies: the Han-Taiwanese and the government. The history of conflict between the indigenous peoples and the Fukien and Kuangtung settlers and between the indigenous peoples and the Japanese has been documented. These people, many of whom, since Japanese times, were inhabitants of mountain reservations, were the most victimized of the island's populations and, while ostensibly protecting them, the government also exploited them and suppressed their attempts to hold on to their traditional ways. Maryknollers and other mission groups might admit that the government tried to improve conditions, but not enough to really change things for this population.

But things have begun to change. While not benefiting as much from the economic miracle as the Han groups, indigenous people were able to make some gains. More important, perhaps they were developing a greater sense of group consciousness and were developing tactics to make their cause known to the Han ethnic groups. Some of the tribal leaders gained seats in the National and provincial legislatures and were able to lobby on behalf of their people. These leaders and those around them used the channels available to them in the political/bureaucratic system to bring about change. Yet these methods were unsatisfying to others within the indigenous community. These individuals, learning lessons from the protest groups that had operated in the 1980s, began to organize a similar group in 1984, the Alliance of Taiwan Aborigines (ATA). This group is considered to be the most important of such indigenous movements—others, working on issues of literature and culture, were also founded during this period. Like other protest groups, the ATA presented its message in the streets of the capital. As it evolved, its leaders developed more defined programs and created tactics to publicize these programs and objectives. In what Hsieh Shih-chung, a T'ai-ta anthropologist studying the culture of the indigenous people and their modern development, has called the third period in their history, members of the group meeting at the ATA's second general assembly drafted a manifesto. This manifesto called for guarantees of basic protections for aborigines, including the protection of their tribal lands. It called for the right to practice local autonomy in traditional lands. It called for state recognition of aborigine social organizations, populations, and regions. It called for aborigine ownership of land and resources and for a return of those lands that the ethnic Han and the state had obtained by illegal means. It called for land rights—including surface, subsoil, and maritime rights. Finally it called for the right to take advantage of aboriginal resources to satisfy basic needs. This was a sweeping statement, and what lay behind it was the development of a strong pantribal body willing to make its people's case known. What also emerged from this meeting was a new term for the aborigine, the *yuan-chu-min*—indigenous people. They demanded that this replace the *kao-shan-tzu*—the high mountain people, a more commonly used term. They were, in effect, recreating their identity.[95]

These steps gave the indigenous people a cause for optimism, and they entered the political arena with high hopes that their demands would be treated seriously. The government made some concessions that were considered window dressing by observers and participants. The key test came in the elections for the Legislative Yuan that took place in 1989. ATA leaders hoped that more representatives who stood for the ATA program would be elected. This did not happen, and ground was lost rather than gained.

Since that election, the leaders have continued to publicize their cause, and their efforts have gained some public attention. One example of this is that in June 1992 *Free China Review* devoted an entire issue to various aspects of the indigenous peoples, including discussion of activism and the forms that had evolved; the government's treatment of the aboriginal people, and the inadequate government attention to these tribal peoples; the pressures for integration with the Han majorities; cultural and linguistic preservation; and history, especially the Wu-she incident, the rebellion of indigenous people against the Japanese in 1930.[96]

This special issue of *Free China Review* marked a new stage in the public perception of indigenous people, as well as indicating the government's recognition of the role of the indigenous people in modern Taiwanese life. The issue was also a wakeup call to the Han ethnic groups to become more aware of and sensitive to the needs of these peoples so long looked upon as enemies. The issue could also be seen as a long note of thanks to the missionary groups, Protestant and Catholic, that had worked with these people during the Dutch period and since the opening of Taiwan in the 1860s. Finally it was a statement that the government—or at least the editors and writers of this very visible government-related publication—recognized the new racial/ethnic consciousness that the indigenous people developed during the 1980s and early 1990s, a consciousness that the government had to take seriously.

On a yet larger and more visible and tangible scale, one witnessed the socio-economic changes on the face of the land, for transformation of the Taiwanese landscape is the most obvious result of the economic miracle that had begun to take shape in the 1960s.

The countryside changed with the increased levels of commercialization and rural industrialization. The major urban areas expanded and this, in turn, helped force the evolution of the suburbs that abutted these seemingly "imperialistic" cities. The central government has played a role in the ongoing and increasingly rapid process of urbanization. Local and county governments have played roles as well. The city and county governments have made a form of urban imperialism possible with land codes that made integration of nearby areas easy to arrange. However, towns with long histories resisted and attempted by a variety of methods to maintain their integrity. While local identity was maintained, the distinct sense of place was not: Suburbanization in population-dense Taiwan is what Westerners would describe as urban sprawl.

The central government attempted to control this process in a number of ways even as it tried to deal with the impact of such growth on urban and country infrastructures. Elements of the Major Projects initiatives have attempted to deal with the related problems of rapid urbanization and what might be called infra-structure-lag. One such project is the Taipei Rapid Transit System now under construction. A second is the development of the "new towns"—the planned communities designed to provide the more middle-class and comfortable population with alternatives to the increasingly crowded and chaotic cities.

In the mid-1990s, Taiwan's major urban centers—Taipei, Keelung, Taichung,

Tainan, and Kao-hsiung—continued to absorb or integrate nearby villages and towns.[97] Even in 1980, for example, the Westerner taking the #270 bus from downtown Taipei to Academia Sinica would have had a hard time discerning just where Taipei ended and such suburbs as Nan-kang began. That task was even more difficult in 1995 as the space of those outlying and once partially rural areas near Taipei city such as Nan-kang to the east or Tam-sui to the northwest filled with high-rise condominium complexes.[98]

The Taipei basin is not the only area affected by this urban growth. Taichung has experienced similar sprawl, with the city taking over more of the countryside each year. By the mid-1990s a new and more modern Taichung surrounded the dense inner core of this city with its park and night market.[99] To the west of the city and the national highway lies Tung-hai University. This private university, with its spacious campus and its famous I.M. Pei–designed chapel, finds itself surrounded by the encroaching city. A few miles farther west lies one of the new towns that have been designed to provide an alternative to the scattershot process of urban expansion. The area around Taichung, especially the area nearest the new Taichung port facilities, will continue to grow and that growth will be rapid if the long-awaited direct trade with the Fukien port of Amoy (Hsia-men) is opened.

Similar patterns of urban growth can be seen southward into the heart of Taiwanese-speaking Taiwan. Classic towns such as Lu-kang, near the metropolis of Chang-hua, and Pei-kang and Hsin-kang, near Chia-yi, have been able to maintain a small-town character, but this is largely due to the recognition by the government and the populace that such towns are major religious and cultural centers and are important in helping maintain links with the island's past and its links with the southern Min culture of Fukien. Yet here, too, one can find evidence of urban expansion, as the short bus ride from Chang-hua to Lu-kang demonstrates.

Even Tainan, the historical heart of Taiwanese Taiwan and a city long treasured for its ability to preserve the island's past, experienced considerable growth between 1971 and 1996. The major educational centers are still in place. Cheng-kung University remains in its attractive sprawling campus and houses one of the old city gates. The Tainan Presbyterian Seminary, perhaps the oldest educational establishment on the island, continues to prepare ministers and teachers for their respective roles in this largest and strongest of the island's Protestant churches. Its campus contains many buildings dating back to the 1860s, when Taiwan was opened to Western trade. Many of the famous temples and historical sites remain well maintained and well publicized by a city government intent upon reminding Taiwanese how important a part the city played in the settlement of the island.[100] Yet Tainan, like Taipei and Taichung, has expanded over the decades. Temples once surrounded by farmland are now surrounded by apartment complexes, factories, or shopping malls. The small-town flavor that was so apparent to the visitor wandering the main streets that radiated out from the rail/bus station complex has faded year by year as the high city has replaced the older low city. The sprawl has even reached the once-pristine coastal lands that surrounded the old Dutch fort at An-p'ing. The grand temples found in this area are busy and well-maintained, but housing developments dot the landscape and even moderate-size high-rises can be found along the canal-side road that leads from downtown Tainan to the coast.[101]

Kao-hsiung possesses a character more reminiscent of Taipei, but is even more aggressive in the never-ending search for modernity. Industry and commerce, not local history and culture, were what made this city come alive. Thus expansion is the norm. While it is a center of Taiwanese nationalism—it became the major site of the *tangwai*/KMT movement in December 1979—it is also the site of Taiwan's new thrust into Southeast Asia. Beginning in the early 1990s, direct flights to Vietnam were available from the Kao-hsiung airport, and during the mid-1990s the city continued to serve as the gateway to Vietnam, Malaysia, the Philippines, Indonesia, and Thailand. In 1995 yet another step was taken as a special international area was laid out in the airport, preparing the way for direct flights to the cities of the mainland. But as in the other major cities, growth seems unchecked, traffic seems ever greater, and the air becomes more unfit to breathe.

Conclusion

Multileveled economic and social changes helped produce a society in Taiwan that was highly trained and well educated, increasingly middle class in values and outlook, and in a position to demand widescale sociopolitical change and greater attention to quality of life issues. This society called for accelerating the pace of integrating the Taiwanese majority into mainland-dominated bureaucratic system and pressured the KMT-dominated regime into creating the broadly based multiparty system put in place in the mid-1990s. These economic and social changes made possible the political and diplomatic changes examined in Chapter 16.

Notes

1. I have used the mid-1960s following the lead of Chu-yuan Cheng, who sees these years as the true beginning of the Chiang Ching-kuo era. See his article, "Taiwan's Economic Development Under Chiang Ching-kuo," *American Asian Review*, 12, no. 1 (spring 1994): 199–224.

2. The nature of the middle class is complex. Like Hill Gates, I see two middle

classes: first, a traditional business-related middle class and, second, a managerial/bureaucratic middle class. In the 1950s and 1960s, these middle classes were divided not only by occupational orientation but also by ethnicity; Taiwanese (*pen-ti jen*) were members of the traditional middle class, and mainlanders (*wai-sheng jen*) were members of the new middle class. However, by the 1970s, while occupational orientation remained constant as a means of definition, ethnicity did not. This Taiwanization explains in some measure the role of the new middle class and the traditional middle class in the post-1971 political process.

3. Wang Chi-hsien, "The Economic Development of Taiwan: Export-Oriented Growth Reexamined" (paper presented at the annual meeting of the Association for Asian Studies, Mid-Atlantic Region, Rutgers University, October 19–21, 1990), 4. A valuable and challenging approach to the development of Taiwan is in Steve Chan and Cal Clark, *Flexibility, Foresight and Fortune in Taiwan's Development: Navigating Between Scylla and Charybdis* (London: Routledge, 1992). A good selection of articles on the island's economic development as seen from the perspective of the early 1980s is in Yuan-li Wu, "Economic Development," in *Contemporary Republic of China: The Taiwan Experience 1950–1980*, ed. James C. Hsiung (New York: Praeger, 1981), 119–217. Wu's introductory article is a model of concision and so is valuable for students in its own right. Finally, one must mention the work of K.T. Li, who was one of the architects of the miracle. In 1976 an English-language edition of his speeches was published, as were articles that give insight into the process of development. See K.T. Li, *The Experience of Dynamic Economic Growth on Taiwan* (Taipei: Mei Ya, 1976) (hereafter, cited as *Experience*). On the economic plans and the early period, see ibid., 87–116. A useful picture of the industrial/technological economy of Taiwan as it existed in 1995 is in *The Republic of China on Taiwan: Partner for Technology and Investment* (Taipei: Department of Industrial Technology, Ministry of Economic Affairs, 1995). This document includes descriptions of the various facets of Taiwan's economy.

4. On the development of agriculture in the 1950s and 1960s, see Li, *Experience*, 379–392. For a perspective on the role of agriculture in Taiwan's economy and society, see Jack F. Williams, "Vulnerability and Change in Chinese Agriculture," in *The Other Taiwan*, ed. Murray A. Rubinstein (Armonk, NY: M.E. Sharpe, 1994), 215–233.

5. Li, *Experience*, 393–432.

6. A provocative piece on this subject is Huan Chun-chieh and Liao Cheng-hung, "The Vanishing Peasant Soul," *Free China Review* (FCR), 39, no. 9 (September 1989): 46–53.

7. On the flower industry, see the special section in FCR for April 1992. The lead article in this section is Winnie Chang, "Big Bloom Theory," FCR, 42, no. 4 (April 1992): 4–17. The section includes related articles by Winnie Chang, Yvonne Yuan, and Emma Wu. On the flower industry and related new developments in the agricultural sector, as well as a telling overview of the state of agriculture on Taiwan, see Philip Liu, "Agricultural Crossroads," FCR, 42, no. 4 (April 1992): 28–33.

8. Huang and Liao, "The Vanishing Peasant Soul," 50. See also Carl Chang, "Eating Hardship," FCR, 39, no. 9 (September 1989): 54–57. A later and equally useful article is Liu, "Agricultural Crossroads."

9. On this industry, see the special section on aquaculture in FCR, 41, no. 11 (November 1991). The various species produced by aquiculture are discussed in Jim Hwang, "Upscale Production," in the same issue, 4–7.

10. A more general look at the industry and its prospects is in Jim Hwang, "From

Success to Uncertainty," in ibid., 8–21. On the role of the research institutes see Hwang Chin-yin, "Old Fish, New Tricks," in ibid., 22–27.

11. Wang, "Economic Development of Taiwan," 6. See also Li, *Experience*, 117–130, 131–144.

12. Li, *Experience*, 131–144, 216–227.

13. Wang, "Economic Development of Taiwan," 7. See also Denis Fred Simon, "Taiwan's Emerging Technological Trajectory: Creating New Forms of Competitive Advantage," in *Taiwan: Beyond the Economic Miracle*, ed. Denis Fred Simon and Kau Ying-mao (Armonk, NY: M.E. Sharpe, 1992), 123–147.

14. Wang, "Economic Development of Taiwan," 8. See also Cheng, "Taiwan's Economy Under Chiang Ching-kuo," 165–166; Li, *Experience*, 359–378.

15. Wang, "Economic Development of Taiwan," 8–9.

16. Ian Skoggard, *The Indigenous Dynamic in Taiwan's Postwar Development* (Armonk, NY: M.E. Sharpe, 1996), chapter 1.

17. Skoggard details the nature of the shoe industry from its origins to its decline in the late 1980s. See ibid.

18. Cheng, "Taiwan's Economy Under Chiang Ching-kuo," 166.

19. Ibid., 167; Li, *Experience*, 352–358.

20. Cheng, "Taiwan's Economy Under Chiang Ching-kuo," 167.

21. Ibid.

22. Ibid., 168.

23. Ibid.

24. Ibid., 168–169.

25. Ibid., 169. For a study of the process of technology transfer, see also Denis Fred Simon, "Taiwan's Emerging Technological Trajectory: Creating New Forms of Competitive Advantage," in Simon and Kau, eds., *Taiwan*, 123–147. Irene Yeung, "PCs Are Only Part of the Action," FCR, 40, no. 12 (December 1990): 4–15; Jim Hwang, "Information Power," in same, 16–23; Chang Yu-wen, "Single-Digit Growth, Triple-Digit Effort," FCR, 42, no. 8 (August 1992): 46–55; Philip Liu, "An Industry in the Chips," FCR, 43, no. 12 (December 1993): 42–47; Philip Liu, "Technological Trailblazing," FCR, 44, no. 12 (December 1994): 49–55; and Wang Fei-yun, "Bright Future," FCR, 45, no. 7 (July 1995), 4–13. On the software industry, see Eugenia Yun, "Hard Sell for Software" FCR, 45, no. 7 (July 1995): 14–23.

26. These comments are based upon personal visits to and observations of these two sites from 1979 to 1995.

27. Cheng, "Taiwan's Economy Under Chiang Ching-kuo," 169.

28. Ibid., 169–170. The Hsin-chu Industrial Park has been covered in segments in many articles in FCR. In the November 1995 issue two articles are devoted to the Hsin-chu complex: Philip Liu, "Blueprint for Success," 50–59; and Jim Hwang, "Model for the Future," 60–61.

29. Cheng, "Taiwan's Economy Under Chiang Ching-kuo," 172–173.

30. Ibid., 173–174.

31. On appreciation of the NT dollar, see Osman Tseng, "Unappreciated Appreciation," FCR, 42, no. 2 (February 1992): 41–43.

32. On this market campaign, see Linda Pennells, "The Making of an Image," FCR, 44, no. 3 (March 1994): 42–45. See also the articles on the marketing of specific products: Linda Pernells, "Turned In, Turned On," 46–47; and Linda Pennells, "A Bicycle Built for Profits," 48–49, both in that same issue of FCR.

33. Cheng, "Taiwan's Economy Under Chiang Ching-kuo," 174. On Taiwan's expanding investment with Southeast Asia, see the special section "Offshore Investment" in

FCR, 45, no. 9 (September 1995): 4–35. This extensive section contains an introduction and articles on Taiwanese investment in Southeast Asian states such as Thailand, Malaysia, Indonesia, and the Philippines.

34. Phillip Liu, "Opening the Door to Competition," FCR, 41, no. 9 (September 1991): 33–37; and Anna Sung, trans., "Mixed Expectations," in same, 38–40. Wang Chien-shien, "Inside Financial Policy Making," FCR, 41, no. 12 (November 1991): 36–39. See also Osman Tseng, "The Heat Is On," FCR, 42, no. 5 (May 1992): 26–29.

35 Cheng, "Taiwan's Economy Under Chiang Ching-kuo," 174–175.

36. Phillip Liu, "Is Manufacturing on the Ropes?" FCR, 43, no. 10 (October 1993): 52–57.

37. The goals of the government in the 1990s are discussed by Shirley Kuo, the chairman of the Council for Economic Planning and Development. See "A Plan for a High Quality Infrastructure," FCR, 42, no. 11 (November 1992): 16–17.

38. Winnie Chang, "True Grit: The Making of the MRT," FCR, 42, no. 11 (November 1992).

39. Amy Lo, "High Speed Ahead?" FCR, 42, no. 11 (November 1992): 25–27. See also Chiu Chin-hsiang, Chen Li-ying, and Hou Chia-chu, "The Choo-choo Brouhaha," FCR, 45, no. 9 (September 1995): 49–55.

40. Laurie Underwood, "This Land Is Your Land, This Land Is My Land," FCR, 42, no. 11 (November 1992).

41. Yvonne Yuan, "Let a Hundred Projects Bloom," FCR, 42, no. 11 (November 1992): 4–15.

42. Phillip Liu, "Who Is Going to Foot the Bill?" FCR, 42, no. 11 (November 1992): 18–21; Amy Lo, "High Speed Ahead?" in same, 25–27.

43. Phillip Liu, "Is Manufacturing on the Ropes?" FCR, 43, no. 10 (October 1993): 52.

44. Osman Tseng, "Steppingstone in the Making," FCR, 43, no. 4 (April 1993): 44–47; Linda Pernells, "Putting Out the Welcome Mat," FCR, 44, no. 2 (February 1994): 46–57.

45. While the Ministry of Education starts its own history of education on Taiwan with events that took place in the decade before the Republic began, that history does not truly reflect Taiwanese educational history. Modern Taiwanese education began in the mid-1860s with the Presbyterian missionaries in T'ai-nan and later in the Taipei basin. These English and Canadians, speaking Taiwanese and writing in a romanized version of Taiwanese, established primary schools, secondary schools, and seminaries. Here they trained two generations of Taiwanese, many of whom converted to Presbyterianism before the Japanese took over the island in 1895. On Presbyterian efforts on Taiwan, see Murray A. Rubinstein, *The Protestant Community on Modern Taiwan: Mission, Seminary, and Church* (Armonk, NY: M.E. Sharpe, 1991), chap. 1.

The Japanese recognized their efforts and allowed them to continue to operate their schools, schools that began an access route to higher education for many Taiwanese during the fifty years that Japan controlled the island that it had taken from China in the wake of the Sino-Japanese War. Many members of the Taiwanese elite who would confront the Nationalists in the late 1940s were products of these schools.

The Japanese occupiers also involved themselves in education, constructing a school system that went from primary to secondary to college levels. On the Japanese system, see Patricia Tsurumi, *Japanese Colonial Education on Taiwan* (Cambridge, MA: Harvard University Press, 197).

While this sophisticated system provided Taiwanese with instruction in Japanese, it limited the number of Taiwanese- and Hakka-speaking peoples able to attend levels above elementary schools. Furthermore, many of the Taiwanese allowed into the higher-level schools were trained in areas that were helpful to the Japanese administrators. For example, many Taiwanese were trained to be teachers and went on to serve in Japanese schools like the ones they had attended.

Many professions were closed to Taiwanese qualified enough to advance to the college level. Certain professions, such as medicine, that did remain open, however, became a professional path that many followed. Others were able to study in other academic areas, doing university work in Japan itself. One of these was P'eng Ming-min, the political scientist, T'ai-ta professor, political exile, and, in 1997, the Democratic Progressive Party presidential candidate.

46. This system has been described in detail in materials published by the Ministry of Education, of which *Education in the Republic of China* (Taipei: Ministry of Education, 1978) is the most useful. An examination of the 1978 issue allows us to see what the system of education was like in Taiwan in the year before both the formal derecognition by the United States and the *tangwai*/KMT conflict.

47. William F. Lew used similar data in his discussion of the educational system on Taiwan. See William F. Lew, "The Educational Ladder," in Hsiung, ed., *The Taiwan Experience*, 82–85.

48. These are the raw figures, but they do suggest how the educational system of Taiwan had grown since the KMT made the island the home of its government (in exile). The authors of *Education in the Republic of China* provide a brief history of the system, describe the organizational structure of the ministry, and then describe each level of schooling. They discuss the nature of the number of years of these levels, the nature of the curriculum, and basic differences between types of schools at the same level.

49. "School Patterns," in *Education in China*, 21–23.

50. Lew, "The Educational Ladder," in *The Taiwan Experience*, 83. See also "School Patterns," in *Education in China*, 21–23. How a student gained entry to such a school and what such a school was like can be seen in the life of the feminist leader Lu Hsiu-lien. See Murray A. Rubinstein, "Lu Hsiu-lien and the Origins of Taiwanese Feminism" (paper presented at the Modern China Seminar, Columbia University, October 12, 1995), to be included in *Men and Women in Modern Taiwan* (forthcoming).

51. Lew, "The Educational Ladder," in *The Taiwan Experience*, 83; "School Patterns," in *Education in China*, 21–23. On questions of curriculum, see "Curriculum, Teaching Materials, and Equipment," in *Education in China*, 34–37.

52. *Education in China*, 19.

53. This author's knowledge of Fujen and Tamkang was obtained firsthand as a member of history/Western studies programs at both schools in 1979 and 1980, while a Fulbright senior lecturer.

54. Lew, "The Educational Ladder," in *The Taiwan Experience*, 84; "International Cultural Interflow," in *Education in China*, 48–49.

55. Rubinstein, "Lu Hsiu-lien and the Origins of Taiwanese Feminism."

56. This author came to know the various facets of the Fulbright Program and the Foundation for Scholarly Exchange from the inside in 1979 and 1980.

57. Li, *Experience*, 247–261.

58. Lew, "The Educational Ladder," in *The Taiwan Experience*, 84; see also the discussion in F.A. Lumley, "The Educational Reform," in *The Taiwan Experience*, 85–86; Eugenia Yun, "Stressed Out System," FCR, 44, no. 9 (September 1994): 4–15.

59. During the past three decades, alternative forms of education have evolved. For those Taiwanese with family in the United States or occupations that took them and their children to the West, there was the Taipei American School. This school was organized to meet the needs of the American diplomatic and military community. For those Chinese families who can afford the high cost of tuition, it provides an excellent point of access to the American academic world. Taiwanese also set up some major alternative schools that, unlike the Taipei American School and the Christian mission–related Morrison School in Taichung, used Chinese as the language of instruction. Examples of these include the Forest School and Caterpillar, which are housed in an unconventional campus, offer a more fluid and creative curriculum, and provide small classes and personalized instruction. They are also very expensive, with tuition between U.S.$4,000 and $5,000. Although the programs are ambitious, campus space is extensive but quite primitive, and the government has yet to give the schools full approval. On these alternative schools, see Yvonne Yuan, "Alternative Study Styles," FCR, 44, no. 9 (September 1994): 24–31.

60. Yun, "Stressed Out System," 15.

61. The reform in the university system is covered in a special section of the June 1995 issue of FCR. On the law and its impact, see Eugenia Yun, "The Road to Autonomy," in that issue, p. 8.

62. Ibid., 9.

63. Ibid., 9–12.

64. Ibid., 12–13.

65. Ibid., 13.

66. On the land reform, see Ching Yuan-Lin, "The 1949–53 Land Reform," in *The Taiwan Experience*, 140–143.

67. See Alden Speare, Jr., "Urbanization and Migration," in *The Taiwan Experience*, 149–150.

68. The transformation of rural society until the mid-1970s is examined in Wu Tsong-shien, *Taiwan's Changing Rural Society* (Taipei: Chinese Association for Folklore/Orient Cultural Service, 1993). See also Hu, Tai-li, *My Mother-in-Law's Village* (Nankang: Institute of Ethnology, 1983).

69. See "Working: People Talk About What They Do and How They Feel About It," FCR, 45, no. 1(January 1995): 4-73. See also Hill Gates, *Chinese Working Class Lives* (Ithaca: Cornell University Press, 1987).

70. "Working," FCR, 45, no. 1 (January 1995).

71. Details on salary scales, job requirements, and duties are spelled out in *Education in the Republic of China* (Taipei: Ministry of Education, 1978).

72. On the stages of sex role development in China, see David C. Shak, *Dating and Mate Selection in Modern Taiwan* (Taipei: Orient Cultural Service, 1974).

73. See the special section "Male-Female Roles," FCR, 41, no. 2 (February 1991): 4–23.

74. On these shifts, see various issues of FCR. On issues related to child care see the special section "Child Welfare," FCR, 42, no. 5 (May 1992): 5–25. See also the special section "Marriage and the Family," FCR, 43, no. 11 (November 1993): 5–31. This special section contains discussions of family life, child-care choices, and divorce. See also Sangmee Bak, "Negotiating the Meaning of Women's Work, Family, and Kinship in Urban Taiwan," in *Harvard Studies on Taiwan: Papers of the Taiwan Studies Workshop* (Cambridge: Fairbank Center for East Asian Research, Harvard University, 1995), 271–285.

75. On Lu Hsiu-lien, see Murray A. Rubinstein, "The Life and Times of a Taiwanese Feminist: Lu Hsiu-lien's Career in the Socio-political Evolution of the Republic of China

on Taiwan, 1944–1995" (paper presented at the annual meeting of the Association for Asian Studies, Washington, DC, March 1995). See also Lu Hsiu-lien, "Women's Liberation: The Taiwanese Experience," in Rubinstein, ed., *The Other Taiwan*.

76. On the changing family in Taiwan, see Chun-kit Joseph Wang, *The Changing Chinese Family Pattern in Taiwan* (Taipei: Southern Materials Center, 1981). See also Hsieh Jih-chang and Chuang Ying-chang, ed., *The Chinese Family and Its Ritual Behavior* (Taipei: Institute of Ethnography, Academia Sinica, 1985).

77. Amy Lo, "Who's Supposed to Take Care of the Kids?" FCR, 42, no. 5 (May 1992): 4–13.

78. Ibid. See also "Marriage and the Family," FCR; special section, 43, no. 11 (November 1991): 4–31.

79. See Hill Gates, "Ethnicity and Social Class," in *The Anthropology of Taiwanese Society*, ed. Hill Gates and Emily Martin Ahern (Stanford: Stanford University Press, 1981), 241–281.

80. Ibid., 279.

81. Ibid., 273.

82. Ibid., 274–275.

83. Ibid., 276.

84. Ibid.

85. Ibid., 277.

86. The Hakka minority that settled the island with the southern Min (Taiwanese)–speaking people from Fukien province are experiencing a similar process of ethnic revival and consciousness.

87. Douglas Mendel, *The Politics of Formosan Nationalism* (Berkeley: University of California Press, 1970).

88. Robert L. Cheng, "Language Unification in Taiwan: Present and Future," in Murray A. Rubinstein, ed., *The Other Taiwan* (Armonk, N.Y.: M.E. Sharpe, 1994).

89. On volunteerism and the organizations the movement has spawned, see the special section "Foundations," in FCR, 41, no. 9 (September 1991): 4–31. On social activism, see the special section "Interest Groups," in FCR, 41, no. 7 (July 1991): 4–35 .

90. Gates, "Ethnicity and Social Class," 278–279.

91. On issues of cultural preservation see the special section "Cultural Preservation," in FCR, 40, no. 11 (November 1990): 4–53.

92. Many of these issues are examined in detail in Alan Wachman, *Taiwan: National Identity and Democratization* (Armonk, NY: M.E. Sharpe, 1994).

93. On literature, see the special section "Contemporary Literature in Taiwan," in FCR, 41, no. 4 (April 1991): 4–47. On film, see the special section "Film Industry," in FCR, 45, no. 2 (February 1995): 4–33. On painting and sculpture, see the special section "Fine Arts," in FCR, 43, no. 3 (March 1993): 4–57. On problems and perspectives of cultural development, see "Cultural Development," FCR, 45, no. 10 (October 1995): 4–39. On the development of Taiwan studies, see the special section "Taiwan Studies," in FCR, 42, no. 3 (March 1992): 4–45. See also a second, more recent section that focuses on the field on Taiwan and in the West, "Taiwan Studies," in FCR, 44, no. 2 (February 1994): 5–45.

94. On the Hakka, see the special section "The Hakka," in FCR, 43, no. 10 (October 1993): 4–39. On the indigenous people, see the special issue "Taiwan's Indigenous People," FCR, 42, no. 6 (June 1992).

95. C.S. Song, ed., *Self-Determination: The Case for Taiwan* (Tainan: Church Press, 1988), gathers together the issues of the journal and offers a detailed look at the process of

suppressing the Taiwanese-speaking Presbyterian Church of Taiwan as well as an attack on this policy and the government of the ROC.

96. I interviewed Shih in 1990 a few weeks after his release from prison in June 1990 and have interviewed him and his former wife, Linda Arrigo, many times since then.

97. Hsieh Shih-chung, "From Shanbao to Yuanzhumin: Taiwan Aborigines in Transition," in Rubinstein, ed., *The Other Taiwan*, 404–419.

98. "Taiwan's Indigenous Tribal People."

99. On the development of these major cities before the 1970s, see Lung Kwai-hai, *Trends of Urbanization in Taiwan: A Study of Five Cities* (Taipei: Orient Publishing Service, 1972).

100. This observation is based on this author's yearly trips to Taipei and these nearby suburbs, the homes of universities and research centers.

101. This author spent considerable time in Taichung while studying the island's Protestant community and returns frequently to visit the chapter house of the Catholic Maryknoll order.

14

Literature in Post-1949 Taiwan, 1950 to 1980s

Sung-sheng Yvonne Chang

The Taipei Fine Arts Museum.

Shifting Literary Trends

Taiwan's post-1949 era began when China's Nationalist government, led by Chiang Kai-shek, retreated from the mainland to settle on the offshore island province of Taiwan after losing the civil war to the Communists.[1] The forty-year period under the rule of two presidents from the Chiang family (Chiang Kai-shek and his son Chiang Ching-kuo) was characterized by remarkable continuity and homogeneity socially, politically, and culturally. Drastic structural changes, however, have been occurring at all levels of society since the mid-1980s, as a direct consequence of the lifting of martial law, the recognition of an opposition party, the removal of the ban on founding newspapers, and the resumption of communication with mainland China at the civilian level. New intellectual and artistic currents have emerged, many with the explicit or implicit motive of reexamining existing orders. Nonetheless, it is undeniable that literary accomplishments of writers from the earlier post-1949 decades laid solid groundwork for Taiwan's vital and pluralistic cultural developments in the 1990s.

Because China split into two political entities with different sociopolitical systems after 1949, the tradition of Chinese New Literature has also been traveling along divergent paths. On the one hand, writers in post-1949 Taiwan have been selective in developing their literary heritage; whereas revolutionary literature and "critical realism" were suppressed, the more inoffensive, lyrical-sentimental strand has enjoyed great popularity. On the other hand, from the anti-Communist propaganda of the cold war decade of the 1950s, through the modernist and the nativist literary movements of the 1960s and 1970s, to the expression of today's pluralism and a burgeoning market-oriented mass culture, literary currents in post-1949 Taiwan have closely mirrored the country's larger sociopolitical transitions.

The elitist, Western-influenced modernist literary movement of the sixties and the populist, nationalistic nativist literary movement of the 1970s may appropriately be regarded as "alternative" and "oppositional" cultural formations in Taiwan during this period, to use Raymond Williams's terminology. As the modernists adopted literary concepts developed in Western capitalist society, they simultaneously longed for an ideological transformation, taking such bourgeois social values as individualism, liberalism, and rationalism as correctives for the oppressive social relations derived from a traditional system of values. The nativist literary movement, in contrast, with its use of literature as a pretext to challenge the dominant sociopolitical order, may be properly considered counterhegemonic. The movement was triggered by the nation's international diplomatic setbacks during the 1970s. It provided a forum for native Taiwanese intellectuals to vent their discontent with the unbalanced distribution of political power between mainlanders and native Taiwanese and with the socioeconomic problems that accompanied the country's accelerated rate of industrialization since the 1960s.

For different reasons, both movements dominated Taiwan's literary scene for only a relatively brief period of time. By the late 1970s and early 1980s, the influence of both the modernists and the nativists had sharply declined, and some of their inherent shortcomings had become obvious with the passage of time. As most of the modernist writers advocated artistic autonomy and were politically disengaged, the subversive elements of their works were easily co-opted by hegemonic cultural forces and their critical impact consequently diluted. The more radical subscription to aestheticism by certain writers, moreover, was deeply at odds with the predominantly lyrical sensibility of ordinary Chinese readers. Even though the essential dynamics of the modernist movement were not entirely exhausted with the loss of popular favor, both critics and general readers received the movement's most mature output in the 1980s with a disheartening nonchalance. In the meantime, the militant political agenda of the nativists both threatened and bored middle-class readers, who were largely satisfied with the status quo. The resistance activities of the more radical nativists, moreover, were increasingly channeled into direct political involvement. The subsiding of these contending literary voices thus paved the way for the rise in the 1980s of a more popular "serious" literature and a resurgence of lyricism and sentimentality. The younger generation of writers of this decade assimilated the technical sophistication of the modernists and displayed social awareness as a result of the nativist influence. Their vocational visions, however, significantly departed from those of their mentors and were much more deeply conditioned by the market logic of Taiwan's increasingly commercialized culture.

Literature of the Mainland Émigrés in the 1950s

After Taiwan was returned to China in 1945, Mandarin Chinese replaced the Taiwanese dialect and Japanese as the official spoken language of the province. Creative activities of middle-aged native Taiwanese writers were then greatly hampered by this language barrier. Political fear also silenced native Taiwanese writers, as many Taiwanese intellectuals were persecuted during and after the "February 28 incident" in 1947.[2] The literary scene in Taiwan during the 1950s was therefore dominated by mainlander writers who followed the Nationalists to Taiwan around 1949. These émigré writers were frequently mobilized in the state-sponsored cultural programs and produced a literature that has often been characterized as anti-Communist.

In addition to their political propaganda, writers of the 1950s are frequently faulted for their amateurism, which is partly the product of a special institution in Taiwan, the *fu-k'an,* or literary supplement to newspapers. The *fu-k'an* undeniably has been the most significant sponsor of literary activities in contemporary Taiwan; nevertheless, because of its large demand for works with immediate popular appeal, it at the same time fostered casual, light-weight writings as well as middle-brow literary tastes. As literary writing became less professional, the distinction between artistic and journalistic genres was often blurred.

Although the general climate in the 1950s was not conducive to the production of serious art, works of considerable artistic merit by a number of writers deserve greater critical attention than they usually receive. Two broad categories of writings by these writers, traditionalist prose and realistic fiction, are representative of literature in this decade.

Traditionalist Prose

Contrary to the situation in the People's Republic of China, where gentry literature of China's feudal past was sometimes renounced for ideological reasons and where numerous political idioms designed to mobilize the masses were added to the vocabulary, the prose style in post-1949 Taiwan tended to be more literary, retaining many more archaic expressions and allusions to classical literature. This phenomenon is apparently a direct result of the cultural policy of the Nationalist government, which promoted traditional culture partly as a means to assert its own legitimacy as a Chinese government. In practice, the dominant culture's selective emphasis on the lyrical strand of Chinese New Literature from the pre-1949 era veered the stylistic development of literary writing in specific directions. The selection of works by such writers as Hsu Chih-mo and Chu Tzu-ch'ing for middle-school textbooks, for instance, contributed to the popularity of the former's exotic, flamboyant, European-flavored aestheticism and the latter's genteel, refined, traditional Chinese sensibility.

The proliferation of traditionalist prose in Taiwan during the 1950s, in the forms of familiar essays and the hybrid genre of essay-fiction, was apparently a continuation of an earlier trend on the mainland during and after the Sino-Japanese war. The decade's best-known essayists—Chang Hsiu-ya, Chung Mei-yin, Hsu Chung-p'ei, Liang Hsuan, and Ch'i-chun—were therefore all mainlander writers.

The wide popularity of traditionalist prose among general Chinese readers was explained by the eminent sinologist Jaroslav Prusek. As Prusek puts it, traditional Chinese literature is a refined, sensitive form of polite writing, one in which "all experiences had to pass the censorship of beauty[;] only what was *wen* or 'beautiful' being allowed to pass into the temple of literature, also designated *wen,* while all evil and ugly emotions were excluded." Although more than half a century has passed since the Chinese New Literature replaced the old, traditional aesthetic assumptions, the "censorship of beauty," is still prevalent among Chinese readers and writers, especially among older people.

Realistic Fiction

Having in their formative years been exposed to works of Lu Hsun, Mao Tun, Pa Chin, and Lao She, mainland émigré writers active in the 1950s and 1960s by and large carried on the Chinese "realist" tradition—a somewhat atrophied version of nineteenth-century European realism—established during the May Fourth era and the 1930s. For political reasons, however, they consciously or unconsciously modified those realistic conventions that might have been offensive to the dominant culture of post-1949 Taiwan: Revolutionary and proletarian themes were taboo, and references to class consciousness were also avoided. Nevertheless, the nature of literary conventions is such that their suppression can never be as complete as it appears on the surface. From a scholarly point of view, the textual strategies employed by these writers to transform subtly highly tendentious Chinese realistic conventions in order to fulfill a different set of ideological requirements are of great research interest.

The 1960s saw the publication of several well-written, "anti-Communist" realistic novels, such as *Rice-Sprout Song* (Yang-ko), *The Whirlwind* (Hsuan-feng), and *Ti Village* (Ti-ts'un chuan). Although they were important in their own right, the fact that these stories were set exclusively in pre-Revolution China and that their authors either never resided in Taiwan (e.g., Eileen Chang), or were marginal to Taiwan's literary scene (e.g., Chiang Kui and Ch'en Hsi-ying) diminishes their significance to Taiwan's post-1949 literary history. Far more relevant are such writers as Wang Lan, Meng Yao, P'an Jen-mu, Lin Hai-yin, Nieh Hua-ling, P'eng Ko, Chu Hsi-ning, Tuan Ts'ai-hua, Ssu-ma Chung-yuan, and Chung Chao-cheng—writers who established their literary reputations around the mid-1950s and who have played prominent roles in Taiwan's literary scene ever since.

Although these writers' fiction works are also filled with nostalgic recollections of the mainland past, they are nevertheless unique products of the contemporary cultural and political environment. On the one hand, unmistakably, the emancipation ethos, a legacy of pre-1949 realist literature, has informed their writings set in the past on subjects such as the oppression of women, the repressive nature of the traditional Chinese family system, and the pathetic condition of working-class people and domestic servants. On the other hand, the realistic codes have been rewritten and the critical messages mitigated or displaced: Rightist political convictions and the active support of the present government frequently caused these writers to domesticate the revolutionary spirit with counterdevices and to shift the thematic focus from the sociohistorical to the private domains.

In sum, although works by writers in this group are not without artistic merit, their ideological outlook is deeply embedded in the conservative, dominant culture of Taiwan's post-1949 era. Extrinsic political motives and conformist spirit have considerably stigmatized their works in the eyes of serious literary critics. The rise of the young modernists, with their liberalism and new aesthetic conceptions, challenged not only these older writers' artistic visions, but also the dominant culture's ideological control over creative writers. The changes brought forth by the modernists in the artistic realm formed the basis for more radical cultural critiques found in later decades.

The Modernist Literary Movement

C.T. Hsia, an eminent scholar of modern Chinese literature who recently retired from his long career at Columbia University, observed in the preface to his *History of Modern Chinese Fiction* (1970, 2d ed.) that "Taiwan since 1961 has enjoyed a minor literary renascence of genuine promise, even though few Western readers are yet aware of its existence" (p. vii). The "literary renascence" referred to here is now commonly known as Taiwan's modernist literary movement, which has left indelible imprints on Taiwan's contemporary literary history.

Since the dominant culture in post-1949 Taiwan carries on many traditions established in China during the Republican era (1911–49), the cultural and intellectual context of Taiwan's modernist literary movement must also be examined with references to pre-1949 modern Chinese history. First, the modernist literary movement may be seen as another instance of Chinese intellectuals' emulation of Western high culture. Ever since the end of the nineteenth century, modern Chinese intellectuals, shocked by the devastating effect of China's encounter with hegemonic Western culture, have continually embarked upon various programs of cultural rejuvenation, the most potent formula for which consists in assimilation of Western culture. Taiwan's modernist literary movement, as one of the latest in a series of such programs, inevitably displays some of its essential characteristics. Second, an important link can be found between this movement and the liberal strand of thought in China's prerevolutionary era, especially that of Anglo-American intellectuals. The ideas of important literary figures of post-1949 Taiwan—such as Liang Shih-ch'iu, a former member of the Crescent Moon Society (Hsin-yueh she); Hsia Chi-an, mentor of a core group of modernists; and Yen Yuan-shu, leading critic of the 1960s, who introduced New Criticism to Taiwan—are all fundamentally rooted in the Western liberal-humanist tradition. Yen Yuan-shu's proposition that "literature has the dual function of being the dramatization and criticism of life," in particular, closely echoes both Matthew Arnold and the Literary Studies Association's (Wen-hsueh yen-chiu she) famous tenet "art for life's sake." Taiwan's modernists particularly stressed the principle of artistic autonomy, among other liberal conceptions of literature, and, by and large, have more thoroughly adhered to this principle than their pre-1949 liberal predecessors.

From the point of view of literary history, however, the epoch-making significance of Taiwan's modernist literary movement rests primarily with its generation of new dynamics among contemporary writers and its redirecting of their artistic mode of expression. A closer look at new artistic formulations of Taiwan's modernist fiction, arguably the movement's most accomplished area, illustrates these points.

New Thematic Conventions

In theme and subject matter, writers of Taiwan's modernist fiction endeavored to explore new spheres of human experience beyond the confines of traditional literature. In doing so, they continued the efforts of their early twentieth-century May Fourth predecessors and even surpassed them. To comprehend and analyze the complexity of human experience in the modern world, they generally favored rationalism, scientism, and serious, if at times immature, philosophical contemplations. We have thus witnessed the establishment of a set of thematic conventions that supposedly incorporate advanced knowledge of human behavior made available by the modern sciences. For example, apparently influenced by popular versions of Freudian psychoanalysis, young writers in the early stage of the modernist literary movement were fascinated in particular with abnormal interpersonal relationships. Most of these writers, such as Wang Wen-hsing, Pai Hsien-yung, Ou-yang Tzu, Ch'en Jo-hsi, Shui Ching, and Ch'en Ying-chen, have written stories featuring imaginary post-Freudian middle-class spiritual dilemmas or have focused on scandalous revelations of some abnormal psychological traits. Most of these stories lack originality in thematic conception; yet, as any writer's fictional imagination necessarily reflects his or her private fantasies (which are rooted in the individual's socialization), even the artistically less mature works by the young modernists reveal serious attempts by individual authors to come to terms with troubling psychological obsessions. These young writers' sincerity and bold, honest self-analysis broke new ground in Taiwan's culture: Such efforts have redefined the boundaries of normalcy in human behavior and thus challenged the conventional ethical prescriptions and the conservative middle-class mentality that have underpinned the dominant culture of post-1949 Taiwan.

Some truly radical cultural examinations are found in the movement's later, more mature stage. For example, sharing the theme of father–son conflict, the most significant novels of two of Taiwan's modernists—Pai Hsien-yung's *Crystal Boys* (Nieh-tzu) (1983) and Wang Wen-hsing's *Family Catastrophe* (Chia-pien) (1973)—bitterly protested the traditional ethical norms that are crystallized in the Confucianist notions of *chung* (loyalty) and *hsiao* (filial piety) and thus called into question the foundations of contemporary Taiwan society. Notably, in both works, the battle against the retention of traditional social values is waged with the aid of Western conceptual frames. *Family Catastrophe* focuses on the conflict between bourgeois individualism and filial piety in a financially strapped modern Chinese family. That the hero is portrayed as a fanatic rationalist shows the degree to which the author is skeptical of the real efficacy of such an ideological transfer. *Crystal Boys* projects a more idealistic vision influenced by the countercultural movement of the 1960s in the United States, with its anarchic assertion of the emancipatory power of the Dionysian impulse, its celebration of youth and beauty in their ephemeral physical forms, and its romantic affirmation of the redeeming virtue of love. The author enhanced the symbolism of this book by including mythical themes from the Chinese classic *Dream of the Red Chamber* (Hung-lou meng). The underground homosexual community of New Park in *Crystal Boys,* like residents of the Garden of the Grand Vision in the famous traditional novel, is ruled by the supreme order of *ch'ing* (sentimentality) and *hsin* (the heart), which can be both salvational and damning. This microcosm, however, is extremely vulnerable, as it is forever overshadowed by the law of the father—the dominant order of the patriarchal, Confucianist society outside the garden. The prominence of the father-quest motif in both *Family Catastrophe* and *Crystal Boys*—heroes in both novels are constantly searching for paternal surrogates—betrays their authors' anxiety over the general corruption of the terms governing human relationships in contemporary Taiwan society, terms that were formerly built solidly on the patriarchal order.

Formal Innovations

Particularly eye-catching during the initial stage of the modernist literary movement was the temporary surge of an "avant-garde" trend. One prominent feature of the self-styled avant-garde writers of the 1960s was their infatuation with the intellectual current of existentialism. As Franz Kafka was introduced early in the movement, the use of obscure plots and bizarre language quickly became a fad, and the basic tenor of works by many young writers—Ch'i-teng Sheng, Ts'ung Su, and Shih Shu-ch'ing among them—was dominated by nihilism, agonism, and an anxiety over the absurdity of existence.

Although the nativist literary movement in the following decade, with its demand for literature's social relevance and mass intelligibility, successfully stemmed the avant-garde craze of obscurantism in literary style, and although many negative critical responses to these young writers' "pseudo-avant-gardism" were justified, the upsurge of "aesthetic iconoclasm" in the 1960s represented a significant moment in postwar Taiwan's literary history. The vigorous dynamics of newly introduced artistic conceptions associated with modernism called into question conventional forms and criteria of literary excellence. The more enduring efforts generated by this initial enthusiasm eventually ushered in a new era of modern Chinese literary history.

Most other modernist fiction writers in Taiwan stayed within the general confines of realism, but they were no less experimental. Their most persevering explorations of language and voice eventually brought forth fundamental changes in the rhetorical conventions of modern Chinese narrative. Since, as some scholars have observed, the attempts of earlier modern Chinese writers to offer realistic portraits of life were frequently hampered by the dominance of the subjective voice in the work's rhetorical structure, the modernists tried to redress this deficiency by introducing a new "objective form." They strove to present an "impartial" picture of reality so that readers could form their own opinions and moral judgments. Viewed from a Western perspective, these ideas are more reminiscent of the realists' concept of literary representation than the modernist view of literature as self-referential discursive practice. Throughout the 1960s, the majority of critical writings introducing Western literary concepts focused on basic technical rules and critical criteria that have long been taken for granted in the West. Authoritative U.S.-trained scholars and critics such as Yen Yuan-shu, Chu Li-min, and Wai-lim Yip systematically expounded the fundamentals of a whole set of Western literary codes, and their influence on creative writing and practical criticism in Taiwan was immeasurable. Such a phenomenon is not difficult to understand, given that the literary genres of the short story and the novel (in the strict sense) have been imported from the West only in the twentieth century. That Chinese writers aspire to excel in these genres on their own terms and are eager to learn about their original formal requirements, is demonstrated not only by writers of Taiwan in the 1960s but also by writers in the People's Republic of China in the 1980s, when "modernist fiction" once again became fashionable there.

It is also true, however, that the appropriation of foreign literary codes always goes beyond the mastery of basic techniques and necessarily involves larger, more complicated networks of artistic and ideological systems. Given that the most noteworthy formal feature popularized by the modernists is widened distance between author and text, their efforts continued the general trend in modern Chinese literary history away from the traditional expressive view toward the mimetic view of literature. With their denunciation of sentimentalism and express interest in the hidden complexities of the human psyche, personal emotions were no longer treated as the source or origin of literature but, rather, as objects of detached observation.

It is arguable that, although Taiwan's modernist literary movement has taken place in a "postmodern" period from standpoint of the West—mainly in the 1960s and 1970s—and many newer artistic trends and techniques have been incorporated by the modernist writers into their work, the dominant tendency of this movement nevertheless is closest to the early phase of Western modernism, in the late nineteenth and early twentieth centuries. In other words, the extremely compressed timetable of Taiwan's modernist literary movement nevertheless contains features such as the reversal of the conventional content–form hierarchy and the radical rejection of traditional writing techniques that results from burgeoning skepticism about language and meaning. Most of the modernists' explorations of language unmistakably reflect Western influences. However, more original experiments have also been undertaken, which followed from a new awareness of the unstable relationship between language and its referents, as well as a reawakened sensitivity toward the ideographic nature of the Chinese language. These experiments—especially those found in Wang Wen-hsing's two novels *Family Catastrophe* and *Backed Against the Sea* (Pei-hai te jen) (1981) and Li Yung-p'ing's story series *Chronicle of Chi-ling* (Chi-ling ch'un-ch'iu) (1986), which mark the apex of the development of modernist aestheticism in contemporary Chinese literature—merit more scholarly attention than they have yet received.

The Nativist Literary Debate

In the late 1960s and early 1970s, as the modernist fiction writers began to mature artistically, the resistance to modernism's dominance of Taiwan's literary scene also began. The precursor to a large-scale denunciation of the modernist literary movement was the 1972 New Poetry debate (*hsin-shih lun-chan*), which involved academic critics and modernist poets who discussed specific Western-influenced features in contemporary Taiwan poetry. The consensus reached in this debate seemed to be that, despite its other merits, the New Poetry suffered from such unhealthy qualities as semantic obscurity, excessive use of foreign imagery and Europeanized syntax, and evasion of contemporary social reality. These features, furthermore, were considered symptomatic of the faulty style generally promoted in Taiwan's modernist literary movement.

While it may not be unusual in literary history for critics and writers periodically to reexamine and revolt against the current dominant style, the New Poetry debate bore a special social implication in that it was closely tied to Taiwan intellectuals' growing consciousness of their endangered Chinese cultural identity. In what was later known as the "return to the native" (*hui-kui hsiang-t'u*) trend around the end of the 1970s, progressive intellectuals criticized the blind admiration and slavish imitation of Western cultural models and exhorted their compatriots to show more respect for their indigenous cultural heritage, as well as greater concern for domestic social issues. Many liberal scholars, especially returnees from the United States, played important roles in igniting this new current, which at first revolved around several universities and intellectual magazines.

Shortly after the New Poetry debate, a group of critics began to renounce publicly the foreign-influenced modernist work and to advocate a nativist, socially responsible literature. This trend reached its apex with the outbreak of a virulent nativist literary debate in 1977 and 1978 and suddenly declined when, in 1979, several key figures of the nativist camp exited from the literary scene and became directly involved in political protests. The tradition of nativist literature as a creative genre—the main features of which are use of the Taiwanese dialect, depiction of the plight of country folks or small-town dwellers facing economic difficulty, and resistance to the imperialist presence in Taiwan—can be traced back to the nativist literary trend during the Japanese colonial period. While inheriting the dominant nationalist spirit from this earlier trend, the nativist literature champions of the 1970s had their own political agenda as well.

Viewed retrospectively, the nativist camp was the first political opposition at a critical juncture in Taiwan's post-1949 history. After two decades of political stability and steady economic growth, the country suffered a series of diplomatic setbacks at the beginning of the 1970s—beginning with its expulsion from the United Nations in 1971, followed by Richard Nixon's visit to the People's Republic of China, and the termination of the country's diplomatic relations with Japan in 1972—which caused not only international isolation but also a crisis of confidence among the intellectuals. The crevice thus created in the Nationalist government's state control provided an opportunity for frustrated native intellectuals to vent the discontent that had been building for years: anxiety over the country's future, which had frequently been glossed over by the "regain the mainland" slogan; indignation about political persecutions of dissidents; and many other grievances against the authoritarian regime.

The nativists also aspired to a noncapitalist socioeconomic system. As the problems accompanying the country's accelerated development grew, long-repressed socialist ideas began to resurface. Unlike the majority of the country's liberal intellectuals, who demanded political democratization but supported capitalist-style economic modernization, the nativists believed that the socioeconomic system of Taiwan must be changed. They launched fierce attacks on the government's economic dependence on Western countries (especially the United States), which allowed the "decadent" capitalist culture to infiltrate the lives of Taiwan's people; feeling indignant on behalf of Taiwan's farmers and workers who paid a high price in the process of urban expansion, they also attempted to draw public attention to adverse effects of the country's economic development as a whole.

Such opposition posed a threat to the government, which was convinced that the logical consequence of the upsurge of socialist ideology would be a Communist insurgency backed by the Chinese government on the mainland. In addition, the regionalist sentiment implied in the nativist project immediately touched on an extremely sensitive issue, the "provincial identity" (or *sheng-chi*) problem. Not only had tensions between native Taiwanese and mainlanders always been a source of disquieting feelings, but the unbalanced distribution of political power was an epicenter on the verge of eruption. As a consequence, even though some of the leading nativist critics were socialists or nationalists rather than separatists who promoted Taiwan independence (Ch'en Ying-chen, for example, has always been a staunch advocate of future reunification with China), the nativist critical discourse as a whole could not but be deeply entrenched in the ongoing political strife between the native Taiwanese and the mainlander-controlled Nationalist government.

It is therefore undeniable that literary nativism was used by a special group of people at a particular historical moment to challenge the existing sociopolitical order. However, it appears that ideological debates in modern Chinese society inevitably generate widespread polemics around literature, as evidenced by numerous such disputes in the May Fourth period, in the 1930s, and during the entire Communist reign on the mainland. The traditional Chinese pragmatic view of literature and the legacy of a gentry ideology, which assigns to intellectuals, especially writers, lofty social missions, have combined to make literary discourse a genuine political arena. As a result, the attacks launched by the nativists on the modernist writers, whose literary ideology is a conspicuously apolitical one, have centered largely on the latter's default of their social responsibilities as members of the intelligentsia.

The home base for the anti-modernist critics was the journal *Literary Quarterly* (Wen-chi), founded in 1966. With Yu T'ien-ts'ung as the central mover, the journal's founding members included several writers already known for their modernist work, such as Ch'en Ying-chen, Liu Ta-jen, Shih Shu-ch'ing, and Ch'i-teng Sheng. The journal had, furthermore, discovered two important writers, Huang Ch'un-ming and Wang Chen-ho, whose fiction significantly departed from the current modernist fads and depicted rural life with unaffected realism. Although both writers refused to label their works as "nativist," the literary reformers on the journal's editorial board were ready to use them as weapons in their fight against the modernist hegemony.

In 1973, T'ang Wen-piao, a visiting math professor closely associated with the *Literary Quarterly,* fired criticism at the modernists' elitist tendency and neglect of the masses. The straightforward accusations so startled the liberal critics that Yen Yuan-shu referred to this critical attack as the "T'ang Wen-piao incident." However, even more vehement militancy was seen when the nativist critics chose individual writers as targets. Almost simultaneously with the T'ang Wen-piao incident, the *Literary Quarterly* organized a series of seminars to examine the thematic implications of Ou-yang Tzu's fiction, and branded it corrupt and immoral. A combatant spirit was aroused, and, by the mid-1970s, writers in Taiwan's literary circle were already split into opposing groups.

The literary climate in this decade became truly unpleasant with the increasing politicization of critical discourse. With the founding of the radical magazine *China Tide* (Hsia-ch'ao) in 1976 and its provocative use of such taboo terms as "proletarian literature" (literally, literature of workers, peasants, and soldiers) and "class consciousness," the deep-seated anti-Communist sentiments of the liberals were incited. In the summer of 1977, the country's leading modernist poet, Yu Kuang-chung, wrote a short essay entitled "The Wolf Is Here" (Lang lai-le) openly accusing the nativists of being leftists. This fatal charge ignited highly emotional responses and retaliation from all sides, and polemical writings about literature and politics began to flood the country's newspapers and literary magazines. This so-called nativist literary debate came to an end only in the middle of 1978, when the government threatened to intervene.

During the debate, intellectuals of different ideological persuasions formed two temporary coalitions. On the one hand, to resist the nativists' leftist dogmatism, the liberal modernists sided with progovernment writers and literary bureaucrats. On the other hand, such older, established literary figures as Hsu Fu-kuan and Hu Ch'iu-yuan allied with the nativists, and defended the intellectual's right to political involvement. New and existing magazines and newspapers also established distinct, partisan alliances. Sandwiched between government supporters and various oppositional factions, the less politically minded modernist writers soon found themselves forced into roles imposed on them by others.

The impact of the nativist literary debate was largely emotional. As the debate involved numerous exchanges of personal insults, it created a schism between the modernists and the nativists that took a long time to bridge. While conservative attacks on nativist literature often included potential political threats, many self-styled nativist critics were overly adamant in their attempts to impose ideological guidelines on creative writers. Some even resorted to distasteful name calling, which only made it doubly clear that the modernists had been used as scapegoats for an unbridled outburst of antigovernment sentiment. Liberal academic critics had ambivalent roles in this dispute. For instance, such respected critics as Yen Yuan-shu and Ch'i Yi-shou always endorsed the nativists' nationalist stance and the notion of socially responsible literature, but they were at the same time disturbed by the confusion of art and politics. Their largely rational, well-informed views on artistic matters, however, fell largely on deaf ears.

Although the nativists took the offensive position in most of the feud, some serious nativist thinkers also found the debate profoundly disappointing. Ch'en Ying-chen, for example, regretted that the discussion never rose to a higher theoretical level and never became a "neo-Enlightenment" intellectual movement. Such activists as Yang Ch'ing-ch'u and Wang T'o, who had intended to use literature as an ideological weapon, also seemed to experience tremendous frustration, which eventually led them to pursue political goals through more direct channels.

Placed within a larger historical context, the modernist–nativist split is part of the continuing struggle in modern Chinese history between liberal and radical intellectuals with different reform programs and different views of literature's social function. The new paradigm of ideological writing as established in the mid-1970s moved in a direction diametrically opposed to that of the introspective, humanist, and universalist approach of the modernists and deliberately focused on the historical specificity of contemporary Taiwan society. In addition to later works by Huang Ch'un-ming on imperialism, such writers as Yang Ch'ing-ch'u and Wang T'o explored capitalist exploitation as it affected urban factory workers and fishermen. These literary efforts were also backed by some serious theoretical thinking, although most of the nativist literary debate itself was virtually divorced from contemporary literary practice.

Wang T'o's 1977 essay, "Shih 'hsien-shih chu-yi' wen-hsueh, pu-shih 'hsiang-t'u wen-hsueh' " (It's "literature of the present reality," not "nativism"), stood out among numerous polemical writings precisely because of its accurate representation of the reality of then-current literary practice. Wang's main argument in this essay is that, instead of writing about rural regions and country people, nativist literature is concerned with the "here and now" of Taiwan society, which embraces a wide range of social environments and people. Nativist literature thus should be defined as a literature rooted in the land of Taiwan that reflects the social reality and the material and psychological aspirations of its people. By using the term "*hsien-shih*" (contemporary reality, the "here and now") rather than "*hsieh-shih*" (realism), and by enlarging the scope of nativist literature to include all levels of society in Taiwan, Wang has disentangled the confused debate over the Western-imported literary term "realism" and has foregrounded the nativists' ideological position by stressing high-priority issues. The essay, therefore, represents an important step in the nativists' self-definition.

The critical evaluation of nativist work produced in the 1970s, however, is in general not very positive. Although the change in thematic conventions since the 1970s met with the approval of most critics, excessive ideological concern is considered an impediment to their literary achievement. Even though Huang Ch'un-ming is often regarded as such an exception, many have felt that his later work, too, deteriorated in direct proportion to the increase in social commentary. However, just as modernist literature continued to evolve after the rise of nativist literature, nativist literature did not come to an end even though the nativist literary debate folded toward the end of the 1970s. The continuing efforts made by such nativist ideological writers as Ch'en Ying-chen, Sung Tse-lai, Li Ch'iao, and Wu Chin-fa in the 1980s show a sharp increase in formal consciousness as well as attempts to experiment with innovative techniques.

The 1980s: A Decade of Pluralism

In a sense, the articulation of dissident views during the nativist literary debate forced the government to exercise greater tolerance and thus paved the way for more intense struggles toward political democratization, which rapidly gained momentum in the early 1980s. Eventually, with the formation in 1987 of an opposition party, the Democratic Progressive Party, literature was largely relieved of its function as a pretext for political contention. It became, however, even more inextricably involved in the country's booming mass media. Most notably, the two competing media giants, the *United Daily News* (Lien-ho pao) and *China Times* (Chung-kuo shih-pao), each claiming the loyalty of a group of writers, invested heavily in their literary pages for marketing purposes. The annual fiction contests they sponsored between the mid-1970s and the mid-1980s gave creative writing a solid boost—an overwhelming majority of the writers of the baby-boom generation rose to literary prominence by winning one of these contests.

The nativist theorists may have felt at once frustrated and vindicated in the 1980s, as the "spiritual corruption" of capitalist society, which they had predicted, became unmistakable with the ascendance of mammonism and a sharp rise in the crime rate. The overall cultural environment also became heavily consumer-oriented. Not without a touch of irony, even the nativist literature itself was largely co-opted by the cultural establishment, especially between the late 1970s and the early 1980s. Newspaper supplements and literary magazines were inundated by pseudo-nativist works, which displayed Taiwanese local color but contained little ideological content.

As public fervor for both the modernist and the nativist causes subsided, the literary scene of the 1980s was dominated largely by the baby-boom generation, whose vocational visions were drastically different from those of their predecessors. Rather than treating creative writing as an intellectual project or a political quest, they were more concerned with popularity and with various problems affecting Taiwan's middle-class urbanites, especially the new social affluence and the relaxation of moral standards. Some writers, such as Huang Fan and Li Ang, with a cynical intellectual pose, offered critiques of materialism and the cultural impoverishment it caused. Others, such as Hsiao Sa and Liao Hui-ying, with down-to-earth pragmatism, examined the new social factors that had changed ordinary people's way of life, showing particular interest in liberated sexual views and the problem of extramarital relationships. Still others, such as Yuan Ch'iung-ch'iung, Chu T'ien-wen, and Su Wei-chen, falling back on the sentimental-lyrical tradition, focused their attention on the personal, with a posture of complacency with regard to sociopolitical issues. Whether progressively or conservatively inclined, the new generation of writers seemed to share a common response to the emergence of new political situations. As knowledge about the Chinese on the other side of the Taiwan strait suddenly became available, and with the public debate over the unification/independence prospects intensifying on a daily basis, many of the writers of the baby-boom generation deliberately stressed their unique cultural identity, rooted in the specific sociohistorical realities of post-1949 Taiwan.

Writers' approaches to literature in this decade were certainly pluralist. While writers of the modernist generation published their more mature works during this decade, literary products of the younger generation were marked by a rich diversity—*chuan-ts'un* literature,[3] works about life in business corporations, political fiction (with a special subgenre on the February 28 incident), neo-nativist literature, resistance literature, feminist works, and science fiction—a phenomenon that may be aptly characterized as an orchestra of discordant "voices." A comprehensive examination of this literature no doubt requires a new analytical scheme. Some strands of literary developments of the 1980s, however, were inevitably tied to what had gone before them.

The broadly defined "return to the native" trend carried over into the early 1980s beyond the modernist–nativist schism. After the nativist literary debate, new interest in an indigenous literary heritage fostered a "cultural nostalgia." Several formerly modernist writers made notable contributions to this trend. Shih Shu-ch'ing and Li Ang, for example, turned consciously to folk traditions and native subject matter in their writing. Lin Huai-min, a former modernist writer who had studied under Martha Graham while in the United States, founded the first Chinese modern dance troupe, produced the well-received "Cloud Gate Dance Series" (yun-men wu-chi), and incorporated both classical Chinese and folk Taiwanese elements in his choreography. Their accomplishments set an important tenor for creative endeavors of the new decade, even while encouraging commercial exploitation of traditional and native cultural signs.

As the indigenous replaced the foreign, becoming the primary source of exotic imagination, and "Chinese/Taiwan cultural identity" came to occupy a prominent place in the public consciousness, the reemergence of a "postmodern" trend since the mid-1980s necessarily reopened the Pandora's box and once again raised issues about Western influences on contemporary Chinese literature. In a pattern closely resembling that by which such earlier Western literary trends as romanticism, realism, and modernism were appropriated by Chinese writers, the postmodern mode of writing has become a new fad and its surface markers—such as double endings, juxtaposition of the factual and the fictional, and the technique of pastiche—have appeared abundantly in works by both greater and lesser writers. Such imitative literary products cannot help but recall works written during the earliest phase of the modernist literary movement and, not surprisingly, were considered of dubious value by some veteran modernists.

Although the younger writers consciously subscribe to the more cynical, "postmodern" ideology—as evidenced by their emphasis on difference, tolerance of pluralistic coexistence of the incommensurable, and, above all, their "appetite" for indeterminacy—which is uncongenial to the modernist temperament, there are also similarities between the two generations of writers: their intellectual disposition, their globalism, and the way they look toward the West—or Western-influenced literary traditions such as those of Eastern Europe and Latin America—for literary models. As prescribed by "postmodern" ideology, however, the younger writers are more keenly aware of the self–other dichotomy and thus do not endorse universalism as the modernists did.

Strictly speaking, except for a selected few, many of the writers of the modernist generation were never fully committed to the modernist ideology and aesthetic. Although they did not concur with the nativists' pejorative view of the modernist literary project as reflecting a "comprador" mentality, they were nonetheless bothered by its derivative, "unauthentic" nature. This uneasiness, after all, is indicative of a dilemma most modern writers in non-Western countries always have to face.

Notes

1. For a complete treatment of the subject and a comprehensive bibliography, please see Sung-sheng Yvonne Chang, *Modernism and the Nativist Resistance: Contemporary Chinese Fiction from Taiwan* (Durham: Duke University Press, 1993).

2. A political incident in Taiwan two years after it was returned to China by Japan. An islandwide riot broke out and was violently suppressed by the Nationalist army.

3. Government housing compounds, built during the early decades following the retrocession, for dependents of military personnel, mostly Nationalists from the mainland. A distinct subculture was developed around such areas and was a shared experience of a large number of the second-generation mainlanders.

15

Aboriginal Self-Government

Taiwan's Uncompleted Agenda

Michael Stainton

**A happy tourist posing for a picture at the gate of the
Formosan Aboriginal Cultural Village.**

This chapter examines the movement for aboriginal self-government *(yuan-tzu-chih)* in Taiwan in the light of Pierre Bourdieu's (1977) conception of the "cultural arbitrary," and knowledge as heterodoxy/orthodoxy/doxa. This is an experiment in testing Bourdieu's ideas to interpret a political movement. To start, some clarification of the key terms "cultural arbitrary" and "self-government" is required.

Cultural Arbitrary

In *Outline of a Theory of Practice* Bourdieu argues, "The theory of knowledge is a dimension of political theory because the specifically symbolic power to impose the principles of the construction of reality—in particular social reality—is a major dimension of political power" (1977: 165). Bourdieu uses the term "cultural arbitrary" to speak of these: "durable constructions of the unconscious . . . an act of cognition and misrecognition that lies beyond—or beneath—the controls of consciousness and will" (Bourdieu 1990: 172). The cultural arbitrary is the symbolic power of constitution, which Bourdieu sees especially in the "somatization" of culture—how one carries the body, how one acts in each situation, or in the meaningful divisions of space in the house. This daily, unconscious rehearsal of cultural constructs—which Bourdieu calls the "habitus"—results in a "ritualization of practices . . . thereby conferring on them the sort of *arbitrary necessity* which specifically defines cultural arbitrariness" (1977: 163).[1] A "cultural arbitrary" thus is any cultural practice that is no longer seen as a choice among many possible human practices, but as natural—"every established order tends to produce . . . the naturalization of its own arbitrariness" (1990: 164). Bourdieu discusses this in terms of gender relations and political orders, in which power and cultural arbitraries reinforce each another. Here we use this schema experimentally to see if it is applicable to an analysis of how social movements and cultural identity reinforce each other, by "naturalizing" a political option.

A "cultural arbitrary" is a form of "doxa"—knowledge that is in the "universe of the undiscussed (undisputed)" (1977: 168). Encompassed by the unquestioned doxa is the "field of opinion (universe of discourse)," in which different ideas compete in a dichotomy of "right" and "left (wrong)" opinion, where debate and disagreement (no matter how stigmatized the heterodoxy may be) are possible.

I suggest that the significance of the idea of self-government among Taiwan's aboriginal people over the past decade can be best appreciated by understanding it as a development from "heterodoxy" to an undisputed "doxa." If self-government has become incorporated (somatized) into Taiwan aboriginal identity, we can say that it has become a "cultural arbitrary" with constitutive power. If this is so, Taiwan's aboriginal people are past the point of debating its merits and demerits with the state as a possible policy—because it is now doxa, aboriginal identity, and an inherent right. A political alternative has become a cultural arbitrary, viewed by aboriginal people as "common sense."

Self-Government

The idea of "aboriginal self-government" is a powerful unit of symbolic capital in the modern marketplace of ideas. Linked to ideas of "autonomy" and "self-determination," it presents a utopian vision of indigenous people in full control of their own lives and future, "freely determining their political status and freely pursuing their economic, social, and cultural development," "maintaining and strengthening their distinct political, economic, social and cultural characteristics as well as their legal systems, while retaining their rights to participate fully, if they so choose, in the political, economic, social, and cultural life of the state" (UN Draft Declaration on the Rights of Indigenous Peoples, Articles three and four). If this sounds like having your cake and eating it too, remember that this is a utopian ideal, against which the sometimes awful realities of the situation of indigenous peoples are measured.

One could argue that "self-government" and "self-determination" are a modern form of ethnic revitalization movement. While it may sound extreme to compare modern political movements clothed in the legal discourse of universal rights with the Handsome Lake longhouse religion, or cargo cults, it is clear that the idea of self-government gains local and personal power among aboriginal people as a way of regaining control over their lives and land, which is what earlier movements clothed in universal religious discourse were also doing.[2]

Our current ideas about self-government, now linked to autonomy and self-determination, are not what self-government always meant. One of the earliest forms of ethnic self-government was the *Millet* of the Ottoman empire, in which religious minorities were allowed internal self-government under religious leaders, whose appointments were controlled by the sultan. Another form was the free city of late medieval Europe—internally self-governing under a charter from king or emperor. Both of these locate "self-government" within the context of empire. The current practice of minority nationality regional autonomy in China could be seen as a twentieth-century expression of this form.

In nineteenth-century Canada, one of the assumptions behind Indian self-government can be seen in the approach of Sir Francis Bond-Head, lieutenant governor of Upper Canada in the 1830s: "Head had an appreciation of native culture that was rare at the time, but also believed that the Indians were doomed to extinction, and would be happiest if allowed to spend their last days free of white interference" (Grant 1984: 85). Bond-Head outraged the churches and uplifters of Indians by proposing a large reservation where the dying race could live as it chose. His policy went out with his term of office.

So contemporary ideas of aboriginal self-government based in the doctrine of universal human rights are a kind of cultural arbitrary. In saying this we affirm the symbolic power of this idea, for as this idea enters into laws, constitutions, declarations, and UN discourse, "The legal consecration of symbolic capital [in this case the symbolic capital of "aboriginal self-government"] confers upon a perspective an absolute, universal value, thus snatching it from a relativity that is by definition inherent in every point of view" (Bourdieu 1990: 136).

The idea of self-government derives its power for Taiwan's aboriginal nationalist movement from two aspects: its utopian nature as an ideal that can never be fully achieved, and its relevance to the daily experience of Taiwan's aboriginal people. We need to look at how this idea developed in Taiwan, from a policy proposal advocated by a few activists, to a cultural arbitrary, which has become a self-evident part of aboriginal identity—so that to say "we are aboriginal" is simultaneously to say "we have the right to self-government."[3] In the chronicle of events that follows, I see an illustration of how: "The self-evidence of the world is reduplicated by the instituted discourses about the world, in which the whole group's adherence to that self-evidence is affirmed" (Bourdieu 1977: 167).

From Imported Heterodoxy to Indigenous Doxa

Bourdieu contends that ideas about reality can be (1) heterodox—dissident ideas that the weight of authority argues against; (2) orthodox—mainstream ideas approved by all authorities, which can nonetheless be contested; or (3) doxa— ideas that, like Gramsci's "common sense," are taken as natural and beyond debate. A review of 17 phases of the aboriginal self-government movement in Taiwan shows an evolution of this idea from heterodoxy to doxa.

Stage 1: Heterodoxy, 1987–1990

On March 15, 1987, the two-year-old Alliance of Taiwan Aborigines (Yuan ch'uan hui, or ATA) elected a new executive. The new president, Yi-chiang Pa-lu-erh (Amis tribe), and vice-president Pa-yen Ta-lu (Tayal tribe), were determined to push the ATA into new political activism. A series of incidents in the period immediately before and after this highlighted the problems of Taiwan Aboriginal People (Taiwan *Yuan-chu-min*). A large demonstration in Taipei that January had made the issue of sale of aboriginal girls into prostitution a national cause. In March the case of T'ang Ying-shen, a young Tsou tribe worker, shocked Taiwan. Unable to find a better job, and cheated of his wages, he killed his employer's family. His death sentence sparked a national appeal by religious leaders and intellectuals for clemency, to no avail. In April the "Tung-p'u Graves incident"—opening of graves in a Pu-nun village to build a tourist hotel—enraged aboriginal people. Meanwhile, the Presbyterian aboriginal churches[4] were pursuing a movement for title to aboriginal church land, which would become the "Return Our Land" movement by the end of 1987. And all Taiwan was in political turmoil, awaiting the end of martial law that July.

1. May 1987. In late 1986 I organized a visit of Presbyterian Church in Taiwan (PCT) aboriginal leaders to the Philippines, where, while visiting Igorot peoples in northern Luzon, they met with the Cordillera People's Alliance (CPA). The CPA shared with them a copy of the Statement of Principles of the World Council of Indigenous Peoples (WCIP). I did an abbreviated translation of that statement as part of the visit report in early 1987. This was presented to the May 25, 1987, meeting of the Mountain Work Committee of the PCT General Assembly. Among its points were that "all indigenous people have the right to self-determination and can freely determine the direction of their own development" and that "indigenous people have the right to determine the structure and jurisdiction of their own institutions."[5] The report was sent to Yi-chiang Pa-lu-erh at the ATA.

2. June 1987. An editorial in *Yuan-chu-min*[6] is the first published call for aboriginal self-government in Taiwan.[7] It was probably written by Yi-chiang Pal-lu-erh and quotes directly some of my Chinese translation of the WCIP Declaration of Principles:

> *"Mountain Restricted Area" and "Aboriginal Self-Government Area"*
> Taiwan Aboriginal People (TAP) have the right of self-determination and can determine their direction of their development. . . . Because of this, the KMT [Kuomintang, or Nationalist Party] government, rather than simply passively choosing to enforce a "Mountain Restricted Area" ostensibly for security reasons, would be better off to plan for the future and actively readjust its current aboriginal policy. In the spirit of the constitution, to guarantee the status of TAP, to build up TAP local self-government efforts (*ti-fang tzu-chih shih-yeh*), develop TAP education, culture, transport, irrigation, health, economy and society, by mapping out a "Taiwan Aboriginal People's self-government (or autonomous) area" (*tzu-chih-ch'u*).

3. January 1988. The Alliance of Taiwan Aborigines issues a "Manifesto of the Rights of Taiwan Aborigines," drawing on the WCIP Declaration. Item 3 states:

> TAP have the right to practice regional autonomy in the area where the aborigines have traditionally lived. To upgrade authorities of autonomy and the competent administrative authorities to the central class. The state shall guarantee to the aborigines the right to exercise autonomy.[8]

Stage 2: Orthodoxy, 1990–1993

By 1990 the desire for aboriginal self-government was no longer simply a dissident opinion of the extremely small and politically marginalized ATA. It moved into the aboriginal mainstream, as a number of concrete policy proposals were made by governing KMT aboriginal legislators. It had become aboriginal orthodoxy.

4. July 1990. Aboriginal legislators Tsai Chung-han and Hua chia-chih propose drafts of a "Law on Fundamental Rights of Aborigines" including self-government rights. Both Tsai and Hua are KMT legislators. Their proposal, though discussed in the Executive Yuan and a committee of the legislature, never gets out of committee.

5. July 1990. "Theory and Practice of Aboriginal Self-Government" article in the *Aboriginal Post* (Yuan Pao)[9] advocates "autonomous areas" as a goal to be achieved by all aborigines at this stage of their political movement. The article gives a detailed plan of geographic scope and administrative structure of such regions, which encompass all thirty-one aboriginal townships in Taiwan and townships along the Pacific coast where the Amis tribe is in the majority. A map of the suggested borders is presented, inscribing this idea in a powerfully iconic way.

6. December 1990. Four aboriginal provincial assembly members make a motion to establish a "Mountain Township" (Kao 1994: 254) in the Taiwan provincial assembly. They are all KMT members. One of them will become the first aboriginal person to be elected county magistrate in Taiwan. Puyuma tribe member Ch'en Chien-nien became magistrate of T'ai-tung county in 1994. One-quarter of T'ai-tung's population is aboriginal.

7. April 1991. The ATA establishes a "Taiwan Aboriginal Autonomous Area Assembly" and calls for a nationalities congress (*min-tzu yi-yuan*) composed of tribal representatives and an autonomous area assembly to be popularly elected. They demand that: "The Nationalities Congress should have the power to decide on all matters concerning Aboriginal People except foreign affairs and defense." Yi-chiang Pal-lu-erh was named convenor of the preparatory committee, with Tayal PCT minister To Au as deputy and Amis PCT minister Ma-yau Ku-mu as secretary-general. Like most of the other organizational initiatives of the ATA, this did not go beyond a few meetings, but for the first time the idea of aboriginal self-government had taken on an organizational life.

8. July 1991. ATA chair Lavakau Rakuraku and Yi-chiang Pal-lu-erh attend the UN Working Group on Indigenous Populations in Geneva. They come back inspired, with more allies, ideas, authority, and energy. Their report especially notes the principles of the "national collective rights of indigenous peoples" in the Draft Declaration on the Rights of Indigenous Peoples, as something that the ATA "has always emphasized" (*Yuan-chu-min*, no. 10, September 1991). Since 1991, Taiwan Aboriginal People, from both the ATA and the PCT, have been present at every meeting of the working group. The ideas and contacts they have made there have given legitimacy and impetus to their own drive for recognition of the right of self-government of Taiwan Aboriginal People. One direct result of the UN contact is the change from using the term "*yuan-chu-min*" (aboriginal people) to "*yuan-chu-min-tzu*" (aboriginal peoples) in their usage in Taiwan.

9. March 1992. Taiwan Aboriginal Self-Government Conference sponsored by the PCT Hua-tung Community Development Center takes place in Hua-lien. The conference brings together more than sixty aboriginal intellectuals and Presbyterian clergy, mostly from Hua-lien and T'ai-tung. The main presentation on "How to promote aboriginal self-government" is given by Yi-chiang Pal-lu-erh, who concludes:

> Under the oppression of rulers from the outside, the collective vitality of Taiwan aboriginal peoples has grown weaker with every passing day, their national (*min-tzu*) consciousness more and more insipid, and their culture almost wiped out. Only sufficient self-government rights can save their race from extinction.
>
> Self-government is not a new or a radical idea. In foreign countries such as the United States, Canada, New Zealand, and even China minority nationalities have already had self-government for a long time, guaranteed by their constitutions. By contrast, how long will Taiwan Aboriginal Peoples have to wait before they enjoy the right to self-government? (Hua-tung 1992: 7)

The conference proposes achieving self-government in five years, along the lines of the ATA proposal of 1991. The conference is reported along with other long articles arguing for the necessity of aboriginal self-government, in *Yuan Pao* (no. 3, April 28, 1992), for example, "Self Government—A Basic Aboriginal Right." The writer of this article argues that self-government is the only road to save TAP from extinction and asserts that in most democratic states, even totalitarian China, aboriginal peoples already have self-government.

10. May 1992. On May 21 a demonstration is held during the National Assembly session, in support of the proposed aboriginal constitutional amendment. A statement issued jointly by the PCT Aboriginal Work Committee and the ATA calls for aboriginal self-government as a solution to aboriginal problems:

> During over forty years of KMT rule in Taiwan, because of the lack of constitutional protection, we see aboriginal people in a situation of loss of land, population outflow, backward education, impoverished economy, sale of young girls (into prostitution), the impending loss of our languages, and each tribe verging on extermination . . . Because of this, we once again present the common demand of all aboriginal people:
> 1. Change the term "mountain compatriots" (*shan pao*) to "aboriginal peoples" (*yuan-chu-min-tzu*).
> 2. Guarantee aboriginal peoples' land rights.
> 3. Guarantee aboriginal peoples' right of self-government.
> 4. Establish a specialized central government-level agency. (Hsu and Shih 1992: 133)

Stage 3: Doxa/Cultural Arbitrary, 1994–present

11. December 27–28, 1993. The Taiwan Aboriginal Policy and Social Development Consultation takes place, sponsored by Ministry of the Interior and the "Republic of China Taiwan Aboriginal People's Cultural Development Association," led by Paiwan KMT legislator Hua Chia-chih. The consultation, held to honor the UN Year of Indigenous Peoples, is attended by more than 130 government official and invited participants, including all aboriginal legislators, National Assembly members, provincial assemblymen, aboriginal township mayors, officials from all levels responsible for aboriginal affairs, academics, and aboriginal church and civic organization leaders. Almost everyone who is anyone in the political universe of aboriginal Taiwan, in both government and opposition camps, is present. The "Statement" passed at the end of the consultation declares:

> Our country is a multiethnic state [*tuo min-tzu kuo-chia*] . . . at present aboriginal people not only face the deep crisis of the extinction of their culture and collapse of their society but also see the gap in development between themselves and the rest of society growing and worsening. . . . In the past decade, the cultural affirmation and desire for autonomy of TAP has grown stronger and stronger. . . . The Consultation has reached the following nine points of consensus, which we ask the government to adopt:. . . .
>
> (4) Establish a Taiwan Aboriginal Affairs Commission under the Executive Yuan . . .
>
> (5) National policies related to aboriginal people should have aboriginal people involved in the planning and policy-making, out of respect for their sovereignty [*tzu-chu ch'uan*].
>
> (6) Implement the right of aboriginal people to self-administration [*tzu-chu kuan-li ch'uan*]. We urge accelerated planning to establish an "Aboriginal Peoples' Autonomous Area" [*yuan-chu-min-tsu tzu-chih-ch'u*].
>
> (9) To confirm the landrights of aboriginal people, we urge the government to make an explicit amendment to the constitution that "Aboriginal Reserve Land" should be managed autonomously [*tzu-chu kuan-li*] by TAP. (Kao 1994: 433–434)

Not only does this represent an unprecedented consensus of all aboriginal elite, but the final statement is much stronger than the original draft, which read "carefully consider the possibility of a policy of establishing an Aboriginal Autonomous Area."

12. May/June 1994. "Aboriginal Constitutional Alliance" campaigns for *Yuan-chu-min* constitutional amendment during the National Assembly session. It holds a large demonstration with the slogan "Taiwan Aboriginal Peoples with their true name, land, and self-government" (*cheng ming ti, t'uti ti, tzu-chih ti Taiwan yuan-chu-min-tzu*). A T-shirt with the slogan sells out and is worn widely in aboriginal Taiwan. President Lee meets with movement leaders on July 1 to discuss their demands. Although he rejects the idea of self-government (still heterodox to the state), the fact of this meeting itself is a consacration of the self-government movement as representing the legitimate voice of TAP and confirms the idea of self-government as the core of aboriginal doxa.

13. July 1995. Yami tribe elite at a government-sponsored "Lan-yu Development Plan Symposium" call for Lan-yu to become a special administrative area (*t'e-pieh hsing-cheng ch'u*). As reported in *Lan-yu Biweekly* (July 28, 1995, p. 1):

> The meeting did not reach any consensus [on the county government's development proposals] because the hopes of Yami intellectuals are not ones that can be met by the local government but, rather, must be met by the central government, because Lan-yu residents hope for the establishment of a special administrative area, under a special law.

Here we see doxa informing and being reproduced in local practice—a remote township council defining a form of self-government as the only solution to its problems.

14. November 1995. The imprisonment of Yi-chiang Pal-lu-erh for leading demonstrations demanding aboriginal rights becomes an occasion for observances by aboriginal legislators, Presbyterians, and human rights groups. Yi-chiang and Ma-yau Ku-mu are the first aboriginal activists ever to be jailed in Taiwan. The movement now has its martyrs. Before his imprisonment Yi-chiang makes a series of speeches around Taiwan, saying, "Our greatest hope is that the aboriginal movement will not shrink back because of our imprisonment, but will grow stronger and more determined" (Yi-chiang letter from prison, November 20, 1995, and report in *Independence Weekly Post,* November 13, 1995).

15. July 1996. The legislature passes first reading of the bill proposed by Tsai Chung-han (with amendments) to establish an Aboriginal Affairs Commission in the Executive Yuan. Budget is approved for a staff of sixty, with a commissioner from each tribe. Former KMT Paiwan legislator Hua chia-chih is appointed the first chair of the commission. Similar commissions are set up in Taipei and Kao-hsiung. The final reading of the bill in November is marked by a near-total evisceration of the proposed powers of the commission. More outrageous to aboriginal people is the attachment of a rider by Taiwanese legislators that all aboriginal reserve land now occupied (illegally) by nonaboriginal holders should be reclassified as ordinary freehold land. This serious setback should not keep us from losing sight of the fact that, at the symbolic level of legal inscription, the establishment of these long-demanded national commissions represents a further confirmation of the legitimacy of the idea of aboriginal people holding a special place in the structure of the state—one of the ideas upon which the doxa of aboriginal self-government is established.

16. August 1996. The Taiwan Aboriginal Self-Government Working Group visits Canada for eighteen days to examine the experience of Canadian First Nations in achieving self-government. The ten-member delegation is led by aboriginal legislators Pa-yeh Ta-lu and Tsai Chung-han. Yi-chiang Pal-lu-erh and Ma-yau Ku-mu, recently parolled from prison, and key PCT aboriginal leaders are also part of the group. They visit Indian reservations and organizations across

Canada, invited by Assembly of First Nations national chief Ovide Mercredi. In their press release on return to Taiwan (September 12, 1996) they state:

> In our visit we discovered that the right of self-government is not given by those who rule but is built upon aboriginal people's clear recognition of who they are. . . . Our visit to Canada has convinced us that self-government is the only road to solve the many problems faced by Taiwan Aboriginal People. From now on our Taiwan Aboriginal Self-Government Working Group will work to promote this approach in Taiwan.

17. December 1996. The National Development Conference and 1997 constitutional revisions represented a major setback for the political program for aboriginal self-government. They remind us that the growing power of the cultural arbitrary of self-government among aboriginal people is not paralleled in the nonaboriginal political field. Both the ruling KMT and the opposition Democratic Progressive Party (DPP) agreed to end elections for township mayors and councils, replacing them by appointed adminsitrators. This proposal was strongly opposed by all aboriginal politicans in each party, as it would end even the minimal self-government of aboriginal townships. They were ignored. Neither party included an aboriginal person as part of its delegation to the National Development Conference. In the end the agreement did not get carried through in the July 1997 constitutional revisions.

However, and more important in the perspective of this argument, the National Assembly did pass an amendment to the constitution, affirming: "The State shall, in accordance with the will of the ethnic groups, safeguard the status and political participation of the aborigines." In addition to the events mentioned here, one could add the annual demonstrations and movements at both the local and national level, which, while not always explicitly about self-government, made aboriginal issues, identity, and demand for changed government policies a part of the habitus of many TAP. Sermons in aboriginal village Presbyterian churches, elite participation in international indigenous conferences, and exchange visits gave continuous input to the "aboriginal movement" in Taiwan, which by 1993 came to focus on self-government. All of this was part of the "ritualization" and "naturalization" of the cultural arbitrary of self-government into *Yuan-chu-min* identity. In this sense the vague constitutional amendment stating "in accordance with the will of the ethnic groups" keeps the political mometum of this idea, even as its practical implementation seems as remote as ever. This discrepency between doxa and reality will continue to have political entailments in Taiwan.

One final bit of evidence of how self-government has become a "cultural arbitrary" is something that struck me as odd in the Taiwan Aboriginal Self-Government Working Group (TASGWG). In Taiwan the most cogent writing about self-government has been done by a Paiwan Ph.D. student and former legislative assistant to current Aboriginal Affairs commissioner Hua Chia-chih. Kao Te-yi has done detailed research on the policy issue of self-government (Kao 1994) and had a part in drafting the proposed Aboriginal Basic Law. Why was he never mentioned by any members of the TASGWG or invited to participate in its visit to Canada? I think it is because Kao discusses self-government as a possible but problematic policy, not an inherent right or issue of aboriginal identity. He points out that the prevailing legal view of the Republic of China constitution (see below) narrowly limits self-government to only two special groups and excludes TAP. As such he has not placed it "beyond the realm of conscious will or critique" (Bourdieu 1977: 76). In short, discussion of alternative possibilities to self-government is of no interest to those for whom it has become a cultural arbitrary. In a sense Kao's pragmatic approach has become aboriginal heterodoxy.

Political Context of Self-Government

The more than 360,000 aboriginal people make up less than 2 percent of Taiwan's population. One might say that whatever a cultural arbitrary, ethnic identity for them is only a matter of those few people, so it is hardly part of Taiwan's political agenda. To see why these few people's ideas will continue to be part of Taiwan's political agenda, I turn to the constitutional and political context in which this movement takes place.

The idea of aboriginal self-government is already present in both the KMT ideology of the "Three People's Principles" and in the existing constitution of the Republic of China:

> *Chapter XI System of Local Self-Government*
> *Section 1 The Province*
> *Article 119*
> The local self-government system of the Mongolian leagues and banners shall be prescribed by law.
>
> *Article 120*
> The self-government system of Tibet shall be safeguarded.
>
> *Chapter XIII Fundamental National Policies*
> *Section 6 Frontier Regions*
> *Article 168*
> The State shall accord to the various racial groups in the frontier regions legal protection of their status and give them special assistance in their local self-government undertakings.

It was on the basis of these articles, defining Taiwan "mountain compatriots" as one of the "racial groups in the frontier regions," that as early as the late 1970s Jen-ai township mayor Kao Shih-shu advocated uniting all thirty-one mountain townships in Taiwan into a "mountain county," a county being the lowest level of self-government in the constitution. This idea, often discussed and often rejected as impractical in the 1980s, took a new life with the self-government movement.

The 1993 amendments to the Additional Articles of the Constitution of the Republic of China made specific reference to Taiwan Aboriginal Peoples, with the term aboriginal (*yuan-chu-min*) replacing the earlier usage "mountain compatriots" (*shan pao*) in 1993. This name change had been stongly opposed by many Taiwanese scholars because of fears of the indigenous rights entailments implied by this name change.

The 1991 amendments 1.2, concerning the National Assembly, and 2.2, concerning the Legislative Yuan, provide that "Three members each shall be elected from the lowland and highland aborigines in the free area." The "free area" is, of course, Taiwan. Aboriginal people are the only status group that continued to have special seats after the constitutional revisions—the only group with special constitutional status.

Amendment 18 (1992) includes a number of provisions intended to serve as a "social charter." One paragraph refers to aborigines:

> The State shall accord to the aborigines in the free area legal protection of their status and right to political participation. It shall also provide assistance and encouragement for their education, cultural preservation, social welfare, and business undertakings.

It is this article that was amended in 1997 with the phrase "in accordance with the will of the ethnic groups" and addition of "transportation, water conservation, health and medical care, economic activity, land . . ." to the items mentioned above.

It should be noted that most of these specific additions are matters that would be central to any form of *territorial* self-government, while the earlier list is of a more general character.

The constitution thus can be interpreted to legitimate and support the goals of the aboriginal self-government movement by putting it within the framework of existing structures and ideology. The opposite interpretation is also possible (Tao 1994: 259–261), but in a situation where ethnic self-government (for Tibet, Mongolia, and "frontier minorities") is already conceded, and in which "self-government" is part of Taiwan aboriginal identity, the broad interpretation must eventually prevail, though the Canadian case shows that actual implementation of a generally conceded principle will not be achieved easily or quickly. This is one implication of setting up the Aboriginal Affairs Commission, implicitly giving Taiwan Aboriginal People status equal to the entitled groups in the constitution.

In keeping with the argument of Bourdieu, I am not saying here that this means there has already been an explicit reinterpretation of the constitution, but, as the habitus of de facto status in bureaucratic practice becomes established, so shall the "cultural arbitrary" assumption of the naturalness of aboriginal self-government following on aboriginal identity. This is what Bourdieu is talking about when he writes about the habitus as a "generative scheme" (1977: 95): "As an acquired system of generative schemes objectively adjusted to the particular conditions in which it is constituted, the habitus engenders all the thoughts, all the perceptions, and all actions consistent with those conditions, and no others." If Bourdieu is right, then we can predict that the cultural arbitrary of aboriginality will engender a broad constitutional interpretation leading to the political necessity of some form of aboriginal self-government. We can also predict that this will take some time—the Canadian constitution (Article 35.1) explicitly recognized inherent and treaty rights of aboriginal peoples in 1982 and we are still negotiating and fighting over their implementation. So we need to look at the reality of political parties in Taiwan as well as constitutions.

Political Parties

The Democratic Progressive Party (DPP)

Much of the movement in nonaboriginal Taiwanese public opinion on aboriginal matters is reflected, and further promoted, in positions taken by the DPP. Indeed, since 1986, it could be said that the dynamic of Taiwan political evolution is that "the DPP proposes and the KMT disposes."[10]

The 1988 Political Platform of the DPP (DPP 1988: 21) included aboriginal self-government as one of its 141 proposals:

> 38. Establish aboriginal autonomy areas in order to protect their autonomous rights in political, economic, and cultural aspects. The rights of aborigines should be specially safeguarded by enacting law.

The platform also suggests allowing "aborigines and minorities to recommend their representatives to take part in formulation and implementation of policies which concern them" (item 37), and "promote the bi-lingual education . . . of every ethnic group in Taiwan" (item 133), and "respect and promote the traditional cultures, languages, religious beliefs of aborigines" (item 140).

In 1992 the DPP Central Committee sent up a Department of Aboriginal Affairs, with Yi-chiang Pal-lu-erh as director. The department was eliminated in the reorganization of 1996, but for three years bureaucratic practice in the DPP bespoke aboriginal rights and special status.

At a December 1993 Symposium Conference on Indigenous People's Rights, DPP chair Shih Ming-teh announced that the DPP Central Committee had voted its support for the principles of the UN Draft Declaration on the Rights of Indigenous Peoples and called for entrenchment of aboriginal rights in the constitution (*Independence Morning Post,* December 9, 1993). DPP county magis-trates in Taipei, Ping-tung, and Hsin-chu have been supportive of aboriginal concerns in their counties, especially in the promotion of aboriginal language teaching in public schools.

Certainly the DPP is a party in opposition, and as such more likely to voice support for things that it does not have to deliver. And indeed, when it had a chance to deliver at the 1996 National Development Conference it did not. However, in its stated party program it gives further political reality to a cultural arbitrary and puts pressure on the KMT to follow with comparable or competing positions.

The Kuomintang Party (KMT)

On July 1, 1994, when President Lee Teng-hui met with the leaders of the Taiwan Aboriginal Constitution Movement, he turned the discussion away from their issues of official name, self-government, and land rights, toward what he characterised as the most pressing need of aboriginal people—"education." Lee here continues the old KMT paternalistic policy of improvement and uplifting of aboriginal people. I consider it more important that he did meet with the leaders of this movement—one of the few, if not the only, street demonstration move-ments whose leaders Lee has met personally.

Note too that all the aboriginal legislators and provincial assembly members advocating self-government or aboriginal counties are KMT members. While aboriginal people have heretofore been "iron-clad votes" for the KMT, this does not guarantee their perpetual devotion, and to gain reelection politicians must align themselves with aboriginal identity, especially as the old methods of pa-tronage and vote-buying begin to lose their power.[11]

The DPP also influences the KMT, first, as the agenda setter (the DPP pro-poses, the KMT disposes), second, as competition for votes at election time, and, finally, as a model as DPP and KMT policies move closer and closer to each other—searching for that political middle in Taiwan, but also in dialogue against their own competitors, the New Party and the Taiwan Independence Party. Ab-original self-government is not something that the KMT explicitly opposes, and when the chair of the party and president of the state meets with aboriginal movement leaders he also gives that movement legitimacy.

As it becomes legitimate, the idea of aboriginal self-government will also become timely. The continuing constitutional revisions in Taiwan have also discussed geographic restructuring of local government, though the interests of incumbent politicians have managed to keep this from ever becoming a concrete project. The National Affairs Conference of 1990 discussed redrawing adminis-trative lines, in which "the dominant opinion among the delegates favored a multi-provincial system and a multi-city system" (Government Information Of-fice 1991: 16). In 1997 the KMT and the DPP pushed through the "freezing" (effective dismantling) of the Taiwan provincial government, despite strong opposition. Eventually the almost annual round of constitutional amendments will get around to the politically sensitive topic of geographic restructuring. At that point the idea of either an aboriginal county or special administrative area will become part of the fights over redrawing and redefining administrative boundaries.

Because this involves half or more of the area of Taiwan, large populations of Chinese residents in aboriginal townships, and loss of territory to existing counties, it seems unlikely that the political support for carving out such a zone would be sufficient to allow it to pass easily through not just the National Assembly but county governments. But in a period when national policies and the political balance of power at various levels are in rapid flux, the votes of six aboriginal representatives in the legislature may be a lever of influence on either the KMT or the DPP. In February 1996 it was the threat of these six votes being withheld from the confirmation by the legislature of Lien Chan as premier that broke through years of delay and established the Aboriginal Affairs Commission.

The Uncompleted Agenda

If collective aboriginal identity is not articulated into the larger Taiwanese identity in an institutional way, aboriginal protest in the name of self-government will continue. While the idea began as an elite self-fashioning of an aboriginal political project, it is now viewed as a right, contiguous with aboriginal identity, which legitimates resistance. This is made salient in the social problems faced by aboriginal people, especially in conflicts over land, which constantly remind aboriginal claimants of their powerlessness in the face of the market, the state, and other Taiwanese interested in getting hold of their land.

As competition over the limited prized good of land increases, in relation to national parks, tourism, mining, forestry, and speculators, we can predict increased conflict in the political arena. As the habitus of defining aboriginal identity and the solution to aboriginal problems in terms of self-government shapes political necessities out of cultural arbitraries, aboriginal legislators will become more aggressive in pursuing this utopian goal, to strengthen their own legitimacy in the eyes of their electorate. Self-government proposals offer a way for the state to establish a new partnership with an aboriginal minority claiming universal and inherent aboriginal rights. Research, debate, and eventually negotiation on aboriginal self-government may be a matter of decades, as they have been in Canada, but aboriginal self-government will be on Taiwan's political agendas as long as there are people who define themselves as Taiwan Aboriginal People.

Notes

1. Many readers see homology between Bourdieu and Gramsci here. Bourdieu's "power" is what Gramsci speaks of as "domination," and "cultural arbitrary" is an idea that has become hegemonic, as "common sense." Bourdieu takes this to a deeper level than Gramsci's "common sense." Bourdieu says that he never read Gramsci until the 1980s (Bourdieu 1990:27).

2. On "revitalization movements," see E.J. Hobsbawm, *Primitive Rebels* (1959); Vittorio Lanterneri, *The Religions of the Oppressed* (1963); and Anthony Wallace, *The Death and Rebirth of the Seneca* (1969). The literature on aboriginal self-government is huge. A good discussion is in Augie Fleras and Jean Leonard Elliot, *The Nations Within* (1992). Brian Slattery, "Aboriginal Sovereignty and Imperial Claims," *Osgoode Hall Law Review,* 29 (1991): 681–703, is also helpful.

3. I have discussed at length this change in the meaning of being aboriginal in Taiwan, using Gramsci's hegemony and counterhegemony, in my "Return Our Land" (M.A. thesis in Social Anthropology, York University, 1995).

4. The Presbyterian Church in Taiwan has played a major role in the modern history of Taiwan aboriginal people. Presbyterians comprise about a third of aboriginal people, but a far higher proportion of aboriginal elite, including many mentioned in this account.

5. I am retranslating my Chinese translation back into English, not quoting the original, and longer, WCIP Declaration. Much of the language of the WCIP document appears almost directly in the 1994 text of the *UN Draft Declaration on the Rights of Indigenous Peoples* (UN Document E/CN.4/Sub.2/1994/2/Add.1), which also was read by Yi-chiang in 1991. The WCIP was founded by Canadian native leader George Manuel and has its headquarters in Ottawa. Someone should write a paper on the important influence of Canadian natives and lawyers on the whole development of the global indigenous rights movement.

6. *Yuan-chu-min* was the publication of the Alliance of Taiwan Aborigines, at that time in a four-page newspaper format. Issue no. 1 appeared in February 1985, and the last issue I saw was no. 10, in September 1991. The most important articles in the first seven issues are collected in *Yuan-chu-min: Pei ya-p'o-che ti na-han* [Aboriginal people: The cry of the oppressed] (Taipei: Alliance of Taiwan Aborigines, 1987).

7. I should add "of which I am aware." However, if there were earlier ones, they were seed that fell on stony soil and were soon forgotten. Not until 1989 did the major aboriginal movement in Taiwan, the Return Our Land movement, make any mention of "self-government" in its seven demands.

8. Reprinted as published in an English-language pamphlet produced by the ATA. The manifesto has seventeen items that are based mainly on the principles of the WCIP.

9. *Aboriginal Post* was published by a group of young aboriginal intellectuals in southern Taiwan, mainly from the Rukai and Paiwan tribes. The 1990 article represented the consensus view of the paper's editors.

10. For a discussion of how this worked in the first round of constitutional revisions, see my monograph *Taiwanese Lambada* (Toronto: Joint Centre for Asia Pacific Studies, 1993). The "social charter amendment of 1993" also represents a weaker version of amendments proposed by the DPP, which made the inclusion of such a charter a political necessity for the KMT.

11. One aboriginal politician complained to me in 1992 about the evil age in which he has to live. In the past, he said, you could depend on 80 percent of the votes you bought actually being delivered, but now you are lucky if you get 50 percent. In keeping with the general trend in Taiwan, the significant growth of an urban aboriginal electorate also reduces the usefulness of vote buying, which depends on the personal relations of a village or other corporate bodies.

References

Alliance of Taiwan Aborigines [Yuan ch'uan hui]. 1987. *Yuan-chu-min: Pei ya-p'o-che te na-han* [Aboriginal people: The cry of the oppressed]. Taipei: Alliance of Taiwan Aborigines.

Bourdieu, Pierre. 1977. *Outline of a Theory of Practice*. New York: Cambridge University Press.

—————. 1990. *In Other Words*. Stanford: Stanford University Press.

Democratic Progressive Party. 1988. *DPP: Democratic Progressive Party/Parti pour le Progrès Democratique*. Taipei: DPP Central Committee.

Government Information Office. 1990. *Summary Reports of the National Affairs Conference*. Taipei: Government Information Office.

Grant, John Webster. 1984. *Moon of Wintertime*. Toronto: University of Toronto Press.

Hsu Hsin-teh and Shih Jui-yun, eds. 1992. *Taiwan Chi-tu chang-lao chiao-hui 1971–1992 tsung-hui she-hui kuan-hui wen-hsien* [General Assembly social concern documents of the Presbyterian Church in Taiwan 1971–1992]. Taipei: Presbyterian Church in Taiwan, General Assembly Resource Centre.

Hua-tung Community Development Center. 1992. "Taiwan yuan-chu-min tzu-chih fa-chan tso-t'an-hui shih-shih pao-kao shu" [Report on Taiwan aboriginal self-government development consultation]. T'ai-tung (mimeo).

Kao Te-i. 1994. "Taiwan Yuan-chu-min shih-hsing tzu-chih te cheng-ts'e: k'e-hsing-hsing fen-hsi" [Taiwan aboriginal people implementing self-government: An analysis of policy possibilities]. In *Yuan-chu-min wen-hua hui-i lun-wen-chi* [Collected papers of the aboriginal cultural conference]. Taipei: Cultural Development Commission, Executive Yuan.

Kao Te-i and Sun Ta-ch'uan, eds. 1993. *Yuan-chu-min cheng-ts'e yu she-hui fa-chan* [Aboriginal policy and social development]. Taipei: Taiwan Aboriginal Cultural Development Association.

Lan-yu Township Overall Development Plan Symposium, *Lan-yu shuang k'an* (Lan-yu biweekly), July 28, 1986.

UN Draft Declaration on the Rights of Indigenous Peoples (UN Document E/CN.4/Sub.2/1994/2/Add.1).

Yan pao (Aboriginal Post). July 1990. "Theory and Practice of Aboriginal Self-Government."

—————July 1990. "Aboriginal Legislators Tsai Chung-han and Hua Chia-chi Demand Self-Government for Aborigines."

—————April 1992. "Establish an Autonomous Area Within Fifteen Years."

16

Political Taiwanization and Pragmatic Diplomacy

The Eras of Chiang Ching-kuo and Lee Teng-hui, 1971–1994

Murray A. Rubinstein

The East Gate in Taipei decorated for the Double Ten Holiday.

Taiwan's political transition from hard totalitarianism to soft totalitarianism to quasi-democracy was made possible, in large measure, by rapid, substantial, economic change and by a set of many-faceted changes in Taiwan's society. This chapter focuses on Taiwan's political evolution and the diplomatic death and rebirth that paralleled the evolving political transformation.[1]

I. The Presidency of Chiang Ching-kuo

In 1971 the government of Taiwan took the first steps on a path that would lead, eighteen years later, to the existence of two political parties competing for power on local, county, provincial, and national levels. This path toward broadened political participation ran parallel to another evolutionary path, one that led to a more open civil society that possessed a greater degree of freedom of the press and freedom of expression.

The dominant figure during this period was Chiang Ching-kuo, the son and heir of Chiang Kai-shek, the president of the Republic of China. The younger Chiang had served as the head of the government of Shanghai during the civil war of the late 1940s and had proven himself to be an effective leader. During the early 1950s he was given the difficult task of cleansing the KMT of corruption, which he did with ruthless efficiency. By 1971 he had become not only his father's right-hand man, but the key figure in the regime; his ascension to the premiership in 1972 formalized his status. His philosophy and style were quite different from his father's. He was more the civilian leader than the quasi-warlord that his father had been, though one of the foundations of his power was the garrison command, and he knew how to create coalitions of bureaucrats who shared his views on socioeconomic modernization. He also recognized that his nation could be torn apart by long suppressed ethnic tensions and worked to defuse this tension by "Taiwanizing" his party and his government, bringing more and more well-trained Taiwanese into the political system. Furthermore, as one who saw himself as a populist, he recognized the need to further democratize the political system, at least at its local levels.

Diplomatic Crisis and Political Activism, 1971–1976

The precipitating events in this period were a linked series of foreign crises that led, in turn to challenges to the authority of the KMT-dominated regime within Taiwan. And in the background, acting to underline the critical nature of each event or set of events was the evolving relationship between Taiwan's strongest ally, the United States, and the People's Republic of China.

As we now know from Henry Kissinger's memoirs and other sources, the roots of the problems for Taiwan began during the late 1960s when Richard Nixon became president of the United States. Faced with the possibility of direct armed conflict with the PRC over the war in Indochina, Kissinger opened secret contacts with the mainland regime.

One result of these talks was that by 1971 the Nixon administration began to take steps to end its policy of isolating the PRC. The all important first step was the U.S. decision to support the PRC in its annual bid for a seat on the United Nations' Security Council. In 1971 the United States supported the PRC and the ROC lost its position. Only in the early 1990s did some Taiwanese, led by Lu Hsiu-lien, attempt to clear the way for the ROC to re-enter the UN, but now as Taiwan.

In 1972 Kissinger made his famous secret trip that paved the way for Nixon's visit to China. That unprecedented event ended with the announcement of the Shanghai Communique. This document defined a series of steps that would lead, in time to the normalization of US-PRC relations and thus to the isolation of Taiwan.[2]

The third diplomatic setback was the dispute over control of a small group of islands claimed by Taiwan, Tiao Yu Tai. While seemingly of little value, it was thought that oil might be found the in the surrounding seabed. Thus the Japanese took steps to occupy these tiny islands. As the dispute escalated, Taiwan's once staunch ally, the United States, backed the Japanese. Taiwan had lost once again in the international arena, this time to a close friend that had invested heavily in its economy. The Tiao Yu Tai dispute was the harbinger of what came next, the Japanese decision to normalize relations with mainland China.[3] Though Taiwan and Japan worked out what became a model for quasi-diplomatic relations in the years that followed, the Japanese action simply added to the impression that the KMT was losing its diplomatic skills and support in the international arena.[4]

In the early 1970s, in the wake of these diplomatic setbacks, Taiwan's growing middle class began to influence the shape of Taiwanese politics. Middle class intellectuals and students, enjoying new status and wealth, began to feel dissatisfied with the frozen political process and the many restrictions on freedom of expression. And the regime, once seemingly a respected member of the world community, was now increasingly losing face. The result was a brief period of political activism highlighted by challenges to the regime in its legislative organs and by actions taken in the street.

On the political front such newcomers as Kang Ning-hsiang and Huang Hsin-chieh began the loosely knit political faction that would come to be known as the *tang-wai*. In the streets a series of demonstrations and open demands for political change, led by college professors, were held. The government was not yet ready to allow such open dialogue, and by 1973 it began to arrest the leaders of the new political movement and fire those professors who openly criticized the regime.[5] Chiang Ching-kuo had become premier in 1971, and it was he who had to deal with this open challenge to the KMT. He was harsh but flexible, as he had been in postwar Shanghai. The iron fist had to be used to warn the opposition, but the velvet glove that hid it also had to be used to show the opposition and those members of the educated middle class still reserving judgment that he could learn the lessons that open dissent signaled.

As premier, Chiang began what can be seen as a process of Taiwanization.

There was precedent for his moves: In 1969 the KMT initiated a rapid turnover of party executives on the county and municipal level. Taiwanese in increasing numbers were appointed to these local committee posts. This process continued after early 1973, in the face of the student and faculty protests, proving that Chiang was willing to continue to push for higher levels of Taiwanese participation. T'ien Hung-ma suggests that even at the top levels such as central party headquarters, more Taiwanese loyalists were being rewarded with very visible posts.[6]

There were other reforms as well, reforms that opened the way for even higher levels of Taiwanese participation. Chiang Ching-kuo urged the government to expand its popular base by increasing the number of seats open to election by the Taiwanese in its major representative organs, the National Assembly and the Legislative Yuan.[7] The administration committed itself to being more accessible and open and there were new attempts to curb corruption. Next, the government provided career planning and sought closer ties with the younger generation. Finally, it addressed social welfare concerns of workers and farmers.[8]

The concessions were limited nevertheless. Seeing the regime attempt to reform itself and open its ranks to Taiwanese, the *tang-wai* thought that it could push things further and in 1975 and 1976 attempted to contest elections and demand even more changes in the basic political structure. This time Chiang responded to the challenge by taking off the velvet glove, making 1976 a year of return to the policy of arrests and repression. Now president (Chiang Kai-shek had died in 1975) Chiang Ching-kuo demonstrated once again that he was willing to play the role of good cop/bad cop, but now as the nation's formal leader and not just the man behind the throne.

Ethnicity, Diplomacy, and the Politics of Resistance, 1977–1979

The issue of Taiwanese identity and the Taiwanese struggle for a larger role in the government of their own country underlay the events of 1971–1976. From 1977 to 1979 the struggle that pitted pen-ti jen (native Taiwanese) against *wai-shen jen* (mainlanders) again was at the center of the conflicts in the political and religious arena. And in the diplomatic sphere, the question of identity—here meaning the formal name that the KMT-dominated state could take—became central and resonated with the issue of Taiwanese identity and Taiwanese power in the struggle between the ruling party and the *tang-wai* upstarts.

There were important questions: Who would control the state apparatus? Would it be the mainlander-dominated KMT or would it be the Taiwanese *tang-wai?* How would Taiwan be viewed in the eyes of the world? Would it be a quasi-fictional Republic of China on Taiwan or the nation that called itself the

Republic of Taiwan? The answer lay in the ballot box, in the streets, and in the hearts and minds of the people. And running through it all: What would Chiang Ching-kuo's response be?

Throughout this period the *tang-wai* and other challengers to KMT power had to face an overarching conundrum: The core basis of the regime's—and its president's—power lay not in titles as given by the constitution and as voted on by the rapidly aging membership of a National Assembly, elected in the mainland in the 1940s, but in its control of the key arm of Taiwan's military and security apparatus, the Garrison Command. This central reality continued to color the actions of all political actors and academic observers well after the events of the late 1970s, and during the freeze and then the dramatic thaw of the 1980s. Most observers felt that ultimately the state would win because it had a history of using force when challenged. Even in the late 1980s, as the regime opened itself up to sweeping change, one could find members of the educated elite expressing bleak assessments of the viability of their increasingly democratic political system.

The last three years of the 1970s found the Nationalist regime being challenged, often successfully, in those political arenas that it had so carefully been opened up in the late 1960s and early and mid-1970s. Members of the *tang-wai,* with a deep and an abiding sense of their Taiwanese heritage, were reluctant to identify with the mainland that the KMT said Taiwan was a province of. They were also reluctant to accept the Nationalist's authoritarian government, a government originally structured to control all of mainland China By the second half of the 1970s the *tang-wai* had been able to win impressive victories in contests for the Taiwan Provincial Assembly. In that legislative body located outside of the city of T'aichung the *tang-wai* candidates were able to win twenty-one out of seventy-seven seats. They also emerged victorious in four of twenty magistrate and mayoral races.[9]

Not all went well however; irregularities in voting and in counting the ballots occurred, as they so often did in Taiwanese elections.[10] Given the atmosphere of confrontation that had been building up, this time the voting public did not let the matter rest. In the northwestern coastal city of Chung-li voters took to the streets in a massive demonstration over discrepancies in the vote count. A clash between the police and the demonstrators ensued; the police station was stormed and burned, and there were casualties.[11]

Little news of that confrontation appeared in the media, but gradually the details leaked out. That resistance could take place and demonstrations held signaled to many that the struggle between the people and the government had now reached a new stage. There was no question now or later about revolution or coherent armed resistance. Everyone knew the power of the state's military apparatus and the general effectiveness of its security mechanisms, but now it was shown that public demonstrations, if carefully planned, might be an effective tactic in the political struggle.

Both the political victories and the lessons of Chung-li affected the choices made by one man who would soon proved to be a major actor in the anti-KMT struggle, Shih Ming-teh. Born into a Catholic family from Kao-hsiung, Shih was educated in a military school until implicated in a youthful and ill-conceived plot against the government. Sentenced to a long prison term and subjected to brutal treatment at the hands of the authorities, he became a self-taught jail house lawyer and scholar for whom confinement became the opportunity for a many faceted education.

Freed in 1977, Shih took the dangerous step of involving himself in one of the campaigns for a Provincial Assembly seat. It was a valuable experience and showed that he could play a role in the evolving political struggle. Shih Ming-teh would emerge less as an ideologue than as a strategist and tactician, a role that he played in the Mei-li-tao-KMT struggle of 1978–79.[12]

The victories of 1977 convinced the *tang-wai* leadership that better days lay ahead, and they were convinced that further gains would be made in the election upcoming in 1978. However, few among their leadership realized how diplomatic events would redefine this optimistic political scenario.[13] In the late fall of 1978, on December 15, President Jimmy Carter announced that his administration was going to formally recognize the PRC.[14] This meant the withdrawal of formal U.S. diplomatic recognition of the Republic of China, abrogation of the ROC/U.S. defense treaty, and withdrawal of military personnel as of January 1, 1979. The shock waves were not as powerful as they might have been. There were carefully staged protests and media criticism of the United States; within a few months, however, a new quasi-formal relationship, generally modeled in some fashion after that with Japan, was in place.[15]

The year from the Carter announcement to the December 10, 1979 Kao-hsiung Incident—a violent clash between *tang-wai* activists holding a demonstration and KMT-hired agent provacatuers and local police in front of the railroad station—was a difficult one for both sides.[16] The inner circle of the *tang-wai,* now publishers of *Mei-li-tao,* a political magazine that became the voice of the *tang-wai* leadership, planned a series of protests.The government tried to keep the Mei-li Tao leaders off balance, harassed them whenever possible, and leaked stories to the press about their personal lives that contained details of prurient interest. Nevertheless, ways were found to meet, convey information, and plan for new demonstrations.[17]

˙The Kao-hsiung Incident, marking the climax of a year of confrontations, is recognized as a pivotal event in modern Taiwanese history and is already legendary. The *tang-wai* leaders were planning a rally of thirty thousand people to be held in the south and another equally large one for Taipei a few days later, on December 16. As it turned out, that second demonstration was never held because of the violent clash in Kao-hsuing.

As the day for the rally drew closer, KMT pressure grew as well, with increased surveillance and constant harassment of core Mei-li-tao members.

Their phones were tapped and their movements followed and noted. This constant pressure concerned the Mei-li-tao leaders for they knew full well that the KMT held real power—and the legal system to justify the actions that the party cadre took. The KMT also controlled the media and was thus able to give its own spin on whatever took place. By the fall of 1979 it was clear to all that the *tang-wai* and the governmental authorities were ready for a large scale confrontation. As a warning of what was to come, a day before the rally in Kao-hsiung a Mei-li-tao staff member in Kao-hsiung was attacked. The core leaders also knew that thugs at the beck and call of the authorities were being mobilized to be used as shock troops and instigators once the rally began.

On the evening of December 10 in Kao-hsiung, when the leaders got word that the police had blocked the original march route, alternative routes were planned. *Tang-wai* activist Lu Hsiu-lien expressed how she felt that fateful night just as the rally got underway

> I sensed that something dangerous would happen that night. Things were out of control. If I were smart enough, I could have left right away, but of course I didn't. I met Chang Chun-nan outside the office and we went next door to get some dinner. He also agreed that something terrible was about to happen. But all we could do was wait and see.[18]

Lu and the other *tang-wai* leaders then got on the platform of a truck that was part of the parade. Events were now set in motion. While she and some of her compatriots expected the worst, no one really knew how far things would go. Their strong resolve to keep matters under control seemed to melt away when it became clear that the government was prepared to use violence in the name of maintaining its hegemony. They made inflammatory and provocative statements, giving the authorities the opportunity to take action.

While important steps had been taken to avoid further confrontation, it was clear that a critical mass had been reached: Those on the truck who saw that they and the marchers were indeed under attack by police with tear gas took microphones and rallied the assembled multitude to stand fast in the face of the challenge. They called on the people to join together but also warned them to avoid violence. Violence did occur, however. After further confrontations and invectives, the demonstrators dispersed and the leaders reassembled. Realizing that the area was swarming with secret police, they traveled north to the old city of Tainan and attempted to reassemble at the Tainan Hotel.[19]

Within a few days, authorities arrested those Mei-li-tao leaders they could apprehend. Among these were Yao Chia-wen, Chang Chun-hung, Lin Yi-hsiung, Lin Hung-hsuan, Ch'en Chu, and Lu Hsiu-lien. Shih Ming-teh, the Lenin of the movement, escaped capture for a few months and his American wife was deported. The government had made its intentions clear. The days of demonstrations by the *tang-wai* were over, as was the period of quasi-liberalism. The regime had to struggle for diplomatic survival and would not allow political activists to give the impression that the Nationalist government was unstable. Chiang Ching-kuo's iron fist put an end to dissent.[20]

Repression and Protest in an Ongoing Struggle, 1980–85

From 1980 to 1985 the Chiang regime attempted to turn the clock back on certain fronts while moving ahead on others. The tang-wai's challenge to the regime was suppressed in the most public manner possible, and the government tried to limit freedom of speech.

But these public actions were not the only story. Without fanfare, the KMT-ruled government was continuing to open itself up to Taiwanese and was taking steps to expand some freedoms even as it attempted to limit others.

The opposition went through a period of disorganization, bitter internal conflict, and considerable soul searching. It was able to develop new tactics, refining the use of street demonstrations, for example.[21] It was able to survive because it had leaders who even from prison were able to keep the faith alive by their very visible martyrdom. Scholars have also argued that he ongoing KMT-tang-wai conflict was in large measure made possible by a surge of demonstrations by the people against the state.

The new middle class and the working class were emboldened to confront the government and demand that the regime take their problems seriously. Farmers held demonstrations demanding that the government deal with the declining state of agriculture and with the problems that the ever diminishing number of small farmers faced in an agrarian world increasingly dominated by large corporate farms.[22] Other groups were similarly emboldened. Environmentalists demonstrated on specific sites, for example Lukang, where a major factory was to be built by Dupont. In this battle the people prevailed and an environmental movement began to take shape.[23] Woman took to the public thoroughfares as well, demanding changes in the law and government action regarding the illicit sex industry. Labor groups became more militant and active, and the forced calm of earlier decades disappeared as workers demanded more rights.[24] Various factions within the opposition took this as their cue and used the tactic of the demonstration to publicize their cause.

During the he early 1980s, many grass-roots organizations and public foundations were created to deal with local issues or specific public policy issues. These were not as dramatic as the larger movements and the more controversial demonstrations, but they did serve to explore issues and raise consciousness even as they helped deal with problems the government had neglected.[25]

This activism suggests that the first half of the 1980s can be seen as a period of middle class activism on Taiwan. This, in turn, provided a context for the political struggles between the two major political players, the KMT and the as-yet-illegal tang-wai.[26]

At the heart of this many-faceted struggle were the key leaders of the Kao-hsiung Incident. Most had been arrested in the early weeks of 1980, but Shih Ming-teh managed to avoid capture. He remained on the run for the next few months with the help of administrative leaders and personnel of the Presbyterian Church on Taiwan (PCT), including General Secretary Kau Chih-min and Joyce Chen, a member of Kau's staff. When Shih was captured and arrested these Presbyterian officials were also arrested and put on trial in court proceedings that followed the public trial of the *Mei-li-tao* leadership.

From mid-December, when they were arrested, until the opening of their trial, the defendants went through periods of psychological and sometimes physical torture and seemingly endless periods of interrogation.[27] The authorities finally got what they wanted—a signed confession from Shih, Lu, and the other defendants.[28]

The trial took place in two phases. The first was a preliminary hearing that lasted about twenty-one days. The formal trial lasted from March 18 to March 28. During the trial, Lu Hsiu-lien and the others retracted their confessions, arguing that they were involuntary and made under great duress.

The trial was covered closely in the Western press and by human rights organizations. The Taiwanese public and foreign observers considered it to be a major event, one with moments of high drama. When all was said and done, the sentences handed out were harsh. Shih Min-teh was sentenced to life. Lu Hsiu-lien received twelve years. Others received similarly long sentences.[29]

Shih-Ming-teh, the convicted leader of the *Mei-li-tao* faction, was treated more harshly than most of the others and was sent to the infamous Green Island facility, as was the Secretary General Kau Chih-min.[30]

Lu Hsin-lien was released from prison in 1985; most of the others were released in 1987, and Shih Ming-teh was released in the late spring of 1990.

Kau Chih-min was not released until the summer of 1984. The government was warning the PCT to keep out of politics and to stop demanding human rights for the Taiwanese. The conflict between the PCT and the Chiang regime had been under way for almost a decade. In the seventies, the church attempted to publish works in Romanized Taiwanese, and when the government confiscated this material, church leaders appealed to the Carter administration then in the midst of its human rights offensive. During the Mei-li-tao period a number of key *tang-wai* members were linked to the church, and church leaders such as John Tin of the Tainan Theological Seminary had been consistent vociferous opponents of the regime. The trial of the church leader and the murder of the Lin family members[31] were evidence that the state would no longer tolerate the church's participation in the secular world of Taiwanese politics.[32]

The government's policy of repression took other forms as well. The small and highly radical New Testament Church had established a community on a mountain in Tainan county, about an hour's drive from the island's western coast. In early 1980 the church, led by a man named Elijah Hong, was driven from the mountain and in the years that followed the government authorities continued to harass it. The church leaders were often intemperate in their remarks and cult-like in their loyalty to their leader, but they posed no real danger to the state, which nevertheless decided to show that any voice of opposition, even one so marginal as this Pentecostal church, would be silenced.[33]

Oppression was not the only policy the state pursued during this period. It continued opening the system to those Taiwanese not committed to a radical course of action. We see this in the role played by Y.S. Tsiang. From 1977 to 1984 he recruited intellectuals to work with the party. On a more local level, Sung Shih-hsuan, who was then the chairman of the Provincial Party Committee, introduced a social service orientation to local-level party work. This may have been to counter *tang-wai* efforts as well as the social activism of the PCT and the equally pro-Taiwanese and socially conscious Maryknoll order.[34] These were important steps, coming as they did at a time when the state was attempting to keep grass-roots political forces in check. In effect it was beginning to set up a system that would pit the Taiwanese intellectuals against those sympathetic to the *tang-wai*. Given the quality of the people recruited, especially young West-ern-trained intellectuals and activists, it seemed to be an effective program.

The government also took steps in the religious arena to show flexibility and openess. The Yi-kuan-tao had been planted on the island in the 1940s and had remained as an underground shamanistic cult with a folk Buddhist and syncretis-tic belief system. The state believed it posed a danger but a number of key figures including Chou Lien-hua and Chu Hai-yuan of the Institute of Ethnol-ogy/Academia Sinica lobbied on its behalf and wrote articles advocating that the organization be legalized, which the state did in the mid-1980s.

The *tang-wai* continued to have internal problems during the early 1980s. The "non-party" seemed to have recovered from the actions the regime had taken in 1979 and 1980 when, in 1981, it fielded candidates under a united nonparty slate. However, by 1982 intra-party conflicts and frictions did surface as intellec-tuals and writers challenged the tactics of the *tang-wai* officeholders. These intellectuals felt that working within the system and thus supporting the state by participating in the political process was wrong. The office holders disagreed and further refined their stand arguing for fighting for votes and seats, developing working relationships with KMT legislators, and attempting to develop contacts with county and local elites, much as the KMT had done in the previous decade. The conflict hurt the party, and it lost ground in the 1983 election.

As a result of the conflict a permanent *tang-wai* office was set up to deter-mine policy and define ideology. It would act as defacto party headquarters and would serve as the nucleus of a formal party center if and when the opposition was given legal status.[35]

The early 1980s was a period of repression and also of confrontation. In the view of contemporary observers, the state could not go too far. The key leaders of the *tang-wai* and Presbyterian Church had been put in prison but the social forces unleashed by Taiwan's economic transformation had led to a new sense of activism outside of the proscribed political arena. This, in turn emboldened the *tang-wai* which readied itself to again challenge the state in a dramatic fashion. That challenge and the regime's response took place during President Chiang's final two years of power.

The Last Years of the Second President Chiang, 1986–1988

By early 1986 there were rumors about President Chiang's health. The questions asked often centered around questions of succession and continuity. Despite this, the president continued to demonstrate that he could still direct policy and transform Taiwan.[36]

In March 1986, Chiang Ching-kuo appointed a twelve man ad hoc committee of ranking officials, all of them members of the party's Central Standing Committee, to recommend reform measures. They were to study the termination of martial law, the lifting of the ban on rival political parties, the reorganization of the national parliamentary organs, the enlarging of the representation of native Taiwanese in these bodies, and the reform of the KMT.

However, some conservatives in the party felt things were going too far and opposed major sections of these proposals. In the summer, the government, perhaps as a means of placating these conservatives, jailed several opposition leaders, including Lin Cheng-Chieh and Chen Shui-Pien, a Taipei city councilman. The opposition responded by holding a number of demonstrations and rallies, which, though illegal under ROC law, were attended by thousands of people. The government took little action, perhaps because, Paris Chang suggests, the events in Korea and the Philippines demonstrated what could happen to regimes that did not respond to the demands of an educated and frustrated middle class.

The *tang-wai* made Chiang's task easier, in a sense, by forcing his hand and making him respond with major changes in policy to the challenge the opposition issued on September 28, 1986—135 leading members of the *tang-wai* "defied a long standing ban on new political parties and announced the establishment of the Democratic Progressive Party. Emboldened by the mood of the public and by their support for change, these leaders decided that they would attempt to dictate the pace and direction of political development. It was they who would pick the issues, choose the arenas, and set the rules, appealing to the masses to support these bold initiatives."[37]

Rather than suppress this step, Chiang held the hard-liners in his party in check and on October 8, 1986, pushed for the Central Standing Committee to face and adjust to the new realities. He was met by opposition, and days past as he pressured the leaders to take the steps he felt were necessary. He argued that he himself had called for major changes and that the CSC had discussed these initiatives and the ways they might be implemented. By October 15 he was able to push through a resolution that lifted the decades-old decree of martial law and relaxed the ban on organizing opposition parties. By taking this step the government legalized the new party the *tang-wai* had established. The DPP could now organize and put up candidates for elections to the major legislative bodies. The KMT, on the other hand, was secure enough in its ability to build a grass-roots base and its quite sophisticated political structure to believe that it could deal with the challenges of the opposition. The KMT had become a very knowledgeable actor in the arena of local politics, and Taiwanese were the key KMT activists on the scene.[38]

On December 6, 1986, the first legal two-party election was held. The DPP fielded forty-four candidates and won twelve of the seventy-three open seats in the Legislative Yuan. More importantly, in key areas, the DPP candidates were top vote getters. The real balance of power was not affected, but the vote getting potential of the candidates of the new party was seen as a warning to President Chiang and the ruling KMT.[39]

In the summer of 1986 further steps were taken to implement other elements of Chiang's reforms. On October 15, 1986, the government lifted martial law. The system of extraordinary measures that provided the government and the ruling party with much of its real power was now taken away. A new, revised national security act replaced it, and although it contained its own restrictions on political rights and freedoms, it was clear that a page had been turned. The long overdue revamping of the constitutional framework of the state's power could take place in the framework of this new and less restrictive document.

The president also took steps as well, steps to transform Taiwan's relationship with China. One step was to allow the citizens of the ROC to convert the national currency (the New Taiwan Dollar or NTs), without limit into foreign currency. The government took another related and even more dramatic step—it lifted its restrictions on travel to the PRC.

These changes opened the mainland to those of mainlander background who still had family there as well as to those Taiwanese who traced their descent from ancestors who came from the Minnan counties and prefectures of Fukien. Mainlanders went home by the hundreds of thousands. Taiwanese took the opportunity to discover their roots and engage in religious pilgrimage.[40]

President Chiang died in January of 1988. He chose as his successor, a Taiwanese Presbyterian named Lee Teng-hui. The Taiwan Chiang passed on to Lee was a thriving economic entity that possessed a sophisticated and stable, but still evolving, political system.

II. Taiwan Under Lee Teng-hui, January 1988– December 1994

Lee Teng-hui was born on January 15, 1923, in the village of Sanchih near Tam-sui, northwest of Taipei He was such a good student that he became one of the relatively few Taiwanese during the Japanese period to go on to university, studying at Kyoto University. When he returned to Taiwan at the end of the war he continued his education at T'ai-ta. Here he received a B.S. in agricultural economics in 1949, the year of the fateful Nationalist retreat to the island, and went on to teach at T'ai-ta and then to earn a masters in the United States. From 1955 to 1957, he taught at T'ai-ta and also served as research fellow at the Provincial Taiwan Cooperative Bank.

He entered public service in 1957 when he began what would be more than twenty year association with the U.S.-ROC Joint Commission on Rural Reconstruction. During the same period he also served as an adjunct professor of economics at T'ai-ta and taught at the Graduate School East Asian Studies at Cheng-chih University (Cheng-ta). During the 1960s he returned to the United States for further graduate studies. In 1968 Lee received a Ph.D. in agricultural economics from Cornell. His return to Cornell in 1995, as an alumni and as the president of the Republic of China, would stir up an international incident.

When Lee returned to Taiwan he resumed his career as a bureaucrat and academician. However, he was gaining a reputation as a skilled politician as well as a scholar-bureaucrat and rising in the ranks of a Taiwanizing KMT. In 1978 he left the JCRR and served as Mayor of Taipei until 1981. He then was appointed governor of Taiwan province, serving from 1981 until 1984. He assumed the vice presidency under Chiang Ching-kuo in 1984 and when Chiang died on January 13, 1988, Lee took over as his successor.[41]

First Steps in a New Domestic Policy, January 1988– December 1990

Lee first gained control of the KMT and then used his power to fight challenges to his programs and policies in both foreign and domestic affairs. This proved to be an ongoing challenge to an ethnic Taiwanese who was fighting to gain authority over a party still dominated by *wai-shen jen* who were, on the whole, more conservative than the Taiwanese technocrats brought in by Chiang Ching-kuo.

Over the course of his first half year in office, Lee demonstrated that he had the ability to build that all-important relationship with the party. He was able to consolidate his leadership authority and demonstrated this at the KMT Congress in July of 1988. At that meeting he received an overwhelming majority of votes from the 1,300 delegates, who endorsed his elevation to the post of chair of the KMT. He went even further in securing his position. He was able to reshuffle the party leadership, naming thirty-one party members to the Central Committee, sixteen of whom were Taiwanese. For the first time in its history, a majority of the party's key decision making body was now held by *pen-ti jen*.[42] As Parris Chang observed, the committee " . . . younger and reform minded, includes the first representative of labor, and includes a woman member for the first time."[43]

Lee was also able to reshape the Executive Yuan in the weeks following this crucial party meeting. He retained the premier, Yu Kuo-hua, a mainlander from Chekiang, who continued to serve as head of the cabinet, but reshuffled the rest of the members of this key administrative/policy making body. He appointed many younger men and chose other Taiwanese to serve as ministers. Key positions in this new cabinet were held by Taiwanese, including the minister of foreign affairs and the minister of finance. Lee's choice for finance minister was a woman, Shirley Kuo. In making this appointment Lee twice shattered precedent. The cabinet that Lee appointed also reflected his own class/educational background, for it included fourteen individuals with Ph.D.s from the United States.[44]

While this was an impressive start, Lee learned in the months that followed that there was more to cabinet and party politics than having one's people in place. He faced a very different KMT from the one his predecessor controlled. The complexion of KMT representatives in the Legislative Yuan had changed. Newly elected, second generation mainlanders formed their own faction, seen by some as "young Turks." They were openly hostile to KMT's hierarchical practices and to the way the party carried out its political affairs.[45] The era of strict party discipline within the KMT was drawing to a close.

That Taiwan had now entered an era of two-party politics was demonstrated by the both the campaign and the results of the of the 1989 elections. The elections were held on December 2, 1989, and were the first multi-party elections in forty years. Being contested were 101 seats in the Legislative Yuan, 77 seats in the Provincial Assembly and 94 seats on the Taipei and Kaohsiung city council, as well as the seats of mayors and county magistrates. The DPP and the KMT went head to head in these races and an estimated 70 percent of Taiwan's registered voters cast ballots. Each party held rallies during the formal campaign period, and the audiences at these rallies increased as the actual day of election neared.[46]

Although the KMT won the elections, the DPP made a solid showing for itself in this first major post-Chiang-era contest. DPP candidates captured 21 seats in the Legislative Yuan and as a result of winning these seats gained the right to introduce legislation. The DPP also won the battle for county magistrate in Taipei County when You Ching beat his KMT opponent[47] James Soong, who was then serving as the KMT's secretary general, and who would in 1997 become the embattled governor of Taiwan Province. The DPP managed to take 7 of the 21 county magistrate seats and altogether won a total of 65 seats. Some observers, mostly those from outside the nation, considered this a victory for democracy, but to the KMT officials, who were not used to an open and competitive system, the results were seen with foreboding: In the opinion of these conservative party members, Taiwan had entered a new and dangerous period, for it seemed to them that the time when the KMT's long-held power would slip from its grasp was approaching.[48]

The election was a clear and direct sign that substantive political change was under way. For the new president, striving to control his party, it meant more worries. Those high in the party ranks who were unhappy with his liberalism and his Taiwanization were all too willing to see the party's loss as a sign of his weakness as leader. Lee recognized this and quickly took the offensive. He set up a party task force that was instructed to implement party reforms. He also ordered that a detailed review of KMT plans for recruiting and training young talent be initiated and that the party examine the results of its new policy of holding primaries as a way of choosing its candidates.[49]

He faced other inter party challenges as well during the late months of 1989. Major disagreements about Lee's foreign policy and initiatives concerning the PRC proved to be the starting point for a new wave of KMT factionalization.[50] These disputes over external policy resulted in the evolution of two different power blocs at the highest levels of the ROC's government.[51]

In early 1990 the process of factionalization and bloc building went even further. Now domestic issues forced the process of faction building. Lee created his own crisis and a new round of inter-party conflict when he announced that Lee Yuan-tsu would become his running mate as he went through the formal processes to become president. The more conservative mainlander faction within the KMT opposed Lee and threatened to run a challenger against him, which was unprecedented. Rather than face such an open challenge to his power at this moment in the late winter of 1990, Lee Teng-hui compromised. Once the election for president was over—an election conducted in the National Assembly, Lee made Hau Pei-tsun—a mainlander, a career military man, a strong supporter of the one ROC's (and the PRC's) one China policy, and a strong advocate of law and order—the new premier.[52]

Hau's ascension was seen by observers as marking the formal creation of two power blocs or factions. The "mainstream" faction, centered around the president and made up largely of Taiwanese, was pragmatic and reformist in nature. Premier Hau was nominal leader of the "non-mainstream" faction. It was made up of mainlanders and its members were more conservative and hard line in their views on both domestic and foreign policy. The struggle between these two factions was central to KMT life during the months from spring 1990 to the months after the dramatic elections for the Legislative Yuan in December 1992.

In March 1990 President Lee learned one of his most important lessons. It was that he needed to make large-scale compromises that would allow him to set the stage for even more dramatic and substantive changes in Taiwan's governmental and political system. The KMT's own factional conflicts helped to precipitate the dramatic and potentially chaotic event. The threat to the presidential election was seen by many people on the island, especially college students, as a bid on the part of some old party types to put a halt to Lee's reform movement. A group of students decided to take dramatic action to push their own sociopolitical agenda, one that was surprisingly in line with Lee's own program.

From March 16 to March 22 students from Tai-ta and other universities engaged in a dramatic act of political theater that reminded many on Taiwan and elsewhere of the student movement in the People's Republic of the previous year.[53] Choosing the location well, the students occupied the area just inside the main gate of the Chiang Kung Memorial Park, taking over the steps of the major concert hall/national theater complex near the very heart of "official Taipei."[54]

The students, like those in Beijing a year before, began hunger strikes, and many wore headbands with political slogans written on them. The shadow of the events of the spring of 1989 in mainland China lay heavily on these students and on the members of the Nationalist government they were demonstrating against. However, they and the members of the KMT-dominated regime had learned much from the shattering events in China and their painful aftermath—the Taiwanese students made clear and realistic demands. They did not expect too much, but aimed for things the regime could and might be willing to do. They were also careful not to cause the government to see the actions they took as a direct threat to social stability and to the established political order.

Their demands centered around matters of political process and were moderate and quite pragmatic in tone. The students called for an end to the National Assembly, retirement of key mainlanders whose position in the legislature was frozen in time and place, a timetable for full democratization, and a general revamping of the constitution. These were demands that, for the most part, members of the government and members of the moderate faction within the DPP could agree to and thus they could be seen as pushing President Lee's government further along a road it was already taking.

But a formal negotiation process had to take place. Chu Hai-yuan, a prominent sociologist, was brought in. He was known by students and by the government as one who could serve in the role of honest broker. And as he had done in the past, he was able to talk to both sides and find common ground.[55]

Then, with his election secured, President Lee visited the students. He told them that he was committed to convening a high level and inclusive conference that would study the needs of the ROC. This was an important statement for it showed the students that he saw their point, agreed with their call for change and was now going to plan a conference that would deal with the specific demands they, the students had made. This settled the crisis in a way satisfactory to all concerned and paved the way for the National Affairs Conference—the Kuo-shih-hui.[56]

The National Affairs Conference took place from June 28 to July 4, 1990. It was a dramatic and highly publicized event that was covered closely by the island's now more open media. Many important figures participated in the conference.[57]

Those chosen as chairs were a diverse group, albeit all male, that demonstrated how wide a net Lee and his regime wanted to cast.[58] Deliberations went on as planned and formal and informal socializing went on as well, breaking the ice between long time political opponents and between the government and its critics. The exchange of ideas was lively, and basic agreements were reached by all parties concerned before the final session was over.

Five large sets of issues provided a core of subjects for deliberation. (1) Substantive parliamentary reforms. The issues of the retirement of members of the National Assembly and the reconstruction of that legislative body were the first to be dealt with. The National Assembly was a hybrid body and can be thought of to Westerners unfamiliar with its role and its functions as the rough equivalent of a U.S. Senate that could act as an annual constitutional convention. (2) The nature of local governments on the island. Questions of the provincial government would be taken up at the Consultative Assembly—a National Affairs Council Part II held in late 1996. Just how these governments might be changed—whether by following the explicit text of the constitution in place in 1990, or by introducing new sets of amendments that dealt with local government as it existed in 1990 and not in 1947—was discussed. This seemingly small issue turned out to be crucial, for there were questions of institutional overlap and over-governance of a place that was both (or either) a small nation or a small Chinese province. (3) The structure of the central government. (4) The constitution. Whether it needed to be revised, amended, or fundamentally rewritten. (5) Relations between Taiwan and the mainland.[59]

The National Affairs Conference gave Lee Teng-hui the opening he needed. He was able use the symbol of the inclusive conference and, more importantly, the results of that conference as a much-needed mandate for reform. He convinced the citizens of Taiwan to see the conference as a clarion call to transform the structure and the role of the National Assembly. The members of the newly reconstructed legislative body would then use their institution's mandated powers to amend the ROC's constitution. These amendments would transform the very nature of presidential, cabinet level, and legislative operations and politics in the Republic of China. The end of the National Affairs Conference signaled an end to a period of relative accord between the two major parties. By the fall of 1990 the intra-party battles began once again with more than their usual fury.

Besides being a foreign policy issue, Taiwan's relations with the mainland were also closely connected with perhaps the most vexing of domestic issues— Taiwanese independence. To talk about reunification with the mainland was to wave a red flag in the face of the many DPP members who openly supported independence. In the fall of 1990, members of the DPP looking ahead to their attempt at securing the gains made at the National Affairs Conference, as well as to those political battles that would take place in 1991, brought the "reunification versus Independence" question to the foreground. The KMT was not simply an observer or a player that reacted to its opposition's tactics. Rather, its leaders forced the DPP to act and make its stance public. In previous months the KMT had developed agencies to deal with the expanding level of PRC-ROC relations and set up a National Reunification Council. Its information agency had also begun to publicize the KMT's hopes for eventual PRC-ROC unification.[60] After a flurry of statements, the Government Information Office lowered the level of rhetoric.[61] However it also announced the results of public opinion polls that showed that the public was against independence and for talks on unification.[62]

The DPP responded to this campaign for unification by stepping up the level of its own rhetoric on the issue. A DPP legislator raised the issue in the Legislative Yuan, knowing what the regime's response would be.[63]

The escalation continued a few weeks later when the DPP announced that it planned to establish a committee to promote the independence movement, suggesting that by taking this dramatic step they were pressuring the government to take action on governmental reforms. The government responded with forceful words. Shaw Yu-ming, then the director general of the GIO, issued a statement condemning this DPP action, taking care to cite ROC laws that prohibited just such a step.[64] The stage was now set for the battle over the independence issue that would take place a year later during the election campaign for the new National Assembly.

Overview: Political Evolution, Political Conflict and Institutional Change, 1991–1994

Each of the four "political years" beginning with January 1991 was dramatic in its own way. Winter and spring were the times that the legislatures met to pass important legislation and the executive's budget. During the summer the legislatures would recess and parties would hold their primaries. With the primaries over, the candidates would plan their fall campaigns for reelection. In the fall the legislatures would reconvene and the election campaigns would gather steam until the day late in the fall when the elections were held. The struggles for institutional change, the infighting within the ranks of the KMT and the battles between the two and, after mid-1993, three major parties would take place in these legislative and executive arenas as well as in the streets, in the print and electronic media. In some years the political conflicts would even spill out into the streets of the capital or other major cities.

On Taiwan, during this dramatic period of four years, the constitutional changes of one year prepared the way for the transformation of the political/governmental process of the next.

Constitutional Reform and the Elections for the New National Assembly, 1991

During the early months of 1991, as the crisis in the Persian Gulf raged on— threatening the ROC's access to oil, Lee Teng-hui and his faction within the KMT pushed ahead to fulfill the promises he had made to reform the island's political system.[65] The first step was to transform the National Assembly. This meant that the current Assembly would have to introduce legislation to dismantle the very legislative body they were members of. A new National Assembly would be elected at years end, an Assembly whose members truly represented the Taiwan of 1991 and not the China of 1947. It was this second incarnation of the National Assembly that would formally make many of the constitutional changes that had been decided on.[66]

By the time the National Assembly adjourned in late April, it had ended the "Temporary Provisions Effective During the Period of Mobilization for Suppression of the Communist Rebellion"—the formal statutes set up to deal with the civil war in China in the late 1940s and the legal foundation of the KMT dictatorship on Taiwan. It had also reduced the size of the National Assembly from 613 to 327 seats, cut the number of seats in the Legislative Yuan from 220 to 161, and reduced the terms of National Assembly members from six year terms to fours years. The newly elected and much smaller body was to be elected in the late fall and was to make further constitutional changes at its sessions in 1992.[67]

The Democratic Progressive Party, however, did not participate in all of the National Assembly's proceedings. DPP members did not like the way the KMT had engineered this special session of the National Assembly, and on April 16 they walked out, boycotting the remainder of the meeting.[68]

In mid-May, the Legislative Yuan rewrote the laws governing sedition. Under the new statutes, sedition was defined as criminal law to be dealt with through regular channels, and was no longer considered treasonous. The legislators, the press, and the public saw this action as a genuine step toward democracy.[69] Changes in the election law and in the way the members of the new National Assembly were to be elected created new inter-party conflicts. The KMT majority in the Legislative Assembly introduced a "one ballot" system of proportional representation. The DPP opposed the new system preferring, instead, a separate popular vote for the special seats. Its representatives argued that the KMT, as an older, larger, and more visible political entity, would get more votes from those voting a straight party ticket.[70]

By September, what had been a lull in the DPP/KMT conflict ended, as both sides looked ahead to the December elections. The government began cracking down on the U.S.-based "World United Formosans for Independence," and other pro-independence organizations.[71]

Matters escalated further in late September. The DPP, testing the new statute on sedition, came out publicly and called itself the party of independence. A few days later the government moved to resolve the conflict over the right to campaign on the issue of independence by setting up a task force to study the sedition statute that was at the heart of the evolving KMT-DPP struggle.[72]

This seeming compromise did not mean that the KMT had lost its taste for battle. On October 2 it announced its candidates, stating that it planned to win three fourths of the seats in the National Assembly with a party slate many saw as formidable.[73]

The DPP's fifth national convention platform called for the establishment of a Republic of Taiwan. In an almost unanimous vote the 350 delegates called for a plebiscite that would allow Taiwanese citizens to vote on the issue, thus making independence the central issue in the vote for the National Assembly.[74]

The battles between the KMT's calls for reform and the DPP's call for an independent Taiwan raged on until election day in December, when the public made it clear that it considered the DPP's campaign, centering as it did on the issue of Taiwanese independence, misguided. Nine million voters went to the polls and gave the KMT 71 percent of the vote and 254 seats in the Second National Assembly. The DPP received only 24 percent and 66 seats.[75]

The New National Assembly, the Process of Constitutional Reform, and the Elections for the Legislative Assembly (li-fa yuan), 1992

The internal struggle between the two factions of the KMT became dramatically evident in the middle of March 1992 when party delegates convened for a meeting of the Central Committee. The topics discussed at this meeting concerned the terms of the president and the members of the National Assembly and the Legislative Assembly, and the way the president and the vice-president were to be elected.

The National Assembly soon began carrying out its mandate for constitutional change by moving ahead on the terms of the Legislative Yuan and the president and vice-president, but went no further: The issue of direct election remained a contentious one.

This lack of KMT action gave the opposition DPP the weapon it needed to attack its rivals. The DPP at first kept its fight in the halls of the National Assembly but then took its battle to the streets. Two days later, DPP leaders called on President Lee to talk to the demonstrators and the DPP leadership.[76]

The DPP dissent was making itself felt on the National Assembly, although the KMT was not yet willing to accept DPP demand for direct elections The assembly did move quickly, however, reducing the twenty-one proposed amendments to nine more workable amendments. Included in these were changes in the terms of office for the president and legislators. Also included were protections of aborigine rights and culture. Concessions had been made to the DPP but these were not deemed sufficient, and it continued its opposition to the KMT's railroading of legislation.[77]

By May 27 eight of the nine proposed amendments had been passed, and these amendments did change the structure of the government. The term changes were the most visible innovation, but other things had been changed as well. For example, the Control Yuan, once considered a branch of government equal to the other branches, was now reduced in power to the role of a semijudicial body. On the other hand, the National Assembly gave itself more power, for it now had the right to nominate members to the Judicial Yuan, the Control Yuan, and the Examination Yuan. The provincial governor and the county magistrates were to be elected by the citizens. Finally a new fifteen member court was set up to review the actions of the political parties.[78]

Domestic politics was one dangerous minefield the president had to traverse. Another was the ethnic antagonism underlying Taiwanese politics. The February 28 Incident still divided Taiwanese from Mainlanders. As a Taiwanese who was head of the government responsible for February 28, Lee Teng-hui was in a good position to confront the ghosts of the past. He did so in the winter of 1992, when the official government report on the incident was issued amid a flurry of publicity and a series of high-profile events.[79]

The release of the February 28 report was part of a larger effort to lift censorship on the media and thus provide for the evolution of viable free press and free electronic media. The government took another important step in the spring by changing the nature of the sedition statute. This was considered a first step toward real freedom of expression in the Republic of China.[80]

That summer when KMT hopefuls announced their candidacy for the new 160–member Legislative Yuan and their decision to run in the party primaries,[81] the DPP responded by presenting a report produced by the party's strategy and policy center spelling out its policy initiatives on a variety of issues.[82]

Presented in the form of a policy "white paper," the DPP's platform dealt in detail with the party's mainland policy, calling for a peaceful settlement with the mainland and assurances from the PRC that no force would be used against Taiwan. It also called for negotiations leading to the creation of direct cross-the-strait transportation links. The foreign policy proposed was simple and powerful—that under the one China/one Taiwan formula, Taiwan should have formal diplomatic relations with major nations. The white paper also contained DPP ideas about domestic issues such as social policy—calling for social security and educational reform, improved labor relations, economic reform, and for selling-off of some of the government's and the KMT's extensive resources. The white paper was a gauntlet thrown at the feet of the KMT leadership.[83]

In the fall, the KMT unveiled its platform, the central tenet of which was the "one China policy"—that China must be unified under a free and democratic system. As a corollary to this, it stated that they opposed the DPP's "one China, one Taiwan" concept or any other form of what they considered to be separation. Their platform contained nineteen other guidelines—or planks—concerning foreign policy, domestic politics, and other major issues.[84]

Distinct styles of campaigning emerged during this election. One DPP candidate in Taipei staged various leisure activities such as chess competitions, softball games and Karaoke contests. Candidates belonging to one party banded together and held joint rallies to reach out to the public.[85] Other candidates realized they needed specialists to run their campaign, opening the door to individuals and firms in the field of public relations and advertising.[86]

The formal campaign that followed was heated, and included fierce attacks and exchanges. Premier Hau Pei-tsun proved to be a lightning rod for criticism and controversy and at times seemed at odds with his own party, defending the old guard, non-mainstream clique and taking a strong law and order stance. The DPP responded in kind, depicting him as a sinister mainlander, out of touch with Taiwan's political realities.[87]

This high visibility national campaign stood in contrast to the quieter but equally serious campaign that took place on the local level. Although here too candidates pulled out all the stops, even holding banquets for voters. One such event was attended by 15,000 people at an estimated cost of $U.S. 40,000.[88]

Taiwan's citizens went to the polls in record numbers. The DPP got the victory it wanted, winning 50 seats. The KMT won 102 seats and received 53 percent of the vote, somewhat less than the party leaders had hoped for.

Lee Teng-hui found that his party had lost some of its strength and that its divisions were clear. However, now politically sophisticated, he realized that his enemies within the party had also lost ground. He could now change the party and find people who reflected his views, furthering the process of Taiwanization his predecessor had begin in 1971.

Taiwan's New Political Environment Emerges, January 1993–December 1994

During the period from January 1993 to December 1994, the expected realignments in the Executive and Legislative branches took place with clear winners and losers. The biggest winner was the mainstream faction supporting President Lee Teng-hui. The biggest loser was his premier of almost three years, Hau Pei-tsun, and his non-mainstream faction.[89]

The year began with President Lee clearly assuming command. In one of his trademark public gestures, Lee laid out his agenda for the new legislature to the nation. On January 4, he gave a wide-ranging address which dealt with constitutional reforms, and mainland affairs—one the most important and vexing issues his government faced—economic development, national defense, and foreign policy.[90]

As the date for convening the new Legislative Yuan drew closer, discussion within the government grew more furious. Premier Hau, who had borne the brunt of the DPP attacks, wanted to leave, but also wanted his opinion heard as he left. Hau and President Lee discussed the issue and asked Hau's cabinet to tender its resignation. Combative to the end, Hau resigned the premiership while retaining positions within the party.[91]

The KMT legislators then acted on a number of key decisions. For the first time, they decided on who should be the president and the vice-president of the legislature. They then attempted to expand their legislative powers, taking on new powers of inquiry and investigation which traditionally belonged to the cabinet. Not surprisingly, the cabinet rejected the idea.[92]

Although the decision to chose a premier was in President Lee's hands, he made another public gesture by asking the legislators for their opinions, thus suggesting that the legislature was no longer merely a rubber stamp.[93] Lee already knew who he wanted—Lien Chan. Lien was a native Taiwanese, like Lee. He was originally an academician, and had risen through the governmental ranks assuming key posts over the years, including a position in the Ministry of Foreign Affairs.[94]

To forestall a fight in the Legislative Yuan over the approval of Lien's appointment, Lee hoped the DPP would play the role of the loyal and responsible opposition. Nevertheless, the DPP announced that it would work to defeat the nomination of Lien Chan. The struggle now began in earnest, and only after a prolonged struggle put up by the DPP and KMT dissidents from all over the island was Lien Chan finally approved by a sizable majority.[95]

One key issue that Lee, the premier, the new cabinet, and the Legislative Yuan all faced was the copyright conflict with the United States. Another issue was a DPP bill designed to ban political parties from running or investing in for-profit companies. This had been a long-standing practice, resulting in party coffers that were usually full. KMT legislators agreed that this bill was a useful step toward substantive reform.[96]

A third issue discussed was disclosure of the assets of high-level government officials and legislators. The DPP and the New KMT Alliance, a coalition of anti-Lee, reform-minded, and pro-reunification KMT legislators, called for the passage of the Sunshine Bill, a bill that would force the legislators and the bureaucrats to disclose their assets. The KMT was not willing to accept the bill as it was written and called for changes. The DPP's Shih Ming-teh continued to press for passage of the bill, threatening legislative deadlock. Finally a newly forged alliance between the DPP and the New KMT Alliance pushed forward. The KMT found it had to bend to the will of the public. Thus, on June 8 a second reading of the bill was held and it passed.[97] The passage of the bill was seen as a yet another major victory for democratization.

The vote on the Sunshine Law was an important victory, but the DPP and other enemies of an all-powerful state, such as the New KMT Alliance, also suffered a major defeat during this same period. The bill reestablishing two major security agencies, the National Security Council and the National Security Bureau, was passed by the legislature after a floor fight.[98]

The New KMT Alliance was now moving closer to breaking away from the KMT. The KMT met this challenge by appointing Hsu Shu-teh as its secretary-general. The government acted again to demonstrate its still potent political clout by appointing James Soong provincial governor.[99]

The DPP realized it had won a major victory when Huang Hsin-chieh was given his seat after a long and tortuous investigation of the election in Hualien. The party spent several months trying to broaden its role in the legislature and in the political process in general. One step it took was arguing that it had a role to play in determining mainland policy. The heads of the Mainland Affairs Council and the Straits Exchange Foundation both responded positively to this new initiative.[100]

Not willing to let their rivals get the upper hand, Lee Teng-hui and his subordinates worked to give themselves and their party positive visibility during the following months. Lee's actions were a prelude to the announcement of the date for the 14th KMT Party Congress. For its part, the KMT Central Committee announced a new party charter which stressed building consensus through democracy and fighting harder for people's interests.[101]

The long awaited formal break of a rebellious KMT faction from the main body of the party took place in late July, when the members of the New KMT Alliance (Six KMT legislators and thirty others) announced that they were officially breaking away from the KMT and forming a party called, simply, the New Party (*Hsin tang*).[102]

The scene was now set for a smaller, besieged KMT to convene its 14th Party Congress. Lee Teng-hui was elected party chair for a four-year term, and. 138 new members of the Central Advisory Committee were also elected, joining the 131 existing members.

The KMT's democratization, as evidenced by the unruly style (name calling, fist fights, etc.) of the 14th Congress, was soon seen within the ranks of the government the party controlled as well. The cabinet, acutely aware of the strong public and bi-partisan support for the Sunshine Law, now introduced its own guidelines of disclosure of assets and set a date for officials to comply— October 31, 1993. Ranking officials were also mandated to place their major assets in trust for the duration of their period of service. The law defining the nature of the trusts had yet to be passed, however, and this had to be done within the year.[103]

By late October, the election campaign shifted into high gear. The KMT, feeling pressure from the other parties, attacked the DPP as radical and the New party as an organization too ready to negotiate immediate reunification with the PRC. The DPP ran a low key campaign, employing strategies that allowed it to undermine President Lee's great appeal to DPP voters. The New Party, calling itself the representative of the common people, attacked both major parties as liars and vote-buyers.[104]

With the election the KMT could see that things were not as bad as its leaders had feared. The party captured 15 of 23 mayoralities and county magistrate's seats in strongly contested campaigns. It did lose a number of key battles, however, most notably in Tainan and Miao-li. The New Party gained no seats and the DPP won six seats, not the eleven they had hoped for, but they did gain over 40 percent of the popular vote. Shih Ming-teh now became the new chairman of the DPP.[105]

The Legislative Assembly's session that had begun in the fall of 1993 finally came to an end in December. In the view of observers and participants, it had been a fruitful one.

Although 1993 ended on a high note, the early days of 1994 proved to be difficult and augured ill for the months to come. As winter unfolded, the government was faced with a series of scandals, including corruption in the Defense Ministry and vote buying in elections for speakers and deputies.[106]

Other branches of the government could not simply sit by as the investigations about the scandals went on and perpetrators were charged. In a new session of the Legislative Assembly, the KMT demonstrated its strength by using its numbers to seat KMT members in key committee chairmanships and on major committees.[107]

The Legislative Assembly began eliminating out-dated laws, and refining those already on the books. This new term was devoted to studying and fine-tuning the ROC's budget as submitted by the premier and cabinet and finding the revenues needed to pay for government expenditures.[108]

By April, the Central Standing Committee of the National Assembly was ready to introduce a series of eight amendments to the constitution. These included the direct election of the president, creation of the offices of a speaker and deputy speaker of the National Assembly, ending the premier's power to countersign presidential appointments, extending the legislators' terms to four years, and limiting parliamentary immunity of speech.[109]

By early July, after a great deal of infighting and violence on the assembly floor, the 112 amendments had been reduced to 22. It was not until July 29 that the National Assembly completed its work.[110]

By the end of July, after much delay and contentiousness, the Legislative Yuan had acted on and passed a series of laws that made possible among other things the direct election of the governor and the mayors of Taipei and Kaohsiung. These laws also determined the makeup of the provincial assembly and allowed the provincial government to levy new taxes.[111]

Other major issues dealt with by the The Legislative Yuan were health care and the funding of a new nuclear power plant. The residents of the fishing village of Kung-liao, 40 km east of Taipei, voted against the construction of the plant. However, representatives of both Taipower and the Economics Ministry stated that the vote was not legal and that they were therefore not bound by it.[112]

The battle over funding of the plant was brought up in the Legislative Yuan, and although there was strong opposition from the DPP and the New Party, anti-nuclear forces did not gain the final victory they wanted—the party-line vote approved funding for the plant.[113]

The Legislative Yuan passed a heath care bill that provided coverage for the 43 percent of Taiwan's population who did not have any health care. This was an important and dramatic and very costly step for the government to take. However, the lawmakers, recognizing the cost factor, made the health-care system voluntary, not mandatory.[114]

Leading up to the December elections, the parties were now preparing to hold their primaries. The New Party was working to separate itself fully from the KMT; it completed its nominations for the post of provincial governor, for mayor of Taipei, and for mayor of Kaohsiung.[115]

KMT leaders nominated Shih Chi-yang to head the Judicial Yuan. Shih's appointment was the first made under the new constitutional amendment giving the president power of appointment without the premier's countersignature. The DPP challenged the step by first issuing a long statement and then boycotting the Legislative Yuan's vote on the new appointee.[116]

The National Assembly took another step which had an impact on Taiwan's judicial system a few weeks later when its members appointed justices to serve in the Council of Grand Justices. This key organ had been increased in size by constitutional amendment and the positions were now all filled. When the vote was taken, only one nominee failed to win a position. This nominee was Lin Chi-shih the wife of Lin Yi-hsiung, a key *tang-wai* figure and a man called the godfather of the DPP. Mrs. Lin's failure to win an appointment was seen as a political act by DPP members.[117]

In mid-September, Premier Lien opened the Legislative Yuan with a speech warning Beijing to work towards better relations with the ROC, and presented the cabinet's list of items it wished the legislators to deliberate and pass. The new session did not begin smoothly, however, for the DPP was protesting a recent crackdown on underground radio.[118]

On September 12 the Central Election Commission ruled that debates between the candidates for provincial governor and for mayors of the key cities could take place, something the public had been calling for.[119]

While the first-time-ever television debates for Taipei mayoral candidates were a step toward greater democracy, the legislature also discussed bills that could be seen as a distinct backward step. The legislature debated ways to make the recall of candidates more difficult. KMT legislators introduced measures that called for more signatures and specified that recall votes take place on special election days, not on days when nationwide elections were held.[120]

As these steps were taken on the legislative and political fronts, the island was rocked by major scandals. The DPP found itself hardest hit by a scandal involving the stock market and another involving the sale of heroin. The KMT was also hit hard, as some of its members were caught up in the stock market scandal.[121]

By November 18 the campaign for governor heated up.[122] Politicians from all parties as well the general public recognized that this would be a historic event marking a new step in the ROC's ongoing process of democratization. The major parties used their extensive clout to gather vast sums of money for the campaign, and each candidate tried to out-advertise his rivals. The public got into the act and Taipei taxi drivers carried on their own mini-campaigns and made Taipei a rather wild place as the election day drew closer.[123] The ROC leaders also decided they had to play their roles. President Lee and Premier Chien made stump speeches and spoke out at rallies, as did Shih Ming-teh, the DPP party leader.[124]

The electorate split the vote in December. Soong won the governor's post and the mayor's seat in Kaohsiung. However, Ch'en Shui-pien, the DPP candidate, was elected mayor of Taipei. The New Party and the DPP did well, gaining seats at the expense of the KMT in the provincial assembly and the city council seats in Taipei.[125]

In the weeks that followed, the KMT-dominated government went into action. The cabinet reshuffled twelve key post. The effort was made in the wake of what were seen as disappointing results in the December 3 election and the party's need to better define its policy toward the PRC. New Party gains probably had some effect on this facet of Lee and Lien's decision.[126]

Lee Teng-hui's Taiwan and the World: Foreign Policy and Cross-the-Strait Policy

By the late 1990s, the Republic of China had been diplomatically isolated for almost two decades and Lee and his foreign minister had to chart a policy to confront this isolation and maneuver around it, working on both the formal/governmental and informal/nongovernmental levels of international relations. When Lee Teng-hui took command of his party in July 1988, he made it clear that a vigorous, effective, and innovative foreign policy, "pragmatic diplomacy," would be central to his new administration.[127]

At the heart of this foreign policy was the realization of the simple truth that money "talked." Thus, an important aspect of the informal foreign policy that Lee and his foreign minister developed involved investment, membership in UN-related nongovernmental organizations (NGOs) and regional economic and trade groups, all areas where Taiwan's large capital reserve could be put to good use. The ROC was able maneuver around the traps and barriers that the regime on the mainland continued to set for them in its ongoing attempt to continue Taiwan's isolation.[128]

This new approach was evident in initiatives begun in 1988 that continued into the 1990s. Taiwan had maintained working relationships with states in various areas of the world and continued to build on them as it strove to take advantage of evolving regional and world-wide diplomatic and political-economic trends—and crises—to broaden its reach and increase its influence overseas.

The central target of ROC diplomacy was Central America, especially Costa Rica, Panama, and El Salvador. The regime worked to improve relations with the region, courting leaders and sending the president and other high ranking officials to visit, and inviting their representatives, to visit Taipei. They also provided large amounts of economic aid to each of these nations.[129]

ROC initiatives in Africa were also quite successful. In 1989, for example, the West African state of Liberia decided to follow a dual recognition policy by maintaining formal diplomatic relations with the ROC while continuing its relationship with the PRC. This made Liberia the first nation to reestablish ties with the ROC since the latter's expulsion from the UN and its PRC-promoted isolation began. This was an important first step in the pursuit of "pragmatic diplomacy." The ROC also maintained ties with states it had long recognized. The visit of the young King of Swaziland, Maswati III, in late October of 1989 was one of those formal occasions that represented the kind of high profile diplomatic initiative the ROC was seeking.[130]

These initiatives continued with new approaches to Swaziland and South Africa, including a visit to Taipei by Nelson Mandela in 1993. Soon the Central African Republic resumed diplomatic relations with the ROC. This was followed a year later by the establishment of full diplomatic relations with Niger in the face of vigorous PRC opposition.[131]

Lee visited South Africa in 1994 to attend Nelson Mandela's inauguration, meeting privately with Mandela and former president Willem DeKlerk. This occasion also gave Lee the opportunity to meet other major leaders including American vice president Albert Gore and Yassar Arafat. The trip demonstrated to other nations that Lee's government was intent on finding a place for itself among the community of nations.[132]

ROC officials also tried to take advantage of the transformation of Eastern Europe and worked to develop relationships with the Baltic states, with other former Soviet client states, and with the nations that had broken away from the Russian-dominated Soviet Union. In 1990, for example, ROC diplomats began discussions with representatives of Poland and Bulgaria at an international meeting on trade convened in Taipei that August.[133]

In 1992, Latvia became the first nation in the area to develop quasi-formal ties with the ROC. In June, a delegation from Belarus, including the mayor of Minsk, came to Taiwan and paid a formal visit to Chiang Ching-kuo's Belarusian-born widow minister to negotiate business deals.[134]

In September 1993, Russia and the ROC agreed to establish quasi-official relations. U.S./ROC-style offices were to be set up in major cities to handle various official services, such as issuing visas.[135] At year's end, Latvia announced its decision to set up direct air links with Taiwan and signed a pact relating to investment and development.[136] Tatarstan sent its prime minister and other officials to the ROC to negotiate business agreements. ROC officials saw links with this resource-rich area as important to strengthening its evolving relationship with the Russian Federation itself.[137] In March 1994, Michail Gorbachev made a six-day visit to the ROC. During his visit it was announced that trade with Russia had reached $U.S. 708 million by 1993.[138]

In the same period, talks with Western European nations began, with the goal of developing stronger economic ties and establishing or reestablishing direct air links. Austria inaugurated direct air links in June 1991.[139] High-level French delegations visited the ROC in January of 1991 to discuss various trade and business issues, including the establishment of a Sino-French coordination council.[140]

However, some gains did not come so easily. Germany, for example, sent a delegation of officials to the ROC in early 1993, in part to compensate for Germany's refusal to sell submarines to the ROC, but it only represented one state in the German Federated Republic, Saxony-Anhalt. Trade was fostered and some bridges were rebuilt. Earlier that year authorities in Great Britain and the ROC signed a similar agreement giving the Taiwanese airline Eva Air the right to fly to England. Step by step the ROC was reconstructing its relationships with European nations.[141]

There were mixed results, too, in the Middle East. In 1989, for example, Taiwan and Saudi Arabia broke off relations. Despite this break in relations, Taipei soon began to work out new quasi-governmental relations with the Saudi government so that the national oil company could continue buying oil from the Saudis and could continue investing there.[142]

During 1992, the ROC developed closer, though informal ties with Israel. Even though earlier that year, Israel and the PRC had issued a joint statement announcing the establishment of formal diplomatic relations, the ROC took no formal action against Israel and set up trade offices in Tel Aviv.[143]

The ROC was most active in Southeast Asia. In the late 1980s and the 1990s, formal or quasi-formal relationships were formed with states such as Indonesia, Malaysia, Thailand, the Philippines, and Singapore.[144]

Perhaps the most dramatic breakthrough made during President Lee's first term was the evolution of an economic and diplomatic relationship with the Democratic Republic of Vietnam. In September 1991, Chen Shen-yi of the Industrial Development Board travelled to Ho Chih Minh City (now again Saigon) with members of Taiwan's land development companies to study sites for establishing export processing zones.[145] A major trade agreement between the two countries that opened the door to the exchange of representatives and to technological cooperation, formalized and strengthened an economic relationship that was reflected in the 600 billion NT that had been invested in Vietnam by the early summer of 1992. In 1994, the United States lifted its trade embargo of Vietnam, paving the way for joint U.S./ROC development of Vietnam and the Vietnamese market. By 1994 the ROC had become the single largest national investor in Vietnam and had also provided Vietnam with loans designed to help improve its infrastructure. The ROC moved into many key areas of the Vietnamese economy including petroleum production and textile production, and by April 1994, four major agreements were signed by Vietnamese and Taiwanese officials.[146]

Taiwan also actively cultivated relations with Australia during this period. In July of 1991, the ROC economics minister was invited to Australia to discuss trade and promote economic ties. He was accompanied by officials of major Taiwanese state-run enterprises such as the Taiwan Sugar Corporation, the Chinese Petroleum Corporation, the China Steel Corporation, and the Taiwan Power Company. This was preceeded by a pact on air service.[147]

On its home ground of East Asia, however, despite some success, Taiwan met painful disappointments. In October 1990, for example, the Tiao Yu Tai Islands dispute flared up briefly. They would prove troublesome again in the mid-1990s as Taiwan and Japan jockeyed for position and each claimed control. Taiwan's quest for a greater share of the Japanese market moved closer to reality in 1992–93.[148] ROC-Japan relations were highlighted by the problem of the Asian Games, i.e., how Japan was to appease the PRC while allowing Taiwan to participate. After much ado, a compromise was finally reached.[149]

Taiwan's relationship with Korea soured when the Republic of Korea recognized the PRC in 1992, followed by the ROC announcement that it was breaking diplomatic relations with its former friend and rival. By 1993 however, the two sides were talking again and progress was being made.[150]

The Taiwan-United States relationship was complicated. There was the quasi-formal relationship the two nations had set up in the wake of the derecognition and the Taiwan Relations Act. There was also the relationship of Taiwan and other certain key agencies within the U.S. government. Thus, when it was to his administration's advantage, George Bush was willing to sell the ROC the F16s it needed to match the PRC.

There were also informal relations between the ROC government and key figures in the United States Senate and House of Representatives. The KMT and the DPP both set up offices in Washington and used these to maintain contact with members of Congress and members of the administration. At key times, such as before the opening of the annual UN General Assembly session, officials and academicians from the ROC would come to the United States to lobby for their cause, in this case readmission to the United Nations, among congressmen and State Department officials.[151]

There were also important ROC initiatives to enter major regional and international organizations and movements, for example, the General Agreement on Trade and Tariffs.[152]

Taiwan's attempt to reenter the United Nations is an example of the workings of Lee's diplomacy in the sphere of international organizations.[153] Taiwan had been out of the United Nations for nineteen years when the cry for re-entry was raised loudly and publicly. This led in turn to a five-year campaign whose failure caused frustration for the ROC every year it took place. The campaign for the UN seat made good press on Taiwan but failed to accomplish much at the United Nations. ROC-officials based in New York suggested that the PRC's reaction was so strong to the now yearly campaign, that such efforts hurt the ROC and made its diplomats more vulnerable overseas.

Mainland Affairs, 1988–1994

Lee Teng-hui faced many challenges from across the strait as he and his government attempted to define the nature of Taiwan's evolving relationship with the People's Republic of China.

When Lee came to office the new cross-the-strait relationship with the mainland had already begun taking shape. In the months after Chiang Ching-kuo allowed *wai-sheng jen* to travel to the PRC, many began to visit relatives they had not seen in almost forty years. *Pen-ti-jen* also took advantage of the lifting of the ban on travel. Leaders and members of some of the larger and more influential Ma-tsu temples sent a delegation to the Ma-tsu ancestral temple (the *tzu-miao*) on Mei-chou island in Fukien. This was only the beginning of what would become a rising tide of tourism and pilgrimages that Taiwanese would make to religious sites in Fukien and in other provinces that were the homes of the ancestral temples of gods prominent on Taiwan.[154]

Businessmen also took advantage of travel opportunities to China. Merchants dealing in religious goods traveled to Fukien to purchase items from shops in Ch'uanchou and Changchou, cities that were the ancestral homes of most of the Minnan (Taiwanese)-speaking citizens of the ROC. Merchants in other types of products also made the trip.

In 1990 the ROC took a major step in developing its relationship with the PRC when it announced the establishment of the Mainland Affairs Commission, which was made a new part of the Executive Yuan. Later in 1990, a new private agency, the Foundation for Exchanges Across the Straits (or Straits Exchange Foundation, as it was later called) was authorized. This agency was designed to facilitate trade development and investment in the PRC and handle other nongovernmental issues. While formally not a part of the government, it was defined as having an intermediary role and could thus be thought of as quasi-governmental.[155]

Once the way to investment-through-joint-venture was paved, an increasing number of industrialists looked for places to build factories. Shoe manufacturers began coming to Pu-t'ien in what was the beginning of the shift of the shoe industry from Taiwan to this coastal county in central Fukien. Industrialists came to the major cities as well, and could be found in Fuchou, the provincial capital, Chuanchou, Changchou, and Hsiamen (Amoy), with joint ventures very much on their minds. Regional and city governments established trade and investment fairs that helped expedite the development of cross-the-strait trade investment.[156]

As 1990 ended, PRC officials made a proposal to hold low-level party to party talks on bilateral relations and reunification under the "one country, two systems" formula the PRC had been pushing. The ROC rejected the plan and proposed secret talks. While the ROC government was wary of the PRC politically, it remained committed to its policy of expanding economic ties with China. One way it expressed its confidence in the evolving relationship was to ensure that the rules promulgated by the Mainland Affairs Council were acceptable to Lee Teng-hui. Lee gave his approval of these regulations in late January 1991; around the same time that the ROC government announced its approval of an indirect joint venture involving a Taiwan-based textile firm. Beijing also approved this pioneering step, demonstrating that at least on some occasions, economics drove international politics and cross-the-strait relations.[157]

During 1991 and 1992, the ROC's relationship with the PRC kept expanding, but each step seemed painful and crises kept occurring that slowed progress. A key quasi-diplomatic mission did go to Beijing in late April to meet with officials in a series of wide-ranging talks that seemed to please both sides. Here business was clearly leading the way, much as the KMT regime hoped it would.[158]

An example of the kind of crisis that occurred during this period happened when three ROC police officers who had boarded a mainland fishing boat they felt was involved in smuggling mushrooms from Taiwan to the PRC were abducted by those on board. A search by ROC ships failed to find the boat. PRC authorities were informed, investigated, and found the men safe in Fukien, whereupon they were released.[159]

This was the first of a series of troubling incidents which forced the ROC authorities to think about the evolving relationship with the mainland. These incidents also caused both sides to consider creating mechanisms which would facilitate higher-level communications. Incidents like these caused both sides to wonder about the feasibility of direct cross-the-strait trade.[160]

Events of a decidedly more positive nature also took place. A delegation of officials and businessmen made an eleven day visit to Canton, Hsiamen, Fuchou, and Shanghai.[161] One positive side effect of these cross-the-strait incidents was that Red Cross organizations on each side of the strait were forced to communicate with each other and this was considered a breakthrough.

During 1992, the relationship evolved, much as it did in 1991, on various levels at the same time. The ROC began the year with some new initiatives that allowed PRC mainlanders to establish private offices in Taipei and for Taiwanese to do so in Beijing.[162]

Premier Li Peng then introduced his own PRC initiative, a forty-four page article regulation that covered cross-the-strait visits. The ROC then made it possible for Taiwanese who had been stranded on the mainland in 1949 to visit or to emigrate. At the same time, a new regulation was issued covering mainlanders working on Taiwan.[163]

From March until May, a wide variety of cultural and academic exchanges were planned and civil servants were now allowed to travel to the PRC, but only as private citizens. This allowed many who had been unable to for so long to make the trip and see the Chinese homeland for themselves. In addition, students up to university level were allowed on exchange programs and trips to the mainland.[164]

As for direct investment, joint ventures were fraught with uncertainty and apt to remain so until the two regimes could work out some system of formal guarantees. Another problem was related to readily available capital for such investments. Taiwanese banks were not yet able to set up branches in the PRC and thus provide the sorts of services the investors and venture capitalists needed.[165]

The first Mainland Affairs Conference was held in September, at which many possibilities for development of PRC/ROC relations were discussed. Three hundred sixty-seven proposals covering several areas were approved to encourage further exchanges across the strait.[166]

By March, the plans for the next round of ARATS/SEF meetings were being formalized. These meetings were to be different as the heads of each organization were to lead the delegations and involve themselves in day to day discussions. The stakes were clearly much higher.[167]

After overcoming a series of minor glitches, the long awaited talks finally got under way in April . Given the rising levels of tourism and investment and the problems caused by high level person-to person and business-to-business interaction, it was imperative that procedures be developed and that protocol for dealing with problems and conflicts be defined. By April 29, the talks had concluded and both sides agreed that they had been as successful as could be hoped for.[168]

Four agreements were worked out. The first dealt with the establishment of systematic communications channels between the two quasi-governmental bodies, SEF and ARATS, the second covered the important issue of notarization of documents, the third covered tracking and compensating for lost cross-the-strait mail, and the fourth dealt with later meetings and the decision to discuss such issues as protection of Taiwanese investment in the PRC and the timing of a cross-the-strait economic conference. This was a watershed moment in the evolving PRC/ROC relationship.[169]

Further talks to consolidate these gains became the major concern of the two governments in the following months. Representatives of SEF tried to meet with those of ARATS to discuss outstanding issues as they implemented those agreements already reached. While concerns about Taiwanese investments continued, other agencies within the government were trying to divert the stream of investment to other areas such as Southeast Asia.

Talks later in the year saw some progress in developing formal mechanisms for easier contact between SEF and ARATS, but broke down again over the issue of air piracy.[170]

In January 1995, the government of the ROC made another important decision concerning mainland affairs by establishing new fields of enterprise that Taiwanese could invest in. These included construction, engineering consultation, and machine leasing. Companies had to apply to the government and decisions were to be made on a case by case basis. The Taiwanese were now poised to provide funds and expertise for the development of the PRC's infrastructure.[171]

In March, the Eighth National People's Congress passed the long awaited law on cross-the-straits contracts. However, it soon came under fire from government officials in the ROC. It did not, in the view of many observers, increase the protection of Taiwanese investment but rather strengthened the PRC government's power over investors and put them under added restrictions. The law did little to shore up Taiwanese confidence in the investment climate in the mainland.[172]

Confidence in the mainland and in the safety of ROC citizens traveling there was shattered almost to the breaking point when in late March a cruise boat on Chingtao Lake was discovered burned, with the remains of 24 Taiwanese and eight others on board. President Lee expressed his great sadness and fury and requested a detailed investigation of what had taken place. The head of MAC and other ROC officials let it be known that all talks with ARATS were suspended until the details of this incident were made available. In one way or another, the Chingtao tragedy dominated ROC/PRC relations for the next few months.[173]

By the end of July, about a month after the executions of the three men sentenced for the Chingtao Lake murders, and after reliable reports of People's Liberation Army involvement, ROC/PRC relations began returning to their pre-tragedy status. MAC had decided to resume cultural and educational exchanges, suspended since April 12, 1994. This step was taken partially because of the desire of many involved to return to normal and partly as an attempt to improve the atmosphere on the verge of the new round of SEF-ARATS talks scheduled for July 30. These new talks were to cover a host of old and new issues. One of the most pressing concerns was the use of mainland fishermen on ROC vessels fishing waters adjacent to Taiwan. Other issues to be covered concerned air piracy and the return of air hijackers and illegal mainland immigrants to Taiwan.[174] The fact that the new talks were to take place at all was seen as the most important sign that the poisoned atmosphere was finally beginning to lift.

By August 8, the new round of talks was concluded and it was announced that a number of agreements had been reached: the deadlocks that had existed on hijacking, piracy, and other issues had finally been broken. The question of notarization was covered and many of the restrictions were eased. Delivery services between the two nations were also to be expedited. Academic exchanges and conferences were to be held as a means of improving cross-the-strait relations and student exchanges were also to be promoted. Other general issues and problems were discussed as a starting point for further changes. There was a general recognition of the differences in society and political culture that divided these two nations, making it difficult to handle a variety of issues such as judicial matters, but at least it could now be said that some level of dialogue had taken place.[175]

By early November, new plans concerning the direct transit of goods and people to the mainland were being discussed. As this point things were still very much in the planning stages.[176]

By the end of 1994 the PRC had raised the possibility of a top level but very private summit between the leaders of the two nations. However, Premier Lien rejected the idea and stated that he wished for an open public meeting. SEF/ARATS talks were discussed with the hope that the chairmen of the two quasi-governmental bodies would meet and deal with substantive issues and bridge their differences.[177]

The year had been difficult, but had ended well. The basis for a stronger PRC/ROC relationship was now set, or so everyone thought. The period from January 1988 to December 1994 had been in many ways a remarkable one in the development of relations between the two governments that claimed to govern China. The years that followed would show just how far things had come and how much further things had to go.

Notes

1. In preparing this section I made use of a variety of sources. One of the most valuable for students of contemporary Taiwan is *Free China Review* (hereafter FCR), a monthly magazine published by the Government Information Office of the Republic of China/Taiwan. The annual conferences on modern Taiwan held at St. Johns University in Jamaica, New York, have proven useful. Each conference has centered around a specific theme. The proceedings of these conferences are published in issues of the *American Asian Review*. A recent volume that contains essays from conferences on Taiwan held in Chicago under the auspices of the International Symposium on Taiwan Studies has been published by the Center of East Asian Studies of the University of Chicago. See Marshall Johnson and Fred Y.L. Chu, eds., *Unbound: Taiwan: Closeups From a Distance* (Select Papers, vol. 8) (Chicago: The Center for East Asian Studies, 1994). A conference volume that has received attention in academic journals is Dennis Fred Simon and Michael Y.M. Kau, eds., *Taiwan: Beyond the Economic Miracle* (Armonk, NY: M.E. Sharpe, 1992). Another useful book with some especially insightful essays on Taiwan in the 1970s is Emily Martin Ahern and Hill Gates, eds., *The Anthropology of Taiwanese Society* (Stanford: Stanford University Press, 1981). Another valuable collection of essays and excerpts from essays for studying the 1970s is James C. Hsiung, ed., *The Taiwan Experience, 1950–1980* (New York: American Association for Chinese Studies, 1981). Articles contained in a book the author of this chapter edited are also useful and will be referred to. See Murray A. Rubinstein, ed., *The Other Taiwan* (Armonk, NY: M.E. Sharpe, 1994). An important volume, that is regarded as a classic in Taiwan studies, is Ralph Clough, *Island China* (Cambridge, MA: Harvard University Press, 1978). Also extremely useful as a starting point for any student of Taiwan's development is Thomas B. Gold, *State and Society in the Taiwan Miracle* (Armonk, NY: M.E. Sharpe, 1986).

2. On the ROC, the U.S. and the UN, see Ralph Clough, *Island China* (Cambridge, Massachusetts, 1978), 149–155.

3. On the ROC's relations with Japan during this period see Clough, *Island China,* 182–189.

4. Clough, *Island China,* 189–200.

5. The best account of this period remains Mab Huang, *Intellectual Ferment for Political Reforms in Taiwan, 1971–1973* (Ann Arbor: University of Michigan Press, 1976). For a liberal/radical critique of the period that is better as journalism than formal political analysis see Marc Cohen, *Taiwan at the Crossroads* (Washington, DC: Asia Resource Center, 1988), 32. See also Clough, *Island China,* 60–63.

6. Hung-Mao T'ien, *The Great Transition* (Stanford, CA: Hoover Institution Press, 1989), 69.

7. Huang, *Intellectual Ferment for Political Reforms in Taiwan, 1971–1973,* 81. On the complex structure of the government of the Republic of China see "Central and Local

Government," in *Republic of China, 1986* (Taipei, 1986), 125–142. This is a basic guide to the republic published for the government. It contains a wealth of useful information but of course does not present an objective picture of conditions of the island.

8. Huang, *Intellectual Ferment for Political Reforms*, 81–101.

9. T'ien, *The Great Transition*, 96. Cohen, *Taiwan at the Crossroads*, 32–33. See also the account in Edwin A. Winkler, "Roles Linking State and Society," in Ahern and Gates, *The Anthropology of Taiwan of Taiwanese Society*, 83–84.

10. On the election process and on the nature of politics on the provincial level on Taiwan see this important if somewhat overlooked book: Arthur J. Lerman, *Taiwan's Politics: The Provincial Assemblyman's World* (Washington, DC: American University Press, 1978).

11. T'ien, *The Great Transition*, 96. Cohen, *Taiwan at the Crossroads*, 32–33. I was given a detailed account the events at Chungli and how it was perceived by the people in another election district by scholar activist Linda Gail Arrigo in part of a long interview that was conducted in Taichung in June 1990.

12. This information was derived from interviews conducted with Shih Ming-teh in July 1991 and in June 1992, as well as from the interviews conducted with Linda Gail Arrigo and other participants in the Mei-li-tao struggle.

13. T'ien, *The Great Transition*, 96. Cohen, *Taiwan at the Crossroads*, 32–33. Also see the account of the *tang-wai* movement in Alexander Ya-li Lu, "Political Opposition in Taiwan: The Development of the Democratic Progressive Party" in Tun-jen Cheng and Stephan Haggard, eds., *Political Change in Taiwan*, 124–126.

14. The most useful survey of Taiwan's diplomatic relations is to be found in T'ien, *The Great Transition*, 217–248. On the role of the US during this critical period in the seventies and eighties see ibid., 232–236.

15. This author became aware of both the deep level of hurt on the part of the mainlander community and others and, at the same time, of the ease of the transition to the new system during this period as I was Fulbright scholar in Taiwan at the time.

16. Linda Arrigo has charted the course of this struggle in articles and in the interviews I conducted with her, and her *tang-wai* sensibility will pervade my own account. I also make use of Lu Hsiu-lien's account in her as-yet-unpublished memoirs.

17. There is a rich and still evolving literature and oral history on the Mei-li-tao movement and on the various principals involved. Shih has published on the subject as has Arrigo. Lu Hsiu-lien has published her own account and Ch'en Chu has provided me with her own impressions in an interview conducted in 1990. See my essay on Ms. Lu presented at the 1995 annual meeting of the Association of Asian Studies: Murray A. Rubinstein, "Lu Hsiu-Lien: the Life and Times of a Taiwanese Feminist,"

18. Reflections on the *tang-wai* movement and the Kaohsiung Incident, in "Autobiography," 5–8.

19. Ibid., 9.

20. Ibid., 9–10, and the Kaohsiung Incident, ibid., 1–3. Another source close to the event is a book of newspaper articles, statements by participants, and court transcripts published in 1988.

21. T'ien, *The Great Transition*, 97. Cohen, *Taiwan at the Crossroads*, 32–33. These books provide short and useful accounts. Such publications as SPEAHRhead, the press organ of the Society for the Protection of East Asian Human Rights, also contain running accounts of the incident and accounts of the trials that followed.

22. See Alexander Ya-li Lu, "Political Opposition in Taiwan: The Development of the Democratic Progressive Party," in Tun-jen Cheng and Stephan Haggard, eds., *Political Change in Taiwan* (Boulder, CO: Lynn Rienner Publishers, 1992), 121–146, for a well-written narrative history and analysis of the DPP.

23. James Reardon Anderson, *Pollution, Politics, and Foreign Investment in Taiwan: The Lukang Rebellion* (Armonk, NY: M.E. Sharpe, 1992). Jack F. Williams, "Environmentalism in Taiwan," in Simon and Kau, eds., *Taiwan: Beyond the Economic Miracle,* 187–210; Jack F. Williams in collaboration with Ch'ang-yi Chang,"Paying the Price of Economic Development in Taiwan: Environmental Degradation" in Rubinstein, ed., *The Other Taiwan,* 237–256; David W. Chen, "The Emergence of an Environmental Consciousness in Taiwan," in ibid., 257–286; Robert Weller, "Environmental Protest in Taiwan," in *Harvard Studies on Taiwan,* 35–63.

24. Hsin-huang Michael Hsiao, "The Labor Movement in Taiwan: A Retrospective and Prospective Look," in Simon and Kau, eds., *Taiwan: Beyond the Economic Miracle,* 151–167.

25. See the special section on foundations in *FCR,* vol. 41, no. 9 (September, 1991), 4–31.

26. Chu Yun-han,"Social Protests and Political Democratization in Taiwan," in Rubinstein, ed., *The Other Taiwan,* 97–113.

27. On this, see Lu, Interrogation, in "Autobiography," 1–4.

28. Ibid., 6.

29. With the help of her lawyer/brother Ms. Lu was able to refute the confession in court on the basis of the fact that it was a confession made while she was being psychologically tortured. Lu, Interrogation part 2, in "Autobiography," 5.

30. Ibid., 8–9.

31. Some old hard liners within the government did not see direct political action—street demonstrations—as a path to be followed and took action to show how they would deal with such resistance. The murder of the mother-in-law and two daughters of Lin Yi-hsiung, a lawyer and a Mei Li Tao leader in their home in a quiet neighborhood near busy Hsin-I Road in east central Taipei was meant to serve as a warning to those dissidents, as did a series of suspicious auto accidents that crippled other members of the opposition. But the dissidents would not be swayed. The PCT, the conscience of the opposition movement, responded to this horrifying attack on the Lin family by converting the Lin family apartment, off Hsin-yi Road into the Gi Kong Church. They also placed a bronze plaque outside the church to remind passers by of what had taken place there. The church that was founded then emerged as the center of church-inspired social action and continued to play that role into the early 1990s.

32. Lu, Imprisonment 1 in "Autobiography," 2–5.

33. On this church see Murray A. Rubinstein, "The New Testament Church and the Taiwanese Protestant Community 1960–1988," in Lin Chi-ping, ed. *Christianity and China: Indigenization* (Proceedings of the International Conference on Indigenization, Taipei, 1988), 644–703. This essay also appears in Rubinstein, ed., *The Other Taiwan,* 445–473.

34. T'ien, *The Great Transition,* 70.

35. Alexander Ya-li Lu," Political Opposition in Taiwan: The Development of the Democratic Progressive Party" in Tun-jen Cheng and Stephan Haggard, eds., *Political Change in Taiwan,* 121–128.

36. Numerous scholars have examined the years from 1986 to 1988 in essays and in sections of recent monographs. One of clearest narratives of this period is found in Alan Wachman, *Taiwan: National Identity and Democratization* (Armonk, NY: M.E. Sharpe, 1995), 142–148. Another is found in Tien, "Elections and Taiwan's Democratic Development," in Tien, ed., *Taiwan's Electoral Politics and Democratic Transition,* 10–12. One can see the period from the perspective of human rights activists in *Yuan,* vol. 4, no. 5, (May/June, 1986) to *Yuan* vol. 5, no. 10 (October 1987). *Yuan* was published by Catholic missionaries in Hong Kong.

37. Parris H. Chang, "The Changing Nature of Taiwan's Politics," in Simon and Kau, eds. *Taiwan: Beyond the Economic Miracle,* 30–31.

38. Joseph Bosco, "Faction Versus Ideology: Mobilization Strategies in Taiwan's Elections" *China Quarterly,* forthcoming).

39. Chang, "The Changing Nature of Taiwan's Politics," in Simon and Kau, ed., *Taiwan: Beyond the Economic Miracle,* 31–32.

40. See Murray A. Rubinstein, 'The Gods Reunited: Pilgrimage and the Renewal of the Fukien/Taiwan Religious Relationship" Panel on Images and Interaction in the Evolving Cross-the Strait Relationship." Annual Meeting of the Association of Asian Studies, 1994.

41. This brief biography is based on the one published in the newsletter of the East Asian Program of Cornell University (Fall 1995). The newsletter also contains an article on President Lee's visit in June of 1995 and articles on the fellowships set up in honor of Lee Teng-hui. A more detailed biography of Lee and other major political leaders on Taiwan appears in Kui Tai-chun, ed., *Taiwan Cheng-chih Chiang-shih Hsiang* (Taiwanese Political Portraits) (Taipei: Independent Daily Press, 1989), 24–47.

42. The party congress is covered in articles in *The Free China Journal* (hereafter FCJ), the GIO's twice weekly English-language newspaper. On the 13th Party Congress see "KMT gets good news to start 13th congress" in *FCJ,* vol. 5, 327 (July 7, 1988), 1.

43. Chang, "The Changing Nature of Taiwan's Politics," in Kau and Simon, eds., *Taiwan: Beyond the Economic Miracle,* 32–33.

44. The person chosen to be finance minister was a woman, Shirley Kuo: In making this appointment Lee twice shattered precedent. The cabinet that Lee appointed also reflected his own educational/class background, for it included fourteen individuals with Ph.D.s from the United States. "All systems go as Lee Teng-hui era is launched," FCJ, vol. 5, 3#3 (July 25, 1988), 1; Chang, "The Changing Nature of Taiwan's Politics," in Kau and Simon, eds., *Taiwan: Beyond the Economic Miracle,* 33.

45. Wachman, *Taiwan: National Identity and Democratization,* 147.

46. "ROC wired with election fever," FCJ, vol. 6, no. 92 (November 30, 1989).

47. "Results to nourish reform," FCJ, vol. 6, no. 94 (December 7), 1.

48. "Election message heard: KMT answers Vox Populi," FCJ, vol. 6, no. 95 (December 11, 1989), 1.

49. Lee sent a high-level delegation to Beijing to attend a meeting of the Asia Development Bank. It was at this time that he also ordered the Ministry of Foreign Affairs to seek dual recognition, i.e., asking friendly states and trading partners to extend diplomatic recognition to the ROC and the PRC. "Kuo says group had no choice," FCJ, vol. 6, no. 34 (May 11, 1989).

50. See Yun-han Chu and Tse-min Lin, "The Process of Democratic Consolidation in Taiwan: Social Cleavage, Electoral Competition, and the Emerging Party System," in T'ien, ed., *Taiwan's Electoral Politics and Democratic Transition,* 84.

51. Ibid.

52. "Hau gets nod," FCJ, vol. 7, no. 40, (May 31 1990), 1.

53. The authors of a book about the movement, *Taipei Hsueh-tung (The Taipei Student Movement)* (Taipei: Yuan Chiang-pien Gung-tz, 1990), suggested that this movement was linked to the social movements and protests that had taken place over the course of the 1980s. Thus they tied into events in Taiwan's recent past, but one can also read as subtext that the events of T'ien-an men were in the minds of all involved, whether they were student activists, intermediaries, or members of the government of the Republic of China.

54. My account of these events is based on published sources such as He Chin-shan, Kuan Ma-chih, Chang Li-chia, Pu Cheng-chih, *Taipei Hsueh-tung (The Taipei Student Movement)* and the relevant sections of Wachman, *Taiwan: National Identity and Democratization.*

55. I interviewed Chu Hai-yuan at his offices at the Institute of Ethnology in June of 1990, a few months after the events had taken place. As I noted in the text, Chu was again

serving contending parties in the role of intermediary, a role he had already played earlier in the 1980s.

56. "Lee Teng-hui 8th ROC president," FCJ, vol. 7, no. 20 (March 26, 1990), 1; "Dissidents OK'd for conference," FCJ, vol. 7, no. 45 (June, 18, 1990), 1. Peng Ming-min, *A Taste of Freedom* (Boston: Houghton Mifflin, 1966).

57. "ROC conference begins," FCJ, vol. 7, no. 48 (June 28, 1990), 1.

58. Lin Ching-wen, "Big changes may be in the wind, FCJ, vol. 7, no. 48 (June 28, 1990), 5. Gabriel Fok, "If 'Ideas Are Events,' NAC was certainly eventful," FCJ, vol. 7, no. 50 (July 5, 1990), 1.

59. "President beats drums for NAC," FCJ, vol. 7, no. 70, (September 13, 1990), 1.

60. "Time 'not ripe' for unification talks says Shaw," FCJ, vol. 7, no. 80 (October 18, 1990), 1.

61. "Poll favors talk against independence," FCJ, vol. 7, no. 80 (October 18, 1990), 1.

62. "No wisdom found in independence talk," FCJ, vol. 7, no. 83 (October 29, 1990), 1.

63. "Government won't tolerate independence moves," FCJ, vol. 7, no. 89 (November 19, 1990), 1.

64. "Gulf crisis won't interfere with president reform pledge," FCJ, vol. 8, no. 9 (January 31, 1991), 1.

65. Ibid.

66. "Kuomintang reaches consensus: ROC constitution in two stages; New assembly to make final changes next year," FCJ, vol. 8, no. 10 (February 4, 1991), 1. "President hails KMT's decision as 'new and definite direction': Lee seeks support of national assembly for reform package to pave the way for new decade of development," FCJ, vol. 8, no. 24, (April 1, 1991), 1.

67. "Extraordinary session of first ROC assembly told of historic task," FCJ, vol. 8, no. 26, (April 1, 1991), 1.

68. "National assembly gets 'well done' for constitutional amendments work," FCJ, vol. 8, no. 31, (April 29, 1991), 1.

69. "Sedition law revised," FCJ, vol. 8, no. 29, (April 22, 1991), 1–2.

70. "ROC election law revised," FCJ, vol. 8, no. 55 (July 19, 1991), 1.

71. "Government cracking down on illegal separatist activities," FCJ, vol. 8, no. 69, (September 6, 1991), 1–2. "Defense proposes Garrison command end police duties," FCJ, vol. 8, no. 69, (September 6, 1991), 2. "Businessmen asked not to back independence movement," FCJ, vol. 8, no. 70, (September 6, 1991), 1.

72."Sedition law studied," FCJ, vol. 8, no. 77, (October 4, 1991), 1.

73. "Majority party out to stay majority in assembly race," FCJ, vol. 8, no. 77, (October 4, 1991), 2.

74. " 'Republic of Taiwan' advocated by DPP," FCJ, vol. 8, no. 79, (October 15, 1991), 2.

75. "ROC voters give KMT whopping mandate, FCJ, vol. 8, no. 98, (December 24, 1991), 1–2. See also DPP's independence platform bombs; "wrong move admitted," FCJ, vol. 8, no. 98, (December 24, 1991), 2.

76. "DPP members clash with MPs in Taipei protest," FCJ, vol. 9, no. 27 (April 21, 1992), 1. "DPP rioters plague the city," FCJ, vol. 9, no. 28 (April 24, 1992), 1.

77. "Ruling party's amendments condensed to 9," FCJ, vol. 9, no. 28 (April 24, 1992), 1.

78. "Lee bemoans the shadow of sadness," FCJ, vol. 9, no. 13 (February 28, 1992), 1. "Legislators want more 2–28 balm," FCJ, vol. 9, no. 314 (March 3, 1992), 2.

79. The report contained sensitive, hitherto classified facts about just what had happened. The report itself was a massive document of 430 pages and 400,000 characters, and there was an appendix of 600,000 characters, all produced by a research task force attached to Academia Sinica.

80. "Law says National Police outrank GHQ," FCJ, vol. 9, no. 51 (July 17, 1992), 1.

81. "December 19 proposed as election date to seat the new legislature by island-wide ballot" FCJ, vol. 9, no. 40 (June 5, 1992) 1. "KMT hopefuls throw hats into ring," FCJ, vol. 9, no. 51 (July 17, 1992), 2.

82. "DPP changing focus for legislative race," FCJ, vol. 9, no. 54 (July 28, 1992), 1.

83. "Election bulletin officially posted—just two months to go," FCJ, vol. 9, no. 78 (October 23, 1992), 2.

84. "KMT, DPP election platforms finalized," *FCJ,* vol. 9, no. 77 (October 20, 1992), 2.

85. "Elections registration complete: 406 candidates for 161 seats," FCJ, vol. 9, no. 87 (November 24 1992), 2. "Democracy taking shape: Wild-card candidates add uncertainty to election," FCJ vol. 9, no. 87 (November 24, 1992) 6. "Candidates must toe one China line," *FCJ,* vol. 9, no. 88 (November 27, 1992), 2.

86. "Candidates try out latest election gimmicks to win," FCJ, vol. 9, no. 88 (November 27, 1992), 6.

87. "KMT, DPP accentuate the negative," FCJ, vol. 9, no. 93 (December 15, 1992), 1.

88. "Voters enticed through their stomachs," FCJ, vol. 9, no. 93 (December 15, 1992), 2.

89. "Political relations making headway in Taiwan," FCJ, vol. 9, no. 91 (December 8, 1992), 8.

90. "President Lee delivers historic address," FCJ, vol. 10, no. 2 (January 8, 1993), 2.

91. "Lee, Hau agree to dissolve cabinet," FCJ, vol. 10, no. 6 (January 21, 1993), 2. A few days later, Hau sent his formal letter to the president. He did not spell out a date, leaving approval of his decision to the party's Central Committee."Hau Pei-tsun to submit resignation," FCJ, vol.10, no. 8 (February 2, 1993), 1. "Premier, cabinet submit resignations, FCJ, vol. 10, no. 9 (February 5, 1993), 1.

92. "Legislative power grab stalled," FCJ, vol. 10, 8 (February 2, 1993), 2.

93. Susan Yu, "Lee seeks counselors' opinions," FCJ, vol. 10, no. 10 (February 9, 1993), 2.

94. "Lee picks Lien Chan for premier," FCJ, vol. 10, no. 11 (February 12, 1993), 1. "Politicians, public rally behind Lien," FCJ, vol. 10, no. 11 (February 12, 1993), 1.

95. "Lee calls for fair, healthy, inter-party competition," FCJ, vol. 10, no. 11 (February 12, 1993), 2 "DPP mobilizes to defeat Lien," FCJ, vol. 10, no. 12 (February 16, 1993), 2. "Premier nominee has the right answers," FCJ, vol. 10, no. 14 (February 23, 1993), 1. "Legislature confirms Lien Chan as next premier," FCJ, vol. 10, no. 15 (February 26, 1993), 1.

96. "Legislature takes on trade dispute," FCJ, vol. 10, no. 18 (March 18, 1993). "Bill aimed at divesting KMT form business empire," FCJ, vol. 10, no. 19 (March 12, 1993), 2.

97. "Sunshine act marches steadily through the legislative process," FCJ, vol. 10, no. 25 (April 9, 1993), 2. "Sunshine law hits a rocky patch," FCJ, vol. 10, no. 27 (April 16, 1993), 2. "Sunshine law breezes through in second reading," FCJ, vol. 10, no. 43 (June 11, 1993), 1. "Assets are listed for top officials," FCJ, vol. 10, no. 62 (October 15, 1993), 2.

98. "Legislature clears NSC, NSB," FCJ, vol. 10, no. 27 (April 16, 1993), 1–2. "New KMT alliance makes waves," FCJ, vol. 10, no. 18 (March 9, 1993).

99. "Hsu Shu-teh KMT Secretary-General) FCJ, vol. 10, no. 19 (March 12, 1993), 1. "James Soong approved as 14th governor," FCJ, vol. 10, no. 21) March 19, 1993), 1.

100. "DPP wants a say in mainland policy," FCJ, vol. 10, no. 21 (March 19, 1993), 2. "DPP against Koo-Wang talks," FCJ, vol. 10, no. 24 (April 2, 1993), 2.

101. President Lee, for example, had the opportunity to give an interview to Lew Dobbs of CNN."Mutual trust first step," FCJ, vol. 10, no. 24 (April 2, 1993), 1. "KMT expands, diversifies delegates," FCJ, vol. X # 37 (May 21, 1993) 2. "KMT congress to vote on charter," FCJ, vol. 10, no. 48 (June 24, 1993), 2.

102. "Alliance says it breaks with KMT to aid reform," FCJ, vol. 10, no. 52 (August 6, 1993), 2. "KMT faction forms new party FCJ, vol. 10, no. 53 (August 13, 1993), 2.

103. "Cabinet espouses rules for disclosure of assets," FCJ, vol. 10, no. 55 (August 27, 1993), 2.

104. "Campaigns readied for Nov. 27 vote," FCJ, vol. 10, no. 64 (October 29, 1993), 1.

105. "KMT captures 15 of 23 posts in three way election," FCJ, vol. 10, no. 69 (December 3, 1993), 1.

106. "Legislature to go on reviewing bills in spite of claim they had passed earlier," FCJ, vol. 10, no. 1 (January 7, 1994), 2. "Defense Ministry seeking ways to halt arms-purchase scandals," FCJ, vol. 11, no. 1 (January 7, 1994), 2. "12 under arrest in case linked to captain's death," FCJ, vol. 11, no. 4 (January 1994), 2. "Naval officers step down in scandal," FCJ, vol. 11, no. 15 (April 22, 1994), 2. "Full inquiry pledged into election charges," FCJ, vol. 11, no. 9 (March 11, 1994), 1.

107. "KMT bolsters control of lawmakers' agenda," FCJ, vol. 11, no. 8 (March 4, 1994), 1.

108. "Budget stalled by debate over funding through sale of bonds," FCJ, vol. 1, no. 14 (April 15, 1994), 2."Lawmakers whittle budget 3.3% from present year's," FCJ, vol. 11, no. 21 (June 3, 1994), 2.

109. "KMT panel proposes direct election, other amendments," FCJ, vol. 11, no. 15 (April 22, 1994), 2.

110. "Constitutional reforms pass, including direct presidential vote," FCJ, vol. 11, no. 30 (August 5, 1994), 2.

111. "Law targets vote-rigging, illegal campaign donations," FCJ, vol. 11, no. 28 (July 22, 1994), 1.

112. "Villages oppose nuclear plant but construction to continue," FCJ, vol. 11, no. 20 (May 27, 1994), 2.

113. "Nuclear-plant budget advances despite demonstrations," FCJ, vol. 11, no. 25 (July 8, 1994), 2.

114. "Voluntary health care plan passes, but drive is on to revise it," FCJ, vol. 11, no. 28 (July 22, 1994), 1.

115. "New Party completes its nominations," FCJ, vol. 11, no. 33 (August 26, 1994), 2.

116. "Assembly approves new Judicial Yuan chief as DPP boycotts vote," FCJ, vol. 11, no. 33 (August 26, 1994), 1.

117. Lin and his wife, as noted earlier in this chapter were the victims of a tragic and still unsolved crime of violence—their twin daughters and Mrs. Lin's mother had been killed in the family apartment during the spring of 1980 as the trials of the Meili Tao defendants was taking place. "Assembly approves 16 grand justices," FCJ, vol. 11, no. 35 (September 9, 1994), 2.

118. "Lien cautions Peking as legislature opens," FCJ, vol. 11, no. 35 (September 9, 1994), 1.

119. Television campaign debates OKed," FCJ, vol. 11, no. 36 (September 36, 1994), 2. "Three Taipei mayoral rivals in live TV debate," FCJ, vol. 11, no. 39 (October 7, 1994), 2.

120."Legislature acts to protect lawmakers from recall movements," FCJ, vol. 11, no. 40 (October 14, 1994), 2. The introduction of the bills was the first step. "Legislature makes it hard for recall of elected officials," FCJ, vol. 11, no. 42 (October 28, 1994), 2.

121. "As election nears blemishes pop up," FCJ, vol. 11, no. 41 (October 21, 1994), 2. See also Confidendence-rattling stock scandal fuels thorough investigation," FCJ, vol. 11, no. 40 (October 14, 1994), 3.

122. "Race for Taiwan provincial governor gets under way," FCJ, vol. 11, no. 44 (November 11, 1994), 1.

123. Extensive and detailed articles on the election of December 3, 1994 were published in what amounted to a special-pre-election issue of the FCJ. This issue, vol. 11, no. 46 came out on November 25, 1994.

124. "Election campaign gets new look," FCJ, vol. 11, no. 45 (November 18, 1994), 2.

125. "KMT takes two top seats; DPP wins in Taipei," FCJ, vol. 11, no. 48 (December 9, 1994), 1.

126. "ROC reshuffles 12 high government posts," FCJ, vol. 11, no. 49 (December 16, 1994), 1.

127. Fredrick Chien, "A View From Taipei," in Jason Hu, *Quiet Revolutions on Taiwan, Republic of China,* 283–296.

128. A basic book on the subject is Frederick F. Chien (Daniel A Mica and J. Terry Anderson, eds.), *Opportunity and Challenge* (Tempe: Arizona State University, 1995); Bernard T.K. Joi, "Pragmatic Diplomacy in the Republic of China: History and Prospects," in Hu, *Quiet Revolutions on Taiwan, Republic of China,* 297–330. On the role of foreign aid in this policy of pragmatic diplomacy, see Lee Wei-chin, ROC's Foreign Aid Policy, in Hu, *Quiet Revolutions on Taiwan, Republic of China,* 331–360.

129. Some sense of the extensive nature of the ROC effort can be found by reading these articles on Latin America and the ROC in FCJ.

130. "Liberia, ROC together again,"FCJ, vol. 6, no. 76 (October 7, 1989), 1. "World's youngest king in ROC," FCJ, vol. 6, no. 82 (1989), 1. De Klerk Tells Chien Taiwan visit planned," FCJ, vol. 8, no. 9 (January 31, 1991), 1.

131. "CAR establishes new relations with ROC," FCJ, vol. 8, no. 53 (July 12, 1991). "Niger rejoins ROC fold," FCJ, vol. 9, no. 44 (June 23, 1992), 1. "Niger gives ROC the official nod," FCJ, vol. 9, no. 54 (July 28, 1992), 1.

132. "Mandela pledges friendly relations with ROC," FCJ,, no. 53 (August 6, 1993), 1.

133. "Poland, Bulgaria send officials to ROC meeting," FCJ, vol. 7, no. 66 (August 30, 1990), 1.

134. This was the first such audience Mrs. Chiang had given and demonstrated here willingness to play a part in the development of this new ROC Belarus relationship. FCJ, vol. 9, no. 42 (June 16, 1992), 1.

135. "Russia and the ROC sign agreement," *FCJ,* vol. 9, no. 67 (September 11, 1992), 1.

136. FCJ, vol. 9, no. 93 (December 15, 1992), 2.

137. "Tartarstan comes calling to improve trade relations," FCJ, vol. 10, no. 9 (February 5, 1993), 2.

138. Gorbachov lauds ROC, while noting key mainland role," FCJ, vol. 9, no. 11 (March 25, 1994), 1. "Trade links with Russia on steady climb upward," FCJ, vol. 9, no. 11 (March 25, 1994), 3.

139. "Austrian smiles," FCJ, vol. 8, no. 45 (June 14, 1991).

140. "French minister's visit lauded," FCJ, vol. 8, no. 3 (January 10, 1991), 1. Ibid., vol. 9, no. 6 (January 28, 1992), 1.

141. "German PM strengthens cooperation," FCJ, vol. 10, no. 9 (February 5, 1993), 2. "Taipei, London forge links; Germany next?," FCJ, vol. 10, no. 9 (February 5, 1993), 2.

142. "Saudi Day Feted Relations Solid," FCJ, vol. 6, no. 75 (October 2, 1989), 1. "Chien offers to 'bite the bullet,' " *FCJ,* vol. 7, no. 56 (July 26, 1990), 1.

143. "Taipei-Tel Aviv relations unaltered by Peking pact," FCJ, vol. 9, no. 6 (January 20, 1992), 1. "ROC, Israel exchange representative offices," FCJ, vol. 9, no. 85 (November 17, 1992), 1.

144. "Lee man of the hour by any name," FCJ, vol. 6, no. 17 (March 13, 1989), 1; "Malaysia opens tourist bureau," FCJ, vol. 6, no. 33 (May 8, 1989), 3; "Philippines inks

pact with ROC," FCJ, vol. 8, no. 52 (July 9, 1991), 2; "Aquino's executive order changes rules," FCJ, vol. 8, no. 61 (August 9, 1991), 1; "President Ramos signs new Subic deal," FCJ, vol. 9, no. 59 (August 14, 1992), 1.

145. Such zones would house Taiwan-financed companies that produced textiles, electronic home appliances, electronics, and processed food products. Chen saw the potential of Vietnam and thus this trip was a necessary first step. "Vietnam scouted as site for firms to set up export processing zones," FCJ, vol. 8, no. 71 (September 13, 1991), 3. "Vietnam offices pact to boost ties," FCJ, vol. 9, no. 47 (July 2, 1992), 1. Questions arose concerning flag carriers and this had halted air service but these issues were settled by August of 1992. See Taiwan, Vietnam air service resuming," FCJ, vol. 9, no. 57 (August 7, 1992), 1.

146. Vietnam, ROC to sign investment agreement," FCJ, vol. 10, no. 12 (February 16, 1993), 2. Now US money would join the mix but with the ROC continuing to lead the way. The ROC was also involving itself in joint-ventures with the government of Vietnam. How sizable the ROC stake had become was explored in a feature article in FCJ in February of 1994. Deborah Shen, "Opportunity blooms in Vietnam," FCJ, vol. 9, no. 6 (February 18, 1994), 3. "Vietnam to sign business pacts: Path cleared for more ROC trade, investment," FCJ, vol. 11, no. 13 (April 9, 1994), 3.

147. "High-ranking ROC official invited to Australia; may ink new agreement," FCJ, vol. 8, no. 57 (July 26, 1991), 1.

148. "Japan militancy over ROC isle sparks outrage," FCJ, vol. 7, no. 82 (October 25, 1990), 1. "Tiaoyutai tensions easing," FCJ, vol. 7, no. 83 (October 29, 1990), 1. "Japan plans to escalate imports," FCJ, vol. 9, no. 47 (July 2, 1992), 1.

149. "Lee invited to attend Asian games but Japan weighs protest by Peking," FCJ, vol. 11, no. 33 (August 26, 1994), 1. "Lee accepts Asian games invitation," FCJ, vol. 11, no. 35 (September 9, 1994), 1. "ROC vice premier, at Asian games backs continued mainland exchange," FCJ, vol. 11, no. 39 (October 7, 1994), 1.

150. "ROC ends ties with dishonest Korea," FCJ, vol. 9, no. 63 (August 28, 1992), 1. See also Seoul extends olive branch; wants talks, FCJ, vol. 9, no. 62 (August 25, 1992), 1. "ROC, South Korea make a good start reestablishing ties," FCJ, vol. 9, no. 59 (July 23, 1993), 1.

151. Murray A. Rubinstein, "Taipei, New York, and the ROC's UN Reentry Campaign," in *American ASIAN REVIEW* 1996.

152. This process can be tracked by examining the runs of FCJ for the years from 1991 to 1994, when the crucial negotiations concerning GATT and concerning Taiwan's role in APEC were taking place.

153. FCJ is a basic source of information on this issue. GIO publications on the UN are also quite extensive and are of value to those who study the UN issue. Proceedings and articles from conferences such as those held at St. Johns University in the 1990s and that held by the DPP in Manhattan in 1994 are other useful sources of information on the UN reentry issue.

154. On cross-the-strait relations see Hsin-hsing Wu, *Bridging the Strait: Taiwan, China, and the Prospects for Reunification* (Hong Kong: Oxford University Press, 1994). See also Tun-jen Cheng, Chi Huang, and Samuel S.G. Wu, eds., *Inherited Rivalry: Conflict Across the Taiwan Straits* (Boulder, CO: Lynne Rienner, 1995); Chang Jih-cheng *Tai-wan, Chung-kuo yu Shi-jieh (Taiwan, China, and the World)* (Taipei, 1990). This would also mark the start of new levels of interaction and cooperation between the ruling committees of temples on Taiwan and temples in the PRC. Funds from these temples would pour in as Taiwanese believers contributed to the rebuilding of temples on various holy sites such those in on Meichou island, and in towns and cities such as Kang-li, Ch'uan-chou, and Hai-tsang. See Murray A. Rubinstein, "The Revival of the Mazu Cult and Taiwanese Pilgrimage to Fujian," Taiwan

Studies Workship (Cambridge, MA: Fairbank Center Working Papers, 1994) and Murray A. Rubinstein, "Cross-the-Strait Pilgrimage and the Reinvention of the Taiwan/Fujian Religious Matrix" (mss. Leiden: Conference on 19th and 20th Century Fujian and Taiwan, July 5–8, 1995). "Taiwan-Mainland Door 'Will Never Be Shut," FCJ, vol. 8, no. 81 (October 22, 1990), 1.

155. "Agency Could Open Door: Official Mainland Contact Possible With Friendly Communist Response," FCJ, vol. 7, no. 90 (November 22, 1990), 1.

156. By 1995 one could find Taiwanese who represented either Taiwan-based or U.S./Taiwan-based shoe manufacturers spending part of each year in Put'ien. A trade organization to help these Taiwanese and foreign investors was located in the city and the major hotels could count on these manufacturers representatives to fill a good number of their rooms on a long-term basis. As a result Put'ien became a boom town. These comments are based upon my observations and discussions in Put'ien in 1992 and again in 1995. In my visits to Fukien in 1990, 1992, and 1995 I met many Taiwanese businessmen. Some were involved in trade while others were involved in setting up joint ventures or were looking for Fukien-based factories to manufacture a their products. What brought them to Fukien was their sense of a common language, a common tradition, and a common culture. What also brought them was the existence of a cheap workforce and an area with few, if any environmental protection laws.

157. "Nothing new in Communist party-to-party talk proposal: Timetable, one country-two systems formula unacceptable; Shaw says reunification should be evolutionary," FCJ, vol. 7, no. 97 (December 17, 1990), 1. "Mainland affairs council rules get president's vote," Gulf crisis won't interfere with president's reform pledge," FCJ, vol. 8, no. 9 (January 31, 1991), 1. "Roc Approves indirect mainland joint venture, Gulf crisis won't interfere with president's reform pledge," FCJ, vol. 8, no. 9 (January 31, 1991), 1.

158. "Straits foundation plans courtesy call," FCJ, vol. 8, no. 19 (March 14, 1991), 1. "Three ROC police officers abducted by mushroom marauders on high seas," FCJ, vol. 8, no. 19 (March 14, 1991), 1. April 28, 1991, in "Chronology," Cheng, Huang, and Wu, eds. *Inherited Rivalry: Conflict Across the Taiwan Straits* (Boulder, CO: Lynne Rienner, 1995), 247.

159. "Negotiations with mainland get underway to get abducted ROC officers nack," FCJ, vol. 8, no. 20 (March 18, 1991), 1. "Abducted policemen safely home," FCJ, vol. 8, no. 26, (April 11, 1991), 1. April 3, 1991, in "Chronology," Cheng, Huang, and Wu, eds., *Inherited Rivalry: Conflict Across the Taiwan Straits,* 247.

160. "Foreign ship, 6 mainland officers held in Taiwan," FCJ, vol. 8, no. 46 (June 19, 1991), 1. See also "Cargo ship detained; prosecutors get case," FCJ, vol. 8, no. 47 (June 21, 1991), 1, and the account for June 13 and 18, "Chronology," Cheng, Huang, and Wu, eds., 247. "Time not right for direct trade," FCJ, vol. 8, no. 51 (July 5, 1991), 2.

161. "SEF delegates on second visit to mainland China," FCJ, vol. 7, no. 52 (July 5, 1991), 2. "SEF reports dialogue problem," FCJ, vol. 7, no. 53 (July 12, 1991), 2. July 5 "Chronology," Cheng, Huang, and Wu, eds., 247.

162. "July 21–22 Chronology," Cheng, Huang, and Wu, eds., 249. For a more detailed account see "ROC prosecutor charges mainlanders with piracy," FCJ, vol. 8, no. 59 (August 2, 1991), 1 and "SEF chief spurs Chinese Communists to cooperate," FCJ, vol. 8, no. 74(September 25, 1991), 2.

163. MAC wants door opened for Taiwan ARATS office, *FCJ,* vol. 9, no. 1, January 7, 1992), 2; January 6, 1992 "Chronology," Cheng, Chi, and Wu, eds., 252. "Taiwan welcoming stranded home," FCJ, vol. 9, no. 7, January 31, 1992), 2. "Law covers mainland's work force," FCJ, vol. 9, no. 7, January 31, 1992), 2.

164. "Cultural and educational mainland visits expanded," FCJ, vol. 9, no. 14 (March 3, 1992), 2. "Students to mainland," FCJ, vol. 9, no. 38 (May 29, 1992), 2.

165. "Taiwan firms to pursue own guarantees in mainland," FCJ, vol. 9, no. 37 (May 26, 1992), 2. "Bank services wanted on mainland," FCJ, vol. 9, no. 39 (June 2, 1992), 3. "SEF prospecting for mainland business ventures," FCJ, vol. 9, no. 42 (June 16, 1992), 1. "Taiwan mainland investments good," FCJ, vol. 9, no. 43 (June 23, 1992), 2.

166. September 18, 1992, "Chronology," Cheng, Chi, and Wu, eds., 253. See also "Hau wants mainland policy expedited," FCJ, vol. 9, no. 69 (September 22, 1992), 1, and "Mainland Affairs Conference spurs exchanges," FCJ, vol. 9, no. 69 (September 22, 1992), 1. And as if to highlight the possibilities of such exchanges, just that week before the conference 18 mainland newsmen had come to Taiwan for a 7–day visit. The MAC idea of news coverage and distribution of news media on both side of the Taiwan Strait was boosted by this visit. September 5, 1992, "Chronology," Cheng, Chi, and Wu, eds., 253.

167. "SEF and ARATs heads plan to meet," FCJ, vol. 10, no. 18 (March 9, 1993), 2.

168. Cross-Straits Koo-Wang talks begin," FCJ, vol. 10, no. 30 (April 27, 1993), 1.

169. April 27–29, 1993, "Chronology," Cheng, Chi, and Wu, eds., 256. See also "Historic meeting produces 4 agreements," FCJ, vol. 10, no. 31 (April 30 1993), 1.

170. "Cross-Straits agencies set high-level session," FCJ, vol. 11, no. 1 (January 7, 1994), 2.

171. "More mainland investment areas," FCJ, vol. 11, no. 4 (January 28, 1994), 3.

172. "Peking's investment law 'vague,' " FCJ, vol. 11, no. 10 (March 18, 1994), 3.

173. "ROC assails mainland China over boat tragedy," FCJ, vol. 11, no. 14 (April 15, 1994), 1. "ROC presses Peking for details of Qingdao Lake tourist deaths," FCJ, vol. 11, no. 15 (April 22, 1994), 1–2.

174. "Taiwan reopens door to mainland exchange," FCJ, vol. 11, no. 29 (July 29, 1994).

175. "Talks break deadlock on hijacking, other issues," FCJ, vol. 11, (August 12, 1994), 1.

176. "Mainland eyed as frontier," FCJ, vol. 11, no. 36 (September 16, 1994), 1. "ROC drawing up blueprint for direct transit to mainland," FCJ, vol. 11, no. 43 (November 4, 1994), 1. "ROC rejects Taiwan-mainland summit in private setting," FCJ, vol. 9, no. 45 (September 12, 1994), 1.

177. "New cross-Straits talks proposed to set the stage for top-level exchange, FCJ, vol. 11, no. 50 (December 23 1994), 1.

Postscript and Conclusion

Murray A. Rubinstein

This concluding chapter examines the year and a half from January 1995 to June 1996, a period in which the president of Taiwan (or Republic of China—ROC) entered the world stage in a dramatic way and the People's Republic of China tried without success to change the direction of Taiwan's political evolution with two very public shows of military force.

The Prelude: January to Late April 1995

The pattern of events that took place in the winter and early spring 1995 foreshadowed the tensions that would evolve from late spring 1995 to late spring 1996. The elections for the Legislative Yuan and the proposed presidential elections were recognized as the major event on the national calendar for 1995 and 1996. However, details had to be resolved and laws enacted before the presidential elections could take place.

The bill regulating the elections was drafted by the Interior Ministry and subsequently introduced to the Legislative Yuan. It came under immediate criticism for what the Democratic Progressive Party (DPP) called the Shih Ming-teh provision, which stipulated the educational level and the occupations for those eligible to run for president. The requirements were very specific—four years of college, and experience as a middle-ranking civil servant, a professor in a junior college, or an official with a private company. Shih, the head of the DPP, had only attended a military academy and had spent most of the next twenty-odd years as a political prisoner. He was therefore ineligible for the presidency, powerful and popular as he may have been at that time. Other provisions limited the number of high-level party members in the major political parties who could run. The target in this case was Lin Yang-kang of the Kuomintang (KMT), who was considering running against Lee Teng-hui. The elite of the ruling KMT had thrown down the gauntlet forcing weeks of negotiations for a mutually accept-able bill.[1]

In late February, a second important event took place: the raising of a monu-ment to the victims of the February 28 incident. This ceremony served as a form of closure, as it prepared the way for the introduction of two dominant subtexts in the presidential election—the role of ethnicity and President Lee's use of the ethnic card, and his identification with the Han-Taiwanese/Han-Hakka majority. The memorial was raised in Taipei's New Park, where a hundred family mem-bers of victims were assembled. They carried yellow roses as they received a formal apology from the KMT leader and ROC president. Lee also suggested that more had to be done to reconcile the two sides—*pen-ti jen* and *wai-sheng jen*—but that the results of a formal scholarly investigation and the monument, as well as compensation for the victims, represented a start. Lee was carefully identifying himself with the KMT, albeit as a *pen-ti jen*, and thus standing between a possible *wai-sheng jen* New Party or mainlander KMT candidate and a possible DPP candidate who advocated Taiwanese independence.[2]

The third significant set of events during this period demonstrated that the two elections being planned were affecting the evolving relationship between the ROC and the People's Republic of China (PRC). Early in the year both sides were discussing the talks planned for 1995, and the ROC cross-strait officials were hopeful that the previous years' progress could be built upon. However, by April it had become clear that ARATS officials were determined to reneg on their decision to sign certain agreements that had been negotiated earlier. Their negoti-ating partners, the ROC officials who represented the CSF disagreed with a new and simplified agenda introduced by the ARATS officials. Talks stalled as each side hardened its position.

Some optimism still remained in late May, as discussions were held in Taipei that raised the possibility of a new round of talks between Koo Chen-fu and Wang Daohan. A date in mid-July was set.[3]

Taiwan, China, and the World in Thirteen Event-Filled Months, May 1995–June 1996

The pace of developments accelerate in the late spring of 1995 and would con-tinue to accelerate until reaching crisis stage early in the spring of 1996. This period started with a singular and most dramatic event—President Lee Teng-hui's visit to the United States and to his alma mater, Cornell University. Lee had been invited to attend the twenty-fifth reunion of his graduating class and was celebrating the granting of his Ph.D. Under considerable pressure from friends of the ROC in both houses of Congress, the U.S. State Department granted him a visa, as a private citizen and not as the head of a friendly state—the United States, of course, did not recognize Taiwan formally. Lee assumed as best he could the role of a private citizen and flew to Los Angeles on June 7. However, as soon as he landed it became clear that, whatever the details of his visa, local officials and members of the overseas Taiwanese community in the United States would not pretend to see him as just another Taiwan/ROC national in the United States on a private visit, nor did many members of Congress. As he landed, he was greeted by government officials in a formal red-carpet ceremony. Natale Bellochi, the head of the American Institute on Taiwan, greeted him as did Benjamin Lu, head of the ROC representative office in the United States. Lee then met a number of government figures from California such as California State Treasurer Mah Fong and State Secretary of Trade and Commerce Julie Wright. The arrival was also heavily covered by the press, as had the discussion over the granting of his visa, and thus the ROC's president made the noon-time news.[4]

He spent the night in Los Angeles, and the next day flew to Syracuse, New York. Here he was again greeted by influential American political leaders, including Jesse Helms, the chair of the Senate Foreign Relations Committee, Alphonse D'Amato, the often outspoken and colorful junior senator from New York, Frank Murkowski, the senator from Alaska, and key members of Congress such as Gary Ackerman from Queens, New York, and a strong supporter of the ROC cause. The mayor of Syracuse, Roy Bernardi, and the president of Cornell, Frank Rhodes, were also there to greet "private citizen" Lee. President Lee took a limousine to Ithaca, where he had spent years as a student of agricultural economics during the late 1960s and early 1970s.

The formal ceremonies that were the reason for his visit were held the day after his arrival on campus. He gave a forty-minute speech called "Always in My Heart," which was widely reported by the print and broadcast media for an American and worldwide audience, especially in Taiwan. Lee's carefully drafted speech dealt with both the Taiwanese "miracle," and his own years at Cornell, and his accomplishments in the years after his graduation. The speech was well received by observers and followers; it demonstrated how effectively Lee—now a consummate politician—was making use of this moment on the world stage.[5]

This trip, and all that it entailed, was seen as significant by observers and officials in the United States, the PRC, and Taiwan. Lee and the officials of the Government Information Office who were based in the United States took maximum advantage of the spotlight cast upon the U.S.-trained agrarian economist who had become the highest official in Taiwan.

The PRC Reaction and the Preliminary Stages of the Presidential Race

The PRC officials were not happy with the publicity President Lee had generated, and began giving their own opinion on Lee and his various policies and positions. Their statements foreshadowed the policies they would follow in the summer and fall of 1995. As they saw it, Lee was assuming a strongly Taiwan-centered and slightly veiled position favoring Taiwan independence. The subtext of Taiwan independence, they believed, lay behind all that he did during the presidential campaign as he and the candidates defined their platforms.[6]

The PRC did more than complain: It decided to teach Taiwan a lesson by holding a series of missile tests in a range located on the Fukien coast and extending into the South China Sea over six days beginning on July 21. The target zone was located about 170 kilometers north of Taiwan itself.

The PRC leadership hoped that the islanders would lose faith in their government and in the focus of the PRC media barrage, Lee himself. However, polls taken during this period showed that he retained his popularity and that people maintained their confidence in his government.[7]

During August and September, presidential politics took center stage as candidates began to enter the race. The front-runner was Lee, but he soon had competition. Before Lee could announce his candidacy formally, on August 17 Chen Li-an, the president of the Control Yuan, announced that he was going to run, thereby forcing Lee's hand. On August 23 he made his announcement at the KMT's party congress.[8]

Lee's actions, in turn, forced the hand of Lin Yang-kang, who declared that he too would oppose President Lee. The KMT now had three candidates and the distinct possibility of a primary. The party's nonmainstream faction wanted a primary in which all KMT members chose the candidate. However, Lee saw the dangers of such an open and public primary and directed the party members faithful to him to support a vote within the party congress itself. His faction won and defeated the motion to hold a primary. However, a more limited party leadership/party congress primary was scheduled for early September.[9] While this move was lauded at the time, some critics saw it as yet another example of what they viewed as Lee's imperial (i.e., nondemocratic) style.

The scaled-down primary was held on August 31 ,and Lee won 92 percent of the vote, as most expected he would. The next day, Premier Lien Chan was chosen as Lee's running mate. The mainstream faction had now fielded the first complete presidential ticket.[10] To reduce the tensions regarding the Taiwan strait, Lee called for both governments to try to resolve their differences by discussing the principles that he and Jiang Zemin had introduced earlier in the year.[11] But the die was cast: Until the drama of Taiwan's democratic elections for the Legislative Yuan and the presidency had been played out, tensions would remain, as would the potential for rash action by the PRC government.

The DPP had pursued another path in choosing its candidate, a long primary campaign. The three resulting candidates represented the spectrum of DPP factions from Mei-li-tao to New Tide: Hsu Hsin-liang, the lawyer and *tang-wai* activist Lin Yi-hsiung, and the famous expatriate activist only recently returned to the island P'eng Ming-min. The fierce campaign was followed by an initial primary vote. The two candidates who received the highest number of votes, Lin and P'eng, then faced each other in a dramatic runoff. Peng won the runoff and then chose Frank Hsieh as his running mate. The DPP had taken a dramatic step designed to show the populace which party was more democratic.[12]

Elections for the Legislative Yuan

By early October the presidential campaign, significant as it was, was overshadowed by the elections for the Legislative Yuan, set for December 2. There were now 164 legislators to be chosen. The new legislature was to have three more seats than the one elected in 1992. Everyone expected that this election would be more hotly contested than the previous one, as path-breaking as that one was, for there were now three major parties fielding candidates. The New Party was now well organized and ready to play its role in the more open Taiwanese political arena.[13]

The DPP announced a formal program and stated its key objectives. By doing so, it positioned itself not just for the presidential and legislative elections but for the National Assembly, which would be elected after the president was chosen. The theme of the DPP's campaign was "Give Taiwan a Chance," and its platform was based on five proposals covering national defense, national sovereignty, government, the economy, and national welfare. In the DPP platform institutional change served as a prelude to the forms of social change that the party had long been advocating.[14]

Multiple levels of campaigning took place from early October to early December. The presidential candidates used this time to campaign and to formally designate their running mates. Chen Li-an picked Wang Ching-feng, a feminist activist.[15] A few days later the KMT dissident Lin Yang-kang chose Chang Fang-shui, a member of the KMT Central Committee involved with the ROC's Olympic program.[16] However, this ticket did not last long. In November, Lin decided that Chang was not a visible enough or strong enough figure. He then dropped him in favor of the controversial and still-powerful Hau Pei-tsun.[17]

While the presidential campaign was proceeding, individuals running for the Legislative Yuan were working on their own local campaigns. Lee used his position as party leader and his visibility to stump for many local candidates. He believed his coattails were long enough to carry local KMT candidates. He also realized that a strong KMT showing in the Legislative Yuan elections would help his bid for the presidency. Lee was the only candidate who could benefit, however. P'eng did not have a strong local base and could not help individual candidates. History worked against the New Party presidential candidates: The New Party had picked KMT mainstays, who could do little to push local New Party Legislative Yuan candidates.[18]

By November 10 the rush to become a candidate had begun. More than four hundred individuals entered the race. Three hundred thirty four entered contests for the local seats while the remaining sixty-six competed for the thirty-six seats apportioned to the political parties based upon their share of the vote. One hundred twenty-three incumbents were running. Many of those who chose not to run were viewed as fat-cat candidates, beholden to corporate interests. The voting system reforms instituted in previous years had created a more open and democratic race.[19]

In mid-November the campaign heated up. This was demonstrated in the southwestern city of Chia-yi, where a strong KMT candidate faced off against equally attractive DPP and New Party candidates. The city came alive during this period with sound trucks driving through the streets, and thousands of posters put up, and with the candidates holding rallies that drew large crowds. In the opinion of Michael Joseph, a Western reporter writing for the *Free China Journal*, the city was a showcase of Taiwan's democratic transformation. Here competitive politics were the rule.[20]

In the opinion of observers, however, the electricity of the 1992 race was not matched, even at the peak of the campaign, even though the stakes were higher and a more democratic, multiparty legislature would result. One reason for this was the economic downturn the ROC suffered during 1995 (which would continue over the course of 1996). The economic problems led to a cutback in the type of lavish spending for banquets and rallies typical of previous years. A second reason for the lack of excitement was the government's effort to control the vote-buying so common in elections. Candidates now knew that they could be arrested, tried, sentenced, and fined for voting irregularities, as many had been the previous year. A final factor was the lack of big-name candidates with the funding and the visibility to put together lavish large-scale campaigns.[21]

Each of the major parties had distinct objectives and entered the campaign with certain advantages and disadvantages.

The KMT wanted to retain as large a majority as possible in the Legislative Yuan. Its candidates ran on a platform of stability in administration, stressing the party's role in creating the prosperous, modern Taiwan which the people now enjoyed. Over the years, it had created strong local organizations and could point to a well-disciplined and loyal membership, but it was vulnerable in certain important ways. Some observers saw the New Party, which had made inroads into its mainlander base in northern Taiwan, as pivotal in deciding the KMT's fate. The DPP declared itself the main proponent of Taiwanese-centered reform and good government, and thus stood to make gains at the KMT's expense.[22]

DPP leaders believed that their party was now ready to take the next step in becoming more than just the major opposition party. The party was defining itself as an innovator of social policy and had entered the realm of foreign and mainland policy. Its leaders knew that they were close to holding national power. The DPP platform addressed issues such as sovereignty in a way that voters would find practical and valid. It also introduced the idea of a "grand coalition," thus holding out the possibility that it would work with its rival, the New Party, in creating a governing coalition. The party did have weaknesses, however: It lacked a cohesive base-level organization, the kind of funding that the KMT had easy access to, and the efficient and sophisticated media exposure the KMT had been able to create.[23]

The New Party's leaders saw their party as the spoiler that would take enough votes from the KMT to force a coalition government upon Taiwan. It stood for reform and against the KMT establishment and its excesses. The party's leaders also saw their organization as one that represented *wai-sheng jen* and defended this hitherto-privileged minority. The New Party wanted a policy of reconciliation with the mainland, a position its candidates defended. Its weakness stemmed from the fact that many of its key leaders had been KMT members and were more conservative in their political stances than many of the candidates representing the other parties.[24]

The days immediately preceding the elections were tense. The PRC again demonstrated its power in the Taiwan strait as it had in mid-summer, holding large-scale military maneuvers near Tung-shan island off the Fukien coast. China's military, the People's Liberation Army (PLA), was testing its methods of amphibious warfare. The representatives of the major Taiwanese parties used the military maneuvers to their advantage, criticizing the PLA for attempting to influence the course of the legislative elections.[25] On the domestic front, the air was tension-filled as well. The major parties hammered away at each other in the press and sometimes on the streets of the major cities. There were, for example, violent clashes between DPP and New Party members in Kao-hsiung, where ten people were injured. The parties then attacked one another in the press, calling each other undisciplined and violent.[26]

Election day finally arrived, and when it was all over Taiwan's electoral politics had been changed. The headlines of the *Free China Journal* summed up the results of the election—"KMT holds edge, DPP grows, New Party surges." More than 9.5 million people had voted and in the end had handed the KMT what had to be seen as a Pyrrhic victory at best. The KMT had won 46.06 percent of the vote and some 85 of the 164 seats. This was a drop of nearly 7 percent from the 1992 elections and marked the first time the majority party had won less than 50 percent of the vote. However the party still held 85 seats. The DPP had won 33.17 percent of the vote and now had a total of forty-three seats in the Legislative Yuan. The New Party had won 12.95 percent of the vote and a total of twenty-one seats. What was more disturbing to KMT leaders was that the party had lost ground to the DPP and the New Party in the core of area of Taipei.[27]

Political analysts assessed the results in the days that followed. Chu Yun-han of Taiwan National University argued that the ROC had now switched from a two- to a three-party system and that the KMT, for all practical purposes, had lost its dominance in the Legislative Yuan. Chen Fang-ming, a professor at Providence University and a former DPP campaign manager, believed that the DPP had lost ground even though it had gained votes because it had not been able to win many of the votes lost by the KMT. A third analyst, Wang Yeh-li of Tung-hai University, thought that the New Party had made the most impressive gains, for it had shown that it had appeal beyond its core mainlander base.[28] The American University president-turned Taiwan political analyst James Robinson was given the final word. In a full-page *Free China Journal* story, he argued that when looked at as a whole, the election had done much to advance and strengthen democracy on the island.[29]

Party Conflicts and Inter-Party Coalitions as Precursor to the Formal Presidential Election Campaign

During the final weeks of 1995, the KMT realigned itself for the presidential race and for the race for the National Assembly. It purged rebel candidates from its ranks by revoking the memberships of Lin Yang-kang and Hau Pei-tsun, the men who made up a rival presidential ticket. This move was not as severe as it might have been, but sent a strong message to these men, party leaders who were outspoken in their criticism of Lee and his handling of KMT affairs. However, Lin and Hau responded in kind and denounced the move as illegal. They refused to curb their attacks. The KMT's high-level move proved to be the first of an ugly presidential campaign.[30] That Lee was able to convince his fellow party leaders to take this step against men who had been key parts of his government was an indication of how far the rift between Hau and Lee and Lin and Lee had widened and how KMT party politics had changed.

The conflicts within the KMT were only one of the problems the party faced. The opposition parties presented a second problem. By late December the oft-rumored coalition of the DPP and the New Party had become a reality. These seemingly antagonistic political entities shared a dislike (perhaps even hatred) of the KMT. The leaders of both parties decided to use their new-found strength to change the existing political system. Many observers argued that by simply creating the coalition and thus demonstrating Chu Yun-han's point, they had already done so. Yet the meeting that forged the alliance was a spontaneous affair held in the Legislative Yuan cafeteria. The two men worked out an agenda of social reform legislation they planned to pass in the Legislative Yuan. They also agreed to work together to decide on positions of leadership in the new legislative session.[31]

The coalition's creation was only the first step, but it proved effective from the very start. Some KMT legislators recognized the potential strength of the coalition and determined to negotiate with the alliance. The plan of one such KMT legislator, Kao Yu-jen, was to apportion the top posts among the three parties. He was putting into concrete terms the conciliatory message that KMT leaders had espoused since the elections, since the action taken against Lin and Hau, and since the DPP and New Party leaders had announced their initiatives.[32]

Politics took center stage during these months, but some observers recognized that the developments in the political realm diverted attention from problems that Taiwan faced, mainly its economy. By late 1995 there were signs that the economy was getting worse, and various indicators, such as unemployment figures, suggested that the nation was slipping into a recession. This became clear as the year ended, when economic indicators pointed to the decrease in the money supply and the fact that business activity had dropped to a five-year low. The *Free China Journal* headline summed up the problem: "Economy officially slips into recession territory." The PRC's reaction to the ongoing development of Taiwan's democratic system was creating conditions that hurt important segments of the economy and fostered an uncertainty that was mirrored in the economic markets. The PRC's aggressive military policy—its scheduling of military maneuvers near Taiwan at the time of the various primaries and elections—had and would continue to have a detrimental effect on the economy.[33] However, the indicators also suggested deep structural problems in the economy that had to be dealt with. Although economists were optimistic that the worst was over by early February, the declining economy would continue to be problematic in the following months.[34] The crisis with the mainland that accompanied the presidential election produced one such shock wave that helped to depress the economy. In late February the PRC held military maneuvers once again, creating an economic downturn and a sluggish stock market, despite government attempts to stabilize the economy with an injection of funds. By early March 1996 the market was down 27 percent from the previous year. Thus the late 1995 indicators had to be taken seriously, even with the occasional hopeful signs.[35]

An unexpected cultural problem arose as the new year dawned. The Palace Museum, working with curators from major American museums, had put together a traveling exhibition that included of 475 pieces from its collection. The ROC wanted to show the world that it was the repository of Chinese culture and that it was the China that respected and gloried in China's artistic past and protected its heritage. This exhibit was scheduled to tour the United States from March 12, 1996, to April 6, 1997. Of the 475 pieces, twenty-seven had been deemed national treasures and were considered extremely valuable and very fragile. Some citizens on Taiwan saw this exhibit as a dangerous step that would put these works at risk and began a series of protests, joined by legislators. As a result, Westerners got mixed signals about what the Taiwanese really thought about this step.[36]

Legislative Battles, Military Exercises, and the Presidential Race

By late January, politics and the upcoming presidential elections once again occupied center stage. Two of the candidates, Chen and Lin, obtained the 201,318 signatures needed to be placed on the ballot. There were now four slates of candidates in the race—two independents, Lin and Chen, the DPP candidate, Peng, and President Lee. Lee Teng-hui did not let these rivals steal the spotlight. On

January 24, he opened up his campaign headquarters with a rally attended by more than 10,000. The two KMT rebels had been campaigning down-island, as had Peng, and now Lee showed that he too was ready to take on the other candidates.[37]

PRC leaders were aware of the upcoming Taiwan elections and were determined to influence them in some way. They leaked the news that they were amassing troops in areas of China near Taiwan and were planning on threatening the island with some sort of military action. At this point, they had not yet formally announced that they again would conduct military maneuvers but, rather, let rumors about their intentions circulate as the four slates of candidates began campaigning in earnest on Taiwan.[38]

Before the presidential battles could begin, important battles had to be waged in the Legislative Yuan. The key struggle was for the speaker's post. The KMT nominated Liu Sung-pan while the DPP/New Party coalition nominated Shih Ming-teh, the chair of the DPP. The first vote ended in a dead heat, but four votes were subsequently declared invalid. On the second vote, Liu beat Shih by one vote. The KMT had survived its first major test. The defeated Shih had only seven years before been serving a lifetime sentence for his role in the Kao-hsiung incident of December 1979, was evidence of how far Taiwan had come on the road to democracy.[39]

Yet another battle had begun in the Legislative Yuan. President Lee nominated Lien Chan, his vice-presidential candidate, to serve as Premier and head of the interim cabinet. The opposition coalition opposed Lien, calling him ineffectual. This was only the start of a battle that would continue until the presidential elections took place.[40] A week later, the coalition formally announced that it would oppose Lien's nomination and, furthermore, would try to block the entire nomination process itself if Lien did not agree to appear in person before the legislature. The idea was simple: Make the vice-presidential candidate and heir-apparent look bad just before the presidential election. While the coalition had lost its bid for the speaker's post, it was showing that it did have power and could make use of it.[41]

The presidential campaign was moving forward. Representatives of the four slates drew lots to determine which position each would occupy on the ballot. The election commission also scheduled a series of debates, three for the presidential candidates and one for the vice-presidential candidates. Earlier in February, an initial debate had been held, attended by the three presidential challengers, but not by Lee. The debate allowed each of the candidates to define his own style in clear terms. A similar debate for the vice-presidential candidates was held in Taichung on February 11, and again the official KMT candidate, Lien Chan, did not attend. Viewers learned from the debate the candidates' basic positions and styles, and Hau appeared, to no one's surprise, the most conservative of the three. The missing man, Premier Lien, was the favorite target of all the candidates.[42]

At this time the military authorities in the PRC confirmed that war games were indeed being planned and that 150,00 troops had amassed along the section of the southeastern coast of the mainland that faced Taiwan. The maneuvers were to be combined efforts but would emphasize airborne training. When the reports of maneuvers were issued, other PRC officials attacked Taiwan for engaging in secessionist activity and described the democratic elections as evidence of attempts to further strengthen Taiwan as a "second China." Both ROC and U.S. officials saw these military training operations and the related announcements as blatant PRC attempts to affect the course of the approaching elections in Taiwan. The ROC officials called for calm, fearing that the announcements would soon drive the stock market into a tailspin, as had happened when the PRC had announced its earlier maneuvers.[43]

The PRC continued to mass its troops in the weeks that followed, as the candidates on Taiwan held rallies and engaged in televised debates. The crisis worked for the incumbent, for it was during this time that President Lee made well-publicized and carefully prepared appeals for calm and for keeping faith in the ROC government. At the same time, ROC military officials expressed their opinion that the maneuvers were just what they appeared to be, and not a prelude to an actual invasion of Taiwan.[44]

In order to demonstrate that everything was okay and that they would not be intimidated by the PRC's threats, all four presidential candidates presented their platforms to the nation in a televised forum marking the formal beginning of the campaign. The forum format was decidedly sedate compared to debates, but each candidate was given the chance to identify himself and his platform to the public. They also outlined their domestic and foreign policy intentions. P'eng Ming-min, the DPP candidate, pushed a domestic agenda that included cleaning up the environment while promoting technological development. He argued for independence of the island and urged cutting links with the mainland. Finally, he wanted a total accounting of the February 28 incident. Chen Li-an criticized P'eng and asked why he was running if he did not recognize the ROC as a political entity. He wanted to shelve any discussion of independence versus reunification because of the hostility the issue engendered on Taiwan and the mainland. On the domestic side, he wanted to clean up Taiwan—to make it once again *mei-li tao* (the beautiful island)—and thus transform it into an Asian Switzerland—an economic power broker as well as a tourist destination.

Lin Yang-kang called for moderation and wanted to maintain the status quo in the PRC–ROC relationship. He also wanted to end Taiwan's yearly campaign to reenter the United Nations. On the domestic front, he wanted to extend the terms of Legislative Yuan members from three to four years. He also wanted to revise the constitution to ensure presidential accountability and restore powers taken from the premier.

Lee Teng-hui then presented his proposed programs and policies. He listed his achievements, including promoting democratization, fostering the economic "miracle," ending cross-strait hostility, and expanding Taiwan's role in the international community. He promised to continue the push toward pragmatic diplomacy and toward the modernization of the economy and society. However, while information had been conveyed in the forum, there had been no direct exchange of views—heated or otherwise. Some analysts suggested that they and the public would have been happier with a real debate, "warts and all."[45]

As the campaign went into higher gear, the PRC kept applying pressure and escalated its efforts. A vice-presidential forum followed the format of the one the presidential candidates held. Each candidate was given the opportunity to present his and his running mate's position on the key issues. The vice-presidential candidates changed the tone of the proceedings and attacked both their rivals and the presidential candidates while presenting themselves in the best possible light. Hau Pei-tsun came off as the attack dog; many thought he was sharply criticizing President Lee and his policies. Lien Chan, however, attacked Hau, the man he had replaced as premier. Frank Hsieh, P'eng's running mate, attacked the KMT for controlling both the Lin/Hau and Lee/Lien ticket. Wang Ching-feng, Chen's running mate, was the only woman in the race. She made the case for her candidacy and for the role of women in the ROC's political process, using the forum to promote her cause and the cause of feminism on Taiwan.[46]

The PRC did not like Taiwan's prominence in world news and wanted to make its presence felt in a dramatic and forceful way. The PRC government announced it would hold missile tests in ranges with target zones situated near Taipei and Kao-hsiung, Taiwan's largest cities. One of the proposed target zones was 35 kilometers northeast of Taiwan while the other was 52 kilometers southwest of Kao-hsiung. Surface-to-air missiles were to be tested. In effect, the PRC had established a near blockade of Taiwan's major urban areas and endangered its sea lanes and airlanes as well. The logic of this action was to influence Taiwanese voters to support those candidates who wanted to maintain close relations with the mainland. The ROC government responded by warning air carriers serving Taiwan about the tests and warning fishermen in the areas near the target zones. Officials also informed U.S. officials about the PRC plans for the missile tests.[47]

The PRC was not done with intimidating Taiwan, however. On March 12, 1996, its forces began nine days of live ammunition military exercises in the seas off Fukien and began firing the missiles as promised. Mainland naval and air forces were involved in these maneuvers near Tung-shan and Nan-ao islands. The maneuvers were a relatively short distance from the two ROC outposts Kin-men (Quemoy) and P'eng-hu. As a result, three hundred commercial flights using the Taiwan strait had to make detours.

Tensions were running high on Taiwan, and both government officials and people in the streets expressed outrage at the PRC's military actions. The Clinton administration then took action, responding to the calls of officials in the PRC and to demands from the many members of the U.S. Congress who had long supported the ROC. The U.S. Navy moved two carrier battle groups into the area to monitor the PRC's military operations. These were the largest U.S. naval forces seen in the area since the end of the Vietnam war—a period when Taiwan and the United States enjoyed a close diplomatic and military relationship and American advisers representing the Military Advisory Group were in many parts of the island.[48]

These PRC actions did not do anything to slow the pace of the two election campaigns in process. However, the military exercises and the threat they posed did become a matter for discussion and argument as the candidates for the presidency again engaged in a forum. All three of Lee's rivals sharply criticized Lee for his diplomacy and his other policies, stressing differences between their mainland policy and his. P'eng took the boldest stand in favor of Taiwan's independence and attacked the very idea of reunification with mainland China. The others pressed the case for a close relationship with the PRC and argued that there was but one China—a China that included the mainland and Taiwan. Lee decided to stay the course and remained calm in the midst of the *sturm und drang* that surrounded him. He stressed what he had achieved during his years in office and presented a clear blueprint for Taiwan's security and continued development. He also laid out a series of five developmental goals. He was determined to act confident and presidential even in the midst of the worst crisis the ROC had faced since the 1950s.[49]

While the presidential election was one that concerned most people on Taiwan and in the West, another important election was going on as well—the fierce, multifaceted contest for the National Assembly. The candidates for the third National Assembly had to, in the words of Christie Sue, "try a little harder these days to get attention." The second National Assembly (the National Assembly was the less powerful of the two legislative bodies) had been elected in 1991. In the years that followed, the members of that body had passed a number of important constitutional amendments that had helped the Republic of China/Taiwan change into a representative democracy. More changes were necessary, and the new assembly would be charged with the task of making them.

During the campaign, the three major parties laid out their candidates' platforms. In these statements, the parties stressed the nature of the constitution and suggested what its party members would do to change and strengthen this fundamental document.

The KMT, for example, promised to protect and to clarify the constitutional system, to promote peace to enhance the relationship with the mainland, and to object to Taiwanese independence and lead the island to unification. The DPP laid out a nine-point program that included the definition of national territory, the abolition of the provincial government, the establishment of a presidential democracy, and the development of a fair and harmonious society. The New Party proposed to keep the existing five-branch government but advocated a parliamentary system in which the premier would be the head of government. The New Party's objective was to create an unwieldy government with more checks and balances, making an imperial presidency all but impossible. The National Assembly candidates worked to get out the grass-roots vote while they discussed high-level constitutional and national issues. The campaigns were privately run, but 370 forums were held where the candidates could exchange their views and present their ideas in given areas.[50]

During the final week, the PRC maintained its pressure and began yet another set of military exercises. These new war games were the closest yet to ROC territory; the PRC's forces simulated a missile blockade, a series of live-fire drills, and finally, simulated attacks on P'eng-hu and Taiwan. The game of Russian roulette was now being played at an even higher and more dangerous level.[51]

The elections for the presidency and the National Assembly were held in the face of this mounting pressure. In the final analysis, the PRC's threats and pressure had the opposite effect of that intended by its leaders: Voters rejected those candidates who had called for even closer ties to the mainland and who rejected in part the democratic changes embraced by the majority of the ROC's voters.[52] The ROC's electorate gave the PRC its answer the next day, March 23, 1996. Lee Teng-hui, the incumbent, won 54 percent of the popular vote. The DPP candidate, P'eng, received 21 percent, the KMT rebel Lin received 14.9 percent, and the other KMT rebel, Chen, garnered 10 percent.[53] However, Lee could not use his influence to help his party gain an equally large majority in the National Assembly. There the KMT won only a relatively slim majority of seats, 183. The DPP won 99 and the New Party won 56. The KMT delegates now wondered whether they could pass the reforms that party leaders had promised. But as James Robinson has pointed out, more work had to be done and additional reforms were needed.[54]

I wish to leave the narrative at this point and move on to a more fitting moment at which to end our epic—the day in May when Lee Teng-hui was inaugurated as the first popularly elected president in the history of China. The day was a triumph for Lee and for his party, the KMT. It was also a day of triumph for his small but increasingly influential country.

In his carefully written inaugural address, Lee charted a course for China and Taiwan's future. He focused not on his victory or the economic "miracle" that he and his party had helped bring about and advance, but on Taiwan's role as a model for all of China. He encouraged the PRC to study what Taiwan had done in developing its economy and in creating a viable representative democracy, and a society that provided its people with both an equitable distribution of wealth and a generally high level of prosperity. He even offered to go to China to work for better relations and closer ties between Taiwan and its brother/rival to the West.[55]

It would be nice to say that all went well after that and that Lee went from triumph to triumph, but that was not to be the case. Taiwan still faces many challenges in its system of governance, economic infrastructure, foreign policy, and relationship with China. The following discussion suggests how these months in 1995 and 1996 can be seen as a culmination of the various streams of development examined here.

Resonating Themes in Taiwan's History

Certain themes—paradigms and patterns of policy, program, and human action—have helped define the very nature of Taiwan in the late 1990s. These basic themes are to be discerned in the modern, democratized, and often embattled Taiwan that is the Republic of China.

Like the People's Republic of China, the ROC remains influenced by its own internal patterns of historical development. So is every country. These patterns of localized evolution have in turn been determined, in good measure, by the relationship between this island and the mainland one hundred or so miles to its west.

The first of these themes (or *leitmotivs*) is the historically grounded antagonism and rivalry among the various groups that now comprise Taiwan's 23 million people. The pattern of racial and ethnic rivalry was further complicated when Taiwan was taken over by what some of its residents saw as two successive waves of imperialist invasion: the Japanese colonization from 1895 to 1945 and the Nationalist retrocession, which (many Taiwanese would argue) in its earliest phase strongly resembled an invasion by an alien and hostile regime.

This process of alien control embedded itself even more firmly after the collapse of the Nationalist regime on the mainland and the Nationalist government's retreat to Taiwan. One can see this complex process of governmental takeover, socioeconomic restructuring, and the imposition of a pan-Chinese culture, between 1949 and 1994.

From January 1995 to May 1996, the ethnic issue emerged again as a major subtheme, highlighted by certain key events. One was a hopeful step—the dedication of the monument commemorating the February 28 incident in Taipei's New Park. This was seen as an act of reconciliation by a regime that had come to represent the population of the island's two Han majorities, Taiwanese and Hakka. The elections for seats in the Legislative Yuan and for the presidency of the ROC can also be seen through the lens of ethnic and subethnic conflict. In this case, the political parties appropriated the theme of mainlander versus Taiwanese as they jockeyed for power. They subsequently attempted—after the December elections at least—realigning themselves for maximum advantage and downplaying the ethnic divisions between the DPP and the New Party, thus cooperating to gain power over their common rival: the increasingly Taiwanese-dominated KMT. Ethnic politics and the issue of an independent Taiwan—whether de facto or de jure—were played out during these intense months.

Ethnic rivalry surfaced again as the presidential election campaign continued. The mainlanders had their candidates, and the Han-Taiwanese (both Southern Min and Hakka) had theirs. The PRC even attempted to use the ethnic and the Taiwan independence issues to their own advantage during the weeks of military pressure before the elections. That bald-faced attempt failed, but it reflected the PRC's leaders awareness of the issue and the way it affected internal Taiwanese politics.

A second, related theme in this book, like one of the *leitmotivs* Wagner used in his magisterial *Ring Cycle,* is the complex and often troubled relationship between the island and its Han population's Chinese homeland. The irony of the decades of separation and verbal and sometimes physical combat is that Taiwan, with its corporatist state and its export-oriented economy, also became a model—a paradigm—and the PRC increasingly recognizes that it needs Western (and Little Dragon) capital and expertise. Finally Taiwan has become a storehouse of Chinese history and a preserver of its long cultural heritage. Taiwan's museums became the best places in the world to study Chinese history, with the Palace Museum and the Museum of History leading the way in the quality of their collections and their clear presentations. A comparison between the Taipei Palace Museum and the Palace Museum in the Forbidden City in Beijing makes this point clear to the Western tourist. Taiwan also became a place where the Chinese religious tradition in all its complexity and diversity was preserved and allowed to flourish. The mainstream traditions of Buddhism and Taoism were able to prosper and to expand their reach, and the present-day Buddhist revival in Taiwan is an example of this vitality of the mainstream, text-centered traditions. The popular tradition has also evolved, and major cults such as those of the gods Ma-tsu, Kuanyin, Kuan Kung, Wang-yeh, and Pao-sheng Ta-ti have been able to play a major role in Taiwanese life. That Taiwan was a storehouse of traditional culture and the home to a living Chinese religious system proved important in the years after 1987.

The opening of direct communication between the ROC and the PRC after 1987 marked the beginning of a new, and in many ways more complex, stage in the four-hundred-year relationship between the mainland and this gradually sinified island. The events of 1995 and 1996 can only be understood against this backdrop and exemplify an even more complex moment in this long relationship. Taiwan has begun to play a major role in helping people in some provinces of China recover history lost during the years of cultural and religious cannibalism that were the Cultural Revolution. Increasingly the people of Taiwan—the followers of the old gods—have helped their brethren in Fukien and other provinces to rebuild their religious sanctuaries. The followers of the Ma-tsu cult have spearheaded this move with pilgrimages to Mei-chou, Kang-li, and Ch'uan-chou, the sites of three important Ma-tsu temples.[56] At the same time scholars of religion in the major Taiwanese research institutes and universities have helped mainlanders to study their own past with confidence and without fear of reprisal by a state that regarded popular religion as superstition and looked with distrust on the leaders and the practitioners of the text-centered faith systems. Today, the publication of books shows the resurgence of religious studies in the PRC. Taiwanese religiously centered tourism and the visits of Taiwanese and Western scholars to the PRC along with the development of joint projects such as the Ma-tsu project of the Chinese University of Hong Kong have all played a part in the multifaceted reappreciation of the Chinese religio-cultural tradition.

A third theme in this book is that of Taiwan as a player in the world arena. Taiwan's entry into the larger world began while the island was a Dutch colony. After its integration into the Ch'ing empire it became a Chinese maritime frontier now isolated, like much of China, from foreign influence; after the treaties of Tientsin (1858) and Peking (1860) were signed, it again mounted the world stage, this time as the site of a treaty port. The years of Japanese domination brought Taiwan into the larger world as both a Japanese-created zone of development and, most painfully, as a target in the Allied war against the Japanese empire. Since 1949, Taiwan—now as the ROC—has continued to play a larger role in the world. It served as a model for U.S. foreign assistance for the next sixteen years and afterward became a showcase for the strategy of export-oriented development. Yet during this period the ROC has been disappointed by its inability to gain diplomatic recognition. The PRC has steadily gained supporters willing to recognize it as the government of all of China. Taiwan's expulsion from the United Nations marked a key moment in this process, and in the years that followed, Taiwan became increasingly isolated. This process reached its climax when the United States in December 1978 withdrew its formal diplomatic recognition. Since then, Taiwan has attempted to rebuild relations with world nations and has gained all-but-formal recognition from many. The former republics of the Soviet Union, for example, have courted Taiwan, and Taiwan also has a close working relationship with Vietnam. President Lee's aggressive foreign policy achieved these new ties and gained a measure of recognition for Taiwan as an economic power and economic-development paradigm.

Lee's visit to the United States in June 1995 can be seen as a demonstration of Taiwan's newly found confidence as an actor on the world stage. Lee Teng-hui became the center of world attention during those few days. The PRC saw Lee's visit and pronouncements as a sign that Lee was a closet activist for Taiwan independence and thus rationalized its aggressive stand toward Lee's policies.

The role played by the United States in the strait crisis of March 1996 demonstrated the success of Lee's policies, for it showed that the United States was not willing to abandon its long-time friend, even if it did not recognize the ROC in a traditional way, through the formal exchange of ambassadors.

There was yet another side to this attempt by Taiwan to play a larger role in the wider world—the reaction of the PRC, which has attempted, sometimes quite effectively, to blunt the ROC's diplomatic initiatives. The PRC countered Taiwan's new pattern of international relations with pressure on nations continuing to deal with Taiwan, and it made life difficult for Taiwanese officials working in UN-related agencies as well as for the Taiwanese press corps covering the UN as Taiwan tried unsuccessfully, year after year to regain admission to that major world body.

A Final Word

Taiwan is continuing to evolve. It is our hope that an understanding of Taiwan's past, and its implications for the future, will be enhanced by the discussions in this book, which illustrate why this small but vital island has become such a source of fascination to this volume's contributors. Each of us has been caught up in the drama and the excitement of Taiwan as we attempt to understand its political, social, and economic evolution. While Taiwan has been influenced by China, it is not China, but a unique, national entity. The central theme of this book is that Taiwan is Taiwan, linked to China, yet forged out of its own unique historical processes. It may yet once again become part of a larger China or serve as an example of what China might become. For the moment, at least, as the twentieth century draws to a close, it is a unique place that has forged its own destiny and created a special role for itself in East Asia and the larger world.

Notes

1. "Bill to Regulate First Presidential Election Under Review," *Free China Journal* (FCJ), 12, no. 3 (January 20, 1995): 1.

2. "Lee Moving to Heal Old Wound, Apologizes for February 28 Incident," FCJ, 12, no. 8 (March 3, 1995): 1.

3. "Agenda Disagreement Stalls Cross-Strait Talk," FCJ, 12, no. 15 (April 28, 1995): 1; "Second Koo–Wang Talks Appear to Be Set for June," FCJ, 12, no. 17 (May 12, 1995): 1; "Taipei Meeting Sets Stage for Second Koo–Wang Talks," FCJ, 12, no. 20 (June 2, 1995): 1.

4. "In a Historic Trip, Lee Arrives in U.S. for Talk at Cornell," FCJ, 12, no. 21 (June 9, 1995): 1. See also "World Press Welcomes U.S. Decision to Allow Lee to Visit," FCJ, 12, no. 21 (June 2, 1995): 1.

5. "Lee, Back from U.S., Says Visit Helped World Recognize ROC," FCJ, 12, no. 22 (June 16, 1995): 1. See also "Text of Lee's Cornell Address," FCJ, 12, no. 22 (June 16, 1995): 7–8.

6. During 1995 and 1996, I met regularly with a member of the PRC's UN delegation. We discussed various matters relating to Taiwan, and he spelled out the official PRC policy toward Taiwan during these dangerous months. As early as July 1995 he began to intimate that in his own opinion as well as his government's Lee was playing the Taiwan independence card as he ran for the presidency.

7. "Lee's Popularity Holds Firm," FCJ, 12, no. 29 (August 4, 1995): 1.

8. "In Bid for Presidency Control Yuan Chief Quits KMT," FCJ, 12, no. 32 (August 25, 1995): 2.

9. "Lee Declares He Will Seek Second Term as President," FCJ, 12, no. 32 (August 25, 1995): 1.

10. "Lee Wins KMT Nod and Picks Lien," FCJ, 12, no. 34 (September 8, 1995): 1.

11. "Lee Strives to Ease Straits Tension," FCJ, 12, no. 34 (September 8, 1995): 2.

12. "DPP Nominates a Former Professor as Its First Presidential Candidate," FCJ, 12, no. 37 (September 30, 1995): 1.

13. "Legislative Election Plan Set," FCJ, 12, no. 38 (October 6, 1995): 1.

14. "DPP Sets Forth Platform as Three Elections Approach," FCJ, 12, no. 38 (October 6, 1995): 2.

15. "Chen Picks Running Mate," FCJ, 12, no. 41 (October 27, 1995): 2.

16. "Lin Opts for Geographic Balence in Choice in Vice-Presidential Choice," FCJ, 12, no. 42 (November 3, 1995): 2.

17. "Lin Names Former Premier Hau as Running Mate for March Vote," FCJ, 12, no. 44 (November 17, 1995): 1.

18. "Parties on Hustings for Legislative Elections," FCJ, 12, no. 42 (November 3, 1995): 2.

19. "Crowd of Candidates Rush for Seats," FCJ, 12, no. 43 (November 10, 1995): 1.

20. "Chiayi Race Showcases Democracy in Taiwan," FCJ, 12, no. 44 (November 17, 1995): 2.

21. "Campaign Purse Straps Tighter This Time Around," FCJ, 12, no. 45 (November 24, 1995): 2.

22. "KMT Hold on Tight as Rival Parties Target Its Majority in the Legislature," FCJ, 12, no. 45 (November 24, 1995): 4.

23. "DPP Makes a Big Power Play," FCJ, 12, no. 45 (November 24, 1995): 4–5.

24. "New Party, in First Legislative Race, Could Be Spoiler," FCJ, 12, no. 45 (November 24, 1995): 4–5.

25. "Taipei Cautions Peking After New Show of Force in the Straits," FCJ, 12, no. 46 (December 1, 1995): 1.

26. "As Millions Prepare to Go to Polls, Legislative Campaign Grows Tense," FCJ, 12, no. 46 (December 1, 1995): 1.

27. "KMT Holds Edge, DPP Grows, New Party Surges," FCJ, 12, no. 47 (December 8, 1995): 1.

28. "Analysts Weigh Impact of Results," FCJ, 12, no. 47 (December 8, 1995): 2.

29. James A. Robinson, "New Election Advances ROC Democracy," FCJ, 12, no. 47 (December 8, 1995): 7.

30. "KMT Outs Two Vice Chairmen as Rift in Ruling Party Deepens," FCJ, 12, no. 48 (December 15, 1995): 1.

31. "DPP and New Party Orchestrate Legislative Alliance," FCJ, 12, no. 49 (December 22, 1995): 1.

32. "Proposal Would Parcel Out Top Positions in Legislature," FCJ, 12, no. 50 (December 29, 1995): 1.

33. "Economy Officially Slips into Recession Territory," FCJ, 12, no. 50 (December 29, 1995): 3.

34. "Taiwan's Economy on Verge of Exiting Recession Territory," FCJ, 13, no. 5 (February 2, 1996): 8.

35. "Fund Unable to Stabilize Bourse," FCJ, 13, no. 8 (March 1, 1996): 3.

36. "Protest Greets Museum's Project to Send Art Treasures on U.S. Tour," FCJ, 13, no. 2 (January 12, 1996): 1.

37. "Lin and Chen Qualify for Ballot; Lee Opens Campaign Headquarters," FCJ, 13, no. 4 (January 26, 1996): 1.

38. "ROC Urges Calm After Reports on Mainland's Military Threats," FCJ, 13, no. 4 (January 26, 1996): 1.

39. "KMT Wins First Legislative Tilt, for Speaker, by One Vote," FCJ, 13, no. 5 (February 2, 1996): 1.

40. "Lee Renominates Lien to Head Transition Cabinet," FCJ, 13, no. 5 (February 16, 1996): 1.

41. "Opposition Parties Collaborate in Bid to Block Premier Nomination," FCJ, 13, no. 7 (February 16, 1996): 2.

42. "Presidential Rivals Draw Ballot Numbers; Three Join Debate," FCJ, 13, no. 7 (February 16, 1996): 2.

43. "Mainland War Games Confirmed; U.S. Calls for Restraint," FCJ, 13, no. 7 (February 16, 1996): 2.

44. "As Mainland Masses Troops, Lee Urges Public to Keep Faith," FCJ, 13, no. 8 (March 1, 1996): 1.

45. "Presidential Rivals in TV Forum Present Platforms to the Public," FCJ, 13, no. 8 (March 1, 1996): 1.

46. "Vice Presidential Rivals Appeal for Votes in Televised Forum," FCJ, 13, no. 9 (March 8, 1996): 1.

47. "Peking Plans to Fire Missiles Close to Two Taiwan Ports," FCJ, 13, no. 9 (March 8, 1996): 1.

48. "Tensions Grow as Peking Extends Military Moves," FCJ, 13, no. 10 (March 15, 1996): 1.

49. "In TV Forum, Candidates Focus on Tensions in Straits," FCJ, 13, no. 10 (March 15, 1996): 2.

50. "Candidates for Assembly Press Partisan Outlooks for Constitutional Reform," FCJ, 13, no. 10 (March 15, 1996): 4.

51. "Peking Begins New Series of Military Steps in Straits," FCJ, 13, no. 11 (March 22, 1996): 1.

52. "In the Face of Threats Millions Set to Elect ROC President," FCJ, 13, no. 11 (March 22, 1996): 1.

53. "Lee Sweeps to Victory in Presidential Poll," *Free China Review* (FCR), 13, no. 12 (March 28, 1996): 1.

54. James A. Robinson, "Little Noticed Assembly Vote May Hold the Key to New Reforms," FCR, 13, no. 12 (March 28, 1996): 7. See also James A. Robinson, "After Key Vote, More Reforms Lie Ahead," FCR, 13, no. 12 (March 28, 1996): 8.

55. "Lee at Inaugural, Offers to Make a 'Journey of Peace' to Mainland," FCR, 13, no. 19 (May 24, 1996): 1. See also "Full Text of Lee's Inaugural Address," in ibid., p. 8.

56. This process of reconnection has been explored by the author and an article on the subject of pilgrimage and reconnection is included in a volume published by E.J. Brill in 1997.

Contributors

Sung-Sheng Yvonne Chang is Chair of the Department of Asian studies at the University of Texas at Austin. She has written extensively on modern Taiwanese literature and is the author of *Modernism and the Nativist Resistance: Contemporary Chinese Fiction* (1993). She has edited, with Ann C. Carver, *Bamboo Shoots After the Rain: Contemporary Stories by Women Writers of Taiwan* (1990).

Chen Ch'iu-kun is a Research Associate in the Institute of Taiwan History of Academia Sinica. He studies and has written extensively on land policy and settlement patterns in Ch'ing Taiwan.

Robert Gardella is a member of the Social Sciences Faculty of the United States Merchant Marine Academy. He is a specialist in Chinese business history and is one of the founders of the Chinese Business Group of the Association of Asian Studies. He is the author of *Harvesting Mountains: Fujian and the China Tea Trade, 1757–1937* (1994) and is coeditor with Jane K. Leonard and Andrea McElderry of *Chinese Business History: Interpretive Trends and Priorities* (1999). He has also published numerous articles in books and major scholarly journals.

Ronald Knapp is a member of the department of geography of The State University of New York/New Paltz. He is a specialist in the cultural geography of China and on the architecture of Central and South China. He is the author of *China's Vernacular Architecture: House Form and Culture* (1989), and the editor of *Chinese Landscapes: The Village as Place* (1992).

Harry Lamley spent many years as a member of the history department of the University of Hawaii at Manoa. He is a pioneer in the western study of the field of Taiwanese history and the history of South China. He is a series editor at SUNY Press and has written numerous articles for major collections. Among his articles are "The Formation of Cities: Initiative and Motivation in Building

Three City Walls in Taiwan," in G. William Skinner, ed., *The City in Late Imperial China* (1977), and "Lineage Feuding in Southern Fujian and Eastern Guangdong under Qing Rule," in Jonathan N. Lipman and Stevan Harrell, eds, *Violence in China: Essays in Culture and Counterculture* (1990).

Steven Phillips has recently completed his Doctorate in Chinese History at Georgetown University. He has taught at Gettysburg College and is now on the staff of the Office of the Historian of the U.S. Department of State. He has done extensive work on the 2–28 period and has presented papers at conferences in the United States and on Taiwan.

Murray A. Rubinstein is a member of the History Department and the Program in Asian/Asian American Studies at Baruch College of the City University of New York. He is also Chair of the Taiwan Studies Group of the Association of Asian Studies. He has done research on Chinese mission history and on the history of Taiwan, Fukien and Kwantung. His monographs include *The Protestant Community on Modern Taiwan: Mission, Seminary, and Church* (1991) and *The Origins of the Anglo-American Protestant Missionary Enterprise in China* (1996). He is the editor of *The Other Taiwan: 1945 to the Present* (1991) and has written articles for books and scholarly journals.

John Robert Shepherd is a member of the department of anthropology of the University of Virginia. He has studied patterns of land ownership, Han/Yuantzu-min relations, and demography in Dutch, Cheng-era and Ch'ing Taiwan. His books include *Statecraft and Political Economy on the Taiwan Frontier, 1600–1800* (1993). He has also written articles for books and scholarly journals, including "From Barbarians to Sinners: Collective Conversion Among the Plains Aborigines in Qing Taiwan, 1859–1895" in Daniel H. Bays, ed., *Christianity in China: From the Eighteenth Century to the Present* (1996).

Michael Stainton worked with the *Yuan-tzu-min* while serving with the Presbyterian Church on Taiwan for over a decade. He is now completing a doctorate in Anthropology at York University, studying the political consciousness and the political activism of the *Yuan-tzu-min*. He has also studied, written about, and organized conferences on the history Protestant Christianity on Taiwan.

Eduard B. Vermeer is a member of the Sinological Institute of the University of Leiden. He studies Chinese socio-economic development. He is the author of *Economic Development in Provincial China: The Central Shaanxi since 1830* (1988). He has also edited, with Frank N. Pieke and Woei Lien Chang, *Cooperative and Collective in China's Rural Development: Between State and Private Interests* (1998). He has also helped organize international conferences on China's development.

Chen-main Peter Wang is a member of the history department of Chun-Cheng University in Chiayi, Taiwan. He has done research on the Ming-Ch'ing Transition, the history of Chinese Christianity, and Sino American relations. His books include *The Rise and Fall of the Wenshe: A Study of the Rise and Fall of Indigenization of Christianity in China in the 1920s* (1993). His articles include "Contextualizing Protestant Publishing in China: The Wenshe, 1924–1928," in Daniel H. Bays, ed., *Christianity in China: From the Eighteenth Century to the Present* (1996).

Robert P. Weller is a member of the Department of Anthropology of Boston University. He has done research on religion and society on Taiwan and China and is the author of *Unities and Diversities in Chinese Religion* (1987), *Resistance, Chaos, and Control In China: Taiping Rebels, Taiwanese Ghosts, and Tianmen* (1994). Among the books he has co-edited is *Unruly Gods: Divinity and Society in China* (1996).

John E. Wills Jr. is a member of the History Department of the University of Southern California. He has done extensive research on the relationship between China and the West in the Late Imperial period. His monographs include *Pepper, Guns, and Parleys: The Dutch East India Company and China, 1662–1681* (1974), *Embassies and Illusions: Dutch and Portuguese Envoys to K'ang-hsi, 1666–1687* (1984), and *Mountain of Fame: Portraits in Chinese history* (1994).

Index